# Theatre Management and Production in America

*Stephen Langley*

# Theatre Management and Production in America

## Commercial •Stock Resident •College Community and Presenting Organizations

**DRAMA PUBLISHERS**
An Imprint of
*Quite Specific Media Group Ltd.*
New York

Copyright© 1990 by Stephen Langley

Other Quite Specific Media Group Ltd. imprints:
Costume & Fashion Press
EntertainmentPro
By Design Press
Jade Rabbit

Library of Congress Cataloging-in-Publication Data

Langley, Stephen.
        Theatre management and production in America: commercial, stock, resident, college, community, and presenting organizations /
Stephen Langley--1st ed.
                p.      cm.
Includes bibliographic references and index.
ISBN 0-89676-143-6:
1. Theater management-United States. 2. Theater--United States--Production and direction. I. Title
PN2291. L29 1990
792'.068--dc20                                        90-42890
                                                          CIP

10 9 8 7 6 5

This book is dedicated to dedication itself,
without which there would be no theatre to manage.

*The author gratefully acknowledges permission to reprint granted from the following:*

Excerpt from *The Performing Arts: Problems and Prospects* is reprinted by permission of The Rockerfeller Brothers Fund, New York, New York.

Excerpt from *Ellen Terry and Bernard Shaw, A Correspondence* is reprinted by permission of The Society of Authors, London, England, on behalf of the Bernard Shaw Estate.

The "Certification Procedure Flow Chart" related to the Approved Production Contract (APC) (Article XVI) is reprinted by permission of the Dramatists Guild, Inc.

The Sample Pre-Production Budget, Weekly Operating Production Budget and Gross Potentials at the end of Chapter 11 are reprinted by permission of Peter G. Guither from "Katz Productions: A Management Residency Report," Unpublished MFA Dissertation, Department of Theatre, Brooklyn College, 1985.

Excerpt from *Light Up The Sky* (Copyright © 1948, 1949 by Moss Hart) is reprinted by permission of Mrs. Moss Hart.

The National Ticket Company, New York, New York (ticket samples).

David Merrick (*Hello Dolly* address form).

The "Love Hurts" newspaper advertisement is reprinted by permission of the New York City Opera: Wallace Whitworth, Director of Marketing; Peggy Pettus, Art Director, McCaffrey & McCall, Inc.,; Jeanie Stein, Copywriter, McCaffrey & McCall, Inc.

The BAM logo is reprinted by permission of the Brooklyn Academy of Music.

The Circle in the Square Theatre logo is reprinted by permission of Circle in the Square Theatre, New York City.

The Lincoln Center logo is reprinted by permission of Lincoln Center for the Performing Arts, Inc., New York City.

The Berkeley Repertory Theatre logo (design by Jerry Haworth) is reprinted by permission of Berkeley Repertory Theatre, Berkeley, CA.

# Table of Contents

# Preface

This book attempts to present a comprehensive approach to theatrical producing and management in America. It provides historical background to shed light on current practice, describes the various methods now used to produce theatre, and explains the managerial systems necessary for successful production.

When I was working on an earlier, altogether different version of this book in the early 1970s, arts management as a certifiable profession was just beginning to gain recognition, and books such as mine were just beginning to create what is today a sizable bibliography related to this field of specialization. Since the early 1980s, when a second edition of the book was published, the field has evolved and changed enormously—which is exciting to observe, although difficult to keep up with in print. While the earlier publications were more or less based on a graduate course I was teaching at the time, this volume is based on an entire graduate program in performing arts management and is at least an introduction to such a program. Each chapter could be expanded into a full volume and examined in much greater depth than is possible here. But it is usually helpful to view the forest as a whole before looking at each tree. Consequently, I have tried to place the different methods of theatrical producing into historical perspective and then to describe current practices in a manner that can be easily understood without any special preparation. Mindful that theatre should be a joyous experience, I have even tried to include a little humor.

Although the historical material in this book deals almost exclusively with live theatre, the contents are otherwise applicable to the management of any type of performing arts company or institution. The preservation of our cultural heritage and the creation of new art is more than ever dependent upon informed management—management that is cognizant of *its* dependence on the art is meant to preserve, facilitate and encourage. I subscribe to the belief that artistic priorities should take precedence over management theories and, sometimes, even over economic realities. The creative process of theatre is a very unpredictable and uncertain one that sometimes must fly in the face of logic and traditional practice in order to succeed. There is no single best way to produce a play or operate a theatre company—and I hope these pages do not give the impression that there is. A good manager is aware of the options and able to make the best choices, which often involve compromise. Theatre is so uncertain, in fact, that it can't even decide how to spell its own name (this work favors *theatre* over *theater, presenter* over *presentor* and *nonprofit* over *not-for-profit* ).

A colleague recently said that the best thing about working in theatre is never having to worry about what to do on a day off—there are none. But despite demanding labor at low pay and twenty-five-hour work days, it could be said that every day working in theatre is a holiday. This is true because theatre is a profession that abounds with an unusually high number of wonderfully kind and interesting people. I have been fortunate indeed to have known many of them. I have avoided footnotes in this book because I wouldn't know where to stop: each and every sentence was, I suppose, inspired by somebody. While it would be impossible to name everyone who has provided me with information, if not with inspiration, I would like to mention a few.

First, of course, I am indebted to my parents, Delma and Marjorie Langley, and my grandparents, Frank and Irene Gould; I miss them very much. While I was growing up, they provided a remarkably supportive household and even the encouragement to create a theatre company of my own when I was in the fifth grade. The actors were only marionettes, but they taught me my first lessons about theatre as well as management—in fact, by the time I finished high school, we had earned enough money to pay a fair amount of my college tuition.

My undergraduate study was mostly done at Emerson College in Boston, where my interest in theatre was redoubled under the stimulating guidance of such teachers as Leonadis Nickole, Elliot Norton and William Van Lennop. Before earning two degrees from Emerson, I spent a year studying in London—thanks to assistance from Dean Richard Pierce and a scholarship from Mrs. Florence B. Pegram. Of the many students and theatre professionals I met there, I was influenced most by the late Stephen Joseph. I remember going on tour with his theatre company as a side kick to Alan Akyborne, who was then stage managing but has since written more plays than Shakespeare and runs the Stephen Joseph Memorial Theatre in Scarborough.

Eventually, I found myself pursuing a Ph.D. at the University of Illinois in Champaign-Urbana. I enjoyed an assistantship under Dr. Joseph W. Scott while he was overseeing the development of architectural plans for the Krannert Center for the Performing Arts. Academically, I am grateful to my advisors, Professors Barnard Hewitt and Charles Shattuck.

Throughout most of my college years and well beyond, I worked summers at the Falmouth Playhouse on Cape Cod, eventually serving as its managing director. This provided an extraordinary amount of valuable experience and an association with a broad segment of the professional theatre world that, given the nature of professional stock theatre at that time, probably could not be duplicated today. So I feel particularly indebted to the former owner and producer at Falmouth, Mrs. Sidney Gordon, as well as to the countless legendary figures, struggling artists, apprentices and staff members who put up with my management. I will mention only three loyal assistants: David Conte, Judith Watson Bailow and the late Jim Fiore, Jr.

As fate would have it, my summer theatre career eventually dovetailed with my academic career. This was because the manager of our closest competition, the Cape Cod Melody Tent, as well as the man who served as the CPA for virtually all New England summer theatres at that time, were both members of the Economics faculty at Brooklyn College when I arrived. T. Bruce Birkenhead and Edward O. Lutz—whom I have regarded as role models ever since I met them—were always willing guest speakers in my Theatre Management class and have also been extremely generous with their advice for this book. In the early 1970s, the three of us formed the nucleus of a faculty for a new M.F.A. Performing Arts Management Program which I had been asked to create. Bruce eventually left academia to work for Emanuel Azenberg on Broadway and became a producer himself, although he still teaches for the program. Ed, who is the founding co-partner of the theatrical accounting firm of Lutz and Carr, was subjected to a crueler fate by getting elected to chair his department, which he continued to do until his retirement. I have also maintained acquaintances with other Cape connections, including the first manager of both Falmouth Playhouse and the Melody Tent, Herman Krawitz—another worthy role model who has been associated with the Metropolitan Opera, the American Ballet Theatre and who recently, I'm pleased to say, taught a course in the Brooklyn program. And I must mention two outstanding gentlemen—Ralph Roseman, now a leading general manager in the commercial theatre and a partner at Theatre Now, Inc., and Charles Forsythe, now the Managing Producer of the Cape Playhouse in Dennis, Massachusetts. Both read long sections of this book in manuscript and made valuable suggestions.

My ten years as General Manager of the Brooklyn College Center for the Performing Arts also provided memorable experiences and I would like to acknowledge the late President Francis Kilcoyne and my immediate supervisor, Dean Dante Negro, who taught me by his own example the definition of a humanist. Of my support staff, I would like to mention Sally Feigen Boodish, Evelyn Lisbin and Margaret Ryan. A highlight of those years was the opportunity to work closely with Sir Rudolf Bing, who was appointed as

Distinguished Professor at Brooklyn College immediately following his retirement as General Manager of the Metropolitan Opera. We collaborated on a highly successful Shakespeare symposium and celebration that was centered around the Royal Shakespeare Company's visit to the Brooklyn Academy of Music, and Sir Rudolf also earned the distinction of being the only person ever to take over my classes while I was on sabbatical leave!

Speaking of the Brooklyn Academy of Music, I must say that it has been a special privilege to have maintained a productive, if informal, relationship with this extraordinary performing arts institution and with Harvey Lichtenstein, its inspired leader. BAM provides a wonderful role model for other institutions. Many of my students have served as interns there and many others have filled full-time positions. Karen Brooks Hopkins, Executive Vice President, and Joseph V. Mellilo, former Executive Producer of the Next Wave Festival, have both taught in the Brooklyn management program, as have two program graduates, Ellen Lampert and Peter Carzasty, who have successively served as BAM's Director of Press and Public Relations. And I must also thank BAM's Vice President for Marketing and Promotion, Douglas Allan, who, together with Mr. Carzasty, provided helpful comments about Part IV of this work.

I feel fortunate that almost all of my nearly thirty years at Brooklyn College of the City University of New York have been pleasant ones. Nothing in my career has given me greater satisfaction than the creation and supervision of the M.F.A. Performing Arts Management Program. For providing the encouragement, support and latitude required for that program's success, I would like to acknowledge President Robert L. Hess, Dean Robert Hickok, Dean Leslie S. Jacobson and, most of all, Professor Benito Ortolani, the longtime Theatre Department Chairman whose unswerving support of both the program and me have been appreciated more than words can express. I would also like to thank Professors William Prosser and John Scheffler for reading sections of the manuscript and, just for being such fine colleagues and friends, I'd like to mention F. Murray Abraham, Herbert Fyler, David Garfield, Samuel Leiter, Margaret Linney, Glenn Loney, Gordon Rogoff and our wonderful department secretary, Shirley Gordon. Adjunct faculty members of the management program who have read sections of the book and made helpful suggestions include Todd Haimes, Managing Producer of the Roundabout Theatre Company in Manhattan; David Kitto, Marketing Manager for Carnegie Hall; and Harry W. Weintraub, P.C.

There's a telling lyric from *The King and I* that says, "If you become a teacher, by you're pupils you'll be taught." Certainly I've learned far more from my students collectively than any one of them has learned from me. And I even get paid for this! I wish I could mention each and every alumnus from the program—an increasingly accomplished body of management professionals working for the arts all over the world. Like a parent, I proudly claim all the credit for their success—although I only had a little to do with it.

While writing this book, I've been blessed with three wonderfully personable and helpful graduate assistants: Mel Black, Patrick Dewane and Judith Kelley. And, of course, I was forever phoning other students and alumni for bits of information, research favors and advice about the manuscript. Hoping that I haven't overlooked anyone, I would like to give special thanks to: Ron Aja (Actors' Equity Association), Jane Bryer (San Francisco Ballet), Diana Fairbanks (Fifth Avenue Productions), John Federico (Theatre Communications Group), Kate Gordon, Dina Graser (Dance Umbrella of Ontario), Thomas Kramer (Attisano Levine, Inc.) James McCallum (Musical America), Paul Tetreault (Berkeley Repertory Theatre), Dolph Timmerman (Columbia Artists Management, Inc.) and Jim Williams (New York City Center). For background material related to theatrical booking offices and presenting organizations, I am grateful to the following former students: Bill J. Cox, Daniel Fishkin, Jan Carol Greenwald, Peter G. Guither, Gary S. McAvay and Jonathan D. Moore, whose dissertations I have listed in the bibliography. Furthermore, Mr. McAvay (now President of CAMI Theatricals, Inc.) together with Alice Bernstein of K-L Management, Inc. made numerous contributions regarding Chapter 10. And for assistance with Appendix L, I am grateful to Marion Kagerer, Terril Miller and Sean Skeehan.

Academia has also afforded me the opportunity to work with colleagues from other institutions of higher education. During my stint as President of the Association of Arts Administration Educators, I became especially well acquainted with other arts management program heads from graduate schools around the nation, and I would like to acknowledge those with whom I worked most closely in organizing the annual conferences. I picked their erudite brains like a vulture: Edward Arien (Drexel University), Stephen Benedict (formerly with Columbia University, now President of the Theatre Development Fund), Joseph Green (York University), Benjamin Mordecai (Yale School of Drama), E. Arthur Prieve (University of Wisconsin/Madison), George Thorne (Virginia Tech), Brann J. Wry (New York University) and Carol Yamomoto (Columbia College in Chicago).

Occasionally, of course, I found it necessary to call upon people who were neither former students nor close colleagues, and I was invariably heartened by their readiness to assist with my research. I must thank Robert and Margery Boyar (R.A. Boyar Division of Marsh and McLennan, Inc. in New York City) for a delightful lunch and crash course in theatrical insurance; Carol Goren, Account Supervisor at Serino Coyne, Inc. in New York City; Steven E. Goldstein of Joseph Harris Associates, Inc.; Richard Grossberg,

General Manager of the Center for the Performing Arts at Brooklyn College; Susan Lee of the League of American Theatres and Producers; Carol Levine, President of Attisano Levine, Inc.; Dorothy Olim, Executive Secretary of the Association of Theatrical Press Agents and Managers; Dana Singer of the Dramatists Guild, Inc.; Willard Swire, former Executive Secretary of Actors' Equity Association; and Ann Leddy of AEA.

I would also like to acknowledge the encouragement that my writing efforts have received over the years from Ralph Pine, my publisher at Drama Book Publishers and a fellow Emersonian who was foolhardy enough to produce an early play of mine in Boston but wise enough in later years to publish four of my books. To paraphrase Mark Twain, as I got older his judgement got better! And now that he has Judith Holmes as a partner, his judgement appears better still.

Finally, I am deeply and eternally indebted to Edelmiro Olavarria, a true companion who, over the decades, somehow managed to tolerate me as well as to provide the support structure upon which I could base my aspirations and my life.

While many people, both knowingly and unknowingly, have contributed to the contents of this book, and my gratitude to them is considerable, any errors, omissions or misconceptions are, of course, my own. This is the third time that I've attempted to describe theatrical producing and management in book form, and I hope that I've finally got it right. In any case, I've tried my best. And until a more definitive book comes along on this subject, I can only hope that mine will assist those people—God bless them all—who labor for the living theatre.

Stephen Langley<br>
Brooklyn Heights<br>
January 1990

# Part I

# Fundamentals of Theatrical Producing

# 1

# The Idea For Theatre

H OW a theatre company or a single theatrical production is organized often determines its success. Why a company was formed or a particular production was attempted in the first place is also of critical importance. Thousands of plays and musicals are produced in America every year. Some employ professionals who earn their livelihood in the theatre, most utilize students and amateurs. Some are successful in that they fully engage the interest of an audience, they achieve artistic excellence, they serve some intended non-artistic purpose and/or they earn a profit; most fail in all these areas. This fact is widely understood, yet people continue to seek careers in the theatre and related fields in fairly staggering numbers. Why? What motivates a person even to attempt to earn a living in the theatre business?

## GETTING THE IDEA

The idea behind a theatrical career, production or organization is the *why* of it. Every theatre, play or production begins as one person's idea. But ideas have a life of their own. They are subject to very unscientific and unpredictable behavior as they are passed from person to person. Yet few projects succeed without the initial impetus of a reasonably clear idea. If a project fails—and failure occurs frequently in theatre—it is probably because the original idea was lost, misguided or compromised along the way. Or, perhaps, the motivation behind the idea was not clearly understood.

### The Motive of Fame

The most visible professionals in the performing arts world, of course, are the performers—those glamorous figures on the stage or screen whose magic can so easily fascinate us. Little wonder, then, that most people drawn to the performing arts start out wanting to be performers—and, almost certainly, famous ones at that.

There is nothing wrong with hoping to achieve eminence in one's profession. In fact, the person who lacks such motivation won't get very far. And for the artist a strong ego is essential, together with a selfless dedication to the creative process. This is particularly true in the performing arts where successful work depends on the collaboration of many people.   It is easier to grasp that a third violinist in a symphony orchestra must perform according to the dictates of the conductor and the score than it is to understand that a supporting actor must function in an equally disciplined and subservient manner. Generally speaking, people expect that actors can perform with much less training, if any, than other performing artists, with a much shorter apprenticeship, if any, and for a much lower salary, if any. Performers who wish to succeed in serious music, opera  or dance must spend an enormous amount of time, money and energy before they even dare hope for an audition with a leading professional organization. The local Barrymores in Peoria, however, can and often do go directly from the lead in a high school play to an audition in New York. Occasionally they may even land a role and become an overnight success. Except for pop music, theatre is the only branch of the live performing arts in which this can happen. But it happens far less frequently than beginners would like to believe; about as frequently, say, as winning a lottery. Most stars and hits that are acclaimed an overnight success are, in fact, the result of long years of hard work, training and self-sacrifice.

Apart from seeking fame in a wide, public sense, a number of people involve themselves in theatre to gain recognition and prestige in more limited ways. Being a Broadway producer, for example, or being cast in a commu-nity theatre production may bring entree into a certain social milieu. More than a few have become "angels," purchased a summer theatre or auditioned for a college theatre production for this reason alone. And many performing arts facilities have been financed by generous gifts from wealthy benefactors who wished to assert their social prominence by seeing their names carved in granite.

Theatre is by nature and necessity a public activity but, paradoxically, when its participants attempt merely to use the public for personal gain, the art of theatre is lost.

## The Motive of Money

If a performer achieves fame, fortune is not usually far behind.  In fact, fame is probably a prerequisite for high income in the case of performers. Managers and producers, however, have often become rich without becom-ing famous—though many have become notorious.

It is safe to guess that at least half of all theatrical productions in America are originated primarily to make money. Yet, profit is not a very good primary motivation if one hopes to produce something of artistic merit. It is also a rather peculiar motivation in light of statistics that prove how few theatrical productions show any real profit, whether on Broadway, in resident theatre, on the campus or in community theatre.

Like gambling on horses, investing in commercial theatre productions involves a high degree of risk. But there is a big difference between the professional investor or gambler and the neophyte. In the theatre there are producers, playwrights, designers, actors and managers whose qualifications are backed by solid accomplishments. This makes their projects a better risk than others, just as some jockeys, horses and racetracks are, to the person who takes the trouble to study them, better than others. Yet both fields are littered with stories of dark horses who have won as well as highly qualified contenders who have lost. Theatrical investors should know that the odds are stacked against them. Yet, at least for the wealthy, such investing may be a more amusing way to lose money than a day at the races. Or it may provide psychic rewards associated with involvement in a creative project, social rewards resulting from acquaintances with interesting and celebrated people or cultural rewards when the project is artistically successful.

If most Broadway shows seek to earn a profit, it is equally true that most community and amateur productions across the nation also aim to make money over expenses—even when the show is organized under the aegis of a nonprofit organization. The aim is often to raise money for a favorite local cause: new uniforms for the football team; instruments for the school band; the senior class trip to Washington; a new dance floor for the Elks Club. Such efforts, of course, are motivated by reasons that bear only the most casual relationship to the art of theatre. Broadway tycoons, then, are not the only people who see theatre in terms of a dollar sign.

## The Motive of Social Service

All art has social as well as educational value, but to qualify as art it must first and foremost communicate a universal truth about the human condition. So, for instance, there should be a great difference between a production of Shakespeare's *Henry IV* and a drama therapy session. The first is presumably motivated by a desire to achieve artistic goals (although a variety of valid secondary objectives is possible), while drama therapy is organized to achieve non-artistic, therapeutic objectives.

Service-oriented theatre includes such diverse forms as the industrial show (intended to demonstrate or promote manufactured products such as cars or shoes), *drama therapy* (intended as a psychologist's device by which patients may express and/or recognize their problems by funnelling their emotions through the portrayal of ostensibly fictional characters), *the role-playing exercise* (in which participants consciously assume roles in order to gain more insight from a lifelike situation than a book or lecture might

5

provide), *the agit-prop production* (intended to disseminate propaganda by theatrically agitating an audience and thereby moving it to take future action), and *guerrilla theatre* (also political in content and propagandistic in purpose). Except for industrial shows, these types of theatre usually don't employ professional actors. Performances do not take place in traditional theatre spaces, and the audiences do not pay an admission charge. These types of theatre, in short, deal primarily in the promotion of products or ideas or they attempt to instruct through the medium of theatrical involvement. Artistic achievement under such circumstances is secondary and sometimes even inappropriate.

## The Humanist Motivation

A humanist is a person who believes that truth can be discovered at least as quickly and well through the medium of a painting, a symphony or a play as it can through the medium of a geological equation. An artist is a humanist who is as passionately committed to the discovery of the truth as is the scientist. While not everyone who works in the theatre need strive to be an artist, everyone should possess a notion of the humanistic nature of art and of its ultimate quest. This is the first requisite for serious theatre and it allows little room for self-centered social, financial or political motivation. Truth is fiercely impersonal. Any person in theatre who is motivated by a passion for truth and a belief in the humanist approach should progress further in terms of artistic achievement than the person propelled by more selfish motivations. If something is not worth doing for its own intrinsic value—such as producing a play or starting a theatre company—then one should be honest about the limiting and probably self-defeating reasons for doing it and seriously question whether it should be done at all.

Americans have traditionally been fond of attaching a monetary, social, or political value both to their possessions and to their activities. Hopefully, new generations will increasingly measure the quality of life according to the beauty, joy and insight it contains as well as the material benefits. In search of a greater realization of life, more and more people may come to understand—as some have always understood—the humanizing force of the arts and their ability to expand our consciousness and sense of being human in a way that is both rewarding and penetrating. A humanist, then, is also a generalist, a person of deep intentions and broad horizons.

# STATING THE IDEA

## Clarity of Purpose

As mentioned earlier, an idea begins with one person. That person may be an impresario whose idea is to organize an annual international theatre festival. That person may be a stage director whose idea is to establish a theatre company devoted to reviving previously produced but critically unacclaimed American musicals. That person may be a successful television actor whose idea is to create the first company of astronaut actors who will relay their performances from outer space to earth-bound audiences. Thank heavens, the possibilities for different ideas are endless. And it is wise to remember that as many "crazy" ideas have proved successful as the "sensible" ideas that have flopped. If you are the person with the idea, you must nurture it, hold onto it with great tenacity and then, when the time is ripe, communicate and sell it to others who can help it grow to fruition. If you are not the person with the idea, then you should search out someone with vision and genius who has an idea to which you can subscribe and associate yourself with that person's project, company or institution.

After the basic, motivating idea for a theatre project has been acknowledged, more specific objectives should be formulated. In commercial theatre, where profit is the motive, the producer finds this to be an unnecessary step. Artistic directors and managers in all types of noncommercial theatre, however, must often concern themselves with clarifying and stating their goals and objectives and, importantly, their plans for achieving them. To ignore the fundamental process of planning (and many organizations do) is to risk the life of a project (or an entire company) and to guarantee confusion. It is also to admit the absence of a plan and the absence of a set of priorities, which may well invite or force other people to set goals and priorities.

While the originating idea for a theatre project is likely to be the brainchild of one person, it must eventually be discussed and agreed upon by others who will play leading roles in its fulfillment. There is bound to be disagreement regarding particulars. Any major goal requires considerable thrashing out before all those who are a party to it arrive at mutual understanding and agreement. Those who remain in fundamental disagreement should be eliminated from the project as soon as possible. Human relations being what they are, such action is difficult and painful more often than not. Philosophical honesty is, unfortunately, rare, and unity of purpose among people is a singular accomplishment. But it can be achieved if one is stubbornly unwilling to proceed without it—even at the risk of losing potential participants, diminishing initial enthusiasm or revising timetables and budgets. Unless agreement about the philosophy, the basic idea and the objectives behind a project is reached and, especially, well understood between the artistic and management leadership, at least half the organization will labor under false or wrongly construed assumptions or under none at all. The operational flaw that results when clarity of purpose is missing is the classic situation of people working at cross purposes. While formulating and communicating a clear statement of purpose may not alone guarantee a harmonious and successful operation, it is a vital first step in that direction.

## Statement of Purpose

Once a tenable idea for theatre has been conceived and a sufficient number of key people who embrace it enthusiastically have been gathered, what is called for is a brief sentence or paragraph that clearly states the central idea or philosophy upon which the project will be built. This is often called the "mission statement" and may or may not include or be followed by a short list of fairly specific objectives. The composition of a mission statement is in fact a legal requirement if and when the group incorporates and applies to the Internal Revenue Code for tax-exempt status, as will be discussed later in this chapter.

The idea that is expressed in a mission statement serves as the standard by which the success or failure of the venture is ultimately judged. The mission statement should be the real tyrant of the group—a henchman, a traffic cop that objectively, unceasingly, impersonally, demands obedience. Suppose that the major purpose of a theatre is to produce new plays of significance, but the directors of that theatre cannot discover any works they feel are significant. Their only honest decision is to produce no plays at all. On the other hand, if they manage to present plays that do measure up to their standards, but these attract only small audiences and disdain from the press, they may consider their theatre a success and those who judge them honestly will respect their integrity.*

While a primary goal of all theatre should be to establish and maintain standards of artistic excellence, the methodology for achieving this will vary. There are many instances in which the success of theatre is best served by compromise, but that does not include compromise in regard to fundamental goals and objectives. If this becomes necessary or desirable, the original project should be dissolved and a new one organized from the beginning.

## Communication of Purpose

To help maintain unity of purpose within a group, to keep a project on the road initially intended for it and to elicit germane criticism from its audience and the press, a theatre group should take every opportunity to proclaim its objectives. The mission and objectives should be frequently reiterated by board members and by the artistic and managerial leadership of the company. This is especially important when discussion centers upon one of the following:

> Long-range planning
> Policy implementation
> Organizational structure

*See also Chapter 6, "The Mission Statement"

Board member recruitment
Recruitment of top staff members
Interviewing potential new board or staff members
Repertory development and play selection
Marketing goals and strategies
Funding goals and strategies
Dismissal of top staff members
Renovation of plant or move to new facilities
Expansion or reduction of activities

In other words, the group's officially adopted mission should be central to the decision-making process at all times. Furthermore, it should be communicated to the public and the press on a regular basis so that the purpose and the goals of the organization are clear to the outside world. Not to do this would be tantamount to turning the company into an ostrich with its head buried in the sand. The most obvious and appropriate places for the mission statement to appear include:

The offering circular
The charter or constitution
Certificate of Incorporation
IRC Application for Recognition of Exemption
Brochures and other promotional literature
Playbills
Major advertisements
Employment applications
Operations manuals
Funding proposals and applications
Annual reports
Newsletters to subscribers
Follow-up reports to donors
In the lobby
Over the proscenium
In the sky

If it is worth turning an idea into reality, it would seem a waste if that idea were kept secret.

## ORGANIZING THE IDEA

When an idea for theatre can be clearly articulated and understood, when the primary motivation for activating the idea is also clear, then an appropriate type of theatre organization must be found (or founded) in which the concept may be produced in a manner consonant with the goals at hand. This is easier to accomplish if one is creating a theatre group from scratch than if one wishes to introduce a new artistic thrust into an existing theatre company. This is also the reason why the appointment of a new artistic director at an existing theatre is fraught with so much anguish and apprehension. If the company is to remain faithful to its stated mission, it must hire someone who will not take it in other directions. But what if the most qualified applicants wish to do exactly that?

This book divides methods of theatre production into six different categories, each with its own implicit goals, standards, motivations. managerial demands, and artistic potential: (1) commercial theatre; (2) nonprofit professional theatre; (3) stock and dinner theatre; (4) college theatre; (5) community theatre; and (6) presenting organizations. Part II deals with each of these in a separate chapter, but it is appropriate here to consider the broad artistic potential of each and how each may best serve an idea for theatre.

## Commercial Theatre

The professional, commercial theatre encompasses any venture or company that employs union actors and that aims to earn and distribute profits to its owners, partners and/or investors. The major types of commercial theatre are:

> Broadway
> Off-Broadway
> National (First Class) Companies
> Bus-and-Truck Companies
> Industrial Shows
> Theatre for Young Audiences
> Cabaret Theatre
> Stock Theatre
> Dinner Theatre

Stock and dinner theatres will be treated separately. Together with productions that might merit any of the above classifications, stock theatre could be produced either as a commercial or a nonprofit venture.

The expertise of producers in the commercial theatre lies mainly in their ability to correctly predict consumer demand for a product and then to acquire and market that product in a way that maximum profits are earned. Basically speaking, they operate like all other entrepreneurs. It is not usually the business of commercial producers to concern themselves with the growth and development of talent or the intellectual and spiritual needs of the artist—not unless such an investment of their time is likely to turn a profit. The commercial theatre industry spends little time and money on what is called "product development." Rare indeed is the commercial producer who maintains a budding playwright on stipend or underwrites a workshop theatre. Instead, such producers wait for nonprofit theatres to develop product and talent and then attempt to acquire it, produce it commercially and make a mint. This is not unethical, but it does seem rather irresponsible. The most common complaints heard from commercial theatre producers today— that costs are too high, that there is not enough product and that we rely too much on British imports—are exactly the same complaints that their predecessors were making over a hundred years ago! Yet now, as then, product development is largely left to the lonely efforts of underfunded theatre groups and impoverished artists. The one relatively recent development that has forced Broadway to help finance serious, nonprofit theatre companies is the enticement of acquiring and transferring a production more or less intact from a nonprofit theatre as David Rabe's *Streamers* was transferred to Broadway from the Long Wharf Theatre, as Lanford Wilson's *Burn This* was brought to New York from the Mark Taper Forum. Or for that matter as *Les Miserables* was brought to London's West End and subsequently to Broadway from the Royal Shakespeare Company. In such cases, although other producers and investors may share in the profits, the originating theatre may also receive a percentage of the show's earnings which it may then use to help finance its on-going activities. Commercial producers may also provide "enhancement money" in the form of contributions which may enable the nonprofit group to develop and stage a particular production.

While stories about profit and loss on Broadway have long been legend, it is true that skyrocketing costs have had a major impact on what and how much is produced and, importantly, what is not produced. Production budgets exceeding three million dollars are now commonplace. An ever-increasing percentage of these budgets is drained by escalating union, legal and accounting costs. As higher expenses drive up ticket prices, consumers in the lower income brackets, including most people under thirty years of age, are excluded from the audience. Non-musical plays with large casts and expensive production requirements go largely unproduced, as do classical plays and others with limited audience appeal. These works have found a home as well as an audience in the nonprofit theatres, but there, too, producers are under constant pressure to keep expenditures low and ticket income high.

Despite problems, the Broadway theatre continues to survive, to maintain remarkably high standards, to bring numerous artists to the attention of the public and the media and to provide product for resident, stock, college, and amateur theatre. The same may also be said of the commercial Off-Broadway theatre, although production has decreased in both theatre communities in recent years.

As one turns a critical eye to the artistic merits found in the other types of commercial theatre, standards are lower—sometimes a little, usually a lot—than they are in the New York commercial theatre. The health of business on the road generally reflects the health of the theatre business in New York. National touring companies are organized and controlled by the producers of the original Broadway production and usually duplicate most of the integrity of that production. The bus-and-truck tours, however, are packaged by production companies on a much more modest scale and are sent on the road to play short engagements in communities that could not support a long run by a first class company.

Industrial shows, by far the most commercial of all types of commercial theatre, really have no artistic aims at all. Rather, they attempt in a sleek and professionally competent way to promote or demonstrate a product or line of products—like cars or shoes—and are usually produced for groups of sales people or wholesale buyers. One might see something similar at a Disney park, where the performers are usually automated robots (and therefore work for less than union scale) or at a world's fair exhibition.

Cabaret theatre, an increasingly popular form of entertainment around the nation, usually adopts a one-person show or musical revue format and may be used to develop new talent or material for transfer to a larger commercial venue. Commercially operated children's theatre companies tend to be low on the artistic achievement scale, as will be discussed shortly.

Perhaps the reason it is so easy to denigrate commercial theatre ventures is that we know that ticket income is not used to support an on-going institution; it is used to make someone rich. Yet that person, that commercial producer, is working just as hard to make a living as is the managing director of a nonprofit theatre. They are simply two people who are approaching the business of producing professional theatre in different ways. There is no right way and there is no wrong way. There are merely good results and bad results, and only an audience can tell which is which. In this sense—and only in this sense—theatre is a very democratic art form.

## Nonprofit Professional Theatre

Any theatre or theatre company that operates as a nonprofit organization and employs union actors is considered to be a nonprofit professional theatre. It may also be called a "funded theatre" because it is legally eligible to accept tax deductible contributions from private, corporate and government sources, and it is also excused from paying property and sales taxes.

Many of the theatres in this category are called "resident theatres" and are members of the League of Resident Theatres (LORT), a management association that, among other functions, negotiates basic labor agreements with Actors' Equity Association and other unions. The nearly one hundred LORT theatres nationwide include the Seattle Repertory Theatre, Washington D.C.'s Arena Stage, and Circle in the Square in the heart of Broadway. Measured by the number of people employed, weeks of work and the number of performances given, LORT theatres now represent the single largest segment of the professional theatre industry. Artistic and managerial standards are high, and there is a great variety of production goals. Some LORT theatres are solely devoted to presenting the plays of Shakespeare (Berkeley Shakespeare Festival and Oregon Shakespeare Festival); one is the only permanent American touring theatre (The Acting Company); some concentrate on an ethnic repertory (EastWest Players, the American Jewish Theatre, INTAR); some on the musical repertory (Goodspeed Opera House, Music-Theatre Group/Lenox Arts Center); and still others on children's theatre, mime, and new plays. The majority of nonprofit  professional theatres (whether they operate under a LORT or other  contract with Equity) present seasons of plays drawn from a broad variety, but with an emphasis on the classics.

During the early years of what is now usually called the resident theatre movement (that is in the '50s and '60s), there was some confusion about what label should be given to this activity. At first "repertory theatre" seemed appropriate, perhaps because this word was contained in the names of many of the companies. Then "regional theatre" came to be used, because most of the companies were located outside New York City (apparently, nobody thought that New York City is also a region). Finally, because most of these theatres had a more or less permanent, resident staff and company of actors, the term "resident theatre" became accepted. "LORT theatre" is also loosely used to label all nonprofit professional theatres. Yet, most of these companies do  not maintain a permanent group of actors on salary—at least not for more than a season. Plays are rarely performed in repertory rotation or repeated after their first run of performances. *And only about one third of all the nonprofit professional theatres in America operate under a LORT contract.* What all such theatres do have in common is:

1. Incorporation
2. Tax-exempt status
3. A board of trustees
4. A managing director and/or an artistic director
5. At least one performer under some type of Equity contract.

Given these five characteristics, any company may be considered a nonprofit professional theatre.

While the LORT members tend to represent the larger theatres with the highest budgets, all nonprofit professional theatres aim for permanence. They aim to be on-going institutions. To succeed at this in a meaningful way, they must acquire professional artistic and managerial directors and pay them a living wage. And then they must do the same for a sizable company of artists and management support staff. While the administrative staff is usually hired for a full season or year, however, the artists (except for the artistic director and, in some cases, the production designers) are often hired for each production from an informal pool of talent—people whose work is well known to the artistic director. This policy has been particularly success-ful as practiced by the late Nikos Psacharopoulos at the Williamstown The-atre Festival, by Marshall Mason during his years at the Circle Repertory Company, by Joseph Papp at the New York Shakespeare Festival, by Arvin Brown at the Long Wharf Theatre, by Gordon Davidson at the Mark Taper Forum and by quite a few others. In fact a number of artistic directors have also formed a professional relationship with one or two playwrights, whose scripts they help to develop in workshops and then in full productions, which sometimes end up on Broadway.

Nonprofit theatre differs from commercial theatre in that it provides more opportunity to experiment, to explore, to work with the same artists on different productions, to undertake more classical or risky or new projects and to have the wonderful security of knowing that the whole thing won't close down tomorrow if a few critics pan the show or if ticket income fails to cover the costs. Of the various methods of producing theatre, then, this type of management structure may offer the best framework for artistic develop-ment.

While America has yet to create a national theatre of the stature of the Comedie Francaise, the Kabuki or the National Theatre in Great Britain, neither have we had the time to build the indigenous cultural traditions that stand behind those great repertory institutions. That would require an end to immigration plus about a millennium to evolve a cohesive cultural heritage! Meanwhile, the nonprofit professional theatre companies collectively form the closest thing we have—and a very precious resource it is—to a national American theatre.

## Stock and Dinner Theatre

Professional stock theatre, which provided more employment weeks annually for Equity actors during the '50s and '60s than any other branch of live theatre, suffered a steady decline during the '70s and '80s that is exactly parallel to the growth of nonprofit professional theatre. Not only may there be some justice in this, there may also be evidence here that American audiences are more discerning than they are usually given credit for. In any case, stock theatres—whether summer or winter, whether they present packaged touring shows with stars or maintain a resident company of Equity actors—are operated on a shoestring with all the attendant compromises in quality. Many a once successful professional stock or dinner theatre around the country now stands idle or is operated on an amateur basis without Equity actors. Nonetheless, as discussed in Chapter 7, stock and dinner theatres still provide many good opportunities both for theatre practitioners and audiences. Unfortunately, these are increasingly on the amateur level.

## College Theatre

College theatre productions are usually organized under the sponsorship of a theatre department or a theatre club of some kind. Such productions offer a mix of faculty and student participation, though it is common for mainstage productions to be directed and designed by faculty members. Smaller facilities, such as a "black box" theatre, may be given over entirely to graduate and undergraduate students with minimal faculty supervision.

Campuses with fairly large, well-equipped theatre facilities (and there are many) also may sponsor a series of professional performing-arts events, such as music and dance concerts and theatre productions. These are usually booked in by an administrator outside the academic departments, although this person may be advised by a student/faculty committee. Sometimes, especially in the case of dance companies, the visiting professional company conducts instructional workshops, provides lecture-demonstrations or coaching for appropriate students.

Whether theatre on the campus involves students or professionals, it is nonprofit theatre (nonprofit nonprofessional theatre, in the case of student/ faculty productions) because all colleges, both private and public, are nonprofit organizations. As the producer is usually the person or entity that provides the financing for a theatre production, in this case the academic institution itself is the producer, because it provides the facilities, the utilities, the faculty and staff that service the production and, very often, it covers the production costs that exceed box office income. So the theatre department alone is not the producer, much less the department chairperson or the stage director. The top of the title page in the playbill, then, should read, for example:

The University of Iowa
Department of Theatre
presents

The person or institution that finances a performance is traditionally the producer.

College theatres may not only offer lavish facilities but also provide a tie-in with a large institution that can furnish an enormous amount of fiscal, administrative, material and human resources found in no other type of theatre organization. But what of the artistic quality of most college theatre productions? Considering the available resources on the one hand and the fact that school plays are performed largely by amateurs on the other, the overall results are often disappointing. The reasons for this apparent paradox are mixed. The campus theatre may be attempting to appeal to too many types of audiences or it may overly compromise its priorities; its obligation to teach may fall victim to its desire to entertain audiences (not to mention its frequent need to maintain and increase a certain level of box-office income).

Due to its position within a large institution, a theatre department may lack the independence required to exercise artistic integrity or it may find itself bogged down in red tape. Perhaps, for example, it has no access to "soft money" and therefore must fill out a purchase requisition even to buy props or to wash costumes at the local laundromat. Theatre chairpeople— who may certainly be considered a type of theatre manager—often spend an inordinate amount of time translating the realities of theatre production into language that college comptrollers, budget directors, deans and presidents can understand.

Fortunately, in the recent past there has been a growing professionalization in the management of both campus theatre departments and campus theatres. It is increasingly common, for instance, to find someone with a graduate degree in arts management who is teaching at least one management course in the department and also managing the department productions, perhaps the theatre facility itself and maybe a summer theatre season as well. Large campus performing arts centers are now usually headed by professionally trained arts managers and staffed by competent, experienced administrators. These centers also, as a rule, employ a number of student interns from the institution and thereby provide valuable, entry-level training for many of the arts managers of tomorrow.

From the audience point of view campus theatre usually provides a chance to see plays not usually performed elsewhere and at low ticket prices. From the faculty point of view, it provides employment opportunities that are not readily available elsewhere. From the student viewpoint, however, the benefits are less focused. Is theatre a trade, a profession or an art? Do theatre studies belong in the humanities or in the fine arts? Do they belong in the liberal arts college or in the conservatory? If an artist can be educated or trained in any traditional sense, is this best accomplished in an institution or by apprenticeship to a master? Definitive answers to such questions have yet to be found.

Nothing will have a stronger impact on the future of the performing arts than how they are treated—or ignored—by our educational institutions. Included in these, although outside the purview of this book, are the almost countless number of primary and secondary schools that comprise our public education system. For a few shining moments during the 1960s there was an infusion of federal money that supported numerous arts programs in the public schools.  But this soon evaporated and once again left arts education entirely at the discretion of local school boards, politicians and voters.  The resulting near disappearance of the arts in public schools is alarming, especially from the viewpoint of developing future audiences.  At least during the late 1980s there was a growing concern and a growing amount of literature in support of arts education.* Perhaps through community action, leadership from both arts and education circles and lobbying in the halls of government, arts education (as well as the arts in education) will find its rightful place in the public school system.  Few areas of arts management offer greater challenges.

## Community Theatre

A nonprofessional theatre is, simply, one comprised of people who do not derive their income from it and do not spend most of their time engaged in it.  There are two distinct categories:  (1) nonprofessional groups that present plays with some regularity; and (2) nonprofessional groups that are organized on a one-time basis to present a play or a show for some special purpose.  The former represents what is known as community theatre, and the latter falls under the heading of amateur theatre (though both types are amateur, or nonprofessional).

In spite of limited resources and volunteer labor, the artistic quality of many community theatre productions can be surprisingly good.  The annual production of Paul Green's *The Lost Colony* in North Carolina, an outdoor historical pageant similar in spirit to the Passion plays presented at Oberammergau, represents community theatre in its truest sense. Often, however, the local theatre club tends to produce recent Broadway musicals and comedies, placing too little emphasis on the continuing development of its individual members, either in terms of their abilities or their knowledge of theatre and dramatic literature.

Children's theatre companies that utilize adult performers, though they are often headed by a full-time director, also fall into the category of amateur theatre.  Even those that earn considerable income and operate under Equity contracts often possess the unmistakable mark of amateurism.  In contrast to the commercially motivated companies are the professional ensembles that present performances specially adapted for children, such as those once

---

produced by the Metropolitan Opera Studio Company, the Joffrey Ballet or the Young Peoples Concerts first popularized by Leonard Bernstein and the New York Philharmonic. And few artists have done more to motivate children to love the arts than dancer/choreographer Jacques d'Amboise and his Emmy- and Oscar-winning network of dance-theatre-in-education programs known as the Dance Theatre Institute. The artistic quality of performances resulting from these and similar efforts is strikingly superior to the trite and condescending quality of most troupes that call themselves "professional children's theatre."

When nonprofessional theatre operates under the guidance of dedicated and knowledgeable leaders, when work is carried out with an honest realization of the limitations at hand, when the group is dedicated to theatre for its own sake and not merely to trying to seek approbation or ape the commercial stage, the result should at least prove satisfactory. Certainly there is nothing heinous about amateur theatre as such. It has the potential for providing a celebration of life that the average citizen may be otherwise missing, and that is justification enough.

## Presenting Organizations

More live entertainment is offered by presenting organizations in America than by any other branch of the performing arts business. Of course, performances include pop music as well as serious music, stand-up comedians as well as ballet companies and acrobats as well as actors. And the performance venues include Carnegie Hall and community centers, the Kennedy Center for the Performing Arts and public schools, The White House and local parks and recreation departments, both commercial and public television networks, the YWCA and the local library. Every private and public organization in America is entitled to present performances of one kind or another and it seems most of them are doing exactly that. Many such productions or performances have been produced (packaged is a better word) by an agency, manager or promoter on a profit-making basis. Yet presenting organizations also sponsor an enormous number of serious music, dance and theatre performances that have been produced by both American and foreign companies. The majority of symphony orchestras and other musical ensembles, as well as classical and modern dance companies, simply could not sustain themselves without the booking fees they earn from presenting organizations. In recognition of the role these venues play in supporting the performing arts, most arts councils now fund presenting organizations directly—which is an indirect way of funding the performance companies that they present.

Presenters are really wholesalers who buy a finished product and then attempt to resell it, either for personal or institutional gain. This eliminates the creativity involved in originating a production, but it may provide the satisfaction of exposing a community to professional theatre of a higher quality than is otherwise available to it. When profit is the primary motive for importing packaged shows—which is more often the case with theatre and pop music presentations than with touring opera, dance and concert events— the presenter tends to engage what is most popular or novel rather than what is artistically viable. And because profit is the motivation much of the time— both from the producer's and the star performer's point of view—an enormous amount of second-rate theatre is packaged and sent to the hinterland. Broadway hits, performed with skill if not always with genius, are transformed into touring vehicles for film and television personalities unused to live audiences and live acting, though their salaries may be so astronomical as to make the presenter's margin of profit negligible.But there are also very worthwhile performers and productions available. The most successful nonprofit presenters recognize a two-fold obligation to cultivate audience support while also cultivating unfamiliar work and new talent.

## INCORPORATING THE IDEA

Certificates of incorporation and legal regulations are not among the most glamorous aspects of theatre, but they represent the structural core of any proposal for a professional theatre production or company. As the type of organization formed should directly relate to the goals of the venture, so the legal structure should be consonant with the motivating idea. It would be hypocritical, for instance, to dedicate a theatre to civic or educational ideals and then to operate it as a profit-taking enterprise. Several Broadway producers are fond of arguing that when nonprofit theatres such as the Vivian Beaumont at Lincoln Center, the Ahmanson at the Los Angeles County Music Center or the Eisenhower at the Kennedy Center present big stars in popular hits, they offer unfair competition to commercial producers, who must operate without the subsidization or tax advantages enjoyed by nonprofit theatres. Similarly, there have been cases of privately owned, commercially operated stock theatres in close proximity to nonprofit stock theatres, both of which were presenting the same star package productions and competing for the same audience. These situations pose some very interesting questions.

Whether the aim is to show a profit for individual owners or investors, or to achieve some higher goal, which kinds of legal structures are most commonly used in the theatre business?

## Profit-Taking Ventures

Anyone wishing to operate a business for the main purpose of earning and distributing profits to its owners and/or investors has the option of organizing as:

1. An unincorporated company, association or partnership
2. A private corporation
3. A public corporation

The unincorporated company, whether it is individually or jointly owned, is financed exclusively by the owner(s), who enjoys full decision-making power and considerable freedom from various legal regulations, excluding the tax laws. However, such owners also assume full personal liability, which means that all their personal assets may be attached in order to settle any debts incurred by their business dealings. Many theatre artists and groups begin in this manner, but few are willing to take the attendant risks for very long.

One type of unincorporated business structure that avoids these hazards and insures legal protection for the investors as well as accountability from its principals is the Limited Partnership Agreement; this is used as the legal instrument for producing virtually all commercial Broadway and Off-Broadway productions.* It is an effective method for attracting investors to such highly speculative ventures as race horses, gold mines, film productions, and Broadway shows. The general partners, or producers, control these ventures fully. The limited partners, also called investors or angels, only earn money or lose money by sharing in the profits or losses according to the amount of their individual investments. The Limited Partnership Agreement was adapted for use by the commercial theatre by the late attorney John Wharton and is sometimes called the Wharton Agreement. It is the simplest means yet devised for producers in this arena to cope with the law and with such agencies as the Securities and Exchange Commission. Aside from the general partners, investors or limited partners in this type of theatrical entity may not themselves be active participants in the project they have financed.

In previous centuries many theatrical companies were financed by means of a shareholding scheme. In early American theatre the investor/partners were usually actors in the company itself. Although this system creates a more personalized business—like being part of a commune—and is still practiced by a few theatre groups today, it is not feasible as a method for financing very costly ventures. Also, as the actor-managers of early American theatre companies learned, when a company is comprised of shareholding actors who possess the right to establish policy and make decisions by vote, the manager or artistic head is denied the autocratic power necessary in most

*See Chapter 5

theatrical endeavors. They learned, as Rudolf Bing once phrased it, that "a theatre should be a democracy—run by one person!" Using the Wharton Agreement, the producers (being the general partners) exercise total control.

A corporation, on the other hand, is legally separate from the lives of its officers, shareholders or participants and has perpetual life unless it is legally dissolved. There are three basic types of corporations: private; public; and nonprofit.

Law stipulates that all corporations must have officers and a board of directors or trustees. Private corporations may only have several officers, who may also be the sole owners of the business as might be the case with a privately owned stock or dinner theatre, a chain of Broadway and road theatres or a talent agency. In contrast, public corporations offer shares to the public through the stock market and are controlled by officers on a board of directors who are elected by vote of the shareholders. While this type of corporate structure is common to huge television networks and film companies, it is a great rarity in the theatre. But there is always an exception, such as the New York musical production *The Little Prince*, based on the widely known novel of the same name by Antoine de St. Exupery. Joseph Tandet, the producer of this vehicle, offered shares to the public through the stock exchange and quickly raised the necessary capital. Although the show never opened on Broadway, the corporation was not dissolved and by means of its other activities has even managed to distribute a few dividends to its shareholders. But this is a singular case.

## *The Nonprofit Corporation*

Nonprofit corporations are not organized in order to go bankrupt or lose money any more than profit-taking corporations. But they do confess to a greater awareness of financial risk. While they endeavor to remain solvent, they vary in the amount of capital and collateral that they maintain—their holdings are also dictated in varying degrees by government regulations. Recent laws, for example, have made it more difficult for nonprofit corporations to be used by wealthy individuals as a tax dodge. They must be active according to their stated objectives, which is to say they must regularly expend a certain percentage of their holdings. All public or tax supported institutions, religious organizations and charities—and hence all theatres operated by them—are nonprofit structures functioning in trust.

Aside from being comparatively selfless in nature, the privately controlled nonprofit corporation possesses numerous advantages as a fiscal and legal structure for serious theatre projects. In contrast to profit-taking corporations, the nonprofit corporation is free from the burden of considerable taxation, can more easily recruit volunteer help, will more likely receive gifts,

21

donations and grants, and stands a greater chance of establishing itself as an institution that will outlive its founders.

The most obvious disadvantage of operating a theatre on a nonprofit basis is that its artistic head will be required to function under a board of trustees. If this usually austere and sometimes uninformed body is willing to allow the director considerable freedom in dictating policy, the enterprise has a fighting chance to run smoothly and successfully. But, as is often the case, if there is a great deal of interference from the board, the result may be friction, fragmentation and a low quality of theatre product.

## WHEN THE IDEA BECOME A WORKABLE PLAN

Any idea for theatre, be it a play, a production, a building or an organization, is a special idea. Potentially, it can enlighten, enhance and expand the lives of many people. But is it a feasible idea?

The hopeful producer or several managers of a project will do well to re-examine the idea behind it before turning to the arduous business of incorporating, staffing, fundraising, financing, casting, marketing, bookkeeping and bootlicking; before getting lost in a hailstorm of decisions about dimmer boards, acoustics, air conditioning systems and computers; before developing ulcers over zoning laws, building permits, fire laws and labor unions. Are answers easily forthcoming to the six W's: *why; what; where; when; who; wherewith?* Has the idea been tested and tried as much as possible without actually being put into full operation? Again, as many good ideas will be disallowed when put to the test as crazy ideas will be proved workable. But no idea has the magical power to translate itself into action. This can only be done by its agents.

# 2

# The Manager
# For The Idea

THE actor-managers who controlled the first century of professional theatre in America, roughly from 1750 to 1850, were too naive about business affairs to effect a successful transition from an agrarian to an industrialized nation. The businessmen who replaced them and controlled the professional American theatre during its second hundred years, roughly from 1850 to 1950, largely deserted live theatre for more lucrative enterprises when theatre ceased to offer easy profits. By the late 1950s—at the dawn of a third century of American theatre—a new breed of manager began to evolve.

## THE THIRD-CENTURY MANAGER

Years ago George Bernard Shaw defined the role of a manager by commenting that every artistic director in theatre should be followed around by a hard-minded businessman, whose main job should be to cut all production budgets by half. And that is essentially what the second-century manager did, thereby creating a villainous, penny-squeezing, Scrooge-like image of theatre managers and producers which, in the commercial sector, retains some validity to this day. But more and more we are coming to the realization that, while economy remains important, the manager must assume other responsibilities if theatre is to survive. To do this it must broaden its base and become more responsive to the spirit and needs of our large, pluralistic society. The Rockefeller Panel Report, *The Performing Arts: Problems and Prospects*, published in 1965, recognizes these new responsibilities by defining a good arts manager as:

> . . . a person who is knowledgeable in the art with which he is concerned, an impresario, labor negotiator, diplomat, educator, publicity and public relations expert, politician, skilled businessman, a social sophisticate, a servant of the community, a tireless leader—becoming humble before authority—a teacher, a tyrant and a continuing student of the arts.

Obviously, this is no ordinary creature! But, of course, art is no ordinary business.

The third-century arts manager must be a person of taste, sensitivity and erudition whose inclinations and education make that person able to seek, recognize, support and develop the genius of artistic originality in whatever guise it may appear. Because the guise is likely to be unusual, if not startling, this process may also require a lot of self-confidence and a lion's share of courage. It may require the person to be a facilitator of fantasies, a mover and a shaker, a Diaghilev, a Margo Jones. Administrative, financial and promotional know-how in the arts are wasted when not complemented by such qualities.

Like a good umpire, a good manager must have the ability to keep an eye on the ball and on the goal lines—and must also believe in the rules and enjoy the game. When leaders of any kind in any field lose their sense of vision and purpose, those below them almost always follow suit. Lack of purpose, an atmosphere of insecurity, pettiness, superficiality, infighting and disunity always reflect absence or failure of leadership. To gain respect and establish authority by consensus, an uncommon amount of fairness, manifested by a willingness to sacrifice personal reward for the good of others and for the success of artistic objectives, is necessary. Only then will the manager be able to function as a convincing translator of policy between the organization and the public, and between factions within the organization itself.

## EDUCATION AND TRAINING
## FOR THE THIRD-CENTURY MANAGER

What type of background, education and training is apt to produce a person with the qualities and capabilities to guide the American theatre successfully in the twenty-first century?

Basic patterns of behavior, sympathies and directions that will eventually comprise a lifestyle are developed early. Formal education can only draw out and broaden one's inherited and acquired inclinations. We can train doctors, musicians and managers in their respective skills, but we cannot create a scientist or a humanist as such. In the arts the widest vocabulary of human sensitivities is desirable, the deepest awareness of the needs and feelings of life, an instinctual response to the heartstrings of humanity. An early and continuing exposure to the arts, and confrontation with a variety of the world's cultures and societies may also broaden the humanist orientation. Such experience and qualities are necessary if the arts manager is to recognize the visionary insights of artistic creativity, feel comfortable in their presence and confident in leading others toward them.

It is not surprising when a child of twelve wants to become an actor or a ballet dancer, but it would be more than precocious if that child wanted to become an arts administrator. In fact, it would seem premature for a person even as a college undergraduate to select a career in arts management. Just as the pediatrician must first learn general medicine, the theatre manager must first learn the arts. The first century of American theatre managers, like the first century of American physicians, had neither the resources nor the knowledge to indulge in much specialization. They were all generalists. Second-century American managers, rather like miracle workers and quacks, were outsiders from the professional point of view. They were specialists without portfolio. Third-century managers must be educated about the profession they serve and committed to its ideals.

High quality education at any level and at any price is difficult to obtain. Up to the college years a broad exposure to the basic disciplines, an accumulation of basic skills and a rough realization of one's intellectual and emotional characteristics are the minimum accomplishments to be desired. Most valuable of all is the development of a compulsive intellectual curiosity, without which it is impossible to live a full and meaningful life. Indeed, curiosity is such a strong motivating force that it can impel a person to hurdle the most overwhelming odds, including those of disadvantaged background and poor education. If it is coupled with energy and determination, then extraordinary achievement is not only possible but likely.

While an undergraduate concentration in theatre management runs the risk of limiting the student's outlook too early, a single course in this subject should be required, if for no other reason than to make students aware that arts management is a viable career option to performing, playwriting and teaching, and that there are graduate programs set up to train professional arts managers. The syllabus in Appendix A suggests what units of study might be appropriate for an undergraduate course in theatre management offered by a department of theatre. Or this course could easily be adapted to fit the needs of music or dance majors or applied to the performing arts field as a whole.

Very few people today achieve a position of leadership—or even professional status—without the benefit of an undergraduate education. Once that has been completed, the basic career options are:

1. Enroll in a graduate program
2. Attempt to gain on-the-job training
3. Serve an internship
4. Attend specialized workshops, seminars and conferences
5. Travel and pursue self-instruction
6. Aim to combine some or all of the above.

Not everyone is ready or able to proceed immediately from undergraduate to graduate school; some will never find this necessary for success. However, if and when this is the choice, decisions must be made about the type of program to enter and the institution to select. MBA programs in graduate schools of business or management and MFA programs that specialize in arts administration are both viable alternatives. In any event, it is now quite common to read as part of a job description in this field: "graduate degree in arts administration preferred."

A master's program in arts management should require two to three years of study and include field work and internship experiences under professional supervision at established arts companies and organizations. The program may include long-established courses in economics, law, business and fine arts. But at least a few specialized seminars that aim to convey the environment peculiar to arts organizations should be taught by adjunct faculty who are practicing professionals. Classroom work should emphasize analytical and original thinking; current practices should be challenged by new and different theories. The list of course titles in Appendix B suggests a creditable graduate program in performing arts management.

Instead of graduate school, one might proceed directly into the job market or even begin one's own business or theatre company. While this approach works for some, it is often the long route to success. It also requires a lot of good luck to learn and to grow without some kind of professional instruction.

Internships in the performing arts world are now an accepted part of doing business. Virtually every company or organization—commercial or nonprofit—has or wants interns working in almost every area of activity. Interns may be high school students or senior citizens, paid or not paid, short-term or long-term, vocationally or avocationally interested in the arts. The internship opportunities themselves may offer go-fer work or meaningful responsibilities; penal-like surveillance or caring supervision; limited or broad access to the organization's files, records, personnel and artistic process. Almost anybody can walk into an arts organization and get some type of internship. Yet it is usually better if the intern has an impartial adviser (an academic program head, a professional counselor or someone from an appropriate arts service organization), who can help place the intern with the right position in the right company, who can mediate any problems that arise and who can assist in the transition from internship to job placement.

Workshops, seminars and conferences that deal with particular facets of arts management (finance, marketing, fundraising, etc.) or with very specific skills (cost accounting, graphic design, corporate grant research, etc.) are offered frequently in many parts of the country by a variety of arts service organizations, membership associations, arts councils and colleges. They provide a way for the neophyte to test the waters, for the arts management student to gain additional instruction, for the practitioner to brush up and for those in leadership positions to glimpse the skills needed by their staff members. These brief sessions, however, do not pretend to replace the more traditional training methods.

Sending young people abroad to "finish" their character has been a traditional part of the educational process for centuries. Travel that includes some kind of formal or informal instruction is still likely to be a memorable if not mind-shaping experience for most young adults. Familiarity with foreign cultures and foreign languages is also a major asset to managers, as the performing arts become increasingly internationalized through touring activities, festivals, cultural exchange and media exploitation.

Finally, there is the matter of continuing education. It is easy for the busy professional to become so wrapped up in day-to-day activities that little time is found to devote to continuing development, both as a professional and as an individual. This requires reading, traveling, attending performances and exhibitions, being active in at least a half dozen national organizations and in numerous local groups, attending seminars and workshops, and otherwise keeping abreast of the times and the profession. While maintaining an objective overview of the manager's own operations is crucial, so also is the matter of nurturing and polishing a viable world view by allowing time for thought and reflection and for a full life emotionally.

## THE SPECIAL ROLE OF THE PRODUCER
## OR BOARD OF TRUSTEES

A producer in the commercial theatre, and a board of trustees for a nonprofit performing arts company or institution, share a common distinction. They both initiate a process that is intended to result in public theatre performances and they both bear the final responsibility for the activities they initiate. The people who work under them—whether it is one person or a thousand—are all filling supportive roles.

Producers and trustees, of course, are also managers in that they are involved (in varying degrees) in such fundamental management functions as planning, organizing, staffing, supervising, and controlling.

As shown in tables of organization in this book and many others, there are always two types of experts who are hired by and report *directly* to the producer or the board. These experts are: (1) a certified public accountant or accounting firm; and (2) a lawyer or law firm. They are usually paid an annual retainer plus additional fees based on services they render over and above those specified in a basic agreement. Of course, nonprofit organizations sometimes receive such services on a pro bono basis (without charge). In any case, the accountant and the lawyer are meant to scrutinize all financial and legal ramifications of the production, corporation and/or institution, and report any real or potential discrepancies to the organizer or owner of the venture (the producer) or the chief officer of the corporation (the chairperson of the board).  So they serve as advisers to the producer or board and as watchdogs over the support managers and other employees. The accountant, for example, conducts regular audits of the books, the bank records and the box office, and the lawyer routinely checks contracts, agreements and policy decisions. All of this underscores the fact that the producer or the board has the final responsibility (and personal liability) for all financial and legal matters pertaining to the company or corporation which they oversee.  Support staffers are literally held accountable for their methods of conducting business, but the producer or the board originates that business in the first place, defines its goals and, in the end, must take final credit or blame for the results.

The commercial producer must raise most of the capital needed for a venture before anything except a small percent can be spent. Most of this money comes from investors (who, incidentally, are prohibited by law from being managers in the venture if it is organized as a limited partnership, which some commercial productions are). The primary goal, of course, is to make as much profit as possible. If, however, there is no profit, and there are outstanding debts after all the capital has been spent, then the producer is personally liable.  No other manager or employee related to the venture bears this responsibility (unless, of course, a criminal offense has been committed).  Although laws pertaining to the fiscal liabilities of trustees for nonprofit corporations are very different, trustees, too, may be personally responsible for outstanding debts under certain circumstances.  And, again, these liabilities are not shared by corporate employees.

Producers and trustees may and often do delegate most duties and responsibilities—but they must always be mindful of the special position they hold at the top of the organizational hierarchy and of the special obligations that go with it.

## BASIC MANAGEMENT FUNCTIONS

In these days of monumental performing arts centers, flashy musicals with automated scenic effects and dizzying budgets, it is easy to forget that theatre is, fundamentally, a very simple process. Only four elements are necessary in order for a theatrical performance to occur:

1. *Creative raw material* (an idea, a scenario, a script)
2. *A person to interpret the material* (an actor, a dancer, a singer, a priest, a witch doctor)
3. *A place to present the material* (a theatre, a church, a barn, a street, a clearing in the woods)
4. *An audience to witness the performance.*

The more this process, this act of theatre, is formalized, the more support personnel, equipment and money it requires. From the first Dionysian theatre festival in Athens in 535 BC, until shortly after World War II, most performing arts companies and ventures—large and small, commercial and institutional—could be organized and managed quite nicely by a single artist-manager and a small staff or, in the case of commercial production, by a thoroughly independent producer or impresario. But with the shift of wealth in our economy from individuals to publicly owned corporations, with complex new tax laws and other government regulations and with the growing power of labor unions, the producer or artistic head of any sizable performing arts enterprise requires a general manager who has the ability to deal with this complicated new world. At first it was possible for a single top manager and limited staff in all but the largest institutionalized companies to run things, though private consultants might be called in to assist with particular problems. But by the early 1970s—encouraged in no small part by the growth of increasingly sophisticated technologies—it became necessary for medium and large size theatre companies to hire a management support staff comprised of specialists in finance, marketing, publicity, fundraising, operations and perhaps other areas such as touring and outreach. A long way from three boards and a passion!

To whatever extent responsibilities are shared with others, a theatre manager is any person who plays a part in bringing together or facilitating two or more elements in the above list, thereby contributing to the realization of a theatrical performance. From the economist's point of view, a manager is any person who helps bring labor and capital together in order to produce an end product. To the sociologist, a theatre manager may be anyone who has influence over the organizational behavior of a given internal and/or external theatre environment or universe. Thus a manager may be an agent who finds performers to interpret a particular script, a publicity director who finds an audience for the performers, a theatre operator who provides the place where the performance is held or a general manager who supervises the entire process from beginning to end. A manager is a matchmaker who helps bring together the idea, the artist, the place and the audience. More specifically, a manager is anyone involved in the following functions:

1. *Planning*
2. *Organizing*
3. *Staffing*
4. *Supervising*
5. *Controlling*

All these functions involve decision-making, which means that a manager is a person who makes decisions as opposed to merely giving advice or opinions. According to this definition, lawyers and accountants are not managers (except in their own offices, if they supervise at least one employee). Similarly, professional consultants are not managers, since they, too, merely provide advice so that managers can make decisions.

What does managerial decision-making entail?

## Planning

The commercial producer decides upon a property to produce (a drama, a comedy, a musical, a one-person show) and a venue in which to produce it (Broadway, stock, tour, cabaret). The board of a nonprofit theatre determines the mission or overall artistic goals, policies and objectives for the company. Taking these factors as usually unalterable "givens," supporting managers must then attempt to devise the best strategies to insure the greatest and most appropriate kind of success. This requires setting priorities, establishing major deadlines and composing a budget. Such actions mark the real beginning of how an idea or a dream is turned into a reality. Staff managers usually work closely with the producer or the board during this initial planning process, to insure that the motivating idea or mission doesn't get lost. Yet, while decisions made at this point may be critical to the life of the project, they should not be written in stone. Creative projects tend to grow organically as they are fed by human energies. In most cases, therefore, plans must be changed as the company's personnel increases and as the production develops artistically.

## Organizing

Once a general battle plan has been drawn up, available resources must be organized in a manner that attempts to maximize their value. How, for instance, should authority and responsibility be delegated? This would be a good point at which to design a line chart or table of organization that shows all job titles connected by lines that indicate the chain of command. This, too, is subject to change. During the hiring and job orientation process, it may be found that one person can do what had been planned as two jobs; that two valued employees work best when they work apart; or that a particular position is unnecessary.

This might also be a good point to draw up work manuals. These booklets are meant to describe how to carry out a set of duties (such as the stage manager's duties of calling a show or the house manager's duties in the event of an emergency), and to describe these so clearly that any idiot could pick up the manual and perform the job without prior training. For this reason a work manual is sometimes referred to as an idiot book. If the project or the theatre is being staffed for the first time, work manuals are usually written by the first person to hold each supervisory position and then revised and enhanced by their successors, though always with top management's approval.

Organizational decisions must also be made in regard to legal and contractual procedures, fiscal recordkeeping and banking procedures; marketing methods, including ticket sales and distribution procedures; operations systems, including computers, stage systems, synthesizers, telecommunications systems; and the latest gizmo just acquired by the competition.

## Staffing and Casting

It is the prerogative of the commercial producer not only to hire a general manager and all the leading artists, but also to have the veto over all hiring and firing in connection with the project at hand. In reality some producers play a very active role while others leave everything except play selection and financing to a general manager. In nonprofit theatres, the board hires one or two people to take the artistic and managerial leadership and, except for giving advice, should then allow that leadership to do the rest of the play selection and the hiring. If the company is not run according to the board's liking over a reasonable period of time, then it should dismiss the management leaders and replace them with candidates more to their liking. Rarely, however, should the board involve itself directly in casting or any kind of decision-making about hiring anyone except the top personnel. The grace period given to employees is considerably shorter in the commercial than in the nonprofit sector of the industry. Perhaps this is because a producer's reputation is based on whether the last *show* produced was a success or a failure, whereas the nonprofit theatre's reputation is more likely based on whether the last *season* was a success or a failure.

Staffing and casting involves what may be a lengthy, complicated and frustrating process. It usually involves job advertising, interviewing and auditioning. It may also involve executive employment agencies or "headhunters," casting directors, talent representatives and personal managers. The first objective in staffing and casting for a theatre must be to establish unity and teamwork, whether on stage or off. In both areas it is advisable to fit people to available jobs and roles rather than to fit overly defined jobs and roles to the people available. In other words, it is much easier and wiser to redefine job requirements or role characteristics than it is to insist upon some set of preconceived qualifications. Naturally, there must be faithfulness to the central, motivating idea.The challenge is to discover a solution that enhances the job in question without compromising the project. Creative energy may well be the most difficult of all forces to place in harness and put to work.

## Supervising

As employees are added to a production or organization, they should be properly greeted, oriented, trained and then given on-going supervision. In a comparatively short time the groundwork that will determine an employee's effectiveness is laid. Yet, as often as not, the few hours or minutes it takes to get a new staff member off to the right start are not provided. This is perhaps the most classic error in personnel management. It is like handing a bag of money to a bank teller and then walking away without having opened an account.

Effective personnel management is aimed at orienting everyone in the same direction, encouraging everyone to embrace the main goals of the project, to understand the product, and, in short, to march to the same tune behind the same piper.

After the major goals have been set, the play or season selected, the financing secured and the staff and cast employed, all subsequent decisions are secondary. Like it or not, by this time the major decisions have been made and, short of starting all over again, are largely irrevocable. Many projects have met failure simply because their primary *raison d'etre* was forgotten or fatally compromised along the way. A good supervisor is able to keep an eye on the final goal and to encourage the teamwork and productivity necessary for achieving it.

While individual department heads in both the artistic and administrative areas must supervise their specialized support staff, the general manager must be concerned with coordinating these departmentalized efforts, nurturing productive interdepartmental relationships and, in short, seeing that all the pieces are being shaped so that they will eventually fit into a single, complete and perfectly solved puzzle.

## Controlling

The business of controlling a project is a matter of analyzing and correcting the weak spots and of perceiving and bolstering the strong spots. It is a matter of checking and balancing, of shifting and adapting, of inspecting and evaluating, of slowing down and speeding up—but always of pushing the project toward its intended destination.

Being in control as a manager means being objective and able to keep one's personal likes and dislikes subservient to the artistic goals of the project. Making changes or corrections in the way an organization is run, unfortunately, usually results in making one or more persons unhappy. Providing constructive criticism, forcing an employee to retrain for a job, demoting an old time staffer to a lesser job for less pay or having to fire someone are not the kinds of responsibilities that most managers savor. Yet they are integral to the process of what is euphemistically called "product control." Because the human condition is central to all artistic work, it is perhaps more painful to hurt someone's feelings in the theatre than in other industries where the end result is seen more coldly to justify the means. However, it *is* sometimes necessary to fire the director or the leading lady, or the marketing manager or the janitor. The real trick is to perceive *when* a project is in trouble, *why* it is in trouble and *what precisely* can be done to correct matters.

The ideal method for managing any project is to organize the fundamental elements so thoroughly and well that, once it is under way, its directors and managers can devote their full attention to coping with minor or unexpected developments—plenty of which are certain to arise.

The ideal manager for a theatre project is not necessarily someone with a Ph.D. in arts management. He or she does not necessarily have a background in economics or management—or, for that matter, in the arts. *The ideal manager for an idea is one who embodies it and makes it work.*

## TYPES OF THEATRE MANAGERS

Having evolved a definition of theatre management in our time, it might be helpful to review the various job titles most commonly given to theatre managers or others who work in the broader field of the arts as a whole. All the titles listed below are held by people who make decisions, who supervise at least one other person and who fulfill the other management functions. In most cases the titles for assistants and support staff members have not been shown, although many such positions exist and many are also managerial.

## VOLUNTEER LEADERSHIP POSITIONS

### Board of Trustees Officer and/or Member

Responsible for the legal, fiscal and overall conduct of a nonprofit corporation, trustees serve without salary, appoint the head artistic/managerial employees, determine long-range policy and provide advice and assistance to key staff members. They may also directly or indirectly contribute money or in-kind services to the organization.

## Government Arts Council Chairperson and/ or Member

There now exists in the United States on the federal, state and local levels a far-reaching network of arts councils whose chairpeople and members are appointed by the President, the state governors and the city mayors, respectively. The President appoints the chair and members of the National Council for the Arts, which oversees the staff and activities of the National Endowment for the Arts (NEA). Another council oversees the National Endowment for the Humanities (NEH). These agencies provide funding for the state arts councils, of which there are fifty-six, including American Samoa, Guam, the Northern Marianas, Puerto Rico, the Virgin Islands and the District of Columbia; these are also members of the National Assembly of State Arts Associations. And there are over fifteen-hundred city, local and community arts councils that receive funding from state councils, as well as from local governments and private and corporate sources. All government-appointed council members serve without salary and have no legal authority. They function in much the same manner as a board of trustees. Their primary responsibilities are to provide subsidies to individual artists, projects and organizations by awarding grants or "contracts"; provide technical assistance; present arts programs to the public and in schools; and disseminate information about the arts.

## United Arts Fund Volunteer Executives

United arts funds are service organizations that raise money through federated or joint appeals to individuals, corporations, foundations and government sources. Volunteer executives often supervise a salaried staff to solicit funds on behalf of its constituents. How funds are distributed and to whom can have considerable impact on arts policy in a particular community.

## Private Foundation Board Officer and/or Member

Organized as nonprofit corporations and governed by a board of trustees, most private foundations are small and administered by a lawyer or other individual on a part time basis. Larger ones have a president or chairperson of the board as well as a professional support staff. Some, like the Rockefeller Foundation, are endowed with funds from the private sector, while others, like like the Ford Foundation, are funded by commercial corporations. Board members in the first type tend to be family members or close associates, while those in the second type tend to be recruited from the corporate world.

## Benefit or Special Event Chairpeople

Most boards for nonprofit arts organizations have auxiliary committees of volunteers who raise money by sponsoring special events. They may run dinners, receptions, tours, benefits, raffles and auctions; they are headed by a volunteer chairperson or director, but may have some salaried support staff; the funds they raise are often vitally important to the arts project or company they are intended to support.

## Union, Guild or Professional Association Officer and/or Board Member

These nonprofit corporations are almost always headed by a board drawn from the organization's membership. Professionals who volunteer their time to serve on such boards usually feel an obligation to "pay their dues" by such service to an industry or career field that has been good to them. Their work includes setting goals for labor-management contract negotiations, overseeing pension and benefit funds, monitoring compliance with existing contracts that apply to members and representing the organization to the industry and the press. Among the better-known theatrical unions and guilds are Actors' Equity Association (AEA), The Association of Theatrical Press Agents and Managers (ATPAM) and the Dramatists Guild. Professional membership groups include the University/Resident Theatre Association (U/RTA), the League of Resident Theatres (LORT) and the International Society of Performing Arts Administrators (ISPAA). It is considered incumbent upon young professionals to become members of the relevant associations in their field and, eventually, to contribute their time and knowledge in a manner that will help sustain and improve that field.

# FREE-LANCE PRODUCING MANAGERS

## Impresario

An outdated term used to describe producers who rarely own their own theatres, who usually concentrate on the serious opera, dance and music field, and who organize and often send on tour performing artists and ensembles of world-class status. The title was applied to such men as Florenz Ziegfeld, Billy Rose and Sol Hurok. While it is rarely used today, it would suit such people as Frank Dunlop (the Edinburgh Festival), Harvey Lichtenstein (Brooklyn Academy of Music) and Martin Segal (New York International Arts Festival).

## Producer

In the British theatre a producer is the person who stages and directs the play; on the continent this position would be that of a *regisseur* or *metteur en scene*. In the American theatre a producer is the person who initiates a theatrical project by finding a property and securing the performance rights to produce it in the desired venue, and then raises the capital necessary to get the project to opening night. In the Broadway theatre the producer works in close partnership with a theatre landlord, who may contribute to the financing of the show and who also shares in labor, advertising and other costs. In institutional nonprofit theatres the term "producer" is inappropriate because no single person is the financier; rather, the institution or nonprofit corporation itself is the producer, because it has accepted the ultimate fiscal responsibility.

## Packager

A packager of productions is a type of producer who usually does not own a theatre but who conceives, initiates and assembles productions that are then sold to theatre operators and presenting organizations. While the packager must absorb certain general, office and rehearsal expenses (which are hopefully earned back), the bulk of the production expenses (cast salaries, transportation, scenery, etc.) are paid directly by the presenter. While the packager enters into a loose agreement with royalty houses, stars and other key personnel, it is the presenter who signs the binding contracts. A packager, therefore, takes few legal or financial risks. The main markets for packaged productions today include presenting organizations (especially college and civic performing arts centers), Equity summer and winter stock theatres, tent and musical variety arenas, dinner theatres, Las Vegas-style casino theatres, promotors of a "Broadway" subscription series and industrial show venues.

## Theatre Operator

Distinct from a landlord who owns, maintains and rents out a theatre facility without necessarily participating in its use, a theatre operator owns or rents a theatre and also produces or books in the entertainment presented in it. This does not always entail initiating the productions, but it does involve taking the lion's share of legal and financial risk, promoting the entertainment locally, hiring and supervising a resident staff, and assuming many other responsibilities that qualify the theatre operator as a producing manager. Most of the Broadway theatres are owned by the Shubert Organization, the Nederlander Organization or Jujamcyn, Inc., all of which are headed by executives who participate very actively in producing and managing the productions in their houses; they are producing managers as well as land-lords. Privately owned stock and dinner theatres may be owner-operated, run by a salaried manager-booker or rented out to a theatre operator.

## Presenter

There are thousands of theatres, civic centers, college and community performing arts facilities that buy or book packaged entertainment of one kind or another and present it for local audiences. The vast majority of these operate under the umbrella of some kind of nonprofit organization and thereby qualify for contributed income (yet arts councils were comparatively late in recognizing presenting organizations' eligibility to receive grant awards). Furthermore, taken as a whole, these venues probably do more to support serious music and dance (and the artists involved) than any other branch of the industry—live or electronic! Without the many weeks of employment on tour which they provide, even our most prestigious orchestras and dance companies would be reduced to part-time operation. Though they seldom originate productions, presenting organizations assume the major business liabilities and play a key role in developing artists' careers, ensembles' repu-tations and audience tastes. For such reasons they earn the title of managing producers.

## Promoter

Like a presenter, a promotor offers packaged events to the public, but is not usually associated with an institution, seeks personal gain and may also incur personal risk by guaranteeing the presentation costs.

## FREE-LANCE GENERAL MANAGERS

## General Manager

Free-lance general managers are peculiar to the commercial theatre. They are independent professionals who are often incorporated, maintain a permanent office and staff, and who are hired by producers and impresarios to take general management responsibility for specific shows or projects. Typically, the general manager negotiates the theatre license, hires the neces-sary staff, formulates a budget, oversees all financial transactions, negotiates all contracts  and serves as the producer's representative and troubleshooter. Most successful commercial producers have been general managers them-selves and some serve in both capacities. In some cases, the producer gives the general manager nearly full control over the production artistically as well as managerially, though this is the exception rather than the rule.

## GENERAL MANAGER EMPLOYEES

### Artistic Director

A person who has full artistic and in some cases also managerial authority over a nonprofit theatre production or company.

### General Manager

A person who has full management responsibility for a commercial theatre season or series, or for a nonprofit theatre company and may also make most artistic decisions.

### General Director

A person with both artistic and managerial authority, most often used in a nonprofit opera theatre.

### Producing Manager

A producer in the commercial sector who also serves as general manager.

### Managing Producer

When the financier-producer in a commercial theatre is usually absent and does not actively participate in the activities of the venture, this is an appropriate title for the person who assumes the responsibilities both of producership and general management.

### Managing Director

This title is used in both commercial and nonprofit theatre to describe someone with overall authority, although a managing director is never the financier of the project or company.

### Executive Director

The chairperson of a board may appoint an employee to serve as liaison between it and the staff of the organization, or the title may be used for other purposes. The word "executive" in front of another title usually implies that the person who holds it has been appointed to serve in somebody else's stead; commonly used in film and television production.

### Actor-Manager

This archaic title is seldom used today, and few people really fit the nineteenth-century definition of an actor-manager as did Henry Irving or David Belasco or, in this century, Eva Le Gallienne and Laurence Olivier. The rarity of actor-managers today may also be explained by the fact that artistic leadership in the theatre has shifted during this century from the actor to the director, and more theatre companies are formed by directors than actors. However, "artist-led company" is a recently coined phrase that would cover either an actor or a director and may gain more common usage.

### Director of Theatre

Academic departments or arts centers that embrace several art forms may appoint someone to head the activity in each, hence a title such as director of theatre.

### Chairperson of Theatre

The head of an academic theatre department in a school, college or university.

## FINANCIAL MANAGERS

### Director of Finance

The chief financial manager in a large nonprofit theatre company or performing arts center.

### Controller

Sometimes referred to in the archaic form, comptroller, this manager has the main accounting responsibility for the organization.

### Director of Business Information Systems

An expert in computer technology, this person may also be called a business systems manager.

### Accountant

While a C.P.A. is usually retained to report directly to the board, a trained accountant who may not be certified is often part of the staff for a large organization.

### Business Manager

The generic term for all finance positions in arts organizations has always been "business manager." In large companies this person reports to the finance director, but in smaller companies this manager may serve as a one-person department.

## Bookkeeper

A person who records all financial transactions into written or computerized journals and ledgers and may also prepare payrolls, tax forms and other routine business items.

## Box Office Manager

This job involves overall supervision and responsibility for a large box office operation without including work in ticket sales.

## Head Treasurer

One box office treasurer, who is also a ticket salesperson, is appointed to supervise other treasurers in terms of day-to-day procedures and routine matters.

# FUNDRAISING MANAGERS

## Director of Fundraising

The word "development" has become a euphemism for "fundraising" and is now in common usage for this title in the nonprofit performing arts world. In the television and film worlds, however, a Vice President or Director of Development is someone who is involved in the creative process of developing a scenario or story idea into a final screenplay. Fundraisers, of course, work exclusively in the nonprofit sector and attempt to attract contributed income from individuals, corporations, foundations and government sources.

## Associate Director of Fundraising

A large organization would employ a number of associates, each with their own support staff, to take charge of such specific areas as proposal writing, grants research, membership, government grants, corporate grants and campaigns aimed at individual donors.

## Special Events Director

This manager usually works within the fundraising department and coordinates a variety of efforts being conducted by a friends' group, a guild or a benefit chairperson, all aimed at raising contributed income.

## Director of Volunteer Services

When a large organization has a lot of volunteers working on different projects, it is obviously wise to hire a salaried person to manage and coordinate all their efforts. Of course, this could be the responsibility of a special events director, or the title might be "Benefit Director."

## MARKETING MANAGERS

### Director of Marketing

In large theatre operations, both nonprofit and commercial, a marketing director conducts research, develops a marketing plan and then supervises a staff to accomplish the marketing goals.

### Marketing Manager or Market Analyst

This person tends to concentrate on the quantitative, scientific and analytical rather than the creative, idea-generating aspects of marketing.

### Director of Membership

Many nonprofit theatres attempt to attract patrons, friends or angels (supporters, all) who contribute money over and above the ticket price. Often they are rewarded for this with special privileges such as invitations to receptions, free parking or restaurant discounts. If this is the case, a salaried manager will be required to supervise the process of membership recruitment and services.

### Director of Audience Development

This title is sometimes given to the head of marketing for a performing arts company. Otherwise, it implies a position responsible for increasing ticket sales in any way possible.

### Director of Marketing Information Systems

An expert in computer technology who expedites the complex research and record-keeping work of the marketing department.

### Director of Public Relations

May also be a Director of Press Relations or Director of Public Information and, indeed, an executive who has one of these titles but does the work implied by all of them. Yet again, the title may be Director of Promotion. This executive may be the head of a department, but it is more common today to find the PR staff reporting to the marketing director. Responsibilities all relate to placing information before the public in a manner that upholds the goals and image that the company is dedicated to expressing.

## Press Representative

This person assists the promotions director by concentrating on the development of good working relations with members of the press. In the commercial theatre, this work is usually done by self-employed press agents who hire out their services to producers and managers.

## Director of Community Relations

This manager may also hold the title of Director of Outreach. In either case, the job entails finding ways to increase audiences and community ties through the development of touring programs, artists-in-the-schools programs, in-house training workshops and the like.

## Director of Advertising Sales

If the theatre distributes a large quantity of playbills, souvenir programs and other such literature, and if advertising space is not sold by an outside agency or publisher—with the theatre earning a percentage of such sales—then an in-house salesperson should be hired to generate what could be a sizable amount of earned advertising income.

## Director of Publications

Again, if a large theatre generates a number of publications on a regular basis, it will be cheaper to hire a staff person to serve as editor-in-chief as well as publications supervisor, than to pay an outside publisher/printer to do such work.

## Ticket Services Manager

A manager to supervise the processing of subscriptions and to deal with complaints, special requests and other matters regarding customer relations.

## Group Sales Manager

When the volume of group sales (multiple ticket orders sold through one transaction) is high, a manager should be hired to encourage such sales and supervise all related activities.

## Subscription Sales Manager

A person who supervises the development, assignment, distribution and follow-up services related to the sale of series or subscription tickets to individual customers.

### Telemarketing Manager

As telephone sales campaigns have begun to rival mail campaigns due to rising postage costs, it is often necessary to hire a manager for telemarketing activities.

### Merchandise Marketing Manager

If a large theatre company creates special merchandise (T-shirts, tote bags, ash trays, etc.) to generate additional earned income, then a manager should be hired to supervise the design, manufacture and sale of such items.

### Concessions Manager

When the theatre itself operates a number of concessions to generate additional earned income (as opposed to merely renting space to individual vendors), then a concessions manager should be hired to oversee the operation of such concessions.

## PRODUCTION AND OPERATIONS MANAGERS

### Literary Manager/Dramaturg

Serves as an advisor to the artistic director in selecting plays, developing new scripts, suggesting performers, doing research to assist in rehearsal and production design; also works with publicity department and writes program notes and any necessary educational materials, like study guides for classroom use.

### Production Manager

Large theatre, dance and opera companies may require a person to control production costs, coordinate schedules and supervise touring productions.

### Facilities Manager

May also be called Operations Manager or Building Manager. A person who oversees maintenance, security, house management, space allocation, rentals, concessions and all purchases related to these areas.

### Office Manager

A person who supervises employee relations, including benefits, compensation and salary reviews, grievances and contract compliance; orders office supplies and equipment and maintains an inventory; organizes internal communication and office systems.

## Stage Systems Manager

When stage and production equipment is complex, and especially when it is largely computerized, a specialist may be required to oversee its installation, operation and maintenance.

## Company Manager

On Broadway and for first class national tours, the company manager is a member of the Association of Theatrical Press Agents and Managers (ATPAM). This position reports to the general manager and is responsible for solving routine problems related to the performers, stagehands and technicians. This position is also responsible for providing payroll information and maintaining good management-employee relations. On tour, if there is no tour manager, the company manager secures housing for the company, makes travel arrangements and serves as the chief on-site executive.

## House Manager

The house manager is also a member of ATPAM on Broadway and on tour. He or she is employed by the landlord to oversee front-of-house staff, verify box office statements and supervise house maintenance. In a nonunion house, this position reports to the general manager.

## Production Stage Manager

A member of AEA when union actors are employed, the stage manager supervises rehearsals, assists the director, monitors compliance with union rules and is in command of stage, performers and crew during performances throughout the run of the show. The stage manager serves as liaison between the acting company and the management.

## Technical Director

A person who supervises all the technicians and craftspeople involved in creating a theatrical production and who attempts to carry out the will of the production designers.

## Tour Manager

When not filled by a company manager, this position entails scheduling, arranging transportation, lodging and meals, overseeing the load-in and load-out of the physical production at each place of engagement and coordinating numerous details.

## Advance Stage Manager

An AEA position used to describe a person who precedes a production as it tours from theatre to theatre and who attempts to make the subsequent load-in, company arrival and opening performance as smooth an operation as possible.

## Internship Director

Large companies that utilize quite a few interns or apprentices in various departments and capacities may employ someone to interview, select, orient and generally supervise the interns in order to insure a mutually beneficial experience.

## School Director or Administrator

A growing number of theatres, mainly in the nonprofit sector, operate a school or training program both as a service to the community and as a means of generating earned income. If this is the case, an administrator or manager will be necessary to coordinate student recruitment and enrollment, faculty appointments and supervision, scheduling of classes and facility usage.

## Director of Security

Supervises on-site security personnel and systems.

## Maintenance Supervisor

Supervises maintenance personnel, supplies and services.

The sixty-six titles described above are the ones most commonly used in the professional theatre to indicate the wide span of managerial positions necessary to this industry. There are many other job titles ("director of audience education" is a recently coined, rather curious example) as well as other specific jobs that qualify as managerial. And there is a wide variety of specialists who offer their services to arts organizations as independent consultants. Titles and job responsibilities will vary, but the fundamentals of management and supervision are salient to all.

# 3

# The Place For
# The Performance

A s the number of Broadway theatres decreased in recent decades, and commercial productions grew more infrequent as they grew more costly, producers and playwrights began to seek professional outlets beyond Times Square. This resulted in the proliferation of Off- and Off-Off-Broadway theatres in the 1950s and 1960s in New York, and similar developments elsewhere, such as the "Off-Loop" theatres in Chicago, and the "Bay Area" theatres in San Francisco. The early '60s also witnessed the toddler period of a nationwide, nonprofit professional theatre movement. At the time, much of this activity was collectively known as "experimental" theatre and much of it was associated with non-theatre spaces: churches, lofts, garages, storefronts, cafes, restaurants and abandoned warehouses. Of course, the experimental aspect of this movement was less often the result of artistic philosophy than of economic necessity. But there was nothing new in this any more than there was anything new in converting any available structure into a perform- ance space. After all, the history of theatre architecture is largely comprised of studies in how non-theatre places evolved into buildings designed exclu- sively as theatres: threshing grounds into the classical Greek theatres, inn yards into the Elizabethan theatres, cathedrals and tennis courts into the eighteenth-century European theatres. It is not surprising, then, that the best contemporary theatre architecture reflects the influence of "loft theatre": the use of open space, the frequent omission of the proscenium arch, the more intimate relationship between performer and audience areas, and the fond- ness for exposed brick walls and other raw materials.

Other recently built theatres, especially the larger ones, merely per- petuate nineteenth-century architecture as if neither theatre nor society had changed in the slightest. As many as two thousand new theatres and auditori- ums were built during the "cultural boom" years of the '60s, or were under construction by the end of that decade. A large majority of these were put up by schools or colleges as multipurpose affairs and include everything from theatres to gymnasiums.Yet a number of new theatres, fine arts centers and performing arts complexes on   campuses are first-rate facilities. Together with the massive civic complexes that range from Lincoln Center for the Performing Arts on the east coast to the Orange County Performing Arts Center on the west coast, these buildings are   manifestations of what has been aptly described as "the edifice complex." At least each auditorium at Lincoln Center—except, most notably, the Vivian Beaumont—was originally designed to house an established performing arts company. In too many cases new theatres have been planned, financed and nearly completed when—almost as an afterthought—it has occurred to someone to think seriously about the performance programs that should or might fill them. Ideally and realistically, this process should be reversed if the results are to be worthwhile.

While governments, architects and the general public may believe that performances can only be held in elaborate and enormous theatres, theatre people themselves know better. Whenever theatre becomes overly formalized and stuffy, creative artists instinctively seek other places to work. Art historian Lord Kenneth Clark once wondered if any great humanist thought was ever conceived in a large room; one might also wonder if a huge auditorium has ever inspired any originality in the theatre. In this age of mass media and electronic entertainment, live theatre is all the more precious for its unique ability to reach people intimately and personally, to address itself to small groups rather than to the masses and to deal with the unusual rather than the conventional.   Most serious dramatists, producers and performers in nonmusical theatre today are wary of bigness in whatever form it appears.

Apart from the reasons why a new theatre space or building is created, however monumental or intimate it may be, there are numerous factors that should be considered before the project gets off the planning board. Most of these will be related to the community in which the theatre is to be located, the building itself and/or the manner in which these elements are likely to influence artistic objectives.

## FEASIBILITY OF THE THEATRE LOCATION

Ideally, producers and artistic directors should be free to select the community and the building in which they believe their productions have the best chance to thrive, both artistically and economically.   But such choices are always limited by circumstances. Yet the brave people who search out performance spaces might come closer to their ideal theatre if they searched a little longer and, perhaps, a little further afield.

Probably the best documented attempt   to suit artistic goals to a community was undertaken by Tyrone Guthrie, Peter Ziesler and Oliver Rea in their methodical search that culminated in the opening of the Tyrone Guthrie Theatre in 1963, and the establishment of the Minnesota Theatre Company at Minneapolis-St. Paul. Its success over the years, even after the departure of its founders, should lend encouragement to producers and artistic directors who are not satisfied with utilizing performance spaces merely because they are readily available. Of course, not everyone has the time and money to invest several years in a nationwide search for the ideal community in which to locate a theatre company. But anyone can scrupulously examine the community in which a desirable theatre space exists and be apprised of the fact that many more potential theatre sites or ways of creating them exist than the most obvious ones. When assessing a potential theatre site—the community, the audience potential, the building itself, the capital and operating costs—the advice of professional consultants is often helpful in gathering information. However, like the business of selecting plays and casting actors, the final decision about the performance place may also, without apology, be based upon a degree of intuition, upon a "feel" one gets from a particular building or community. Consultants, feasibility reports, architects, and the rest are helpful and often necessary adjuncts to the process of creating new theatres, but they should never be allowed to dominate the process. Final decision-making should always rest with the artistic leadership of the project. In fact, artistic directors who attempt to establish their own theatres can often serve as their own consultants by undertaking some simple field work and by getting free advice from the right experts.

Whether the plan is to buy, build or lease a theatre—or a more creative alternative is found—what factors regarding the theatre site and the community in which it is located should be taken into consideration?

## Audience Potential

Statistical surveys have shown that somewhere between one and three percent of our population attend live theatre performances and that the ratio of theatregoers to non-theatregoers is higher in metropolitan areas. It is a simple matter to determine the population of a given city and the area immediately around it: compute one to three percent of the total figure and then see whether or not that number of people would be sufficient to fill all the seats of all the performances of each anticipated production. Of course factors other than mere numbers will also impact on the percentage of the local population that attends a particular theatre or production. It has been found that the typical American theatregoer is white, college educated, middle-aged or older, a current or retired white collar worker in a middle or upper income category. This may be a valid profile of audiences for large conventional productions. It would not, however, fit many audiences in resort areas, those that attend experimental, campus, ethnic or special-interest productions.The profile is also radically altered when there is a free-admission policy—a practice made feasible when subsidization is available and made desirable by the alarmingly urgent need to attract a wider and younger segment of the population.

If a theatre wishes to attract a particular kind of audience, it should usually be located as close to that audience as possible; however, if a particular theatre or production offers a potent enough lure, people will come from hundreds of miles away, often by the bus load. The lure may be the performers, the material or the marketing strategy. Nonetheless, the theatre building and its locale will always be a powerful influence upon who and how many people attend performances there.

## Proximity to Transportation

Is a theatre site easily accessible to the public? If located in a large metropolitan area, accessibility to public modes of transport—subways, buses, trains—may take precedence over private transportation routes.Can a majority of the potential audience reach the theatre easily, quickly and safely? If not, will authorities cooperate to improve transportation systems? Are parking facilities available or will costly provisions be required to handle a maximum number of automobiles? Can cars be accommodated equally well for both evening and matinee performances? Is the theatre located on a major thoroughfare or is it off the beaten path and difficult to find?

Generally, it has been found that theatregoers in the eastern states are not willing to drive as far to places of entertainment as those in the rest of the nation, but in any case the process of finding one's way to a theatre should not take on the mysteries of a treasure hunt. What are the federal and local regulations about placing directional signs on nearby roads and highways? As a public service, and in order to facilitate a safe flow of traffic, many cities and townships are willing to cooperate with theatre managers by allowing at least a few regulation-size road signs; however, signs for commercial operations are outlawed on federal highways and state and local governments continue to tighten regulations that deal with outdoor advertising. Special permits are always required, unless a sign is located on the business site itself and meets local specifications. When a theatre is located in a remote area, even road signs may not always be sufficient to guide many of the patrons. In such cases the local and state police as well as neighboring merchants and businessmen should be well informed about the location of the theatre, in the event they are asked to give directions. Every attempt should be made to have the name of the theatre appear on as many road maps as possible—

those distributed through official channels, as well as smaller, more local maps such as those printed on restaurant place mats, motel bath mats, in tourist guides and in chamber of commerce literature.

Transportation will affect the operating cost of a theatre as well as its patronage. Large professional operations find it necessary to transport everything, from scenery to actors. Costs related to the transportation of people and materials will be smallest for theatres located in New York, Chicago, Los Angeles and San Francisco simply because, aside from being supply centers for most theatrical materials, each of these cities also serves as a home or branch office for Actors' Equity Association as well as other theatrical unions, which means that professional theatres may (though they may choose differently) hire performers locally and thereby avoid transporting them over long distances. On the other hand, metropolitan theatres are not necessarily free from high transportation costs. When scenery is constructed in studios away from the theatre, for example, trucking costs can be appreciable—especially for repertory theatres that lack adequate scene storage space. The problems of moving scenery in and out of the old New York Metropolitan Opera House on Fortieth Street and Broadway, where the sidewalks provided the only storage space, contribute to the legends that, however amusing, stand as a warning to anyone who is assessing a theatre site (like the stories of getting the circus elephants in and out of the old Hippodrome for performances). Blue laws that limit trucking on Sundays or after dark, freeways that restrict commercial traffic, interstate trucking laws, and other such factors can easily upset both the schedule and the budget for theatres located in somewhat remote regions of the country. All bear close examination when plans for a theatre are being laid.

## The Competition

Contrary to general opinion, competition in the performing arts is a healthy thing provided, of course, that it does not involve an overly frequent duplication of similar entertainment or programming. Theatregoing is a habit. It can be cultivated by school and community theatres and eventually applied to professional theatregoing. The opposite is rarely true, because high quality entertainment leads patrons to demand more of the same high standards. But theatregoing is not a habit that people acquire quickly. Long and continuing availability of theatre in a given area is desirable. Without question, the new theatre that locates itself in a community already accustomed to playgoing has a more ready audience potential than others; it is easier to share an audience than to create a new one from scratch. But there is an obvious difference between sharing and dividing. If, for example, two Shakespearean repertory theatres are located within fifty or even one hundred miles of each other, one will doubtless hurt the other at the box office.

How large is the potential audience for a particular kind of entertainment? Can metropolitan areas that possess numerous performing groups of a similar type work more diligently to coordinate their programming? On a given night in New York, for instance, one might find twenty groups that are performing a Mozart recital and not one of them playing to capacity. Even in a city the size of New York, there are probably not eight to ten thousand people who would go out on a given evening to attend a Mozart recital. Did the New York productions of *Dracula, Count Dracula* and *The Passion of Dracula,* presented simultaneously in 1978, help or hurt each other? What should be said about having three or four major performing arts summertime festivals all trying to attract the same type of ticketbuyer? While such duplication should be avoided, there are exceptions, among the most interesting being those times when two outstanding performers choose to appear at the same time and in the same role, as when both John Gielgud and Leslie Howard were playing *Hamlet* in 1936, or when the Metropolitan Opera and the New York City Opera present the same work during the same season next door to each other at Lincoln Center. But such competition is rare as well as risky. It is much better policy to coordinate programming with the competition, when this is possible, and work to share rather than divide an audience. For example, when the Cameron Mackintosh production of *The Phantom of the Opera* became a new smash hit at Broadway's Majestic Theatre in 1988, David Merrick, producer of the aging hit production of *42nd Street* at the St. James across the street, announced a new performance schedule. His curtain would go up fifteen minutes later than *Phantom,* his hope being that people turned away from the sold-out box office would come across the street and buy some of the unsold tickets to his show!

Most ways of benefitting from the competition are more obvious: advertising in each other's playbills; sharing mailing lists; sharing costumes, lighting equipment, properties and other available items when possible; joining constituent arts groups or competitors in a united fundraising campaign; and, importantly, joining other arts groups in lobbying for better regulations and support from elected officials at all levels of government. Learning to cooperate with what is misnamed "competition" in the theatre world is really proving the old adage that there is strength in numbers.

## *The Local Media*

Finding a community with a good potential audience is one thing; reaching that audience with a message that stimulates it sufficiently to attend the theatre is something else. If audience potential is extremely high, and people are in the habit of theatregoing, perhaps the job of selling tickets is as simple as disseminating minimal information about the play, the prices and the curtain times. But this is unusual. More often, people have to be enticed to attend a performance or, at least, strongly impressed about the existence of a theatre and the rewards of playgoing.

The most efficient way of reaching an audience will differ with each community. Direct mail, telemarketing, the distribution of posters and hand-bills, newspaper advertising, television or some other channel of communication may prove successful at one theatre, but unimportant at another. First, the size of the potential audience must be estimated and, second, its profile must be understood as clearly as possible. Only in this manner can high-potential customers be "targeted" to receive advertising messages. Not to undertake market research would be like skeet shooting in a blindfold. If the habits and living patterns of typical theatregoers in a particular community are known, it will be easier to reach them. What newspapers do they read? What radio and television stations capture their attention and at what times of day? What stores do they patronize most frequently? Advertising is expensive, and few theatres can afford nearly as much of it as they would like, so decisions about where and how to advertise are important.* Perhaps even more important is the amount of free space or time the local media is willing to provide. To secure such vital publicity, a theatre must establish and nurture a cooperative relationship with the media. Most editors and program directors recognize that a theatre is an asset to the community, to its economy and its culture, and they are apt to welcome theatrical copy or programming material because it is often more interesting and colorful than other copy they receive.

Theatres located outside large metropolitan areas may find themselves in a community that has no local radio or television station, and no local newspaper with a distribution reaching a majority of the potential audience. This situation requires a wider and more expensive advertising campaign and creates greater difficulty in determining the audience profile and communicating with that audience. And, of course, the further away a newspaper or radio station is from a theatre, the less likely it is to provide free publicity space or time. Communicating with potential theatregoers in resort areas also presents special problems: the year-round residents follow the local newspapers while the tourists ignore them and buy the big city papers or none at all. Fortunate indeed is the theatre that can reach most of its audience through one or two media outlets.

## Local Organizations

What groups exist within a given community that might offer assistance to a theatre? Helpful in the area of publicity and promotion, for example, are chambers of commerce, tourist bureaus, information centers, and travel

---

*See Chapter 15

agencies. Senior citizen and service clubs, civic and charitable organizations can be a good source of volunteer personnel for nonprofit theatres. From the standpoint of financial assistance, what sort of philanthropic record is generally maintained by local individuals, businesses and corporations? Is there a community arts council, and what is the record of the state arts council? Do nearby schools and colleges represent potential sources for group ticket sales?

## The Local Economy

Another yardstick for predicting the success of a theatre is to determine whether potential playgoers can easily afford the price of admission. What is the average income in the area? How much are people currently spending for live entertainment? How much can they afford to spend? Can group sales be anticipated from large businesses, schools and religious organizations? Has there been growth or decline in the general economy of the area over the past decade or so? Some communities can support a theatre that charges comparatively high admissions prices; others can afford no admission charges at all. The records in the local tax assessor's office will provide answers to some of these questions, as will interviews with chamber of commerce officials, managers of local movie theatres and other businessmen. Long before a theatre opens its doors, the producers should take a hard look at the local economy and ask whether or not its planned ticket prices are within a range that the market can bear. Even though the answer may be positive, of course, it does not mean that a community *will* buy tickets. If the answer seems doubtful, can high-priced performances be alternated with low-priced or free-admission performances? How much income is it reasonable to expect from nonadmission sources?

If the local economy will affect theatre business, then theatre business will also affect the local economy. This fact may provide a selling point and help to rally local support, including hefty concessions and subsidies from local government and business. For example, Cleveland's Playhouse Square Center, a mixed-use development that includes three beautifully restored theatres seating 6,829 people, was able to show that 660,000 tickets were sold in 1986, generating $9.9 million; and, impressively, that patrons spent an additional $10.6 million on meals, transportation, parking and retail purchases; that seventy-nine new businesses opened, bringing 1,400 new jobs to the area; that taxes, property values and rental rates increased; and that occupancy rose from 75 percent to 90 percent during that year. Such statistics are powerful ammunition in combatting local lethargy and rallying support for a theatre. They should be compiled and publicized on a regular basis by theatre companies both large and small, because all are having a positive impact on their local economies. In fact it may be claimed that the arts are a key factor in successful community development or redevelopment, as the case may be. The presence of numerous individual artists in places like Greenwich Village and Soho in lower Manhattan stimulated real estate values (so that fledgling artists soon could no longer afford to live there, unfortunately). Severely dilapidated metropolitan waterfront sites such as Baltimore's Inner Harbor and Toronto's Harbor Front have been transformed into tourist meccas with the arts as an  attraction.  And whenever a major new theatre or performing arts center is constructed, surrounding real estate values invariably increase.

The corporate world is also coming to realize the importance of the arts. More and more, large buildings that house a corporation's headquarters are designed to include a theatre, a museum or art gallery. And corporations located away from the nation's so-called cultural centers are finding that it is less difficult to attract top executives, scientists and other professionals when the community in which they are located can offer high quality leisure time activities, such as theatre and dance. For this reason it is often possible for a theatre group to gain major support from a local corporation.

Having to justify the arts because of what they contribute to the economy is, of course, regrettable.  The arts are their own justification. Yet artists and theatre people have been made to feel like poor relations for so long that they might take heart in knowing that this is not at all the case. The arts have a lot of political and economic clout in corporate America and they are finally learning to take advantage of it.

## The Local Climate

Weather conditions can seriously affect the business of theatre. How dependent is the tourist trade on climate fluctuations? What will general weather conditions mean in terms of heating and cooling an auditorium? What will this cost in terms of energy? Many a summer theatre has been bought during the winter when it is easy to forget or underestimate summertime weather conditions. No theatre can be easily tested for comfort until it is in use.

Weather conditions are, of course, most germane to tent and outdoor theatres. Not a few open-air amphitheatres are standing idle because it was discovered, too late, that the local climate was either too unpredictable or too uncomfortable to use them with any regularity. "Good ideas," such as theatre-under-the-stars, need careful scrutiny!

## Local Attitudes

Even when all other conditions for theatre appear favorable, local attitudes toward the presence of a particular theatre may determine its success or failure. What, it must be asked, is the sum of all the information that has been gathered about a community? What is the general reaction to the idea for a theatre? Is it hot, lukewarm or cool? What is the history of previous theatre projects in the community, and have these projects encouraged or discouraged local attitudes?

Communities comprised largely of well-educated and cosmopolitan people may be more ready to support a theatre than others; but it should be remembered that such communities may also have more deeply entrenched concepts of what theatre should be and how a theatre should be operated. That is all well and good for the more traditional or commercial types of theatre, but a decided liability for experimental groups. Taking theatre to the hinterlands is a noble gesture, but it is fraught with difficulties—largely those concerning local attitude—that should be studied carefully. While a majority of the people in the community may possess negative attitudes toward theatre, strong community leaders (politicians, religious leaders and the like) may be able to turn the tide of local opinion. Once in the habit of theatregoing, the newly found audience may prove to be an extremely loyal and exciting one.

Finally, it is important for the people who will be associated with a theatre to ask themselves whether or not they will be comfortable and happy working in a particular community. If it is fair to ask that a community accept the theatre and its workers, it is equally fair to expect the theatre workers to accept the community. Many theatres, especially those with a resident company of actors and those located outside our largest cities, have been justly criticized for treating their community in a condescending or isolationist manner. Totally opposed to the humanistic mission of theatre, such attitudes only reinforce negativism within the community and obstruct the kind of empathy that should lie at the foundation of all theatre work.

# THE REAL ESTATE ALTERNATIVES

## To Build a Theatre

Before building a new theatre a number of questions should be asked, the most important ones pertaining to artistic needs. If the theatre is being designed to house a particular acting company, every effort should be made to provide that company with an ideal working plant. How can the architecture complement the working style and habits of the actors and directors? It is usually preferable to aim for a good amount of structural flexibility that will facilitate various methods of staging and production. On the other hand, when this requires complicated machinery (such as stage lifts, an automated proscenium and the like), the machinery may dictate the style.

What are the motivations for constructing a new theatre? Does the desire stem from artistic needs or merely from an urge to have a new building for the sake of newness? Have the alternatives been considered? Could the use of an existing building offer the same solutions as the construction of a new one? Can the anticipated income for a theatre comfortably support the costs of a new building? Will a new theatre complement the abilities of the acting company or does it run the risk of being more impressive than the productions on stage? Will a new building inspire more local support and interest or, conversely, will it damage the loyalty and romantic associations that the community feels toward an existing theatre? However impractical and outdated an old building may be, it may have established a large following of its own and attract many customers to its box office regardless of the performance being offered. (Witness the hue and cry every time Carnegie Hall is threatened with destruction.)

After the decision to build a new theatre has been made, an architect must be found to translate artistic and economic needs into the permanent reality of a building. Unhappily, most architects are unfamiliar with theatrical needs and structures, but a local chapter of the American Institute of Architects can be of assistance in locating one who is. When a selection is made, a strong working relationship should be established between the architect and the artistic directors of the theatre. Although artists in their own right, architects must not be allowed to design structural elements that impose unnecessary limitations on the artistic work of the theatre.The architect willing to collaborate with theatre artists, however, can be an enormous help in facilitating theatrical goals.

## To Buy a Theatre

Any piece of real estate should be considered first for its general use. In terms of size, structure, location, age and history, and regardless of whether or not the building is used as a theatre, what is its fair market price? What is its potential resale value? Is it structurally sound, or will major renovation and repair of heating, cooling, plumbing, electrical and physical support systems be necessary? Few buyers are sufficiently expert to judge these matters for themselves, so a detailed report in writing from a professional building engineer is always wise. Among the things that are seldom what they appear to be, old buildings are high on the list. And it is not always true, as is generally believed, that it is cheaper to renovate than to build from scratch. Also, every attempt should be made to discover the reasons why the building is for sale. The records of the business that previously occupied the building

57

should be studied; past owners, managers and employees should be quizzed about it, as should neighboring business people and others in the community. Does the building have a reputation or image that will affect future business? This is a serious matter, since the restoration of a reputation can take a lot longer than the restoration of a building!

## To Rent or Lease a Theatre

Before signing a lease, one needs to consider the building in question almost as if one planned to purchase it. Indeed, if the lessee hopes to operate for a long period of time, an option to buy the property at a stipulated maximum price and, if possible, with the past rent serving as some type of concession in that price, should be written into the lease. Negotiating a lease is complicated and usually requires legal counsel, but everything in a lease will be related to one of two questions: what does the landlord provide and what must the tenant provide? As with all contracts and agreements, *that which is not specifically withheld is given away.* This means, for example, that if the lease doesn't stipulate that the landlord provide the theatre seats, there may be no theatre seats when the lease goes into effect! Many prospective tenants  look at a theatre when it is occupied and in full production, so they simply assume that what they see is what they will get. But when a lease is being drawn up, the best advice to follow is: *assume nothing* !

The agreement between producers and landlords of Broadway theatres is not called a lease but, rather, a license. Instead of rent, it calls for a percentage of the gross box office receipts to be paid to the landlord (as much as 40 percent). However, the landlord pays a number of the necessary employees, house insurance, utilities and other such items. In effect, the producers and the landlord are partners, because both benefit from the highest grosses. Of course, the laws of supply and demand impact upon the terms of a Broadway theatre license. During poor theatre seasons, when there are more theatres available than productions to fill them, more favorable terms may result. Or, when a production itself has already proved to be successful in London or Los Angeles, the landlord may offer more generous terms in anticipation of a long and lucrative tenancy. Or, if the producer is willing to occupy what tradition and superstition regard as undesirable theatres (such as those below 42nd Street or east of Broadway), then better terms may result. When Broadway is booming, however, or when the producer is waiting for a particular theatre to become available, the deck is stacked in the landlord's favor. Some productions, when this is the situation, originate on the west coast and then keep seeking limited engagements in various cities until the desired Broadway theatre becomes available—rather like an airliner being held in a flight pattern until airport traffic conditions permit it to land.

The Off-Broadway theatre lease, also written on a per-production basis, is also unusual in that it typically requires around six weeks of guaranteed payment, even if the tenant production is a flop and vacates after one week. And it is usually a simple "four-wall lease," meaning that terms provide the tenant merely with the space inside the four walls of the property and nothing else in exchange for a flat, weekly rent. This is in sharp contrast to the agreement that would be made by outside producers or performance groups to rent a college theatre or civic auditorium. Here, almost everything and everyone necessary to the operation of the facility may be provided (for a price, of course), except for the artists and the physical production.

When negotiating to occupy a nontheatre space, such as a loft or warehouse, one may have the option of signing a short-term, one-year rental agreement after which one could be evicted or face a sharp rent increase, or a longer term three-to-five-year lease, which would offer more property control, tax benefits and a fixed cost with minor built-in increases.   Or one may be able to negotiate a lease-option in which payments go toward a stipulated purchase price for the building at some future date.   Another favorable arrangement for a tenant would be to establish occupancy payments as a percentage of the box office gross without a minimum guarantee, though this would require a very sympathetic or very desperate landlord. Whatever the terms, it is critical that  the written occupancy agreement state clearly what both parties must provide: what is the fine print, and how easily may the contract be broken or extended?

## To Share a Theatre

Producers and theatre companies just starting out rarely have the resources to buy, build or even rent the theatre of their dreams. This leads them to examine less obvious alternatives and, invariably, it leads them to compromise. But creative solutions to their space needs may be found without altering the primary mission and artistic objectives of the project. Sharing a space is one such solution. It is not unusual today to find a theatre group offering performances in a church, a public or private school, or in commercial establishments such as hotels, restaurants and cafes. The landlord-host may charge very low usage fees, feeling that the theatre will attract new people to its own establishment and that cultural or entertainment activity enhances its own image. But, as with any liaison, there are risks. How does the image of the host establishment reflect upon the theatre's image in the mind of the public? Will the host place restrictions on the type of productions the theatre wishes to present? What restrictions will be placed on the scheduling of rehearsals and performances?

The theatre company with a space dilemma should search out theatres, auditoriums and other potential performance places in the community that are not being fully utilized. Museums, for example, may have such space available and also be very happy to include theatre performances among public activities. Many office buildings today have large ground-level atriums open to the public, and noontime theatre might be welcomed and subsidized by the corporate landlord.

If theatre is about sharing, which it is in more ways than one, then it has certainly shared some unusual places: Vietnam veterans performing at war memorials; a socialist troupe performing for striking auto workers in Detroit and migrant workers in the vineyards of California; AIDS patients performing for hospital audiences; and the inmates performing at the State Correctional Facility at Ossining, where the late Miguel Pinero honed his talents as a playwright. Recently, environmental or participatory theatre has become popular. With this type of theatre, the audience participates in the action, and the line between fantasy and reality is intentionally blurred, and it is often staged in places that are also used for other purposes. *Tony 'n Tina's Wedding*, for example, begins in a real church and then takes its audience off to a mock reception in a real catering establishment with cast and audience freely interacting  throughout. The production company, then, pays rent to share nontheatre spaces.

Yet another concept of shared space is that of the consortium, which merely entails several arts groups pooling their resources to mutual advantage. For example, both The Kitchen and P.S. 122 in Lower Manhattan occupy buildings acquired by experimental artists who needed space to create and perform, and who soon brought other artists into their company, thereby offering many opportunities for interdisciplinary experimentation in performance art. Choreographer Michael Bennett acquired a large industrial building on Broadway and converted it into dance studios, which he then rented at favorable rates to American Ballet Theatre and other groups and productions in rehearsal. Even an institution like Lincoln Center, comprised as it is of a half dozen major performing arts companies sharing real estate as well as some fundraising, marketing and administrative costs, is a consortium. But the concept can be applied with great advantage to much smaller and much more impoverished groups of arts companies and individual artists.

## To Be Given a Theatre

Incredible as it may sound, an increasing number of nonprofit theatre companies are having theatre facilities built for them according to their own specifications and are then allowed to occupy them on very favorable terms; or they are given free rent in an existing theatre building. Municipalities have many real estate holdings, and these often include unused movie theatres, cultural facilities and other buildings suitable for conversion into theatres. And local governments, like real estate developers, realize the positive impact that an arts facility can have on land values and the economy. In New York City, for example, both the Brooklyn Academy of Music and the New York Public Theatre—huge, multi-theatre facilities—are rented to their nonprofit corporate operators by the city for one dollar a year. In addition, the city provides most of the maintenance and security needs for these buildings. In 1987 the Academy was given—by means of a complicated funding package from the City and the State—an additional building, the Majestic Theatre, located just a few blocks from its main facility. A legitimate theatre built in the nineteenth century, then a vaudeville and movie house, the Majestic was renovated at a cost of $5 million in a style similar to Peter Brook's Les Bouffes du Nord theatre in Paris. It opened with Brook's nine-hour production of *The Mahabharata* and subsequently provided, among other things, a venue where small and nontraditional opera productions could be mounted. Brook also continues to work there. Similar, if less grand, examples exist across the nation. Cities are allocating increasing portions of their budgets to support the arts.

Private developers in New York City have been encouraged for several decades to include theatres in their high-rise office structures in exchange for permission to construct additional stories. The Circle in the Square and the American Place Theatre, among others, owe their facilities to this ordinance. For other reasons, developer William Zeckendorf, Jr. agreed to give a $1 lease for a space valued at $850,000 in his new Union Square high-rise building to a small theatre company in the vicinity, mainly because its forceful founding director had asked him for it and had the community's backing.

There are several tax advantages that a developer or landlord may realize by donating a space or a whole building to a nonprofit organization. Even individual property owners may find that there is greater financial advantage in giving a property away than in selling it. If the possibility of such a corporate or private gift appears on the horizon, a good tax lawyer should be retained to explore the most attractive alternatives.

## Assistance in Assessing and Acquiring a Building

As one of the four requirements for theatre, the place for the performances is a fundamental element that will deeply and unequivocally influence every other aspect of the operation. Every precaution should be taken to guarantee the best possible theatre place and design. While producers and artistic directors know the general architectural and physical requirements for their project, they should seek the advice of others who, depending on the nature of the real estate situation, can provide valuable technical assistance.

## MARKET RESEARCH CONSULTANTS

Many market research firms, both small and large, local and national, experienced in theatre consultation and inexperienced, are available to conduct broad surveys in a community that result in a feasibility report and deal with such factors as audience potential, community attitudes and the local economy. Such studies may be helpful both before a theatre is opened and after it has been in operation.

## FACILITY AND MANAGEMENT CONSULTANTS

Assistance may be required in facility planning and construction (as well as arts planning and long range programming); in the physical and usage development of an existing property; in planning for facility operation and management; and, of course, in planning a capital funding drive.

## FINANCIAL CONSULTANTS

Before plans are finalized, it will be necessary to determine the full cost of acquiring and/or renovating the real estate in question. Furthermore, it would be wise to determine what it will cost to operate the theatre once it has opened. Drawing up a realistic capital budget and operating budget at this early stage may show that the project is financially impractical, that production plans need to be altered or that everything is within the realm of possibility.

## ARCHITECTS AND ENGINEERING CONSULTANTS

Theatre architects may be contacted directly, with the assistance of the local chapter of the American Institute of Architects, or a number of architects may be invited to submit designs or proposals for a building or renovation. If the building already exists, building engineers or consultants of various kinds may be hired to analyze facility operations, make recommendations for changes or submit renovation plans. Consultants might include specialists in acoustics, plumbing, electrics, and the like. Such specialists may be contracted by the producing organization, by the landlord or by the architect.

## ACTUARIES

In assessing a property for its real and special values an actuary may be requested to submit a report directly to the producing organization, or to banks and financiers for the purpose of establishing a loan or mortgage value. Such reports are meant to be objective appraisals of the building's worth in terms of the current market value.

## REAL ESTATE BROKERS

When buying or leasing a building, one usually prefers to avoid paying broker commissions, either directly or indirectly. But real estate brokers can be of great assistance in locating a desirable building in a particular area and are also likely to know a considerable amount about the building's history and the community's profile.

## INSURANCE BROKERS

The cost of insurance policies is often a major item in a theatre's operating budget. Brokers will have to be dealt with eventually,as discussed in Chapter 18,  but in the planning stages of a project a consultant may give valuable advice about the types of insurance available—which are necessary and which merely desirable—and where to buy the best coverage at the lowest cost. Some buildings, due to age, construction, wiring, lack of emergency equipment such as fire doors and sprinkler systems, simply cannot be insured at affordable rates. It would be best to know this before a deal is signed.

## LICENSING BOARDS AND INSPECTORS

All public buildings must be approved and licensed by certain agencies of the local and state governments. Theatres must be located on property zoned for business. Such zones are determined by public vote and then controlled by the local board of selectmen, town council, city council or government office. Because zoning laws change and special permits pertaining to noise, construction, renovation, historic landmarking and business operation may be needed, the appropriate officials should be contacted before a site is finally negotiated. Permits must also be obtained concerning public safety conditions, such as the accessibility of emergency exits, public elevators, fire-proofing, absence of asbestos and the like. If not approved as safe and sanitary, a building may require extensive and costly work.

## LABOR UNION INSPECTORS

Most unions concerned with employees who work in theatre buildings have a variety of rules and regulations pertaining to the working conditions for their members. Actors' Equity Association, for example, requires minimum safe and sanitary conditions in dressing rooms, a certain temperature range during working hours, specific rest room and shower facilities, stage and rehearsal area flooring specifications and so forth. Union officials should be consulted about such building requirements before a theatre is designed or acquired.

## TAX SPECIALISTS

The city tax assessor can provide information about local land values, who owns the surrounding property and what property tax would be imposed if the theatre is to operate on a commercial basis. Tax accountants and tax lawyers would be very helpful advisors if the theatre is to be donated or if some other type of tax advantage is being sought by the owner, the user or both.

## BANKERS

When a mortgage or other type of loan is necessary, bank officials should be consulted to determine the cost and availability of such money. They may also be a good source of information about the previous owners and operators of a building. Investment brokers might also provide creative financing solutions under certain circumstances.

## LEGAL CONSULTANTS

Lawyers, preferably specialists in the type of contract or problem being negotiated, are both necessary and desirable. Their assistance may be for a specific purpose or they may be retained for a long period to perform a variety of specified services at a set fee—otherwise clients are billed per service performed and the time it consumed.

Because there is no official certification of consultants and because they are found under every stone, care should be taken in hiring one. It is standard form to request a consultant's qualifications in writing together with a sample report or proposal from one of the consultant's previous projects. Then an interview should be arranged, references requested and checked and, finally, services and fees spelled out in writing. Consultants charge by the hour, the day or the project. It is not considered proper to base fees on a percentage of money raised (such as in a fundraising campaign), money saved (such as construction bids under cost estimates) or money earned (such as box office income).

Consultants can appear to be a very expensive luxury. And it is true that one does not need to be hired every time there is a difficult set of decisions to be made. But when a board of trustees or a manager walks into truly unknown territory, a consultant's fee might be money well spent. It would be a lot more costly to discover a major error when it is too late to bail out.

## Estimating Capital and Operating Costs

(See Chapter 11.)

## THEATRE DESIGN OPTIONS AND REQUIREMENTS

When a major renovation job or a new building is being planned, an architect must be chosen and will begin by producing a set of schematic drawings that show the basic interior layout as well as the exterior design and the juxtaposition of the structure to abutting properties. As these drawings are discussed and developed with the client and also perhaps with consultants, they become increasingly detailed and eventually specify what type of materials and building systems will be utilized and what the dimensions are for each room and surface. Finally, architectural elevations and detailed drawings are prepared and given to a contractor for implementation. The process can be time consuming and frustrating, but fine results can be achieved if architect and client work closely and communicate well with each other. Design plans should be studied repeatedly by the people who will eventually work in the building, and those people should attempt to visualize just how well the place will function when actually in operation. One should "walk through" the design plans—as an audience member, an administrator, an actor, a technician, and so forth. When problems are encountered, they should be discussed and solved, hopefully before construction has begun. As the rest of this chapter suggests, a theatre building is a unique type of real estate which, like the performance of a play, must bring together a complex and diverse number of elements and make them work as a unified whole.

### Central Operating Systems

Among the most costly and essential aspects of operating any building are plumbing, heating, cooling and electric systems. The first consideration in regard to the engineering of these utilities is whether or not they should be centrally operated and how much flexibility of control they should permit. When speaking in terms of furnaces, water pumps, water towers, hot water tanks, compressor units, electrical generators and the like, it is usually less costly and more efficient to maintain and operate one large mechanical unit rather than numerous smaller ones. But this assumes that most of the plant is in operation most of the time. When large areas of a building are not used for long periods, utility systems that service them should possess the capability of controlling those areas separately. Is it necessary, for example, to provide heat and electricity for an entire theatre during times of the day or year when the auditorium isn't in use? Do scene shops and storage areas require heating or cooling when only the auditorium is in use? Most new buildings today provide built-in fire protection, but older buildings require fire hose or sprinkler systems that are always operable. To avoid failure in the event of power losses, both fire alarm and pumping equipment must be supplied with electrical power independent from outside power sources. Like all plumbing, sprinkler pipes that contain water must be kept above freezing temperatures (a so-called dry system only involves piping water to the source of the system where the generators and pumps are also located). Emergency power and light systems are required by law in all public buildings and may receive their power either from a central generator or from individual, battery-operated units that are tied into the regular electrical system so they automatically cut in when normal power is interrupted.

Many problems arise when a theatre is part of a larger complex of buildings and its utilities are operated from a central system. Heat or air conditioning for a campus theatre, for instance, might be supplied from a heating plant as far as a mile distant, requiring troublesome and expensive arrangements at times when other campus facilities are not in use. Many architects and engineers, it seems, assume that theatre rehearsals, performances and preparations all occur during a normal forty-hour week, excluding weekends and holidays.

Central communications systems offer other problems and advantages. A telephone switchboard, for example, may provide communication efficiently within a building complex and control over the use of each unit, but it may not be fully operable at all times of the day and week. To obtain the greatest efficiency at the lowest cost, one has to shop carefully for the best available telecommunications services and equipment.

## Audience Seating Capacity

The seating capacity and size of an auditorium will greatly influence both the business and artistic potentials of a theatre. Audience capacity will determine the total potential box office income (although this will vary depending on how tickets are priced) and therefore the total theatre budget, and it will dictate appropriate types of productions and artistic goals. This does not mean, of course, that a great deal that is inappropriate is not attempted in certain theatre buildings or that the entire question of what is appropriate in a particular theatre is not a matter of opinion. Nonetheless, it would be generally agreed that to play *Hedda Gabler*, for example, in a twenty-five-hundred-seat theatre would be about as inappropriate as to perform *West Side Story* in a two-hundred-seat theatre. Unfortunately, circumstances often tempt producing organizations to make drastic compromises in suiting a particular production to a particular theatre. It is not always understood that the theatre itself, the performance place, is an integral element of the art. Change the place of performance and the performance also changes—a principle not far removed from Marshall McLuhan's theory that the medium, not its message, determines what is communicated.

As the result of much trial and error, and as the outgrowth of long tradition, most theatre practitioners concede that each style of play production dictates some ideal in terms of audience size. Laboratory or workshop theatres usually seat from one to three hundred people, although the avant-garde theatre director Jerzy Grotowski prefers an audience of forty or less. Theatres seating from two to eight hundred seem ideal for most non-musical presentations and about one thousand to eighteen hundred seats is the norm for musical plays, chamber operas, tent theatres and commercial houses. Auditoriums seating about twenty-five hundred are acceptable for large musical productions, opera, symphony, dance, and certain concert presentations. Naturally, acoustics, sight lines, decor and general comfort contribute substantially to the appropriateness and desirability of any performance place.

From a purely numerical point of view, theatre managers like to have lots of seats to sell for popular attractions but, on the other hand, are sorely embarrassed by a large expanse of empty seats when ticket sales are slow. An intriguing strategy for obtaining the best of two worlds is to design the audience area so that it contains a large transverse aisle (an aisle that runs parallel to the stage and separates one price of seats from the price of the section behind it). The wide transverse aisle reduces the seating capacity of the house. But when ticket sales are brisk, additional seats can be placed in such aisles to increase the capacity. Best of all, these additional seats can be priced much higher than if they had been placed at the back of the house or if standing room had been sold in lieu of actual seats.

## Types of Stages

Concepts of performer-audience relationships have varied greatly over the centuries, but forward-looking theatres today favor a more intimate relationship than the one offered by traditional, nineteenth-century proscenium theatres. Partly because the cinema can accomplish these effects so much better than live theatre, fewer and fewer productions aim for lifelike illusions or the fishbowl look of a stage encased by a proscenium arch. Also, realistic styles of drama and theatre production are common only to a small portion of the total writing and staging output in twenty-five hundred years of theatrical history. Most often, theatre has been admittedly theatrical; but it has not always tried for as intimate a performer-audience relationship as it often does today. Briefly, what types of stages are commonly in use today and what kinds of performer-audience relationships do they establish?

*Proscenium Theatre*—The stage is behind a picture frame arch with the audience located directly in front of it.

*Thrust Stage*—An Apron is projected into the audience area and may or may not extend out in front of a proscenium arch.

*Arena Stage or Theatre-in-the-round*—The stage is surrounded on all sides by audience areas.

*Center Stage or Two-Sided Arena*—The audience is placed in two sections on opposite sides of the performance area. The least common type of staging.

*Open Stage or Three-Quarter-Round*—The audience is arranged around three sides of the stage.

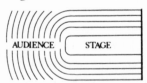

*Flexible Stage*—A theatre designed and often automated in such a manner that a combination of several different types of stages may be used.

Any play or presentation can be adapted to any type of stage, although many plays intrinsically dictate an appropriate method of staging. Each type of stage, therefore, will suggest a certain repertory of dramatic literature and certain styles of production, just as it will suggest certain scenic and technical embellishments, certain staff positions to create and operate these embellishments and certain budget lines to pay for them all. For instance, a fully staged production of a musical like *Oklahoma!* will require a greater bulk of scenery when produced in a large proscenium theatre than when produced in a theatre-in-the-round seating the same number of people. However, a theatre-in-the-round might require twice as many stagehands to get its limited scenery on and off the stage in the same amount of time, as fewer stagehands can move twice that amount of scenery in a proscenium theatre. From a budgetary viewpoint the size of the building and the seating capacity will have a much greater impact than the type of stage it contains. However simple and uncluttered a production may appear, it is a mistake to jump to the conclusion that it is less costly than a heavier looking production.

## The Audience Areas

"Going to the theatre" is an experience that begins when   playgoers leave their home and ends when they have returned to it. In this sense, every place along the way during the evening is part of the audience area. Theatre managers and publicity directors cannot overestimate this fact. Ease and comfort of theatregoing are not only major factors in encouraging habitual theatregoing, they are also major factors in determining how the audience will respond to the performers. A primary goal of house management and theatre planning is to organize things in a way that enables the audience to give its full attention to the performance. Theatregoers are strongly influenced not only by such factors as convenience in getting to the theatre and securing tickets and being greeted by the house staff but by the physical setting in which they find themselves while attending a performance.

Although Broadway theatres are notorious for their limited lobby space, their small rest rooms and their narrow aisles, there is a psychological point to be made in favor of crowding people in order to create an emotional and intellectual togetherness, ordinarily a desirable audience characteristic. (The "crowding effect" can also be accomplished by means of architecture and decor, without physical crowding.) The other extreme, that of arranging the performance place so that each member of the audience always has an abundance of empty space around him, polarizes the audience and impedes the performer-audience relationship, making communication difficult if not impossible. Open-air theatres are especially susceptible to this problem. The focal point in any performance place must be the performer himself and he, in turn, should be able to feel a unanimity of audience response, which depends upon the audience feeling and responding as a whole.

The general atmosphere that a theatre generates by virtue of its lighting and decor can strongly affect audience reaction. Since warmth and intimacy are complementary to most live theatre experiences, an effort should be made to promote these feelings. The use of warm colors, surfaces and textures that are soft in appearance, a limited amount of empty space, and architecture that focuses attention toward the stage are usually desirable. The bland, impersonal, cool and sterile look common to many public or institutional buildings should assiduously be avoided. (This is exactly the look for which the Kennedy Center for the Performing Arts in Washington, D.C. is most criticized.) The emphasis in live performing arts should, after all, be on the living performer. If surroundings dwarf humanity, either physically or psychologically, by stressing a larger-than-life or other-than-human atmosphere, the entire perspective of live performance can be distorted. There are, of course, experimental theatre companies that, in pursuing their aim of creating "total theatre," have unusual requirements for theatre decoration and audience engineering. In most cases, however, theatre directors are desirous of an audience that is prepared to give its full attention to the performance, that is ready to respond as a whole, and whose surroundings are in all ways sympathetic to the encouragement of these responses.

When planning or renovating an auditorium, rows containing odd numbers of seats should be avoided because most theatregoers buy tickets in pairs. Continental seating (in which there is no center aisle running down the middle of the orchestra and each row contains many seats) may require fewer ushers but would necessitate a wider distance between rows to allow people to get in and out; hence, the elimination of aisles may not mean a greater number of seats.

The following checklist contains items related to the audience areas of typical theatre buildings. Each item, of course, suggests that its condition, its presence or its absence, and its arrangement in a given theatre will contribute to the value of the building, either as an asset or as a liability, and to the success or failure of artistic objectives.

1. *THE THEATRE EXTERIOR*
Proximity to public transportation
Automobile parking facilities
Access to streets and highways
Visibility from public highways and byways
Identification on the building
Marquee and display advertising provisions
Exterior lighting on and in front of the building
Street and highway lighting
General security risks and provisions
Proximity to fire hydrants

## 2. *THE THEATRE LOBBIES*

Size

Location and size of entryways

Door bars and emergency exits

General appearance and decor

Ability to isolate when not in use

General lighting

Flooring and carpeting

Ease and economy of temperature control

Security provisions

Emergency lighting

Potential for multipurpose use

Box office in relation to audience traffic flow

Coat-checking facilities

Concession spaces (bar, shops, restaurant, etc.)

Space and provisions for display advertising

House-to-lobby speaker or television systems

Curtain signaling devices

Elevators to upper levels

Gallery areas

Patrons' lounge areas


## 3. *THE PUBLIC REST ROOMS*

Accessibility from audience areas

General appearance and decor

Ability to isolate when not in use

General lighting

Flooring

Ease and economy of temperature control

Ventilation

Emergency lighting

Size

Sanitary conditions in relation to public health laws

Plumbing conditions

Number of toilet units (both men's and womens' rest rooms should
   contain at least one unit per hundred of potential audience capacity)

Public water fountains

Disposal provisions

Vending machines for sanitary napkins

Soap vending units

Paper towel and water cup vending units

Automatic hand-drying devices
Number of sinks and mirrored areas

4. *THE AUDITORIUM*
Accessibility from street and lobby areas
General appearance and decor
Ability to isolate when not in use
General lighting
Flooring and carpeting
Ease and economy of temperature control
Emergency lighting
Emergency exits, fire escapes, etc.
Size and number of doors
Acoustics
Air conditioning and heating systems
Security provisions
Number of seats
Potential for increasing or decreasing seating capacity
Space for standing room
Comfort of seats
Condition of seats
Sight lines from house to stage
Elevation of floor and seats
Potential for altering audience-stage relationship
Aisle, row and door lights
Stairway lights and railings
Seating and aisle arrangement in terms of traffic flow, ticket taking,
    ushering, etc.
Seat, row and aisle numbering system
Ease and economy of cleaning, maintaining, replacing light bulbs or
    fixtures, etc.
Provisions or space for house-to-stage lighting and projectors
Access for the handicapped
Access to backstage
Ability to separate audience from performer areas
Potential for multipurpose use

## *The Performers' Areas*

It is probably safe to say that a majority of existing theatre buildings
contain backstage and dressing room facilities that range from inadequate to
deplorable. Even when the audience areas are outstandingly lush and attrac-

tive, it often seems that the architects ran out of space, money, imagination and all respect for comfort when it came to constructing facilities for the performers. Dressing rooms are frequently several flights up and a good jog from the stage, contain inadequate heating, plumbing and ventilation systems, have an insufficient amount of space and totally lack anything aesthetically appealing. On the other hand, certain new theatres (especially, it seems, those associated with educational institutions) contain dressing rooms with an atmosphere of sterility reminiscent of surgical scrub rooms. A pleasing medium between these two extremes would seem desirable.

When a building that was not originally intended as a theatre is converted, some unfortunate compromises will probably be necessary when it comes to designing the backstage area. In locations such as Broadway, where every foot of space is a precious commodity, conditions can never be ideal. Examples of buildings poorly converted into theatres are numerous and sometimes almost unbelievable. One theatre in New York has a stairwell located stage center around which all scenery and action must revolve. The absence of a fire escape makes the balcony section of another New York theatre completely unusable. The tiny doors leading into many Off-Broadway theatres render it impossible to carry in pre-constructed scenery and set pieces. But much more unforgivable are the glaring errors built into new theatres because an architect was unfamiliar with theatre operations and failed to inform himself about basic production requirements. One new theatre in the Midwest was constructed with permanently installed stage lighting instruments that were wired into the circuits and dimmers, thereby necessitating the same lighting scheme for a big musical production as for a one-man concert. An expensive new dinner theatre in the South provided only one set of rest rooms, which had to be shared by audience and performers. A new campus theatre in Texas offers less than a 55 percent view of the stage from a majority of seats in the auditorium. Architects, engineers and administrators should do their homework early and thoroughly.

The amount and type of backstage area required is determined by the type of presentation a particular theatre is designed to accommodate. Is the stage too large and costly to operate in relation to potential box office income? Are rehearsal rooms necessary or will the theatre seldom house a resident group of performers who will need them? Does the same rehearsal and dressing room space have to service more than one performance or production at a time? Can rehearsal areas be utilized during performance hours? Can the stage itself be used for rehearsals during nonperformance hours and can it be heated, cooled and lighted independently from the auditorium? What are the most desirable and efficient types of stage machinery for the types of productions a theatre is designed to accommodate? Larger and more sophisticated facilities are required when the plan is to perform in repertory style or to produce numerous different productions in rapid succession. The Mark Taper Forum in Los Angeles (which has accommodated a busy resident production schedule since it opened) was built with virtually no rehearsal space and no administrative office space. The Vivian Beaumont Theatre at Lincoln Center, on the other hand, was designed to accommodate a repertory company which, it was expected, would rotate its productions each season. For this reason, an enormous amount of space was provided behind the acting area so that the scenery for two or three productions could be stored intact and simply moved into place when required. But a repertory policy was not practiced at the Beaumont. The large amount of unused space in the building has periodically prompted calls for the installation of a cinema theatre and a film library, among other things.

Most of the space in most theatre buildings sits idle most of the time—a startling fact that explains why theatrical real estate is such a costly and impractical holding. While there are disadvantages to multipurpose theatres, every reasonable attempt should be made to utilize theatre buildings as fully as possible and thereby to decrease the horrible necessity of having to support a twenty-four-hour plant operation with a mere two hours of income producing usage. When multipurpose use can be accomplished without detriment to the operation of the theatre, the supplementary income accrued can comprise the best and most reliable kind of subsidization.

Whether building, buying or leasing a theatre, what is the essential checklist to ponder in regard to the performers' facilities? The following points include many that are required or regulated under Actors' Equity Association rules pertaining to safe and sanitary employment conditions, and these will be inspected periodically by an Equity representative whose approval is prerequisite to the employment of Equity actors.

1. *STAGE*
Size (depth, width, height, flexibility)
Ability to isolate when not in use
General lighting
Ease and economy of temperature control
Security provisions
Emergency lighting and emergency exits
Potential for multipurpose use
Accessibility from dressing rooms
Accessibility from scenic-loading areas
Fire curtain
Act curtain

Teasers, pipes, lines, rigging systems

Fly space, catwalks, etc.

Automated versus manually operated equipment

Wing space (preferably as large as stage on both sides and /or behind stage)

Quick-change dressing areas in wings

Cross-over wing space (minimum of three feet)

Well-marked and lighted steps to stage

Stage flooring (must be of wood)

Floor traps

Stage revolves

Apron space

Stage wiring and lighting systems

Footlights

Back-of-house projection and control booth

Facilities for motion picture projection

Space and facilities for rear projection

Cyclorama

Upstage wall

Ability to isolate from street noise

Ability to seal from daylight and other light sources

Stage manager's control booth and area

Stage manager's communication systems (with front of house, dressing rooms and stage hands)

Stage-to-dressing-room amplifiers

Sound systems

Orchestra pit (size, flexibility, etc.)

Orchestra pit entrances (below stage level)

Orchestra lift or elevator

2. *THE DRESSING ROOMS*

Size (minimum of sixteen square feet per actor)

Number of rooms

Ability to isolate when not in use

General lighting

Ease and economy of temperature control

Ventilation

Security provisions

Accessibility from stage and stage door

Space for doorman near stage door

Call-board and mailbox facilities

Flooring

Corridors and stairs to stage (wide enough for passing actors in
   large costumes)

General appearance and decor

Communication systems with stage and front of house

Water fountains

Elevators to stage (if more than two stories above or below stage
   level)

Chorus dressing rooms (for approximately fifteen actors)

Musicians' dressing rooms (for approximately thirty people)

Ballet dressing rooms (for approximately thirty people)

Star dressing rooms (with private rest room, for one actor each)

Conductor's dressing room (with private rest room for one person
   each)

Makeup lighting

Mirrors

Overhead shelving and wig racks

Clothing racks in well ventilated area

Stage-to-dressing room sound system

Dressing room sinks

Showers (required for all musical productions)

Rest room facilities (distance from dressing rooms, number of;
   should be for exclusive use of performers, etc.)

Safe and sanitary conditions in relation to public health laws and
   union regulations

Green room facilities

Wardrobe room (preferably with washers, sinks, dryers and ironing
   equipment

Wig and makeup storage facilities


3. *THE REHEARSAL AREAS:*

Stage-size rooms available for rehearsal

Flooring (preferably same as stage)

Other space available for rehearsal

Ability to isolate from rest of building

General appearance and decor

Ease and economy of temperature control

General lighting

Ability to adapt to multipurpose usage

Access to stage, orchestra pit, dressing rooms

Musicians' warm-up rooms

Ballet warmup rooms

Dance barres, mirrors, etc.

Security provisions

Rest room and shower facilities

Locker facilities

## *The Scenic Production Areas*

Space and facilities for the construction of scenery, costumes and props is a decided asset in any theatre building intended to support resident productions. Commercial theatres in New York and on the road do not require such space because the physical production is usually a temporary tenant. But in cases where the landlord (whether an individual or an organization) is also a producer who originates productions from the beginning, facilities for the construction and rehearsal of productions will be necessary either in the theatre building or elsewhere. If located away from the theatre, scenic construction areas may be more costly due to scenery transportation requirements and more difficult to control from the administrative point of view. The operation that is centralized under one roof is always the more desirable.

Like the auditorium itself, adequate scenic production facilities require an enormous amount of space and a large capital investment in machinery and supplies, which makes such facilities impractical for organizations that do not offer a number of different productions on a regular basis. Scenic construction areas are also difficult to utilize for non-theatrical purposes. In cases where the theatre building does not contain such facilities, it is possible to rent lofts, bowling alleys, warehouses or other low cost spaces. Some amateur and stock theatres find it necessary to construct most scenery out of doors or in neighboring barns and garages. Some educational theatres utilize the industrial arts workshop in their school or college. Whatever solutions are found, the place and the cost for scenic construction should be studied carefully when plans to build or utilize a theatre are being formulated. The following list should serve as a working guide:

1. *THE SCENIC CONSTRUCTION SHOP*

Size

Accessibility to stage

Space available exclusively for construction

Ability to isolate when not in use

General lighting and electric power facilities

Ease and economy of temperature control

Humidity problems (in relation to the drying of painted flats, drops, etc.)

Flooring

Fireproofing (and adequate space to fireproof set pieces)

Ability to use during performance hours

Lumber storage provisions

Scenery storage and dock areas

Loading docks and ramps

Scenic painting docks and convenient slop sinks

Scenic construction areas

Work tables

Tool storage cabinets

Paint and brush cleaning and storage facilities

Tool inventory: hand and power tools

Stock scenery and platform inventory

Muslin and fabric inventory

Security provisions

Office space for designer and technical directors

Public and interoffice communication systems


2. *STAGE ELECTRICS SHOP*

Lighting designer's office space

Stage electrician's office and work space

Size

Security provisions

Accessibility to theatre and stage

Inventory of stage lighting instruments

Inventory of gels

Inventory of light projectors and special effects equipment

Inventory of tools

Inventory of lamps, bulbs, etc.

Inventory of electrical cable, plugs, etc.

Storage space

Fireproofing


3. *THE PROPERTIES SHOP*

Size

Accessibility to theatre and stage

Security provisions

General lighting

Office and work space for properties supervisors

Storage space for hand props

Storage space for furniture and large props

Provisions near stage for storage and preparation of perishable
props, food, etc.

Inventory of properties

Inventory of fabrics and supplies

4. *THE COSTUME SHOP*

Size

Accessibility to theatre and stage

Security provisions

General lighting and adequate power source

Office space for costume designer

Work space, cutting tables, etc.

Inventory of sewing machines, irons, etc.

Inventory of supplies

Inventory of fabrics

Inventory of costumes (clothing, hats, wigs, shoes, jewelry, etc.)

Storage cabinets

Storerooms for costume collection

Fitting rooms

Library of resource books

Fireproofing

Laundry and dyeing facilities

## *The Administration Areas*

As with the space and facilities provided for performers, many theatres
also fall short when it comes to the areas in which its administrators must
work. The members of a management staff in a fairly active theatre are
usually required to work long hours in places that often resemble the cells of
a maximum security prison rather than places designed to encourage efficient work and pleasant attitudes. What, then, is an appropriate checklist of
items and factors to consider when it comes to planning office space for an
executive staff?

1. *THE MANAGEMENT OFFICES*

Size

Number of separate offices available

Physical relationship of offices to each other

Accessibility to theatre and rest of operation

Need for branch offices away from theatre

Ability to isolate when not in use

Security provisions

General appearance and decor

Ease and economy of temperature control

Flooring

Soundproofing

General lighting

Inventory of furniture, equipment, supplies

Storage space for records and supplies

Communication systems (with public, with other departments in theatre, between offices)

Reception space

Secretarial space

Executive space

Board room or conference room space

Library and archive space

Press office space and facilities

Reasonable privacy for executives


## 2. *THE BOX OFFICE*

Size

Security provisions

General appearance and decor

Ease and economy of temperature control (ability to isolate from exterior weather conditions)

Fireproofing

Soundproofing

General lighting

Proximity to business offices

Number of customer windows or spaces

Number of treasurers who can be accommodated

Communication systems (with public and offices)

Ticket storage space

Storage space for equipment and supplies

Inventory of equipment and supplies

Need for theatre-operated agencies away from building

Accessibility to general public

Safe

Work space away from public view

Convenience of telephone to ticket window

Each item on the preceeding checklists can be translated into a considerable amount of money when purchase or alteration of it is necessary. Its condition and how close it comes to being ideal and serviceable will contribute to the value of a theatre both as a physical asset and as a factor that contributes to or detracts from operational efficiency. While no theatre is perfect, most theatres could come much closer to achieving optimum conditions if more time were spent on detail in the planning and organizing stages of construction or renovation.

# SUMMATION

From the time an idea to build or acquire a theatre is conceived until opening night and throughout the life of the organization, it must be kept in mind that the performer is central to everything else. We build theatres primarily for actors to act in, not primarily to display scenery, to exhibit architecture or to memorialize an individual. Throughout every phase of planning and producing a play, the acting company, its repertory and its artistic objectives must be the dominating influence in all decision-making. Of all the raw materials available to the theatre today, perhaps the most important one, as British director Peter Brook has pointed out, is empty or open space. It is space, pure and simple, that the actor can best mold according to the unlimited dimensions of the imagination.

When contracting for a theatre, then, every precaution should be taken to insure that artistic policy will be established by the theatre personnel and not by the architecture and the physical surroundings or, at least, that these elements—the human and the physical—complement each other. A strong sales resistance must be developed against architects, designers, consultants and technologists who are more interested in form than in function, in methods as opposed to results, in efficiency as opposed to effect, in machinery as opposed to people. A newfangled stage lighting system, for example, may be a wonderful thing for a large professional theatre but a foolish luxury in a high school theatre where no one has the knowledge or ability to operate it. Traditional methods of doing things must always be weighed against those that are new and revolutionary. The methods finally adopted should be the ones best suited to the needs and objectives of a particular producing organization. Many people want the "newest and the best" while others merely want "a theatre that looks like a theatre." It is up to those who will work in a theatre building to exert their influence in securing what they believe comes closest to being ideal for them.

# 4

# The Personnel
# For The Theatre

A FTER defining the artistic goals of a theatre project or company, the most basic decisions regarding its organization relate to the following questions:

Will it be incorporated, unincorporated or a partnership?
Will it be commercial or nonprofit?
Will it be union or nonunion?
Will it be professional or nonprofessional?

This chapter deals with the last two of these questions by discussing general principles of personnel management, then turning to the special problems of managing unsalaried workers as well as the more complex problem of managing union workers. But first, let's clarify the difference between a professional and a nonprofessional.

If a member of Equity was asked to define a professional actor, the answer would be "a professional actor is a member of Actors' Equity." And most unions and their members would agree with such a qualification. However, there are many skilled and talented theatre people—directors, designers, managers and actors—who earn a living from their specialization and yet do not belong to a union. For this reason, a "professional" may better be defined as someone who earns money from his or her work. A nonprofessional, then, would be someone who works without receiving money for it, although there may well be other types of reward. "Professional" also implies that the work produced is of high quality. Humphrey Bogart had another definition, once stating, "A professional is a guy who does his job well—even when he doesn't feel like it !"

## DIVISIONS OF THEATRICAL LABOR

The upcoming six chapters discuss the different types of theatre in

America and how each is usually organized and staffed. But no matter how or why a theatre is organized, the work that needs to be done falls into three distinct categories: artistic, production and administrative. Each category requires workers who possess definably different sets of skills, attitudes and interests. It may even be said that each requires a certain temperament. Some people are just not happy sitting at a desk, and others are nervous wrecks when facing an audience. So an important objective of personnel management is placing or replacing workers into the jobs they will do best.

Above the staff or cast level, of course, there are managers or supervisors. And above this level of personnel there is the top leadership of the project or organization: the producer in commercial theatre, the board of trustees in nonprofit theatre, the college president or department chairperson in campus theatre. According to guidelines set by the National Labor Relations Board, management cannot be unionized. The general manager of Circle Repertory Company cannot work as a member of the Association of Theatrical Press Agents and Managers (ATPAM), nor can the college president work as a member of a teachers' union. This is contestable, however, and not always followed in practice. Theatrical producers and general managers, for instance, often join ATPAM early in their careers and maintain active membership. To gain and build upon union benefits, many general managers work under ATPAM contracts—though far above the ATPAM minimum wage—and producers sometimes sign themselves to a company manager's contract for shows they are producing in order to earn a salary, to which the role of producer alone does not entitle them. So theatre productions and companies are comprised of three levels of personnel and three divisions of labor:

*Leadership Level*
(Producer, Landlord, Board)

*Management Level*
(General Manager - - - - Artistic Director)

*Staff Level*
(Administrative, Production, Artistic)

In nearly all cases the chain of command in the theatre—clearly progressing from top leader down to the lowest staffer—is just as vertical as it appears in the above chart. But there are alternatives. Historically, many eighteenth century European and American theatres were operated as shareholding companies in which the actors were the main shareholders, and decisions were made by vote. Today, a few theatre companies are organized as collectives in which all matters—both artistic and managerial—must be discussed and agreed to by most or all members. The Living Theatre and Mabou Mines are two examples. But what may sound enchanting in theory can be very inefficient and very boring in practice. In fact, after thirty years as a self-managed company, The Living Theatre finally gave in to time-tested tradition and hired a general manager. Similarly, Chicago's Steppenwolf Theatre Company abandoned its collective play selection process and appointed an artistic director from within its own ranks to handle such decision-making.

## DEFINING STAFF REQUIREMENTS
### Organizational Structure

Each basic type of theatre organization—commercial, nonprofit, educational and community—dictates its own peculiar personnel requirements. Unlike a commercial enterprise, for example, a nonprofit theatre must have a board of trustees, is likely to have an artistic director as well as a managing director and should also employ fundraising personnel. If the theatre hires union workers, certain jobs will be mandated and union employees will be limited in the hours and types of tasks they are permitted to perform. This may require more personnel to accomplish things than would be the case in a nonunion situation. If the theatre is a constituent of a larger institution, personnel requirements may vary greatly from those in an independently operated theatre. This is especially obvious in the case of a college theatre, for which virtually all salaried positions may be paid for by the college budget and filled by people such as instructors, technicians and custodians whose main jobs are something else.

A good way to begin defining what jobs must be created and how the operation will function in terms of its chain of command is to draw up a table of organization—also called a "line chart," because it clearly shows the lines of authority and who will report to whom in the following fashion:

When the line chart is developed, each job title is shown, often in a little box, with a line connecting that position to a supervisor above and, perhaps, staff people below. To inform personnel how the organization is structured and exactly where each person fits in, the line chart could be distributed with job orientation material or even displayed in the reception area. The danger is that such charts can encourage an overly rigid style of personnel management. They do not take the human element into account and may tempt management not to see creative solutions in combining several jobs into one, or redefining job titles and responsibilities or changing the chain of command. And from the employee's point of view, let's face it, people don't want to be put into a box except as a very last resort! So personnel charts are a useful planning tool but should probably be kept in the manager's desk drawer most of the time.

## Minimum staffing requirements

What size and type of staff does a theatre need to fulfill its purpose efficiently? The following chart demonstrates that as professionalism increases so do the number of jobs required to produce the final product.

New York producers often complain about having to hire unnecessary union workers, yet production quality on Broadway is equalled only by that found in major opera houses, which, incidentally, deal with even more unions than the Broadway houses.

The type of production(s) being produced also has a major impact upon staff requirements. Musical theatre almost always requires more artistic and production personnel than nonmusical theatre. Repertory theatre requires more personnel than nonrepertory. Similarly, Shakespearean or classical theatre may require more actors and staff than contemporary theatre. And the larger the performance facility, the more people will be needed to operate it efficiently.

In reality, most commercial theatres are somewhat understaffed due to financial constraints, especially in terms of administrative personnel. More help is almost always needed in promotion and marketing, for example. Many college theatres are overstaffed, largely due to faculty and staff tenure systems, although this does not increase their production efficiency or quality. The well-established, nonprofit professional theatres—except during times of a budget crisis—seem to achieve the most reasonable staffing efficiency. Too many people on the job can be just as detrimental as too few. However, it is better to be slightly shorthanded than to be conspicuously overstaffed. No employee should be truly indispensable, but each person should feel and, indeed, *be* needed.

## AN 800 SEAT, NON-MUSICAL THEATRE: TYPICAL STAFF REQUIREMENTS (Excluding Performers)

| | Non-professional community theatre (multi-production season) | | Stock theatre using AEA company (multi-production season) | | Broadway theatre (one production) | |
|---|---|---|---|---|---|---|
| | Full-time operating staff (non-salaried) | Part-time or on fee, royalty or optional | Full-time operating staff (non-union) | Part-time or on fee, royalty or optional | Full-time operating staff (union) | Part-time or on fee, royalty or optional |
| | Artistic Director<br>House Manager<br>Box Office Treasurer<br>Stage Manager<br>Master Electrician<br>Properties Master<br>Stage crew<br>Makeup crew | Board of Directors<br>Committees<br>Executive Secretary<br>Business Secretary<br>Publicity Chairman<br>Ticket Sales committees<br>Legal Counsel<br>Director<br>Author*<br>Scenic, Lighting and Costume Designer<br>Scene and costume construction crews<br>Ushers<br>Ticket takers<br>Prompters<br>Maintenance crew | Producer or Artistic Director<br>General Manager<br>Business Manager<br>House Manager<br>Secretary<br>Box Office Treasurer<br>Assistant Treasurer<br>Publicity Director<br>Janitor(s)<br>Production Stage Manager*<br>Scenic Designer<br>Lighting Designer<br>Costume Designer<br>Properties Master.<br>Technical Director<br>Carpenter<br>Stitcher and Wardrobe Supervisor<br>Master Electrician<br>5-15 technicians or apprentices | Board of Directors (if nonprofit)<br>Attorney<br>Accountant<br>Director*<br>Author*<br>Group Sales Manager<br>Ushers<br>Ticket takers<br>Doorman<br>Poster crew, etc.<br>Security Guard<br>Hairdresser and wig specialist<br>House Physician<br>Matrons | *(Producer's Staff)*<br>General Manager<br>Company Manager*<br>Stage Manager*<br>Assistant Stage Manager*<br>Stagehands*<br>Fly crew*<br>Light crew*<br>Makeup artist*<br>Hairdresser*<br>Wardrobe Supervisor*<br>Press Agent*<br>Dressers*<br>*(Landlord's Staff)*<br>House Manager*<br>Treasurers*<br>Ushers*<br>Doormen*<br>Carpenter*<br>Electrician*<br>Property Master*<br>Cleaners*<br>Matrons*<br>Heat, air-conditioning and other maintenance<br>Fireman*<br>Watchman*<br>Porter | Director*<br>Author*<br>Scenic Designer*<br>Costume Designer*<br>Lighting Designer*<br>Scene builders*<br>Scene painters*<br>Costume builders*<br>Wig makers*<br>Prop builders*<br>Scene transporters*<br>Attorney<br>Accountant(s)<br>House Physician<br>Ad Agency<br>Group Sales |

*Working under union or other collective bargaining association contract.

## Job Combining

Combining several jobs into one position may be frowned upon by large institutions or may be forbidden by labor unions, but it is a practice common to many theatres, because of limited finances or because it encourages greater efficiency. For example, an employee should be able to assume more work and responsibility as time goes on. And most people respond well when they are given new challenges on top of familiar routines. Big industries have recognized this factor and many have reassigned the one-task assemblyline worker to multi-task, beginning-to-end production work.

It would not be wise in the theatre, however, to combine a backstage with a front-of-house position, a leading performance job with any other, any two jobs that involve similar hours or require being in two difference places at the same time or any two jobs that require full-time work. When it is permissible, what are some of the most frequent and successful job combinations?

Producer and Director
Producer and General Manager
Producer and Business Manager
Producer and Publicity Director
Director and Designer
Stage Manager and Lighting Designer
Assistant Stage Manager and Properties Master
Scenic Designer and Costume and Properties Designer
Scenic Designer and Lighting, Costume and Props Designer
Lighting Designer and Electrician
Designer and Technical Director
Publicity Director and House Manager
Publicity Director and Assistant Box Office Treasurer
Publicity Director and Assistant to the General Manager
Publicity Director and Assistant to the Producer
Business Manager and Box Office Treasurer
Business Manager and House Manager
Business Manager and Associate Producer
Business Manager and Assistant Manager

Job combining is frequently a good device for offering a person the highest possible salary, the fanciest job title and the greatest set of challenges. Successful job combinations, however, always depend upon the interests, qualifications and abilities of the individuals for whom they are designed. Because one person may perform several jobs simultaneously in a superb manner does not mean that a replacement with the same ability can ever be found or, necessarily, should even be sought. Jobs must be suited to people, not people to jobs.

## Who Will Hire Whom?

Employees always reflect the people who hired them in some way. And hiring and casting decisions will go a long way in determining the success or failure of an organization or production. In the commercial theatre, the producer contracts all the leading artists and may even veto casting decisions made by the director. The general manager hired by the producer usually hires the administrative personnel, except those hired by a Broadway landlord. In professional nonprofit theatre, hiring power is usually split between the managing director and the artistic director. And in campus and community theatre, outside of the casting process, hiring is usually done by a committee. However, in large nonprofit theatres, presenting organizations and performing arts centers, hiring power may be given to department heads. The marketing director, for instance, may hold both hiring and firing authority for the entire marketing staff. This will probably mean that the staff will feel more loyalty and perhaps respect for the marketing director than, say, for the general manager. There is a potential danger here for divisiveness, for the creation of a little fiefdom, but the advantages of delegating hiring authority to department heads in large organizations outweigh the disadvantages. In small organizations all staff members are best hired by the top manager in order to create unity and the singleness of purpose, style and character that will help determine the public profile of the organization.

# ATTRACTING APPLICANTS

## Writing the Job Description

The first step in finding the right employee is composing the right job description. No matter how familiar the hiring agent is with the organization and the job in question—perhaps the position has been filled and refilled four or five times during the past year—it is always wise to put the job description in writing, even if it's not going to be published or distributed. This forces the employer to review what the job has entailed in the past, what different tasks and responsibilities it might now entail and what qualifications are necessary. Salary range, title and benefits should be listed. Once written, the job description should be discussed with appropriate employees in the organization and, perhaps, with the person who is leaving the position. Does it reflect the true nature of the job? Has anything been left out? Overly vague or misleading job descriptions, if published, will waste the time many of applicants as well as that of the hiring agent. While a salary range is commonly omitted because the employer hopes to hire someone for less than can actually be afforded by the budget, this tactic should be avoided. Too many greatly overqualified or underqualified applicants will apply, and it may be tempting for the employer to make a salary offer much higher than originally intended. The following sample presents a job description that is sufficiently detailed and that is also worded in an honest style:

## ART'S ADMINISTRATION POSITION AVAILABLE— LORT B THEATRE

### Assistant to General Manager/Company Manager

Responsibilities include assisting General Manager in all areas of operation for a LORT B regional theatre in Houston, Texas; supervise building maintenance, coordinate special events, handle purchasing of equipment and supplies and other unglorious duties. Position also entails making travel and housing arrangements for visiting artists and others. Salary low 20s plus benefits. Must have own car, computer skills a plus together with theatre experience. Send resume to Jack Sprat, Box 1000 GPO, Houston, TX 00000.

When a theatre is preparing a general or seasonal announcement of job openings, the aim once again should be completeness of information and honesty. For example:

STAR PLAYHOUSE: Located near Aspen, CO, Star Playhouse is a nonprofit summer theatre producing an annual season of six plays performed by non-Equity actors and offering college credit through the University of Colorado summer school. Auditions held in April in Denver, Chicago & LA for 6 resident actors ($200. per week) and 10 apprentice actors (nonsalaried). Other openings for technical and administrative positions (salary range: $50. to $200. per week). Send pictures and/or resumes to: Michael Boulder, 000 Vale Ave., Denver, CO 00000.

If the above listing were published in the appropriate theatrical periodicals, Mr. Boulder could expect to receive dozens, even hundreds of applications from many parts of the country. While resumes and photographs are helpful, it is even better in such cases to have all applicants complete a

standard application form. This insures that the exact information of greatest interest to the employer will be put in writing, and it provides a uniform
device by which to compare many applications quickly and intelligently.
The following standard items should be included on most application forms
for administrative positions:

Applicant's name
Present address and zip code—if temporary, until what date
Permanent address and zip code, if different from above
Present home and work telephone numbers
Education:
  High school and year completed
  College: degrees and when completed, major subjects
  Professional training, workshops attended, etc.
Driver's license?
Owner of automobile?
Office skills (typing, computer, etc.)
Date available for employment?
Date when applicant must terminate employment (if seasonal)
Statement of career goals
Listing of theatre experience and positions (or attach resume)
Names, addresses and phone numbers of three people who may be
  requested to provide statements about the applicant
List of hometown and college newspapers (for publicity department)

It should be noted that questions regarding race, age, sex and marital
status are inadmissible. The application form should be accompanied by a
covering letter (a Xeroxed form letter will do) that describes the goals of the
theatre company, its artistic accomplishments, the type of employees it is
seeking, the nature of the working and living conditions and other details
that may generate the applicant's interest. But, again, the information should
be honest. If, for example, "apprentice actors" are really used only on
production crews and never permitted to act in the main productions, this
should be clearly stated, as should salary range, special housing problems
or costs and other such matters.

## Broadcasting the Job Opening

Most job openings are first announced in a person-to-person manner,
usually by the employer contacting known and trusted colleagues who may
be able to refer qualified applicants. This explains why, by the time a job
announcement is mailed out or published, the job may already have been
filled. All government and tax-supported employers, however, must adver-

tise openings and process applications according to equal opportunity employment guidelines. And all employers are bound by federal anti-discrimination laws pertaining to hiring, work conditions, promotion and firing. Additional laws of this type vary according to the city and state in which the business is located.

Outlets for listing job openings common to most employers, such as the classified sections of local newspapers and the state employment agency, are seldom a good source for theatrical workers. But trade publications, such as *Backstage* or *Variety* may work. And a number of national arts service organizations provide job listings and referral services, including the Association of Performing Arts Presenters (APAP), and Theatre Communications Group (TCG), which publishes *ArtSearch*. This is similar to *National Arts JobBank*, published by the Western States Arts Foundation (WESTAF) in Santa Fe, New Mexico. Listings carried by such groups pertain mainly to administrative, technical and teaching positions with nonprofit organizations.

Perhaps the most time honored way of broadcasting a job opening is simply to mail a brief announcement to an appropriate list of places, such as college theatre departments or theatre companies. These may then be posted on bulletin boards or given to appropriate faculty and students.

## Search Firms and Employment Agencies

Search firms, or "headhunters," as they are also called, may be engaged to conduct a search that will end by filling a particular job opening. These companies work for and are paid by the employer, usually to find top-level executives as opposed to junior staff. The most established search firms that specialize in finding management personnel for arts organizations are Opportunity Resources for the Arts, in New York; Management Consultants for the Arts, in Greenwich, Connecticut, and Los Angeles; and Boyden International, in Madison, New Jersey. But more generalized companies may also be used.

While search firms are hired by the employer, employment agencies work for the job-seeker and are utilized by the hopeful employee, who pays them a percentage of the first year's salary if a job is secured through the agency. Rarely are specialized top management jobs found or filled in this way in the theatre, but a theatre may, for instance, find both private and state employment agencies a good source for clerical and custodial help.

## Talent and Casting Agents and Contractors

Talent agencies are a specialized type of private employment agency that represent such artists as performers, writers, directors and musicians.

They must be licensed by the state in which they do business, and some must also be franchised by the labor union to which their clients belong, such as Actors' Equity Association. There are many talent agencies throughout the country and they have long been recognized by producers and directors as a primary source of artist employees. Their compensation is a percentage of the salaries received for jobs that they arrange. Large agencies that represent a diversity of talent may offer a producing organization a "package" in which they represent the playwright as well as a director, and perhaps also the leading performer.

Casting agents, like search firms, work for the producer/employer to identify and secure all the performers required by a particular script. They are a common and influential presence in film and television production today and are also used by some Broadway producers. While professional nonprofit theatres often use talent agencies or in-house casting directors, there has been a growing reliance on resident dramaturgs rather than casting agents or directors. A dramaturg, of course, advises the theatre company primarily about matters of repertoire and dramatic literature, but is also concerned with all artistic elements including the casting.

A contractor is a private businessperson who supplies union performers—mostly musicians—to Broadway shows, road shows, cabarets, nightclubs, orchestral groups and others. They are located in every major city and might be the best source of certain talent in the event that a musician or specialty performer must be replaced on short notice.

## THE HIRING PROCESS

When an organization invites resumes and applications from potential employees—whether the job is administrative, production or artistic—it should be prepared to answer each and every response it receives. It is inconsiderate and unprofessional to invite applications and then to ignore them. Of course, not every applicant need be interviewed or auditioned, but all should at least be acknowledged.

### Interviewing the Applicant

A person's first visit and personal contact with an organization and its directors creates an impression that, if hired, will last throughout that person's employment and serve as a positive, negative or fuzzy foundation for it. Few theatres are so large that every interviewee cannot be given a personal tour of the building and an introduction to the appropriate department heads. If the job opening is for a leading position, the interview should be spread over several days, to allow the applicant to meet a number of people and become better known to future colleagues. Before such an applicant is hired, a conference should be held between the hiring agent and employees who have met the applicant. The job candidate's qualifications and personality should be discussed, especially in regard to how he or she might get along with others in the operation. When interviews and conferences go badly, it is generally because too little thought is given to seemingly minor details, or because too little time is allowed.

## Auditioning the Performer

It is easy for seasoned producers and directors to become jaded about auditions and treat performers little better than cattle. But even the most seasoned performer may always find that auditioning causes acute anxiety, at best. Auditioning is a very uncertain, risky and personal exposure of ego and ability upon which depends a job, if not an entire career. People who conduct auditions should always keep this in mind and treat the auditioning performers accordingly. This means a polite greeting, a few words of encouragement to help the performer relax and a pleasant "thank you" at the end. More time is usually required to audition nonprofessionals, because they are unaccustomed to the audition process and often uncertain of how best to demonstrate their talents and abilities. But courtesy and sensitivity should always be shown to nonprofessional and professional auditioners alike.

While auditions for the majority of theatrical productions are just held locally, and just for that particular production, this is not always the case. Some professional resident theatres hire a company of actors to perform in a series of different productions throughout a season of many weeks. If that theatre is in Minneapolis, for example, it may hold auditions in New York or Los Angeles or both, and these might be comparatively lengthy and complex, since the artistic director is seeking actors who can play a number of roles and also work well as an ensemble. Other large theatres hold regional auditions each year in four or five cities throughout the country. This enables them to see a great amount of talent (usually nonprofessionals) in a short time. Also, several professional associations, such as the University/ Resident Theatre Association (U/RTA), arrange regional auditions together with interviews for administrative and production jobs for their member theatre groups. Two or three dozen artistic directors and managers may attend the audition held in their region of the nation and watch auditions and oral presentations by hundreds of hopeful participants. It is a very efficient hiring technique and could be adopted by more groups of theatres than presently use it.

## Checking References

Before an applicant is hired it is always good policy to check his or her qualifications with others familiar with them. When the hiring agent knows a colleague who also knows the applicant well, this will usually provide the most dependable reference. The next best thing is knowing the reference by reputation. But even checking with unknown people whose names were provided by the applicant can produce information that will eventually be helpful either in supervising the employee or avoiding a mistake by hiring this person in the first place. Rarely should any staff position be filled based only on the hiring agent's intuition about a candidate. Casting decisions, however, are often based largely upon a director's intuition about a performer. The perception of talent is a gift in itself and, if it is unproved talent, not something that any two people might agree upon. So casting decisions tend to be lonelier and more private decisions than most others in a hiring process. Of course, there is also the question of a performer's work habits. In the professional theatre, it seldom takes long for bad reputations to become widely known among directors and managers, and not a few casting decisions take such knowledge into account.

## Handshakes, Letters of Agreement, Job Contracts

While countless employees have worked many years in a job without having any written agreement with their employer, such an arrangement is nonetheless an invitation for the distress of one party or both. Far better to define, even loosely, such basic terms of employment as salary, scheduled increments, promotion, hours, duties and responsibilities, title, benefits, severance notice and pay, and the like. This may be done briefly in a letter of agreement from the employer to the employee. In the case of important, high-salaried positions with performing arts companies or institutions, a formal agreement would be drawn up and checked by lawyers for both parties. Members of Actors' Equity, most employees on Broadway, on the road, in large civic or campus performing arts centers, work under a collective bargaining agreement of some kind. This provides the most detailed terms of employment and the strongest guarantee that such terms will be upheld. In addition to a basic agreement between a union and an employer, there may also be a contract that specifies additional terms between the employer and each individual employee, as is the case with members of Equity and most other theatrical unions. While the employer has no choice but to sign such contracts (short of union busting), much of what they contain (such as salary, billing in the program, payment of royalties or percentage of box office income) is highly negotiable.

## Determining Job Title, Salary and Perks

Employees who work under a collective bargaining agreement are guaranteed a minimum rate of pay and various minimum benefits and working conditions. Those minimum terms, then, mark the starting point for negotiations between the hiring agent and the job candidate. The employer, whether in a commercial or nonprofit operation, generally hopes to give no concessions above the union minimums, and the candidate hopes to get as many concessions above them as possible. Academic and civil service positions provide the most rigid job protection (often including tenure), while nonprofessional and largely nonunion professional companies offer the least. In the latter case, whether it's a civic opera company where the only union contract is with the American Federation of Musicians (AFM), or a summer theatre where the only union contract is with Equity, management has the greatest latitude in its hiring and employment practices.

Often, a salary demand may be negotiated downward from what the applicant requests in exchange for certain benefits and opportunities. Or a lower salary may be accepted in exchange for a particular job title, job location, prestigious company, working hours, travel benefits, entertainment allowance or whatever. In short, money is not the only type of payment for labor.

Some theatre personnel are traditionally paid on a fee basis, including directors and designers. Minimum per-production or per-design fees have been set by the Society of Stage Directors and Choreographers (SSDC) and United Scenic Artists (USA) respectively. When such artists work on or off-Broadway, they frequently receive a fee plus a small percentage of the box office income. When they are hired to be in residence and work on a series of productions, however, they are usually paid by means of a weekly salary. A few staff members might also be offered a percentage above their salaries: telemarketing people, who sell tickets by phone, or group sales people might be given a percentage of their sales receipts.

Just as the job applicant must remember that the salary offered will not be the amount taken home after taxes and other deductions (unless salary is paid as a fee on an independent contractor basis) so the employer must remember that the salary offered is less than that employee will actually cost. Over the base salary, the employer must pay matching social security taxes that are based on the gross salary and the worker's deductions. Further payroll costs may include payments for medical insurance, unemployment insurance, disability insurance, worker's compensation, pension and welfare funds, and other standard benefits. Generally, payroll taxes and benefits will add an additional 20 percent to the base salary. The promise of royalties or percentages could add considerably more, as could food and housing allowances, per diems, travel reimbursement and expense accounts. But there is another hidden cost involved in hiring certain people that must also be kept in mind. A theatre company may be able to afford to pay a person's salary or fee, yet be unable to support the style or manner in which that person works. Just as it would be foolish to buy a car without having enough money for gas, so it is foolish to hire a top flight costume designer, say, without having the facilities, staff and budget to buy fabrics and build the costumes. This type of management mistake, which happens often, can be avoided by checking on a person's work habits before a contract is signed and then by realistically computing what those habits and approaches to the work at hand will cost the organization. Some workers require an assistant or a whole staff while others may not. Some may require more work space than others, more equipment and materials, more sophisticated technology, more phone calls, more travel or whatever. Experience, professionalism and high standards are usually accompanied by high quality results *and* high costs.

## JOB TRAINING AND ORIENTATION
### Staff Orientation

Some managers simply plunge new employees headlong into the work; others prefer to put them through a period of special training. Off-site training paid by the employer might include a short course in computer skills. Usually, however, all training is done on the job. If the position is a new one, the employee may have to learn by trial and error. Otherwise, the departing staff person may train the incoming employee—providing that the departure is amiable and that the employer wants the job done as it has been in the past.

Most nonartistic jobs in a theatre—from general manager to building custodian—should be clearly and specifically outlined in an effective work manual that describes all the responsibilities and peculiarities of a particular job or department. The Sample Manual for Box Office Treasurers in Appendix G provides an example. At the very least, every on-going theatre operation should maintain periodically-updated manuals that cover general management, business management, marketing and promotion, fundraising, box office operations, house management, company management, production supervision (costumes, scenery, lighting, props, makeup), technical supervision (tools, supplies, stage equipment), and facility maintenance and operation. In outline form, each manual should deal with work hours, supervisory responsibilities, procedures to follow under both normal and emergency conditions, lists of relevant vendors and service companies with their phone numbers. Each department head should update the appropriate manual at least annually and submit it to the general manager, perhaps with recommendations for improvements and purchases. Manuals make the orientation of a new employee much easier and more efficient than verbal orientation alone. Supervisors should remember, however, that no two people work in the same manner. A given system may suit one person well but not another, and there is always a better way of doing something. Procedural flexibility is desirable, and a work manual should be used as a guide and history of operations, not as a bible.

When an entire staff has been hired to begin work for the first time, as in the case of a new theatre or at the beginning of a new season, a general orientation meeting involving all personnel is essential to clarify and restate goals and objectives, to set the right tone, to establish a sense of unity, to introduce people to each other and to establish the chain of authority. This should be followed by break-out meetings for each department or area in the operation and finally by one-on-one discussions and instruction among supervisors and staff members. When a new employee comes into a functioning operation, the same process should be followed more informally. It always pays management to spend a little extra time and effort with new employees so they will become an integral part of the team as soon as possible.

## The Rehearsal Process

Rehearsing is a unique form of job orientation invented to avoid the embarrassment of on-the-job training in front of an audience. As discussed in the next chapter, Equity members rehearse under a very stringent set of rules. While the director of the production is the overall rehearsal supervisor, the production stage manager attends to the details, monitors the union rule book and assists the director.     Because the stage manager on Broadway puts together the prompt book that contains the stage directions, he or she may later work with a publisher in creating the acting edition of the script that will be used in future non-professional productions. Also, the stage manager often rehearses replacement cast members once the show is in production and may even direct road versions of the show; and so it is that many stage managers become directors themselves.

When a theatre or production has a company manager, this person serves as management's representative in dealing with cast and rehearsal needs and problems. When this is not the case, the theatre's general manager, the producer or the college department's chairperson must fill this function. Most directors prefer that rehearsals be kept closed to everyone not directly related to the production.   However, the producer or the management should make its presence known by being supportive of the artistic process. All Equity actors, including stars, are paid at the union's minimum salary rate during the rehearsal period and only receive their contractual salary as of the first public performance. Nonetheless, performers probably work harder during the rehearsal period than any other time and they probably feel most vulnerable at that time. Management and staff need to keep this in mind.

## GOALS AND TECHNIQUES OF
## PERSONNEL SUPERVISION

Three of the leading goals in personnel supervision are the economical organization of the workers' time, control over the quality of their work and the achievement of optimum output. How each employee is judged according to these goals differs according to that person's job. For example, a time-quality-output-efficient box office treasurer would be one who can process fifty to sixty telephone and window ticket sales per hour without making a mistake.    A time-quality-output-efficient Equity actor is one who performs a given role with equal brilliance eight times a week. The manager's efficiency is judged by the fact that he or she hired and supervised that terrific treasurer, just as the director's success is judged by that brilliant actor. The success of the theatre organization as a whole, however, will be measured either in economic terms (how many tickets were sold and how much profit was made) or in terms of its stated goals (to produce outstanding new American plays), or a combination of both. The more efficiently each employee performs, the more likely the whole organization will succeed.

### Leadership

Leadership goes beyond management, beyond merely figuring out how to accomplish something. Effective leadership understands why something is being done and inspires people with the value of what they are doing. Good leadership qualities are desirable in anyone who holds a supervisory position, from the office manager to the board president. Employees appreciate a supervisor who displays common sense, fairness, humor and who also keeps them mindful of the why and the value of their labor. Poor leadership or the lack of leadership at the head of an organization or production almost always leads to malaise, if not malfunction. The effective leader is able to inspire and enthuse, to teach and explain and, importantly, to share both power and responsibility. This last quality is perhaps the most difficult to learn and so is a rarity in ambitious, young supervisors. Sharing requires great    self-confidence but, when done in good faith, generates respect and    indebtedness from others. The writer Lawrence Durell put it another way: "We can never really possess anything until we have given it away."

## Delegating Authority and Responsibility

All employees should understand from day one the limits of their authority and responsibilities and should also feel secure that no one is going to usurp them. There is no quicker way to convert a productive worker into a careless drone than by subverting that person's authority. Supervisors may do this by making decisions or taking actions that fall within the worker's purview, by dealing directly with that worker's support staff or crew or by being critical of that worker to others. Any decision, problem or policy should be forced up or down a ladder of responsibility, one step at a time. This procedure not only respects the authority of each staff member, it also insures the most thorough examination and treatment of the matter at hand.

As workers grow in experience and ability, they should be given additional authority and responsibility or be promoted. An important part of a supervisor's job is to assess continually when and how rewards of this type should be made and, of course, to whom. When a job offers no possibility of growth and when this begins to take its toll on the person holding it, which it inevitably will, that person should probably be placed in another job or encouraged to leave the organization. Whether or not workers in a hierarchy tend to rise to their highest level of incompetence, as Laurence Peter and Raymond Hull suggest in their book *The Peter Principle*, is debatable. But it does seem true that few people today are satisfied to remain very long in a job. Job mobility within the organization helps maintain the nucleus of a permanent staff and avoid excessive turnover. Non-union and low-salaried workers are particularly apt to be tempted away, as are volunteers. The first step in retaining such people is to treat them well and reward them frequently with appreciation and special privileges, such as tickets to a dress rehearsal.

## Communicating

As we all know, but often forget, communicating is a two-way process. It involves receiving signals as well as sending them. Indeed, the successful manager probably spends more time listening than talking. Sound decisions are informed decisions. It may also be said that information is a form of power, so the ability to gather it well and share it astutely is important.

Lines of communication within an organization should follow lines of authority, with systems put into practice that insure that information will be sent up the ladder as well as down. No worker or department in the organization should feel isolated, as can happen in a theatre operation. Do the box office treasurers have a chance to see the productions? Do they see the press releases that describe the upcoming productions for which they are selling tickets? Does the stage carpenter know the show he is building? Have the actors been greeted by the producer or general manager?

While meetings can be a boring waste of time, they can also be informative, productive and even stimulating, when they are well organized and conducted. The key to running a successful business meeting—whether the group is large or small—is advance planning. An agenda should be drawn up, perhaps discussed with an assistant, revised and then followed closely with as few diversions during the meeting as possible. A little humor should be encouraged and those present should feel they have made a contribution. At the end, the discussion leader should instill the group with a sense of accomplishment by summarizing what progress or decisions have been made (even agreeing to disagree is a decision).

Position papers, announcements and memos, written in a succinct but friendly style, should be distributed on a regular basis. Mail and information received in the front office should be shared with or referred to appropriate staff members.

And, of course, social events are a proven way to encourage and improve communications within an organization. Parties and receptions are a good way to bring together artists and staff members who would otherwise never meet, a good way to relax tensions and reward hard, usually underpaid labor. However, there can be too many parties, and nonprofessionals in particular can begin to believe that the theatre is all play and no work. Also, care must always be taken to insure that no one is overlooked when the invitations are made.

The idea of holding a staff retreat is also popular. The object of a retreat is to have a group meet away from its usual environment, often for several days, in order to brainstorm in a think-tank atmosphere that will produce more clear-headed results than might otherwise emerge. Sometimes a consultant or discussion facilitator is hired from outside the group or organization to lend objectivity and serve as a neutral moderator. Retreats are especially helpful for a board of trustees or a group of executives when long-range planning is the business of the hour.

The most skillful supervisor is the one who can prevent trouble before it begins. Early and minor corrections of some problem—perhaps just apologizing for a perceived slight—are always easier than having to cope with a problem that has festered and grown into a crisis. To recognize problems early on, supervisors must be sensitive to what is going on among the staff :

what is the power structure among the employees; who are the instigators; how are loyalties being divided? The more dominant, aggressive employees should be guided so their energies will be channeled in a positive way and the weaker so their opinions and abilities will be more fully utilized. A negative attitude is always very dangerous to the health of group efforts and should always be squelched, even when it means firing someone. Factions or cliques within the staff should be similarly discouraged. Such problems can quickly corrode the morale and productivity of a group.

Employees will always respect steadiness and a good degree of predictability from their superiors, factors that contribute greatly to a sense of job security. Conversely, the surest way to abdicate authority is to practice back-stabbing, hypocrisy or favoritism. And supervisors should remember, too, that criticism is constructive only when it helps the person at whom it is directed to work more happily and efficiently. People should not be expected to accomplish things that are beyond their training or capabilities— they simply should not be given such assignments in the first place.

Of course the main purpose of communicating effectively from the management viewpoint is to keep the ship sailing smoothly on course toward its intended destination which, hopefully, it will reach on schedule. This can only happen if the entire crew pulls together. It may appear somewhat Machiavellian to claim, but managers and supervisors aren't always nice to employees because they like them, they don't always hold their criticism because they have none to voice, and they don't always tolerate temper tantrums because they're masochists or have no egos of their own. Effective, controlled personnel supervision aims at getting the work done. To achieve this, arts legislation champion Senator Claiborne Pell offers sound advice to managers everywhere, "Always let the other fellow have your way!"

## Job Reviews

In the corporate world and in academia, job reviews are common practice. The CEO, area head or department chairperson looks through the employee's personnel records (letters of commendation, critiques, absentee reports and so forth) and then arranges a private meeting with the employee, which may result in an evaluation report written by the supervisor and placed on file. The meeting allows the employee to express grievances, discuss problems and make observations about the work and the organization. This may provide the basis for a promotion, a raise or, of course, termination. It also offers the employee a sense of being valued and it invariably provides the supervisor with useful feedback. All managers of on-going theatre companies should consider adopting some form of the job review process, however informally it may be conducted. It assures that the door between staff and management is open and that at least a little time will be set aside to recognize, analyze and evaluate the people who are trying to make the company work.

## Job Termination

Union employees, as discussed below, work under contracts that provide a considerable amount of job security, including protection against being fired unjustly. Employers who hire nonunion personnel should usually provide them with some kind of written agreement that states the terms for resignation, layoff, retirement and involuntary termination. What are the grounds for termination? How much notice must be given, if any? What is the severance pay, if any? There may also be special stipulations. For example, department heads at stock and resident theatres who are hired on a seasonal basis may be asked to maintain a written inventory of equipment, tools, supplies or whatever and then be held accountable for those goods before being given their final paycheck.

Ideally, all jobs should come to a happy ending, and every effort and precaution should be made by both employer and employee to insure that this will be the case. The theatre world is a small one and most of its workers hold many different jobs in the course of their careers. Taking care to leave each job with good feelings all around can greatly help to extend those careers.

## THE FUNDAMENTALS OF U.S. LABOR LAW

A majority of professional theatre productions in America employ the members of at least one labor union—namely, Actors' Equity Association. Broadway theatres, large opera, dance and symphony orchestras, as well as large presenting organizations, may have agreements with a dozen or more unions. It is prudent, then, for professional managers in the performing arts to understand the basis for labor law in this country, as well as the collective bargaining agreements of specific theatrical labor unions (will be discussed in Chapters 5 through 10).

Labor legislation enacted by the United States Congress is essentially aimed at strengthening the rights of (a) employees, (b) employers, and/or (c) labor organizations that are guaranteed to all citizens by the Constitution and the Bill of Rights. These include freedom of speech and assembly, equal rights, and the right to sue, among others. While the Norris-LaGuardia Act (1932) outlawed the use of injunctions in labor disputes for a time, and the Wages and Hours Act (1938) established minimum work hours and pay in basic industries, the three congressional acts most germane to organized labor practices are the National Labor Relations Act, also called the Wagner Act (1935), the Taft-Hartley Act (1947), and the Landrum-Griffin Act (1959). Although greatly modified by the two subsequent acts, the Wagner Act established the National Labor Relations Board (NLRB), which continues to serve an important function today. The NLRB resembles a court that hears complaints that cannot be settled by other means and that are brought to it by a union, an employer or an employee. It does not deal with matters pertaining only to supervisors or managers, although it now handles complaints filed by employers against unions. With nearly fifty offices around the country, its main function is to investigate charges of unfair labor practices by employers and unions and to render decisions. If the parties concerned disagree with NLRB rulings, they may take their complaint to the U.S. Court of Appeals. The NLRB is authorized to issue cease and desist orders against unfair practices affecting interstate commerce (not until 1961 did a federal ruling establish that the theatre industry is interstate commerce), insure the right of workers to bargain collectively and arbitrate labor disputes. Although the NLRB has been a frequent target of criticism, its success in settling countless labor problems over the years has been remarkable.

The Taft-Hartley Act introduced an eighty-day injunction procedure in labor disputes that affect the national welfare. It also prohibits the closed shop, permits employers to sue unions for breaking contracts, forbids union contributions to political campaigns and requires unions to provide sixty days' notice before going on strike. The closed-shop provision, incidentally, means that a person does not need to belong to a union to be offered a job in a union shop. But once the job is offered, that person must join the appropriate union within thirty days.

The Landrum-Griffin Act strengthens labor legislation by permitting criminal charges to be brought to the U.S. District Court in union and labor affairs. It also attempts to assure that unions will be run democratically, by stipulating that the union membership has the right to vote on all decisions made by its officers. Of course, no law can guarantee this, so an active and vigilant membership is always required to enforce it.

There are also a variety of labor laws on the state level that may affect labor practices, but these are always superseded by federal law.

## LABOR AND MANAGEMENT ORGANIZATION

Labor unions were born of necessity: workers the world over were being exploited into starvation, illness and early death by greedy overlords. This had been the case throughout history, but labor conditions became particularly bad with the spread of the Industrial Revolution. In recognition of this, and in an early attempt to organize the world's workers as a force in their own right, Karl Marx established the International Workingmen's Association in London in 1864. Soon dissolved, this was followed by the Socialist International, organized in Brussels in 1889; the Third International in 1943, in Moscow, also dissolved as did Trotsky's failed Fourth International, in Mexico. This association between communism and organized labor helps explain why capitalist America often viewed union members as "reds" and helped Senator Joseph McCarthy to brand many, especially from Broadway and Hollywood, as traitors.

Broad efforts to organize workers in the United States and Canada began in 1881 with the formation of the American Federation of Labor (AFL), a fairly loose combination of craft unions that initially opposed organization by industry. As a result, a splinter group formed the Congress of Industrial Organizations (CIO) in 1935, to unionize mass-production workers by industries rather than by crafts. The CIO often criticized the NLRB for favoring its AFL rival. However, these two organizations were united in 1955 to form a single, national labor union organization: the AFL-CIO. This body grants charters for different categories of craft  and industrial workers to form a national labor union. Actors' Equity Association is a national labor union. The national, in turn, can establish branch offices wherever it may have sufficient membership.

Membership through a branch office or local means automatic national membership in most cases. So if an actor "gets into Equity" in Chicago, it means that actor can also work as a union member in New York or anywhere where the union has jurisdiction and can enjoy the hard-won benefits for which that union has bargained. No branch or local is permitted to strike without permission from its national headquarters, which also negotiates all basic contracts with management.

As unions grew in strength, people who represented the ownership of the service and manufacturing industries—collectively known as "management"—had to devise strategies for dealing with them. Huge companies with huge profits, like General Motors or General Electric, could hire expensive lawyers to negotiate with the unions and could even sustain strikes and lockouts periodically. In the theatre industry, only the Shubert producing organization was in this league during the early years of union growth. But as workers learned that there is strength in numbers, so did employers. So numerous employer/management associations were formed expressly to negotiate collectively with labor unions on behalf of a segment of an industry—like resident theatre or stock theatre—in which no single employer had any clout. Only for this reason, namely to provide mutual protection against cost increases imposed by new union agreements, do we have such management associations as the League of American Theatres and Producers and the League of Resident Theatres. Their main purpose, quite unashamedly, is to do battle with the unions. Alone, each member of such associations would be helpless against the collective strength of an Actors' Equity Association. But by uniting, they are able to pool their resources, hire an attorney and negotiate new labor agreements with more balanced authority.

## COMMON LABOR RELATIONS TERMINOLOGY

Most of the following terms are in common usage, but some also have specific meaning in labor-management parlance. Certainly, they are used frequently on both sides of the negotiating table.

*Arbitration*: Both parties in a dispute agree in advance to abide by the decision of a single arbitrator or board of arbitrators. A board is often comprised of three people—one chosen by the union, one by the employer or management association, and a third by the other two.

*Boycott*: When people refuse to work or patronize a place of business, picket that place and encourage others to act as if there were a strike in progress.

*Closed shop*: A place or type of employment in which only members of a particular union are eligible to work. This was outlawed by the Taft-Hartley Act.

*Fact-finding*: A form of arbitration that ends with a ruling being given but without the legal clout of an arbitration panel.

*Featherbedding*: Payment for services that were never performed and never will be. Certain Broadway theatres, for example, have agreements stipulating that they will hire a minimum number of union musicians, called "walkers," whether or not the production in residence requires them. The unnecessary workers report regularly for work but just sit around or play cards. Unions argue that this practice is required in order to assure employers that there will always be an available pool of experienced, specialized workers when they are needed.

*Fire for cause*: Terminating employment on grounds specified in the union contract, such as failure to appear for work, failure to perform work, gross abuse of discipline, cheating or dishonesty. Firing for artistic reasons is rare and difficult to justify. When proof of misconduct can be produced, the employee need not be given notice or severance pay.

*In good faith*: A genuine attempt to resolve differences.

*Injunction*: A temporary restraining order.

*Local*: The branch of a national union.

*Lockout*: When the employer refuses to permit its employees to work.

*Mediation*: An attempt to make peace between two opposing factions.

*"To serve"*: To start legal proceedings by giving someone a subpoena.

*Settlement*: When an agreement is reached or work resumes.

*Sidebar*: When both parties in a dispute or negotiation authorize representatives to go off alone, to explore what each side really wants and what they will settle for.

*Strike*: A concerted refusal by employees (approved by the union, if there is one) to work until certain labor demands are met by the employer.

*Strikebreaker*: A person who attempts to break up a workers' strike by supplying scabs or intimidating the strikers. It is illegal for an employer to participate in such activity or otherwise impede workers' attempts to organize and to bargain collectively.

*Unfair labor practice*: Any attempt to interfere with the rights of employees to organize, select representatives and bargain collectively. Any form of discrimination in hiring, employment or firing policies.

*Union busting*: An attempt to subvert the jurisdiction of a union, as when President Reagan fired the striking air traffic controllers nationwide in the mid '80s and had new ones outside the union receive training.

*Union shop*: A place of employment where all workers of a given type must belong to the appropriate union.

*Wildcat*: A worker who is on strike without permission from the union.

# THE COLLECTIVE BARGAINING PROCESS
## *Labor / Capital / Management*

The three most necessary ingredients in any economy—whether that of a nation, an industry or a single company—are labor, capital and management. Without the direction supplied by management, labor and capital (workers and money) are merely untapped resources. But when management attempts to bring them together for the purpose of producing some service or commodity, a dynamic peculiar to the human species comes into play. This evolves around a system of give and take, of bartering time, skill and talent for personal income, on the one hand, and of investing time, thought and capital for private or public profit on the other. It is easy to believe that money alone will determine the strength of an economy, yet economies are also fueled by such intangible resources as inspired leadership, human energies and strongly shared goals. Trade unions attempt to equalize the balance of power between employee and employer. Some economists argue that unions have gained a disproportionate share of power. Most employers who hire union workers would probably agree with this position, while most union employees would probably take the opposite view. It is traditionally difficult for the two sides to agree on anything, which is why a formal system that permits both sides to present their arguments, flex their muscles and test the limits of the other's endurance makes sense. This system is politely known as the collective bargaining process.

## *The Negotiation*

All labor-management basic contracts have a limited life once they are ratified—three years is the norm, though shorter periods may be negotiated under especially difficult circumstances or in periods of high inflation or economic instability. It is customary, of course, to begin negotiating a new contract before the old one has run out. How soon before that date may itself be a negotiated point, because the less time allowed the more pressure may be felt by management to reach a new agreement and thereby avoid costly job action. A strike or lockout, incidentally, is almost never in the best interests of management. Aside from being costly in terms of lost income and perhaps lost subscribers, work stoppage costs a great deal in terms of lost morale, team spirit and momentum. When negotiations fail to result in agreement, it's usually because one or both sides simply do not understand the needs or resources of the other.

Both parties at a contract negotiation are usually represented by a delegation of people headed by a chief negotiator, who may be an attorney, a union officer, a corporate officer, someone appointed to the task by a trade association or the head manager of a particular company. At least several other officers, association members or managers are usually selected to complete the negotiating team. Then there may also be present silent witnesses from the union's council of members or from the trade group's membership. The press and the public are usually excluded and, in fact, those present may be admonished not to discuss the proceedings with anyone outside. Negotiations are easily derailed by attention or pressures from without. When the media is involved, negotiators often try to mislead or intimidate their adversaries across the table by what they say to the public. Both sides usually like to look and act tough, so that the people they represent have faith in them. But such posturing can waste a lot of time and energy and even lead to a deadlock. When this is the case, a fact-finding team or outside mediation may have to be used to settle the issues.

Contract negotiations traditionally begin with each side presenting a list of demands to the other. These have been discussed and developed by a union council or management leaders. The demands usually exceed expectations and usually include at least a few that are, for practical purposes, really "off the wall." But these permit the bargainers to throw something away as easy concessions and look sensible. The question of pay increases is almost always the biggest and most difficult to settle, but other union demands may also involve new costs to employers: increased time off, increased pension contributions, increased travel reimbursement— whatever. Throughout the bargaining process, it is always a matter of how much management is willing to give and how little the union is willing to accept.

Many negotiations are helped along when a representative from both sides is authorized to meet privately and quietly to try to settle the differences. Often, too, negotiations drag on for many hours, permitting the bargainers little time to sleep, eat or relax. Then, when they've all had enough, issues may be settled within minutes so that everyone can go home to bed.

## Ratification and Implementation

Once a new contract—the terms of which always build upon the previous contracts—has been approved by the negotiating teams, it must then be put to a vote of the union's council or its full membership for ratification. Approval is not automatic and there may also be serious objections from the management side. Several landlords and producers on Broadway, for example, categorically refuse to accept the terms of the Production Contract that the American League of Theatres and Producers periodically negotiates with Equity on their behalf. So these mavericks negotiate individually with Equity, as is their right. Of course, their agreements bear remarkable resemblance to the League's, but egos are stroked, and the show goes on.

When the union membership ratifies a contract, then management must implement it as of the expiration of the old contract. If that has already expired, the terms of the new contract are retroactive to that date, so that pay increases, for instance, would have to be given retroactively. The implementation of a new contract should also involve informing both workers and supervisors about changes that have been made. Because the jargon in official union contracts and rule books is steeped in confusing legalese, simplified summations that can be easily understood are helpful. It is easy for someone to accept increased pay, but not so easy to change a familiar routine or forget a familiar work regulation. Both workers and supervisors, then, must understand the rules of the game and insist that they be carried out to their own best advantage.

## Maintaining Union-Management Relations

When employees are unionized, it is tempting to allow the creation of an adversarial atmosphere: "Them against Us," "Union vs. Management." Of course, the role of employer is different from the role of employee. But the more successful operations tend to encourage at least a sense of cooperation and partnership between the two. This may merely involve bringing employees into the managerial decision-making process, or it may go all the way to employee ownership of the company. But some form of partnership is desirable because it is usually productive.

General principles of personnel supervision discussed earlier in this chapter should not be forgotten when dealing with union members. Every group of union workers (the actors in a particular production, the carpenters in a particular scene shop) must elect a deputy or steward to represent any grievances they may have either to management or to the union. It is very important, then, that management establish the best possible working relationship with these people and cultivate good feelings to withstand the thorny problems that are certain to arise. Unions also periodically send inspectors for on-site visits with their members to see if contract provisions are being upheld. Management should also develop good relations with these people.

All too often, there is little or no communication between a particular management and the unions, except when it's time to negotiate a new contract or when problems arise. Yet, by keeping in more frequent touch, and by extending a few amenities such as inviting union officials to receptions, to sit in on personnel meetings or to attend performances, managers could greatly ease tensions and increase good will. They would also increase their understanding of union positions and needs, while at the same time helping the unions to understand their own. Good union-management relations, then, depend most heavily upon mutual understanding.

## MANAGING UNSALARIED PERSONNEL
### *Volunteers*

Volunteers range all the way from the board chairperson of a prestigious nonprofit institution to young people helping to drum up support for their favorite cause. Volunteers are people who provide labor without receiving financial compensation, but who expect to receive other kinds of rewards for their efforts. When those rewards are not forthcoming, neither is the labor. This is the main point that supervisors of all unsalaried personnel must remember: labor must be rewarded if it is to be productive. Money is the easiest resource with which to reward labor. Gratitude, appreciation, psychic and emotional rewards are among the most difficult. In other words, the managers and supervisors usually have to work harder to extract the desired labor from volunteers than from salaried employees.

The paradox involved with volunteer leadership positions, such as the trustees or board members of all nonprofit organizations and, especially, the officers within such boards, is that they must manage themselves. They alone are ultimately responsible for the fiscal and legal conduct of the organization they serve. They may hire professional managers to carry out their objectives, but such managers do not manage the board, try as they may. They are hired to manage the board's policies and organization. So board members of nonprofit corporations, as discussed in Chapter 6, are a special breed of volunteer.

The majority of volunteers, however, work at the low end of the totem pole. And, of course, most work in the nonprofit sector. Unlike students, they are not involved primarily to learn about something. Unlike apprentices, they are not involved primarily to advance their careers. They are involved because they believe in the cause or the institution at hand. Their greatest reward would be to see the goals of that cause or institution advanced. But their next greatest reward is to feel that they are a meaningful part of that advancement process so they must be supervised with the kind of parental devotion that elicits loyalty as well as obedience. No easy job, as any parent will attest.

The leading national organization devoted to the encouragement of volunteering, giving and nonprofit initiatives is The Independent Sector, headquartered in Washington, D.C.

## Interns and Apprentices

Apprentices have been a fixture in the theatre business, especially in stock theatres, for many years. While some may receive free room and board, most work for no salary or even pay tuition or housing fees. Many successful careers began on the apprentice level and, indeed, this can offer an opportunity to learn a lot in a short time. Most theatre apprenticeships center around long hours of production work, both in the scene shop and on running crews. But distributing posters, ushering and serving as a go-fer may also be part of the work. The danger is that supervisors may treat apprentices as little better than slave labor. Yet, they can be of great value to an organization when treated with respect, given the necessary training and rewarded with appreciation.

A number of states have special laws that may prohibit the use of volunteer workers in certain jobs, such as ushering or administrative work. Other laws restrict the number of nonsalaried apprentices an organization may utilize, and all states observe child labor laws.

Interns are apprentices, though "internship" has come to imply a somewhat more responsible position, usually in one area or department and usually in administration or management. The Ford Foundation helped to establish the acceptance of trainees with its arts management internship program, begun in 1959. Since then, virtually all nonprofit arts organizations and, more recently, many commercial arts companies and offices, have eagerly incorporated interns into their salaried staffs. Some are paid a small stipend, most are given specific responsibilities at least of entry-level weight and receive professional supervision. Interns may be undergraduate or graduate students in arts management programs or others, or they may seek out this type of learning experience independently. Because most are fairly mature and seriously hoping that their internship may lead both to a job and a career—perhaps even where they are interning—others on the staff may feel threatened by them. The primary compensation they seek, of course, is training and a high quality learning experience. When supervisors provide this for them by allowing them to sit in on meetings and go though the files, for example, interns tend to return such opportunities with loyalty and meaningful job performance.

## Students

Students at all levels are also trainees in a sense. Certainly, their participation in campus theatre productions provides hands-on, practical experience. This is often designed to enhance classroom instruction and study, thereby adding another dimension to the learning process. Since students either pay tuition or attend tax-supported institutions, they have a right to expect more expert and valuable instruction than they would receive in the workplace. The ramifications of supervising students in campus theatre departments are discussed in Chapter 8.

## MANAGING THE ARTISTIC TEMPERAMENT

Although often protected by unions and collective bargaining agreements, artists in the performing arts are perhaps the most uncharacteristic of all unionized workers. Despite all the rules and regulations, artistic creativity and output itself cannot be regulated. The performer, for instance, does not turn off his or her creative energy when Equity says the rehearsal time is over. The scenic designer who met great success with designs for *Othello* cannot be ordered at any price to design an equally brilliant *Saint Joan*. The stage director cannot be expected to inspire a good production of a script that is anathema to him or her. Rules must sometimes be bent or broken to accommodate the artistic process. Always, the producer or manager or artistic director—whoever may have the responsibility—must be aware of the artists' backgrounds, work styles, tastes, levels of accomplishment and promise, mood swings, and even their physical and mental health. Knowledge of all such matters is often necessary for finding the right artist for the right project at the right time in that artist's career. And just as important is putting the right collection of individual artists together in close collaboration. This can be especially difficult in professional theatre, where job opportunities for the artists tend to be few and far between. So when the playwright has a production offer from a producer, the playwright naturally wants to do everything possible to insure that a production will actually occur. Thus, the director and the designer suggested by the producer are greeted with open arms by the playwright, and the director is madly in love with the script (because the director is also anxious for work), and the designer agrees with every design concept that is suggested. Obviously, it is very difficult to judge people under such circumstances. And it would not be unusual if, after the contracts are signed and the rehearsals begin, the director decides that half the script needs to be rewritten, and the macho

113

playwright discovers that the director is gay and refuses his advice on those grounds and the designer begins dating the ingenue, who is also the playwright's daughter. What promised to be a love-in has suddenly developed into a cat fight that threatens to turn a five-million dollar production into the proverbial disaster.

The biggest problems related to theatre management and production will not have to do with money or unions or even critics, they will have to do with people—very special people known as artists. All the money, rules and good press in the world cannot guarantee artistic achievement. They can, however, help to form a support system for the artist, a system constructed and maintained by good management. This excludes behavior that is patronizing, indiscriminate or condescending. In theatre circles, for instance, one sometimes hears expressions like "actors are children" or "mindless chorus boys" or others. Such comments and attitudes tend to isolate artists against management, if not against society at large, and are never productive. Management has an obligation to nurture and protect meritorious talent, as it is one of humanity's great resources. Too often, however, the artist has been treated as the servant rather than the master in his own house. Managing artistic talent well means respecting it, if not loving it, for the insight and the joy it provides for others. It means understanding the artists' fears of taking risks. It means, even when such understanding and respect are not present, putting the artists' concerns above those of all others. When this perspective is lost, everything else can be lost along with it.

# *Part II*

# Methods of Theatrical Production

# 5

# Commercial Theatre

THE term "commercial theatre" is anathema to some people, while others use it to assert pride in the rather dubious ability of professional theatre to function without subsidy. It remains, however, the best term to indicate one of several economic systems of theatrical producing. Commercial theatre is centered in New York City—on Broadway and Off-Broadway—and its behavior in terms of product, talent and box office influences all other theatre activity in America; it even impacts on film and television production. Before discussing how the commercial theatre functions, it might be helpful to review how this curious species evolved, to remember some of its leading figures and to look at its profile today.

## BACKGROUND

### The Beginnings: 1752 to 1792

One of the earliest known professional theatre companies in the Western Hemisphere was headed by Francisco Perez de Robles, who brought a company from Spain to Peru in 1599. But the first professional company of any consequence to reach North America was headed by Lewis Hallam and arrived in Williamsburg, Virginia, in 1752; the 21-year-old George Washington may have seen the troupe during his visits there. Both theatre companies were organized as profit-sharing or shareholding ventures. A common means of financing theatre companies since before the Elizabethan period, this system provided that each actor own a specific percentage of the company, thus entitling that actor to a proportionate share of any profits. The organizer of the venture, usually its leading actor and general manager as well, held the greatest number of shares usually by virtue of having made the largest initial investment or because of the extra managerial duties. The number of shares allotted to actors might also be determined by issues such as the number of costumes they could provide, whether they could play leading as opposed to supporting roles, whether they owned and played musical instruments, whether any children who might be travelling with them could also be pressed into serving the muse, and even family or romantic ties with the head of the company. Occasionally, playwrights and musicians were also shareholders.

Although many European companies were organized on a shareholding basis, the system presented several disadvantages and was not long favored by either American actors or actor-managers. Actors disliked the arrangement because it meant an uncertain income, when providing any at all; and actor-managers disliked the system because it created a situation that deprived them of absolute authority and control. Virtually all theatre managers at that time were also actors. The roles of actor, manager, director, and producer did not emerge as clearly separate positions in the theatre until the twentieth century. Until then, both managerial and artistic control usually rested with the leading actor in the company, the so-called actor-manager.

Despite Calvinist and Quaker resistance to stage plays, and despite the fact that public theatres were officially closed by Congress from 1774 until 1783, professional theatre managed to establish a foothold in America by the end of the eighteenth century. Generals on both sides of the Revolutionary War produced theatrical performances to keep their troops entertained; David Douglass (who married Hallam's widow during the war) built the nation's first permanent brick theatre in Philadelphia in 1776; and George Washington, when President, attended theatre two or three times a week, sometimes accompanied by John Adams, who had picked up the habit in Paris.

A 300-to-400-seat playhouse at that time, admittedly a rather flimsy structure, could be built for a cost of less than $2,000, an investment that could be recovered from the box office receipts of four performances. Nor did other expenses begin to approach what they are today: actors were required to provide their own costumes, the scenery and props were meager, and there were no royalties, fees or accountants to pay! And, during the first forty years of professional theatre in America, theatrical real estate was regarded as no more important than scenery. So actors shared both the profits and the losses of their company, and very few attempts were made to conduct the business of theatre in a businesslike way.

## *The Era of the Independent Stock Companies: 1792 to 1860*

By 1792 the shareholding system appears to have died a natural death. Until after the Civil War, the actor-managers and their investors took full financial and managerial responsibility for the theatre company, while other actors received set wages (ranging from ten to fifty dollars per week) together with the proceeds from occasional benefit performances. The heyday of the independent stock company—with its relatively permanent resident actors, stock supply of scenery, and repertory of classical plays and current melodramas—occurred during the first half of the nineteenth century. Edwin Forrest, the nation's first great, native-born actor, made his debut in 1820. Some companies wandered from town to town playing short engagements; others remained in one city and operated from their own theatres. While those who stayed home often met with lethargic audiences overly familiar with their bag of theatrical tricks, those who traveled encountered other problems. When Joseph Jefferson and his company tried to play Springfield, Illinois, in the late 1820s, for instance, a local ordinance prevented them because there was a religious "camp meeting" in progress. But a young lawyer pleaded before the city council on their behalf and got the law repealed. His name was Abraham Lincoln.

Like the scenery in stock productions, character portrayals were also, in a sense, drawn from stock. Most actors specialized in character types, or "lines," which varied only slightly during their entire career. Describing the nineteenth century stock system in England, which largely paralleled the American system, George Bernard Shaw observed:

> To begin with, the playgoers of their towns grew so desperately tired of them, and so hopelessly unable to imagine them to be any but their too familiar selves, that they performed in an atmosphere of hatred and derision that few of their members had talent or charm enough to conciliate. The modern practice of selecting for the performances actors and actresses suited to the parts they had to play was impossible; the stock company was a ready-made cast that had to fit all plays, from *Hamlet* down to the latest burlesque; and as it never fitted any of them completely, and seldom fitted them at all, the casts were more or less grotesque misfits. This system did not develop versatility; it destroyed it. Every member of the company, except the utilities, as they called the worst actors who got parts that did not matter, had his or her specialty or "line." Thus there were leading juveniles with an age limit of fifty. There were walking gentlemen, first and second light comedians, first and second low comedians, first and second old men, heavies who played all the villains, and, as aforesaid, utilities. There were leading ladies and walking ladies, singing chambermaids (soubrettes), and heavies to whom Lady Macbeth was all in a night's work, a pair of old women of whom one played the great ladies and the other the comic landladies, and, of course, female utilities. Each claimed as of right the part which came nearest to his or her specialty; and each played all his or her parts in exactly the same way.*

---

*Christopher St. John, ed., *Ellen Terry and Bernard Shaw, A Correspondence* (New York: G.P. Putnam's Sons, 1932).

Nonetheless, stock companies often provided the only organized entertainment in town, and most actors developed a cadre of fans who returned week after week to cheer them on—much as TV viewers today follow their favorite characters in soap operas or weekly sitcoms.

To breathe more life into the local stock company and increase business, managers began to engage touring stars from abroad. From roughly 1820 to 1860, American stock companies were visited by a veritable parade of highly touted English actors: Edmund and Charles Kean, Charles Mathews, Charles and Fanny Kemble, Junius Brutus Booth, William Charles Macready and others. Nor did the language barrier dampen the touring success of such stars as Sarah Bernhardt, Adelaide Ristori and Ernesto Rossi. Together with many others, they came across the Atlantic in the wake of their managers and advance men, whose main task was to whip the American press and the public into a fury of anticipation that would translate into ticket sales at the box office. Many made considerable profits, primarily because they had so little competition from the natives. But if the stock system was less than ideal for both actor and audience, the advent of visiting stars only made matters worse. Stars became so numerous that their appearances with a company were almost essential for drawing an audience. The public was encouraged to ask, "Who's in it?" rather than, simply, "Shall we go to the theatre?"

Because the salaries and percentages demanded by stars were so high, the salaries granted to resident actors had to be lowered to meet expenses, much less to show a profit. In short, the appearance of stars, however more skillful they may have been than the local talent, did not do much to improve the overall integrity of theatrical production. Imagine a performance of *Romeo and Juliet* in preparation for which the star, playing Juliet, meets her supporting cast only hours or minutes before curtain and spends less time rehearsing than instructing everyone, including Romeo, to stay away from center stage! It may be assumed, moreover, that Juliet did not enjoy the incongruities and foibles of a provincial American Romeo any more than he could have enjoyed having his theatrical territory invaded by a foreigner who was fast making his professional life untenable.

## The Era of the Combination Companies: 1860 to 1896

The development that changed the single travelling star system, and virtually killed resident stock companies, was the sudden growth of the American railway system. In the decades immediately following the 1848 Gold Rush, thousands of miles of rail track were laid, connecting the major cities of the nation and presaging an era of previously undreamed mobility. During the first half of the century, it would have been impractical for a star to travel with a complete supporting company plus all the necessary costumes and scenic appurtenances; but by the 1880s, the "combination company" dominated the industry. Some historians credit actor-manager-playwright Dion Boucicault with having organized the first combination company sometime around 1860. In any case, the idea caught on quickly and soon undermined the century-old stock system. For the first time, actors were not tied to a particular resident company, had no control or interest in the theatres they played and performed for long periods in a single play.

As more and more towns and cities sprang up on the American frontiers, the demand for entertainment became larger and covered more territory. It has been estimated that there were only about forty theatres of a permanent type at the time of the Gold Rush, but that the nation possessed over five thousand theatres by the end of the nineteenth century! About one-fourth of these were primarily vaudeville houses, while the others played host to resident companies, touring combination troupes and touring stars playing with resident companies. Theatres along the frontier sometimes doubled as saloons or brothels (talk about mixed-use facilities!), while the larger western cities anxiously sought to establish their respectability by constructing elaborate opera houses and engaging some of the world's most celebrated performing artists. It was a period of wild and woolly extremes in the American theatre, and a time of phenomenal expansion. Aside from the broad appeal of such uniquely American family entertainments as minstrel shows and vaudeville (the precursor of the television variety show), live theatre experienced an unprecedented increase in attendance during this period thanks to two vastly different attractions: *Uncle Tom's Cabin*; and the operettas of W.S. Gilbert and Arthur Sullivan. The first appeared in 1852 when George Aiken dramatized Harriet Beecher Stowe's novel—he didn't need her permission in those days, nor did he have it. Suddenly, God-fearing Christians who had been brought up to believe that the theatre was "the devil's own drawing room" were being encouraged to see this production by their own preachers, no less. There were literally hundreds of companies performing *Uncle Tom's Cabin* across the country, and thousands of people were converted to regular theatre-going. Meanwhile, the manager of New York's fashionable Niblo's Garden adopted an entire French ballet troupe that had been booked into the Academy of Music (which suddenly burned down) and inserted it into his new melodrama, *The Black Crook*. This is regarded as the first American musical. Of course, Stephen Foster was already writing for the minstrel stage, and other American composers had been gaining great popularity. But, beginning with the 1878 Boston premier of *H.M.S. Pinafore*, Gilbert and Sullivan took the country by storm. Soon there were three hundred companies performing the piece. Then came *The Mikado*, which inspired both the Britons and Americans to buy everything Japanese that they could get their hands on. There was to be nothing like it again in terms of Western fascination with the Far East until President Richard M. Nixon visited China during the 1970s. And, incredibly, there was no British-United States copyright agreement until 1905, so that no royalties were paid for producing these extremely popular works. Imagine the profit gains if Broadway producers today didn't have to pay Andrew Lloyd Webber a single penny for the production rights to *Evita* or *Phantom of the Opera* !

## The Centralization of Power: 1896 to 1914 *

In both England and America, the nineteenth century actor-managers who were also stars were mostly impractical businessmen and women; their inflated egos fostered such traditions as the long-running engagement, an emphasis on contemporary comedies and melodrama, productions that were often tasteless, and a financial structure that usually teetered on the threshold of bankruptcy. The most common method they used to avoid the debtor's prison was to revive a particular tour de force that had become their trademark and that audiences always turned out to see.

If famous stars were ill equipped to cope with the new demands of the modern age, so were the small town actor-managers. The growth of touring combination companies, the continuation of the star system, the advent of vaudeville and the striking proliferation of playhouses during the closing decades of the nineteenth century necessitated more than haphazard planning and management. With the disbanding of local resident companies, theatre buildings fell under the ownership of local bankers and investors whose primary concern was to utilize the property in a profitable way. This situation placed a local manager, usually a non-actor, in charge of selecting and booking touring performers and productions. It also made play producing clearly separate from theatre managing.

Because of complexities in routing companies from one city to another, local managers welcomed the appearance of centralized booking offices, which began to spring up in New York City around 1880. Before long the booking agents were also selecting and producing the plays—long the prerogative of the actor—as well as serving as the actors' agents and establishing themselves as distinct functionaries in the emerging entertainment industry. Because they often took fees and commissions for services not rendered, and because employment was nearly impossible without their assistance, actors disliked them from the beginning. And, initially, these agents maintained a three-sided advantage, since they could extract a booking fee from the local manager, a casting fee from the producer and a job-finding fee from the actor. Despite signed contracts and agreements, booking agents were notoriously unscrupulous. Companies were rerouted at the last minute, leav-

*See also Chapter 10: "Background."

ing the local theatre manager without an engagement; tours were canceled midway, leaving actors stranded without return fare to New York. (The famous story about the lost company of *Blossom Time* is no myth—the Shubert brothers canceled the show when it was playing in the northwest, and it took most of the actors years to work their way back home!) Actors never received a salary for rehearsal time and were required to furnish their own wigs and costumes—which sometimes cost more than they could expect to earn during their engagement. In this lamentable fashion, New York City became the nation's theatre capital; theatrical booking, producing and casting became highly centralized, and profits were taken by a middleman rather than by the actors and playwrights. The era of the business tycoon in the theatre had begun.

In 1896, three of New York's booking offices merged into one and thereby created the infamous Theatrical Syndicate (also called the Theatrical Trust), a partnership comprised of Sam Nixon, Fred Zimmerman, Al Hayman, Charles Frohman, Marc Klaw and Abraham Erlanger. Less interested in standards of production than in making large profits, these gentlemen set out to gain absolute booking control over the nation's theatres and, within a few years, succeeded. Such extreme centralization naturally fostered numerous evils, and the monopoly was bound to meet opposition. In 1902, the well known actress Minnie Maddern Fiske and her husband, Harrison Grey Fiske, established the Independent Booking Agency, which attempted to break Syndicate control. Comparatively few actors of note were willing to join the Fiskes, who were often forced to perform in barns and skating rinks because the Syndicate controlled most of the theatres. David Belasco also waged a valorous campaign against the monopoly, but the people who finally *did* manage to topple the Syndicate were the Shubert brothers. Beginning modestly in upstate New York and following the untimely death of Sam in 1905, Lee and J.J. Shubert proclaimed themselves the liberators of the American theatre, demanding "open door" booking and casting policies. Enough people in the industry swallowed this bait to make the Shuberts successful. But everyone soon woke up to the fact that they had simply replaced the Syndicate partners as ruling tyrants of the American theatre. There was, however, one difference. The Shuberts also amassed an empire in theatrical real estate, thus making their power more complete.

Today the founding brothers are dead, many Shubert-owned theatres have been sold for profit and demolished, others were sold when the Shuberts lost a federal anti-trust suit in the mid-1950s. It should be mentioned that while the Syndicate and the Shuberts certainly took advantage of a business opportunity and milked it for all it was worth, they did not create that opportunity. They did not engineer the westward movement of America's population or encourage the demand for entertainment and the initial growth in theatre construction. Nor did they invent the star system or combination companies. They did not destroy the independence of resident stock companies and they did not build the railway system. They simply grasped an opportunity that few actor-managers saw or cared about.

Rather than fighting for artistic and economic control over their profession, actors embroiled themselves in a more fatalistic battle for workers' rights. By doing so they sealed their own status as mere laborers and simultaneously established the "right" of business people to control the theatre and its artists. Thus began the labor-management syndrome that haunts the theatre to this day. It is interesting to wonder what the industry might be like had George M. Cohan and others succeeded in their efforts to prevent theatrical unionism. But attempts to organize a collective bargaining association for actors persisted. The first was the Actors' Society of America, formed the same year as the Syndicate, in 1896. Then the American Federation of Labor chartered the Actors' International Union, which fell under the control of the White Rats, a union of vaudeville performers. (Its curious name came from the word "star" spelled backward and from the performer who founded the group, George White, who was once rescued from poverty in London by a society of actors known as the British Water Rats.) Vaudevillians had formed the White Rats to fight a five percent kickback of their salaries to managers that had been imposed through the Vaudeville Managers Protective Association, an organization formed by Keith and Albee, who came to monopolize vaudeville at the same time the Shuberts monopolized the legitimate. Since the AFL can only grant one charter for any given trade or craft, a conflict arose when legitimate stage actors organized under the banner of Actors' Equity Association in 1913. But, after a three-month strike in 1919, when the union won its first meaningful contract with producers, it eventually won a charter.

Playwrights and composers were also busy securing protection for their creative output. After the turn of the century, Victor Herbert was dining in a fashionable restaurant when the orchestra began playing some of his music, for which he was not entitled to a cent in royalty payments. Deciding that he did not wish to die penniless in the Bowery, which had been Stephen Foster's fate, he began a four-year court battle that ended when the Supreme Court ruled in his favor. In 1914, Herbert helped to organize the American Society of Composers and Publishers (ASCAP), which is today the world's largest music licensing organization, having agreements with over 300,000 music users in the U.S. and with music societies in forty countries. Its primary function is to monitor music use on behalf of some 43,000 members and to collect and distribute royalty payments. Of course, this would not be possible without the copyright protection guaranteed by the Congressional legislation that began in 1909 and covers all types of creative work. Playwrights began to organize in 1878, when Steele MacKaye helped establish the American Dramatic Authors' Society; this was followed in 1891 by the American Dramatists Club, although neither made much progress. In 1911 the Authors League of America was established, and playwrights were included in its membership. Finally, following the Equity strike, a playwrights' committee at the League grew into the Dramatists Guild, which signed its first contract with producers in 1921. Ironically, as theatre artists began to gain better compensation and working conditions, their prospects for employment were rapidly diminishing.

## The Decline of Commercial Theatre: 1914 to 1960

The phenomenal growth of electronic entertainment got substantially under way in 1915 with D.W. Griffith's film, *Birth of a Nation*. By that time there were approximately ten thousand movie theatres scattered across the country, a figure that doubled by 1920; the average price of admission was fifty cents while the cost of the average theatre ticket was two dollars. The advent of network radio shows around 1925, and of talking pictures in 1927, greatly increased the competition that threatened live theatre. Furthermore, during World War I America mobilized its railroads for the war effort and, while shipping a can of film was easy, rail travel for theatrical companies was often impossible.

Statistics vary greatly, but it seems feasible to claim that between 1900 and 1932 the number of theatres presenting live entertainment decreased from about five thousand to as few as one hundred—thirty-two of which were located in New York City. And only six of *those* were operating at one point in 1932! The stock market crash in 1929, and the subsequent depression, also contributed to the near demise of commercial theatre in America. Together with increasing union costs and royalty payments—not to mention the insidious growth of income taxes—this left very few producers rich enough to finance a commercial production solely out of their own pockets, which had been the rule before the Great Crash. Afterward, most producers had to seek outside investors or "angels" or, as we'll soon discuss, invent other financing schemes. The days of the truly independent producer, as typified by Florenz Ziegfeld, Arthur Hopkins and Jed Harris, had come to an end.

Fortunately for the future of American theatre, several developments outside the commercial arena during this period—the growth of the "little theatre movement," the first federal assistance to theatre, the growth of college theatre and other factors that will be considered in later chapters—did much to kindle both our theatre and our written drama. Beginning as noncommercial and largely experimental ventures, such groups as the Provincetown Playhouse, the Theatre Guild and the Group Theatre uncovered an impressive amount of talent as well as a new audience to support it, much of which was soon fed into the mainstream of commercial Broadway theatre.

While Greenwich Village had long provided the space for experimental theatre, the history of the Off-Broadway movement is usually traced from Jose Quintero's 1952 production of Tennessee Williams' *Summer and Smoke*, which starred Geraldine Page at the Circle in the Square on its original site in the Village. This is the case simply because that was the first downtown production to receive a major review in *The New York Times*. The Off-Broadway movement subsequently received increasingly greater publicity (which didn't escape the attention of Actors' Equity), and soon the union won its first contract with the League of Off-Broadway Theatres and Producers, an event doubtless hastened by the 1960 opening of the first big money-making Off-Broadway hit, *The Fantasticks*. Originally offering a showcase where producers could operate without union employees and at low cost, in less than two decades most Off-Broadway productions, both in content and economic structure, belonged to the commercial genre. Nonetheless, the comparative economy and freedom offered by Off-Broadway brought new blood to commercial theatre and encouraged a new generation of producers and playwrights. But with the unionization of Off-Broadway came the inevitable: increased production costs and increased commercialization. Just as inevitable, perhaps, was the subsequent birth and development of Off-Off-Broadway—small, nonprofit, nonunion theatres that began in the early '60s with groups like Ellen Stewart's Cafe La Mama in lower Manhattan and proliferated rapidly in New York and other cities. Once again, actors, directors, playwrights, and producers (many with professional credentials) had comparatively easy showcase opportunities for their talents. And, once again, beginning in the mid-1970s, Equity began to push for jurisdiction over these theatres—first by the introduction of the Showcase Code, which only gained carfare for its members, then by attempts to establish minimum weekly salaries. But this time, illustrating how much things can change in fifty years, Equity's own membership questioned the wisdom of forcing union regulations onto such a fragile, yet productive, workplace for developing talent.

## Retrenchment: 1960 to the Present

During its first hundred years, the professional theatre in America was dominated and controlled by actor-managers, by men and women of the theatre. During its second hundred years, professional theatre in America was largely controlled by businessmen and speculators, people with only a secondary interest in the art of theatre. In the final analysis it must be concluded that neither group managed very well to solve the fundamental economic problems of theatrical producing or create a viable national drama. Both merely exploited a situation as they found it, doing little to improve that situation and less to prevent its disintegration. Actor-managers of the 1800s were no more aggressive at protesting the take-over of their theatre companies by travelling stars and combination companies than producer-landlords of the 1900s were at avoiding turning their theatres over to the movie industry.

Bread and butter for theatre employees of both periods were provided by the proceeds from meaningless farces, melodramas and operettas, although the best companies and playwrights were also presented in both periods—as long as they had commercial value. Ironically, the most productive and important period of American drama occurred during the '30s when the American theatre was at its lowest ebb economically, yet it brought forth the works of Eugene O'Neill, Maxwell Anderson, Lillian Hellman, S.N. Behrman, Robert Sherwood, Elmer Rice, and Kaufman and Hart. The leading playwrights of the '40s and '50s—Arthur Miller, Tennessee Williams and William Inge—kept alive the promise of serious American drama, but the next generation could only boast the somewhat uneven works of Edward Albee, who may also be considered the last major American playwright to write serious pieces expressly for the commercial theatre—unless one counts Neil Simon. Audiences were turning more and more to comedies and musicals, with an emphasis on the latter. At least this was the case on Broadway and the road. In part because this commercial situation frustrated so many theatre artists—especially directors—the '60s and '70s saw the nonprofit resident theatre companies not only grow in numbers but actually surpass the commercial theatre in terms of jobs and professional theatre production. The remarkable thing about this, historically, was that for the first time two distinctly different methods of producing professional theatre in America were being practiced concurrently: the commercial method and the nonprofit method. Until the '70s the nonprofit sector often borrowed plays, stars, directors, and designers from Broadway. Perhaps significantly, it rarely borrowed Broadway producers or managers. But by the mid-1970s, the balance of payments, as it were, had shifted so that Broadway was relying heavily on the nonprofits for both product and talent, not to mention managerial innovations. Virtually all serious dramatists today are nurtured and sustained by the nonprofit theatre: David Mamet, August Wilson, Christopher Durang, Sam Shepard, John Guare, Marsha Norman, Terrence McNally, David Rabe and Landford Wilson, among others. And when their plays *are* produced on Broadway, one of the nonprofit theatre companies is often the producer or co-producer. It's a little like practicing capitalism in a communist country— only difficult to justify until the profits start coming in!

While the nonprofit theatre has developed new artistic and managerial leadership—people like Joseph Papp, Gordon Davidson, Lloyd Richards and Gregory Mosher, who come from theatre backgrounds and place artistic integrity above all else—the commercial theatre in New York continues to be dominated by businessmen/landlords, people like Gerald Schoenfeld and Bernard Jacobs of the Shubert Organization, and James Nederlander. However, there has been discussion of ways to revitalize Broadway attendance and to support the development of new product: flexible ticket pricing, a city-sponsored theatre trust fund to subsidize productions in empty Broadway theatres, schemes to provide Broadway theatres at little or no rent for low-admission productions, plans to permit nonprofit companies to operate on Broadway with greatly reduced union requirements and hopes to subsidize the theatres by income from selling the air rights above them. And there have been some actual accomplishments in recent years. For example, the Theatre Development Fund was formed to buy blocks of tickets for worthwhile but faltering shows and to sell these back to the public at discounted rates through several "TKTS" box office locations. Or producers could make half-price tickets to their shows available for sale through TKTS. New York State legislation was introduced to permit investors to put money into blind pools, which producers may use to invest not in just one production but in many. Rocco Landesman of Jujamcyn, Inc., which operates three Broadway houses, hired Jack Viertel from the Mark Taper Forum—the first dramaturg to work for a Broadway landlord. The League and the Dramatists Guild agreed to a contractual arrangement between producers and writers that replaced the 1926 Minimum Basic Production Contract with the 1985 Approved Production Contract.

In fairness, it must also be said that Broadway executives are hampered in their efforts to sustain and improve the commercial theatre. To begin with, most would argue that the industry is over-regulated in terms of such areas as investing, financing, insurance, ticket sales and distribution, ticket pricing, union jurisdiction and regulations, and other such matters that escalate costs, especially the cost of lawyers and accountants. Most commercial theatre executives argue that the nonprofit theatres benefit from an unfair tax advantage. And Broadway landlords bitterly resent the fact that over two-thirds of the existing thirty or so Broadway theatres have been given landmark designations, thereby preventing their demolition, and in some cases even their interior renovation to accommodate production requirements of certain shows. The development potential of the Broadway theatre district was further limited in 1988, when the city reduced allowable building density, due to the Times Square development project. In fact, the Shubert, Nederlander, and Jujamcyn concerns joined forces that year and filed suit against the City to revoke the landmarking status. A landmark theatre housing an empty stage, they claim, serves nobody. Many would disagree with that characteristically commercial attitude, because for every landmarked theatre in America there must be a hundred demolished ones, and the craftspeople necessary to rebuild them are as rare as the giant Wurlitzer organs in bygone movie palaces. And for every aggravating regulation there must be a hundred victims of wrongdoing whose experience mandated the regulation.

While serious drama has been sadly lacking, Broadway has largely survived in recent decades on the comedies and memory plays of Neil Simon, limited engagements by foreign troupes—such as the Royal Shakespeare Company's productions of *Nicholas Nickleby* and *Les Liaisons Dangereuses*; American musicals like *Hello, Dolly!* and *A Chorus Line*; and, more recently, the mega-musical hits from abroad such as *Les Miserables, Cats* and *Phantom of the Opera*, imported by British producer Cameron Mackintosh. While the Broadway musical can reflect artistic merit of the highest order, audiences must usually look elsewhere for serious, nonmusical theatre. Fortunately, both in New York and in other cities, they don't have to look far.

## FINDING A PROPERTY TO PRODUCE

Anyone, given the somewhat crazy urge, can produce for the commercial theatre. One needn't have a lot of money, free time, connections in high places, experience, taste or even a knowledge of how the commercial theatre works. Other people can and usually are hired to provide those elements. All that a person must have to be a producer is something in theatrical form to produce and, of course, the legal right to produce it. This may begin merely as an idea in the producer's mind for translating some nondramatic work into a piece for the theatre. It may begin with performers (Marlene Dietrich, Whoopi Goldberg, Lily Tomlin), whom the producer wants to present on stage in one-person shows. It may begin as an idea for presenting an historic or literary personality in monologue form (Harry Truman, Mark Twain, Gertrude Stein). Or the producer may be lucky enough to obtain the right to produce a finished, original play. From the performer's point of view, a script is a "vehicle," a medium that allows ability to be displayed before an audience. From the producer's point of view, a script is a "property," a piece of theatrical-literary real estate that has the potential for making money. Perhaps it is indicative of how deeply commercialism has pervaded the theatre that in no other branch of the arts is the artist's creative work referred to as a "property." The term is a striking reminder to playwrights and producers that a script has financial as well as artistic potential.

The business of finding a property to produce, then, is the producer's first and most important responsibility. Rarely does a promising script appear unsolicited on a producer's desk. The producer must usually do a lot of reading, travelling, theatregoing, moviegoing and specific searching before a viable idea or property shows up. Or, in some cases, commercial producers have nurtured a working relationship with a writer, such as Emanuel Azenberg has enjoyed with Neil Simon, or Cameron Mackintosh with Andrew Lloyd Webber. In any case, from the time a producer decides upon a property until the first day of rehearsals, many months, and sometimes many years, can pass.

## Federal Copyright Law

When searching for material to present on the stage, the producer should be mindful of laws that pertain to literary ownership. However, copyright laws and their application are among the most complex in the entire legal field, and an attorney should always be consulted when one is attempting to purchase or protect literary rights of any kind.

Copyright law in the United States is now based on the Copyright Act of 1976. Very simply, this stipulates that any creative work or expression of an idea is the property of its author or creator for the duration of that person's life plus fifty years. The 1909 copyright law that was previously in effect stipulated that a work would enjoy copyright protection for only twenty-eight years. But, if the copyright was renewed during the twenty-seventh year, protection could be extended for an additional twenty-eight years and, at a later point, this extension was increased to forty-seven years for a maximum of seventy-five years. As a result of that bothersome condition, many works fell into the public domain (they could be used freely by anyone) at the end of the first twenty-eight years.

In 1988, federal legislation approved American participation in and conformity with the Berne copyright treaty. This extended protection to American copyright holders in nations with no direct treaties with the United States so that pirated American works could no longer be reproduced in these nations with impunity. The treaty also eliminated previous requirements for obtaining a copyright. Because a copyright now occurs at the moment of creation, the work no longer needs to be registered with the Library of Congress, nor must copies of the work be deposited there. However, in order to invoke protections of certain copyright laws in court—copyright infringement litigation, for example—the work must be registered. Also, copyrighted works no longer need to display the copyright symbol, ©. Other points that may be helpful to bear in mind include:

1.  All literary rights are extinguishable and cannot be owned by anyone in perpetuity.

2.  Ownership of a basic property is not divisible; one may own, sell or give away all of it or none of it.

3.  The copyright holder, however, may grant or sell licenses giving others the right to use the copyrighted material in a particular way, as in the case of granting the dramatization and attendant performance rights for a novel, and to share income generated from those particular uses with the holder.

4.  Copyrights cannot usually protect the title of a work nor may one copyright an idea (Broadway, for example, has seen three or four productions titled *South Pacific*, two titled *Speed-the-Plow* and there were two different versions of the same story, both titled *The Elephant Man*, one a Broadway play and the other a film). However, titles *may* be protected under tort law and under the Lanham Act if they have acquired secondary meaning.

5.  Only the *expression* of an idea may be copyrighted, not the idea alone.

6.  The Library of Congress merely files copies of work when these are submitted to it, unlike the U.S. Office of Patents, which verifies that an invention of some kind is original and unique before it issues a patent. Any copyright dispute, therefore, must be settled in a court of law.

7.  When obtaining any license, agreement or permit, it should always be remembered that anything not specifically withheld is given away. (For example, if the license does not state that the producer controls the television rights to his or her property, then these rights have probably been forfeited by default, and the producer has no control over the property as far as television production of it is concerned.)

Theatre-related works that enjoy copyright protection include: plays, lyrics, musical scores, directors' notes, choreographic notations, scenic, costume and lighting designs and/or plots, and photographs.

## Types of Theatrical Property

The most usual types of theatrical properties in both the commercial and nonprofit sectors are:

An original copyrighted work (*Our Town* and *The Odd Couple* when they were first produced)

An adaptation of a copyrighted work (*Cats* from a poem by T.S. Eliot and *La Cage Aux Folles* from a French film)

An original copyrighted work that was commissioned (as *A Chorus Line* was developed, in effect commissioned, by the New York Shakespeare Festival, and *Nixon in China* commissioned by the Brooklyn Academy of Music and its underwriters)

A revival of a work in the public domain (such as *Hamlet* or *The Pirates of Penzance*)

A revival of a copyrighted work (*42nd Street* or *Anything Goes* in their second Broadway productions)

An adaptation of a work in the public domain (*Dracula,* adapted from the 1897 romance novel by Bram Stoker and *West Side Story,* adapted from Shakespeare's *Romeo and Juliet*)

A translation of a foreign language work in the public domain (*The Cherry Orchard* from the Russian or *Cyrano de Bergerac* from the French)

A translation of a copyrighted work (*Six Characters in Search of an Author* from the Italian or *Irma La Douce* from the French)

But the work of discovering a property such as those mentioned above, or rediscovering it, or commissioning it to be written, and then of putting the property together with the right interpretive artists at the right time in the right theatre is very difficult to accomplish, as is proved by how few commercial producers have become millionaires.

## SECURING PRODUCTION AND SUBSIDIARY RIGHTS

Once a producer has decided to present a particular script or commission a script to be written, adapted or translated, legal action must be taken to secure the necessary production and subsidiary rights. (It may be necessary to hire an attorney to conduct a title search in order to determine who, if anybody, owns the copyright of the basic property.) Since 1921, playwrights, bookwriters, lyricists and composers working on Broadway have usually been members of the Dramatists Guild and have usually negotiated with producers through what became in the late '40s the Dramatists Guild Minimum Basic Production Contract (MBPC). With rapidly rising production costs, however, it became increasingly difficult to attract investors, especially since the terms of the MBPC meant that angels could not earn back their investments for months or years. Hoping to sweeten the pot then, producers began dreaming up ways to pay back their investors sooner and the idea of the "royalty pool formula" was born. This is also known as "profit pooling." Why should playwrights, the reasoning went, be earning full royalties if the production was breaking even, when investors had yet to see a dime returned? During the early '80s there was serious threat of legal action between the Dramatists Guild and the League of American Theatres and Producers on the basis that the the other group violated the Sherman Antitrust Act. But the matter was dropped when both parties agreed upon the Approved Production Contract (APC) in 1985. This agreement is now the basis of most contracts between producers and writers for all live, first class productions on the speaking stage in the United States, its territories, possessions and in Canada. Essentially, this boils down to Broadway and first class productions in other major cities and on tour. Importantly, however, the APC is rarely used if the authors are deceased or of a foreign nationality.

Today, the Dramatists Guild is an independent corporation open to anyone, although there are two classes of members, active and associate. Guild members automatically become members of the Authors League of America. In exchange for 2 percent of the author's weekly royalties (3 percent if these exceed $3,000 per week for a dramatic work or $4,000 for a musical), the Guild monitors the terms of the playwright's contract with the producer, insuring certain minimum terms. It then continues to act as the playwright's protector in other ways. For example, it mediates differences that the producer and the playwright cannot resolve between themselves, checks box office grosses to insure that the playwright receives the correct royalty, and negotiates any sale of the play to a motion picture company, for which it receives two percent of that sale price.

## *The Dramatists Guild Approved Production Contract (APC)*

The APC, as originally published by the Guild, is a forty-five page document that ostensibly has a provision for every aspect of the relationship between a producer and the writers for a production. In fact, there are really two APCs—one for plays and one for musicals. Just as salaries are at the heart of all employee contracts, so option and royalty payments are at the heart of contracts with creative (nonemployee) artists. The APC sets these payments as follows:

|  | **Plays** | **Musicals** |
|---|---|---|
| Option Payments | $5,000 for first six months<br>$2,500 for next six months<br>$5,500 for second year | $18,000 for first year<br>$9,000 for second year<br>$900 per month for third year |
| Advance Payments | 3% of capitalization<br>up to $35,000 | 2% of capitalization<br>up to $60,000 |
| Pre-Broadway &<br>Previews | 5% of weekly gross | $4,500 a week aggregate |
| First 3 Broadway<br>weeks | $1,000 a week | $4,500 a week aggregate |
| Minimum Broadway<br>Pre-Recoupment<br>royalty | $1,000 a week<br>5% weekly gross | $3,000 a week aggregate<br>4.5% weekly gross<br>aggregate (can vary) |
| Pre-Recoupment<br>royalty adjustment | Guarantee plus 25% of<br>wkly profit when gross<br>is 10% or less above wkly<br>break-even point, but not<br>to exceed 5% of gross | Same as for plays |
| Post-Recoupment<br>royalty adjustment | $1,000 plus a % of wkly<br>profits based on a sliding<br>scale in relation to the<br>wkly break-even, but not<br>to exceed 10% of gross. | Guarantee plus 35%<br>of wkly profit when<br>wkly gross is 15% or<br>less above wkly<br>break-even |

It should be noted that all advance and option payments for plays and musicals are deductible, but only after recoupment of production expenses and only from fifty percent of the royalties. "Recoupment" means that the show has earned back its capitalization (the cost of getting to and including opening night on Broadway). In theatre jargon this is also known as "re-couping the nut." It is said this term dates back to the middle ages when troupes of actors travelled from village to village in wagons, which also served as their stage. At the end of each performance they would take a collection from the audience. But to prevent them from skipping town without paying the requisite permit fee, the local mayor or burgermeister would remove all the nuts from the wagon wheels and return them only when the fee was paid—hence, "recouping the nut"!

As a rule, of course, authors should not sell an option on their work without reasonable certainty of a production, nor should producers buy an option without reasonable certainty of being able to raise the necessary capital required to produce it. And the more quickly the optioned work can be produced, the less "front money" will have to be paid to the authors *and* the longer everyone with royalty rights will earn money from the project.

From the artistic standpoint, the Dramatists Guild (and the APC) exist in order to insure the writer's integrity and intent. They serve to prevent unapproved changes being made in the script or performance without an author's consent, unapproved additional authors being brought in and other unapproved decisions being made that might alter the creative intent. These are mighty hard matters to regulate. It is very likely that both the Guild and the League are in violation of antitrust laws. Yet, until somebody comes up with better solutions, they are the best service organizations for their constituents.

As the APC Certification Procedure Flow Chart illustrates, the process of negotiating the terms of this contract and then of gaining the Guild's certification can be complex, although the Flow Chart is a worst-case scenario. Most of the time the contract approval process is quite simple.

## Subsidiary Rights

The APC stipulates that the producer has until midnight on the first day of rehearsals to select one of four alternatives for sharing the income from certain subsidiary uses that the property may eventually enjoy. If the producer fails to notify the Guild of this choice, then the author may make the selection or, if both ignore the decision, then one of the alternatives automatically goes into effect. However, all such income will belong to the author unless the production runs for a certain number of performances and thereby permits the production company to share in any subsequent profits. The APC covers the following subsidiary rights:

1. MEDIA PRODUCTIONS: Audio-only recordings and radio use, plus those uses covered below;

2. AUDIO-VISUAL PRODUCTIONS: Motion pictures, television, video cassette, video disc and all other types of audio-visual production excluding foreign local television production outside the U.S. and Canada;

3. COMMERCIAL USE PRODUCTS: Wearing apparel, toys, games, dolls figures, novelties, books, souvenir programs and any other physical property in any way associated with the play, its title or characters;

APPROVED PRODUCTION CONTRACT (APC)
CERTIFICATION PROCEDURE FLOW CHART

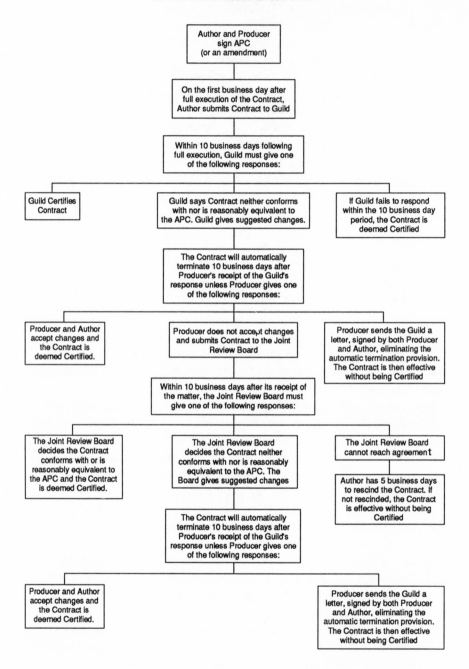

Author and Producer
sign APC
(or an amendment)

On the first business day after
full execution of the Contract,
Author submits Contract to Guild

Within 10 business days following
full execution, Guild must give one
of the following responses:

Guild Certifies
Contract

Guild says Contract neither conforms
with nor is reasonably equivalent to
the APC. Guild gives suggested changes.

If Guild fails to respond
within the 10 business day
period, the Contract is
deemed Certified

The Contract will automatically
terminate 10 business days after
Producer's receipt of the Guild's
response unless Producer gives one
of the following responses:

Producer and Author
accept changes and
the Contract is
deemed Certified.

Producer does not accept changes
and submits Contract to the Joint
Review Board

Producer sends the Guild a
letter, signed by both Producer
and Author, eliminating the
automatic termination provision.
The Contract is then effective
without being Certified

Within 10 business days after its receipt of
the matter, the Joint Review Board must
give one of the following responses:

The Joint Review Board
decides the Contract
conforms with or is
reasonably equivalent to
the APC and the Contract
is deemed Certified.

The Joint Review Board
decides the Contract neither
conforms with nor is reasonably
equivalent to the APC. The
Board gives suggested changes

The Joint Review Board
cannot reach agreement

Author has 5 business days
to rescind the Contract. If
not rescinded, the Contract
is effective without being
Certified

The Contract will automatically
terminate 10 business days after
Producer's receipt of the Guild's
response unless Producer gives one
of the following responses:

Producer and Author
accept changes and
the Contract is
deemed Certified.

Producer sends the Guild a
letter, signed by both Producer
and Author, eliminating the
automatic termination provision.
The Contract is then effective
without being Certified

4. STOCK PERFORMANCES: All performances of the work in English presented under an AEA agreement for stock, resident theatre, university resident theatre, dinner theatre or guest artist agreement and the equivalent of such performances outside the U. S.;

5. AMATEUR PERFORMANCES: All performances in English performed only by non-professional actors who are not members of a performers' union or guild either in or outside of the U.S.;

6. ANCILLARY PERFORMANCES: Any performances in English presented in a condensed or abbreviated version, so-called concert tours, plus any musical version based on the work, plus foreign language performances of all kinds both here and abroad, plus performances presented under AEA agreements for theatre for young audiences, small professional theatre, nonprofit theatre code and their equivalents outside the United States;

7. REVIVAL PERFORMANCES: All performances of the play in New York City after the producer's rights to present that work have expired, plus all performances outside the city after the producer's rights have expired, providing there are revivals in at least three different cities.

If the APC is not used, as when the writer is foreign, deceased or not a Guild member or the play is not being produced on Broadway, the producer or producing organization will want to make certain that its attorney draws up an agreement with the authors that covers the above subsidiary rights. But if that production subsequently moves to Broadway it can convert to an APC at that time. Subsidiary rights are of vital concern to both producers and their backers as well as to playwrights because they may eventually bring in a tremendous amount of money. In fact, a number of shows have failed to break even on Broadway and yet have earned high profits for their participants due to subsidiary earnings. Depending upon which alternative formula is selected, the APC specifies that producers may share with the author from zero to fifty percent of subsidiary earnings for a period of time ranging up to forty years, and much longer in the case of media rights.

While the original producer also usually produces the first class national touring companies of the show—as well as the initial first class productions in foreign capitals—other producers may buy the rights to present subsequent productions of the show.* The rights to publish an "acting edition" of most remotely successful plays that have received first class productions either in New York or elsewhere are bought by a play publishing company, such as Samuel French or Dramatists Play Service, Inc., which in turn administers the stock and amateur rights, collects royalties and then turns over the appropriate portion of these to the Dramatists Guild, which extracts its fee and gives

---

the remainder to the author or author's agent (who would extract yet another fee). The rights to the majority of Broadway musicals are administered by such publishers as Tams Witmark, Inc., Music Theatre International, and the Rodgers and Hammerstein Music Library. These companies also rent or sell scripts and musical scores for the properties they control.

It is not unusual for a media company such as Warner Communications to make a substantial investment in a Broadway production in exchange for the recording, film or television rights to that production. In any case, when there is a cast recording of a Broadway show, the cast and musicians must be reimbursed in the amount of one week's salary, although the recording session seldom takes more than a day or may even be done at a regular performance and require no extra cast time.

## FORMING A PRODUCTION COMPANY

While Chapter One discusses the characteristics of unincorporated companies as opposed to corporations, let's quickly review the options currently open to a commercial producer who is about to set up a production company.

### Sole Proprietorship

Prior to the stock market crash of 1929, the sole proprietorship of a production company was a common method of producing. It provides the greatest independence for a producer, who puts up all the capital and takes all the risk along with full, personal liability. This has virtually disappeared as a method of producing on Broadway, although it may still exist as a method for operating a few stock or dinner theatres.

### Private Corporation

Offering the advantage of limited personal liability and perpetual existence, a private corporation is theoretically controlled by a board of directors (although they may be family members or friends who, in reality, exercise no say whatever). Private corporations are commonly used as the legal structure for commercial stock and dinner theatres, companies that package road shows and tours of all kinds, and by theatrical service and production companies. Individual artists and managers sometimes incorporate themselves in order to gain certain tax advantages.

### Public Corporation

The possibility of financing a Broadway show through the device of a public stock offering has intrigued producers for years. It was finally put to the test during the '70s by Joseph Tandet as the method for producing a musical adaptation of *The Little Prince*. Unfortunately, the show was not a hit, so it doesn't provide much of a case study, although a successful million-dollar law suit against the Nederlander Organization has kept the company active to this day. However, advantages of this approach include the ability of the company to enter easily into other ventures, to raise money in one fell swoop (through block stock sales to an underwriter), and to tap a vast number of small investors whose risk is minimal and who ordinarily wouldn't invest in theatre. The company can also take advantage of retained earnings, since profits need not be distributed as they come in. Disadvantages include locking the production into a set budget (there is no "overcall"); high start-up costs for attorneys, accountants and underwriters, having the Securities and Exchange Commission acting as a watchdog, and making stockholders subject to double (corporate and personal) taxation, which is not the case in a partnership.

### General Partnership / Joint Venture

The joint venture arrangement is not unusual today and provides one of the quickest ways to launch a Broadway production company. It typically involves two, three or four entities—corporations and/or individuals—who provide the full capitalization, somewhat like a sole proprietorship with several owners. The diffusion of control, however, can present a danger as it is always more complicated when decisions are shared by a group than when made by an individual. To determine how decisions will be made and by whom, the amount of capital needed, how much each party will contribute, how profits will be distributed, and the conditions under which a party may withdraw, a Joint Venture Agreement must be drawn up by an attorney. It is not necessary to become involved with the Securities and Exchange Commission (SEC). Each of the three major Broadway theatre landlords has often entered into joint ventures with independent producers and corporations as the most expedient way to keep their theatres occupied.

### Investment Pooling

In 1988 a new bill was introduced in the New York State Legislature that provided an alternative to the way in which Broadway and Off-Broadway productions could be financed. Previously, producers were only permitted to raise money for a specified production and had to repeat the process for each new production they hoped to stage. The new law permits producers to set up a "blind pool" (somewhat like a mutual fund) into which investors put money that can then be used for a number of unspecified productions. Unfortunately, the original law required that all investments in a pool be spent within two years, making the scheme highly impractical without lots of money in a pool and, even more unlikely, lots of potential hits to produce. While new legislation may eventually correct this problem, only those few producers with solid track records are likely to attract such investors. And the profits from a hit show could easily be lost on a succession of flops. Nonetheless, investment pooling is a creative attempt to revitalize commercial production.

## Limited Partnership Agreement

Commercial New York theatre productions are also—although with diminishing frequency—organized around a Limited Partnership Agreement, the terms of which differ from agreement to agreement but have basic similarities that appear to offer the best legal and tax advantages for both producers and investors when shares are offered publicly through the SEC. For example, investors in a partnership can deduct the full amount of any loss in the year it occurs, whereas corporate shareholders can deduct only a part of the loss in each of several years and may never be able to deduct the full amount lost. Similarly, profits from a partnership are taxed only to the individual partners, while corporations pay taxes on their profits, and then shareholders are taxed when the same profits are distributed as dividends.

A Limited Partnership Agreement provides for two types of partners: general partners and limited partners. The former, who are the producers, assume all control over the affairs of the partnership and all the legal risks and liabilities. The limited partners are liable only for the dollar amount of their investment plus, in most cases, an additional amount or "overcall" (usually 10 to 20 percent of their initial investment). Ordinarily, the limited partners collectively provide the total capital required to finance the production but share only 50 percent of the profits, with the other 50 percent going to the general partners. In practice, this means that if a limited partner has paid (invested) 10 percent of the total cost (capitalization), that person will share in only 5 percent of the profits. The producers (general partners) of the company start out with 50 percent ownership but seldom retain that amount, because they usually deem it advisable or necessary to sell or otherwise forfeit a portion of it. If, for instance, a higher capitalization is required than originally stated in the Limited Partnership Agreement, the general partners may have to sell part of their share in the company, because they are not allowed to issue more limited shares and thereby decrease the value of the original limited partners' shares. Or portions of the general partners' percentage may be given away in order to obtain a certain star, director or theatre. Perhaps it is decided during the tryout period to build a whole new set of costumes or scenery. Or the hydralic turntable breaks down. Or a new computerized light board has to be ordered. Such costly decisions are frequent along the road to opening night. And when such costs cannot be covered by the budget printed in the Limited Partnership Agreement and, furthermore, the overcall is insufficient to cover them, then the general partners have little choice but to sell off some of their own shares to raise the additional financing. To sell *more* than 100 percent of the original shares would, of course, be fraudulent.

The limited partners' chief obligations and benefits are:

1. To contribute a specified amount of money to the company;
2. To contribute a further specified amount if requested to do so, provided this is stated in the investment agreement;
3. To have no other financial or legal obligation or liability in connection with the company;
4. To share 50 percent of any profits with the other limited partners according to the amount of their investments (profits usually include money earned from the sale of subsidiary rights though, again, such matters must be spelled out in the agreement).

The general partners' chief obligations to the limited partners and to the company are:

1. To guarantee that they have the legal right to produce the property in question;
2. To guarantee that they actually intend to produce the property, provided the necessary capital is raised;
3. To guarantee the safekeeping and legitimate expenditure of all invested capital;
4. To return all invested capital in full if the amount specified in the agreement is not raised within a stated length of time;
5. To desist from spending any invested capital until the full amount required has been raised, unless otherwise stated and specifically agreed to by the investor;
6. To guarantee that the total capitalization stated in the agreement is sufficient to finance the production and that, for the purpose of determining the value of each share, it shall not be changed;
7. To repay the limited partners' investments before the general partners begin to share in any profits;
8. To assume all legal and financial responsibility for the proper conduct of the partnership and the company.

Because they possess full control over the company, the general partners may dissolve it at any time provided they can show reasonable cause for so doing.

Now let's make up some simple figures to illustrate how the Limited Partnership system works:

| | |
|---|---|
| An Off-Broadway show organized as a Limited Partnership is capitalized at: | $500,000 |
| There are 100 units offered, each valued at: | 5,000 |
| The total potential weekly gross of the theatre is: | 125,000 |
| The total weekly operating cost of the show is: | 50,000 |
| How many weeks of capacity business are required to break even? (The difference between operating cost and full gross for as many weeks as it takes to pay back the $500,000 capitalization) | 6.75 |
| If an investor bought 10 shares or 10% of the capitalization, that person's weekly share of the profits (after the show breaks even) is: | 3,750 |
| Due to the 50/50 split (and assuming they still own their full 50 percent) the general partners' weekly share of the profits is: | 37,500 |

It may appear at first glance that a 50 percent share in a company is excessive for a person who doesn't invest a cent in it. While the producer is entitled to be reimbursed by the company for option money advanced to the playwrights, for office expenses and other such costs, there are no provisions for reimbursing that producer for all the time, travel and entertaining that were necessary to obtain the property in the first place. Nor may producers (general partners) be reimbursed for expenses incurred to attract investors. Several years often elapse from the time a play is optioned until it opens in New York, and it may take another year or more of capacity business before it begins to realize a profit.* Whatever money a producer may finally earn is, indeed, well earned.

## RAISING THE CAPITAL

How a production company is organized, as suggested in the preceding section, also determines how it will be financed. When just a few individuals and/or corporations are supplying all the needed capital, then the

*See Chapter 11.

process is a simple one. But, as in the case of most Limited Partnership Agreements, it is often necessary to attract dozens of investors. After obtaining a property, then, financing the venture is the producer's most important function.

When a show is financed as a public offering, law requires that a prospectus of the production company, together with a copy of the Limited Partnership Agreement and other documents, be filed with the office of the Attorney General of the State of New York and with the Securities and Exchange Commission. After the total capitalization for the production has been raised, the general partners of the agreement must file a Certificate of Limited Partnership in the County Clerk's office of the county in which the company is operating. Then notice of the partnership must be published in two different newspapers or periodicals consecutively for a period of six weeks.

The prospectus, or offering circular, distributed to potential investors provides a synopsis of the play and short biographies of the producer, author and any leading artists who have committed themselves to the project. It must also describe in detail the financial and legal organization of the company and contain a statement about the risks of theatrical investing, even giving the percentage of Broadway (or Off-Broadway) shows that failed during the previous New York season. Legal requirements such as these are designed to protect investors from unknowingly taking extraordinary risks by investing in highly speculative ventures (like gold prospecting) or from phony ventures—and nobody can deny that producing for the commercial theatre is highly speculative.

An offering circular is often accompanied by a promissory letter that the producer hopes the potential investor will sign and return. The sample that follows shows its typical content. However, it should be emphasized that this form letter merely precedes or accompanies a Limited Partnership Agreement and is not a substitute for it; nor should it be used until the Agreement has been filed with the Attorney General. The great care that a producer must take when attempting to comply with the numerous laws and regulations related to producing for the commercial theatre cannot be overstated.

A few reference works, like the four volumes edited by Donald Farber, *Entertainment Industry Contracts* (Mathew Bender and Company, Albany, New York, 1987) describe these regulations in greater detail than is appropriate here; but the producer is best advised to retain a reputable attorney with experience in the field of theatrical law.

One method often used to sell shares in commercial theatre production is the so-called backers' audition. This entails inviting potential investors to a rented theatre, hall or private home to witness the informal presentation of scenes read from the script or songs sung from the score by profes-

HY HOPE PRODUCTIONS, INC.
000 BROADWAY
NEW YORK, NEW YORK

RE: <u>Romeo and Juliet</u>
by William Shakespeare
an Off-Broadway Production

Dear Sirs:

I hereby state that I would like to be an investor and Limited Partner in the "R & J" Company, which will produce William Shakespeare's <u>Romeo and Juliet</u> Off-Broadway. Accordingly, I hereby invest a total amount of $       which shall entitle me to       units of 50 percent of any net profits based upon a total capitalization of $500,000.

$10,000 shall represent one unit or percentile.* I enclose my investment check in the above amount (or, upon demand, I shall deliver my check to you). You shall hold my funds in trust in a special account until such time as $425,000 is raised, after which you may utilize the funds for production purposes.

In the event that capital contributions total at least $425,000, and you believe that the production can commence, then the capitalization of the Limited Partnership shall be reduced to the amount determined, and the Limited Partners' proportional shall be increased accordingly.**

You shall hereafter forward to me the Limited Partnership Agreement for this production, which has been filed in the office of the Attorney General of the State of New York. I shall promptly sign and return it to you.

In the event that the Limited Partnership is not formed within twelve months from the date of this letter, then the money advanced shall be returned to me in full. There shall be no overcall.

Sincerely,

_____
(Signature)

_____
(Name, printed in full)

Please initial one:
My investment may___
may not____
be used as front money.

_____
(Full legal address)

*Traditionally, fifty limited partner shares are offered, each representing 1 percent of the capitalization and .5 percent of profits, although, of course, an investor may buy part of a share or more than one.

**This is the usual procedure when a production comes in under the stated capitalization; it is safest to overestimate the required capital than to increase the value of shares.

sional performers (not necessarily the ones who will appear in the actual production). The producer, author and others are present to answer questions and help promote the venture. Scenic design models or sketches may be displayed, and generous amounts of food and drink may be served. Few investors are capable of judging the commercial value and theatrical effectiveness of a play merely by reading the script, so a backers' audition can help them to visualize better what the production may eventually be like and, of course, when well stage-managed, can also help them part with their money. However, few producers wish to take investments from people who cannot afford to lose that investment in full.

## NEGOTIATING FOR A THEATRE

The success or failure of a production is at least partially determined by the theatre in which it is performed. Is the city, the neighborhood and the address of the theatre "right" for the production at hand? The annals of theatre are filled with examples of intimate plays that got lost in huge theatres and of more flamboyant plays that were stifled in small houses. When considering the alternative for a theatre space, whether on Broadway or in Toronto, the selection should be based first upon artistic considerations and only second upon economic reasons.

New York commercial theatre is basically divided into two categories: Broadway and Off-Broadway; and each designation is determined by the seating capacity of the theatre and usually by its location. Most theatres located in the general area of Times Square that have more than 500 seats, operate as Broadway theatres under the Actors' Equity Production Contract, and also have contracts with the other theatrical unions discussed later in this chapter. However, there are a few exceptions, such as the Lambs Theatre and the Helen Hayes Theatre,which are located in that district but have 499 or fewer seats. They operate under what is called a "middle theatre" or Special Production Contract with AEA. The AEA Off-Broadway contract generally applies to the theatres below 34th Street in Manhattan that seat fewer than 499 people. Showcase and "mini theatre" contracts have been devised by AEA to cover runs limited to four weeks (Showcase) or commercial productions (mini) in theatres with less than one hundred seats.

Before going too far with contractual commitments to actors and others, the producer or the general manager must begin negotiating to rent a theatre (the rental agreement is actually a license rather than a lease). The Off-Broadway producer has the advantage of being able to choose from a variety of theatres and often has considerable bargaining flexibility in the type of license that is concluded with the landlord. Many Off-Broadway theatres are rented according to a "four-wall" agreement. This simply provides the building, with no personnel, no special equipment and no operating costs paid by the landlord; the producer pays only a fixed rental fee. The producer may also be required to pay a minimum of six or more weeks rent, even if the production closes during the first week. The League of Off-Broadway Theatres and Producers negotiates the minimum Off-Broadway contract terms with AEA.

In other Off-Broadway houses and most Broadway theatres, the relationship between the landlord and the tenant-producer is more like a partnership, in which both may share in the box office income and both gain from a successful, long-running production. Most terms in a theatre license are negotiable and will depend upon the potential success that the landlord sees in a certain show and, equally important, upon how many different shows are seeking to use that theatre. When a new show proves to be a great hit in London, for example, New York landlords may bid against each other to offer the producer the best terms—which may even include extensive interior renovation of the theatre, as production requirements demanded for the musical *Cats*. While various union employees are contracted to the landlord, the producer pays for their salaries plus the other operating costs for the theatre. These may be included in a flat rental fee negotiated between the producer and the landlord, or the parties may negotiate a minimum guaranteed rent plus a percentage of the gross over a stipulated break-even figure. With sell-out business a Broadway landlord can receive as much as 40 percent of the total gross. With ticket prices at their current levels, that's not chicken feed!

Another unique characteristic of the Broadway theatre license is the stop clause, a weekly box office gross amount that is agreed to in the license. If the show fails to realize this amount (usually for a period of two consecutive weeks) the landlord has the right to evict the production and the tenant may vacate without cost or penalty.The agreement may exempt the show from the stop clause stipulation for certain periods, like the two weeks before Christmas or the first three weeks of January. The producer cannot logically arrive at a figure for the stop clause, however, until the total capitalization *and* the weekly operating cost for the production have been determined.*

Producers with an established record of success or those who own a "hot" property or one that will feature artists of known commercial value are in the strongest bargaining position. The star (or lack of one) is a primary factor in negotiating with Broadway landlords, and a license frequently requires the producer to use a certain star as promised. The landlord in many cases has the right to terminate the license if a particular star fails to appear or leaves the production for any reason; or the landlord may have the right

---

*See Chapter 11: "Setting the Stop Clause in a Commercial Theatre License"

to veto the hiring or replacement of the star and certain featured players. For reasons such as these, the producer cannot effectively begin negotiating for a theatre until the production plans are well under way and leading artists' contracts have been signed. But the producer also does not wish to sign too many contracts until the license for a New York theatre is assured In other words, a commercial producer must often play both ends against the middle; time, luck, and shrewd judgment are critical, to say the least.

## CONTRACTING UNION EMPLOYEES

Before discussing the jurisdiction of Actors' Equity Association and its regulations (which generally pertain to all Equity companies both in and out of New York), a descriptive listing of all theatrical unions and collective bargaining associations related to Broadway productions might be helpful.

The only person allowed to sign contracts with union employees is the one who has posted a bond with the union or that union's authorized representative. Questions regarding union jurisdiction, contracts and regulations should be addressed directly to the appropriate union office, since many contractual terms involving salaries, benefits and working conditions change each year and special concessions may be negotiated by direct contact with a union. In any case, producers and managers are well advised to establish cordial relationships with union representatives. The following organizations maintain their headquarters in New York City, though some also have offices in other major cities.

## Contracts Made by the Producer

1. *Dramatists Guild, Inc.* Not a union, but a professional association to protect the rights of authors (playwrights, bookwriters, lyricists and composers) of dramatic and dramatico-musical works. Most works by living American playwrights presented on the New York stage, except those in public domain, are performed under a Dramatists Guild Approved Production Contract, as negotiated by the producer and author(s) with Guild guidance and certification;

2. *Actors' Equity Association (AEA)*. Equity derives its charter from the Associated Actors and Artists of America (known as the 4 A's) which in turn is chartered by the AFL-CIO. Its jurisdiction covers all professional actors (principals, chorus members and extras) as well as stage managers and assistant stage managers;

3. *Society of Stage Directors and Choreographers (SSDC)*. Not a union, but a society to which virtually all directors and choreographers active

147

in New York legitimate theatre belong. It sets minimum fees, royalty percentages, and employment conditions for its members, although each contract is negotiated individually by the producer and the artist before seeking SSDC approval;

4.  *United Scenic Artists of America (USA), Local 829B.*  Most scenic, costume and lighting designers working in New York legitimate theatre belong to this union. It requires all members to pass a lengthy and difficult examination before gaining membership, although producers may hire nonmembers who must then join the union, but are exempted from the exam;

5.  *Wardrobe Supervisors and Dressers, Local 764.* Although producers or stars may hire whomever they wish in these two job categories, such people must join the union within thirty days if they are not already members.

## Contracts Made by the Theatre Landlord

1.  *International Alliance of Theatrical Stage Employees (IATSE), Local 1.*  Representing all carpenters, stagehands, electricians, sound technicians and property crewpeople, this union is contracted to the theatre. The number of employees required is determined by the theatre's agreement with the union and the type of production in residence. This union is also known as the "IA". And the term "yellow card" means that the IA member holding it must be paid for a certain job, whether services are rendered or not;

2.  *Treasurers and Ticketsellers, Local 751.* This union is also contracted by the theatre, and the number of employees required depends upon the theatre's seating capacity;

3.  *Porters and Cleaners—Service Employees in Amusement and Cultural Buildings, Local 54.* Includes all cleaners, matrons, elevator operators and porters;

4.  *International Union of Operating Engineers, Local 30.* Includes all heavy equipment maintenance personnel, heating and air-conditioning engineers;

5.  *Ushers and Doormen—Legitimate Theatre Employees Union, Local B-183.* Includes jurisdiction over all ushers, directors of ushers, and front and back doorkeepers.

## Contracts Made with Both the Producer and Theatre Landlord

1. *Association of Theatrical Press Agents and Managers (ATPAM), Union No. 18032.* The producer contracts with the company manager and press agent (both of whom must be employed in conjunction with every Broadway and first class touring production for the full length of its engagement). The landlord contracts with the house managers. The number of employees is determined by whether the production is musical or nonmusical and where it is playing;

2. *American Federation of Musicians, Local 802.* Some theatres have agreed to employ a minimum number of musicians whenever there is a musical production in residence or when more than four minutes of taped music is used. Additional musicians required, if any, are determined by the demands of the score and are contracted by the producer.

All collective bargaining agreements with the above organizations are conducted between them and the League of American Theatres and Producers every two or three years on average. Even so, producers and landlords can and often do negotiate independently for special concessions or modifications in regard to a particular employee or production. Rarely, however, do such concessions reduce the minimum terms as spelled out in the standing collective bargaining agreement.

Authors and composers receive royalties from the income generated by their work on Broadway, as we have discussed, as well as all subsequent uses of that work, such as road tours and television adaptations. Other leading artists—directors, choreographers, designers and star performers—may also negotiate a contract in which they earn a percentage of a show's Broadway box office income in addition to their fee or salary. While actors and designers must negotiate any such percentage from scratch, SSDC contracts stipulate minimum royalty payments of 1/2 to 1 percent for its members. And some leading artists also negotiate terms whereby they share in subsidiary income that the show may generate beyond its Broadway run.

### Profit Pooling

For many years the creative artists connected with a Broadway production negotiated contracts with the producer that stipulated they would receive a percentage of box office income from the very first performance week, or at least the first after opening night. This meant that these people would be earning royalties long before the show reached its break-even point and, therefore, long before the investors earned back a penny's worth of their

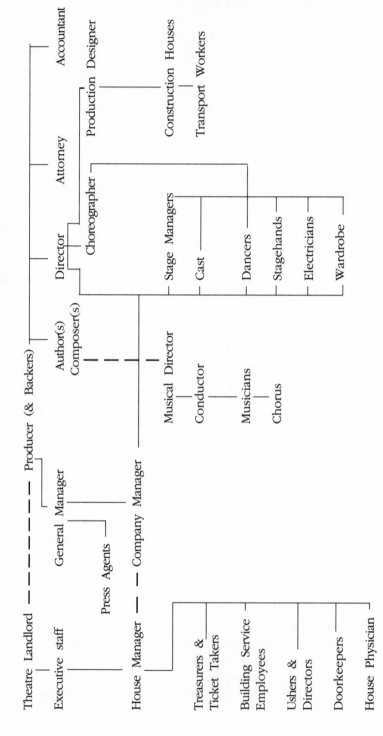

TABLE OF ORGANIZATION
FOR A TYPICAL BROADWAY MUSICAL

investments. As the cost of Broadway production skyrocketed, it became increasingly urgent to devise ways for shows to break even faster so that investors would not desert the industry. This is when profit pooling was introduced in the commercial theatre.

A profit pool is an agreement between the producer and each person who is entitled to receive a percentage of the show from net box office receipts. Each negotiates a fixed amount that is tied to his or her percentage points. For example, each point may be valued at $500. If that person has a 2.5 percent royalty agreement, the payment will be $1,250 per week until the show reaches its break-even point, at which time the actual percentage deal goes into effect. Thus, royalties become a fixed cost while the income is on the down side and a variable cost when it is on the up side. And, because the fixed payments are lower than actual percentage payments would be, the show can break even sooner, the investors can get paid back faster and everybody can share in the profits longer.

## UNDERSTANDING THE ACTORS' UNION
### Actors' Equity Association Jurisdiction and Membership

Equity is an open union in the sense that no one can be denied membership if offered a job under a standard Equity contract. Nonetheless, it is difficult for nonmember actors to gain access to directors, agents and casting directors, although Equity auditions are now somewhat more open to nonmembers. In 1988, the union was called before the National Labor Relations Board and told that its audition system discriminated against nonunion members and was therefore illegal. An agreement was finally reached that admits non-Equity members to Equity auditions, providing they can prove a minimum amount of professional employment as actors during any *one* year. This is defined as two weeks of salary and benefits at the Theatre for Young Audiences contract minimum (the lowest among standard AEA contracts) as a performer in theatre, radio, television or film. Aside from gaining employment through the audition process, one may join Equity by being hired as a stage manager or assistant stage manager for an AEA production, or through the Equity membership candidate program in which one becomes a full member after fifty weeks of work. Finally, there is a "side door" membership by which members of other performers' unions (AGVA, SAG, etc.) who have belonged to that union for at least one year and can document at least three days work under contract, may then gain Equity membership. Once a member, a person may work either as an actor or stage manager regardless of how membership was gained.

From its beginning in 1919 until 1956, the Chorus Equity Association—generally independent from AEA—represented chorus performers. The two organizations merged in 1956 under the single banner of Equity, which now represents both principal and chorus performers. Both enjoy the same basic employment protection and benefits, although there remain a few minor differences between a "white contract" (used for principals) and a "pink contract" (used for chorus). One area of jurisdiction that is sometimes challenged concerns vaudeville-like performers in burlesque shows or revues where both Equity and the American Guild of Variety Artists (AGVA) might claim authority. Equity is only vested with jurisdiction over live and so-called legitimate stage productions, even though it shares the 1919 AFL charter (granted to the Associated Actors and Artists of America, or the 4 A's) with the following unions:

AGVA  The American Guild of Variety Artists, covering performers in nightclubs, vaudeville, special acts, burlesque, etc.;

SAG  The Screen Actors' Guild, covering cinema and certain television performers;

SEG  The Screen Extras' Guild, covering cinema performers who do not have speaking roles. Jurisdiction is only on the West Coast;

AFTRA  The American Federation of Television and Radio Artists, covering most performers, newscasters and participants on the television screen or in front of a television or radio microphone;

AGMA  The American Guild of Musical Artists, covering performers in dance, opera, concert, and the serious music field;

IAU  The Italian Actors' Union, for actors who perform in Italian;

HAU  The Hebrew Actors' Union, for actors who perform in Yiddish;

APATE  Asociacion Puertorriquena de Artistas y Technicos del Espectaculo, with offices in San Juan, for actors who perform in Spanish.

Geographically, Equity's jurisdiction extends throughout the United States. Until 1976 it also extended throughout Canada, but as of that date an independent Canadian Actors' Equity Association was created to represent English-speaking actors and the Union des Artistes was formed in Montreal to represent French-speaking actors in Quebec, although special reciprocal membership privileges continue between these unions. However, there is no reciprocal agreement with British Equity or actors' associations in other foreign countries, so American Equity cannot guarantee or assist its members in gaining employment abroad. Indeed, labor unions both here and abroad always favor contracts for their own citizens over foreign nationals. If a Broadway producer wishes to employ a performer who is not a U.S. citizen, Equity usually requires proof that the role in question cannot be played by an American. The same would be true, in reverse, in England. When certain star performers bring unique talents and personalities to a role, then the union is likely to permit their employment despite their alien status, but usually with the stipulation that they must be replaced by a native performer within a few months' time. Non-resident aliens are never permitted to replace American actors. In other cases, when a British actor is allowed to work in the United States, for example, either the producer or British Equity is made to promise equal employment of an American actor in England. In the best of all possible worlds, artists would be able to work wherever they wish, and international cross-fertilization in the arts would be common, but that won't happen soon. Meanwhile, unions do at least permit whole ensembles, or "unit companies" from foreign lands to perform wherever they earn bookings, as artistic ensembles often represent a whole unit that cannot be separated without destroying its character. So the union does not attempt to force American performers into a visiting Kabuki, Teatro Picolo or Royal Shakespeare production—thank goodness!

Numerically, Equity has a membership of around forty thousand, although not much weight should be given to this figure. Many people maintain their membership for a lifetime, although they may have only worked under an AEA contact once for a few weeks (teachers, students, whomever); or worked in legitimate theatre only infrequently (film and television actors).

## Common AEA Terminology

*Actor* Any member of Actors' Equity Association;

*Principal Actor* Any AEA actor-member signed to a contract, excluding those signed to a chorus or extra contract;

*Chorus*   Any AEA member signed to a chorus ("pink") contract and performing chorus work, as determined by the union;

*Extra*   One who provides atmosphere and background only. Not a definite character, not permitted a make-up change or more than one costume change, may not speak except *in omnes*, may not tour except for eight weeks or less with a pre-Broadway tryout and usually receives one half of minimum salary for principals;

*"As Cast"*   If this appears in a principal actor's contract and no part(s) is designated, the actor is only required to perform the part(s) performed at the first public appearance. Or, if the actor is to be cast in multiple parts, at least half of these must be designated in the contract and these may not subsequently change. This rule is especially applicable to LORT (League of Resident Theatres) and CORST (Council of Resident Stock Theatres) contracts;

*Understudy*   An understudy is usually, although not always, a member of the performing company who receives additional compensation for being prepared to assume another role or roles in that production, in the event of which additional compensation is provided. The specific role(s) an actor understudies must be determined no later than two weeks after the New York City opening or four weeks after the out-of-town opening, whichever is sooner;

*Alien*   To employ an alien, the producer must get special permission from AEA and also conform to laws and regulations of such agencies as the U.S. Immigration Bureau;

*Part*   Each character, specialty or function for which the actor is responsible;

*Role*   The sum of all characters, specialities or functions for which the actor is responsible;

*Producer*   For the purpose of AEA contracts, the producer is the person who posted bond with Equity and who is ultimately responsible for complying with union rules. The term "manager" is used to mean the same thing in some contracts;

*Deputy*   A member of the performing company, elected by the company to serve as representative on its behalf both to management and the union;

*Council*   The Council of Actors' Equity is its governing body, which has the power, among other things, to settle certain disputes between actors and managers, to define and redefine terms and to render interpretations of Equity rules and regulations;

*Juvenile Actor*   Any actor under the age of sixteen to whom special rules apply—such as not disrupting his or her school day for certain rehearsals more than once a week, providing a guardian while at the theatre and providing a tutor while the production is on tour;

*Point of Organization (Origin)*   The producer may designate New York, Los Angeles, San Francisco or Chicago as the city that will appear on the contract, otherwise the union will decide. This will especially influence such matters as casting, and reimbursement to AEA members for travel and out of town expenses;

*Rider*   Any clause attached or added to a contract.

## Types of AEA Contracts and Agreements for Commercial Theatre

There are six or eight collective bargaining agreements between Equity and different segments of the commercial theatre. The figure is vague because some of these segments include both commercial and nonprofit theatre operations—stock and theatre for young audiences, for instance. The latter will be discussed here, while the different types of AEA stock agreements are covered in Chapter 7. However, it bears repeating that Equity, unlike the IRS, recognizes no difference between commercial and nonprofit operations, except that the LORT agreement is restricted to the nonprofit sector. Equity has also devised a number of standard contract forms for use in segments of the theatre industry where there is no collective bargaining process—in cabaret and industrial shows, for instance. And, finally, there are many cases when Equity tailors an agreement to suit the needs and circumstances of a particular production or company: the Special Production Contract and the Letter of Agreement (LOA) are two such cases.

All Equity contracts are subject to the Constitution and By-Laws of the union. Most of the rules and regulations are essentially the same for all segments of the industry; the items that vary most, not surprisingly, are those related to salaries, benefits, and the use of nonprofessionals.

155

## The Production Contract

The AEA Production Contract is normally negotiated every three years by the League of American Theatres and Producers. It dictates the terms of the Standard Production Contract and the Run of the Play Contract, to which all principal and chorus actors, and all stage managers, are signed on Broadway. It also governs AEA employment for first class and bus and truck tours and sit-down (open-ended) runs in any of the Equity office cities. The Production Contract is the basic agreement from which all other Equity contracts and agreements are derived. Familiarity with the Production Contract, its terminology and types of regulation, greatly assists in understanding any type of Equity contract. The producer members of the League, incidentally, negotiate the Equity contracts, while the landlord members negotiate with those unions that represent treasurers, building service employees and others.

## The Off-Broadway Contract

The contract between Equity and the League of Off-Broadway Theatres and Producers provides minimum salaries based on five different sets of potential box office grosses as well as five different seating capacities. The more money a production can earn at the box office, the more the actors must be paid until a certain maximum gross is reached. Minimum salaries for Equity members are, of course, lower Off-Broadway than on Broadway. Nonprofessionals may not be used under either contract. The Off-Broadway Contract applies only to productions in the borough of Manhattan, but may not be used in any theatre located in the area bounded by Fifth and Ninth Avenues from 34th to 56th Streets, or from Fifth Avenue to the Hudson River between 56th and 72nd Streets, or in any theatre having a seating capacity of more than 499.

## Stock Contracts (See Chapter7.)

## The Dinner Theatre Contract (See Chapter7.)

## The Theatre for Young Audiences Contract

During the 1975 negotiations for the AEA contract governing children's theatre, the official name of the agreement was changed to Theatre for Young Audiences and the name of the management association representing producers in this field became the Producers' League of Theatre for Young Audiences (PLOTYA). Equity defines young audience productions as those presenting material expressly prepared or adapted for children up to and including the eighth grade (excluding Shakespearean adaptations), with performance time not exceeding an hour and a half, including intermissions. Several Equity companies that perform only on the high school level have also been signed under this contract. Actors may work by the week or by the performance, but in both cases minimum salaries are comparatively low, although additional compensation is required when the actor:

1. Performs in a theatre seating more than 300;
2. Is required to travel beyond points that can be reached by one fare via local public transportation;
3. Is required to travel to more than one theatre during the same day;
4. Is required to sleep away from home.

Except when agreed to in writing with AEA, nonprofessionals are no longer permitted in Theatre for Young Audiences productions. Due to the special nature of children's theatre, this is one of the most flexible AEA contracts, and modifications are often granted to producers by the union.

Before the first agreement was negotiated in 1953, Equity had kept its eyes closed to children's theatre, because so few were profitable. But when more or less permanent children's theatre companies comprised of adult actors were formed, and their organizers began to realize sizable profits, Equity began making an effort to guarantee basic rights and wages that most actors in this branch of the business were being denied. Of course, there remain a great number of nonprofessional children's theatre companies and productions that continue to work outside union jurisdiction.

### The Showcase Code

In order to deal with Equity members who choose to work without salary in Off-Off-Broadway theatres in New York or similar theatres in other cities, the union developed what has come to be called the Showcase Code. This permits producers to collect contributions from the audience or charge a limited ticket price, but restricts the size of the theatre to less than one hundred seats, and the number of performances to twelve. While unsalaried, Equity members must be reimbursed for basic expenses during the rehearsal and performance periods. There are no restrictions on the number of nonprofessionals who may be used in a showcase production.

While there is no Off-Off-Broadway producers' association as such, there is a service organization called the Alliance of Resident Theatre/New York (ART/NY, formerly the Off-Off-Broadway Alliance or OOBA) in which many such producers are members. The vast majority of Off-Off-Broadway companies are nonprofit, yet works that are showcased may end up in the commercial sector. For this reason, Equity stipulates that if a Showcase (or other Equity Code or other-than-standard contract) production is produced under a standard contract within five years of the showcase, all Equity actors in that showcase must be offered the same roles or paid four weeks' salary at the minimum rate of the contract under which the new production is playing.

## Workshop Productions

Usually organized as a method of trying out and developing a property for eventual commercial production, the AEA-approved workshops stipulate that only union actors may be used, that they may receive a smaller than standard production salary, that the workshop consist of six to twelve weeks of rehearsal (during which twelve rehearsals may be played before an invited audience), and that rehearsals may be interrupted for as much as two weeks to permit rewriting time. Then there may be three weeks of limited performances, again without admission charge. The hitch is that actors are to receive a percentage of any income the property may generate for the next eighteen years!

Needless to say, both the Showcase Code and the Workshop provisions have stirred up a terrific amount of controversy. A number of prominent playwrights refuse to allow their work to be produced under either arrangement, because the cost (which is paid from their royalties) could eventually be too high. And factions of Equity's own membership have loudly protested the union's growing jurisdiction over developmental production projects. Actors want opportunities to perform and be seen. Playwrights want opportunities to get produced and develop their work based on actors' input and audience reaction. The union, on the other hand, is trying to protect its members from being exploited. The controversy is not likely to go away soon.

## Cabaret Theatres

Equity has devised a standard cabaret theatre agreement to cover its members who perform in a nightclub or cafe setting. Unlike dinner theatres, the price of admission (or minimum or cover charge) is separate from the cost of any food or beverages that customers may purchase or that cabarets are permitted in Equity office cities. Cabaret productions may be no more than ninety minutes in length (excluding intermission) and must present their shows in the same room where beverages are being served. Like the Showcase Code, if a cabaret production is transferred and produced under a standard contract, the actors must be offered their original roles or compensated with special payments. However, there are cases in which actors work in cabarets without salary or future production agreements, because this is their wish and because the union does not find any evidence of exploitation. Under an AEA cabaret contract, a week's work may include ten performances on six consecutive days.

The Cabaret contract is used nation-wide and, like other AEA contracts, is monitored by the regional union office that has jurisdiction over the territory in which the production is originated. There may be three or four dozen cabaret productions under AEA contract at any one time. Associations of cabaret operators have been formed in some cities, like the Manhattan Association of Cabarets (MAC) in New York City, although these are not collective bargaining groups. A number of theatre companies throughout the nation operate a cabaret theatre apart from their main performance space. In such cases, performances are usually scheduled after the mainstage curtain has come down or at other nontraditional times. Such programming can provide desirable performance opportunities—especially for performers, playwrights and composers—while also earning additional income for the theatre company.

From the producer's point of view, the cabaret format may (for the right property or material) offer a comparatively inexpensive method of trying out and developing a production. This is especially true because cabaret operators rarely demand to share in any future profits that the production may earn—as would be the case if the same production were done at a nonprofit professional theatre, for instance. Instead, the cabaret operator only asks to keep 50 percent or less of the admission price (or gate), while keeping 100 percent of food and beverage sales. Another, perhaps unique, aspect of cabaret contracts is that actors sometimes produce their own cabaret shows, so the union ends up dealing with a person who is both employer and employee!

Such productions as *Ain't Misbehavin'* and *Forbidden Broadway* originated in cabaret theatres, and a number of solo performers like Whoopi Goldberg, Lily Tomlin and Michael Feinstein developed material in cabarets that they later performed on Broadway.

## Industrial Shows

An industrial show is a device dreamed up by Madison Avenue to promote or demonstrate the products or ideas of a particular industry. "Industrials" are produced for conventions sponsored by manufacturers at which franchised managers and salespeople gather to learn about new products or new sales techniques. Industrials have also been produced for public expositions of an industrial nature (like auto shows and boat shows), at world's fairs, at theme parks and at political conventions. An industrial show is a theatrical gimmick for increasing an audience's excitement about a particular product, person or idea—and it can work as potent propaganda. In essence, it is an elongated television commercial and it costs a very pretty penny to produce. For many years the best known example was the annual Milliken Breakfast Show, produced for fashion and garment buyers in New York for thirteen days, at a cost of around two million dollars.

The Equity regulations covering industrial shows generally follow those in the Production Contract. There are no provisions for nonprofessionals. Actors must receive additional compensation for overtime and travel, and the minimum salaries are rather handsome as, perhaps, they should be, in this most commercial of all live theatre activities.

Industrials are produced by companies that specialize in this activity, by talent agencies, and by advertising and marketing firms. Equity members may only perform in industrial shows produced by companies or individuals who are signators to AEA's Industrial Shows Basic Agreement.

## Special Contracts and Agreements

While the contracts and agreements mentioned above, together with the LORT contract to be discussed in Chapter 6, are those most commonly used to employ Equity actors, the union has devised many others to accommodate special productions and circumstances. For example, there is a contract for outdoor symphonic drama; a special production contract; a Letter of Agreement; special waivers; and so forth. Producers should contact the nearest Equity office whenever a new production or theatre company is being planned and begin exploring how much the union is willing to accommodate the management of the project. Such producers or managers should also join the appropriate bargaining association (if there is one) and compare notes with their colleagues in the profession.

## GENERAL ASPECTS OF
## EMPLOYMENT REGULATED BY AEA

The following regulations, with minor exceptions, apply to all Equity productions, whether in New York or not, whether produced by commercial or nonprofit organizations, and regardless of the budget or box office gross entailed.

## Auditions

Auditioning and casting for a production is one of the director's most important responsibilities, although producers and playwrights often have veto power over casting decisions, and professional casting directors have recently diminished directors' involvement in this process. The union mandates that interviews/auditions be held for all Equity productions and that these be open to all AEA members as well as nonmembers who can prove professional credentials.* However, as with the other labor organizations in theatre, Equity is opposed to its members doing any extensive work until a contract is signed. Actors should not be required to polish a character interpretation, designers should not submit renderings, and company managers should not prepare a payroll for a production without compensation. There are separate interviews/auditions for principals and chorus, and no stars or other actors may be summoned or sent by agents until the open auditions (sometimes referred to as "cattle calls") have been completed. Auditioning cannot be delegated to a stage manager or minor functionary; at least one person with casting authority must be present (producer, director, choreographer, casting director, etc.) as well as an AEA representative. The Equity Audition and Interview Code spells out a number of conditions that must be met regarding audition facilities and conduct, and the Code also requires that liability insurance be provided.

Auditions for AEA productions are held in the Equity office city that the producer indicates as the "point of origin" (New York, Los Angeles, San Francisco or Chicago). Despite the inconvenience, and that it may cost more to transport actors to a theatre far removed from New York, many producers and artistic directors prefer holding auditions in New York, as opposed to a closer Equity office city; they believe the quality and variety of talent based in New York is greater. It is dangerous to characterize "Chicago actors" or "L.A. actors" or "New York actors," but many experienced producers and directors swear by such generalizations.

Because it is so crucial to the success of a production, the casting process is likely to be difficult and time consuming, often because the opinions of so many people are involved; and no matter how clear the character descriptions may be, or the director's vision, actors cannot be ordered to exact specifications. In fact, such clarity may only serve to frustrate casting decisions. As actors audition for roles, the original concepts about those roles might better be allowed to change as the actors bring new insights and dimensions to them and, after all, that is what actors are trained to do.

## Agents

Equity maintains a list of actor agents and personal representatives in good standing, whom it has franchised to seek and oversee employment for its members; actors who do not use such representatives may be suspended from the union. Actors are not required to pay an agency commission if they settle their terms of employment directly with the producer; and agents traditionally don't accept commissions from performers holding a chorus contract.

---

## Rehearsals

If signed to a standard minimum contract, performers may find that the rehearsal period serves as a probationary trial period during which they may be replaced, if they receive the proper notice and severance pay. Or actors may receive a Run of the Play contract, which carries a higher minimum salary but perhaps one not so high as the actors will demand if they prove to be a big hit after the play has opened. Stars are usually signed to a long-term contract from the outset, making it more expensive to replace them before the termination date. Musical plays usually rehearse for five or six weeks, and nonmusicals for four weeks, although there are exceptions. All performers, including stars, work for the union minimum salary during rehearsal periods.

Rehearsals for Broadway productions are conducted in rented studios, and only a few days are set aside for dress and technical rehearsals in the theatre where the show will open, although Off-Broadway productions are likely to get more rehearsal time in the theatre. New York companies rehearsing for stock, dinner theatre or other productions away from the city may be required to rehearse at the first out-of-town theatre, since this is less expensive for the producer. The stage manager is charged with enforcing union rules both during rehearsal and performance periods, although if rules are broken the producer is liable for any overtime or penalties imposed by Equity.

## Salaries and Benefits

The minimum salaries that producers are required to pay AEA members in the various job categories (principal, chorus, understudy, stage manager, etc.) are usually negotiated every three years between the union and an association of producers from the appropriate branch of the industry. Salary increments are granted each year, and salaries may also be increased annually to cover rises in the cost of living, based on the Cost of Living Index compiled by the U.S. Bureau of Labor Statistics' revised Consumers' Price Index.

Provisions in AEA contracts stipulate that actors and stage managers must receive extra compensation or insurance coverage for the performance of special tasks or feats, such as being responsible for the transportation of costumes, performing a risky feat on stage or playing a second role. Overtime payments are mandated when Equity members exceed specified time limits for rehearsals, performances, picture calls, and travel. Except for Cabaret, Industrials, and Young Audiences, AEA contracts state that, in exchange for a week's salary, the actor is obligated to provide eight performances in six days and must be paid full salary even if the producer reduces the number of performances. An additional pro-rated performance salary must be paid when an extra performance is added, when a performance begins before 2:00 P.M. or after 11:00 P.M. on any day, when more than two performances are given on the same day, or when actors are required to work seven days out of seven.

All Equity contracts provide that members will receive illness and hospitalization insurance, Worker's Compensation, pension and health contributions from the producer, and, of course, matching Social Security contributions. Those contracted under the Production Contract also receive life insurance and are required to perform without salary in a performance to benefit the Actors' Fund of America, a nonprofit organization that assists aging and infirm Equity members.

## Costumes and Makeup

While actors must provide their own conventional makeup, the producer foots the bill if special makeup (body makeup, face masks) is required. Under the Production Contract, the producer provides all stage clothing and its upkeep, although actors may get permission to wear their own clothing when this is appropriate. But this ruling is less stringent under other contracts, when actors earning over a stipulated weekly salary may be required to furnish their own street clothing and footwear, although the actors receive a rental fee from the producer for each item they themselves provide. Management is always responsible for cleaning and maintaining all clothing, footwear and wigs on a regular basis, and paying expenses involved when actors are required to change hair color or style.

## Transportation and Travel (See Chapter 7.)

## Conversions and Transfers (See Chapter 6.)

## Publicity, Photographs and Billing (See Chapter 16.)

## Safe and Sanitary Working Conditions (See Chapter 3, "The Performers' Area")

## SUPERVISING THE PRODUCTION
### Tryouts and Previews

During the nineteenth century, nearly all shows opened first in New York, if only for one or two performances, and were then sent on the road so they could use the magical phrase "direct from New York!" in their advertisements. Later the situation was reversed and nearly every commercial show began outside New York. It now seems safe to say that neither "prior to Broadway" nor "direct from New York" attracts many ticket buyers. For this reason, and even more because of the high cost of touring, a less frenzied method of trying out a show became popular during the 1960s: the New York "preview." Of course, eliminating the pre-Broadway, out-of-town engagement meant that many shows would never be seen outside New York, and that "the road" would be diminished to a noticeable degree. But lower operating costs, and the belief that preview audiences in New York are more representative of post-opening Broadway audiences, soon made the preview system the choice of many producers. Of course, this method tends to exclude theatrical properties that are being developed over a fairly long period of time, usually by a nonprofit theatre company. Out-of-town tryouts seldom earn enough revenue at the box office to pay the expenses of the tour. Nonetheless, they do permit the production company to work away from the glare of Broadway publicity and potentially damaging word of mouth.

The purpose of tryout or preview performances is to examine a production as it plays to a live audience and make whatever adjustments are deemed necessary and possible. Like casting, this kind of artistic analysis and decision-making is difficult—producers and directors who have mastered it are at the top of the profession. When a show is "in trouble," it is rarely a simple matter to figure out exactly what the problem is—the writing, directing, designing, performing, or perhaps even the marketing. In some cases a "play doctor" or consultant will be brought in to make changes. In other cases, the producer may have to "buy out" the contract of one or more of the leading artists. This may be very costly, since the producer might have to pay both a weekly salary and a percentage of the gross throughout the New York run, as in the case of dismissing a star who signed a Run of the Show Contract. A dismissed director would be entitled to the full contractual fee plus a percentage of the show and subsidiary rights, as specified. Or it may be deemed necessary to scrap the scenery or costumes and build anew.

Pressure is always intense during tryouts, because the fuse is burning and nobody is really certain whether it will set off a fireworks celebration or a bomb. Ego and anxiety can easily blur judgement. For example, there is a wonderfully telling story about a famous Broadway producer who decided he didn't like the color of the stage floor on the set of his latest show, which was in previews. So he ordered the designer to have it repainted. But the show's director, who had been out of town when this happened, ordered the designer to have it painted back to the original color when the producer was out of town. This happened several times and always incurred the considerable expense of a union crew on night shift and overtime. When the perplexed designer related this story to a colleague after the successful opening of the show, the response was: "But, baby, didn't you know? They're both color blind!"

## The Opening Night

On Broadway, as in the community theatre in Sioux City, the opening night of a production is likely to be the least typical night the show will ever enjoy or regret. The house is usually packed with well-wishers, relatives, critics and, perhaps, backers and celebrity hounds. Little wonder that "opening night jitters" have become part of the tradition. The performances can easily suffer and the perception of audience members may be equally off balance. From the first preview performance to the opening night and beyond, it is the role of management to do whatever is reasonable to create a stable and secure workplace for the company, while also helping the audience and the press to feel that they're having the time of their lives. But there are no union rules that stipulate how this can be accomplished.

## Maintaining a Production

Because so much energy and anxiety go into opening night, the second night's performance may well be the most difficult. Seasoned professionals understand that they must go on night after night and maintain a uniformly high level of performance. Nonprofessionals tend to relax their efforts and lose their concentration as time goes on (and this is true on both sides of the footlights). Keeping a production alive and fresh for an extended number of performances is an obligation shared by both the artists and the management. If the price of admission remains the same, so should the quality of the production.

On Broadway, SSDC requires that directors and choreographers attend performances of their productions approximately every eight weeks, and redirect or re-rehearse it without additional compensation if they find this to be necessary. They may even forfeit half of their royalties if they fail in this responsibility. It is difficult to win judgements against performers on artistic grounds, but not impossible. Most serious complaints leveled against actors by producers are likely to be leveled against stars, whom the union is not as disposed to protect so vigorously as supporting players. Stars, after all, earn a great deal of money and don't require minimum levels of salary, housing, transport and other such conditions. More likely, they require protection against exploitation, harassment, anxiety, self-aggrandizement, boredom, alcohol, hangers-on or drugs—and that is a management function.

Fortunately, most professional actors work hard at keeping their performances fresh. Many take ongoing lessons, develop daily memory or sensory exercises and spend considerable time "getting into character" before each performance. Others just seem blessed and, as was once said about pianist Artur Rubinstein, never need to practice. Whatever the case may be, the integrity of the theatre profession hangs on its ability to engage the full attention and admiration of an audience. So everyone seriously involved in theatre is committed to maintaining this integrity.

## Dissolving a Production Company

Once the media critics' views are known, the New York commercial producer must decide almost immediately whether to continue the production or not. If the reaction is unfavorable, a closing notice might be posted after opening night (or even before) in order to terminate all contracts and other financial obligations as quickly and inexpensively as possible. But when the critical reaction is mixed, when there is a large advance sale or when audience reaction appears to indicate the possibility of extending the run, then the producer may decide to absorb a degree of loss in order to "turn business around." In the event of rave reviews, of course, the producer's decision is both obvious and easy.

When closing a commercial production in New York and dissolving a joint venture or Limited Partnership Agreement, the producer must dispatch all obligations as quickly as possible and render a final accounting of the enterprise to all partners. Nowhere is the sad business of closing a show more goodheartedly recorded than in Moss Hart's classic comedy about show business, *Light Up the Sky*. Listen as the star's mother, Stella, explains it to the producer's wife:

> STELLA. This the first show you put money into, Frances?
> FRANCES. Yes.
> STELLA. Well, I'll tell you about the scenery first. You can't sell it—get that out of your mind right now—and what's more, you can't even walk away and leave it here.
> FRANCES. All that scenery?
> STELLA. All that scenery! You can't even make believe you forgot about it. No, dear. First you have to pay somebody to have it carted away from the theatre—and then you have to pay somebody to burn it.
> FRANCES. Pay somebody to burn it?
> STELLA. Pay somebody to burn it. You and Sidney want to run about the city dump lighting matches? You have to pay someone to burn it. Regular union rates, and it's my impression this scenery is going to burn real slow.
> FRANCES. Listen, Stella—don't rib me about this. My stomach just turned over.
> STELLA. I'm just telling you what happens, Frances. You might as well

know it.

FRANCES. Yeah. I can tell Sidney. I'll tell him nice and slow—for about two years. Go on, Stella. What happens with the costumes?

STELLA. Well, in an ordinary show, Frances, a costume that cost two hundred dollars they buy back for about two dollars but this is an allegory, dear. The costumes in this show are mostly rags the survivors of the world are walking around in, right?

FRANCES. Right! So we get about a dollar apiece for 'em.

STELLA. Oh, no! I wouldn't think so, Frances. What are they going to do with 'em? Can't even cover chairs with 'em!

FRANCES. Can't leave 'em here, either.

STELLA. That's right.

FRANCES. Cart 'em away. Burn 'em. Union rates. Pray for a windy day on the dump so they'll burn fast. Do people who put money into shows know about this, Stella?

STELLA. Well, usually a backer gets at least some kind of souvenir for his dough, Frances. Say, he puts up five thousand dollars—he gets a lamp to take home, or his wife gets a pocketbook. But you're dealing with an allegory here, Frances. You see anything in this show you can take home?

FRANCES. I got no use for a wind machine. That I know right away.

STELLA. You got any place in your house for the mountain with the faces of Washington, Jefferson and Lincoln carved on it? Or the rain effects?

FRANCES. Sidney's bedroom. He should wake up every morning and look at it, and the rain should pour down on him. So, actually, Stella, it's going to cost more money, even to close it.

STELLA. Oh, sure. It would be wonderful if you could just stick up a sign saying "gone to lunch" or "if not called for in thirty days, forget it"—but it just doesn't work that way,

FRANCES. How did you figure my interest was worth eleven dollars, Stella? That's pretty high, isn't it?

STELLA. Well, I wanted to slip it to you easy. This is your first show.

FRANCES. Yeah. Boy, I can't wait now to run into Irving Berlin. "There's no business like show business." He ought to be arrested.

©Copyright by Moss Hart 1948, 1949.

A conversation similar to this must still take place with every failure in the commercial theatre. So let's hope for more hits than flops!

## PUTTING THE SHOW ON THE ROAD*

National touring companies, also called first class touring companies, are generally organized and controlled by the original producer. This may

---

*See also Chapter 10: Theatrical Presenting Organizations

be a commercial Broadway producer, such as Cameron Mackintosh or Emanuel Azenberg, or a nonprofit institution, like the New York Shakespeare Festival or Lincoln Center Theater. When ticket demand is high, two or three national companies of the same show may be sent on the road simultaneously while the original production is still playing in New York. In such cases, each company will perform in a major city like Boston, Los Angeles or Chicago for many months. National companies are signed to the AEA Production Contract, which spells out all the rules and regulations regarding actors away from home.*

Unlike national companies, bus and truck companies often give only a few performances at each theatre they visit. National companies are usually under the supervision of the original producer, director and creative team whose aim is to stage carbon copies of the New York hit, but bus and truck tours tend to be more modest, though not necessarily less effective.

During the years just before and after 1900 there were usually three hundred to four hundred commercial theatre productions touring the country at any given time. Today there are seldom more than three or four dozen. Still, profits earned from tours of commercial productions have long been important to New York producers. Increasingly, touring has also become a regular activity for nonprofit theatre companies, as will be discussed in the next chapter.

## SUMMATION

The commercial theatre in America has always been a speculative business. In some periods it has just managed to provide a living for people who work in it. At other times, the commercial theatre has made large profits, most of which have been distributed to people other than theatre artists. Ostensibly, commercial theatre has continued to exist without the benefit of subsidy, but a closer look reveals that it is ever dependent upon the noncompensatory time and energy invested by nearly everyone who has worked to be a part of it, and by many fortunes in private capital that have been invested and lost. The most positive force working in favor of the commercial theatre is the autonomy it provides both producers and artists, allowing them to fly, as it were, without the board members, donors, government agencies, and institutional delays that usually encumber nonprofit companies. While few commercial productions offer little of lasting significance, commercial theatre continues to function as an influential marketplace, in terms of both audience and talent.

*See Chapter 7.

# 6

# Nonprofit Professional Theatre

T HE comparatively sudden existence of nearly three hundred nonprofit professional theatres located from coast to coast—most founded after 1960—has radically altered the map of the American theatre, in terms of both where and how theatre is produced. While many of these theatres may resemble the resident stock companies of the 1800s, they sprang out of a completely different tradition; indeed, they have created their own tradition in American theatre.The nonprofit theatres are governed by boards of trustees and artistic directors who, unlike the actor-managers of yesteryear, have their sights fixed on artistic rather than commercial goals.

This chapter will consider governmental structures and special concerns of nonprofit theatres, and then look at the different types of Equity contracts under which they may or may not operate.

## BACKGROUND
### The Seeds are Planted: "47" to '47

The foundation upon which today's nonprofit professional theatre rests was put down between 1912, when George Pierce Baker first offered an influential playwrighting course numbered "47" in the Harvard catalog, and 1947, when Margo Jones' Theatre '47 in Dallas and Nina Vance's Alley Theatre in Houston provided models for many of the "serious" theatre companies that were to follow.

The early drama courses and theatre programs that appeared on college campuses grew simultaneously with what is called the Little Theatre Movement. Both were stimulated by an interest in the drama of Ibsen, Strindberg, Chekhov, Shaw and others, and by the innovative productions their works were receiving in Europe under the stage direction of such men as Antoine, Stanislavsky and Meyerhold. The first important, nonprofessional theatre companies here were the Washington Square Players (1914) and the Provincetown Players, which produced O'Neill's *Bound East for Cardiff* on Cape Cod in 1916, during the group's first season; subsequently they set up permanent headquarters in New York's Greenwich Village. On a professional level, the Theatre Guild (1919) was founded to produce serious plays for subscription audiences in a number of major cities. Americans such as Kenneth Macgowan, Robert Edmund Jones, Joshua Logan and Elia Kazan traveled abroad to observe the work of Stanislavsky and others, while Europeans such as Lee Strasberg and Herbert Berghof, who had been exposed to the Free Theatre Movement abroad, migrated to America and became its proponents here. In both playwriting and staging, two essentially new styles were developed—realism and expressionism—which by the '40s gave the theatre an altogether new look, even transforming the operetta into distinctly American musical theatre.

Eva Le Gallienne attempted to revive the repertory system with her Civic Repertory Theatre, which she founded in 1926; and the Group Theatre was established in 1929 by several defectors from the Theatre Guild. Outside New York, the most ambitious pioneering groups included the Cleveland Play House (1917), Jasper Deeter's Hedgerow Theatre (1923), the Pittsburgh Playhouse (1933), and Robert Porterfield's Barter Theatre (1933).

Between 1935 and 1939 the administration of Franklin D. Roosevelt provided indirect subsidy for the arts through the Works Progress Administration, the main purpose of which was to create jobs for a nation in the throes of the Depression. Several million dollars were earmarked for four arts programs, intended to benefit painters, writers, musicians and theatre workers respectively. Theatre artists were organized under the Federal Theatre Project, headed by Hallie Flanagan. Aside from the well-documented productions and talents that came to light as a result of the Federal Theatre, the project also inspired the creation of the National Theatre Conference, a collection of theatre people (many inspired by George Pierce Baker) who sought to reduce the dominance of commercial Broadway theatre and encourage quality work, without being tied to the profit motive. The Conference also sought to create a network of community theatre centers across the country and lay the groundwork for a national federation of theatres. But the Federal Theatre Project became entangled in a web of political controversy, and federal support was abruptly withdrawn. Still, while most of its ambitious plans were never realized, the Project helped plant the seeds for the growth of serious professional theatre in America, as well as for more meaningful and direct government subsidy of the arts.

Much of the hope and passion engendered by Federal Theatre Project activities seems to have taken root in the work of Margo Jones and her Theatre '47 in Texas, helping to inspire the subsequent proliferation of professional theatres outside New York City. Having worked for the Federal Theatre Project in Houston, taught at the university level and directed on Broadway, Jones combined the attributes of intelligence, professionalism and dedication to artistic integrity that remain the cornerstones of the nonprofit theatre today. Aside from presenting the first productions of plays by such writers as William Inge and Tennessee Williams, her theatre was also important as a model for arena-style staging, which has been adopted or adapted by so many of the nonprofit theatres that followed.

## *The Birth of the Nonprofit Theatre Movement: 1950 to 1965*

The Arena Stage in Washington, D.C. was founded in 1950 by Zelda Fichandler, who was a disciple of Margo Jones, by Fichandler's husband Thomas and by Edward Mangum. From its humble beginnings in a converted movie house, the Arena Stage eventually moved into its own, multi-million dollar facility, to become one of the most venerated of the nonprofit companies. The nonprofit model upon which many of the Off-Broadway companies were based was Circle in the Square (1951), which eventually moved from Greenwich Village to Broadway and became one of the first nonprofit companies to invade the citadel of commercialism. Rising production costs also prompted the growth of another alternative to the commercial theatre, Off-Off-Broadway, which was fueled by the experimental energies of such innovators as Judith Malina and Julian Beck and their Living Theatre, Ellen Stewart, Maria Irene Fornes, Al Carmines, and Joseph Chaikin, among others. But the catalyst that turned all this considerable activity into what could soon be identified as a nonprofit theatre movement was the commitment of the Ford Foundation in 1957 to give almost sixty million dollars to the arts over a short period of years—the first such philanthropic undertaking in American history. As director and later vice president of this program, W. McNeil Lowry conceivably influenced twentieth century theatre in this country more than any other individual. While money was also given to opera and dance companies, symphony orchestras and schools, these had already been long established both as "serious" endeavors and as nonprofit institutions. The theatre, however, was still regarded for the most part as a frivolous form of entertainment that could and should pay its own way—not an uncommon attitude even today. Nonetheless, the Ford Foundation arts program made one thing very clear for the first time: If a theatre wished to receive a philanthropic gift, it had to operate as an on-going, nonprofit organization. In other words, it had to be an institution, like the Cleveland Symphony Orchestra, the Lyric Theatre of Chicago or the Boston Museum of Fine Arts. Furthermore, it had to be professional (both in terms of its objectives and its employees). To this end, Ford also funded an arts management internship program, probably the first attempt to provide professional training in this field.

As a result, theatre groups that had been loosely structured began incorporating and applying for nonprofit status, and groups springing into existence for the first time began to use the nonprofit model from the outset. Then, in 1961, again at the instigation of Lowry and with additional money from the Ford Foundation, Theatre Communications Group (TCG) was established in New York to provide networking and support for the increasing number of diverse nonprofits, which soon included the Guthrie Theatre in Minneapolis (1963), Trinity Square Repertory Company in Providence (founded in 1964 by another Margo Jones disciple, Adrian Hall), the Actors Theatre of Louisville (1964), and the American Conservatory Theatre (ACT) in San Francisco (1965).

Needless to say, all this new activity did not escape the attention of Actors' Equity, which soon felt that a new contract should be drawn up to "accommodate" this new category of theatre—not because such theatre was nonprofit, but simply because it made different demands upon actors than theatres in the stock or Off-Broadway categories, for example. To negotiate with the union, a group of managers from the larger and most established nonprofits formed the League of Resident Theatres (LORT).

The year 1965 is a landmark for the arts in America, due to President Lyndon B. Johnson's signing of legislation that created the National Endowment for the Arts (NEA). The establishment of NEA had followed the publication of the Rockefeller Panel Report, *The Performing Arts: Problems and Prospects* , which had made a compelling case in favor of federal subsidy for the arts. Now subsidy had become a reality, with state and local arts support just around the corner. But, as with private and corporate contributions, only nonprofit organizations were eligible to receive government funding.* So it was that the nonprofit professional theatre movement in America was first nurtured, then formalized.

## *The Dominance of Nonprofit Theatre: 1966 to the Present*

Beginning in 1966 with a meager congressional allocation of $2.5 million, the NEA began its grant-giving process. The first AEA/LORT contract went into effect. William J. Baumol and William G. Bowen published *Performing Arts: The Economic Dilemma*, which documented the inherent inability of the arts to become cost efficient, and in that way reinforced the argument in favor of subsidy. To encourage the further professionalization of nonprofit theatres (and their employment of union actors), Equity established the Foundation for the Extension and Development of the American Profes-

*See also Chapter 14.

sional Theatre (FEDAPT) in 1967, although this organization eventually became independent of the union and served emerging nonprofit dance companies as well. The movement continued to grow, and very soon the nonprofit professional theatre was the largest branch of the American theatre industry, offering more productions and providing more weeks of employment each year than any other.

While it is outside the purview of this volume to document all the activities and accomplishments of the nonprofit theatre during recent years, these successes have been impressive. It has even been said that nonprofit professional theatres, collectively, form a national American theatre—since they represent all the cultural, social, ethnic, political, aesthetic and philosophical diversity that constitutes America in a way that no single national theatre company ever could.

Most ongoing nonprofit companies grew from modest beginnings and had time to resolve fundamental artistic goals and build a local support system, before plunging into a fully professional and high-budget status. Most were founded by a singular, dynamic artist who possessed both a vision and the ability to lead. However, as groups evolved into institutions, and as founding artists departed, the leadership role was sometimes up for grabs, and the company's survival was often threatened when this role was not filled well.

## ORGANIZING A NONPROFIT THEATRE COMPANY

If there was a standard textbook formula for putting together a nonprofit theatre company, it might look like this:

$$\text{Idea = Mission = Board = Policy} = \frac{\text{Artists}}{\text{Management}} = \text{Production} = \frac{\text{Box Office}}{\text{Contributions}}$$

$$\text{Production = etcetera ad infinitum}$$

It would be lovely if, as the above formula suggests, the original idea always led to a clearly articulated mission statement, which then stimulated a terrific volunteer board of trustees to jump on the band wagon and sing out such a rousing medley of policies that top artists and managers would sign on and produce brilliant works, which would then attract sell-out business and unlimited contributions for ever and ever! Unfortunately, there is no formula for producing theatre successfully in the nonprofit sector any more than within the commercial sector. But there are guidelines that can be followed, and common mistakes that can be avoided.

## Leadership

As discussed in Chapter 1, most theatre companies begin as one person's idea, and that person is most usually an actor or director who is motivated either by career frustrations or by a consuming need to create theatre according to a certain vision. At other times, a theatre company is formed in order to fill a vacant or planned facility; this can be rather like the cart drawing the horse, but it can work. And some companies have been formed in order to celebrate a particular playwright, such as Shakespeare, Shaw or O'Neill. Even more difficult than forming a company from scratch may be the task of reorganizing and revitalizing a failed company, or one that is in serious trouble. Each of these different scenarios will require different types of leadership, of which there are four prototypes:

1. An artist-driven company
2. A board-driven company
3. A management-driven company
4. Shared leadership

Any of these may or may not work in a given set of circumstances. As theatre owner James Nederlander once said, "Every theatre has a policy, the only trick is to find it!" For twenty years, the Vivian Beaumont Theatre at Lincoln Center, for example, seemingly defied the efforts of some of the most successful producers and directors in the American theatre, including Robert Whitehead, Elia Kazan, Jules Irving, Herbert Blau and Joseph Papp. Only when a newly constituted board of trustees hired Gregory Mosher from Chicago's Goodman Theatre, under the strong leadership of former New York City Mayor John Lindsay, and Bernard Gersten, formerly of the New York Shakespeare Festival, as artistic director and executive producer, respectively, did the Beaumont "find" its policy.

When a company is firmly controlled by one dynamic and capable person—whether artist, board chairperson or manager—then everyone else becomes subservient, and the chain of authority is clear. However, when authority is shared, and no one person can say, like Harry Truman, "the buck stops here," problems are bound to arise. The Metropolitan Opera, like the Soviet Union, once attempted a troika-style leadership. It didn't work in either case. Titles and salaries may be equal, but people's ambitions and abilities rarely are. Still, like it or not, there are three essential components in the structure of a nonprofit theatre company, and it is difficult not to think of them in a triangular relationship:

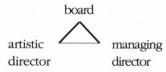

board

artistic director    managing director

Of course, the artistic director might also be the board president or chairperson, or the artistic and managerial leadership might be combined in one person. But usually a different person fills each of the three leadership functions. The managing director may report to the artistic director who, alone, reports to the board. In many cases, both report to the board and have equal status; this situation mandates a true partnership based on mutual respect—not easy to arrange! Extreme examples of shared leadership, as noted earlier, are found in companies such as The Living Theatre and Mabou Mines which are organized as collectives.

No matter how authority is assigned in a nonprofit theatre company, none of the above three components can be neglected. Law requires a board of trustees; theatre production requires artistic direction; and the process requires management. It seems insulting to ask trustees to take fiscal and legal responsibility for a company, yet require them to keep their mouths shut about the art part; or to ask a managing director of twenty years experience to report to a young, unproved genius just appointed artistic director; or ask the proven genius to play second banana to a finance manager. Yet, people in nonprofit theatre *are* frequently asked to accept such relationships. When that is the case, it would be wise for the board to monitor relationships closely and permit them to evolve in terms of position, salary, title and authority based on what seems to work best for the company and the people in it.

## *The Mission Statement*

Chapter One talks about the importance of a mission statement, or statement of purpose, and when it is most useful. But what characterizes a good mission statement? Ideally, it should:

1. State the company's central philosophy, thrust or goal in one concise sentence or brief paragraph
2. Be unique and recognizable, not suitable for any other company
3. Be exciting and inspiring, especially to company participants and to the targeted audience
4. State the company's primary objectives so that its progress and success may be measured according to its own terms.

Yet, one must bear in mind that the mission statement or something close to it will appear in the company's papers of incorporation and its IRC tax determination, both of which are bothersome and expensive to change after they have been filed and accepted. If anything a company does is written in stone, this is it. So particular care should be taken. And, based on this statement, not only will the IRC decide whether or not to grant nonprofit status, it could take away that status at a later date if it determines that the company is not living up to the statement. For example, if the statement declares that the company is organized on a membership basis (as with a collective or a community theatre), or that a primary goal is to tour in the schools, and then company policy changes, there is a real possibility that the 501 (c) (3) status will be forfeited. A theatre company must be very certain of its basic goals before beginning the process of incorporation.

Here is a possible mission statement for a dance theatre company:

The Spanish Dance Theatre is committed to reviving Spanish dance as a theatre art and to bringing this art to all sectors of the American public. The goal is to create ballets, that is, theatre works with a story line, using the Spanish dance idiom. The Spanish Dance Theatre also seeks to establish itself as the "premiere" Spanish dance company of the City of Miami.

This sample would seem to meet the four characteristics of a good mission statement, as discussed above. But the company may decide to delete the last sentence in its corporate papers—because it might eventually decide to make its home in another city.

The next sample shows a rather general statement for use in corporate papers, followed by a few specific objectives to be promulgated in-house, on grant applications and at fundraising events:

The Black Caravan Theatre is dedicated to the support of a professional theatre company, the presentation of works that dramatize and enrich the Black experience, and the development of a broad-based audience.

Objectives of the Black Caravan Theatre include:
1. To establish and maintain at least ten artists/technicians/administrators on a full-time basis each season
2. To present at least four full-length productions each season
3. To perform for audiences in the City of Detroit at a permanent theatre space as well as through a touring program in parks, schools, churches and social centers

Notice that this statement does not restrict the company only to Black participants, audiences or to a narrow repertory of plays. And, of course, the specific objectives can be changed or adapted to suit the purposes at hand.

It is also common for nonprofit theatre companies—especially the larger ones—to operate under a very broad mission statement: "To present classical and modern drama in a way that is relevant to contemporary audiences." And, in fact, this is just what many of the best nonprofit companies do. But, as with libraries, there is a public need for both general and specialized collections of human expressions from the past and/or the present. So that general statement is appropriate for some institutions, but a highly defined image can also serve a company well. For example, the Second Stage Company in New York City is dedicated to giving a second chance to scripts that did poorly in their premiere productions; other companies are dedicated to developing playwrights, actors or directors; and still others are dedicated to presenting only the plays of Shakespeare or some other dramatist.

The *raison d'etre*, or mission, of a theatre company is important. It tells participants, audiences, grant-givers and critics what to look for and how to judge the company's performance.

## Forming a Corporation and Gaining Nonprofit Status

To gain permission to operate under the 501 (c) (3) provision of the Internal Revenue Code and qualify as a nonprofit organization, the group in question must state that its primary purpose is not pecuniary, although it may aim to make money in order to further its nonpecuniary goals. Excluding salaries and other normal operating costs, no assets or income belonging to the organization may be used to benefit its participants. The law recognizes four types of nonprofit corporations (A, B, C, and D), each determined by such factors as the organization's declared purpose and whether it is a membership or nonmembership group. To gain nonprofit corporate status, an attorney should be engaged to:

1. Choose, clear and reserve a corporate name
2. Prepare a Certificate of Incorporation (which must give the organization's stated goals, among other items)
3. Secure approvals from the appropriate administrative and judicial state officials
4. File the completed Certificate of Incorporation and the necessary supporting documents with the Secretary of State.

Because law firms accept a limited number or *pro bono* clients for whom they do legal work without charge, fledgling nonprofit theatre companies should always seek out such an arrangement. Corporate laws vary from state to state. But once corporate status for a group has been legally recognized in a particular state and its goals can be established as nonpecuniary, it should immediately proceed to apply for tax-exempt 501 (c) (3) status. This process will again require an attorney to file applications with the appropriate finance and tax departments of the city and state in which the organization plans to make its headquarters. On the federal level, the attorney must file a Treasury Department IRS Form 1023, "Application for Recognition of Exemption." Again, there are different exempt categories, as determined by the Internal Revenue Code. And the organization is not entitled to tax exemptions until the applicable determinations have been granted. However, it is important to note that exemptions may eventually be retroactive to the date of application (not to the date of incorporation, which is why it is advisable to apply for tax-exempt status as soon as the corporate status has become official).

Legal counsel should also be sought to assist with the preparation of an organization's constitution and by-laws and to provide advice regarding a variety of other legal obligations to which an organization must conform.

## Developing a Board of Trustees

The terms "board of directors" and "board of trustees" are used interchangeably, although the title of "director" is more appropriate at for-profit corporations and seems to imply a much more active role than "trustee." The latter term may help to foster a more benign board, if that is the goal.

The first question in forming a new board concerns its size. The law may only require three or four members to fill the roles of president, vice president, secretary and treasurer. There are no limitations on how large the board may be beyond those imposed by its own by-laws. For most theatre organizations with an annual budget under $5 million, a board of fifteen to twenty-five members is common as well as sensible. However, many artist-led companies begin with a small board comprised of the artist's friends and relatives who are merely asked to lend their names to the papers of incorporation and then serve as a rubber stamp board when necessary. These could be called "paper boards" or "funny boards." If the company grows and begins to require comparatively sophisticated leadership, especially in regard to fundraising, then such boards are usually replaced or increased in size.

Traditional wisdom dictates that board membership should reflect the organization's main areas of concern: finance, marketing, fundraising, operations, planning, artistic development, education and so forth. At least one person who is an expert in each of these areas would then be invited to join the board and head a committee that advises and supports the corresponding staff director. When the new marketing director needs contacts in the media world, for example, someone on the board's marketing committee presumably could provide them. While this method of board development provides a very clear structure, it may also encourage board interference in the day-to-day management of the company. Small companies with fairly small boards may dispense with the formality of the committee structure and allow its board to function as a committee of the whole. But boards of more than eight people should have an executive committee empowered to act on a variety of matters without obtaining full board approval.

While aiming to include successful and influential members of the community, a board should also reflect the character of the theatre company and the fact that it is an artistic endeavor. At least a few board members should either be artists themselves or understand the arts well enough to interpret their special needs to board members who may not have an arts background. Even the presence of a local eccentric or unusual personality is sometimes useful for representing certain viewpoints that don't ordinarily get expressed at board meetings.

Another key question in board development is length of service. Most experts agree that membership should be limited to three-to-five years, although many nonprofit organizations impose no limitation. But this risks stagnation and the inability to change policies when that is desirable or necessary. Also, once trustees have tapped their best contacts, especially potential contributors, they are less and less likely to repeat this effort.

But the biggest question concerns the responsibilities of board members, especially in terms of the amount of money they are expected to raise or contribute each year. Most small and developing arts organizations are much too sheepish on this matter and fail to clarify or even mention it when recruiting new board members, fearing that potential members will be "turned off" and decline. Yet, insuring the fiscal health of the organization is a primary responsibility of trusteeship, and a trustee who does not contribute to this health is usually dead weight. Trustees should be required to bring in a certain dollar amount each year, and this should be made a clear condition of their service. In addition to this, typical board responsibilities include:

1. Making and/or approving policy (executive committee and full board)
2. Approving large capital expenditures and leases (executive committee and full board)
3. Developing long-range plans (planning committee)
4. Hiring artistic and managerial staff heads (executive committee and search committee)
5. Approving and monitoring the budget (finance committee)
6. Seeking and nominating new board members (nominating committee)
7. Raising the needed unearned income (fundraising committee)
8. Assisting with special events and benefit functions (special

programs committee)

9. Promoting ticket sales and other sources of earned income
(marketing committee)

10. Helping to keep the organization solvent and within the
law according to prudent management strategies and
helping to support the artistic goals of the company.

A trusteeship, then, is not an honor to be accepted lightly. It carries with it real obligations, including personal liability under certain circumstances. In fact, some board members take out insurance to protect themselves against possible damages. The law requires that trustees act with diligence, care and prudence. If they are negligent and cause loss or damage to the institution, they may be held personally liable and may even be prosecuted, unless they dissented against board actions and this dissent appears in the board minutes, or the suspected illegality was reported to the state's attorney general.

While the first board of trustees for a new nonprofit corporation is handpicked by the organizers of the enterprise, future members are generally nominated and elected by the sitting board. Of course the artistic director, manager or someone else may also suggest nominees. The original organizers also have the luxury of writing the by-laws (usually with an attorney's guidance) that will determine the structure and governance of the board and the organization. Future boards, of course, may amend these, but the basic character of an organization is very difficult to alter after its "birth certificate" has been put on record and its profile has been shown in public.

## Junior Boards and Advisory Groups

Considering the obligations and liabilities that most trustees must assume, it is hardly surprising that many are socially and/or professionally well-established people. Their status may even seem to contradict the work and the audience of the theatre on whose board they sit, especially in the case of ethnic, experimental and developing companies. But rather than weaken the board by bringing in younger and less established members, it may be more effective to create a junior board or advisory group of some kind. This has no legal decision-making power and may not even have any relationship to the regular board; but it is a device for involving more people (young or old) as volunteers in the work of the company—not as interns or go-fers, but as people who will attend performances on a regular basis and get their friends into the same habit, often with postperformance social gatherings as a lure. Junior boards should hold regular business meetings to plan such events; they may also plan and help run telethons, benefit parties and other special events. While the organization and supervision of such groups is labor-intensive, the investment may be worth the effort. During a time when sources of government and corporate support for the arts are diminishing along with young and new audiences, any strategy that engages fresh converts is a good one. Professional opera companies and symphony orchestras have a long-established record of success with junior boards, and nonprofit theatre companies are beginning to follow suit. Aside from providing an avenue along which new audiences can be brought in, these groups are perhaps the best way to train and identify future leadership for the regular boards of trustees.

# ORGANIZATIONAL STRUCTURES
## Large Theatre Company Organization

Large nonprofit theatre companies with annual operating expenses of more than $3 million usually have a board comprised of several dozen people, who are often divided into committees, as discussed above, to best harness their expertise for the benefit of the institution. Of course, this is not the only method of executive organization, and the relationship between the artistic director and the general manager often depends upon the caliber of the people who hold those positions, as much as any predetermined job description. Every artistic decision, of course, carries a price tag; and every financial decision impacts upon the artistic product. Hopefully, if two different people hold these positions they will be able to develop a symbiotic relationship; however, paradoxically, while the manager must be concerned with all the production and artistic elements, rarely does the artistic director care to become more than superficially involved with such managerial elements as fundraising and marketing. So in practice, while the managing director may report to the artistic director, the former may have a very free hand over all nonartistic departments or areas.

## Medium-Size Theatre Company Organization

Nonprofit theatre companies with an annual operating budget of more than $750,000, but less than $3 million, lack the resources for the large number of specialized personnel found in companies with higher budgets. They are less likely to occupy large multi-operational facilities, produce a mini or workshop series, sponsor a school or touring program or other such activities often found at bigger institutions. There may also be a less formal board structure.

## Small Theatre Company Organization

The majority of nonprofit professional theatre companies have annual

SAMPLE TABLE OF ORGANIZATION: LARGE NONPROFIT THEATRE COMPANY
BUDGETED OVER $3 MILLION ANNUALY

Chairperson & Board of Trustees

Attorneys

Accountants

Executive Committee: President, Vice-President, Secretary, Treasurer

Nominating Committee

Planning Committee

Education Committee

Operations Committee

Finance Committee

Development Committee

Marketing Committee

Special Committees

Managing Director

Artistic Director

School Director

Faculty

Artists-in-Schools Coordinator

Internship Coordinator

Dramaturg

Stage Directors, Choreographers, Music Directors, Conductors

Designers

Performers

Production Manager

Production Technicians

Stage Managers

Stage Crews

Road Manager

Facilities Manager

House Manager

Building Engineers

Maintenance Staff

Finance Director

Systems Analyst

Business Manager

Staff

Development Director

Staff

Marketing Director

Box Office Manager

Subscription Manager

Group Sales Manager

Press & Public Relations Manager

Tour & Booking Manager

Special Events Director

Benefit Chairpeople

Staff

SAMPLE TABLE OF ORGANIZATION:
Medium-Size Theatre Company
Budgeted Between $750,000 & $2 Million

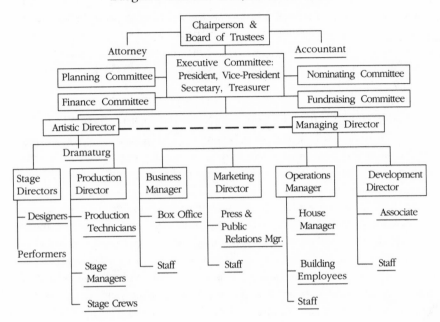

SAMPLE TABLE OF ORGANIZATION:
Small Theatre Company
Budgeted Under $750,000 Annually

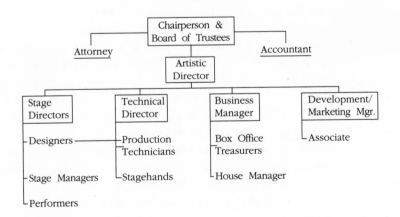

budgets under $750,000. As they grow from having no budget to $100,000 and more, such companies must frequently agonize over how to divide up their limited payroll resources. For instance, whether to hire a technical director or a development director, whether to increase seating capacity and/or ticket prices and thereby graduate into the next higher category of Equity salaries, or whether to continue business as usual; whether the time has come for the artistic director to share, actually share, the power and the glory with a managing director. Growing pains are difficult, but always more fun than old age!

## ARTISTIC POLICY CHOICES IN NONPROFIT THEATRE

Some of the issues discussed below are of concern to stock, college and community theatre groups, but they are especially important to nonprofit professional theatres in terms of setting artistic character and direction. While policies should only be put in place after careful study and deliberation by the leading participants who will be principally responsible for their execution, policies should also be given sufficient time and support to prove themselves. If they do not prove successful, then they should be dropped or altered. And, of course, policies must be flexible enough to accommodate the abilities and desires of their leading exponents. For example, when a new artistic director is brought in, it is reasonable to assume that he or she will bring along a few policy changes, although these should be made clear to the board in advance.

### Production Policy

In the early years of the nonprofit professional theatre movement, many artistic directors believed that serious theatre should follow the model of ballet and opera companies (not to mention the great theatre companies of Europe) and adopt the repertory rotation method of production. This means that after a production is directed, constructed and premiered, all the costumes and other physical elements are kept in storage, and the cast is kept under contract (at least for a season), so that the piece can be performed alternately with others. A resident company of actors performs in all productions, although guest performers may be jobbed in for some roles (many American companies still contain the word "repertory" in their title, although most no longer practice this system of production).

There are several advantages to performing in repertory: visitors to the community can see three or four productions in as many days, extra performances can be scheduled for popular productions and reduced for unpopular ones, rehearsal and production costs can be spread over many performances and, perhaps, over many seasons. But the greatest advantage is

an artistic one; for repertory is the ideal system for nurturing ensemble acting and speeding the growth of individual acting talents. The big *dis*advantage of repertory is that it is the most expensive system of production: there
must be a resident company, extensive storage space, extra personnel are
required for the frequent set-up and break-down of productions, trucking
costs from a warehouse may be high, costumes and scenery must be maintained in fresh condition and cast changes require costume alterations. Nonetheless, repertory is a time-tested and highly regarded system of production
and it adapts well to small, permanent companies that place little emphasis
on physical production elements; it also adapts well to touring. The Metropolitan Opera, the New York City Opera and American Ballet Theatre are
among the largest repertory companies in America, both in terms of personnel and the number of productions in their repertories. But a major, professional nonmusical repertory theatre has eluded the attempts of numerous
organizers for over a century.

The opposite of repertory rotation, of course, is the single, open-ended
run as usually practiced in the commercial theatre. Fortunately, few of the
nonprofit professional theatres have yet succumbed to this temptation, however successful a particular production may prove. Instead, such "hits" are
often transferred from the nonprofit theatre to Broadway or sent on tour and,
in both cases, converted to an Equity production contract.

Most medium to large-size nonprofit companies produce a three-to-
eight-month annual season of five-to-twelve different productions that are
performed in sequence, one after the other. Like repertory, this system is
aimed at attracting a large, permanent audience of subscribers, though there
is less scheduling flexibility. However, an extra performance or two may be
added each week (at extra cost), or it may be possible to revive the most
successful production for a nonsubscription audience at the end of the regular season. A season comprised of a set number of limited runs may also
employ a resident company and provide ample opportunity for actor and
ensemble development.

Quite a few nonprofit companies have two production facilities, usually a 500-to-1000-seat theatre and a smaller studio, or black box space. This
permits certain works to be tested in simple, workshop productions in the
small space and then, if successful, transferred to the larger space and given
a full production. The largest nonprofit outfits, like the New York Shakespeare
Festival, may have a number of performance spaces at several different locations, operating under different ticket policies for different types of audiences: subscription, membership, free theatre in the park, subsidized performances for public school students and so forth.

The artistic goal of production policy is to create high quality performances; the management goal is to match the policy with the largest audience for the production.

## Play Selection Policy

Perhaps the most recently created position in the American professional theatre is that of the dramaturg. While the job has a long history in European theatre, it earned particular distinction and publicity during the '60s with Kenneth Tynan's work as literary manager of England's National Theatre. Many nonprofit companies in this country now employ a full-time dramaturg, or literary manager, to assist the artistic director in searching for works to produce; to research all matters that pertain to selected works for the purpose of enhancing their interpretation; to assist the marketing department in the preparation of publicity material and program notes; to assist the touring and schools programs in the preparation of special educational materials. In fact, companies that have recently acquired the services of a dramaturg may soon wonder how they ever managed without one. But while a dramaturg's contributions to the work of a company can be varied, his or her primary value lies in the play selection process. And this may often include the identification of artists who are available and interested in certain projects and who might bring some special quality to those projects.

Most stage directors have a genre, an historic period or an interpretative style in which they more or less specialize and attempt to make the hallmark of their reputations. After all, one cannot be all things for all productions. To mention names like Elia Kazan, Franco Zeffirelli or Peter Brook is immediately to conjure up certain types of work done in certain styles. Lesser known directors of repute have also learned to cultivate fairly specific interests and skills. This is to say that the artistic director of a theatre company will impose his or her tastes upon that company and, indeed, cannot do otherwise. And these tastes will be most obviously reflected by the plays chosen for production: classical, modern, contemporary, new. Or by the style of production the plays are given: presentational, realistic, expressionistic or experimental. Of course, large institutions can afford to be more universal in their appeal than smaller ones—or this may be mandated by their need to attract a wide patronage. In the public mind, the largest theatre companies may represent nothing more specific than "quality" and "diversity," which would certainly fulfill an important mission. But the smaller theatre companies often succeed best with an audience-specific mission that evolves around a particular genre, style, culture, philosophy or movement. The artistic director usually has final say on which plays will be selected to comprise a season, but rarely does the same person direct all of these if there are more than three or four. Then it is a matter of finding guest directors who are available, suitable for the productions at hand and enthusiastic about directing them.When this is not the case, selections should be changed or postponed. The availability of particular actors might also cause changes to be made.

Some theatre companies follow a play scheduling tradition that dictates, for example, that each season will begin with a comparatively light piece and end with a musical. Or, just as many ballet companies present *The Nutcracker* during the winter holiday season, so resident theatre companies have found that *A Christmas Carol* is a reliable money-maker each year. Other productions must then be scheduled around these.

The artistic goal of play selection is to choose works for which the best interpretive artists can be employed; the management goal is the efficient organization of the selections both in terms of production and marketing.

## Casting Policy

Nonprofit theatres that employ Equity actors must first select one of the four cities with a union office in which to hold auditions. Actors may then be hired according to the rules of the contract under which the theatre is operating. LORT contracts allow the theatre to choose between signing actors to standard contracts (for the length of a production's run) or to seasonal contracts (which must offer between twenty-four and fifty-two consecutive weeks of employment). When hired on a seasonal contract to perform in up to six productions, at least two roles must be specified. If the actor is to be used in more than six productions, at least 50 percent of the roles must be specified. The other roles would be "as cast," meaning that these decisions may be postponed until the actor has arrived at the theatre and rehearsals get under way. However, roles may not be changed after the first public performance of a play without special negotiation and agreement.

These and other union regulations have a direct impact on casting policy and, of course, on payroll costs. If there is a resident Equity company, then seasonal contracts are the most economical, providing that all actors on such contracts are utilized in all productions. When the proposed list of productions for a season is studied from the casting viewpoint, changes or substitutions may again be required. Such casting questions may arise as, "What roles other than Hedda Gabler can be performed by the actress we have in mind?" "Shouldn't we schedule the three-character play at the beginning or end of the season so that contracts for the other actors can be written for a shorter season?" "Should not the guest directors sit in on the seasonal auditions?" "Should the actor whom director X wants to play Hamlet be signed to a seasonal contract?"

None of the nonprofit professional theatres in New York City sign actors to seasonal contracts because there is always such a large pool of available talent, and transportation costs are so negligible. However, the artistic directors of these theatres and others elsewhere that do not maintain a true resident company often hire many of the same actors over and over and thereby create a sense of "company," even without the seasonal contracts.

Beginning in 1985, the AEA/LORT agreement has carried a resolution to encourage nontraditional casting. This is defined as the casting of ethnic minorities or female actors in roles where race, ethnicity or sex is not germane. Of course, the casting process is by nature a highly subjective one that cannot be strictly regulated by union rules. But the League of Resident Theatres was the first to formally encourage its members and their employees to regard nontraditional casting as a desirable alternative. This could eventually have broad ramifications on casting throughout the entertainment industry, not to mention on audience perceptions.

Casting policy at many nonprofit theatres must also consider whether or not to engage "name" performers. In terms of box office it is often believed that name actors will sell more tickets, though this often turns out not to be the case.* Also, training audiences to attend theatre because of stars rather than the overall quality of production can lead to a "catch-22" situation that is difficult to alter. On the other hand, many performers have established their names because they are very, very talented and, for that reason alone, it is not surprising when directors wish to engage them.

While discrimination in casting is prohibited by the union, "preference" in casting may nonetheless be a policy when a theatre also operates a school or conservatory, for example, and wishes to reward its best students with a professional contract. Or, as mentioned, when a director casts from a pool of actors with whose work he or she is familiar and who may achieve an ensemble effect more readily than talent unknown to the director and to each other.

The audition process by which casting decisions are made is described in both Chapters 4 and 5.

The artistic goal of casting is to bring together a group of performers who will illuminate the playwright's script both through their individual work and as an ensemble; the management goal is to provide the resources and environment in which this will be possible.

## Outreach Policy

Most activities that fall outside the business of producing and performing one or more productions yet involve the theatre company's personnel may be classified as "outreach" programs. These include sending artists into schools, sending the whole company on tour, running special workshops or running a whole conservatory. Such activities are discussed in the appro-

*See also Chapter 7.

priate sections elsewhere in this volume. But as a matter of policy they must be considered in terms of the amount of personal energy and other resources they will cost the organization. How will such activities affect the quality of the company's primary mission and production schedule? Do available personnel really have the expertise to perform these activities in an acceptable manner? (For example, a person who is a good technical director is not necessarily good at teaching a course in stagecraft.)

The temptation to sponsor outreach activities usually arises from the need for more earned income. But running a school or going on tour are demanding projects and, if they are not done well, the company's mission and public image could be seriously tarnished. Nonetheless, nonprofit professional theatres have a greater responsibility than commercial theatres to provide community service. After all, most receive grants from public tax monies. The nonprofit companies are also organized as institutions that presumably hope to function for many years. To do this, they must think about educating future audiences, future employees, future trustees and future donors, and this is best accomplished through outreach programs of various kinds.

The artistic goal of outreach policy is to elevate standards of theatre practice and appreciation in ways that are inappropriate or impossible through regular stage productions alone; the management goal is to cultivate future audiences for the institution.

## TYPES OF EQUITY CONTRACTS
## USED BY NONPROFIT THEATRES
### LORT: A, B+, B, C, and D

The League of Resident Theatres negotiates an agreement with AEA every three years. Five categories of theatres are covered in the agreement: A, B+, B, C, and D. The category is determined by the weekly gross of the theatre averaged over the previous three-year period, with "A" theatres having the highest gross and "D" the lowest. Salary scales covering actors, stage managers, assistant stage managers, and Equity professional interns are adjusted downward from the "A" to "D" categories. Actors may be signed to a standard or a seasonal contract. A limited number of nonprofessional actors may be used (except in "A" theatres in New York and Los Angeles), according to a formula based on the LORT category and the number of full Equity members under contract for the production in question. A similar formula exists for the employment of "professional theatre interns." These are actors who can prove professional training and/or experience, and who are then signed to a standard Equity contract at 75 percent of the minimum salary in the appropriate theatre category.

## Off-Broadway (See Chapter 5)

The Off-Broadway contract is most frequently used for commercial productions, although some nonprofit theatre companies such as Circle Repertory Company in New York have also used it. It serves as the model upon which special agreements are designed to accommodate other nonprofit companies.

## Theatre for Young Audiences (See Chapter 5)

## Stock Contracts (See Chapter 7)

## The Showcase Code (See Chapter 5)

## Workshop Productions (See Chapter 5)

## Cabaret Theatres (See Chapter 5)

## Small Professional Theatre Contract (SPT)

This contract was designed mostly for nonprofit theatres that have a seating capacity of less than 350 and are not located in an Equity office city. They may not serve food or beverages in the manner of a dinner or cabaret theatre and they may not have operated under a standard Equity contract during the previous year. There are ten categories of SPT theatres ("1" through "10") based on different ranges of box office income. The "1" theatres, for instance, may earn from zero to around $5,000 per week, while the "10" theatres earn around $30,000 weekly. In the first three categories, the rehearsal time is limited and performances are limited to four to six a week. Categories "4" through "10" may rehearse a full forty-two-hour week and give seven performances.

Until recently, many theatres now operating under the SPT contract merely had a letter of agreement with Equity (see below). It was the union's hope that such theatres would graduate in terms of size and income into a LORT category. But this happened so infrequently that SPT was conceived.

## 99-Seat Theatre Plan

During much of the '70s and '80s, Equity more or less ignored the sizable number of theatres in Los Angles that had under one hundred seats. After a great deal of controversy, the local Equity membership voted to institute a 99-Seat Theatre Plan to replace what had previously been called the Equity Waiver Theatres. The plan is modelled after the Off-Broadway contract, although, like the SPT, it features ten salary categories based on ranges of box office income and it may be applied to single-unit productions or a full season.

### Chicago Area Plan (CAP)

This is similar to the 99-Seat Theatre Plan that is in effect for the Los Angeles area. Here again, Equity had waived jurisdiction over theatres with less than one hundred seats, then beginning in 1988 gained an important foothold in this territory.

### Letter of Agreement (LOA)

The LOA was designed for small, developing theatres with very limited income and resources and it requires a minimum weekly salary of one hundred dollars plus benefits.

While the SPT and CAP have now been applied to many theatres that previously had a LOA, the latter is still used by the union for certain new and developing theatre groups. Theatres operating under this agreement are not required to observe any restrictions on seating capacity or ticket prices. LOA theatres in New York City have formed the League of Letter of Agreement Theatres (LLOA) to negotiate with the union.

### Funded Nonprofit Theatre Code

This agreement limits ticket prices to ten dollars each and the seating capacity must be under one hundred.

### Visiting and Guest Artist Agreements (See Chapter 9)

### Special Contracts and Agreements

Again it should be stressed that special arrangements may often be negotiated with AEA by individual theatres or producing companies. This may involve adapting one of the standard agreements to suit individual production or company needs, or it may involve writing a special letter of agreement. In either case, the possibility of special concessions should be explored and discussed thoroughly with the union.

## SPECIAL AEA REGULATIONS
## PERTAINING TO NONPROFIT THEATRES

### "As Cast"

As discussed above under "Casting Policy," there are special AEA provisions designed to accommodate the special needs of companies that produce a multi-production season. While roughly 50 percent of the roles an actor is to play must be specified in the employment contract, the others may be left open and the contract may simply read " John Doe" and "as cast."

## Seasonal Contract

Actors may be hired under a multi-role seasonal contract for twenty-four to fifty-two weeks. This may be more economical for the theatre than hiring different actors for each role on standard contracts.

## Second Theatre

When a company has a second theatre facility in the same city as its other facility, the category of Equity contract will be determined by the weekly box office gross of the second theatre. When productions from the second theatre go on tour, they are governed by the rules that apply to the main theatre. Actors are permitted to "cross over" from one theatre to the other while under a seasonal contract, but the salary of an actor moving from a large theatre to a smaller one may not be reduced, and the salary of an actor moving from a small theatre to a larger one must be increased to the minimum salary for the larger facility. Similar provisions apply when there are more than two performance spaces operated by the same theatre company.

## Repertory Work Schedules

For theatres that perform in repertory rotation or hire actors under seasonal contracts, AEA provides that actors may rehearse and perform during the same day. Generally, actors may rehearse for forty-five hours during weeks in which there are no performances; however, when the actor is also performing, the total work week cannot exceed fifty hours.

## Local Tours

Many companies sponsor outreach programs that send a company of actors to schools or community centers. The union regards these as local tours when the actor is within a specified amount of travel time from the home theatre and not required to spend the night away. In such cases actors are permitted to give ten performances per week, providing each performance does not exceed one-and-one-half hours in length. This and other rules pertaining to local tours are similar to those in the Theatre for Young Audiences Contract.

## Professional Theatre Intern (See "LORT A, B+, B, C, D")

## Conversion and Contingent Rights

Actors employed under Production, Off-Broadway, LORT or Stock contracts rarely have any claim on subsequent productions or income in regard to the particular production for which they were hired. However, under the contracts and agreements for which actors receive what the union considers substandard compensation, there are somewhat complex provisions giving actors the right either to recreate their roles, if the production is subsequently produced under a standard contract, or to receive four or five weeks of minimum salary under the Production Contract. Such actors must receive similar compensation in the event that the property is subsequently produced in a different medium, such as film or television, within a specified number of years after the original was performed. Similar rules also apply when an independent producer (who owns an option on the work and/ or a controlling financial interest in the production company) uses a LORT theatre in lieu of some other tryout venue prior to producing the work under the Production Contract.

Regulations covering conversion and contingent rights are found in Showcase, Workshop, 99-Seat Theatre, SPT, LOA, and Funded Nonprofit Theatre agreements as well as special agreements. Regulations may vary somewhat and are subject to change; details should be obtained directly from AEA.

## TRANSFERRING A PRODUCTION

One of the first productions transferred from a LORT theatre to Broadway was Howard Sackler's *The Great White Hope*, which opened in 1968 after a successful premiere at the Arena Stage in Washington, D.C. Unfortunately, there was no provision for Arena to share in the play's subsequent earnings—an oversight almost certainly never repeated by any nonprofit company. In recent years, the transfer of productions from nonprofit theatres to Broadway, Off-Broadway, and the road have been relatively common. Yet, there are many factors to consider before a production is moved, assuming that its popularity at the box office warrants such action.

The first alternative to be studied is the possibility of extending the run right where the production is playing. This is by far the most economical solution and, in fact, may require no additional costs at all, outside of increased marketing expenses. The most usual problem with this is that the company is locked into a production schedule that is already sold to a subscription audience. Or certain actors who are considered indispensable to the play's success aren't available for a longer run. In 1988, for example, the Circle in the Square hosted the Abbey Players in a highly popular production of Sean O'Casey's *Juno and the Paycock* which could easily have run for a season on Broadway. Yet some of the actors had commitments in Ireland, so that was that. Conversely, Lincoln Center Theater presented an African company in the musical *Sarafina* in its small Mitzi E. Newhouse Theater. Not only did the company remain in this country under special Equity dispensation, but it transferred with the hit show to Broadway and later went on tour. However, the hit revival of *Anything Goes*, which originated in the large Vivian Beaumont Theater, was kept in that space because transferring it to a Broadway house would have been too expensive. Instead, the Lincoln Center Theater negotiated special terms with unions and landlords and produced its regular 1988/89 season in Broadway theatres, while its hit musical continued to earn nice revenues at home! But there is no subscription plan for the Beaumont; instead, there is a membership plan by which patrons pay an annual fee and can then pick and choose tickets at low prices for whatever Lincoln Center Theater produces.

If it is decided to move a production intact to another theatre, the faster this can be done the more money will be saved; and, perhaps, less artistic momentum and energy will be lost. Ideally, the curtain would fall on Sunday at one theatre and rise on Tuesday at the new one. This avoids lay-off and rehearsal costs, as well as an interruption in publicity, audience interest and ticket sales.

There are several methods by which a nonprofit professional theatre may go about transferring one of its productions:

1. The nonprofit company may license the first class production rights to a commercial producer, who then takes on all the responsibilities in exchange for a royalty payment or percentage of the gross, a cash advance and, perhaps, payment for any physical elements that will be used in the new production

2. The nonprofit company may act as producer of the production at the new venue but hire a professional general-management firm to execute the details

3. The nonprofit company may go into partnership with an independent producer or theatre landlord and become a co-producer in exchange for certain services, financing or concessions in the theatre license

4. The nonprofit company may serve as both its own producer and general manager for the production at the new venue.

There are, of course, possible variations on these methods. For example, commercial producers sometimes "invest" in nonprofit companies by providing what is called "enhancement money." This is in the form of a contribution to help develop a particular property that the producer hopes will transfer to Broadway; of course, he or she also hopes to share in any future revenues as a participating producer, co-producer or investment partner.

The object of transferring productions from nonprofit theatres to Off-Broadway or production contracts is twofold: to share the company's artistic achievement with the widest possible audience and to gain additional revenue for the institution. So long as such revenue is invested in the furtherance of the nonprofit company's stated goal, there is nothing illegal or unethical about making money as "the big guys" do in the commercial sector. And think how much healthier the nonprofit sector would be—and the performing arts as a whole—if, like the New York Shakespeare Festival, each company had *A Chorus Line* doing hit business on Broadway—year after year after year!

## CO-PRODUCTIONS, SHARED PRODUCTIONS AND COMMISSIONS

By the mid-1980s, it became apparent to most nonprofit professional theatres that neither earned nor contributed income could keep pace with rising costs, at least not for long or not without certain fairly drastic changes in production policy. Some theatre companies transferred their "hit" productions to other venues, where they could enjoy an open-ended profitable run, or they permitted such a run in their home theatres. Other companies cut back on their production schedules or cut back on their more daring work and increased the productions of popular works; however, such policy changes seriously compromise artistic standards and risk letting the nonprofit theatres backslide into stock-company tactics. Still, hard times require creative economic solutions.

One solution that has become increasingly common is for two or more nonprofit theatres to share the costs of productions that also share their stages. Sometimes a production originates at one theatre and then, for a fee, another theatre picks up and transfers the production more or less intact. Or the originating theatre may offer one or more of its productions as a touring attraction. A true co-production, however, is one that is a cooperative endeavor among several producing companies from the beginning. The theatres share the artistic decisions as well as costs. Or a production may be co-produced by a nonprofit company and a commercial producer in an attempt to develop the property for a Broadway run, as was the case when the Cleveland Playhouse entered into a joint venture with several commercial producers that resulted in the Broadway revival of Garson Kanin's *Born Yesterday*, starring Ed Asner and Madeline Kahn. A different kind of example is provided by August Wilson's *Fences*, which originated at Yale Repertory Theatre. After a year's lay-off, it was reassembled with the original cast at Chicago's Goodman Theatre and then moved to the Seattle Repertory Theatre and subsequently into a commercial tryout in San Francisco and an award-winning run on Broadway.

But commercial success is not always the goal. Production costs are sometimes shared simply to make a project possible. For instance, the Brooklyn Academy of Music, the Houston Grand Opera and the Kennedy Center joined forces to coproduce *Nixon in China*, which they commissioned for $100,000. This not only made the production feasible but also generated seventeen performances, rather than the one or two given to most new operas. (Eventually, it was also shown to a wide television audience.) Similar cooperation between BAM and other institutions yielded such productions as Peter Brook's *Mahabharata*; the Robert Wilson and Philip Glass opera *Einstein on the Beach*; the Lee Breuer and Bob Telson spectacle *The Warrior Ant* as well as their *Gospel at Colonus*, the last of which *did* make it to Broadway. Most shared productions and co-productions,of course, are much smaller in scale and never receive national or media attention. Whatever the case, they all enjoy the same advantages:

1. Sharing costs is cheaper than picking up the full tab
2. Sharing a production increases the number of performances it can be guaranteed and, therefore, the size of the audience
3. Increased performances bring increased work weeks for the performers and production staff
4. By moving a production to several theatres, rehearsal time can be increased and also given more flexibility; and dark periods between engagements can provide the creative team valuable time to rework the project
5. Sharing production costs may permit larger, more ambitious works than would otherwise be possible.

The disadvantages of sharing productions include loss of autonomy in decision-making, conflicts in scheduling and the dilution of any revenues the project generates over expenses. The conflicts that commonly plague shared productions are usually costly, both artistically and economically. For example, the stage director may have to move on to another project after opening night and not be available for needed rehearsals, major reconstruction may be required to move the production to another venue, or the company may have to be paid while waiting for the next available performance date.

But co-producing, as implied above, can also make the commissioning of new works much more feasible. Of course the process involves considerable risk, because it involves buying something that does not yet exist. Before a commission payment of any kind is extended, therefore, the producer or institution should draw up a contract with the artist that spells out what must be delivered or shown and when, and this contract should allow payments to be stopped or a performance denied at various points in the development of the creative material. The contract must also stipulate any future rights that may be enjoyed by the signators.

Co-producing among different institutions and even between the commercial and nonprofit sectors of the industry provides a viable economic alternative to suffering penury alone.

## SUMMATION

The nonprofit professional theatre today encompasses the largest and most dynamic activity in the profession. Its growth since the early 1950s has amazed even those who helped to pioneer the movement. Its accomplishments in terms of discovering, supporting and developing theatrical talent of all types have been outstanding. In fact, without the nonprofit companies, it is doubtful that in recent decades there would be a body of work worthy of being called "the American drama" or a record of production worthy of being called "the American professional theatre."

The nonprofit professional theatre movement was nurtured and helped by contributions from government, corporate and private sources, which created fairly reliable patterns of support during the '60s and '70s. But the combined reduction of government support and tax incentives for private and corporate giving, enacted during the Reagan Administration of the '80s, threatens the health of this movement in the '90s and beyond.

# 7

# Stock And Dinner Theatre

THE majority of stock theatres, dinner theatres and outdoor drama productions are nonprofessional—that is to say, they do not employ Equity actors. And few of those that do deal with any of the other unions discussed in this book. Many of these theatres are nonprofit organizations, although most dinner theatres and many of the Equity stock theatres are commercial ventures. There are both summer and winter operations in all three categories, although we tend to use the phrase "summer theatre" or "summer stock" as a general label. While this chapter takes into account the role that AEA plays with some of these theatres, it is also relevant to the operation of those that are nonprofessional.

## BACKGROUND
### *The Rebirth of Independent Stock Companies: 1914 to 1935*

Chapter 5 outlines the story of independent stock companies during the nineteenth century and tells how, during the years prior to World War I, they virtually disappeared due to travelling stars, combination companies and the over-centralization of the professional theatre. Chapter 6 outlines the growth of nonprofit professional theatres as encouraged by academics and others interested in giving a high quality of production to serious drama. The stock theatre companies that came into existence after World War I were more in the tradition of nineteenth century stock theatres, except that most were located in resort communities and only operate during an eight- to twelve-week summer or winter season. Most began as amateur efforts of the kind immortalized by Mickey Rooney and Judy Garland ("Let's put on a play!"/ "Gosh, d'ya think we could?"). While serious drama was sometimes included in a season of plays, the emphasis was decidedly on light entertainment and on providing young people with opportunities to learn the craft of theatre. Like the Lakewood Playhouse, which was established in 1901 in the resort town of Skowhegan, Maine, the "born again" stock theatres were independent operations that utilized a resident company of amateur actors under a resident director and staff, operated on a seasonal basis and produced a different play every week or two; usually in a humble, wooden playhouse that resembled or actually was a converted barn. Such companies were often organized and run by enthusiastic college students, like the University Players Guild that operated during the summers from 1928 to 1932 in Falmouth, Massachusetts, under the leadership of several Princeton students. Few other summer stock theatres included so many young talents who would later become famous: Henry Fonda; Joshua Logan; Myron McCormick; Mildred Natwick; Kent Smith; James Stewart; and Margaret Sullavan!

During the '20s, men like Richard Aldrich, Milton Stiefel and Guy Palmerton, who later became the scions of a summer theatre establishment, were searching among the resort communities of New England for hospitable places to establish amateur resident companies. Aldrich founded the Cape Playhouse on Cape Cod in 1926 and later also operated the Falmouth Playhouse and the Cape Cod Melody Tent. The Ivoryton Playhouse in Connecticut opened in 1930 (and gave Katharine Hepburn an early opportunity). The Westport Country Playhouse was founded by Lawrence Langner as an informal laboratory for Theatre Guild activities in 1931, and the Ogunquit Playhouse was started in Maine in 1932. By the '30s there were hundreds of stock companies that, collectively, served as about the only training ground for future Broadway and Hollywood actors. And the movement spread from its New England beginnings to the South and Middle West. Some stock theatres lasted only a season, others continued for years on an amateur basis, and yet others negotiated with Equity and began hiring professional actors and stars. And winter stock, typified by the elegant Royal Poinciana Playhouse in Palm Beach and the Coconut Grove Playhouse, also in Florida, further expanded the activities.

## The Heyday of Stock; History Repeats Itself: 1935 to 1975

Most of the better-known summer theatres were started during the '30s and '40s and followed similar patterns of development. They progressed from amateur-resident companies to Equity-resident companies, to Equity-resident companies with visiting stars, to roadhouses for Equity-nonresident-touring-package productions—exactly the same pattern as that followed by the independent stock theatres of the nineteenth century!

When the Stock Managers' Association negotiated its first contract with Actors' Equity in the early '30s, only about a dozen summer theatres were under union jurisdiction. By 1950, that number had increased to about 130 and continued to grow. As always with the unionization of a new branch of the industry, minimum salaries were low at first and Equity also permitted a rather liberal use of nonprofessionals.

It appears that the first "star" in this century hired to perform with a resident stock company was Jane Cowl, whom Richard Aldrich paid $1,000 in 1935 to appear for a week in *Romance* with his company at the Cape Playhouse. Many stock managers were horrified by such extravagance but, since the experiment paid off at the box office, the idea soon caught on; once again, audiences were asking, "Who's in it?" before buying their tickets. And, once again, the shady townships of rural America were brightened by the seasonal visitation of theatrical luminaries: ZaSu Pitts; Billie Burke; Bea Lillie; Gertrude Lawrence, Cedric Hardwicke, Helen Hayes, Lillian Gish and the perennial Tallulah Bankhead were among the atypical tourists. Star salaries climbed as high as $5,000 per week, forcing managers to pinch pennies in other areas. Providing something of a vacation for the star, if no one else, the system usually required the star to spend several weeks rehearsing with the resident company before the performance week. Soon, however, stars began travelling with several feature players, and by the 1950s they generally carried their entire company—which was cast, directed, rehearsed and costumed in New York City and spent only the performance week itself at each theatre. The "package system" had begun and was just like the combination companies of the previous century, except for the name and the fact that package shows seldom travelled with the necessary scenery. This was constructed at each theatre in order to accommodate greatly different stage dimensions and production capabilities. As a result of packages, the professional resident stock system once again virtually ceased to exist.

Other theatrical unions, such as the Association of Theatrical Press Agents and Managers (ATPAM) and the International Alliance of Theatrical Stage Employees (IA) also attempted to organize stock houses. However, they succeeded only in those theatres near New York City and other large cities where their jurisdiction was already established. Only the Society of Stage Directors and Choreographers succeeded on a wide scale among stock and dinner theatres (directors and choreographers had previously worked under Equity contracts).

While stock theatres never fell under the control of a syndicate (although some producers operated several theatres simultaneously), the stock managers who opted for the package system lost most artistic control over their product and, in effect, became presenters rather than producers. Only a limited number of top attractions—that is to say, big-name stars or hit shows fresh from New York—became available each season. Most managers wanted the same attractions and therefore booked almost identical seasons. The Stock Managers' Association was replaced in the '50s by a similar organization of summer and winter theatre managers, the Council of Stock Theatres (COST), which negotiated the Equity agreements and also served as a central booking exchange. Stock companies that still maintained a professional resident company formed the Council of Resident Stock Theatres (CORST) and also negotiated with Equity. The resident theatres, of course, have retained full casting and artistic control over their productions. Some, like the Hampton Playhouse in New Hampshire and the Totem Pole Playhouse in Pennsylvania, present recent commercial hits, while others like the Peterborough Players in New Hampshire produce European and American classics. Perhaps the best known of the CORST operations is the Williamstown Theatre Festival in Massachusetts, operated for thirty years under the artistic direction of the late Nikos Psacharopoulos. Its tradition of bringing stars in to play with a resident company harks back to the earlier days of stock but is also similar to the policy of other nonprofit professional companies, especially since Williamstown also strives for artistic excellence. During its heyday, stock often provided a testing ground for new plays, a function now filled by the nonprofit professional theatres. Some managers originated productions in their stock theatres and then produced them on Broadway: Michael Ellis (Bucks County Playhouse) and Zev Bufman (Coconut Grove Playhouse) are examples from the '60s. In other cases, a New York producer who had no affiliation with a stock theatre would offer a stock tour of a new play before it opened in New York. Among the many plays that traveled through stock on their way to becoming hits were *Life With Father*, *The Fourposter*, *A View From the Bridge* and *Barefoot in the Park*.

The most obvious attempt to cash in on the popularity of stock theatre took the form of the large tent theatres, which began operations in the 1950s using real tents or more permanent structures. A number of so-called tent theatres seating one thousand to two thousand people were put up from Boston Harbor to San Francisco Bay, and another stock managers' organization was formed to deal with Equity: the Musical Theatre Association (MTA). Initially, the tents presented popular musicals and operettas, which were performed by a largely resident company, chorus and orchestra, and aimed to please the entire family at low prices. The prototype of all tent theatres was the Music Circus in Lambertville, New Jersey, founded by St. John Terrell; the largest and most successful operations involved the simultaneous management of several tent theatres, such as John Lemar Price, Jr.'s Musicarnival, Inc., begun in 1954, which controlled a summer theatre in Cleveland and a winter theatre in Palm Beach. Messrs. Guber, Gross and Ford operated five tent theatres just south of New York City during this period. But the popular appeal of such attractions as *The Student Prince* and *My Fair Lady* began to dwindle as they were revived for the third or fourth time, and

Broadway simply wasn't keeping up with the demand for new hit musicals. Not surprisingly, tents began to engage stars in their productions and to supplement their seasons with special performances by rock groups or nightclub and TV personalities. Ticket prices went up, and tent theatres found themselves ensnared in the star-package system and all the attendant problems. Furthermore, because of the large potential grosses at the tents, many stars adjusted their salary demands upward and became unavailable to the smaller, proscenium stock houses. By 1975, it was not unusual for a Victor Borge or a Liberace to receive close to $10,000 a week plus a percentage of the gross. And some stars, like Frank Sinatra and Bob Hope, received considerably more. In effect, the larger stock and tent theatres had to compete with the kind of performer fees being paid in Las Vegas, and in fact, a spectacular stage show built around a star performer became known as a "Vegas show." The weekly operating costs for a 1500-seat tent theatre rose from around $8,000 in 1950 to as much as $75,000 in 1975.

Another novel approach to commercial theatre is the dinner theatre format, in which food and beverages are served in the same room where the production is performed, somewhat like a nightclub.

In the '60s and '70s dinner theatres like Chicago's Ivanhoe sprang up throughout the nation. Most operate like nonresident stock theatres, except for their food policy and the fact that their shows usually run longer than one or two weeks. Like professional stock theatres, they declined in number during the '80s and also suffered from the lack of new hit comedies and musicals. The management association that negotiates with Equity is the American Dinner Theatre Institute, headquartered in Cockeysville, Maryland.

Completing the spectrum of largely tourist-oriented theatre operations are the outdoor drama festivals and productions. Only a handful of these operate under an Equity contract of some kind, but many pay salaries to all or some of their participants nonetheless. Of the nearly one hundred companies in this category, most are members of the Institute of Outdoor Drama, headquartered in Chapel Hill, North Carolina, although this association does not involve itself in collective bargaining. Outdoor drama productions—which have been popular in all sections of the country for much of the twentieth century—often center around an American folk hero such as Daniel Boone, Abraham Lincoln, Mark Twain or Stephen Foster; many are passion plays or are based on religious themes; some are pageants,such as *Champoeg: The Birth of Oregon* and *The Mormon Miracle Pageant*; others, such as the Starlight Theatre in Kansas City and Starlight Musicals in San Diego, present Broadway musicals; and yet others like the Oregon Shakespeare Festival, the Kentucky Shakespeare Festival and the Berkeley Shakespeare Festival present the classics. As may be imagined, the quality of production varies enormously from outfit to outfit. But outdoor drama companies represent the closest thing this country has to grassroots theatre and many have maintained their success while other tourist-oriented theatres have fallen by the wayside.

## Decline and Retrenchment: 1975 to the Present

The weekly operating cost for a typical 600-to-800-seat summer theatre employing Equity actors rose from around $3,000 in 1935 to about $10,000 in 1950 and to $60,000 in 1975. During those same years, resort communities from Cape Cod to the Florida peninsula evolved into year-round communities with largely stay-at-home populations. And tourists from Minneapolis, Providence, Dallas, Baltimore, Little Rock and other nonresort localities had learned to recognize the difference between good theatre and a tourist trap. Serious-minded talent—both artistic and managerial—was moving into the nonprofit professional arena. Money-minded talent was moving into the film and television arenas. Broadway was becoming the kind of stepping stone to success that stock used to be, and Actors' Equity had upped the ante by a large amount in terms of minimum salaries for its members who worked under stock and dinner theatre contracts.

By the end of the 1980s, a once-thriving branch of professional theatre had been pruned back to a few twigs. Rather than increasing the number of Equity stock theatres, the union's increasing contract demands and other escalating costs caused many to close or revert to amateur status. Of those still operating under an AEA contract, there were only five COST theatres, nine CORST theatres, thirty-three dinner theatres and six outdoor theatres. Touring package productions were so scarce that some COST theatres began to "buy" productions from nonprofit theatres to fill out their seasons. And tent theatres that presented book musicals—together with the Musical Theatre Association—had disappeared altogether!

## TYPES OF PROFESSIONAL STOCK, DINNER AND OUTDOOR THEATRES

### Nonresident Dramatic Stock (COST)

The remaining stock theatres in AEA's nonresident dramatic category are all located in the Northeast, all have less than 850 seats and all book in package productions, supplemented by shows they produce for themselves when necessary. COST managers also sometimes package shows that then tour the other theatres. They all belong to the Council of Stock Theatres (COST), which negotiates the basic agreement with Equity every two or three years.

When it is less expensive, the COST theatre that originates a production may rehearse it at the theatre rather than in New York (usually two weeks for nonmusicals and three for musicals). More often, the new company arrives at the theatre already rehearsed on a Sunday or Monday afternoon, holds a technical or dress rehearsal either that night or the next day and opens that night for one or two weeks of eight performances each. This process is then repeated throughout the season. To facilitate the transfer of a package from one theatre to the next, an advance stage manager arrives a week ahead of the company to advise about production design, properties, housing, travel and other matters. Otherwise, each theatre maintains a resident staff (including a resident AEA stage manager), who carry out all nonperformance duties and responsibilities. Many COST theatres also engage a number of non-salaried apprentices or interns who spend long hours each day in the scene shop, on stage crews and doing front-of-house chores. Because the shows usually change each week, with only one "dark" day between productions, the work, and the learning experience, can be intensive. In fact, apprentices accustomed to the leisure of college or community-theatre production schedules are initially amazed that a multi-set show can be built, painted, clad and propped in five or six days, then assembled and lighted in one day.

## Resident Dramatic Stock (CORST)

Those theatres that maintain a resident company of actors—at least five principle actors and one stage manager signed to an Equity Minimum Contract for Stock are required—and present a season of consecutive productions are represented by the Council of Resident Stock Theatres (CORST). Salary minimums are somewhat lower than at COST theatres, and there are slightly more liberal rules pertaining to the use of nonprofessionals. There are three categories of CORST theatres ("X," "Y" and "Z"), determined by the potential, weekly box-office gross of the theatre.

The CORST contract carries provisions similar to those in the LORT contract in regard to actors' working hours when they are both performing in one play and rehearsing another. Directors and choreographers work under SSDC contracts.

Most of the CORST theatres employ non-salaried apprentices and low salaried technicians. Williamstown operates a sizable theatre school that is essentially separate from its professional operation, but the students present their own production toward the end of the season. As with other types of stock theatres, the work is very demanding, but a great deal may be learned in just a few months.

## Resident Musical Stock

The Resident Musical Theatre Association negotiates with Equity on behalf of only three members. Their agreement is similar to the CORST contract, with additional provisions regarding the use of chorus, understudies and nonprofessionals.

## Dinner Theatres and Theatre Restaurants

Equity defines a dinner theatre as one that presents consecutive productions in conjunction with dinner service, each production playing no less than three weeks on a year-round basis (an occasional hiatus notwithstanding). Dinner and theatre must be offered in the same room and the only advertised price of admission for at least 75 percent of the weekly performances must include both the meal and the show; 25 percent of weekly performances may be offered on a "show only" basis.

A theatre restaurant meets all the above qualifications except that dinner and theatre are offered in separate but adjacent rooms. If the rooms are not in the same building, they must be connected by a covered walkway, and both parts of the operation must be under the same ownership. Seating in theatre restaurants may not exceed one thousand.

Dinner theatres and theatre restaurants that engage Equity actors, as well as many that don't, belong to the American Dinner Theatre Institute. Except with special AEA permission, those that use union actors may not operate within twenty-five miles of Times Square in New York City or the Chicago loop or within the cities of Los Angeles or San Francisco. There are five categories, based on seating capacity:

> 0 - 199 seats
> 200 - 329 seats
> 330 - 449 seats
> 450 - 649 seats
> 650 - 1200 seats

The category determines such matters as minimum salary levels and the use of nonprofessionals.

## Outdoor Theatre

Perhaps the most uncommon type of stock theatre that employs Equity actors is the one that presents its productions out-of-doors. Some of these are highly professional and well established; the New York Shakespeare Festival's summer productions at the Delacorte Theatre in Central Park; those presented by the St. Louis Municipal Theatre Association or the Starlight Theatre in Kansas City. At one time, several such theatres formed the Association of Civic Musical Theatres to negotiate with Equity, but this is no longer in existence, and today each theatre deals directly with the union. Rules concerning the use of nonprofessionals are quite liberal.

In the field of nonprofessional outdoor theatre there are many well-established community groups that perform annual pageants and historical dramas. Together with the professional outdoor companies, many belong to the Institute of Outdoor Drama, located at the University of North Carolina in Chapel Hill.

# PACKAGE PRODUCTIONS

## *The Role of the Packager*

A packager is a producer who initiates a production and then sells it to a number of theatres in exchange for a packaging fee. Because this is usually a nominal amount, the packager may also serve in some other capacity, such as director, performer or advance stage manager for the production. During the '60s and '70s when there were dozens of stock theatres that booked in package productions, it was possible to put together a number of tours that would play for ten to twenty weeks—usually in a different theatre each week. A number of people, including Harold Kennedy, Ralph Roseman, Carlton Davis and Charles Forsythe, became experts at the process. This often entailed being personally acquainted with a number of stars, independent producers and managers, so that the stock rights to recent New York hits could be obtained, and actors with name value could be enticed into spending a number of weeks on the road. Before rehearsals began, packagers tried to elicit enough verbal commitments from stock managers to make their productions worthwhile. Stock theatres that booked packages (except for unit packages, which are discussed below) signed all the Equity contracts and took full responsibility for the production (outside of casting, directing, rehearsing and costuming) and full liability for any losses that were incurred at the box office. Nonetheless, packagers had to lay out a fairly substantial amount of money to get shows into rehearsal, and some lost thousands of dollars as a result of irresponsible stock managers and failed operations.

## *Booking Package Productions*

Today, there are no big name stars touring what is left of the stock circuit, because their salary demands are too high. Nonetheless, COST members still gather in New York City each spring to meet with the surviving packagers, to discuss their own package proposals and consider any new plays or projects that may be available for their theatres. They vie with each other for the most promising packages, trade engagement weeks to better accommodate themselves and spend considerable time wracking their brains to come up with sufficient product. Several stock operators have acquired four or five theatres, with the idea of creating a little circuit that would engage all the productions that they themselves produce. But this idea only worked with the Guber, Gross and Ford music tents in the '60s—perhaps because their facilities were large and similar to each other, and the timing was right. Later in that decade, actor-turned-theatre-operator Eddie Bracken acquired the Falmouth, Lakewood, Hyde Park, and Coconut Grove playhouses, but lost them all to bankruptcy. In the '80s Ralph Miller acquired the Falmouth, Pocono, Woodstock and New Hope playhouses and converted them from Equity to non-Equity houses; and soon after let them all go dark except for Falmouth (the venerable Woodstock Playhouse was destroyed by fire in 1988). A chain or circuit of stock theatres is not feasible for several reasons: each one is sufficiently different in terms of its stage-house that scenery cannot be traveled, and productions may even have to be restaged; and each one is likely to have a different audience (again, success means matching the right production policy with the right audience). One community may be very conservative, for example, while another, just a few hundred miles away may be more daring and cosmopolitan.

Stock rights for Broadway and Off-Broadway productions are usually not released until the play has completed its New York engagement and until the national touring companies have also completed their engagements— at least in the general geographic area of the stock theatre that is seeking performance rights. But stock rights generally precede amateur rights to give the professional theatres first crack at a production, and generally precede the release of any film version of the play. However, any stock manager or packager is free to negotiate directly with the New York producers of a show to obtain exclusive permission to present it, to book in a national company or a bus and truck company or to insure that performance rights will not be given to other theatres nearby. Finally, some packages have been put together by independent New York producers as an inexpensive method for trying out a script before deciding whether or not to produce it in New York; however, beginning in the '80, such producers were more likely to work with professional nonprofit theatre companies for tryouts and script development.

As with all other theatrical producing, the business of selecting which play to package or which package to book is highly speculative. Anyone, no matter how experienced, can guess wrong. Perhaps the most disastrous opening night in the history of stock occurred when Bert Lahr and Tom Ewell performed the American premiere of Samuel Beckett's *Waiting for Godot* for a fashionable, late-arriving audience at the Coconut Grove Playhouse in Miami—hardly the ideal theatregoers for avant-garde European drama. However, in deference to the folks who were there, it should be added that the production had been advertised as "the laugh sensation of two continents," and, when asked, even Bert Lahr confessed that he had no idea what he was doing!

## The Package Agreement

Once the packager knows that enough theatres are willing to book a production to make it worthwhile, a package agreement is drawn up for the theatre operator to sign. This follows a standard format provided by COST and requires the packager to provide the following items to each theatre on the tour in a timely fashion:

1. Contracts and biographies for each cast member
2. Photographs of each cast member
3. A property list and plot
4. A scenery floor plan and elevations, when necessary
5. A lighting plot and cue sheet
6. A costume plot
7. A master script with cue sheet
8. All necessary tape recordings and a list of necessary sound equipment
9. An itemized list of packaging and preproduction expenses
10. The transportation route and housing requirements for the company

The cost of a package is determined by expenditures which the packager makes for office, telephone, postage, rehearsal hall, rehearsal salaries, director's fee, choreographer's fee and other such standard items. The total of these preproduction costs is then divided by the number of performance weeks on the tour (a theatre that offers the same package for two weeks obviously pays twice as much as a theatre that offers it for only one week). The more weeks that a package is booked, the lower its cost for each week.

As mentioned above, the theatres and not the packager sign the actor and other contracts and pay the salaries. This means that the first theatre on each tour is responsible for paying rehearsal salaries, although these are eventually divided among all the theatres on the tour.

The actors, of course, sign separate but identical stock-jobbing contracts with each theatre on the tour. And each theatre posts a bond with Actors' Equity (an amount of money usually equivalent to two weeks' cast salaries), which is why the union does not recognize the packager as a bona fide producer. Each theatre must also secure the performance rights and pay the royalties.

Because stars can and do change their minds about appearing in a stock tour or at one of the theatres where it is booked, it behooves the manager to secure the star's signed contract before signing the others. Regardless of any circumstances that might cause a star not to appear in the production, the theatre must still honor all other contracts it has signed. Each theatre may attempt to change contractual provisions that have been made by the packager, but any concessions are usually minor.

## The Unit Package

In rare cases, a producer or packager may wish to take full control and responsibility for a touring package and personally post bond with Equity, sign the contracts and pay the actors. This arrangement is called a "unit package" or a "unit attraction." Equity permits unit attractions to perform in non-stock theatres, providing that the actors receive at least the minimum salaries for nonresident dramatic stock.

The unit method of packaging may appear efficient at first, but it is fraught with potential problems for the packager, who must make up and distribute the weekly cast payroll and pay all the benefits and federal, state and local taxes mandated by the union and the law. Also, it makes packagers responsible for contractual terms that theatre staffs beyond their control must uphold.

## AEA REGULATIONS PERTAINING TO ACTORS "AWAY FROM HOME"

The general aspects of employment under an Equity contract as discussed in Chapter 5 apply to union actors wherever they may work. But when actors work outside New York City (or one of the other Equity office cities, provided the audition was supervised by that office), the theatre manager has further contractual obligations pertaining to transporting, housing and feeding the actors. These invariably consume a lot of management and staff time, have an impact on the budget, and sometimes create problems that end up in arbitration.

## Transportation for the Actor

Management is always responsible for arranging and paying an actor's transportation from the doorstep of the actor's home to the doorstep of the lodging provided in the vicinity of the theatre—and home again!   During the regular run of a production in an Equity office city or, when away from home, if the place of lodging is within a half mile of the theatre, the actor must get back and forth to rehearsals and performances without assistance or reimbursement from management.   Transporting actors to a theatre where they will remain for a season or a protracted run is usually a simple matter because time is seldom pressing. Rail transportation is the mode preferred

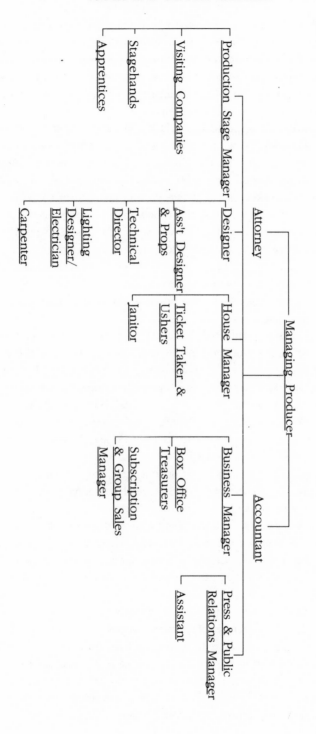

TABLE OF ORGANIZATION:
Medium-Size Commercial, Nonresident Stock Theatre

by AEA, though bus service is permitted where trains are unavailable. If travel exceeds ten hours, a Pullman sleeping accommodation must be provided or, if not available, the actor must be reimbursed for its equivalent cost. When first class rail transportation is not used, it is wise for the manager to check the appropriate Equity rulebook or to apply to Equity directly for permission to use some other type of transportation.

Actors may not be required to travel by air against their wishes; when such travel is necessary to meet a time schedule, managers should protect themselves by entering such an obligation in the actors' contracts. Whatever mode of travel is used, actors must be notified in advance about departure times and given paid tickets at least three days in advance. If the actor elects some other mode of transportation, the tickets may be redeemed by the actor—who must always receive the equivalent of first class rail travel, unless management has prior AEA permission to transport the company as a group (for example, on a chartered bus). Only then do actors who elect to travel otherwise not receive equivalent compensation.

Most actors working away from home are signed to one contract by one producer, who takes care of all the travel arrangements and payments. But with most package productions, the actors hold a number of different contracts with different producers. In this case, the theatre *to which* the actor is traveling is responsible. Of course, there are exceptions. If there is a period of three or more days between contracted performance dates, then the *last* theatre must transport the actor back home and the *next* theatre picks up again from there. Also, the next theatre is obligated to pay *no more than* the fare from the Equity home city to its own doorstep. Any amount over that must be paid by the last theatre.

When travel time and conditions do not meet the standards set by the union, actors must be compensated with special payments over and above the regular fare. Management must also reimburse actors for taxi fees, porters, tips and, in the case of air travel, flight insurance, providing that an itemized breakdown of such expenses is provided. There are also AEA regulations regarding the use of excursion or group fares, chartered buses, limousines, and when actors must be accompanied during travel by a stage manager or assistant stage manager.

The business of transporting large or numerous wardrobe trunks, boxes of stage properties and scenery is often more expensive and complicated than that of transporting actors. For extra compensation, an actor or stage manager may agree to be responsible for the transfer of such items from one place to another. But when these are large or numerous, other arrangements will have to be made. If time is not a factor, then arrangements may be simple. But before booking any touring show, a manager should be aware of the items that are traveling and what kind of problems and expenses will be involved. Ignorance about such matters has caused some theatres to cancel performances, because it was physically impossible to transfer the production in time from its last place of engagement.

Once a company is in residence at a theatre, management must arrange for the actors to be transported from their lodging to the theatre and back via well-lighted thoroughfares. If the distance is more than half a mile, specific pickup and departure times must be set, and any properly insured theatre car, taxi or limousine may be used. Ideally, lodging will be close to the theatre or close to inexpensive public transportation, so that actors can get back and forth on their own. When this is not the case, it helps if the entire company is lodged in the same building or complex.

## Housing for the Actor

When employment requires actors to live away from home, the union stipulates that lodging expenses may not reduce salaries below certain levels. Specifically, lodging may not cost more than 15 percent of weekly salaries under $500 or more than 20 percent for weekly salaries between $500 and $1000. Over that point, management need not be concerned. Equity actors must be offered a choice of accommodations at different locations in advance of their arrival at the theatre, may not be required to share a room but may be offered housing in private homes. When lodging costs exceed the limits set by the union, management must pay the difference. If management fails to list the housing choices in advance (both with the actor and with AEA), the actor must be reimbursed for the lodging of his or her choice. However, as with transportation, if actors reject what management offers, then they are fully responsible for their own lodging costs and for their own local transportation. At least, management is not responsible for housing, feeding or transporting relatives or pets of the four-legged variety that are not under contract!

Obviously, housing a company of actors—not to mention the administrative and production staff—can be an expensive proposition. In the nation's larger cities, it may not be difficult to make reasonably low, discount deals with local hotels, guest houses and restaurants, especially if there is a guarantee of a goodly volume of such business. But in resort areas and out-of-the-way places, local businesspeople are loath to discount their prices when it might mean forfeiting business at full price. And, let's face it, housing *anyone* for, say, one hundred dollars per week *anywhere* these days is almost impossible. The best solution may be for the theatre to operate its own housing and dining facilities. This would require extra personnel, costs and liabilities, but it could be less expensive than subsidizing such costs or paying salaries high enough to cover them. Of course, non-actors in resort or regional theatres are seldom protected by a union, but it may be impossible to attract the necessary personnel unless room and board are provided for a reasonable amount.

## Meals for the Actor

Equity requires that actors have at least one hour to rest between performances on the same day, exclusive of half-hour call. When the time between two performances is less than one-and-a half hours, management must provide each actor and stage manager with the choice of a hot or cold meal at the expense of the theatre. This rule applies most often to dinner theatres and those that offer "twilight" performances followed by a later performance on the same evening.

In most cases there are restaurants or cooking facilities in or near the actor's place of lodging. When this is not true, the theatre is responsible for transporting actors to and from eating places for every meal. Other AEA rules regulate the number and frequency of meal stops actors must have while traveling, when transportation must be provided to local shopping centers and the like.

## International Tours

While international tours of performing arts companies are increasingly common—whether these are foreign companies booked into American theatres or American companies booked into foreign theatres—the subject is beyond the scope of this volume. The advent of international exchange in the performing arts is considered at greater length in the Conclusion. But such tours present a whole new array of problems to challenge the abilities of theatre managers—on both sides of the border. Unions like AEA expect the same away-from-home rules to be upheld whether their members are working in Minneapolis or Moscow, although, needless to say, it's quite a bit easier for American managers to arrange things like meals and local transportation in Minneapolis!

## SPECIAL CONCERNS OF STOCK AND DINNER THEATRE MANAGEMENT

### The Use of Nonprofessionals on Stage

Theatres that do not hire anyone under an Equity contract, of course, use nonprofessionals exclusively. Broadway productions and others that operate under the AEA production contract, as well as certain LORT theatres, are rarely permitted to put *any* nonprofessional on stage. But between these two extremes there are union formulas that allow nonprofessionals to be cast with professionals. Such formulas are particularly lenient under the special AEA agreements, like the 99-Seat Theatre Plan and the Letter of Agreement. But many categories of stock and dinner theatres are also permitted to use nonprofessional actors. Economically, of course, it is cheaper to use as many nonprofessionals as possible. Artistically, this policy can be detrimental.

In LOA and other small, developing theatres, Equity has considerable clout in regulating the use of nonprofessionals. As with LORT, stock and dinner theatres, the union's aim is really to convert as many amateurs into union members as possible. So when full members are not used, one of three types of nonprofessional actor is encouraged: AEA membership candidates, students, and local jobbers.

A membership candidate is a nonprofessional who is interested in a professional acting career and who has registered with Equity. Such people may earn AEA membership by working (not necessarily on salary) as an actor, understudy or production assistant to the stage manager for a cumulative total of fifty weeks at theatres participating in the AEA Membership Candidate Program. A maximum of ten weeks of credit may be earned for doing purely technical theatre work, and candidates who successfully complete an education program as devised by the union are eligible for membership after only forty weeks. Candidates are eligible to join Equity for up to five years after completing their forty or fifty weeks of work. But they may not be employed by any Equity theatre during this period—unless they are signed to an Equity contract.

Local jobbers are defined by AEA as residents of the community in which the theatre is located and as nonprofessionals. The management, of course, may only engage as many such people as the union formula permits. But they must be offered the option to enroll as an AEA membership candidate. If they do not, they may only be used twice in their first season and once in any season after that unless—you guessed it—they are signed to an Equity contract.

## Apprentice or Intern Systems

Any type of theatre may utilize apprentices providing they do not overlap the jurisdiction of any unions that are contracted by the theatre in question. The apprentice system (as old as craft jobs themselves) is meant to teach someone a set of skills by allowing that person to work under the supervision of a master craftsperson. Apprentices have long been a feature of American stock theatres and, when the work and the supervision are meaningful, an apprenticeship can provide a valuable learning experience. Of course, there have always been both good and poor apprentice programs. Appli-

TABLE OF ORGANIZATION
Musical Stock or Outdoor Theatre Company

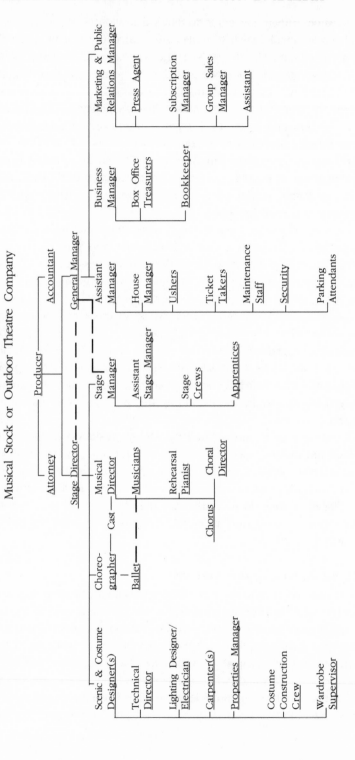

cants for such programs should closely examine whether or not the program will give them what they are seeking. Many, for example, do not offer any acting opportunities, others mainly involve go-fer work and still others use apprentices only as ushers and janitors.

From the theatre's point of view, apprentices are, at first glance, a source of cheap labor. But managers should be aware of the hidden costs of apprentice labor. For instance, the theatre may have to absorb some or all of the apprentices' room and board expenses; it may have to hire someone to supervise the apprentices; it may find that too much valuable staff time is taken up with supervising and teaching the apprentices. Also, beginners are prone to make mistakes, have accidents, lack discipline and good judgement and, in short, be unprofessional. Because of such factors, many stock theatres have abandoned the traditional apprentice system and, instead, have hired "interns" or "technicians." While such employees may earn only a small salary or stipend, they tend to be more mature and, importantly, more interested in specializing in a particular area (such as scene building or marketing) than young apprentices who are shifted from one job to another every week or two. Also, a salary or stipend permits the employer to demand a higher level of accomplishment while also giving the employee a greater sense of obligation.

Some theatres have experimented with apprentice programs that offer college credit, or with apprentice schools that actually offer formal classes. These are fine when they are well-run and when they are part of the theatre's mission, as opposed to being merely a gimmick to earn extra income. Any apprentice or intern policy needs to be thought out carefully in terms of the time, expense and energy it will require compared to the benefits that may or may not accrue.*

## The Mix of Professionals and Amateurs

If professionals are people who earn their living at what they're doing, they are also people whose earnings could decline if they're not doing it well. The quality of each person's work, especially in theatre where team effort is so critical, is invariably affected by co-workers. It doesn't matter how much a star is getting paid, for instance, when an apprentice has failed to place the necessary properties on the set and the curtain is going up. For just such reasons, many professionals are extremely wary of working with amateurs or nonprofessionals. And, indeed, it is difficult to argue that using nonprofessionals will not lower the standards of an otherwise professional operation. However, if this mix of workers is the policy, management should take time to familiarize the nonprofessionals as thoroughly as possible with pro-

---

*See also Chapter 4

fessional standards and etiquette. This can be more difficult than expected. Department heads should hold orientation meetings, work manuals and instruction sheets should be prepared and distributed, and the nonprofessionals should be supervised and corrected until the desired level of competence is achieved. When professionalism is compromised, this will be reflected in the production or in the organization.

## SUMMATION

Stock theatre in America has enjoyed two lives, both of which were largely provincial geographically and largely commercial artistically. The star system and overcentralization contributed to the demise of the nineteenth century's professional stock theatres. The star system, escalating costs, and changing tastes led to the near demise of professional stock theatres in the twentieth century. However, a remarkable number of nonprofessional stock theatres continue to thrive across the nation, and a sizable amount of new theatrical activity has allowed the near disappearance of professional stock to go almost unnoticed. Summer theatre directories, for example, are now filled with productions given by nonprofit professional companies, or presented at international festivals, produced by college and community groups, as well as by the nonprofessional stock theatres. So there is still a healthy amount of activity, many opportunities for nonprofessionals to gain experience, and a much wider variety of productions than when "the straw hat circuit" was the main event.

# 8

# College Theatre

POETS, philosophers, and educators since Plato and Aristotle have been concerned about the educational and moral values of theatre. Does the drama have an obligation to teach and enlighten its audiences? How deeply and in what ways can the living theatre influence its audiences? Questions such as these have pragmatic as well as academic relevance. Until the twentieth century, schools and colleges in the Western world were concerned with theatre almost exclusively as an instrument for teaching, especially in connection with classical subjects. In other words, educational theatre for the participant and not for the audience. The first plays written and performed in English were the products of British schools like Oxford and St. Paul's. In the eighteenth and nineteenth centuries, theatre was only recognized as an extracurricular school activity and as an appropriate addition to commencement and assembly programs; not until the twentieth century were theatre courses as such included in British and American college curricula, and not until recently have American theatre programs begun to recognize an obligation to campus and community audiences as well as to student participants. The history of educational theatre, therefore, is largely modern history.

## BACKGROUND

### Early Theatre Schools: 1871 to 1914

Nearly forty-five years elapsed between the establishment of the first schools to train professional actors in America and the introduction of the first four-year theatre program in an American college. Among those who had an early impact upon the growth of professional schools was Steele MacKaye, one of the most inventive and innovative men the American theatre has ever known. Influenced by Francois Delsarte and the Paris Conservatorie, MacKaye established a school of acting at the St. James Theatre in New York in 1871. Although it failed after several months, he founded the School of Expression on Union Square in 1877, the declared purpose of which was "to instruct and elevate society beyond merely entertaining it." MacKaye was the school's only teacher and again the venture collapsed. But in 1884 he was the major force behind the establishment of the Lyceum Theatre School, an institution that evolved into the present American Academy of Dramatic Arts. Early management of the Lyceum School was assumed by Franklin Sargent, with Charles Frohman as business manager and a faculty that included David Belasco.

During the 1870s other schools offered classes in acting, such as the New York Conservatory of Music and James E. Frobisher's College of Oratory and Acting. Subsequently, many more acting schools opened, especially in the eastern part of the nation. Most were privately sponsored and a few were affiliated with a producing theatre, such as the Lyceum, the Empire, and the Madison Square schools.

Early theatre schools were founded to provide students an alternative to the traditional method of learning theatre by joining a stock or repertory company. As stock companies disappeared early in the twentieth century, formal school programs became increasingly accepted and influential. At first, curricula included such courses as body movement, mime, vocal expression and, later, diction, stage effect, makeup, elementary dance, ballet and fencing. Many schools adopted the Delsartian "Life Study" approach to acting, which advised the student to look to life and nature as a basis for dramatic characterization—a method well suited to the contemporaneous plays of Ibsen, Chekhov and Shaw. Little if any attention was paid, academically, to technical aspects of theatre, and schools of elocution that emphasized the verbal and oral elements of interpretation continued to be popular.

As the little theatre movement increased its activity, the new European drama became known to Americans and people grew more dissatisfied with commercial theatre, the nation's colleges slowly began to pay lip service to the dramatic arts. The Wisconsin Players was founded in 1911, though it was only unofficially identified with the state university. George Pierce Baker began his '47 Workshop at Harvard University in 1912, and in 1914 the first four-year program in theatre leading to a baccalaureate degree was inaugurated at the Carnegie Institute of Technology in Pittsburgh.

## The Growth of Theatre Programs on the Campus: 1914 to 1950

Theatre courses and performances on the campus increased tremendously after World War I and again after World War II. Part of this increase—like so many other changes in American life—can be attributed to the liberalizing effect that foreign military duty had upon young Americans. This is not to imply, however, that college theatre programs in America are designed after European models. The performing arts are still treated either in an extracurricular or in a highly academic manner in the majority of European colleges and universities. The business of training performers abroad is done in a conservatory, a special school, or through apprenticeships with professional performance organizations. College degree programs in theatre are uniquely American.

At the outbreak of World War I and in the following two decades, American theatre schools could be divided into four categories: (1) professional training schools, (2) schools of expression, (3) community and art theatre-affiliated schools, and (4) college theatre programs. The first type, similar to the Lyceum School, was often affiliated with a professional theatre or designed to offer specialized training in some aspect or method of theatre. Examples include the National Dramatic Conservatory of New York, the American School of Playwriting, founded by William T. Price, and Richard Boleslavsky's Laboratory Theatre School, founded in 1924 and modeled after the Moscow Art Theatre School. Those affiliated with regularly operating theatres included the Henry Jewett School of Acting in Boston and the Detroit Civic Theatre. Both the Washington Square Players and the Theatre Guild operated schools for a brief period of time. Schools of expression, offering a slightly more refined and "respectable" approach to the drama, were, predictably, concentrated in Boston. Inspired by Professor L. B. Monroe of the Boston University School of Oratory, Charles Wesley Emerson founded the Boston College of Oratory (later Emerson College) in 1880; Anna and Samuel Currey founded Currey College, and the Leland Powers School was founded in 1904. All were schools of expression which, nonetheless, reflected the influence of Delsarte and the Lyceum School.

Noncommercial community and art theatres that operated schools included the Pasadena Community Playhouse, founded by Gilmore Brown in 1917; the Cleveland Playhouse, organized in the late '20s under the guidance of Frederic McConnell; the Goodman Theatre, which was affiliated with the Chicago Art Institute; and the Neighborhood Playhouse in New York. Following upon the heels of the first college theatre department at the Carnegie Institute of Technology, other institutions of higher education began to offer special courses in theatre, among them, New York University, Iowa, Northwestern, Cornell and Yale. Often a department was inspired by the activities of a campus theatre club, such as the Carolina Playmakers, which started in 1918 at the University of North Carolina.

From the beginning the trend was to offer college courses that emphasized theatre practice as well as history and theory. The study of dramatic literature and playwriting, rather illogically, generally continued under the domain of English departments. Practical training required the use of actual theatres and the presentation of plays before an audience, a fact that took many notable professors many years to establish: Brander Matthews at Columbia, Alexander Drummond at Cornell, Edward Mabie at the University of Iowa and Frederick Koch at North Carolina, among others.

The first large campus playhouse opened in 1926 at Yale, which enticed George Pierce Baker to join its faculty. Like European colleges, Harvard refused to create a separate theatre department and, after a fire destroyed his laboratory theatre, it also refused to provide Baker with a new theatre for his '47 Workshop students. When Baker transferred his energies from Harvard to Yale, the headlines in the Harvard *Crimson* read "Yale 47, Harvard 0!"

During the 1930s, large and well-equipped theatres were constructed on one campus after another: Iowa, Stanford, Amherst, Indiana. Also during the decade, theatre began to emerge as a separate academic discipline. Organizations such as the National Theatre Conference, the American National Theatre and Academy and the American Theatre Association (ATA) gave voice to the standards and goals of campus theatre and provided an important wedge that helped make theatre study distinct from other disciplines, such as English and Speech. To this day, however, many theatre programs both in colleges and high schools remain tied to nontheatre departments, budgets and regulations.

## *The Professionalization of College Theatre: 1950 to Present*

Theatre came into higher education through the back door. A major justification for the study and practice of theatre was that it offered the best approach to drama appreciation and, under the guidance of college dons, a far more responsible approach than that of attending commercial theatre productions. Little wonder that the academic world long disassociated itself (rather snobbishly, at times) from the commercial and professional theatre. But as higher education in general came to recognize and use the knowledge of professionals, first in the sciences, then in all disciplines, its attitude toward professional theatre began to change. Ivory towerism faded as practice was mixed with theory, the practitioner was heard alongside the professor and the laboratory was used as well as the library. More and more theatre programs became vocationally oriented. More and more they replaced instruction that had previously occurred in independent schools and institutes. The professional became a frequent lecturer on the campus. Visiting artists, entire theatre companies, and professionals-in-residence became almost commonplace.

In 1962 the Association of Producing Artists (APA), under the direction of Ellis Rabb, took up residence at the University of Michigan. With a large grant from the Rockefeller Foundation, New York University established a professional theatre training program and, with another Rockefeller grant, Stanford University hired nine professional actors to form two resident companies to work with its students. The University of Minnesota offered credit-generating internships for its theatre students at the Tyrone Guthrie Theater; Indiana University operated a showboat on the Ohio River; the University of Kansas established an exchange program with acting students from Yugo-slavia; the University of Missouri (Southwest Missouri State campus) oper-ated an annual summer tent theatre; the University of Missouri at Kansas City inaugurated a summer repertory program, as did many other colleges.

Several campuses even established a professional LORT theatre to pro-duce plays on a regular basis and to supplement the instructional programs by providing work experiences of various kinds. As Dean of the Yale School of Drama, Robert Brustein founded Yale Repertory Theatre in 1966 but even-tually left that institution and in 1979 founded the American Repertory The-atre at Harvard—providing a nice turn-around to the George Pierce Baker defection over fifty years earlier. Meanwhile, the new dean and artistic di-rector at Yale Rep, Lloyd Richards, brought considerable distinction to the company with the transfer to New York of such productions as Athol Fugard's *The Road to Mecca* and August Wilson's *Fences*. As a result of having pro-ducer Emanuel Azenberg on its faculty, Duke University in Durham, North Carolina, has hosted Broadway tryouts of Neil Simon's *Broadway Bound*, O'Neill's *Long Day's Journey Into Night* with Jack Lemon, and Lee Blessing's *Walk in the Woods*. Another producer, Roger L. Stevens, previewed *Meta-morphosis*, starring Mikail Baryshnikov at Duke.

The list of professionally-oriented theatre programs offered by colleges today is a long one. Most were inaugurated during the '60s and '70s and many were accompanied by ambitious plans for the construction of new campus theatre facilities, of which the Krannert Center for the Performing Arts at the University of Illinois is among the largest and most elaborate. Such facilities were often built as a result of the dreams and labor of senior faculty mem-bers, long frustrated by inadequate theatres and budgets, and by theatre pro-grams still tied to other departments. Once a new campus theatre or per-forming arts center had become a reality, however, it often required profes-sional management of a kind that faculty members were not prepared to provide. Not unlike the manner in which actor-managers lost control of their profession to businessmen, many academicians and theatre departments lost considerable autonomy when they moved into shining new facilities and found themselves "under new management," as it were. Centralization and bigness often create an identity crisis among constituents.

Shortly after the American Theatre Association went bankrupt in 1986, several dozen educators founded the Association for Theatre in Higher Edu-cation (ATHE), which attracted a large membership and now sponsors an annual convention. The University/Resident Theatre Association (U/RTA) continues as an independent organization to service campuses that operate resident, often professional, acting companies.

## TYPES OF COLLEGE THEATRE PROGRAMS

### Extracurricular Theatre Activities

Support for the arts in public education has never been very great, although the Title I and II programs of the Johnson administration are notable, and several states, especially California and Texas, have at times made meaningful budgetary allocations for this field. More often than not, the arts take a back seat to athletic activities; and public schools provide little if any money, faculty expertise or special facilities to promote the arts in education, much less arts education itself. And without strong arts programs at the secondary level, fewer promising students will appear as arts majors at the college level.

Theatre production can serve young people in a number of unique ways. Aside from demonstrating the importance of teamwork and coordination, theatre provides insight into literature and history, as well as into the student's own personality. When properly guided, it can also teach self-confidence, self-awareness and sensitivity.

When guided badly, it's merely another channel for extroverted students to show off or for others to develop fantasies about becoming stars.

Extracurricular theatre clubs and productions are common on the college campus, where they may or may not coexist with an academic theatre program. There should always be faculty guidance to insure continuity from year to year and to provide a liaison with the faculty and administration. The success of such organizations, however, always depends upon student leadership and involvement. The first test of this may well be the ability of the student officers to gain a fair budget allotment from their student government organization or whoever administers the student activities fees that are collected by most colleges precisely to support extracurricular initiatives. Again, sports activities are usually favored. When there is a theatre department or program, an extracurricular club can help encourage interest in theatre courses and in becoming a theatre major. It may feed volunteers into departmental production crews and it can also serve as a helpful safety valve that permits students a place to get rid of any complaints they may have with the department. They may, for example, not like the department's choice of productions or its casting policy. The student theatre organization might also be the best venue for producing experimental, original or unusual material. There have also been educationally creative instances when students have cast faculty members in their productions and otherwise reversed traditional relationships—usually to everyone's advantage.

## Elective Theatre Course Offerings

While over fifty percent of the nation's accredited colleges offer a "major" in theatre arts, over seventy-five percent offer a limited number of elective courses in drama, theatre history, practice and criticism. Theatre production is usually extracurricular on campuses where there is no major and emphasis in the classroom is placed on scholarship, with little thought that the student may enter theatre as a profession or pursue graduate work in the field. Courses and productions on these campuses are designed to complement a liberal arts education or concentration in some specialized field of study. Only one or two faculty members are needed, but they should have a special background and experience in theatre.

## Liberal Arts Theatre Programs

A liberal arts program offering a bachelor of arts degree with a concentration in theatre is often the best undergraduate study plan for students interested in this field. This assures a broad-based education, while also introducing the student to theatre and, hopefully, the wide range of dramatic literature. Although the student unrest of the 1960s prompted academia to loosen or drop many curricular requirements and make course content more "relevant," many such changes were reversed in the '80s with the reintroduction of a required core curriculum at many institutions. Theatre courses in this type of program are usually open to majors and nonmajors alike, as are department stage productions. Two or more full-time theatre instructors will be necessary and they should also be qualified to direct the productions.

## Vocationally Oriented Undergraduate Theatre Programs

A number of college theatre programs offer a bachelor of fine arts degree in theatre. This allows the student more theatre courses (usually of a more pragmatic, vocationally oriented nature), fewer course requirements in the humanities and sciences, no foreign language requirement, and perhaps more production opportunities than in a B.A. program. Yet the student receives a broader education than would be the case at a professional theatre school and a more intense exposure to theatre than would be the case in a B.A. program. In short, B.F.A. programs attempt to adopt a conservatory approach to professional training, such as that used by the Juilliard School and Oberlin College. The faculty for such a program should be comprised of four or more full time instructors as well as guests and part time adjuncts from the professional theatre. Concentrations in acting, musical theatre and design as well as theatre education are appropriate for B.F.A. programs. Concentrations in directing and theatre management, however, are inappro-

225

priate at the undergraduate level, because students interested in these areas must first gain broad knowledge of theatre and its repertory.

## Vocationally Oriented Graduate Theatre Programs

Graduate schools offer theatre programs that lead to the master of arts, master of fine arts, doctor of education, doctor of fine arts and doctor of philosophy degrees. The M.A. is usually a one- or two-year program and serves as a stepping stone toward a doctoral degree. The M.F.A., however, is considered a terminal degree, which means that it is considered the highest degree necessary for professional certification in fields such as acting, directing, design and arts management. Most colleges, for example, accept it in lieu of a doctoral degree for purposes of hiring and promoting faculty. M.F.A. programs are two-to-three years in length and in theatre, as with the B.F.A., aim for an intensive, conservatory approach to training that provides a great deal of laboratory, workshop and production work. Students may also work as interns on campus or with professional theatre companies and organizations off-campus. In fact, the strongest graduate theatre programs are associated with one or more professional groups, include established theatre professionals on their regular faculty, and make frequent use of visiting guest artists and lecturers from the profession.

Doctoral theatre programs (the Ph.D. is the degree most commonly offered) are primarily designed for students interested in education, history, criticism and/or dramaturgy, although graduates who hold a doctoral degree have a wide variety of other career choices as well. Doctoral programs emphasize research and scholarship as opposed to practice and application.

Information about both undergraduate and graduate theatre programs is published by Peterson's Guides, Inc. (Princeton, NJ), or one may consult the *New York Times College Directory* or *The Directory of American College Theatres*. Graduate programs in the field of arts administration are described in the *Survey of Arts Administration Training*, published periodically by the American Council for the Arts.

## MANAGEMENT OF THE COLLEGE THEATRE DEPARTMENT
### The Department's Position Within the Institution

The manner in which an academic department is positioned within the overall structure of the institution will determine a great deal about its programs, its faculty and its students. The weakest theatre programs are those housed within a department of another discipline, such as Speech or English. Fortunately, this type of situation is not nearly so common as it used to be. The strongest theatre programs are those housed in their own school of theatre and headed by a dean who has direct access to the college president and the college budget. But few universities are willing or able to elevate the study of theatre to such a lofty position in the academic hierarchy. A number, however, have established a school of the arts to embrace departments in both visual and performing arts disciplines. Others have a school of fine and applied arts or a school of communication arts and sciences that includes departments of television and journalism, as well as the visual and performing arts. Smaller institutions may make similar configurations within a department rather than a school. While such arrangements may not seem important at first glance, in fact they can have a very significant and far-reaching impact. Structuring an academic institution is somewhat like creating a family out of a group of strangers, or having the opportunity to pick all one's relatives. It mandates that certain people and disciplines will have to learn to live and work together and, just as important, that others won't. Academic planning must answer such questions as: Should theatre majors be required to take film and television courses, and vice versa? Should dancers study acting? Can actors and singers be combined in the same voice and diction classes? And so forth. Similar questions emerge in regard to inter-disciplinary faculty relationships and the shared use of performance, production, studio, classroom, office and other campus facilities.

Theatre departments within a more general structure, like a school of humanities, or an institution where there is no school structure at all, may find it more difficult to defend their interests because they must compete directly with larger and therefore more powerful departments, such as economics or education. (Size and power in academia are almost always based on numbers of students and the faculty-student ratio. As in the theatre business, the economics of education is based on the price of admission and the number of fannies in the seats!) Of course, personalities and campus politics can also contribute greatly to how a department is treated by the administration and the college community at large. In other words, it would help if the president were a theatre buff.

The degree to which a theatre department controls the appropriate facilities is also of major importance. Lucky indeed is the department that has exclusive use of a fully-equipped theatre. More often, it must share performance, rehearsal, classroom and production spaces with other departments, if not also with outside bookings and special events. This tends to be the case when there is a large auditorium or a performing arts center on campus, as discussed in the previous chapter. When facilities are controlled by the administration and its appointed managers, faculty must often battle to see to it that academic priorities take precedence over all others.

Finally, the department's position within the college budget and its control over the money it generates from box office receipts are major factors. As a general rule, the more hands money must pass through on its way to the project or purpose for which it was originally intended, the less will arrive there. So the department or school head wants to be as close as possible to the original source—the state legislature, the board of trustees, the college president, the provost, the dean—whoever. And control over box office income is critical to campus theatre production because this often represents the only "soft money," money that can be spent immediately without having to go through the lengthy and uncertain requisition process. Many items and services related to theatre production require immediate or quick payment, although few college budget officers are able to grasp this.

## Faculty vs. Student Control

The sudden explosion of campus riots during the 1960s, ethnically oriented demonstrations and forceful student demands had a measurable effect on higher education. This is characterized by greater student participation in such fundamental areas as curriculum planning and development, faculty hiring and promotion, budgeting, grading and admission procedures. During this period, there was a huge turnover of college presidents (many out the door and many others, no doubt, in their graves), a widespread change in college admission policies, and a general move toward community service and away from research and employment relationships with the so-called military-industrial complex. While there has been a recent trend to restore a more traditional curriculum, campus governance continues to require student representation in most areas and levels of decision-making. Many faculty members and administrators have been pleasantly surprised to find that such student involvement has actually been helpful; certainly it bespeaks a new partnership on the campus. College professors are no longer the autocrats they used to be.

Due to the collaborative and close nature of putting together a production, student-teacher relationships in a theatre department have always tended to be less rigid and more personal than in most others. Yet lines of authority must be drawn and maintained. Faculty members must often work hard to keep the learning process to the fore, as opposed to the production, entertainment or gratification process alone. Students may have control of an extracurricular theatre organization and participate in campus and department management, but faculty must control the teaching as well as maintain its leadership in campus governance.

## The Committee System

A giraffe, it has been said, is a horse designed by committee. Then who, we must ask, designed the horse, so we can hire that person as a consultant to talk to our committee!

228

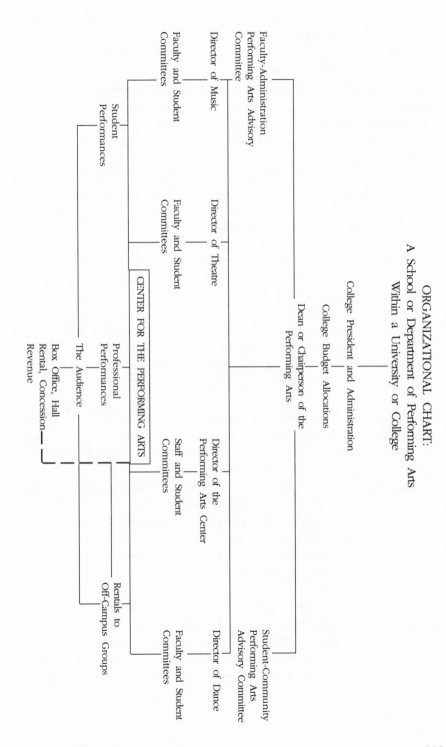

ORGANIZATIONAL CHART:
A School or Department of Performing Arts
Within a University or College

College President and Administration

College Budget Allocations

Dean or Chairperson of the
Performing Arts

Faculty-Administration
Performing Arts Advisory
Committee

Director of Music

Faculty and Student
Committees

Director of Theatre

Faculty and Student
Committees

CENTER FOR THE PERFORMING ARTS

Director of the
Performing Arts Center

Staff and Student
Committees

Director of Dance

Faculty and Student
Committees

Student-Community
Performing Arts
Advisory Committee

Faculty and Student
Committees

Student
Performances

Professional
Performances

The Audience

Box Office, Hall
Rental, Concession
Revenue

Rentals to
Off-Campus Groups

Most colleges and universities operate though a system of committees. This may hamper individual decision-making and initiative because it makes it so easy to avoid personal responsibility; one can always "defer to the decision of the committee" or hide behind the cloak of anonymity provided by group membership. But from another view, while committees may give the appearance of democratic distribution of power, very little democracy or government by consensus may actually be at work.

Department chairpeople in large institutions usually inherit an administrative structure that they are powerless to change, while at small institutions chairpeople may have the ability to establish a system of their own choosing. However, in both cases some type of committee system will be necessary. The advantages of management by committee should include:

1. Decentralization of political power
2. Majority rule
3. The guarantee that minority opinions will be heard

The usual disadvantages include:
1. Time-consuming delays
2. The discouragement of individual initiative and responsibility, which of course retards action, change and development
3. Decisions often lack the personal commitment of the people who must carry them out

Any system for managing an academic department should aim at clarity of purpose and reasoned leadership, with a fair representation of faculty and students on all committees and fair weight given to their collective voice.

There are some aspects of a theatre department's work that obviously defy management by committee. A committee may select the plays that will be produced, for example, but it cannot direct those plays. This must be done by an individual director who has autocratic authority over the production. And there are times when a chairperson must stand alone and make decisions like a commercial producer: to cancel a production before it opens, to replace the set designer, to bring in a play doctor or to cancel a performance because of some emergency.

The principles of personnel management discussed in Chapter 4 are as applicable to college theatre as to any other, although the college administrator may be burdened with more bureaucracy and institutional red tape. And on top of all the details and responsibilities that go into play producing, the managers of college theatre programs must add the challenges of teaching.

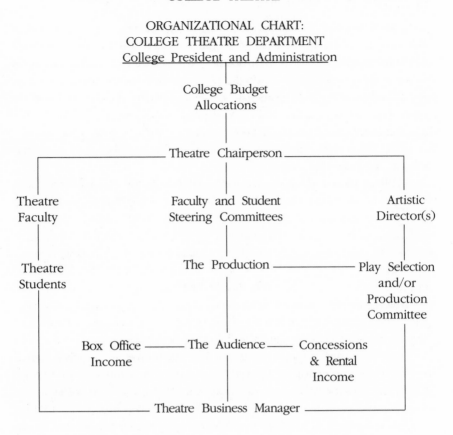

ORGANIZATIONAL CHART:
COLLEGE THEATRE DEPARTMENT
College President and Administration

College Budget
Allocations

Theatre Chairperson

Theatre
Faculty

Faculty and Student
Steering Committees

Artistic
Director(s)

Theatre
Students

The Production —————— Play Selection
and/or
Production
Committee

Box Office ——— The Audience —— Concessions
Income                              & Rental
Income

Theatre Business Manager

## PLAY PRODUCTION IN COLLEGE THEATRE

*Play Selection*

Chapter 6 defines certain criteria that may be applied to play selection and the business of planning a season. Decision-making in this area is surprisingly casual for many theatres. It is especially unfortunate when college theatres engage in random methods of play selection, because in no other branch of theatre do the people involved enjoy such job security and leisure for planning. Most students are in residence for three or four years, and most faculty members are likely to have tenure or long-term contracts. The problems of paying the rent, breaking even or showing a profit are seldom urgent, although they may be a factor in budgeting. A college theatre faculty is in a unique position to analyze its strengths and weaknesses, formulate policy and activate long-term projects. If a campus theatre program is primarily extracurricular or avocational, its major obligation is to the audience. If it is vocational and aimed at training students for the profession, the student participants must receive high priority in terms of play selection. In ei-

231

ther case, four years is a natural cycle due to the length of time most under-graduates are in residence. What, it should be asked, will be produced over each four-year period? How well do the plays selected represent the reper-tory of world drama? How well do the plays selected suit the talents and abili-ties of student and faculty participants? What experiences, both as audience and as participants, will the student walk away with at the end of four years? In commercial, resident, stock and community theatre, four years usually seems like an eternity, four months is a long season, and four days can make or break the entire operation.

College theatre departments traditionally favor the classics: Sophocles, Shakespeare, Congreve, Wilde, Ibsen, Shaw, Strindberg, Brecht; and, of the American dramatists, O'Neill, Miller and Williams. This is as it should be, because academia has an obligation to protect the masterworks of civiliza-tion and to encourage each generation to rediscover them. But new, obscure or controversial plays also have a place on campus. While the classics oc-cupy the main stage or theatre facility, most theatre departments of any size also have access to a smaller performance space. This may simply be a large room with its walls covered with black velour (thus the term "black box" theatre) and with flexible staging and seating possibilities.

College theatre seasons can easily lend themselves to a festival format in which play selection is related to a particular dramatist or theme: Shakespeare's history plays, the American musical theatre, new voices in the theatre, whatever. A few colleges have even announced in advance four-to-five-year main-stage production schedules. This approach has the advantage of enabling other departments and the local schools to adapt course content to the study of plays in production. Background materials, production infor-mation, study kits and teaching aids can be prepared well in advance and made available to teachers whose students will attend the performances. Generally, college play production could do much to coordinate productions with classroom study and utilize them as teaching opportunities for theatre and nontheatre majors on campus and off.

Whatever standards for play selection are applied, students should be involved in the decision-making, educational priorities should be honored, and immediate as well as long-range goals should be set and understood by both faculty and students.

## Casting

The casting process presents special problems in nonprofessional the-atre, where favoritism, real or imagined, is often a factor. Yet what do fac-ulty directors do when the number of really capable student actors is limited to just a few? Or when academic policy requires that acting majors be cast a certain number of times each year, even to the exclusion of others who give better auditions? Or when a faculty member is cast instead of a student? The solution often lies in adopting a standard departmental casting policy, of making this well-known to the students and then sticking to it. If policy *requires* teachers of acting to take on roles in campus productions periodically, then students will accept such casting.

Many theatre departments hold annual or semestral auditions in which all its majors are required to participate and nonmajors may also be invited. From these general auditions, faculty and students who are directing upcoming productions call back the actors of their choice to audition again for specific roles. Before casting is finalized, all directors meet to discuss their choices and resolve the inevitable conflicts. This system helps insure an even distribution of acting opportunities and, importantly, permits the student actors to integrate their academic work and other activities accordingly.

A card or computer catalog system that indexes all the current department majors and keeps their production credits up-to-date can be an indispensable casting and crewing device. It can also be consulted before play selections are made, not for precasting but as an indication of talent and crew resources. It can serve as a record of student activities and accomplishments that may be consulted when a letter of recommendation is requested, when a grievance is being voiced, or when award time rolls around. It is also a helpful resource for new faculty members and for student counseling purposes.

Double or alternate casting can substantially increase the number of acting roles available to students. Of course, directing two casts for the same production is difficult and time consuming, costuming is more expensive and time consuming, and so on. But some educators feel that the advantages of alternate casts performing on alternate nights far outweigh the disadvantages. Another valuable educational technique is to switch the roles that actors in the same cast are to perform, to give them experience in different roles on different nights. While such policies may bring about somewhat uneven or inconsistent performances, the actors' development—at least in a professional training program—must be considered at least as important as the audiences' reactions. Most campus audiences, even when they pay admission, understand this.

As a final note about casting, it should be said that college theatre is in the best position of all to avoid typecasting. Indeed, training programs for actors have an obligation to provide students with roles and experiences they might not gain elsewhere. As a rule, more is learned by taking risks than by playing it safe—provided that there is a purpose to the experiment and that good coaching and some kind of safety net are available.

## Managing the Campus Theatre and Production Personnel

When the theatre or performing arts department does not have exclusive use of the campus theatre, which is often the case, then that facility is usually managed and staffed by professionals who are accountable to the administration rather than to an academic department. Most such facilities also offer professional performing arts companies and performances to the general public. These facilities, together with other types of presenting organizations, are discussed in Chapter 10.

Small campus theatre facilities, however, are often staffed entirely by faculty and students, in which case management and production may be less professional, but life and learning are likely to be a whole lot easier! Even when there is a large performing arts center on campus, where the theatre department stages its major productions, a sizable department would benefit from another, smaller performance space that it can call its own.

Whenever possible, productions should be related to class work and student participants should be drawn largely from such classes. All theatre majors might be required to work on a certain number of productions each semester. Students in the theatre management class, for example, would serve in box office and publicity jobs. Students in a stagecraft class would be assigned to set construction jobs, and so forth. In order for this system to work well in relation to a busy production schedule, a crew coordinator will have to be appointed to visit classrooms, describe the personnel needs, sign up the crews, monitor crew performance, keep time sheets, collect grades or other assessments of each student from the crew supervisors, and hand all such information back to the classroom instructor, who may use it as part of the final grade determination.

Some theatre departments also grant credit exclusively in exchange for production work. This is justifiable when such work is meaningful and accomplished under direct faculty supervision. It is similar to fieldwork that might be conducted for credit in any academic discipline. The only drawback is that the more credits a student earns this way, the fewer he or she will earn from classroom coursework.

When the department operates a theatre facility, obviously it must assign faculty members to take responsibility for the primary functions. These usually include:

PRODUCTION COORDINATION   In charge of scheduling of space, coordinating efforts of design and technical personnel, assigning student crews, supervising production purchases, supplies and inventories, serving as liaison with department chairperson and college administration in appropriate areas, assigning personnel and supervising stage and house management, faculty supervisor in charge of all performances.

*BUSINESS COORDINATION* In charge of long-and-short-term budgeting, preparation of production budgets, annual financial reports, individual production reports, box office operation, banking, production requisitions, payment orders, account ledgers, and departmental grants administration.

*TECHNICAL COORDINATION* In charge of all personnel and activity in the technical production shops; oversees requisition, purchasing, and maintenance of all production equipment and supplies; able to operate all power equipment, as well as sound and lighting equipment.

*MARKETING COORDINATION* In charge of working with appropriate campus and performing arts center offices to coordinate information gathering and distribution in regard to theatre productions: playbills, posters, on-and-off-campus advertising, press releases, seasonal brochure design and distribution, subscription sales, group sales.

Such responsibilities must be taken into account when the theatre department is hiring new faculty and should be included in job descriptions. Some institutions make it possible to excuse instructors from a full teaching load in exchange for nonteaching duties, such as those listed above. When this is not the case, faculty must simply volunteer to take on extra responsibility in order to make theatre production possible. Faculty and administrators outside the department rarely understand the time, expertise, energy, talent and money required to produce good theatre. Getting a new budget line to hire a technical director, or an electrician, or a professional guest artist can be a major battle. College administrators will understand the need to build a well-equipped chemistry lab, but won't see the need for a well-equipped theatre. They will understand an accounting class with seventy-five students, but refuse to permit an acting class with fewer than twenty students. And they'll view box office income with the greed of a Silas Marner and wonder why the theatre department can't always use the same six-to-ten-week requisition process like everyone else.

The four job functions listed above could, of course, be handled by nonfaculty personnel, but the use of faculty insures that the facility will be used more fully as a teaching laboratory and that production work will have a close tie to classroom instruction.

In addition, many of the duties described can and often should be executed by students as a learning experience,which would allow faculty to perform major functions such as directing, designing, choreographing and conducting the productions as part of their regular duties. A department chairperson usually serves as something like the artistic director of a nonprofit theatre company.

## THE PROFESSIONAL ON CAMPUS

As mentioned earlier, the use of experts, professionals and celebrities in the college classroom has increased tremendously in recent years. Some institutions have even been accused of being overloaded with big names and short on professors of substance. As a marketing ploy, there is little doubt that star performers attract attention and often sell seats; and so as long as their academic credentials and teaching abilities are acceptable, there is nothing wrong with including them on the faculty. However, if they are given favored treatment—especially regarding their appointment, promotion or tenure—other faculty will have legitimate grounds for complaint.

### Professionals As Full-Time Faculty

Because they are committed to providing the best professional training possible, many academic departments—especially on the graduate level— hire well-known, established professionals with the belief that such people's success in "the real world" will be a valuable learning resource. In most cases it probably is. But there is a difference between hiring a professional who is still working and one who has effectively retired. The difference will be the amount of service the college receives from the professional. Because few successful people in the performing arts ever retire by choice, special problems arise when the theatre department hires an actor, director or designer who is still in demand professionally. What happens when a major film offer comes through in mid-semester? Or a directing offer comes from Europe? Or involvement with professional or government committees requires frequent trips to the other coast?   In these cases, a department's solution is often to hire the professional on a part-time or half-time basis, or to compress that person's teaching schedule into a short period or even interrupt it. But all of these scenarios usually present complications. It would be preferable to hire retired professionals only on a full-time basis, even though they are not always the most glamorous choices available.

### Adjunct Faculty

Adjunct faculty have been hired to teach one or two courses instead of a full-time load. They are brought in because the regular faculty is either insufficient or unqualified to teach the courses or sections being offered. Adjuncts are sometimes hired from another department on campus, from another campus altogether or from the profession. They are the best solution to limited or short-term teaching needs, and the college administration regards them as a bargain because they often get paid less and receive fewer benefits than the regular faculty. And when they are respected experts, they lend a professional tone to the department and may also provide valuable job contacts to students. The disadvantage of adjuncts is that they are not so available to students outside the classroom as the full-time faculty and some have little real interest in the ongoing work of the department or the institution.

## Guest Lecturers

Campuses that want to attract top professionals to their classrooms but are located more than a few hours' drive from one of the nation's major cities sometimes hire such people for just one lecture or for a day or two. The person might run a day-long workshop for selected students or deliver several lectures and also, in the role of a consultant, prepare some special report for the department or the college administration.

Wherever a campus is located, the faculty and chairpeople should always keep their eyes open for special guest opportunities. What successful professional could they personally invite to the campus? Who is visiting the area on other business? Who are the local experts in a given field? What members of the faculty and administration might provide an interesting guest lecture? The possibilities are endless although, of course, guests should not be overused nor should they distract from good, solid instruction.

While it is always correct to pay guest speakers a fee or an honorarium, this may not always be possible or necessary. Most people feel honored to have the opportunity to teach or lecture at a college or university. And there is also the psychic reward from sharing one's hard-earned wisdom with an eager group of listeners. For the very successful people who have received all the money, awards and acclaim they could hope for, teaching may offer special gratification that is its own payment.

## Artists-in-Residence

Artist-in-residence programs entail that an individual artist or whole company of performing artists be contracted to spend anything from a day to several weeks at a campus conducting lectures and workshops with students and often also putting on a public performance. This practice is now a major source of income for most American dance companies, which generally try to arrange such residencies as a regular part of their touring schedule. It is less common for theatre companies, because so few are available to tour in the first place. However, it is not unusual for a theatre department to arrange for a playwright to be in residence while his or her work is being produced on the campus, and there are many cases where a professional

237

director has been brought in to stage a production. In fact, most leading actors and directors have a few plays they are itching to do but will probably never get the chance in the professional theatre. They might grab such an opportunity on the campus—and for a very reasonable fee!

## The AEA Actor-Teacher Contract

Members of Actors' Equity who accept teaching positions of any kind can do so without AEA involvement. Equity members who wish to appear without salary in campus productions should request permission from AEA in order to avoid union penalty. Permission is rarely denied. However, when an Equity member is hired by a college as a performer or as a performer and teacher, both parties usually sign one of two agreements, devised primarily to insure that actors would receive compensation and treatment equal to those of the institution's faculty and receive also the minimum guarantees of an Equity contract.

The University Actor-Teacher Agreement is a simple form that specifies the following terms of employment:

1. Preknowledge of the productions and courses the actor will be assigned
2. All rights and privileges accorded to the college faculty will be accorded to the Equity member
3. Agreement to length of employment (no week to exceed an average of forty hours of work and to include at least one full day of rest)
4. Agreement on salary (no less than the minimum salary for faculty members of comparable status)
5. Agreement on pension, medical and insurance coverage (the actor is covered by Equity provisions in these areas until such time as the university coverage becomes effective).

## The AEA Guest-Artist Agreement

Equity members who are hired exclusively for performance duties on a campus are signed to an AEA Guest-Artist Agreement, which is issued on a quadruplicate contract form similar to other Equity contracts. Such actors usually perform with a student cast. The same agreement is used when an AEA member is hired to perform with a community theatre cast. The list of college and community theatres that have employed Equity actors is a long one, numbering hundreds of organizations from nearly every state.

## Resident Performing Companies

If a college wishes to maintain an entirely professional resident theatre company on its campus—as has been done at the University of Michigan, in Ann Arbor; at the University of Texas, in Fort Worth; at Yale and at Harvard— it may employ the actors on a Guest-Artist Agreement or, more likely, it may operate under a League of Resident Theatres (Lort) Contract.* Sometimes the professional or partially professional company operates within the university structure; at other times it is a separate corporation with greater autonomy.

Maintaining a professional theatre company of any kind is an expensive proposition that also risks some bad press for the host institution, but the educational opportunities it affords students in affiliated academic programs can be considerable. Students can observe and work with accomplished professionals who may also serve as classroom instructors. Professional theatre companies on campus also reinforce the future of resident, regional theatres that concentrate on a serious repertory. It is interesting to speculate about the possibility of numerous professional theatre companies on numerous campuses. If that were ever the case, a student of theatre could secure both an undergraduate and graduate education, an internship, preprofessional training and a long professional career all on a single college campus!

## SUMMATION

During the years that have elapsed since the creation of the first college theatre program in 1914, the study of theatre has become an accepted part of higher education, vocationally oriented theatre programs have increased tremendously, colleges have allocated many millions of dollars for performing arts facilities and instruction, and many campuses have become important centers for the professional arts. There is increased dialogue and understanding between the educational and professional branches of the theatre—an encouraging trend away from the old academic attitude that theatre is an extracurricular plaything, and a move toward professional recognition of the validity of academic training. And hundreds of campus productions each year entertain college and community audiences and help keep the breath of life in the world's drama.

Yet the arts continue to be treated inequitably when budget allocations are made, whether in the halls of government or the halls of ivy, whether in public or private education. The challenge of making politicians, bureaucrats and administrators understand the life-sustaining value of the arts and their need for subsidy is a supreme challenge to arts educators at all levels. But this should become easier as campuses become entrenched as the cultural centers of their communities, as communication increases between the academy and the professional world, and as a new generation learns about the essential value of the arts.

---

*See Chapter 6

# 9

# Community Theatre

A LL theatre, from ancient times to the present, has been rooted in amateur activity that reflects people's urge to imitate and their delight
in watching others engage in this activity.

The amateur in theatre is a person who does not receive financial remuneration, although amateurs may be highly knowledgeable about their
theatre work and even gifted. They have simply not chosen to earn their living in the theatre. Community theatres, or civic theatres, are either largely or
exclusively comprised of nonsalaried amateurs who usually represent a cross
section of residents in a given area and perform only in that area, for its other
residents.

## BACKGROUND

Amateur theatricals unrelated to a distinct theatre organization have long
been common in America. Judge Samuel Sewall, the Pepys of New England
puritanism, wrote in his diary in 1687 that a maypole had been set up in
Charlestown, Massachusetts, that public dancing was seen, and a stage fight
occurred in the streets. During the same year, Increase Mather noted "much
discourse of beginning Stage-Plays in New England." By the early 1700s
amateur theatricals were being offered in the southern colonies and one Tony
Ashton, the first professional actor to perform in the colonies, was paving
the way for the arrival of Lewis Hallam's company in 1752. When public theatres were inactive during the Revolution, the spirit of theatre was kept alive
by amateur theatricals performed in military camps and organized by such
eminent "producers" as Generals Howe, Burgoyne and Clinton. So began the
nation's tradition of amateur theatre. The purpose of this chapter, however,
is to consider organized community theatres which, like today's college theatres, did not really evolve until the present century.

Both community and educational theatre sprang from the same urges
and sources of inspiration. Both began at about the same time, in the years
immediately before and after World War I, and both had considerable influence upon the development of resident and Off-Broadway theatre, which in

turn influenced the commercial theatre. The little theatre movement (also referred to as the "tributary theatre" or "nationwide theatre" or, simply, "community theatre") was a reaction against the quality of the flagging commercial theatre, a vote in favor of the European Free Theatre movement and, not insignificantly, an indication that, as average Americans gained leisure time, they lost certain puritanical standards for using it.

Inspired by the genius of men like Reinhardt, Stanislavsky and Craig, by the example of the Abbey Theatre in Dublin and American tours by the Irish Players, countless little theatres began to organize in communities throughout the nation. Initially, their resources were slight, their leadership was lacking and their activities were primarily aimed to please participants rather than audiences. By the mid-twenties, however, many community groups could boast a salaried, year-round director and, perhaps, several other salaried workers. Many had acquired or constructed a permanent home for their productions and achieved sizable membership and audience support. Unfortunately, the growth of community theatre was curtailed by the depression that followed the stock market crash of 1929 and by the diversion of energies into World War II. But with the creation of the Federal Theatre Project in 1935, as discussed in Chapter 6, there was renewed theatre activity nationwide. Many audience members in the forty states where Federally-sponsored theatres were located were exposed to live performance for the first time. This helped establish the idea and the feasibility of local theatre.

As community theatre found its own voice through the meetings and publications of organizations like the Drama League and the National Theatre Conference, its standards and goals became more ambitious and well-defined. Although there are many ill-guided and selfishly-oriented community theatres, there can be little question that many maintain standards and resources that are the highest in the world for amateur activity.

The fundamental principles that should govern community theatre organizations are discussed in Part I. Later sections deal with specific factors of administration. This chapter is concerned only with areas unique to community theatre or those that need special emphasis and attention.

## CENTRAL ELEMENTS OF A COMMUNITY THEATRE
### Leadership

A successful community theatre depends no less on strong, imaginative leadership than does a commercial theatre production, a resident theatre or a college theatre. Theatrical productions don't simply spring out of the ground, nor do they result merely from good intentions. They result from the hard work of many people under the guidance of a clear-minded leader. Because an energetic, knowledgeable theatre director is not always available to a community, there may be frequent gaps in local leadership. This is especially true when the organization does not employ a salaried director. To avoid the problem, every attempt should be made to groom directors before some crisis necessitates a changeover. When events conspire to leave a group without effective leadership (a situation, when it occurs, that is readily obvious to everyone), the organization should consider a temporary suspension of major productions. This might dampen membership enthusiasm and weaken audience loyalties, but it is a more honest and ultimately more rewarding policy than that of presenting productions that are inferior to established standards. The membership, during such times, can remain active in other areas or can present less ambitious productions. And meanwhile, of course, it should search for a new artistic director who is able and willing to assume leadership.

## Membership

When there is talk about forming a new community theatre or about reactivating one that has been dormant, the leading organizers should question their motivations to be certain that they wish to establish a long-term venture. Perhaps they are merely enthusiastic about producing a particular script for a particular cause, in which case they should limit their sights accordingly. Or, they might produce a play as a trial venture *preceding* the formation of a community theatre group in order to test local support, attract potential leaders and participants, or serve as a rallying point. A trial production uncovers problems and factors that, subsequently, can be dealt with intelligently when writing the constitution and bylaws for a new organization.

Most community theatres provide for several types of membership. Full members usually pay annual dues, serve on committees, work on the productions, and are eligible to serve as officers and directors. Associate members may be comprised of all those who buy a season ticket or a block of tickets but are not eligible to vote in the organization unless they also pay dues and thereby change their membership status. Patrons or sponsors may constitute a third class of membership, comprised of people or businesses who donate money or materials to the group or who purchase program advertising.

The important thing is to maintain a large nucleus of enthusiastic and active members. To do this, the organization must offer a range of activities sufficient to satisfy the diverse abilities and desires of its membership. Not everyone will want to perform on stage, and those who do should not be regarded as so "special" that other workers and activities are made to seem unimportant or unnecessary. It must become known throughout the community that the organization can serve the interests of many individuals and that it welcomes the nonactor as readily as the actor.

## Capital

Before writing bylaws and planning productions, the organizers of a community theatre should estimate how much their activities will cost. Where will the money come from? Ticket sales, patrons, donations, membership dues, advertising revenue? How much money can be reasonably expected from each source? Does the anticipated revenue indicate that the proposed activities of the group are too costly for it to support? Should ticket prices and dues be increased? How much money will be required before any ticket income is seen? What provisions can be made for a reserve fund? Whatever the answers to these questions, they will determine the early activities and plans of the organization. To realize the best legal and financial advantages, a community theatre should be formed as a nonprofit organization.

## Forming a Nonprofit Corporation (See Chapter 1)

## Theatre Facilities

Like the availability of capital, the availability of physical plant facilities will dictate a great deal about what a community theatre can produce, how frequently and at what cost. Often, the organization may negotiate for free or low-cost usage of a school or civic auditorium. Or it may use a professional theatre during its off-season or nonperformance periods. The owners of such theatres may welcome off-season usage for several reasons: the rental income, the fact that it may introduce new audiences to the theatre building, the fact that it may reduce the landlord's maintenance and security problems. Some community theatres are sufficiently established and resourceful to own a theatre. Chapter 3 is especially pertinent in regard to the plant facilities operated by community theatre organizations.

## Constitution and Bylaws

After stating the goals and objectives of the organization, the constitution and bylaws of a community theatre should spell out carefully-determined specifics. Legal counsel should be obtained before the document is finalized. While basic operating rules and organizational structure should be defined, enough flexibility should be provided to accommodate changes and future developments. The bylaws for a typical community theatre should probably include details related to the following:

1. GENERAL
   Name and location
   Preamble
   Legal counsel
   Bookkeeping and audit procedures
   Corporate status
   Amendment and repeal procedures
   Rules of procedure
2. OFFICERS AND BOARD OF DIRECTORS
   Election procedures
   Terms of office
   Powers
   Duties
   Replacement during absences and vacancies
   Indemnification
3. MEMBERS
   Definitions
   Types of
   Dues
   Obligations
   Powers
   Privileges
4. MEETINGS
   Annual
   Special
   Purposes of
   Quorum requirements
   Advance notice for
   Order of business
   Time and place requirements, if any
5. COMMITTEES
   Standing committees
   Types and purposes of
   Membership of
   Quorum requirements
   Chairmanship of
   Membership change in committees
   Appointment or election to
   Powers of
   Duties of
6. AMENDMENTS

The revised edition of *Roberts' Rules of Order* is generally recognized as the authoritative guide for parliamentary procedure, a system of discussion that is highly efficient and democratic, especially for large meetings or those that are meant to result in formal, important actions.

It is possible to conduct an organization without any official constitution or bylaws, simply letting things develop casually and using the precedent of past actions as the basis for governance, and this kind of common-law technique may be suitable for some organizations. But when the goals, objectives and nature of the organization assume a different character each year, these matters should be discussed by the membership frequently so they are understood by everyone.

## ADMINISTRATIVE ORGANIZATION
### *The Board, The Officers and The Committees*

When a nonprofit corporation is established as the legal base of an organization, there must be a board of directors (or trustees) and a set of officers to control it.*   If the board is a large one, it may appoint an executive committee comprised of a few of its members, together with the president of the group and its leading managers. An executive committee can help to facilitate the rapid transaction of routine business. The fundamental responsibilities of a board of directors in a civic or community theatre should include the following:

1 .To set long-range goals and objectives
2. To safeguard and improve physical and financial assets
3. To insure the legality of the organization's activities
4. To approve annual budgets
5. To receive annual reports from all leading officers and standing committees
6. To ratify the appointment of salaried personnel, especially the artistic director.

A board of directors should not officially concern itself with any of the routine, day-to-day business of the organization. If a salaried artistic director is employed, he or she should be given a great amount of power and flexibility in all areas of artistic decision making. If the board is unhappy with the results, it may decide not to renew the artistic director's contract at the end of the year.

While the following tables of organization show typical structures for community theatre groups, many different schemes are possible. The number of standing and special committees will be determined by the number of active members and, of course, by their interests. Sizable groups should

*See also Chapter 1.

attempt to operate a publications program which, among other projects, should write and distribute frequent newsletters to keep the membership informed about activities and, more important, maintain a high level of membership support and enthusiasm.

When a production is being prepared, the artistic director must organize workers under his or her immediate supervision, as shown in the second chart. Some of these workers may come from standing committees if the group is sufficiently active. For example, there might be a standing "design" committee that studies problems and techniques in scene and costume design and then applies its knowledge to the organization's productions. The same could hold true in the areas of publicity, makeup and house management. When there are groups of people permanently working in such areas, it is much easier to organize a production staff and it guarantees more knowledgeable and better-prepared workers. Following each production, the appropriate committees and workers should analyze the results to learn as much as possible from their experiences. Suggestions and written reports should then be submitted for the benefit of future production workers. Too many community groups virtually disband between productions. Unless there is loyalty to and participation in the organization itself and not merely in its productions, little growth and development will be possible. Each production will have to be staffed anew, each will make the same mistakes as the last, each will face the same ponderous difficulties.

## AFFILIATION WITH OTHER ORGANIZATIONS

To strengthen theatre activities and standards on the community and amateur level, local organizations should devise both informal and official methods of working together. Sometimes a community arts council or some other umbrella group can serve to coordinate, sponsor or fund broad-based community programs. However it is done, the community theatre should benefit in terms of material and personnel resources when it works with local school, college, or civic groups in appropriate ways.

### Public Schools

Members of the high school theatre club and members of the community theatre probably face many of the same problems. This may be especially true in regard to such areas as scene design and construction, makeup and publicity. Some high schools give credit or out-of-school time to students who participate in community projects and this type of work deserves encouragement.

High school and community theatre groups may find it possible to coordinate their productions and thereby create a local "theatre season" for

## TABLE OF EXECUTIVE ORGANIZATION

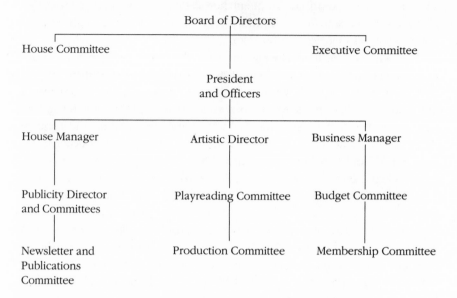

## TABLE OF PRODUCTION ORGANIZATION

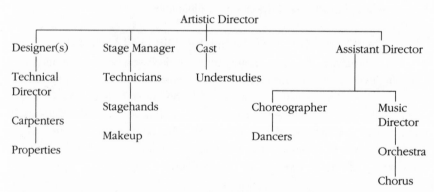

which tickets can be sold on a series basis. Or the community theatre, assisted by a budget allocation or fee from the school, might present special performances for public school audiences. Whatever the affiliation, cooperative efforts between local arts organizations are important to strengthen the arts and to strengthen the community itself.

## *Colleges*

Formalized programs may be arranged between college and community theatres to share facilities, audiences, materials, personnel and experiences. The community theatre may be pleased to accept student workers (who should receive credit for their field work) and in some cases may be able to provide such students with a small fee or salary. And, conversely, the college theatre may welcome and benefit from the involvement of community theatre members.

## Civic Organizations

Many community theatres are forced into an affiliation with a civic agency or organization in order to secure their theatre facilities. When a town or city operates a recreation center, this may include a theatre, auditorium or some other space suitable for stage productions which the local theatre club can use at a low cost. By working under the umbrella of a city agency, the theatre may be able to benefit by utilizing the agency's personnel, fiscal resources, mailing lists, public information services and space facilities. Conversely, such a marriage may also detract from the desired image and independence of the theatre group, force many compromises in regard to space usage and, if the town fathers are especially conservative, may force compromises in regard to the plays selected for production.

A community theatre may affiliate itself with a local service club, business or charity organization that offers it some kind of sustaining support. Although security of this kind is always tempting, it is likely to be accompanied by compromises in the theatre's policies and attempts by outsiders to impose their vested interests upon the theatre organization.

## RELATIONSHIP OF COMMUNITY TO PROFESSIONAL THEATRE

The quality of work produced by community theatres reflects the quality of interest its members have toward professional theatre and, indeed, toward life itself. If the membership of a group is comprised largely of people who are seeking mere ego satisfaction, the productions are unlikely to satisfy the audiences. Nor, in the long run, are they apt to provide much personal satisfaction for participants. It is not contradictory for nonprofessional groups to aim at professionalism. People who join ongoing community theatres should have an ongoing interest in the arts as well as a desire to develop as individuals. There is a big difference between the dedicated amateur and the dabbling dilettante. To keep the standards and goals of professionalism ever before it, a community theatre may establish varying types of relationships with professional artists and organizations.

A standing or special committee should be formed within the community theatre organization to assist and encourage its members to attend professional plays and events. This committee should negotiate with professional theatres for group rates, arrange for backstage tours and lectures and invite professionals to speak at membership meetings. When the community theatre is located many miles from professional theatres, it should arrange annual trips to visit distinguished professional theatres. Most professional managements are extremely gracious about providing backstage tours, will frequently arrange for groups to be addressed by leading artists or craftspeople and willingly make special arrangements when requested to do so. The same may be said of college theatres, which also stand ready to receive touring groups and provide special lectures.

When members of a community theatre attend outside productions and activities in groups, follow-up discussions should analyze and evaluate the productions seen and the experience gained. Also, thank-you letters should be sent to the host theatre—a matter that is often overlooked.

## Sponsorship of Professional Events

There is no reason why a community theatre should not sponsor a professional series of public events together with its own productions. This may take the form of a lecture series featuring well-known speakers, a poetry and play-reading series or a series of seminars. If there is strong membership and local support, events like these can be self-sustaining and, if they are tied in with the sale of tickets for the organization's regular productions, may increase general ticket sales. Guest speakers and individual guest performers may be engaged through direct negotiation or, more simply, through agencies like the American Program Bureau (Boston) or the International Platform Association (Cleveland), which offer nationwide bookings.

An ambitious community theatre might also sponsor or cosponsor the presentation of professional touring companies, such as those produced by Columbia Artists Theatricals Corp or American Theatre Productions (both New York City firms).

## Employment of Professional Guest-Artists

While a civic theatre organization can hire professional stage directors, designers, conductors, choreographers and others without necessarily negotiating a union contract (though some type of formal agreement should *always* be employed), professional actors who work with community groups must be contracted according to the terms of the Actors' Equity Association Guest-Artist Agreement. This is designed for use by individual actors who appear with an otherwise amateur company. The Guest-Artist Agreement carries the standard AEA stipulations regarding work conditions, travel, living accommodations and the like. The salary minimum and other information can be obtained through an Equity office.

The Guest-Artist Agreement permits the actor to work only as a performer and his role(s) must be specified in his contract. A professional's association with an amateur group will afford considerable opportunity for its members to learn about professional attitudes and techniques. Not all actors are anxious or suited to engage in this type of association, and an effort should be made to avoid the employment of guests who are interested only in the salary they will receive. The community theatre group should know why it wants or needs the services and talents of a professional, and the professional should have good reason for working with a community organization. Perhaps it offers the artist a role that he or she might not play elsewhere, an opportunity to experiment in some way or the gratification of teaching and assisting nonprofessionals.

## Cooperation with Professional Competitors

As mentioned earlier, theatregoing is a habit and, generally speaking, the more that theatre is available to the public the more theatregoing will take place. Provided that good sense is applied to performance scheduling, play selection and related matters, a number of different theatres and performing organizations can live comfortably together in the same community and, furthermore, contribute substantially to each other's success.

Obvious areas for desirable cooperation between theatre groups include the sharing of mailing lists, fundraising campaigns, plant facilities, material resources and personnel resources. Mutual endeavors can be organized without loss of image or independence to any of the participating groups. On the other hand, no group should merely "use" another for its own self-centered purposes. By keeping lines of communication open between various arts organizations in a community, many opportunities for joint endeavors and benefits will be discovered. An energetic community arts council can be especially helpful in promoting such activities and increasing audience support.

## SUMMATION

There is no area in which more theatrical beginnings can and should be made than in the community, among novices and dedicated amateurs. Community theatre is grassroots theatre that offers many of the nation's audience members and artists their first theatre experiences. The higher the quality of community theatre, the higher the demands will be on the professional theatre.

Community theatre in America has long passed the blushing rigor of youth, but it has yet to reach full maturity. Indeed, due to the living (and moving) patterns of Americans and the resulting impermanence of American communities, civic theatre may never reach its full potential. In addition, limited financial and personnel resources make many community theatres dependent on assistance and cooperation from educational and professional theatres and organizations. So a primary responsibility of community theatre leaders is to secure the best outside help available. Do-it-yourself craftsmanship should not mean working from ignorance—there are too many experts, books and services available to excuse such an approach. There are also local or community arts councils ready to give assistance *and* financial support to serious community theatre groups that have good track records.

# 10

# Theatrical Presenting Organizations

T HIS book focuses on the process of *producing* theatrical productions, but there are literally thousands of theatres and administrators who concern themselves almost exclusively with *presenting* productions that have been produced by somebody else. The managers of such theatres, or the corporate entities that they represent, are known as presenters (or "presentors"), licensees, sponsors, local managers, promoters, or, collectively, as presenting organizations. The people or outfits that sell the artists and/or attractions to presenters are known as producers, impresarios, booking agencies, licensors, or production companies.

More live, professional performances in America today are financed by money earned from presenters' fees than from any other source. As a result, the salaries and fees paid to artists and support personnel in the presenting branch of the performing arts business represent a major portion of all earnings in this field. Also, presenters collectively generate the greatest percentage of the total box office gross in the entire live entertainment industry. This means that they exert the greatest influence over what the American public will see in terms of live performances.

In the nonprofit arena, presenting organizations include private, campus and civic performing arts centers, museums, religious organizations, libraries and community centers. Commercial presenting organizations include certain stock theatres, cabarets, casinos, hotels, nightclubs and so-called road houses. There are also countless independent promoters and presenting organizations that rent rather than operate their own performance facilities. Clearly, then, "the road" is shared by nonprofit presenters and commercial promoters, although both deal with the same booking agencies and producing companies. This chapter will use the generic label, "presenting organizations," except where there are notable differences between nonprofit and commercial entities.

The majority of performances that are presented across the land fall into the music category—everything from pop, folk, jazz and rock concerts to symphony, choral and solo performances. Yet presenting organizations also sponsor a considerable amount of theatre—including serious drama, musical comedy, children's theatre, modern dance, ballet and opera. For most institutions involved in this activity, like colleges and museums, presenting performances is a secondary activity; however, there are hundreds of other fully professional presenting organizations, like the Brooklyn Academy of Music (the nation's oldest, dating back to 1861), Baltimore's Mechanic Theatre and the Washington (D.C.) Performing Arts Society, for which presenting is the primary activity.

While this chapter concentrates on theatrical presenting, there are several points that should be understood at the outset:

1. Many presenters sponsor all types of performing arts events and some present films, closed-circuit TV events, visual arts exhibitions, lectures and demonstrations as well

2. While removed from the artistic elements of producing, the managers of presenting organizations should be just as skilled in finance, marketing and personnel supervision, among other areas, as the managers who work with producing organizations

3. Some of the larger and more ambitious presenting organizations occasionally commission and actually produce a production that is included among their presentations*

4. Some of the producing organizations that supply product to various presenters are themselves presenters

5. Some producing organizations present themselves by offering their productions to presenters away from their home theatres, or by simply renting a theatre on a "four-wall" basis and absorbing all the costs themselves.

To untangle this seemingly contradictory branch of the theatre business, let's back up and consider how it got that way.

## BACKGROUND
### The First Presenters: 1830-1900

The American tradition of presenting live entertainment that has been produced by somebody else can be traced back to the lyceum bureaus, the Chautauquas and various theatre circuits that fostered touring stars and companies during the nineteenth century. Touring, of course, has been a necessary part of the presenting process since the system began.

Popular for several decades prior to the Civil War, lyceum groups sought

*See Chapter 6: "Commissions"

to disseminate information for adults about history, politics, science and the arts by offering lectures, concerts and other presentations. The lyceum bureau in a given community would select which speakers and events to offer from those available. Derived from a French word meaning "school" and from a Greek word meaning "gymnasium," such as the one in which Aristotle taught in ancient Athens, American-style lyceums gained respectability during the 1830s—even in such puritanical cities as Boston. In fact, a lyceum or "musee" offered the *only* form of theatre or dance presented in many communities, usually under a pious-sounding title that promised instruction rather than, heaven forbid, entertainment. Theatre performances, for example, might have been Shakespearean tragedies rearranged to illustrate a moral lesson and "dance" recitals were often little more than a series of *tableaux vivants* in which well-draped performers stood stock-still in a formation meant to depict some edifying moment, real or imagined.

The Chautauqua institutions, like the lyceums, were devoted to adult education in both religious and secular subjects. The first was established in upstate New York in 1874 as an annual summer activity, and thousands attended this eight-week event, taking courses in religion as well as in the arts and humanities. Chautauqua publications were written to accommodate groups of people who could not attend the institute, and lecturers were sent on the road to enhance such literature. Eventually, several hundred Chautauqua institutes were formed around the country, and each engaged speakers, musicians and various types of entertainment. In 1912, the movement was organized as a commercial enterprise: entertainers and speakers were offered on a contractual basis, touring circuits were formed and the system enjoyed considerable popularity until the mid-'20s.

While the advent of Chautauquas encouraged the careers of many local promoters and community lyceum (or booking) bureaus, they were a comparatively unsophisticated forerunner of today's professional presenting organizations. A Chautauqua program was comprised of both lectures and entertainments, the participants traveled together by train and the whole event usually took place in a tent—something between a revival meeting and a country fair. However, parallel with the growth of the Chautauqua movement was the growth in popularity of the touring combination companies,* organized to present full-length theatre productions with professional actors, including a number of stars from England and the continent. These troupes also traveled by rail, but they performed in permanent theatre buildings that had been vacated by resident companies forced out by the demand for visiting stars and companies. In essence, landlords of such theatres became presenters who were dependent upon the offerings put together by booking agencies in New York City.

---

*See Chapter 5.

Aside from the theatre managers on the road and the booking/producing agencies in New York City, there was also a kind of hybrid promoter-presenter known as an impresario. One pioneer in the art of promoting, touring and presenting on a grand scale was Phineas T. Barnum, who in the 1850s made a fortune managing the American tour of the Swedish singer Jenny Lind. While his other attractions were hardly artistic ventures, Barnum proved there was a vast American market for foreign attractions and unusual spectacles. In the 1890s, after failing as a theatre operator, a German emigre named William Morris opened the performers' agency that still bears his name and also served as a leading booking agency for vaudeville acts. Morris thus established a link between artist representation and booking that is still practiced. Impresarios of later times purveyed offerings that were somewhat more refined, but their taste for profit was equally keen: Florenz Ziegfeld; Billy Rose; and the quintessential impresario of the twentieth century, Sol Hurok. Yet impresarios are a breed apart, because they usually combine the functions of booking and presenting and, therefore, do not share profits or losses with another party.

## Booking and Producing Monopolies: 1900 - 1955

Given the uncertainties of travel, as well as a general attitude of mistrust, the first booking offices often made simultaneous engagements, and local theatre managers for their part would book two or three attractions for the same date, to cover themselves. This practice caused a chaotic situation that was partially addressed when three New York booking offices joined forces in 1900 to form the Theatrical Syndicate and soon controlled most of the nation's legitimate theatres and bookings. A similar situation developed in the field of vaudeville.

An immensely popular form of entertainment from the 1880s until 1932, when New York's Palace Theatre closed, vaudeville performances consisted of unrelated songs, sketches and acts. A number of different vaudeville circuits, each comprised of a string of theatres, were eventually absorbed into the Keith-Albee circuit, just as legit theatres fell under Syndicate control. The vaudeville monopoly did business out of B.F. Keith's United Booking Office (UBO), which was managed by E.F. Albee, whose adopted grandson was the playwright Edward Albee.

By the time the Shubert Brothers began to gain prominence both as producers and theatre landlords, theatre production in America was on the decline. By the mid-'20s, the Shuberts had secretly become a majority shareholder of UBO and also controlled well over half of all legitimate theatre bookings in the nation. And they produced about 20 percent of all road shows. By the early '50s, they had gained control of virtually all theatres still operating outside of New York, and the UBO had become their central booking office. Even when they merely booked a theatre, they took as much as 50 percent of the box office; and when box office receipts fell below a minimum, they simply booked in a new attraction and avoided any serious loss.

## Organized Audience Support: 1920-1960

Methods for organizing audience support on the road—as opposed to merely organizing control over theatres and bookings—were pioneered during the 1920s in the theatrical field when the Theatre Guild invented a subscription plan that guaranteed support for its productions. Aside from being the dominant producing company on Broadway during the '20s and '30s, the Guild could boast 30,000 subscribers in cities outside New York. In the concert field, two far-sighted promoters in Chicago, Dema Harshburger and Ward French, came up with a subscription plan that was eventually adopted by literally thousands of local music clubs. A permanent, nonprofit concert association in each city ran an intensive, annual, one-week membership drive directed by a professional organizer. The money raised became the budget for that year's attractions. Single admissions were not sold, and only members could attend the concerts. The plan was first tried in Battle Creek, Michigan, in 1920; by 1930 it had been successfully introduced in numerous cities and its operation became centralized when the two leading artist management organizations of the day, Columbia Concerts Inc. and National Artists Service, gave it both financial and artistic support. Operated today as a division of Columbia Artists Management, Inc., Community Concerts has presented countless soloists and ensembles over the years and served as a highly successful inspiration for the development of subscription audiences in all branches of the performing arts. In a later decade, the Ford Foundation became so convinced that subscription audiences were the key to a stable performing arts economy, that it hired a special consultant, Danny Newman, to help a number of nonprofit companies develop a ticket sales plan. This plan is outlined in his book *Subscribe Now!*

The history of theatrical road tours was abruptly altered in 1955 when the federal government began its anti-trust action against the Shuberts. By the next year, the courts put an end to the Shuberts' monopoly by forcing them both to sell a number of their theatres and also to stop operating the United Booking Office. When that office was closed in 1956, it created a wide-open opportunity in the theatre industry. Several groups jumped into action, notably the League of New York Theatres and Producers; the Legitimate Independent Theatres of North America (LITNA), a group of theatre mangers from outside New York City; and Columbia Artists Management, Inc. (CAMI).

The Independent Booking Office (IBO) was incorporated by the League in 1956 as a central booking office for touring legit shows. The hope was that all theatre owners and operators would join IBO, but instead, LITNA attempted to conduct its own booking activities: it charged 5 percent of the gross as its booking fee, while IBO introduced a rather modest flat fee to be paid both by the presenter and the producer. After inevitable conflicts, in 1957 the two organizations consolidated their booking interests under the IBO banner. It served the road business by booking and contracting shows as well as collecting and sharing pertinent information with its client theatres. There were twenty board members, ten from the League and ten from LITNA. While the number of playing weeks on the road experienced wide fluctuations in the '60s and '70s, IBO continued to function primarily as a booking agency until the early '80s, when its main work evolved into serving as a computerized national clearing-house for performing arts touring information. In 1985, however, IBO was dissolved, and its assets were transferred to the League for the purpose of forming a professional resource center to assist producers and presenters both on Broadway and the road. To reflect this change in its membership and services to the industry, the League of New York Theatres and Producers became the League of American Theatres and Producers—a national membership organization, not a booking agency. That work has been taken over by others.

In 1955, anticipating the demise of IBO and just twenty-five years after its founding by Arthur Judson, CAMI created the Columbia Artists Theatricals Corporation (CATC). Modelled after Community Concerts, CATC maintained a professional central staff in New York to work with volunteers in seventy-eight cities, people who were usually members of such service organizations as the Junior League. Prior to each season of four productions that CATC sent on the road (typically, there would be two musicals, a comedy and either a serious drama or a mystery), a representative from the New York office would visit each city. The season would be announced at an annual dinner, and assistance would be given in terms of publicity and ticket sales. Each volunteer group was comprised of a nucleus of members who chaired committees dealing with such areas as finance, publicity, facility rental, hospitality and, of course, subscription sales. Furthermore, each member was expected to bring ten other volunteers into the organization to assist with sales.

CATC's primary responsibility to its local constituents was to contact the services of producers who would organize the four necessary productions each year and provide the volunteer presenters with the necessary support material and information. In 1958 Ronald Wilford was invited into CAMI as general manager of this network or circuit of theatrical presenters, known by this time as the Broadway Theatre Alliance (later renamed the Broadway Theatre League). CATC never intended to produce its own productions, although it was eventually forced into this activity in order to fulfill its commitments. Perhaps because of such complications, in 1961 CATC sold its interest in the national subscription series it had created to an independent producer, Harlowe Dean, and became a temporarily dormant corporation. After a single season, the Broadway Theatre League was acquired by Julian Olney, who renamed it the National Performing Arts Company. By the mid-'60s, however, the circuit members no longer paid annual fees to a central booking agency and were free to develop their own series. For the first time in the history of touring in America, the road became decentralized. Individual presenters were free to pick and choose whatever attractions they wished from the agencies or producers they chose.

## Diversity and Expansion: 1965 - Present

A significant factor in the decentralization and growth of the road was the construction of thousands of new performing arts facilities in the '60s and '70s, most on college and university campuses. As these were often too lavish and expensive to maintain on the basis of student use alone, they opened their doors to professional performing arts presentations of every kind in order to generate needed revenues. As a result, the campus often became the cultural center of its community. And, predictably, many new booking agencies and producers anxious to cash in on a quickly widening national audience eventually sprang into operation.

In 1965 Tom Mallow founded American Theatre Productions (ATP) and quickly gained preeminence in the theatrical touring market. Operating under the banner of the American Theatre League, Mallow worked closely with local promoters and presenters without attempting to centralize road management. Then ATP created a subsidiary corporation, Janco Productions, which served as the production arm of its booking operation, thus eliminating the middleman position of the booking agency and strengthening control over both product and contract flexibility. By 1970, APT was virtually the sole bidder for the touring rights to Broadway shows. Shortly thereafter, however, CAMI decided to revive its theatrical touring activities, in part because it happened to own the touring rights to the Tony Award-winning musical, *1776*. Kenneth Olsen, who had worked with Tom Mallow at APT, was recruited to head CATC and soon revitalized its reputation by importing such prestigious companies as The Young Vic, The Royal Shakespeare Company, and the Comedie Francaise, while also vying for the rights to New York hit shows.

By the 1980s, several dozen booking agencies and/or producing companies were offering theatrical tours to presenting organizations around the country. These included CATC, ATP, Kolmar/Luth Entertainment, Katz Productions, National Artists Management Company (NAMCO), and Roadworks Productions, as well as individual producers. Like virtually all booking agencies and producers of touring productions, these are commercial, for-profit outfits, even though they often sell their products to nonprofit presenting organizations.

While the producers of touring productions and booking agencies have no membership organization of their own, the most active belong to the League of American Theatres and Producers. As discussed in Chapter 5, this organization negotiates with Actors' Equity Association and other unions. Most theatrical touring productions that employ AEA members are governed by that union's Production Contract, which includes provisions for first class touring companies as well as bus and truck companies, although some tours go out under stock, LORT or experimental bus and truck contracts. Members of the League's Road Committee are actively involved in appropriate contract negotiations. Its Department of Road Resources publishes a semimonthly newsletter and offers a variety of services to members, including computerized data regarding such matters as gross receipts for touring shows, seating and stage specifications for many venues nationwide, Broadway show statistics and the like.

On the other side of the coin, presenters have also become increasingly legitimatized in recent decades through the creation of their own professional associations and through the recognition that the nonprofit presenters among them have been recognized as a separate funding category for government, corporate and private grants and contributions.

Formerly the Association of College, University and Community Arts Administrators (ACUCAA), the Association of Performing Arts Presenters (APAP), headquartered in Washington, D.C., is the largest national membership organization for managers and administrators in the presenting field. It holds an annual conference in New York City, provides workshops there and at other locations around the country and supports research and publication. The National Association for Campus Activities (NACA) and the International Society of Performing Arts Administrators (ISPAA) also represent presenters; this last has an international membership and holds conferences both in the U.S. and abroad. Regional associations and consortia devoted largely to management issues and block-booking for presenting organizations include Arts Midwest, in Minneapolis; Mid-America Arts Alliance, in Kansas City; Mid-Atlantic States Arts Consortium, in Baltimore; Southern Arts Federation, in Atlanta; SWAP Northwest, in Seattle; and the Western Alliance of Arts Administrators (WAAA), in Santa Fe.

Until the 1970s few funding agencies regarded nonprofit presenting organizations as eligible for grants; most awards went directly to the artists and nonprofit producing companies. Finally, however, the NEA, state arts councils, and others came to realize that without the theatres, audiences and fees provided by presenting organizations, few ongoing performing arts companies could survive. After all, about one-third of most presenting organizations' budgets is spent on artist fees. To support presenters, then, became a way of supporting the companies they presented, but in a more democratic manner than direct support, because the "most presented" companies, those with appeal in many communities, benefited most. Commercial presenters, of course, are not eligible to receive grants or contributions.

By the 1980s, the business of presenting theatre and other types of performances had become a major part of the entertainment industry. And the nation's sprawling performing arts centers, from Lincoln Center to the Kennedy Center to the Los Angeles Music Center, had become the jewels on what is a very impressive "presentation" crown sitting atop the performing arts colossus in America. This is due in no small part to the fact that major performances at such centers are sometimes broadcast by both commercial and public radio and television networks. With their big budgets and even bigger audiences, the networks have become, ironically, the most sought-after sponsors ever known in the history of presenting "live" performances.

## TYPES OF THEATRICAL TOURS*

Touring was invented as a means for increasing audiences and revenues for productions beyond what they could attract by staying in one place. Summer stock packages, cabaret acts and out-of-town tryouts for Broadway shows all qualify as types of touring productions and have been discussed in previous chapters. This chapter is concerned with productions that are originated primarily for sale on a fee and/or commission basis to commercial and/or nonprofit presenting organizations.

### National Tour

Also called a national company or a first class touring production, the national tour of a New York production that has received critical acclaim or audience interest is usually sent on the road concurrent with the New York run or right after its close. It is almost always organized and controlled by the original New York producers. If one of these producers is the Shubert or Nederlander Organization, which owns theatres in several major cities, the first national company or companies may be obliged in the production agreement to play in those theatres, if they are available. Otherwise, it may be booked into another first class road house, such as the Colonial Theatre in Boston or the National Theatre in Washington, or it may play at a major presenting organization, such as the Kennedy Center or the O'Keefe Center in Toronto.

---

*See also Chapters 5 and 7.

National companies are booked into theatres according to one of two schemes:

1.   *Open-ended run*: the production will continue at the theatre as long as it earns a minimum weekly amount at the box office, similar to a Broadway theatre license

2.   *Sit-down run*: the production is booked into the theatre for a limited run, usually from four-to-twelve weeks.

## Bus and Truck Tour

A bus and truck tour may also be called the second or third national company. Its name is obviously derived from the tradition of transporting the performers by chartered bus and the scenery and costumes by rented trucks, although air travel is sometimes used for the performers. Such companies (less well-paid and less lavishly-produced than their first generation cousins) are booked into venues according to one of three schemes:

1.   *One-to-two week runs*: these might be in cities such as Seattle or St. Louis or they might play major cities some time after the first national company has departed

2.   *Split-week runs*: the production plays in two venues during the same week, usually in such secondary markets as Austin and Scranton

3.   *One-nighters*: one or two performances in a single day, often with "lay-over" periods of several days or more between performances in such markets as State College, PA, or Madison, WI, or another one of the campus venues.

## International Tour

First class productions of Broadway hits outside the United States, like first class national tours, are usually organized and controlled by the original producers. These occur in foreign capitals and often  employ performers who are citizens of those nations. Sometimes, however, fully American productions are sent on foreign tours as part of a cultural exchange program or for the purpose of performing at an international festival.

## Company-Booked Tour

Nonprofit, institutional performing arts companies have become increasingly dependent upon revenues earned from both national and international tours. Fortunately, the growing number of touring opportunities has enabled many companies to keep pace with their growing costs. Large institutions like the New York Shakespeare Festival and Lincoln Center Theater have sent out national tours of their more successful productions. More often, theatre companies organize limited tours or support special small or junior troupes that perform for public school and community audiences. Most companies whose mission is to perform almost exclusively for young audiences, like the Paper Bag Players, tour constantly. And there is a professional repertory company for adult audiences, The Acting Company, that tours exclusively. Like professional dance companies both large and small—American Ballet Theatre and the David Gordon Pickup Company are two of several hundred examples—each of these ensembles operates its own in-house booking department, which sells and manages what may be extensive annual tours produced by the company itself.

## TYPES OF VENUES

### Commercial Road Houses

There are numerous commercially-operated theatres across the nation that book national and bus and truck companies of Broadway hits and other attractions that have a perceived potential for making a profit. These facilities include the Royal Alexandra Theatre, in Toronto and the Fisher Theatre, in Detroit.

### Major Performing Arts Centers

Multi-facility performing arts centers like the Los Angeles Music Center and the Brooklyn Academy of Music may be owned by a municipality and leased to a nonprofit operating corporation; they often have constituent performing arts companies in residence, such as a symphony orchestra and a theatre group, and they usually operate as presenters at least part of the time. They may also make their facilities available to outside groups on a rental basis.

### College and University Performance Facilities

Campus facilities may be large performing arts complexes equipped with state-of-the-art technical systems, like the Krannert Center at the University of Illinois; or more modest, single-use theatres, like the Spingold at Brandeis University. Many are used jointly for student productions and booked-in professional attractions.

### Civic Centers, Auditoriums, Halls, and Other Facilities

Built by a city or county and operated with civic funds, these facilities are usually part of a civic complex of some type and usually service a variety of functions: town meetings, conventions, public performances produced by amateur groups or professional performances booked in by local promoters or community arts bureaus.

## Public School Facilities

Many auditoriums, gymnasiums and cafeterias in public schools are used for student activities, as well as for community meetings and public performances.

## Mixed-Use Noncommercial Facilities

Hospitals, clinics, libraries, community centers, museums, war memorials, ethnic and multicultural centers, religious facilities, and social-service clubs often make their buildings available for both amateur and professional performances, especially in small or developing communities.

## Mixed-Use Commercial Facilities

Gambling casinos and hotels, like those in Las Vegas and Atlantic City, are famous for their lavish entertainment. Mixed-use developments like Toronto's HarborFront, as well as cabarets, cafes and restaurants also present performances.

## Festivals

There are several hundred annual performing arts festivals in the United States and Canada alone, including the Spoleto Festival USA in Charleston, South Carolina, and the Chicago International Theatre Festival. These may operate as producers or presenters or both. Internationally, there are thousands of such festivals, and American artists and companies are becoming increasingly involved with them. Until recently there had been virtually no financial assistance available to support such activity, although the United States Information Agency (USIA) and such organizations as the International Theatre Institute (ITI) have provided nonmonetary help for selected touring projects for some time. In 1988, however, USIA, NEA, the Rockefeller Foundation and others entered into partnership to create the Fund for U.S. Artists at International Festivals and Exhibitions, the resources of which are largely administered by Arts International in New York City. This aims to provide about $1 million each year to help support selected applicants at foreign festivals and exhibitions. A modest sum, but it should help to make the arts in America more visible abroad.

# THE ROLE OF THE BOOKING OFFICE

## Acquiring the Product

Assuming that the booking agency and producing company are not part of the same operation, the former must acquire the rights to represent a particular attraction on the road for a specified length of time. In terms of a current or recent Broadway or Off-Broadway show, this usually involves negotiating with the New York producer for the bus and truck rights. Booking agencies can acquire such rights because the original producer often lacks either the expertise or the inclination to organize road tours and would rather sit back and collect royalties, which are usually based on the road company's share of the box office income. This figure includes a minimum guarantee plus any overages plus royalties. For example, the deal might call for a $195,000 guarantee plus 12 percent royalties (on net adjusted gross box office) plus a 60/40 percent split of net adjusted gross, after local documented expenses, and a $10,000 promoter profit have been paid. So on a net gross of $550,000 with $150,000 in local expenses exclusive of the guarantee and royalties, the company share will be $338,400. Royalty participants are then paid on the basis of that figure. Here's another way of looking at it:

| | | | |
|---|---|---|---|
| Net gross | $550,000 | | |
| 12% royalty | 66,000 | | |
| Local expense | 150,000 | | |
| Promoter profit | 10,000 | | |
| Guarantee | 195,000 | | |
| Overage | 129,000 | 60% to company | = 77,400 |
| | 40% to promoter | = 51,600 | |

Total company share:  $338,400
Total promoter share:  $211,600

When there is no producer with whom to negotiate, as in the case of an original production or a new production of a revival, the agent negotiates with whoever owns the copyright or touring rights to the property in question. This might necessitate dealing with a licensing agency, such as Samuel French or the Tams Witmark Music Library, which would add another fee to the costs and further dilute any profits. In the case of one-person shows, like Hal Holbrook's *Mark Twain Tonight*, the agent usually negotiates with the artist. When hoping to arrange a tour for an established ensemble company, like Ireland's Abbey Theatre, the agent would negotiate with that company's top management. Or some independent artist, producer or packager might approach the booking agent about a revival or some special attraction that could be put together for the road. Quite a few projects are born because a particular star wishes to go on the road. The reason for this is seldom magnanimous; usually it has to do with the star's desire to revitalize a sagging career or bank account or both. The road is often used as a means of persuading producers that a performer still has what it takes, despite all kinds of rumors and evidence to the contrary; and either a booking agent or some other party might initiate the proposal. Most never come to fruition, because usually it is decided that the star lacks sufficient commercial viability.

In short, it is the booking agent's job to keep abreast of product availability (including stars, hit shows and new projects) and, just as important, to know the road markets ("Will it play in Dubuque?").

The agreement between the booking agency and the party that controls the touring rights (called a managerial agreement) is usually drawn up either on a "best efforts" or "minimum guarantee" basis. The former is used when there is a very uncertain market for the product and it gives the agency time to drop the project without penalty if a profitable tour does not appear likely. Conversely, the latter agreement is used when the show or star has known value at the box office and it guarantees a minimum number of performances and/or minimum revenues. When such minimums are not met, the booking agency must still pay the fees that were lost as a result. Standard items contained in the touring rights agreement include:

1. The period of time during which the booking agency has permission to book the property
2. The geographical territory in which the property may be booked
3. How any fees, percentages and/or royalties will be determined, collected and paid
4. Artistic conditions, if any, related to such matters as direction, casting or script revision
5. Travel, technical and performance requirements.

## Selecting a Producer

Once the touring rights have been secured, the booking agency must find a producer to organize the production and manage the tour. Several New York companies, like K L Management and Pace Theatricals, specialize in producing and/or general managing road productions. Other companies, like ATP/JANCO, serve as both producer and booking agency. Or, of course, the original New York producer may also produce the touring versions of a show. When two different parties are involved in the process—which is usually the case—a managerial agreement is drawn up between them. This assigns the production rights to the producer while permitting the agent exclusive rights to sell engagements of the production to local promoters, theatre managers and presenters. It is also likely to cover such points as:

1. Financial obligations of both parties to the agreement regarding such costs as travel, production design and construction, company lodg-

ings and food, publicity and promotion

2. Financial compensation to be received by both parties and the method used to compute such payments (i.e. flat fees or percentages of box office revenues) and how these may be increased after the tour has reached its break-even point
3. How payments will be collected and distributed
4. What artistic rights will be controlled by each party (such as selection of a star or director)
5. How penalties and/or losses will be absorbed.

This last point requires further comment.

Despite the best attempts of the most brilliant booking agent, no bus and truck tour is going to end up filling every available date as well as complying with every union rule and regulation. The most common infractions involve AEA and its regulations concerning travel, extra performances and overtime. IATSE overtime for load-ins and load-outs is also common when travel time between venues is tight. The booking agency may decide to schedule an extra performance in a given week for which the union will require additional compensation for its members. The booking agent, of course, should be aware of all such penalties before contracts are signed and should be certain that they will be more than offset by increased earnings. In other cases, penalties and loss of performances may be caused by the production company. The managerial agreement between the producer and the booking agency, then, must stipulate how costs and losses related to such matters will be covered. Sometimes both parties split them, but often there is an uneven split. This can make the final computation of the agency's commission and the company's share a rather complex matter.

## Budgeting the Tour

The party that fills the role of producer must hire a general manager to work with the booking office for the purpose of estimating the costs of the production and tour. An initial budget is drawn up long before the show goes into rehearsal. This is used to determine the preproduction costs and the weekly operating costs. Based on these figures, the booking agency will decide how much to charge each presenter. Of course, the sooner a tour earns back its preproduction costs while also earning its weekly operating costs, the sooner it will become profitable. This may take a few engagements, many engagements over a few months, or the tour may never show a profit.

The three parties involved in the touring process (producer, booking agency and presenter) usually divide expenses according to the following formula:

1. The producer's costs include all of the normal preproduction and weekly operating expenses for the production itself:
   a. artists' salaries, benefits, per diems
   b. salaries, benefits, per diems of general manager and touring staff (company manager, stage manager(s), press agent, etc.
   c. sets
   d. costumes
   e. lighting designs
   f. rental of touring sound and lighting equipment
   g. royalties and fees
   h. company and production transportation
   i. advertising, press and promotional material
   j. refundable bonds.

2. The booking agency's costs include a prorated share of its general, fixed operating expenses plus the expenses of selling and booking the production in question:
   a. office rent
   b. overhead
   c. staff salaries and benefits
   d. telephone
   e. postage
   f. printing of booking sales material
   g. travel costs for sales representatives

3. The presenter's costs, aside from a production fee that represents a prorated share of the above expenses and, usually, a commission and/or percentage of the gross, include all the expenses involved in promoting and presenting the attraction in the local venue, such as:
   a. theatre rental or operation costs
   b. box office staff
   c. front-of-house staff
   d. stage crews
   e. wardrobe and loaders
   f. local musicians
   g. security
   h. all local advertising and promotion costs
   i. hospitality
   j. workshops, demonstrations or residencies led by members of the visiting company

The tour budget, as implicit in the above lists, only takes into account the producer's and booker's expenses. The presenter must then add all of the local costs to determine the actual amount that the attraction will cost for the local engagement.

## Selling and Routing the Tour

When the rights, the production deal and the budget have been worked out; the booking agency prepares promotional material about the attraction and sends it to potential presenters; then sales people from the booking office begin to contact local presenters by phone.    It is no coincidence that booking and touring came of age with the invention of the telephone—ever since, managers at both ends of the line seem to have been surgically affixed to the instrument!

When the attraction is a recent New York hit or features one or two popular stars, presenters basically accept whatever engagement date they are offered, thus making the booking agent's job an easy one. More often, the box office potential of the attraction is "ify," and the job of putting together a profitable tour is a nightmare. As the booking agent begins talking with various presenters, potential performance dates and locations are penciled into a calendar or routing sheet. Or, of course, bookings can be entered into a computer that is programmed to provide detailed information about each venue, such as seating capacity and stage specifications. The initial schedule of engagements is called a "ghost route," because it is very tentative and will be changed a number of times. Paradoxically, when a presenter is trying to lock in a date so it can be announced to local ticket  buyers, the booking agency cannot make a firm commitment because not enough dates are firm enough to determine the final route. Then, when the agency is ready to firm things up, the presenter wants extra time to decide between different dates or attractions.

Agents who are routing extensive tours that will play split weeks or one-night stands usually begin the routing process by assigning a specific time period for each geographical market where the attraction will tour: four weeks in Texas, for example, or six weeks in the southern states. Large booking agencies may assign a different sales agent to each of the nation's regions (the northeast, the midwest, the south and so on). This permits salespeople and presenters to develop an informed, personalized relationship. As with routing any tour, the goal is to gain as many bookings, in as many high-grossing venues, in as small a geographical area, as possible. So the shorter the travel distance between venues the better. Actors' Equity, of course, places limits on travel between engagements, both in terms of time and distance. And these limits are shorter on days with matinee performances than on those without. A performance-free day is required each week, and a day free of both travel and performance is required twice each month. The amount of load-in and load-out time required for the attraction will also dictate the necessary time lapse between performances in different venues. National tours playing sit-down runs of one to twelve weeks may allow two days for a load-in, whereas bus and truck tours must usually limit this process to eight or ten hours.

In 1986, Equity and the League of American Theatres and Producers established a joint Bus and Truck Committee to monitor the implementation of a Bus and Truck Experimental Contract that was, in effect, appended to the Production Contract. Typically, the regulations are very specific and provide booking agents and tour managers little latitude for miscalculation. For example, the contracts gives the following schedule of maximum hours and miles that a bus and truck company is permitted to travel each day, depending on the number of performances it gives:

Double performance days:     3 hours or 165 miles,*
Single performance days:     7 hours or 385 miles
Non-performance days:     9 hours or 495 miles

*Or the number of permissible travel hours by road multiplied by the current legal speed limit.

The contract goes on to stipulate how travel time will be calculated and what penalties will be imposed when the rules are broken. A company manager must usually travel with the company and be present for hotel check-ins and check-outs to deal with complaints and, on behalf of the producer, clock the travel time. Company managers for national tours, incidentally, must be members of ATPAM, while others need not. The pay is usually high for this job—and so is the burn-out rate.

Aside from sponsor interest, availability of playing dates, distance, union regulations, and, sometimes, grant money to help support a booking, the human element in routing and booking a tour also plays a key role. Virtually all the deals made in this business begin as verbal agreements over the phone. The several weeks that may elapse between that agreement time and the time when a formal contract is signed and returned is crucial. If one party backs out of a verbal agreement during that time, an entire tour or an entire season of attractions may be placed in jeopardy. For this reason the reliability of agents and presenters is highly valued, and those who build up a reputation for being unreliable seldom remain in the business for long.

Once key engagement dates have been locked in with signed contracts, the tour becomes inevitable, and the booking agency must do everything possible to fill in the open dates, even lowering the booking fees as a last resort. Only when all available dates have been booked and the last contract signed and returned—sometimes as much as a year before the engagement or as little as a week—is the sales process complete.

## Contracting the Tour

When the booking agency has received a reasonable number of assurances from presenters, and when ghost routes look as if they will materialize into a visible tour, the agency begins to negotiate specific terms with specific presenters and then sends out contracts that contain those terms. From now until the tour is complete, routing and contracting proceed apace.

In cases where the booking agency has assigned the touring rights for a given attraction to an independent producer, all booking contracts are basically an agreement between the presenter and the producer. The booking agency acts as an intermediary between those two parties and may even sign contracts on behalf of the producer but disclaims any legal responsibility or liability in the event that contractual terms are not upheld by either. A crucial factor in any type of contracting process is that of accountability—knowing what a contract contains and where it is at every moment. Any number of hand-written or computerized systems to monitor the contents and whereabouts of various contracts may be used; all should leave as little to chance and human error as possible. This will require a system that records each step in the contracting:

1. What was done (contract sent to accountant to verify terms, contract sent to sponsor for signature, contract held for decision, etc.)
2. When it was done (indicate the full date)
3. Who did it (signature or initial).

Most booking agencies have devised a basic form contract that has been printed and bound together with four to six carbon duplicates. These provide blank spaces where specific names, dates and conditions may be filled in. Copies of the fully executed and signed contract will go to the booking agency, the presenter, the producer, the general manager, the company manager, and, in large agencies, to a publicity department, a financial department and a legal department.

The basic form contract contains numerous fairly standard items related to the presenter's obligations to the booking agency and the production. Attached to this contract there may be a lengthy and detailed rider or addendum that relates to the particular needs of the attraction and specifies further presenter obligations, such as sound equipment, space in the house for a lighting console and the like.* Each and every item in a contract and its attachments is subject to negotiation. Each and every item should be care-

---

*See Appendix C for sample contract and addendum.

fully scrutinized. So many changes may be negotiated, in fact, that it could be necessary to destroy the original contract and issue superseding ones until everything is clearly written in and agreed to by both parties.

## Negotiating Booking Fees and Commissions

As discussed earlier, the managerial agreement between the producer and the booking agency will specify the tour's break-even point, which is the minimum amount that the agency must pay the producer each week, either through a "best efforts" or a guarantee arrangement. The asking fee for the attraction, however, is determined by the agency and then negotiated with the interested presenters. The financial terms finally agreed upon in most booking contracts employ one of three basic formats: (a) the payment of a flat fee or guarantee; (b) the payment of a negotiated percentage of the box office gross; (c) a combination of both (a) and (b); and (d) a straight four-wall arrangement in which the producer pays for *all* production as well as local operating costs and then takes *all* the revenue.

The flat fee arrangement is, of course, the simplest possibility and is used when limited seating capacity, the nature of the potential audience or the reliability of the presenter casts serious doubts about the profitability of a percentage deal. As with all negotiations, the booking agent's knowledge of the presenters and their audiences is important.

When negotiating a percentage deal there are any number of possibilities. It is a process that always involves a gamble by both parties, because one party inevitably comes out better than the other. Neither party need necessarily lose—but one will do better. Knowledge (especially of product, market and mathematics) is the key to profitable negotiation. The most common percentage agreements include:

1. A straight percentage of the total box office gross
2. A minimum guaranteed fee against a percentage of the gross, whichever is higher
3. A minimum guaranteed fee plus a percentage of the gross.

There are also arrangements that guarantee the local presenter against losses, although these are less common. For instance, the contract might stipulate that the artist or attraction will receive the entire box office gross after local expenses have been deducted, or a percentage of the gross after expenses.

Whenever the financial arrangement calls for more than a flat fee, the seating manifest, ticket scale, potential gross, discount policy, ticket taxes, and allowable complimentary tickets all become part of the contract, because they will impact on the percentage earnings that were negotiated.

In some cases, the booking agency collects the production fees from the presenters, deducts its own commission and delivers the rest to the producer on a weekly basis. In other cases the producer collects the fee (it is actually paid to the company manager who is traveling with the production) and sends the booking commission along on a weekly basis. Any advance payments made by the presenter, of course, must be figured into the final settlement.

## THE ROLE OF THE PRODUCER

### Mounting the Production

Equity shows that are sent on tour directly after some type of regular run and require few cast or production changes may need almost no extra rehearsal time, all of which greatly reduces the cost of the tour. However, most tours under an Equity contract rehearse from three to six weeks before starting their travels, depending upon whether or not they are musicals. But the rehearsal and production process does not begin until shortly before the first road engagement.

As the subsequent chapters of this book deal with the managerial aspects of theatre production, such as budgeting and advertising, it is not necessary to discuss those matters here; the tour producer must follow the same steps as other theatrical producers. But there are a few matters unique to tour management that do deserve mention. Especially germane are the duties and responsibilities of three key managers who work for the producer: the general manager, the company manager and the production stage manager.

### The General Manager

The producer's first lieutenant in the battle to win profits from the road is the general manager. This position may be filled by an associate or employee of the producer, by an independent general manager or, in rare cases, by the producer in a double role. In any case, the general manager works with the booking agency early on to determine what costs and other obligations are demanded by the attraction in question. If the attraction is a current or recent theatre production, this process may begin with a check on the initial set of production contracts to discover which, if any, of the original creative team have the right of first refusal to work on subsequent productions and to determine the size of the royalty package those contracts mandate in terms of road performances. Other factors that may have a major influence on the cost of a tour include:

1. The size of the physical production and the number of trucks necessary to move it, and the number of stagehands necessary to load, unload, assemble and operate it

2. Whether or not existing sets and costumes can be used
3. Whether or not the orchestrations can be adapted to fewer musicians without losing the desired effect
4. Whether or not the number of performers can be reduced
5. The costs involved in designing and building scenery that can withstand the necessary travel, set-up and break-down
6. Star salaries and percentages (often the largest single expense) and other royalties, fees and commissions.

The general manager or a production coordinator may also work with designers and a master carpenter to put together a production rider or technical addendum to the booking contract; this will give local presenters a clear idea of the hidden expenses related to such matters as dressing room requirements, star amenities and the number of stagehands and musicians who must be hired locally. The former must often be members of IATSE, in which case the show is called a "yellow card" attraction. The producer informs the presenter about how many IATSE workers must be hired with skills in such areas as electrics, props, wardrobe and carpentry for the load-in, performances and load-out. The appropriate union members are then pulled from the card files of the local IATSE and sent on the job. Musicians not touring with the show are usually AFM members and are often hired through a local contractor who specializes in supplying talent for visiting shows and who may also be a promoter.

When time is at a premium, as it always is on tour, the more advance, detailed notice given to the local presenter the better. Of course, some presenting organizations and local promoters are oblivious to advance information—the mere mention of their names can make experienced "roadies" cringe. In these cases especially, seasoned producers phone ahead frequently or send a production coordinator ahead to help prepare for a smooth load-in and engagement.

As the tour develops and contracts begin to come in from local presenters, the general manager checks them on behalf of the producer, particularly in regard to financial terms and touring logistics. Then, when the time is ripe to organize the touring production itself, the general manager must oversee and often execute all of the production contracts and agreements with performers, director, choreographer, conductor, designers, company manager, stage manager(s) and any others who will travel with the tour. Also, arrangements must be made to construct the costumes and scenery, rent the necessary trucks and buses as well as any traveling sound and lighting equipment, buy insurance, rent rehearsal facilities and, finally, send the whole motley mess on the road and hope that, by opening night, it metamorphoses into something worthy of applause!

Whatever happens on stage, the general manager continues as an active off-stage player throughout the tour. All of the traveling personnel—artistic, technical and managerial—must be cared for, managed and paid. Fees and royalties must be collected, adjustments dictated by penalties and lost performances must be made, disbursements must be handed out, and disagreements with the unions as well as the presenters must be resolved. And all such responsibilities must observe deadlines dictated by curtain times and union rules, even though the general manager is sitting in an office thousands of miles away.

## The Company Manager

As soon as engagements look firm, someone must begin to make housing arrangements for the traveling company. This responsibility is taken over by a company manager as soon as this position is filled. Union rules determine many factors that must be taken into account when hotel rooms or other accommodations are being booked.* Fall bus and truck routing is considered the most difficult because the company is often competing with university football weekends for room reservations. The company manager may also book airplane tickets when these are necessary.

Once the production is actually on the road, the company manager is the producer's top on-site representative. Whoever is hired must be very familiar with contracts in order to represent accurately the producer's interests at settlement time. There may be daily phone contact between the general manager and the company manager. Financial settlements, box office statements, programs, check registers, petty cash reconciliations and media reviews must be sent to the general manager weekly. Conversely, the general manager must send out payroll and other checks together with updated routing and technical information. Weekly payroll preparation is never a routine matter. Factors such as percentages, overtime, additional services, and missed performances always prevent any two payrolls from being identical.

With so many of the company manager's responsibilities pertaining to money, the producer obviously hopes for an honest employee in the job. Unfortunately, this has not always been the case. In fact, the word "ice" (which in the theatre business has come to mean money stolen from company funds) originated on the road. Dishonest company managers, the story goes, would routinely write "incidental company expenses," or "I.C.E.," in their account books for amounts they had put into their own pockets!

## The Production Stage Manager

The production stage manager who travels with the show also serves as a vital link with the producer and general manager, especially in regard

---

*See also Chapter 7, "AEA Rules Pertaining to Actors Away From Home."     275

to artistic and technical matters. Together with the company manager, the stage manager helps to set and maintain company morale. Often the grueling and narrowly focused life on the road causes people to lose perspective. Tempers flare up, grudges grow into feuds, and suddenly the company is divided into factions. Obviously, it pays to have someone on board the bus who can prevent this from happening.

## Promotional Support and Marketing

The booking contract usually states a minimum amount of money that the producer agrees to absorb for the local "media buy." The producer's office or press agent works with the local presenter or marketing director to coordinate this buy. In addition, the producer supplies heralds, posters, logos, advertising copy and copy for news releases, radio and television commercials—the latter may be actual prerecorded audio or video tapes. The star may also record telephone interviews with local radio stations well before the show arrives. On tour, the press agent works closely with the company manager and stage manager to maximize the limited amount of time the star gives for interviews and promotional appearances. Reports on box office "wraps" (money taken in each day) and advances from the venues where the attraction has been booked are used to determine where additional advertising and publicity are necessary. Promotion experts either from the producer's or the booker's office may then be sent to venues where single ticket sales need beefing up.

The marketing process for a touring production may involve researching population demographics in order to select the prime venues for a particular show; for example, communities with high Black populations might be considered ideal for *The Wiz*. The process may involve putting together corporate sponsorships for an attraction either in underwriting or in media trade-offs. These arrangements may be made by a marketing firm working on a percentage basis; by the press agent; or by another of the producer's employees.*

## THE ROLE OF THE PRESENTER

### Management

Presenters are theatre managers who, as a rule, are not directly involved in theatrical production, although they should be familiar with all other aspects of theatre management (these are discussed elsewhere in this book). A few words might be said, however, about the special skills that presenters should possess in regard to negotiating their booking contracts and hosting their attractions.

*See Chapters 15, 16 and 17.

## Contract Negotiation

Before starting to negotiate with booking agents, the presenter must know that a particular performance space is available and must also know its exact seating and production specifications. In addition, the presenter must be very familiar with the audience potential. This is easiest with many seasons of experience and when there is a subscription audience. Knowing what the scale of ticket prices will be (and whether or not this may be raised or lowered to suit particular attractions) means knowing the gross potentials for each performance or series of performances. Finally, the presenter must have a close approximation of all the expenses required to operate the venue and manage the season. Only when armed with this information is the presenter ready to begin negotiating for the most promising attractions.

As noted earlier, the booking agent sets an asking price for the attraction and this is the starting point for contract negotiations. To the local operating costs the presenter now adds the basic cost of the attraction, which is most often set as a minimum guaranteed fee. Potential income from house-operated concessions such as food, drink, parking and coat checking operations might then be added, although the sum is usually negligible. (Other concessions, like souvenir book and record sales in the lobby, may be operated by the production company without any potential revenue for the presenter.) At this point the presenter should be able to decide if there is enough margin for profit between the anticipated income and the anticipated expenses to warrant booking a particular attraction. If so, this is when percentage terms might enter into the negotiations. The most common types of percentage deals have been discussed earlier in this chapter. But, just as agents should not negotiate percentage deals with presenters with whom they are unfamiliar, neither should presenters negotiate such deals unless they are very familiar with their audience tastes and potential. Negotiating percentage agreements takes a skill for quick figuring and fast thinking.

The most frequently-heard complaint among presenters concerns cancellations and the near impossibility of protecting one's organization against them. Several of the presenters' membership associations are addressing this problem and may one day be able to improve the booking system in this regard.

## Block-Booking

When a number of different presenters in a particular geographical area share similar programming interests that are normally limited to one-night or split-week engagements, they sometimes negotiate with booking agents as a group and strengthen their bargaining clout. By giving agents a block of time that can be booked solid within reasonable traveling distances, such a consortium can usually buy attractions at reduced rates and also have more assurance that the dates will be firm. Quite a few presenter consortia exist around the nation.

## Covering Losses

Most nonprofit presenting organizations are connected to a larger institution, such as a university, or are themselves an on-going institution, like the Kennedy Center, and can absorb a reasonable amount of unexpected loss in ticket revenues. But independent promoters, who often operate without any real capital, are not as prepared to meet such losses; one serious failure at the box office might put them permanently out of business. To protect themselves, such promoters find a company or an individual to cover any losses for specified attractions in exchange for 50 percent of any profits. Unlike investors in a limited partnership agreement, these backers need not advance any money unless there is a loss, yet could also realize a considerable gain. Nor do promoters advance any money to booking agents, as most expenses are paid after the curtain is up and the money is in the box office. Given such arrangements as these, it is easy to understand how promoters can operate without reserve capital.

## Hosting the Attraction

A very large part of the management function in the performing arts field is that of hosting. But, as with society in general, there are very few good hosts or hostesses within the performing arts management profession. Yet making visiting artists and support personnel feel "at home" and even loved in a particular theatre is at the core of good management. When such reactions are achieved, it is always much easier to conduct business. The presenting organization, the presenter, the manager, the venue—all become favored in the eyes of producers, bookers, stars, tour managers and roadies. And, of course, the audience benefits most of all.

What are some of the things a presenter can do to insure the happiness and tranquility of a visiting attraction?

1. Study all advance information about the attraction, request more when necessary and try to provide more than is required
2. Personally greet the arriving company with as many "hands on deck" as possible—never leave this obligation to underlings
3. Be certain that all contractual promises are met. If the star is supposed to make personal appearances, if a workshop or lecture is part of the deal or if there is a shared concession deal, be certain that these terms are upheld, or reduce what is paid in the final settlement

4. Remember that artists are special; remember that they would rather be home than staying in a strange motel; and remember not to over-burden them with unnecessary introductions or appearances

5. Provide whatever amenities are affordable: flowers in hotel and dressing rooms; fruit; champagne; or just a hug and a "hello." But provide something meaningful and personal

6. Workshops, demonstrations and lectures can often be arranged with visiting artists; this may bring them some welcome additional income and may bring the organization additional grants. It may also serve to relate the presenting organization to other, local institutions such as schools and hospitals and thereby enhance its esteem and value in the community

7. Be just as courteous in saying "good-bye" as in saying "hello"

8. Follow up each engagement by communications with the booking agent, the producer's office, the star, the media and the audience—this will provide valuable feedback and help to cement relationships.

## SUMMATION

There are different types of presenting organizations, and as wide a range of venues in which performances may be presented as there are different kinds of attractions. Theatrical productions probably represent less than 20 percent of all performances presented in America, but that is still a significant amount of production. Just as there is a whole network of artists, managers, agents and promoters who are involved in presenting serious music and dance performances, and another involved in presenting popular music events, so there is a network of specialists and a professional schema that has evolved around the tradition of presenting theatre performances.

Although there are important exceptions, the presenting process usually entails a three-way relationship among a producer, a presenter and a booking agent. The unique role played by the booking agent is what most distinguishes the presenting process from other methods of producing. The booking agent is, of course, a "middleman." But the complexities of getting a particular attraction to perform at a particular venue at a particular time for a particular cost apparently require skilled matchmakers. In any case, booking agents have been operating more or less as they do today for about a hundred years and are likely to continue doing so for as long as there are roads to travel.

# Part III

# Financial Management of the Theatre

# 11

# Budget Planning

A budget is a financial estimate of *future* expenses and revenues. It attempts to predict how much something will cost and how much it will earn and/or attract from all possible sources. In other words, budgeting is guessing.

A financial statement is documentation of *past* expenses and revenues. It attempts to record actual financial performance. In other words, financial statements show history. But, as we have learned, figures do not always add up to the truth.

So if budgets cannot be written in granite, and if financial statements are not to be taken as proof positive, why bother with them? Because they are among the best tools we have for the exercise of sound yet creative management. Hence, this chapter will discuss the two opposites in the budgetary process: costs and revenues—or, how it takes one hand to wash the other!

## GENERAL BUDGETARY CONSIDERATIONS
### Planning and Using a Budget

Financial planning is a process that should be indulged soberly, conservatively and even pessimistically before serious work begins on the project at hand, before contracts are signed, before commitments are made. Accurate financial planning depends on the experience and expertise of the person or people who devise it. Generally speaking, everybody within an organization who will eventually have an impact on expenditures or earnings should be involved in the budget-planning process; this will increase both accuracy and control. While methods for doing this are discussed in the next chapter, it ought to be said here that, once adopted, no budget should be adhered to with fanatic zeal. As policies, plans, costs and income change, the figures in the budget must be revised. And, of course, a budget must be flexible enough to deal with unanticipated emergencies and unforeseen expenses. Nonetheless, when used as the well-informed and intelligent guess that it should be, a budget is a good thermometer for measuring the fiscal health of a particular project or organization.

## Zero-Based vs Incremental Budgeting

Many ongoing companies and institutions begin the annual budget process by digging out the previous year's budget or financial statement. Then, figures for the new budget are simply based on last year's figures, plus an increase that takes inflation and operational growth into account. Such incremental budgeting is fine when the financial climate is steady, and when the company wishes to continue the same policies and methods of operation as in the past. But when this is not the case, zero-based budgeting probably offers a better approach. This requires that every dollar be justified from the first—it requires annual, *full* dollar justification. This tends to encourage deeper analytical thinking about finances and, hence, about policies and priorities.

Because the largest budget area for a performing arts company is that of production, and because each production is unique, most of the budgeting in this field is zero-based due to the nature of the product. Ongoing operating budgets might be designed incrementally, but only when the theatre organization operates under the umbrella of a secure parent institution or a huge endowment fund. Production budgets, such as those illustrated later in this chapter, are often problematic in that a series of productions is being budgeted for the same season. This encourages comparative analysis and also, as we will see, permits more flexibility than if each production were planned independently.

## The Contingency

Most budgets should contain a "miscellaneous" contingency or reserve fund. It would be even safer to include both a miscellaneous and a contingency fund. And the dollar amount in such funds should represent no less than 10 percent of the total budget estimation. A miscellaneous fund is intended to provide money for minor but unexpected costs: overtime payments to workers, increases in costs due to inflation, minor unanticipated expenses and other factors that are easy to ignore or underestimate. The contingency fund, on the other hand, is intended to provide financial insurance against costly emergencies that may and often do occur in the theatre: cancelled performances, unexpectedly poor box office receipts, fire, flood and other such major factors. The absence of such reserve money can spell big trouble when disaster strikes. Unfortunately, many budget allocations—such as those from college, university and government institutions or agencies—do not recognize or provide contingency funds. In this case, the organization or department making budget requests is virtually forced to overestimate its costs and thereby create a built-in contingency. Once such allocations are received, if the amounts were *not* purposely inflated, the recipient must usually readjust budget commitments to provide for miscellaneous and unexpected costs. When every dollar is closely and specifically budgeted, slavish adherence to the budget is a likely—and undesirable—result.

## Deficit Spending

While it usually "takes money to make money," it is a peculiarity of fundraising that it may take a deficit to gain more revenue. Many nonprofit organizations believe that if they maintain sizable cash assets and are therefore known as a "rich" organization, they will not easily be able to attract contributions. After all, who gives charity to the rich? And, while it might be possible for a nonprofit company to build up its cash reserves by economizing, what would this do to the quality of its work? The money that comes in, after all, is meant to further its stated mission and goals, not to compromise them. The line between solvency and bankruptcy is often a very thin one; the line between quality and mediocrity is a very broad one. Deficits, consequently, are a fact of life for most serious, nonprofit theatres. And most have the ability to carry a limited deficit all of the time and a large deficit some of the time. The seriousness of deficits is frequently exaggerated by the press, which may even be encouraged in this view by the deficit organization itself because it is seeking to dramatize its financial need and thereby attract grants and contributions. After all, one must usually prove a *need* for subsidy before one is going to *get* subsidy. On the other hand, if the organization cannot prove its value to society as well as its financial need, then fundraising efforts will seldom be successful. Also, there is the old danger of crying "Wolf!" once too often.

## Cost-Averaging

Theatres that offer a season or series of different productions often plan in terms of *average* box office income and *average* costs so that popular shows can "carry" less popular ones, and expensive productions are balanced by inexpensive ones. This permits a greater range of production than is possible on Broadway, where each show is a completely separate enterprise. It is also a practice that emphasizes the overall picture rather than each production. And it provides an average weekly or per-production operating figure that may sometimes serve as a break-even point for the purpose of paying royalties and percentages, or for the purpose of estimating profits, which are also called "marginal revenue." Royalties and percentages are variable costs determined by the actual box office gross. Let 's say that a star is guaranteed a weekly salary of $2,000 against a percentage of 25 percent over the break-even point. If the theatre determines its break-even (weekly operating cost) at an average of $18,000, this means that the star will earn a percentage of box office income only when it exceeds $18,000, but that a $2,000 salary is assured whatever the box office gross turns out to be. And if the average operating cost for that week was higher than the actual operating cost, then management got a bargain.

Cost-averaging helps to show a general profile of projected or actual costs and revenues. Figures are averaged over a series of units, which may be performances, weeks, productions or whole seasons.

## The Variable Cost

In large commercial operations and presenting organizations especially, many costs—such as rent, performer fees, booking fees and royalties paid to the creative team—are tied to the actual box office gross and cannot be determined until that figure is known. Small professional companies and most nonprofessional groups pay flat royalty amounts simply determined by the number of performances; rarely are they involved in any percentage deals.

Variable costs dictate that there will be a difference between the fixed weekly operating cost and the actual weekly operating cost for a production. Basically, this means that the higher the box office gross, the higher the royalties and percentage payments will be. So the estimated weekly operating cost is not a static figure. The fixed costs *plus* the variable costs at the actual box office gross are what finally tell the true story.

## The Marginal Cost

An operating budget is always based on the assumption that the producing organization will present a certain number of productions and a certain number of performances per production and per week. When the cost of doing this is averaged out among all the performances, the resulting figure represents the "per-unit cost" of producing a product (in theatre the unit is either a single performance, a week or a season of performances). As any manufacturer knows, it is cheaper to produce one hundred units of the same product than one hundred different products. Live theatre's inability to do this is the core of its economic dilemma. Hollywood can produce one hundred different prints of the same film for showing in one hundred different movie houses simultaneously, and all for about the same investment and the same number of employee hours it would take to produce a single print of the film. Live theatre, on the other hand, cannot even approach such mass production. Yet, there are several ways live theatre may be able to decrease its per-unit cost. One of these, when business warrants it, is to increase the number of performances presented in a given week or the number of productions presented in a given season at the same theatre. Capital, operating and production expenses remain essentially the same whether a theatre presents four or eight performances per week. If the budget is based on a schedule of eight performances per week, and the show is a smash hit, the producing organization may wish to know how much extra cost would be involved to present a ninth performance during that week. The figure that answers this question is called the marginal cost, as illustrated in the budget for a twelve-week community theatre season at the end of this chapter. It shows how the per-unit cost decreases as production of the units increases.

## FOUR BIG VARIABLES IN COST-ESTIMATING

The most common variables that should be taken into account when drafting a budget for a theatrical project are:

1.  Whether or not it operates under union contracts
2.  Whether it is independent or affiliated with some other group or institution
3.  General overhead and maintenance costs
4.  Whether it plans a single production or a series
5.  Whether it rents or operates its own facility
6.  The seating capacity of the facility
7.  Whether it is commercial or nonprofit
8.  The physical condition of the facility
9.  The location of the facility
10. The nature of the production(s) being offered
11. The number of performances (per day, week and season)
12. The total anticipated revenues from all sources.

Theatre budgets also possess some similarities. For instance, all federal withholding taxes are computed in the same manner as are union benefits.

But for the moment let's look at four of the variables in the preceding list that deserve special attention.

### *The Larger the Capacity, the Higher the Cost*

The dollar amount of many budgetary items will be influenced by the volume of space contained within the physical plant. Larger buildings require more maintenance, more heat and air-conditioning, greater repair and renovation costs, more powerful and extensive machinery and electronic systems and, of course, a larger staff and more complicated security provisions. As a general rule-of-thumb, this principle dictates that the front-of-house staff (box office, ushers, maintenance, security, parking attendants, ticket takers, etc.) should be at a minimum number for a one-hundred-to-five-hundred-seat theatre, and then doubled for each additional five-hundred seats contained in a given facility. The larger seating capacity also requires that more programs and tickets be printed; marketing costs also increase proportionately with the seating capacity, so that more seats will be sold.

## The Newer the Theatre, the Higher the Cost

Old buildings invariably present operating problems that account for high costs, especially in the areas of maintenance and repair. Poor plumbing and wiring, leaking roofs and aging equipment often inspire the tenants of an old plant to lease or build a new one, believing that it will be less expensive to operate. And a new building *should* offer greater operating efficiency than an old one, but only for a price. A new building will probably contain more telephones, more electric wiring, more plumbing and more computer technology than an older building. New surroundings and new gizmos can be wonders, but are they assets or liabilities? A new facility, like a new employee, must be broken in—which requires both time and money. Perhaps it will be necessary to correct the acoustics in the auditorium, enlarge the box office or hire pole climbers from the circus to change the light bulbs in the chandelier. In short, replacing the old with the new can sometimes amount to little more than swapping one set of frustrations and expenses for another.

The new or beginning organization may also be more costly to operate because, as it will get less of the automatic public attention given to more established organizations, it must spend more on marketing to inform the public where it is located, what it is doing, and to build a nucleus of loyal customers. A young organization will also make unavoidable and sometimes expensive mistakes which can only be written off as growing pains: mistakes in staffing, in production policy, in the selection of vendors. Inexperience is an expensive item.

A new building or newly established operation also brings down upon its shoulders myriad inspectors and officials who may ignore or go more gently with established operations. Labor unions may demand that more of their members be used where nonunion employees were previously hired. Building, health insurance and public safety inspectors will almost certainly make thorough investigations of the building, and these may result in unexpected costs. Building codes and operating regulations are often more stringent for new buildings or for extensively renovated ones than for existing structures.

## The More Geographically Remote, the Higher the Cost

Theatres located off the beaten path may spend many dollars merely to call attention to their existence and to direct customers to their doors. They may also have high transportation costs for personnel and supplies, and it may be difficult to find convenient housing for artists and staff. If located away from shopping centers, a simple errand may become a time-consuming safari.

## *The More Unusual or Esoteric the Fare, the Higher the Cost*

Because the general public is hesitant about what is new or unfamiliar, extra marketing is usually necessary to promote unique or esoteric types of entertainment. Generally speaking, opera is more difficult to sell than musical comedy, Shakespeare more difficult than Simon, the new play more difficult than the established hit, the unknown actor more difficult than the star. Unusual productions often require employees who possess special skills or training and who therefore command higher salaries: opera singers, instrumentalists, acrobats, technicians, animal trainers. Novelty, sophistication or extravagance may also require special or additional equipment in terms of stage lighting, scenery, sound systems, costumes and properties. The extra expenses may pay off at the box office, but rarely unless the elements that mandate them can be justified artistically.

## THREE IMPORTANT "DON'T'S"
### *Don't Spend Your Income Before You Earn It*

Most earned income in the theatre business is derived from the sale of tickets. A theatre ticket is a rental agreement that entitles the buyer to a particular seat in a particular theatre, at a particular time and date, for a particular performance at a particular price—possibly featuring particular performers. Those are a lot of particulars! If for any reason the producer cannot deliver every one of them as promised on the ticket, the price paid for that ticket may have to be refunded. Owing to this possibility, ticket revenue (1) should be held until the performance for which it was paid has concluded; (2) should thereafter be spent only for operating costs until all these have been paid; and (3) should never be regarded as money earned until the performance has occurred. In other words, one should recognize the fundamental difference between earned revenue and deferred revenue (money that has been received but not yet earned). This distinction is especially clear in regard to Broadway productions, because the law requires that producers and their backers (limited partners) provide all the capital necessary to finance the production up to and including its opening night. Advance ticket revenue—which may be considerable—is held in order to pay for post-opening, weekly operating costs. If weekly ticket sales are insufficient to cover weekly operating costs, the show is usually closed—fast. Money for advance sales is refunded. But if weekly sales *do* cover costs, any excess ticket revenue is used to pay back the investors. Only after all investments have been paid back can money earned over the operating costs be distributed as profit. Yet, the wisdom of this practice is not always apparent when a theatre company is not regulated by law, as Broadway is.

When advance ticket revenue is spent *before* production operating costs have been paid, the producing organization is courting danger if not bankruptcy. One stock theatre producer, for example, used the advance season ticket income as the down payment on the purchase price of the theatre where the season was to be presented. But by opening night there was no money left to meet the payroll and there were no more tickets to sell for additional income!

It is always tempting to dip into deferred revenue. Season tickets or subscriptions may be sold as much as a year in advance, the income may be earning interest (which *may* be safely spent as it is earned) and the amount could be substantial. But the most prudent policy is to regard such income as money being held in trust, to keep it in a safe and separate savings or investment account, and to transfer it into an operating account only as the daily or weekly box office reports show that it has been earned. The problem is that, unlike Broadway, most theatres commit themselves to a minimum number of performances, regardless of what they may earn at the box office—a policy that incurs considerable risk. Whether or not tickets are sold, the show goes on. In the case of commercial ventures, the producer or promoter should have the personal resources to underwrite any losses, or find another person or company that agrees to assume this risk in exchange for a percentage of any profits. If the theatre operates as a nonprofit organization, it should arrange to cover anticipated losses with contributions of various kinds. Few corporate, foundation or government funding agencies, however, will long support a theatre that fails to earn at least 50 or 60 percent of its costs at the box office. But revenue from such sources as well as from individuals (as long as it is promised in writing), is like money in the bank and may be spent immediately, within the limits of any conditions attached to it. Although concessionary income may supplement box office receipts, caution should be used in estimating potential revenue from such sources as program advertising, parking lots, food and beverage concessions; profits rarely meet expectations.

When a theatre company has estimated its cost and sees that it will need its contributed income plus more than 60-percent-of-capacity business in order to break even, it is usually a sign that its costs should be reduced, its revenue increased or its plans abandoned.

## Don't Spend or Budget the Same Dollar Twice

There is always a need to stretch a dollar as far as possible, but there is a limit to how much this can be done. Optimism or inexperience sometimes leads people into the illusion that the same dollar can be spent twice. For example, many theatre companies must post bonds with unions before they can sign contracts with members of those unions. The bond may be in the form of cash, a savings account book or some other security. Although the person or company posting the bond is entitled to receive any interest it earns, the principle itself will not be returned until after the production or the season has concluded. And, if there is unfinished business or a dispute between the two parties involved, the bond will be held until everything is settled. Bonds are returnable and represent a cash asset, but they do not represent readily available cash and, indeed, may eventually be lost due to arbitration or litigation.

Sales tax collected as part of ticket or merchandise sales—or payroll tax withheld from salaries—belongs to the government. If spent by the organization, it would be money spent twice. And budgeting for labor costs also holds possibilities for spending the same dollar twice. For example, it may be assumed that one employee can fulfill the functions of both receptionist and box office treasurer—but handling box office and front office traffic simultaneously may prove impossible for one person. Another case: Equity or another union may require that two of its members be hired, although the budget has only provided for one.

## Don't Get Into the Boat Unless You Can Afford to Sink

If a project is initiated and financial commitments made before there is good assurance that the necessary capital will be forthcoming, a lot of money is likely to be lost, and a lot of reputations ruined. Because theatre is so highly speculative as a business and because so many unexpected things can happen to increase expenses or prevent productions from taking place as planned, producing organizations must always keep the possibility of financial disaster in mind and protect themselves, their investors and the ticket buyers accordingly. The manner in which promoters often find someone to underwrite any losses which their presentations may incur is a good example of this. Of course, it is sometimes necessary to take calculated risks. The New York producer may never be compensated for time and money spent trying to secure an option on a certain property. The organization trying to establish an acting company or construct a new theatre building may never see its efforts pay off. The late Lawrence Langner liked to relate how he broke ground for the construction of the Shakespeare Festival Theatre in Stratford, Connecticut, without having the slightest idea of where the construction money would come from. Such risks are often necessary to attract attention to a project so that, in turn, funding may be found. But one must be able to afford to lose the seed money (or initial investment) in a project.

## ESTIMATING THE EXPENSES

Most theatre operations must absorb four basic types of expenses and these are traditionally reflected by four different types of budgets:

1. *Capital Budget*: one-time business and facility expenses (such as incorporation, board development, feasibility studies, facility design, construction, renovation, new equipment)

2. *Annual Operating Budget*: ongoing business and facility expenses that continue over an entire season or year without being greatly influenced by what productions are offered (such as utilities, real estate taxes, in-house staff, insurance and office supplies)

3. *Pre-Production Budget*: one-time expenses related to the preparation of a theatrical production (such as auditions, rehearsal salaries, director's fee, costume and scenic construction, seasonal or pre-opening marketing, nonartistic production personnel, opening night party)

4. *Production Operating Budget*: ongoing expenses per week or per performance that are directly related to the stage show itself (such as royalties, performers' salaries, advertising, stagehands, company transportation, per diems, equipment rentals).

While a single production company or organization may have to absorb all the items covered in all four budgets, it may not have direct responsibility for estimating and controlling them. For example, the cost of operating a Broadway theatre and the corporation that owns it is paid as rental fees by the tenant production company to the landlord, who controls the capital and annual operating budgets. Or, from an opposite viewpoint, the preproduction and production operating costs for a bus and truck company are paid as production fees by the promoter or presenting organization to a commercial producer. The presenting organization may control its own facility and therefore control its own capital and annual operating budgets, or it may rent a facility and pay for such costs indirectly in the form of rental fees. Or, to cite a third possibility, a resident stock company or a LORT theatre that operates its own facility and originates its own productions would have control over all four budgets listed above. But because this is not always the case, and because the separation of these types of expenses greatly clarifies the planning process, such budget categories are often maintained even when all are controlled by the same company or organization.

## Capital Budget

Virtually all producers or groups that seriously intend to organize a professional theatre production or company must soon form a legal partnership or corporation of some type. This process is discussed in Chapter 1. Not surprisingly, it requires money and the services of an attorney, as does the process of drawing up a limited partnership agreement, an offering prospectus, a set of bylaws and other one-time obligations related to setting up a business. Such start-up costs are shown in the capital budget or, in the case of a commercial production, in the preproduction budget (which is the capital budget for the show as well as for its single-purpose production company).   Most ongoing theatre companies must also find a more or less permanent theatre space in which to present their work. As discussed in Chapter 3, there are a variety of possibilities when it comes to real estate such as buying, renting or sharing a facility. Many a theatre company starts out in a modest, rented space and years later acquires its own home. So initial start-up costs may be minimal—limited, perhaps, to the cost of incorporation— and easily absorbed into the first annual operating budget; or they may be very high—including, perhaps, the cost of buying and renovating an old movie theatre. Or, a theatrical entrepreneur may begin by purchasing an existing theatre and then producing or booking the productions that will perform in it.

The resources and budget related to building, renovation or construction costs should be separate from those related to production and operating expenses. The acquisition of a new facility may require a separate public relations and funding campaign, as well as consultants and experts on staff who are not directly related to regular production activity. But the producing organization that is already presenting plays should not endanger its production activity by committing its operating capital to other uses—that would be like selling the baby to pay for the bassinet!

Eventually, of course, construction, renovation and other capital costs will appear in the operating budget in the form of plant amortization. If a mortgage or loan has been secured, the payments will constitute the organization's rent or "occupancy cost." Organizations that operate in campus or civic facilities may not be required to contribute directly to capital expenditures, since these are often paid by the institution or the city. But when financial responsibility for facility acquisition and renovation does rest with the producing organization, then a capital budget must be written. While this will be based upon as much expert advice as possible and contain detailed figures for numerous items, it will still be only an estimate,

Using the hypothetical example of a professional nonprofit theatre company, let's look at sample budgets of the four basic types and then see how each contributes to the total annual cost of the operation. Later in the chapter, we'll examine how this company might also estimate its income and thereby determine whether or not its plans are realistic. The sample budgets that follow cannot provide the full detail of actual circumstances, but they show the major items and should suffice to illustrate the budgetary process.

## SAMPLE CAPITAL BUDGET
### (Nonprofit Professional Theatre)

| | |
|---|---:|
| Capital fundraising drive | $175,000 |
| Purchase price of building | 1,230,000 |
| Title search, legal fees, etc. | 12,000 |
| Permits, licenses, etc. | 7,900 |
| Consultant fees | 30,000 |
| Architect's fees & costs | 45,000 |
| Renovation costs (interior) | 500,000 |
| Renovation costs (exterior) | 115,000 |
| Landscaping | 64,000 |
| New, permanent stage equipment | 562,100 |
| New, permanent office equipment | 109,000 |
| Miscellaneous | 50,000 |
| Contingency | 100,000 |
| | |
| Total Estimated Capital Expenses | $3,000,000 |

## Annual Operating Budget

Once the occupancy cost has been determined, whether in the form of mortgage or loan payments, or rent payments to a landlord, then the organization must estimate its annual operating expenses. How much will it cost to operate the facility, including an amortized portion of the capital cost?

Chapter 4 discusses the matter of personnel and staffing, which will account for a large portion of ongoing, annual expenses. These and the other items in an annual operating budget are all inflexible. Most of them will be essentially the same whether the theatre presents five or eight performances a week, or six or sixteen productions during the year. Like the rent or occupancy cost, the total of all annual operating costs may eventually be amortized or averaged over each week in the year or season, or into the cost of each production, whichever will better assist the planning and evaluation process.

## SAMPLE ANNUAL OPERATING BUDGET
(Nonprofit Professional Theatre)

| | |
|---|---|
| Mortgage payment | $25,000 |
| Interest | 2,500 |
| Salaries: | |
|     Artistic (annual contracts) | 92,000 |
|     Administrative (annual contracts) | 165,000 |
|     Technical (annual contracts) | 90,000 |
|     Security & Maintenance (annual contracts) | 55,000 |
| Payroll taxes & benefits | 68,400 |
| Company vehicles expense | 6,200 |
| Utilities | 46,500 |
| Insurance | 24,000 |
| Legal & auditing | 16,500 |
| Licenses & permits | 900 |
| Maintenance & repair | 18,000 |
| Telephone & fax | 29,000 |
| Plant opening & closing | 5,000 |
| Office & building supplies | 45,000 |
| Travel & transportation | 10,000 |
| Seasonal marketing expenses | 200,000 |
| Seasonal development expenses | 34,000 |
| Equipment rentals | 12,000 |
| Board meetings & expense | 1,500 |
| Postage (general) | 3,500 |
| Miscellaneous | 50,000 |
| | |
| Total Estimated Annual Operating Expenses: | $1,000,000 |
| | |
| AEA & ATPAM Bonds (returnable) | 55,000 |

## Pre-Production Budget

A pre-production budget contains the one-time expenses involved in mounting a production, which makes it the capital budget for that production.

Thus far, we have estimated the cost of acquiring a facility and operating that facility—but the theatre is still dark. Now a third budget must be drawn up in order to estimate the cost of putting together a stage production. In fact, there should be a separate preproduction budget for each show that is being planned. Items included in such budgets will be determined in part by how goods and services are contracted. If production supplies such as lighting gels, scene paint and muslin are purchased annually in order to take advantage of bulk-rate discounts, they may be shown in the annual operating budget. The same might also be true for personnel (including directors and designers) hired for a whole year or season rather than for a single production. Again, the budgeting and accounting system that most helps the decision-making process is the one to use.

Productions being mounted on a one-time basis—as for Broadway and the road—are budgeted as independent, one-time ventures. This makes it comparatively easy to isolate the cost of each item, because the full cost of virtually all items can only be charged to one production. Budget items for ongoing, multi-production companies or institutions, on the other hand, can more easily be manipulated in order to create a particular impression. In fact, the same set of figures can and sometimes is reorganized into several different budgets for different eyes—those of the press, those of the state arts council, those of the IRS. The same may also be done with financial reports. Computerized business systems have made such statistical exercises as easy as child's play.

The budget sample that follows reflects the costs for a professional nonprofit theatre that does not maintain a resident acting company.

### SAMPLE PRE-PRODUCTION BUDGET
(Nonprofit Professional Theatre:
Nonresident, nonmusical, five-character, one-set show)

|  | *Fees:* |
| --- | --- |
| Director | $6,000 |
| Set designer | 2,500 |
| Costume designer | 1,500 |
| Lighting designer | 1,500 |
| | |
| *Salaries (Rehearsal):* | |
| Actors (5 x 5 wks x $398) | 9,950 |
| Stage Manager (5 wks x $425) | 2,125 |
| Ass't stage manager (5 wks x $380) | 1,900 |
| Ass't set designer | 1,000 |
| Ass't costume designer | 800 |
| Ass't lighting/sound | 800 |
| Ass't director | 500 |

| Payroll taxes & benefits | 3,450 |
|---|---|

*Rehearsal & Audition Expenses*:

| | |
|---|---|
| NYC audition studio | 2,000 |
| Audition stage manager | 500 |
| Stage manager's rehearsal expenses | 200 |
| Scripts, parts & duplicating | 200 |
| Rehearsal props | 225 |

*Per Diems*:

| | |
|---|---|
| Director | 1,500 |
| Designers & assistants | 3,000 |

*Company Travel*:

| | |
|---|---|
| R/T from NYC | 750 |
| Local transportation | 600 |

*Physical Production*:

| | |
|---|---|
| Scenery | 38,000 |
| Properties | 2,000 |
| Costumes & accessories | 4,100 |
| Electrics | 400 |
| Sound | 200 |

*Marketing/Promotion:*

| | |
|---|---|
| Advertising | 6,500 |
| Brochures, flyers, mailings | 2,100 |
| Press kits | 200 |
| Graphics, design | 1,500 |

*Miscellaneous*:

| | |
|---|---|
| Box office expenses | 1,000 |
| Departmental | 1,500 |
| Opening night party | 1,500 |
| Contingency | 10,000 |

| Total Estimated Pre-Production Expenses: | $100,000 |
|---|---|

## Production Operating Budget

A production operating budget estimates the costs directly related to the performances of a theatre work after it has been designed, constructed and rehearsed. Naturally, the production that requires twenty rather than two union actors will be more expensive. Musicals and recent hits carry higher royalty costs than other shows, while works in the public domain (excluding recent translations, adaptations or revised versions) carry no royalty charges at all. The use of accomplished and well-known actors, directors and designers not only requires high fees or salaries but may also require other expenditures for them to work at their highest levels of achievement. In short, the *manner* in which an organization chooses to produce its productions—the quality and the results it wishes to achieve—are the most flexible budget elements of all.

Ongoing theatre productions from Broadway to nonprofit professional theatres are budgeted on a weekly basis, perhaps because standard AEA contracts define employment this way. Touring productions that play split-week or one-night engagements, of course, are sold to presenters on a per-performance basis—although the company's producer still must deal with ongoing weekly contracts and expenses.

The production operating budget is designed to suggest how much performances will cost, apart from capital, annual and preproduction expenses. By isolating this part of the overall operation, it is easily possible to compute the cost of extending the performances of a certain production—by one more performance in a given week, by one more full week or whatever. As most standard AEA contracts cover eight performances per week, it seldom makes economic sense to offer fewer than that number. Capital, annual operating and pre-production budgets, as outlined above, all involve fixed or inflexible dollar estimations. This is to say that the amounts spent on each item can be determined in advance with reasonable accuracy. The advertising expenses, for instance, may go up and down depending on the show and the advance ticket sale, but those expenses can nonetheless be controlled and determined in advance. Production operating expenses, on the other hand, often include variable or flexible costs, such as royalties, that are directly tied to the box office gross and can only be determined once the actual gross is known. While the following operating budget shows only fixed costs, a method for computing the break-even point that takes variable costs into account is discussed later.

No two preproduction or production operating budgets are ever the same, because no two theatre works are the same. The budget sample that follows might be for a nonmusical, five-character play with one set.

## SAMPLE WEEKLY PRODUCTION OPERATING BUDGET
(Nonprofit Professional Theatre: Show #1
five-character, one-set nonmusical)

*Salaries:*

| | |
|---|---:|
| Actors (2 x $5,000 & 3 x $1,750) | $15,250 |
| Stage managers | 850 |
| Stagehands | 2,000 |
| Wardrobe/makeup | 400 |
| House staff | 1,090 |
| Payroll taxes & benefits | 3,918 |
| | |
| Royalties | 13,280 |
| Local transportation (company) | 240 |
| Maintenance of physical production | 200 |
| Laundry & cleaning | 132 |
| Marketing/promotion | 1,340 |
| Printing & postage | 500 |
| Playbill printing (commission deal) | 0 |
| General entertainment | 300 |
| Box office expenses | 500 |
| Contingency | 2,000 |
| | |
| Total Estimated Weekly Production Operating Expenses: | $42,000 |

Of course, a typical nonprofit theatre company would produce more than one production per season. Let's say that our sample theatre company is planning four major productions, each with a five-week run for its upcoming twenty-week season. The first of these is budgeted above: a five-character, one-set, nonmusical play. Assuming that there are no variable costs and that the remaining three productions have been budgeted in detail, the budget summation for this theatre's upcoming season might look something like the following:

| Production | PreProduction Expenses | Wkly Production Operating Exp. | Total Wkly Production Exp. | Total Production Expense |
|---|---|---|---|---|
| Show #1 | $100,000 | $42,000 x 5 wks = | $210,000 | $310,000 |
| Show #2 | 43,000 | 39,000 x 5 wks = | 195,000 | 238,000 |
| Show #3 | 83,000 | 41,000 x 5 wks = | 205,000 | 288,000 |
| Show #4 | 50,000 | 35,000 x 5 wks = | 175,000 | 225,000 |
| Totals | $276,000 | $157,000 | $785,000 | $1,061,000 |
| Average Cost | $69,000 | $39,250 | $196,250 | $265,250 |

One can see at a glance that not all productions are equal in terms of their demands on the budget. While show #1 is a five-character play, its budget indicates that two of these are played by high-salaried stars. Perhaps show #2 is a revival of *A Christmas Carol* using sets and costumes from storage and no stars; Show #3 could be a contemporary comedy, and Show #4 could be a five-character expressionist play with virtually no scenery. But, again, if different scripts mandate different costs, then different artistic approaches to the same play also generate different—even wildly divergent—costs, thus underscoring an essential principle in regard to theatrical budgeting: *the budget figures must reflect the standards and goals of the leading artists involved with the production.* This presents a challenge to the business manager because it requires translating what a designer or artistic director is saying into probable dollar amounts—or the contractual demands of a performer into likely costs, or the desire for live dogs on the stage into the costs which they will incur (no pun intended). Production plans conceived in the artistic imagination, in short, must soon be costed out in the business office—and this is the point at which artistic-managerial dialogue often begins to heat up.

## Computing the Annual Estimated Expenses

Now that all the cost estimations are in (let's call them "preliminary estimates"), and dollar figures have been entered next to all the items in our four basic types of budgets, there are several ways these costs can be summarized:

*COST SUMMATION A*: Estimated Weekly Operating Cost, Show #1

| Capital Expenses: | $3,000,000 | $2,500,000 | offset by municipal bond & corporate contributions |
|---|---|---|---|
| Annual Operating Expenses: | | | |
| Mortgage payment | 25,000 | 500,000 | financed by a 20-year mortgage |
| Interest | 2,500 | | |
| Other annual expenses | 972,500 | | |
| | $1,000,000 | | |
| Preproduction Expenses (Show #1) | 100,000 | | |

Weekly Production Operating
Expenses (Show #1)          42,000

                            20,000    Preproduction, amortized over 5
                                      performance weeks

                            50,000    Annual operating costs amortized
                                      over 20 weeks of the season


                          $112,000    Estimated weekly operating cost,
                                      Show #1



*COST SUMMATION B*: Estimated Total Cost, Show     #1

Preproduction Expenses      $100,000

Weekly Operating Expenses    210,000

Annual Operating Expenses
($50,000 x 5)                250,000

                            $560,000   Estimated Total Cost,
                                       Show #1

*COST SUMMATION C*: Estimated Total Annual Expenses,
  Including Shows 1 through 4

Annual Operating Expenses
(including mortgage & interest)     $1,000,000

Preproduction and Production
Operating Expenses: Shows 1 - 4      1,061,000

                                    $2,061,000

AEA & ATPAM Bonds (Returnable)          55,000

                                    $2,116,000   Total Annual
                                                 Estimated Expenses

With all the production plans set, and cost estimations listed for every-thing and everyone necessary to carry them out, it might be tempting to hold auditions and begin rehearsals. But the projected costs only represent one side of the budgetary coin. Now the organization should also devise a de-tailed estimation of all the income it can prudently anticipate during the same season. Actually, income can be estimated first and expenses second—it doesn't matter in the least, so long as both are based on sound judgement.

## ESTIMATING THE INCOME

Commercial ventures do not as a rule receive contributions; they rely exclusively on earnings to fuel their activities and, hopefully, to distribute as profits. Nonprofit companies, however, usually engage in activities that gen-erate earnings while they also initiate appeals which they hope will attract grants and contributions, also called "unearned income." Also, there are many types of nonmonetary contributions: in-kind services, volunteer labor, do-nated land, corporate tie-ins that provide free advertising, free housing for visiting artists and so forth. But this chapter is only concerned with mone-tary income. What are all the different sources of earned and unearned in-come that an organization can reasonably count on? In the case of a theatre production or an ongoing theatre company, the first source of income that comes to mind is the box office.

### Ticket Pricing

Capitalist thinking dictates that goods and services should be sold at the highest price the market will bear, and that when prices are set below this level, income is diminished and the producer is either a philanthropist or a fool! But, of course, the purely capitalist approach tends to exploit the moment and the ready resource. More conservative economic thought con-cerns itself with the future and with long-term exploitation—such as the danger of covering arable land with asphalt, or the danger of pricing young audiences out of the theatre. But whichever school of thought is applied, the piper in the pit must be paid.

In point of fact, ticket prices are often based more on intuition than on economic logic. A producer may simply "feel" that certain prices are right for a particular theatre and community. And, in truth, it is difficult to judge whether or not there will be price resistance until tickets are actually on sale. For many years it was believed that there was a psychological advantage in pricing a ticket at, say, $19.95 rather than $20.00; but today the round dollar amount is more common—and making change for cash sales is much eas-ier.

Another somewhat unique aspect of the theatre ticket as a marketable commodity is that some states, including New York, make it difficult at best, and illegal at worst, to sell theatre tickets at any price except the advertised one that is printed on them. This puts the theatre producer at a severe disadvantage in comparison to most other retailers. After all, booksellers and furniture stores can run sales during slow periods and have specials on unpopular items. But theatre producers generally lack such pricing flexibility, although they may sell two tickets for the price of one (in the legal sense, this means giving one away, which is permissible) or allow charitable organizations and ticket agents to add a surcharge and keep the difference. Yet, these exceptions merely serve to underscore the wide gulf in pricing flexibility that separates the theatre operator from the bookseller and the furniture retailer. For the purpose of investigating this disparity, the League of American Theatres and Producers once commissioned attorney John Wharton to investigate such regulations and come up with a few suggestions. His 1965 report to the Legitimate Theatre Industry Exploratory Commission still deserves attention. It recommends, at least for Broadway, a system of flexible ticket pricing based on supply and demand rather than upon laws concocted by the state's attorney general. If tickets for a particular production can bring a price of $500 each, that would be the established price. As the production becomes less popular, the price would go down. Also, customers would be offered low prices on tickets purchased before opening night, as well as sharp discounts on tickets that remain unsold at curtain time. Such policies could greatly increase advance ticket sales, on the one hand, and last minute, walk-in business on the other. "Floated" ticket prices would be similar to the manner in which stock prices are determined on the stock exchange. The recommendation was designed to eliminate ticket scalpers, place all ticket revenues into the hands of the industry, and bring in more money sooner than is usually the case. Later in a successful run, of course, prices would be very low to encourage a younger and less affluent audience. Theatre tickets are a luxury that brings harm to no one, the report argues, and politicians have no business regulating their cost as if they were food or utility prices.

Unfortunately, the Commission's recommendations have never received a fair trial, but they remain a challenge to forward thinking managers in the performing arts—a challenge based on the simple, indisputable fact that few items are more worthless than a ticket to a past performance. While other retailers can list their unsold items as assets, unsold theatre tickets to past performances—like unrented motel rooms for nights past—aren't worth zip.

Decisions about ticket pricing generally boil down to an estimation of the elasticity of demand for tickets as opposed to the fixed demand. What is the top price the consumer market will pay? How many consumers will pay it? Assigning ticket prices which answer those questions correctly will result in optimum ticket sales for the production being priced.

## Scaling the House

The diagrams in Chapter 3 showing different theatrical seating arrangements suggest that ticket prices might reflect such differences: for example, one price for the orchestra, another for the mezzanine, and another for the balcony. Assigning different prices to different sections of the theatre is known as "scaling the house," and the result is the price scale that is usually posted next to the box office.

Some theatres have a long stretch of uninterrupted rows of seats, in which case it may be necessary to select an arbitrary point where the price changes. If rows of orchestra seats proceed from A to Z, for instance, the producer may decide to decrease ticket prices beginning at row N. To make such an arbitrary decision obvious to customers and ushers, different colored seat covers or some other indication might be used. No theatre, incidentally, should include a row "I" when designating its row and seat numbers; the letter "I" is too easily confused with the number '1.' Many theatres label the first few rows of the orchestra by using double letters (row AA, row BB, etc.) and commence anew with row A further back in the orchestra. Or the first ten rows may proceed from A to K, and the next ten from AA to KK. The psychology of this system is that ticket buyers are less hesitant to purchase a seat in row KK than in row U; but, of course, there is an element of deceit involved here.

Pricing tickets for a theatre-in-the-round offers special problems. Since it is a comparatively unusual type of audience seating, the public is likely to be confused about which seats are the best ones. The answer given by producers and treasurers at such theatres is, invariably, "They're all good."

If there are less than five-hundred seats, perhaps there should be a single ticket price. Otherwise, prices should diminish as the rows of seats get further from the stage. However, when sightlines are poor in certain sections of the house (often the case in arena theatres that have an elliptical stage), ticket prices should be adjusted accordingly.

Because auditorium and ticket terminology varies from one theatre to another, it is not surprising that many customers are confused when it comes to ordering tickets. How, then, should the various sections of a theatre be labeled? Some terms are preferred because they may sound more elegant than others: "terrace" instead of "first balcony," "family circle" instead of "second balcony." While the fancy labels may be desirable for some theatres, more accurate terms are probably a better choice in most cases. Almost any box office treasurer will attest that a surprising number of ticket buyers don't even understand the term "orchestra." Suffice it to say that theatregoing should be made as easy as possible. The following are the most commonly used seating terms:

| *Front Auditorium* | *Middle Auditorium* | *Rear Auditorium* |
|---|---|---|
| Orchestra | Mezzanine | Balcony |
| Stalls (England) | Dress Circle | Rear Orchestra |
| | Front Balcony | Family Circle |
| | First Balcony | Second Balcony |
| | Boxes | Rear Balcony |
| | Side Terrace | The Gods |
| | | (England) |
| | Side Balcony | Second Tier |
| | Loge | Second Terrace |
| | Parterre | |
| | Galleries (England) | |
| | First Tier | |

## Estimating Potential Box Office Income

Once the seating arrangement has been determined, and the various sections have been labeled, a price is assigned to each seat and the potential gross determined as follows:

| Section | # of Seats | | Price Per Ticket | Total |
|---|---|---|---|---|
| Orchestra | 500 | x | $25.00 | $12,500 |
| Mezzanine | 200 | x | 20.00 | 4,000 |
| Balcony | 100 | x | 15.00 | 1,500 |

Total Potential Gross for a
Single Evening Performance: $18,000

When matinee or twilight performances are offered, ticket prices are traditionally lowered. (While there is great precedent for this practice, it is not altogether logical. Most theatregoers who attend matinees do so for reasons other than the lower price and would probably not resist paying evening prices). To simplify advertising and ticket sales, matinee prices should simply drop the top evening price category and continue the other prices downward:

| Section | # of Seats | | Price Per Ticket | Total |
|---|---|---|---|---|
| Orchestra | 500 | x | $20.00 | $10,000 |
| Mezzanine | 200 | x | 15.00 | 3,000 |
| Balcony | 100 | x | 10.00 | 1,000 |

Total Potential Gross for a
Single Matinee Performance: $14,000

If the production is scheduled for a limited run of less than a week, the total potential gross for the entire run can be computed and then set aside for study, once the estimated production costs have been determined. But if the same or different productions are offered as an ongoing policy, then a weekly potential gross can be determined as follows:

6 evening performances x $18,000 = $108,000
2 matinee performances x 14,000 =      28,000

Total Potential Weekly Gross              $136,000

Total Potential Season Gross
         ( $136,000 x 20)            $2,720,000

As well as having different price scales for evening and matinee performances, a theatre may also elect to increase its ticket prices for weekend and holiday performances, for musical productions, or for those that feature an especially popular (and expensive) star.

But before one imagines putting that total gross amount into the bank after each performance, it would be wise to remember that the potential gross will almost never be reached due to:

1. Complimentary tickets
2. Press seats
3. Discounted season or subscription tickets
4. Discounted group sales tickets
5. Commissions paid to ticket agents and other salespeople
6. Unclaimed and unpaid reservations
7. Difficulty in selling single, scattered seats
8. Service charges imposed by credit card companies

The only way to offset such revenue losses is to sell standing room or additional chairs that are not included in the potential gross estimations. And as if the above list isn't sufficiently discouraging, ticket sales can also be diminished by:

1. Lousy reviews
2. Poor word of mouth
3. Adverse general publicity
4. Illness and/or nonappearance of leading performers
5. Interruptions in public transportation

6. Interruptions in media coverage
7. Severe weather conditions
8. National emergency

Is it any wonder that seasoned producers and theatre managers usually plan on taking in no more than 50 to 60 percent of the total potential box office gross?

In states that impose a sales tax on theatre tickets, price scales and estimates of gross must take this into account by providing "net" and "tax" categories for each price. And the taxable portion of all income should be deposited separately into a special escrow account, until paid over to the appropriate tax collector. This practice helps to avoid the temptation of spending those tax dollars for other purposes.

## Income Earned Outside the Box Office

There are countless ways a theatre organization may earn money apart from the sale of tickets. These are discussed in Chapter 13, but here it is necessary to show how income that is earned outside the box office might fit into the budget process. Sometimes this income is called "subsidiary" or "concessionary" income. While it has become increasingly important for the survival of many professional theatres, it is nonetheless unwise to count on such revenue when it is minimal.

Just as capital and operating expenses must be estimated in regard to acquiring and running both a facility and a theatrical production, so they must be estimated in regard to stocking and running a concession—although inexperienced theatre groups are often tempted merely to anticipate the earnings and forget that there are usually expenses involved! For example, a "simple" little soft drink concession might entail the following costs:

SAMPLE CONCESSION BUDGET: Soft Drink Bar

*Capital Costs:*

| | |
|---|---|
| Electric 100-cup coffee maker | $ 95 |
| Double hot plate | 50 |
| Four carafes | 65 |
| Small refrigerator | 215 |
| Large cooler chest | 275 |
| Caps & aprons for employees | 100 |

Total Capital Costs    $800    amortized over
20 operating weeks

*Weekly Operating Costs:*

| | |
|---|---:|
| 1000 paper napkins | $10 |
| 1 gross swizzel sticks | 5 |
| 1 gross hot drink cups | 20 |
| 1 gross cold drink cups | 30 |
| 2 cases half-&-half cream containers | 17 |
| 20 pounds of coffee | 60 |
| 200 tea bags | 10 |
| 25 cases of cola | 250 |
| 25 cases other soda & juices | 250 |
| 12 lemons | 5 |
| 6 limes | 3 |
| Amortized Capital Costs | 40 |
| Wages for part-time concession operators (2 x $125 + 15% tax) | 288 |
| | |
| Total Estimated Wkly Costs | $988 |

One can see at a glance that, if both hot and cold drinks are sold for one dollar each, it would take 988 sales each week just to break even—which means that, if this 800-seat theatre plays to 50 percent capacity for eight performances, every 2.2 customers would have to buy a drink. Furthermore, sales for this concession will fluctuate greatly due to such factors as:

1. Outside weather conditions
2. Changes in the inside temperature
3. General age of the audience
4. General affluence of the audience
5. The nature of the stage production

If the air-conditioning system malfunctions, if the audience includes five hundred children from local day care centers or six hundred senior citizens, if the play is a high-spirited comedy in which champagne is frequently served or a serious drama about alcohol abuse or—heaven help concessionaires and people with weak bladders—if the play is performed without any intermission, then certain concessions will suffer a sudden drop in revenues. Spoilage, theft and embezzlement are also common problems in concession management. And don't forget that any losses may have to come out of the hard-earned box office revenue. So before going into the wet goods business, experienced theatre managers should carefully weigh the alternative of leasing concession space to private operators on a flat fee basis. And even in that situation, a percentage deal in which the theatre shares a portion of any profit with the concessionaire requires almost as much surveillance of the operation as if the theatre ran the juice bar itself.

Only when concessions have been in operation over a period of weeks or, better still, seasons, should a theatre feel reasonably confident in estimating the revenue—unless this is purely rental income. For example:

## SAMPLE CONCESSION EXPENSE & INCOME SUMMARY

| Concession | Estimated Expense | Estimated Revenue | Differential |
|---|---|---|---|
| Soft drinks | $988 | $700 | $288 |
| Parking | 200 | 1,600 | 1,400 |
| Coat lockers | 50 | 75 | 25 |
| Souvenir programs | 425 | 1,200 | 775 |
| Estimated Totals | $1,663 | $3,575 | $1,912 |

Projected Season Total ($1912 x 20 weeks)     $38,240

Aside from concessions, there may be other important sources of earned income. Again, any operating expenses must be figured in before profits (or losses) can be projected:

## SAMPLE INCOME PROJECTION OTHER THAN
## BOX OFFICE & CONCESSIONS

| Other Earned Revenues (Annual) | Est. Income After Expenses |
|---|---|
| Endowment Fund Interest | $6,000 |
| Savings Account Interest | 2,100 |
| Income from Rentals | 23,500 |
| Tuition from Acting School | (4,600) |
| Fees from Artists-in-the-Schools Program | (1,500) |
| Total Annual Other Earned Revenues | $25,500 |

If the above figures cover all sources of potential income, and if the prudent manager of our hypothetical theatre company plans on taking in 50 percent of the potential box office gross, the income summary so far would appear as follows:

## SAMPLE INCOME SUMMARY (ALL SOURCES)

Est. season box office income
($136,000 x 20 wks = $2,720,000 @ 50% =     $1,360,000
Est. concessionary income after expenses          38,240
Est. other earned income after expenses           25,500

Total Annual Estimated Income          $1,423,740

Remembering that the total cost for our season is projected at $2,116,000, it is obvious that we have a shortfall of $692,260. Fortunately, this is a nonprofit theatre company that can not only sell things to earn money but can also appeal to a variety of sources for grants and contributions. At this juncture in the budgeting process, then, it is clearly time to call in the company's fundraiser.

## Estimating Potential Contributed Income

The basic types of unearned or contributed income, and the methods for gaining such resources, are discussed at length in Chapter 14. Once again, we are at present only concerned with illustrating how such revenue figures into the financial planning process.

Because the cost of raising most of the money needed to cover the capital  budget was included in that budget, and the cost of raising funds to offset operating and production expenses is included in the salary and development items in those budgets, we need not concern ourselves with fundraising costs again at this point—unless, of course, they have increased over earlier estimations.

Fundraising activities are generally conducted well in advance of opening night. In fact, when contributed income is necessary to fund a particular project, work on that project should not begin until such funds are assured. So the fundraiser is likely to begin work at least a year or more prior to the time when it is hoped that the project can be initiated. While there will be many turn-downs, it will eventually become clear whether a few funding sources are interested in the project or not and then it will become clear how much money they are willing to promise. The results of a fundraising campaign aimed at numerous individuals for small donations is also difficult to predict, although experience with such appeals lends validity to any estimations.

Let's say that contributed income estimations—based on past success and careful projection of increases based on new initiatives—can be summarized as follows:

## SAMPLE SUMMARY OF PROJECTED ANNUAL CONTRIBUTED INCOME

GOVERNMENT:

| | |
|---|---:|
| Municipal Agencies | $10,000 |
| City Arts Council | 5,000 |
| State Arts Council | 8,000 |
| NEA | 4,000 |

FOUNDATIONS:

| | |
|---|---:|
| Foundation A | 6,000 |
| Foundation B | 24,000 |
| Foundation C | 2,500 |

CORPORATIONS:

| | |
|---|---:|
| Corporation A | 125,500 |
| Corporation B | 30,000 |

INDIVIDUAL DONORS:

| | |
|---|---:|
| Subscribers | 16,000 |
| Trustee Donations | 75,000 |
| Friends Campaign | 10,000 |
| Major Benefactors | 15,000 |

| | |
|---|---:|
| Total Annual Projected Unearned Income | $331,000 |

Of course, a sizable portion of contributed income is likely to be earmarked for specific purposes, such as a particular production or tour, or a project to hire minority artists. Similarly, budget allocations from a parent institution, such as a civic center, a university or a municipal agency, are usually limited to specific types of expenditures, like office supplies, full-time salaries, part-time wages, equipment and so forth. Such encumbrances, which limit the manner in which an organization can spend its money, are discussed in the "cash flow" section of the next chapter.

## PROJECTING PROFIT (OR LOSS)

Commercial managers talk in terms of profit and loss, while nonprofit managers use the terms surplus and deficit. From a bookkeeping standpoint, such distinctions mean little. The bottom line in a budget shows whether a given company or project is expected to come out with a profit or a loss, and the bottom line in a financial statement shows whether or not it did. The following budget summation for our hypothetical theatre company projects a troublesome, though hardly gigantic, deficit for an operation of its size.

## SAMPLE PROJECTION OF EXPENSES & INCOME
### (Nonprofit Professional Theatre, 20-Week Season)

PROJECTED EXPENSES

| | |
|---|---:|
| Annual Operating Budget | |
| (Including Amortized Capital Costs) | $1,000,000 |
| Pre-Production Expenses (4 shows) | 276,000 |
| Production Operating Expenses | |
| (4 shows, 5 weeks each) | 785,000 |
| Total Bonds (returnable) | 55,000 |
| | |
| Total Projected Annual Expense | $2,116,000 |

PROJECTED INCOME

| | |
|---|---:|
| Total Box Office Income | |
| (50% of $2,720,000) | $1,360,000 |
| Total Concessionary Income | |
| After Expenses | 38,240 |
| Total Earned Income from | |
| Other Sources | 25,500 |
| Total Grants & Contributions | 331,000 |
| | |
| Total Projected Annual Income | $1,754,740 |
| Income Less Expenses | (361,260) |
| Plus Refundable Bonds | 55,000 |
| | |
| Differential | ($306,260) |

The bottom line for this make-believe company doesn't look too bad—providing that the board of trustees and the management have faith in the veracity of the planning process that was used. But it may still be too soon to move the productions from the drawing board to the scene shop and the rehearsal hall. Alternative plans should first be explored, and proposed revisions should be studied in terms of their impact on production standards and goals.

## BUDGET BALANCING ALTERNATIVES

The basic alternatives to a projected deficit are very simple:

1. Increase earned income
2. Increase contributed income
3. Decrease expenses

Yet balancing a budget can be tricky, largely because it is tempting to make false assumptions. For example, it is easy to assume that if ticket prices are raised, the theatre will continue to draw 50 percent of its capacity, which may not be the result. Or perhaps the decision is made to produce three rather than four productions over the twenty-week season, thereby lowering pre-production costs. But this makes the dangerous assumption that more ticket buyers can be found to support the additional performances of the remaining three productions and thereby maintain revenue at the same level estimated from four shows.

Most budgeting involves a certain amount of robbing Peter to pay Paul. Money for one item is reduced so that money for another can be increased. But realism must be brought to bear. For instance, if it is decided to hire only two box office treasurers rather than three, can the box office still service customers without a loss in ticket sales? If the set designer is told not to construct a revolving stage unit, will additional stagehands have to be hired to move scenery manually?

While commercial ventures aim to make profits, nonprofit organizations, as mentioned, may be embarrassed by a surplus and find that it hampers their fundraising efforts. And theatre projects or departments supported by a larger institution may actually be penalized for a surplus by subsequent cutbacks in budget allocations. Such realities make it tempting to adopt a somewhat cynical viewpoint and say that budgets for commercial ventures should produce a little surplus, while budgets for nonprofit endeavors should produce a little deficit!

Substantial revisions of estimated expenses or income almost always translate into substantial revisions of policies and priorities. Managers and boards must be mindful of this fact when looking at the budget-balancing alternatives. How much financial compromise is possible before the artistic mission and integrity of the project are mortally threatened?

### Increasing the Earned Income

The first budget-balancing alternative that might be considered is an increase in ticket prices. A computer program can quickly provide data about any number of different pricing schemes. Let's look at our hypothetical theatre company to illustrate the point:

## SAMPLE ALTERNATIVE PRICING SCHEMES
## VS TOTAL ANNUAL EXPENSES

| Top Ticket Price | At 100% Capacity | Differential After Est. Annual Expenses (of $2,116,000) | At 50% Capacity | Differential After Annual Expenses (of $1,226,000) |
|---|---|---|---|---|
| $25.00* | $2,720,000 | $ 604,000 | $1,360,000 | ($756,000) |
| 30.00 | 3,360,000 | 1,244,000 | 1,680,000 | (436,000) |
| 35.00 | 4,000,000 | 1,884,000 | 2,000,000 | (116,000) |
| 40.00 | 4,640,000 | 2,524,000 | 2,320,000 | 204,000 |

*Original Scheme

But the above chart only shows estimated box office income. Once other sources of earned and contributed income are programmed in—which total $394,740 in our sample—it is clear that with a $30.00 ticket top at 50 percent capacity there would be a projected surplus of $41,260. But what are other alternatives for increasing income, if the board of trustees adamantly refuses to increase ticket prices above the present $25.00 top?

1. Increase prices or sales in relation to other sources of earned income (i.e. charge $2.00 for a soda or add a T-shirt concession)
2. Increase the number of performances for the planned production(s) (this would also increase expenses, but the marginal revenue could be worth it); additional performances might be given at the home theatre, another theatre or on tour
3. Increase the number of productions and performances (this would usually entail the greatest extra costs, unless such productions were revivals using costumes and scenery from storage and, perhaps, actors already rehearsed in their roles).

Some alternatives obviously carry a higher degree of risk than others. At least some experimentation with alternatives, however, can provide valuable lessons for future planning.

## Increasing the Contributed Income

While the fundraising director may already feel overburdened, necessity may inspire increased productivity in this area as in others. Present donors, from board members to subscribers, can be asked to donate more. Funding agencies can also be asked for additional money, although many of them are locked into annual budgets themselves, which they cannot exceed. And new funding sources of all types may always be approached. Factors such as urgency and merit are important in seeking additional or new funding. But as with the business of increasing sales, the business of increasing contributed income will also entail added expenses.

## Decreasing the Expenses

Nobody likes cutting back or having to economize, much less being downright impoverished. But unfortunately most arts organizations, and the dedicated people who work for them, have had to function under such circumstances. Many never rise above them. Doing more with less is a well-known exercise.

If we look at the production budgets and the programming plans which these budgets seem to imply for our hypothetical theatre company, it's clear that many cost-saving measures could be adopted, as is almost always the case. What remains the big point of conjecture is how such measures will affect production activities and results. Artistic considerations aside, let's make a few cuts, feed this information into a computer and see how it affects the bottom line.

Merely by not using stars in the first production and thereby reducing actors' salaries to $7,500 per playing week (saving $9,300 in weekly salaries and payroll taxes) and by substituting two plays that don't carry royalty payments for two that do, thereby saving a total of, say, $60,000, the season's costs are reduced by $69,300. Any number of changes and combinations of cost reductions can be fed into the computer and the results seen instantly. Each new set of results will stimulate new discussion between the artistic and managerial leadership, or at least this is how it should be. Each new budget cut will threaten somebody's territorial imperative; each will affect the quality and standards of the operation in some way; each will alter the navigational direction of the operation, even if this is only perceptible to the keenest observer.

## The Free Admission Policy

Ironically enough, the policy of eliminating box office revenue is sometimes the best way to balance the budget. Of course this policy could only be adopted by a nonprofit organization because it is based on the theory that if audience size can be substantially increased by giving all tickets away, contributed income will be increased proportionately. From a per capita standpoint, free tickets may actually reduce losses (a good argument to use in grants applications). For example, if the weekly operating costs for a production are $10,000, and 1,000 people per week are paying $2.50 each to see that production, then each person is being subsidized in the amount of $7.50. But if no admission is charged and, as a result of this policy, the production plays to 5,000 people weekly, each person is then being subsidized by only $2! This is a logical rationale, providing that the goal is not to make money. Also, the larger the audience served by a theatre group (regardless of ticket policy), the more favorably that group is likely to be regarded by potential funders. If many libraries, parks and museums are free to the public, another argument goes, why shouldn't free theatre also be made available? Experiments with this policy, such as Joseph Papp's Shakespeare in the Park productions each summer in New York, and others around the country, show that free theatre in accessible places attracts hundreds of thousands of first-time theatregoers—a phenomenon that makes politicians as well as government and corporate funders sit up and take notice.

### Pay-What-You-Can Policy

From California's La Jolla Playhouse to Baltimore's Center Stage, many nonprofit theatres have successfully experimented with a "pay-what-you-can" ticket policy. This permits patrons to buy two seats for specially designated performances at whatever price they can afford. In many cases these tickets sell out within hours after being offered for sale and, best of all, a majority are usually purchased by first-time theatregoers who will hopefully become regular, full-price ticket buyers in the future. So this policy is a promising technique for audience development. It can also attract corporate sponsorship to subsidize the voluntary admission income.

## TWO SPECIAL EQUATIONS

### Setting the Stop Clause in a Commercial Theatre License

Most tenants who rent a building negotiate a lease that allows occupancy for a specified length of time at a specified rental. A Broadway theatre license, however, calls for a percentage of the box office gross *against* a minimum guaranteed rental fee. Rarely is there a specified date when the production must vacate the theatre, unless the attraction is truly locked into a limited engagement. The date when the production will actually vacate the theatre is usually determined by the so-called stop clause.

The stop clause is a provision in the theatre license stipulating that when weekly box office revenue falls below a certain figure (usually for two consecutive weeks), either the landlord or the producer may terminate the lease. Termination notice must be give within so many days after the gross has dropped below that predetermined figure. The question is, what box office figure should be used in the stop clause? If the weekly break-even point is projected at $94,340, perhaps that figure should be used, because the producer doesn't wish to lose money. On the other hand, what if bad weather or illness of the star or some other occurrence results in business that is only temporarily bad? The producer obviously doesn't wish to give the theatre owner the right to close the production. In most cases, therefore, the Broadway producer selects a figure slightly below the break-even point. The reasoning is that, while poor business can be sustained for a few weeks, if business is going to be permanently bad, it will probably get worse quickly; if receipts fall to $80,000 one week, for example, they will probably fall much lower the following week. But the producer who must sustain a continuing weekly loss that is above the stop clause figure is in serious trouble. After the capitalization has been exhausted, and previous profits spent, further losses probably have to come out of the producer's own pocket. Hence, the importance of setting the right stop clause amount.*

## Computing the Break-Even Point When There Are Variable Costs

When all operating costs are fixed, as earlier examples in this chapter illustrate, it is a simple matter to estimate that revenue dollar amount at which there will be neither profit nor loss (that amount being the so-called break-even point). But what if there are also variable costs in the form of percentages, the dollar costs of which can only be determined by the exact revenue earned? In this case, the point at which the fixed *and* variable costs equal the gross income is the break-even point. Furthermore, if revenue exceeds the break-even point, expenses will increase due to the percentage payments. If revenue is less than the break-even point, then the actual operating cost will be lower than the break-even point. How, then, can a break-even point be determined without first knowing the actual revenue? To illustrate the equation that provides the answer, let's isolate the items in a Broadway production weekly operating budget that involve both fixed and variable costs. For the sake of clarity, the following figures have been lowered and rounded off:

| Item | Fixed Cost | (plus) | Variable Cost |
|---|---|---|---|
| Theatre rent | $ 4,000 | | 25% |
| Star | 2,500 | | 10% |
| Lyricist | 750 | | 2% |
| Composer | 1,000 | | 3% |
| Director | 500 | | 2% |
| Author (book) | 1,000 | | 5% |
| Total of all other weekly operating costs | 40,250 | | 0% |
| | | | |
| Total weekly operating costs | $50,000 | (plus) | 47% (of the actual gross) |

---

* See also Chapter 5: "Negotiating for a Theatre."                                    317

This budget shows fixed weekly operating costs at $50,000. But the producing company would have to take in well over that amount in weekly revenue in order to show a profit, due to the 47 percent variable cost. The formula below provides a way to compute the actual operating cost (the break-even point). It divides the fixed cost by what may be called the marginal income ratio (meaning the margin of profit that can be gained after variable costs are paid. In this example the producer has given away 47 percent of every dollar that will be taken in at the box office, leaving a 53 percent marginal income).

$$\frac{\text{Fixed cost (\$50,000)}}{\text{Marginal Income Ratio (53\%)}} = \text{Break-even Point}$$

or:   $50,000 / .53 = $94,340

| Proof: | Gross Income | | $94,340 |
|---|---|---|---|
| | Variable Cost (47%) | $44,340 | |
| | Fixed Costs | 50,000 | |
| | Total Costs | 94,340 | |
| | Profit or Loss | 0 | |

If the total potential weekly gross at the theatre where this show is playing is $106,000, then at capacity business it can earn a $6,180 weekly profit—but only after the capitalization, or pre-production expenses, have been paid off. If this pre-production amount is $250,000, then the show must play at capacity gross for over forty weeks before any true profit can be realized. Under this scheme the producer and backers must wait until the capitalization is repaid before they earn a profit, although the theatre landlord, the star and others begin to earn their percentages from the first ticket sold. (Under the Dramatists Guild Approved Production Contract percentage payments to the creative team are lower prior to recoupment of capital costs, so that the investors can be paid back sooner and begin to share in profits earlier.)*   Notice that actual operating costs of a production vary according to the actual box office income. If the total weekly potential gross is $106,000 but the actual weekly gross is $95,000, then the *actual* cost for that week will be $94,650 (47 percent of $95,000 plus the $50,000 fixed cost), which leaves a fat $350 in weekly profit! If the show opens at and maintains this $95,000 weekly gross, it will take over 714 weeks merely to pay off a $250,000 capitalization. Once the weekly gross falls below $94,340 the show is losing money. Is it any wonder that so few commercial productions ever "recoup the nut"?

To reduce these figures in terms of profit dividends (assuming that the producer is sharing profits equally with the limited partners), at a $95,000 weekly gross the producer can earn no more than $175 per week after 714 weeks or 14 years of waiting (plus all the time spent before the show even went into rehearsal). And the person who bought a 10 percent investment in that show (providing $25,000 of the total $250,000 capitalization) will earn only $17.50 per week (10 percent of $175). Let's hope they both share in a multimillion dollar sale of the show to a film company!

The length of time it will take to pay back the capitalization for this commercial production is pictured more graphically in the chart that follows. The accompanying graph show's the cost-revenue relationship for a college or community theatre production. Here the basic unit of measurement is not a week but a single performance valued at $1,000 in total potential revenue. With $4,000 in production and operating costs, this production has the potential to break even after four performances, after which all revenue will represent a profit. Both graphs are based on the assumption that variable costs may be computed from the first dollar of revenue—in other words, the playwright and others all earn a flat percentage from the bottom dollar. In some circumstances, however, percentages are paid on a system of graduating revenue: 5 percent of the first $10,000 in revenue, then 7 percent of the next $15,000 and so forth. When this is the case, the marginal income ratio may be estimated by using the *average* of all the percentages that are involved.

SAMPLE COST-REVENUE RELATIONSHIP
FOR A COLLEGE OR COMMUNITY THEATRE PRODUCTION

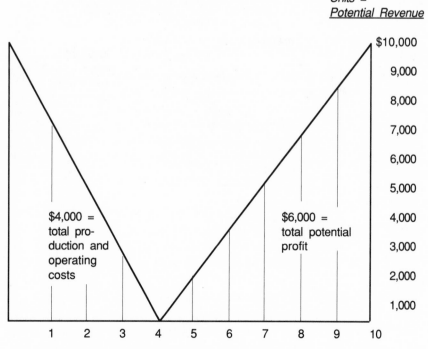

*Units =*
*Potential Revenue*

$4,000 =
total pro-
duction and
operating
costs

$6,000 =
total potential
profit

*Units = Performances*

SAMPLE COST-REVENUE RELATIONSHIP
FOR A COMMERCIAL NEW YORK PRODUCTION

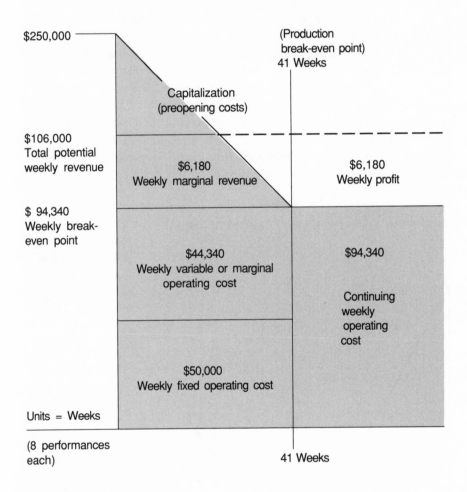

$250,000

(Production
break-even point)
41 Weeks

Capitalization
(preopening costs)

$106,000
Total potential
weekly revenue

$6,180
Weekly marginal revenue

$6,180
Weekly profit

$ 94,340
Weekly break-
even point

$44,340
Weekly variable or marginal
operating cost

$94,340

Continuing
weekly
operating
cost

$50,000
Weekly fixed operating cost

Units = Weeks

(8 performances
each)

41 Weeks

SAMPLE OPERATING COSTS (ASSUMING BASIC 12-WEEK SEASON, 7 REGULAR PERFORMANCES) SMALL MUSICAL PRODUCTION

| | 1st WEEK of 7 PERF. | 2nd WEEK OF SAME SHOW | Addl. Cost 8th PERF. IN WEEK | Addl. Cost 9th PERF. IN WEEK [5] | MARGINAL COST OF ADDITIONAL (13TH) WEEK SAME SHOW | NEW SHOW |
|---|---|---|---|---|---|---|
| *SALARIES:* | | | | | | |
| Cast (principals) | $ 2,200 | $ 2,200 | $ — | $ 275 | $ 2,200 | $ 2,200 |
| Cast (rehearsal) | 500 | — | — | — | — | 500 |
| Chorus ("Parts") | 1,300 | 1,300 | — | 165 | 1,300 | 1,300 |
| Performers (over-time) | — | — | 205 | 300 | — | — |
| Director and choreographer | 500 | 500 | — | — | — | 500 |
| Orchestra[1] | 1,400 | 1,400 | —[3] | 100 | 1,400 | 1,450 |
| Stage Manager and technical[2] | 650 | 650 | — | 20 | 370 | 650 |
| Box office and office | 700 | 700 | — | — | 700 | 700 |
| Parking and ushers | 300 | 300 | 40 | 40 | 300 | 300 |
| Maintenance | 175 | 175 | — | — | 175 | 175 |
| Press department | 225 | 225 | — | — | 225 | 225 |
| *TOTAL SALARIES* | $ 7,950 | $ 7,450 | $ 245 | $ 900 | $ 6,670 | $ 8,000 |
| Advertising and press expense | 1,000 | 900 | 200 | 200 | 900 | 1,000 |
| Ground and equipment rental | 300 | 300 | —[4] | —[4] | 300 | 300 |
| Royalty and rental materials | 1,600 | 1,600 | — | — | 1,600 | 1,600 |
| Costume rental and shoes | 750 | 500 | — | — | 500 | 750 |
| Wardrobe costs and freight | 100 | 50 | — | — | 50 | 100 |
| Scenery, lighting and props | 150 | 20 | 10 | 10 | 20 | 150 |
| Cast (travel pay) | 100 | — | — | — | — | 100 |
| Office supplies and expenses | 700 | 650 | 10 | 20 | 650 | 700 |
| Box office tickets and supplies | 60 | 60 | 10 | 10 | 60 | 60 |
| Light, water and heat | 100 | 100 | 10 | 10 | 100 | 100 |
| Maintenance, repairs and auto expenses | 150 | 150 | — | — | 150 | 150 |
| Payroll taxes, HIP and W/C Insurance | 450 | 420 | 15 | 50 | 400 | 450 |
| Package deals and production expenses | 40 | — | — | — | — | 40 |
| *TOTAL OPERATING COSTS* | $ 13,450 | $ 12,200 | $ 500 | $ 1,200 | $ 11,400 | $ 13,500 |
| *TOTAL OPENING/CLOSING COSTS AND CAPITAL COSTS AMORTIZED OVER 12 WEEKS* | 3,500 | 3,500 | — | — | — | — |
| *BREAK-EVEN POINT* | $ 16,950 | $ 15,700 | $ 500 | $ 1,200 | $ 11,400 | $ 13,500 |

[1] Includes musical director, choral conductor, rehearsal pianist, union tax and contractor fee.
[2] Includes set designer, carpenter, scene shifters, props master.
[3] Assumes musicians contract calls for eight performances at no additional pay.
[4] Assumes no percentage rent or royalties based on gross receipts.
[5] Assumes ninth performance in week does not interfere with day off.

321

## SAMPLE PREPRODUCTION BUDGET
### (Small Off-Broadway Musical)

| | | |
|---|---:|---:|
| **PHYSICAL:** | | |
| Scenery | $20,000 | |
| Costumes | 10,000 | |
| Props | 500 | |
| Electric and sound | 5,000 | |
| Instrument rental | 400 | |
| | | $ 35,900 |
| **FEES:** | | |
| Authors | 6,000 | |
| Director | 7,000 | |
| Scenic designer | 5,000 | |
| Costume designer | 4,000 | |
| Lighting designer | 4,000 | |
| Choreographer | 3,000 | |
| Casting | 500 | |
| General manager | 8,000 | |
| Orchestration | 1,000 | |
| | | 38,500 |
| **SALARIES:** | | |
| Equity | 21,400 | |
| Crew/wardrobe | 4,000 | |
| Musical director | 3,000 | |
| Musicians | 3,000 | |
| Press agent | 4,200 | |
| | | 35,600 |
| **REHEARSAL EXPENSES:** | | |
| Audition/rehearsal hall | 3,000 | |
| Scripts and scores | 500 | |
| Departmental | 500 | |
| | | 4,000 |
| **PRE-OPENING:** | | |
| Hauling | 1,500 | |
| Take-in and out | 3,000 | |
| Box office | 1,000 | |
| Opening night party | 1,500 | |
| | | 7,000 |
| **ADVERTISING:** | | |
| Newspaper and radio | 50,000 | |

| | | |
|---|---:|---:|
| Posters, printing, etc. | 12,000 | |
| Radio spot | 1,000 | |
| | | 63,000 |
| ADMINISTRATION: | | |
| Office fee | 500 | |
| Legal | 600 | |
| Accounting | 500 | |
| Payroll/fringes | 10,700 | |
| Insurance | 2,000 | |
| | | 14,300 |

| | |
|---|---:|
| TOTAL PRODUCTION COSTS: | $198,500 |
| BONDS/DEPOSITS: | 21,700 |
| CONTINGENCY | 25,000 |
| CLOSING COSTS: | 5,000 |
| TOTAL CAPITALIZATION: | $250,000 |

## SAMPLE WEEKLY OPERATING PRODUCTION BUDGET
### (Small Off-Broadway Musical)

FIXED COST
SALARIES:

| | | |
|---|---:|---:|
| Cast | $4,400 | |
| Stage managers | 600 | |
| General manager | 1,000 | |
| Press agent | 700 | |
| Stagehands | 1,500 | |
| Wardrobe/makeup | 500 | |
| Musicians | 1,800 | |
| | | 10,500 |
| PHYSICAL PRODUCTION: | | |
| Light/sound rental | 500 | |
| Physical prod. maint. | 200 | |
| Instrument rental | 400 | |
| | | 1,100 |
| ADVERTISING: | | |
| Print and radio. | 3,500 | |
| | | 3,500 |
| ADMINISTRATION: | | |
| Office | 125 | |
| Legal | 50 | |

| Accounting | 50 | |
| Insurance | 100 | |
| Payroll Taxes, etc. | 2,100 | |
| | | 2,425 |

THEATRE OPERATING:

| Rent | 1,800 |
| House staff | 1,250 |

| | 3,050 |
| TOTAL FIXED COSTS: | $20,575 |

## VARIABLE COSTS
Rent: 5% over 12,000, 10% over 15,000
Royalties: 7% plus 10% over 24,000

## BREAK-EVEN POINT
($S$ = sales at break-even)

$$s = 20,575 + .05 + .05(s\text{-}12,000) + .05(s\text{-}15,000)$$
$$s = 20,575 + .07s + .05s - 600 + .05s - 750$$
$$s = 20,575 + .17s - 1,350$$
$$.83s = 19,225$$
$$s = 23,162.65$$

BREAK-EVEN POINT: $23,162.65

To further illustrate the computation of the break-even point when there are variable costs involved, let's examine the previous budget (Sample Weekly Operating Production Budget), using the following formula:

Sales at Breakeven = Fixed Operating Costs + (Roylaty Percentage x
Sales at Break-even)

Given the fixed costs of $20,575 and a straight 7% royalty, this translates into the following ($S$ = Sales at Break-even):

$$S = 20,575 - (.07 \text{ x } S)$$
$$S = 20,575 + .07S$$
$$.93S = 20,575$$
$$S - 22,123.66$$

But often percentages are contracted in a more complex manner and are tied to different levels of sales income, as illustrated by the rent percentages in the preceding sample budget. So, when we take the same $20,575 in fixed costs and the same 7% straight royalty and then add a rent percentage of 5% for all sales over $12,000 and 10% for all sales of $15,000, the formula would be:

| | |
|---|---|
| S = | Sales at Break-even equals |
| 20,575 + | Fixed operating costs, plus |
| .05(S - 12,000) + | Percent times (Sales at Break-even exceeding $12,000), plus |
| .05(S - 15,000) | Additional Percent times (Sales at Break-even exceeding $15,000) |

Note that the rent is figured in two formula steps: 5% of all sales over $12,000 and *an additional* 5% for all sales over $15,000. This computes as follows:

$$S = 20,575 + .07S /.05S - 600 + 05S - 750$$
$$S = 20,575 + .17S - 1,350$$
$$.83S = 19,225$$
$$S = 23,162.65$$

After computing the break-even point one should be certain that none of the sales levels at which a percentage begins are higher than that break-even figure. If that is the case, the break-even figure will be inaccurate. For instance, if the above example were changed to add an additional 10% royalty for all sales over $24,000, this would invalidate the break-even figure that is shown. Because many contractual percentages (or increases) are negotiated after the break-even point has been figured, it is important to bear this point in mind.

## SAMPLE GROSS POTENTIALS
(For an 8-performance week in a 248-seat house
with a $23,162.65 weekly break-even point)

GROSS POTENTIAL
Capacity: 248
Performances/Wk: 8
Weekly Break-even: $23,162.65

| Average Ticket Price | % Capacity | Gross Potential | Weekly Profit (Loss) | # of weeks to pay off Capital of $200,000 | # of weeks to pay off Capital of $250,000 |
|---|---|---|---|---|---|
| $25.00 | 100 | $49,600 | $19,383 | 11 | 13 |
|  | 65 | 32,240 | 6,710 | 30 | 38 |
| 22.50 | 100 | 44,640 | 15,762 | 13 | 16 |
|  | 65 | 29,016 | 4,355 | 46 | 58 |
| 20.00 | 100 | 39,680 | 12,141 | 17 | 21 |
|  | 65 | 25,792 | 2,001 | 100 | 125 |
| 17.50 | 100 | 34,720 | 8,520 | 24 | 30 |
|  | 65 | 22,568 | (494) | — | — |
| 15.00 | 100 | 29,760 | 4,899 | 41 | 52 |
|  | 65 | 19,344 | (3,171) | — | — |

| Average Ticket Price | Weekly Break-even as % of Gross Potential |
|---|---|
| $25.00 | 47 |
| 22.50 | 52 |
| 20.00 | 59 |
| 17.50 | 67 |
| 15.00 | 78 |

## SUMMATION

It is impossible to illustrate here how much time and effort must be invested if financial planning is to result in a budget that will bear a reasonable approximation to the final financial report. But what everyone involved in the planning process and subsequent cost control should remember is this: variances between estimations and actual figures will almost certainly influence which employees and/or artists are retained or rehired for another season, and which are not; which productions are sent on tour, transferred or kept in the repertory, and which are not; which audience markets are targeted and courted in subsequent seasons, and which are not; and, indeed, whether or not the theatre company or organization will even continue to operate. So there is a great deal at stake when budget strategies are adopted and put into action.

People who can successfully project profits and losses do not depend on occult powers or magical formulas. They depend on experience, knowledge and a degree of intuition. An intelligent projection of costs and revenues for a project should provide the basis for intelligent decision making. Measured against such projections, one should be able to classify each decision as (1) reasonable, (2) cautious, or (3) risky. There is certainly no law against making risky decisions—and many success stories are based on such action—but it is stupid and needless not to know just how risky a decision may be.

There are many factors, some obvious and some hidden, that influence costs and revenue. The best budget manager for an organization is the one who is familiar not only with general business practices but, perhaps more importantly, with the art, and the organization that is being managed, and the community in which it is operating. Business managers and finance directors frequently provide facts and projections that nobody wants to hear. But, as with physicians, one would be foolish to ignore their findings.

# 12

# Cost Control Strategies

ONCE the artistic mission of a theatre production or company has been
set, and financial planning has evolved into a budget projecting the
expenses and income that will facilitate the mission, a system of checks and
balances should be put in place to safeguard the project. While accountants and bookkeepers have devised cost control systems to suit every type
of theatre organization, such systems are only as trustworthy as the people
who supervise and operate them. Perhaps most important is the comptroller. In the theatre this person may also be the producer, the general manager, the executive director or it may be someone who holds the title of business manager or finance director. Whichever the case, it is the person with
overall responsibility for the income and outflow of company funds.

## THE BUSINESS MANAGER

The person whose daily routine is keeping financial records, paying
bills, making deposits, or supervising such activities, usually has the most
accurate and up-to-the-minute picture of the organization's fiscal health.
Obviously, this person's advice should be sought and heeded on a variety
of matters. A business manager should not merely be a bookkeeper, but
someone regarded as a partner in the enterprise. A good business manager
is able to give valuable assessments about what is and is not possible from a
financial viewpoint, without being negative or throwing up road blocks. For
example, if the producer asks if a certain actor can be paid by certified check,
the answer should not include a discourse on the inconvenience of doing
this. To be certain of giving sound advice, the business manager must at all
times have a clear idea of the current assets and liabilities of the organization and of the many factors that may affect them in the near term. While
small operations may combine the position with that of producer or general
manager, it is not wise to assign business management functions to a stage
director, as often happens in community and campus theatres where one
person has assumed all the leadership responsibilities. Good business management requires an overview and objectivity that the person intimately in-

volved in directing a production is usually unable to provide. A good business manager is interested in the financial as well as artistic workings of the theatre, skilled at dealing with the myriad details that make things run smoothly and desirous of being a facilitator whose efforts will support the artistic mission and make everyone's job easier and more secure.

Aside from being an assistant and adviser to the general manager, producer, artistic director or board of trustees (depending on how the organization is structured), the business manager is usually responsible for the following aspects of the operation:

1. The box office
2. Banking
3. Insurance
4. Budgeting
5. Purchasing
6. Taxes
7. Payroll
8. Accounting , bookkeeping and financial reporting
9. Fulfilling contract and license obligations
10. Union negotiations and contracts

The business manager should be the direct supervisor of staff members concerned with the above areas, although union negotiations are sometimes conducted by a higher authority or an attorney, and box office personnel may be under the marketing department.

The business manager serves in many ways as a public relations representative. It is important to establish and maintain good will with unions, vendors, bankers, creditors, insurance companies, funding organizations and local authorities, just as it is to have the good will of the audience. In fact, the audience will include many people with whom the theatre conducts business. The business manager, more than most others in the organization, serves as a day-to-day spokesperson to the local power structure upon which the theatre depends. When leading merchants or bankers, for example, are disinclined to do business with the local theatre, its ability to operate may be seriously impaired. It is important that theatres project an image of sound fiscal responsibility, precisely because many businesspeople outside the arts tend to be skeptical about theatre companies, about their seriousness as business enterprises, their chances for success—about their very worth. In fact, it is probably safe to say that a factory or a plumbing service would automatically receive a higher credit rating from a bank or retailer than would a professional theatre. So the business manager often starts off at a disadvantage and must usually work hard to gain the trust and goodwill not only of the business community but of the artists in the theatre community as well.

## THE BUSINESS OFFICE

The business office of any ongoing theatre operation should provide a pleasant work environment. Yet, in a great many cases, the administrative offices—even in newly constructed performing arts facilities—are windowless, overcrowded, undecorated, claustrophobic and downright depressing. This is not the type of space likely to inspire a high level of efficiency from employees who may be spending ten hours a day, six days a week in it. If such an office cannot be substantially improved through renovation, it should be abandoned for storage purposes, and a more congenial space should be found. Increases in productivity will repay even a sizable expense many times over. And it is not usually necessary to locate the administrative offices in the theatre building itself, although this may save steps and help communications.

The business office of a theatre should provide privacy, security and quiet. Privacy is required due to the confidential nature of discussions about personnel, finances and policy matters. Security is an important factor for safeguarding expensive computers and other business equipment, as well as financial records and any cash that may be on hand from the box office. People who are required to work with figures should, at the very least, be located away from noise and interruption. If the business office is not located next to the box office, money should be counted in the box office itself and then transported directly to a bank to minimize the security risk.

Because there are so many different computer business systems and programs, many theatres hire a consultant to advise them about which hardware to purchase. The same consultant is often paid to train employees to use the computers. And large theatre organizations usually hire a full-time person with a title like "business systems analyst" just to oversee the purchase and use of computer hardware and software.

Other equipment and supplies required by a business office for an active theatre organization are obvious to any person qualified to work in one. But the cost of doing business has increased sharply with technological advances. Fax machines, remote or relay telephone-message devices and computerized ticket systems are all terrific; but will such technology decrease expenses and/or increase income? If the answer to that question is not a positive "yes," then the acquisition of that technology is not necessary.

## METHODS OF BUDGET CONTROL
### Budget Meetings and Conferences

At the beginning of each year or season, managers of ongoing theatres should hold a general business meeting at which the business manager instructs the entire staff about business, payroll, purchasing, payment, inventory and budgetary procedures. Who is authorized to make purchases? How will supply inventories be protected? What checks and balances have been devised to control expenses and safeguard income? Answers to these and other questions should be known to the entire staff. As provided in an early pre-season or preopening meeting, they are a strong, frontal attack against such enemies of cost control as ignorance, negligence, complicity and downright dishonesty.

Additional, smaller meetings should also be held as a matter of policy for planning discussions that will lead to budgets for each production or project. Budgets should not be composed in secret, much less by one person. They should result from the thoughts, suggestions and experiences of all people eventually responsible for accomplishing a project. If the supervisor of some department (which is to say, some part of the budget) believes that the project cannot be accomplished for less than a certain dollar amount, this should be made known to the business manager, who must then reexamine both the budget and the supervisor's plans: one of the two is unrealistic and must be changed in some way. If a person does not believe that a task can be accomplished within certain limitations, it's fairly certain that this same person will either exceed those limitations or do a poor job.

Different people have different idiosyncrasies about the use of money. Some have little concept of thrift; others jeopardize the project to spare the penny. Some work best with clearly-defined budget allocations, others do not. Some spend everything allocated to them, on general principle, others do not. Some consistently overestimate costs, others underestimate them. The business manager must analyze the work habits of each department head and establish a business relationship based on that person's outlook toward budgeting and spending. Different supervisors in an organization may be treated in different ways, with some given more leeway and trust in financial matters, and others less.

One of the most important factors in cost control is that of time. The less time allowed between the planning and the execution of a project, the less control there will be in relation to that project. (This applies to controlling the quality, the personnel, and the organization of the project, as well as the expenditures related to them.) In all cases, the business manager must maintain contact with the people responsible for spending budget allocations. When emergencies or unexpected expenses arise that change cost and revenue projections, then special business conferences must be arranged to discuss possible adjustments. The business manager must establish credibility among staff members in order to gain trust and exert control. In short, everyone in the organization should feel that the door to the business office is open to them—that the business office is a friendly place, and the people in it are there to help.

332

## *Internal Control*

As a precaution against both errors and embezzlement, every business enterprise involving more than one person should establish internal control. This entails introducing a variety of devices to safeguard the company's assets, the most important of which is the separation of duties so that more than one person is involved in each transaction. While cash is the most vulnerable asset, methods to protect inventories of goods and supplies should also be put in place. Many theatre organizations are run by just a few administrators, so a reasonable balance must be struck between the division of duties and effective internal control. Among the most common internal control practices are:

1. An annual audit conducted by an outside CPA who reports directly to the owner or the board. This should include both an audit of all the books and financial records, and the box office
2. Bonding employees, especially those who work in the box office and handle cash. Fidelity insurance should be reviewed annually with an insurance company
3. Separation of personal and business funds to clarify record keeping and reporting—especially tax reporting
4. Daily cash deposits in which cash, checks and credit card slips are sent to the bank exactly as they were received and on the same day. Cash, checks and credit slips should be received and recorded in some way by one person and later recounted and rerecorded for deposit by another person
5. Check signing should not be authorized for employees who handle cash or keep the financial records
6. Reconciliation of bank accounts should also be done personally by the owner or top financial officer, or reconciliations should at least be checked against bank statements to maintain ongoing knowledge of cash assets, and assurance that reconciliation is being conducted properly
7. Treat all tax money received, withheld or owed as a liability, so it is not counted as an asset and is not budgeted or spent as if it were
8. Disburse payment for an original invoice only to avoid duplicate payment
9. Use Purchasing Requisition and Purchase Order Forms (discussed below)
10. Use Tax Exempt Forms when permitted (discussed below).

Requisition and purchase orders should not exist merely to frustrate people. They should serve as tools of planning, cost control and record keeping. A requisition is a request for the purchase of something and should be submitted sufficiently in advance to allow time for the business manager to shop around and secure the best price. Large institutions do this by inviting bids from different vendors, while small companies simply get prices over the phone. Price reductions for many items and services can be negotiated before a commitment to buy has been made. But the business of haggling over the price once payment is due is unsavory and should also be unnecessary if the purchase was properly negotiated and, of course, if it was delivered as bargained. A signed purchase order form is an actual offer to buy something. Only the business manager should be authorized to sign purchase orders. All vendors with whom the theatre conducts business on a "charge" basis should be informed in writing that no charges will be honored unless made on the authority of a purchase order. These forms should be in triplicate, allowing a copy for the purchaser, a copy for the vendor to keep and a third for the vendor to mail back along with the bill. The use of purchase orders tends to eliminate hasty expenditures.  In the heat of dress rehearsal, for example, a designer or properties person may be tempted to rush out and buy items that are later left unused. While quick purchases are sometimes necessary, a system  that requires approval in advance helps to make people think twice; it also gives the business office the chance to suggest the best or least  expensive vendor, to point out that the item is already on hand, that another item may be substituted, or that it may be borrowed at no cost. Standard requisition and purchase order forms are available at stationary stores, or special forms may be designed to suit a company's bookkeeping system.

Most public, tax-supported organizations and private nonprofit corporations are legally exempted from paying state and local sales taxes. To qualify for these exemptions, however, the organization must have been granted official tax exempt status from the appropriate local and state departments of taxation. To gain exemption from certain federal taxes (payroll taxes are excluded), nonprofit organizations must file a Treasury Department IRS Form 1023, called "Application for Recognition of Exemption." After exemption from sales taxes has been granted, and an identification number assigned to the organization, tax-exempt forms should be acquired for presentation to vendors so they, in turn, have proof for their own tax records. The form must show the name, address and ID number of the exempt organization, as well as an authorized signature and the person's title. People who make cash purchases for a theatre may have to be reminded repeatedly to carry exemption forms with them, as the unnecessary payment of sales taxes can soon add up to a tidy sum.

# purchasing requisition
BROOKLYN COLLEGE

DEPARTMENT INSTRUCTIONS FOR USE OF THIS FORM
SEND ALL COPIES TO PURCHASING

PLEASE PRESS FIRMLY
YOU ARE MAKING 5 COPIES

HAND BUSINESS FORMS, INC., P.O. BOX 196, SPRINGFIELD, MASS. 01101

**BROOKLYN COLLEGE REQUISITION NO.**

| OVER $250 ☐ | SOLE VENDOR ☐ | F.O.B. |
| UNDER $250 ☐ | DEPT. MUST ATTACH | ☐ BROOKLYN COLLEGE |
| | LETTER OF JUSTIFICATION | ☐ SHIPPING POINT |

DEPARTMENT & NO.

DATE SUBMITTED

REFER QUESTIONS TO

PURCHASE ORDER NO.

P.O. DATE

TRAN. NO.

REQUIRED DELIVERY DATE

DELIVER TO:
ROOM #
BLDG
ATTN

TELEPHONE NO.

FEDERAL I.D. NO.

| COMPANY NAME OF SUGGESTED VENDOR 1 | COMPANY NAME OF SUGGESTED VENDOR 2 | COMPANY NAME OF SUGGESTED VENDOR 3 | COMPANY NAME OF SUGGESTED VENDOR 4 | COMPANY NAME OF SUGGESTED VENDOR 5 |

ADDRESS | ADDRESS | ADDRESS | ADDRESS | ADDRESS

| CITY | STATE | ZIP | CITY | STATE | ZIP | CITY | STATE | ZIP | CITY | STATE | ZIP |

PHONE NUMBER | PHONE NUMBER | PHONE NUMBER | PHONE NUMBER | PHONE NUMBER

ATTN: | ATTN: | ATTN: | ATTN: | ATTN:

| ITEM NO. | DESCRIPTION | QUANTITY | UNIT | UNIT PRICE | TOTAL |
|---|---|---|---|---|---|

**CODING BELOW TO BE FILLED IN BY DEPARTMENT**

| DEBT | COST CENTER | VAR | YR | OBJECT | SUB. PURP. | SUB. OBJ. | PROJECT | CUM. TOTAL |
|---|---|---|---|---|---|---|---|---|
| 7 0 4 5 | | 1 A 8 | | 2 | 0 1 | | | ▲ |

REMARKS:

I hereby certify that the items above are necessary for dept. use.

APPROVED BY:

AUTHORIZED SIGNATURE

**PURCHASING COPY**

335

# PURCHASE VOUCHER

Nº 8903

Date _____

FROM _____

TO: SUPPLIER

Name _____

Address _____

This voucher issued to _____

Furnish the following:

Your Invoice
Must Show
Our Order
Number

| Quantity | DESCRIPTION | |
|----------|-------------|--|
|          |             |  |
|          |             |  |
|          |             |  |
|          |             |  |
|          |             |  |
|          |             |  |
|          |             | TOTAL |

Show: _____

Account: _____

Approved by _____

## Comparative Budget Analysis

At the very least, a budget should be examined and analyzed (1) before it is adopted, (2) during the period when it is in effect and (3) after all the actual costs are known. Computer programs, of course, make it possible to conduct such analyses virtually on an hourly basis if that is desirable.

Once preliminary cost estimates are in, these should be checked against current retail prices and services to be sure they are realistic. Department heads should be given an opportunity to think about their estimates and be certain they can work within those figures—or within revised figures. Once the project is under way and purchasing has begun, a comparative budget should be drawn up to show actual costs subtracted from budgeted costs and also show the unexpended balance. Does this appear sufficient to cover the necessary remaining costs? Do the original estimates appear too high or too low? Can the organization anticipate a budget surplus or deficit? Is it necessary to take corrective measures? The sample budget analysis sheet that follows could also provide columns to show "final outcome" and "final difference between budgeted and actual costs." Original, interim, and final budget reports such as these are usually requested from nonprofit theatres by foundations and government agencies that fund them.

### SAMPLE BUDGET ANALYSIS SHEET

| ITEMS | (A) Original Estimation | (B) Actual to Date | (C) Balance | (D) Estimate to Complete | (E) Difference |
|---|---|---|---|---|---|
| 1. Box Office Income | | | | | |
| 2. Concessions Income | | | | | |
| 3. Grants and Contributions | | | | | |
| TOTAL REVENUE | | | | | |
| 4. Less: Total Operating Expenses | | | | | |
| 5. Surplus (or Deficit) | | | | | |

## Variance Analysis

An effective management tool for evaluating the financial performance of a business organization and its component departments is to make a comparison between actual costs and budgeted costs; this is called a variance report. Like the comparative analysis above, its purpose is to compare budgetary projections with actual costs and revenue, to determine a variance, or differential, and thereby judge the accuracy or inaccuracy of earlier estimates.

In large and complex business organizations, management often decides where to focus its investigations by locating the greatest variances. For instance, a general variance report (estimated vs actual costs) might show that overall costs for an operation are currently exceeding the overall estimates (see Chart A). One would then wish to see detailed variance reports for each area or department in the operation. Then it will become obvious exactly where the greatest variance occurs. Let's say that the cost for scenery was estimated at $1,000, but $1,800 was actually spent. Perhaps the scenery budget included funds for lumber, muslin, paints, hardware and lighting equipment. By examining the costs in each of these specified areas, it is seen that the overage occurred largely in regard to lumber, which cost more than anticipated (see Chart B). The set designer and technical director might then be asked why this happened. Perhaps it was because lumber prices were misjudged, because lumber was stolen from the scene shop, because costly mistakes were made in set construction or because the original set designs proved detrimental to the director's concept of the play and were replaced by new designs and sets. Based on such a budget analysis, management can identify the employee who should bear the greatest burden of blame (the business manager, the security guard, the technical director or the stage director) and take whatever corrective measures are deemed appropriate. In any case, management should know the reasons for budget over-runs and any employees who may be responsible for them.

CHART A
SAMPLE VARIANCE REPORT
(*College Theatre Production*)

| ITEM | ESTIMATED COST | ACTUAL COST | DIFFERENTIAL |
|------|------|------|------|
| Tickets | $    45.00 | $    47.63 | $      2.63 (over) |
| Publicity | 150.00 | 162.00 | 12.00 (over) |
| Programs | 200.00 | 150.00 | 50.00 under |
| Costumes | 350.00 | 164.32 | 185.68 under |
| Scenery and Props | 1,000.00 | 1,800.00 | 800.00 (over) |
| Trucking | 50.00 | 21.59 | 28.41 under |
| Lighting | 25.00 | 0 | 25.00 under |
| Royalty | 130.00 | 130.00 | 0 (-) |
| Makeup | 50.00 | 18.47 | 31.53 under |
| Scripts | 30.00 | 28.19 | 1.81 under |
| House Manager | 100.00 | 85.80 | 14.20 under |
| Sound | 2.00 | 0 | 2.00 under |
| Reserve Fund | 200.00 | 200.00 | 0 (-) |
| TOTALS | $ 2332.00 | $ 2,808.00 | $ 476.00 (over)* |

*Note: While scenery costs were $800.00 higher than estimated, savings in other areas and the use of the $200.00 reserve fund brings the final differential to only $476.00.

## CHART B
## SAMPLE VARIANCE REPORT ON SCENERY EXPENSES
### *(College Theatre Production, as per Chart A)*

| VENDOR | ITEM | Est. Cost | Actual Cost | Differential |
|--------|------|-----------|-------------|--------------|
| ABC Lumber Co. | lumber | $ 155.00 | $ 313.60 | (158.60) |
| ABC Lumber Co. | lumber | | 472.00 | (472.00) |
| Acme Color Co. | scene paint | 25.00 | 25.50 | ( .50) |
| J & J Rental Co. | prop rentals | 200.00 | 325.00 | (125.00) |
| Joe's Hardware | nails, braces, etc. | 58.70 | 61.20 | ( 2.50) |
| Lighting Assoc. | gels | 15.80 | 15.80 | ____ |
| Local Electrics Co. | projector rental | 200.00 | 200.00 | ____ |
| B & B Fabrics | muslin | 75.50 | 75.50 | ____ |
| Transfer Assoc. | prop transport | 100.00 | 100.00 | ____ |
| Miscellaneous | | 170.00 | 211.40 | ( 41.40) |
| | | $1,000.00 | $1,800.00 | $800.00 (over) |

## Cash-Flow Budget

If a theatre began its season or fiscal year with all the income for that period safely in the bank, it would be an easy matter to spend that money whenever necessary. But rarely is annual income accumulated all at once, so the business office must usually plan ahead to insure that money will be available when it is needed. The best device for doing this is called a cash-flow budget or, simply, a cash budget. It attempts to project when income from all sources will be received, and when payments for all expenses will fall due. Companies that do not utilize this type of planning are often in crisis—always, for example, scrambling around just to meet the weekly payroll. Cash budgets can predict cash shortages and thereby provide time to secure a loan, cut expenses, change plans, speed up the subscription campaign or take other measures that will avert a crisis. The sample that follows in Chart C could, of course, show the expense categories in greater detail, but it serves to illustrate how a cash budget can be designed. It might, for instance, be helpful to show payroll, tax and loan payment obligations for each month since these cannot usually be postponed.

## Inventories

Everything that belongs to a theatre organization should be listed in an inventory, copies of which should be kept in the business office and in a fireproof safe. For insurance purposes, it is helpful to send inventories of all insured items (together with the dollar value of each item) to the insurance company, which should also be notified when expensive new items are acquired. Especially when the physical assets of a theatre are extensive, or when items are stored in a variety of places, appropriate inventories should be available to department heads who may then easily check to see what is on

CHART C
SAMPLE CASH-FLOW PROJECTION
(Professional Nonprofit Theatre Company)
4 productions, 5 weeks each, November through March)

| | JULY | AUGUST | SEPTEMBER | OCTOBER | NOVEMBER | DECEMBER | JANUARY | FEBRUARY | MARCH | APRIL | MAY | JUNE | PROJECTED ANNUAL TOTALS |
|---|---|---|---|---|---|---|---|---|---|---|---|---|---|
| Capital & Annual Operating Expense | $83,333 | $83,333 | $83,333 | $83,333 | $83,333 | $83,333 | $83,333 | $83,333 | $83,333 | $83,333 | $83,333 | $83,333 | $1,000,000 |
| Pre-Production Expenses | 0 | 0 | 40,000 | 75,000 | 75,000 | 16,000 | 40,000 | 20,000 | 10,000 | 0 | 0 | 0 | 276,000 |
| Production Operating Expenses | 0 | 0 | 0 | 0 | 126,000 | 120,000 | 133,000 | 164,000 | 121,000 | 121,000 | 0 | 0 | 785,000 |
| Bonds (returnable) | 0 | 0 | 0 | 55,000 | 0 | 0 | 0 | 0 | 0 | 0 | 0 | 0 | 55,000 |
| Total Expenses | $83,333 | $83,333 | $123,333 | $213,333 | $284,333 | $219,333 | $256,333 | $267,333 | $214,333 | $204,333 | $83,333 | $83,333 | $2,116,000 |
| Box Office Income* | $ 0 | $ 0 | $405,000 | $270,000 | $380,000 | $250,000 | $175,000 | $150,000 | $50,000 | $ 0 | $ 0 | $ 0 | $1,680,000 |
| Concessionary Income After Expenses | 0 | 0 | 0 | 0 | 10,000 | 10,000 | 2,500 | 7,500 | 7,500 | 740 | 0 | 0 | 38,240 |
| Grants & Contributions | 0 | 0 | 25,000 | 31,000 | 50,000 | 75,000 | 100,000 | 50,000 | 0 | 0 | 0 | 0 | 331,000 |
| Other Earned Income | 500 | 500 | 5,500 | 2,000 | 2,000 | 2,000 | 2,000 | 2,500 | 2,500 | 1,500 | 500 | 4,000 | 25,500 |
| Total Income | $500 | $500 | $435,500 | $303,000 | $442,000 | $337,000 | $279,500 | $210,000 | $60,000 | $2,240 | $500 | $4,000 | $2,074,740 |
| Differential | ($82,833) | ($82,833) | $312,167 | $89,667 | $157,667 | $117,667 | $23,167 | ($57,333) | ($154,333) | ($202,093) | ($82,833) | ($79,333) | ($41,260) |
| WORKING CAPITAL ON HAND (Income minus Expenses with surplus or deficit carried forward) | ($82,833) | ($165,667) | $146,500 | $236,167 | $393,833 | $511,500 | $534,667 | $477,333 | $323,000 | $120,907 | $38,073 | ($41,260) | ($41,260) |

*With a $30 ticket top and a total potential annual gross of $3,360,000--shown here at 50% capacity

Bond returns: $55,000

Projected Year-End Balance: $13,740

hand and what is not. The properties department, for example, should not have to rummage through five cluttered storage rooms to determine whether or not the theatre owns a seltzer bottle. Each department head should be responsible for keeping its inventory list up to date. At the beginning and end of each season, the department head, together with a representative from the business office, should check the inventory. Then department heads should be held responsible for all items on the list, within the boundaries of common sense. A master carpenter, for instance, is more likely to worry about retrieving shop tools and locking them up at the end of each day when the cost of any missing tools may be deducted from that carpenter's next paycheck. Even when no financial penalty is imposed for missing or broken items, it is good business practice to verify the inventory with the appropriate staff member before that person receives a final paycheck.

Expendable and salable items should also be inventoried: the cash on hand in the box office, postage stamps, theatre tickets, candy and soda in concession booths and so forth. Remaindered items (unsold tickets, unused money, unsold candy bars) should be checked periodically against cash receipts. Obviously, when the records don't balance, an investigation should be conducted. A method of auditing the box office (with an inventory control technique for theatre tickets) is provided in the appendix. If a theatre operates a concession of some type, it should utilize a concession sales form maintained and checked not by sales personnel but by the theatre's business office.

## METHODS OF PAYMENT

Once an item or service has been selected, there is often a choice of ways to pay for it. Delayed payment may involve interest or service charges that amount to a considerable sum over a period of time. Prompt payment may be rewarded by special discounts taken off the purchase price (often the case with advertising bills). Other considerations, such as the interest being earned on cash assets, also help determine when payments should be made.

### A Tickler System

A good management technique for being certain that things are done in a timely fashion is to establish some type of tickler system. For example, one could set up a file drawer that contains a separate folder for each work day of the year. As invoices are received, they might be filed under the date on which they should be paid. Memos about loan repayments, tax and budget deadlines, and even personal reminders to call a particular vendor or attend to some other matter might be similarly filed. At the beginning of each work-

## SAMPLE CONCESSION INVENTORY & SALES REPORT FORM

Concessioner _____

Week Ending _____

| ITEM | MERCHANDISE RECEIVED | | | | | | | | Opening Inventory This | Less Closing Inventory | Allow-able Credits | Total Unit Sales | Unit Selling Price | AMOUNT OF SALES |
|---|---|---|---|---|---|---|---|---|---|---|---|---|---|---|
| | Mon | Tues | Wed | Thurs | Fri | Sat | Sun | Total | | | | | | |
| | | | | | | | | | | | | | | |
| | | | | | | | | | | | | | | |
| | | | | | | | | | | | | | | |
| | | | | | | | | | | | | | | |
| | | | | | | | | | | | | | | |
| | | | | | | | | | | | | | | |
| | | | | | | | | | | | | | | |
| | | | | | | | | | | | | | | |
| | | | | | | | | | | | | | | |
| | | | | | | | | | | | | | | |
| | | | | | | | | | | | | | | |
| TOTALS | | | | | | | | | | | | | | |

day, one simply takes out the folder for that date and there are all the chores that must be accomplished on that day. And this system not only "tickles" the memory of the person who ordinarily maintains it, but it also enables another worker to step in and take over, if necessary.

## Processing the Payment

When the business office receives a bill (original invoice), it should proceed as follows:

1. Check the bill for mathematical accuracy
2. Check the bill against the purchase order (did the vendor supply what was ordered?)
3. Check the purchase order against the requisitions (did the order request what was requisitioned?)
4. Check to be certain the merchandise or service was received in proper condition (to accomplish this in a large operation, a "receiver of goods" form may be sent to the appropriate theatre employee who must then verify or disclaim that the merchandise or service was actually received)
5. Issue a check in payment of the invoice, or file it for future payment.

As mentioned, payments should only be made from original invoices or bills, never from statements sent by the vendor. Payment by check allows more time than cash payments to study bills, examine merchandise and correct mistakes. And mistakes in billing are much more common than might be thought. This is as true in regard to bills written on computers by huge utility companies as for those scrawled by hand at the local pharmacy.

## The Petty Cash Fund

A petty cash fund is a separate imprest (or advance) fund set up to cover small expenses. It might be, for example, a fund of one hundred dollars to pay for postage, delivery charges or carfare. While it may be a temptation to pay for such items with box office money (placing a chit in the box office cash drawer whenever money is removed), this increases the possibility for error in accounting for ticket income and should be avoided. The better method is to keep a petty-cash box from which small amounts are paid in exchange for signed and itemized receipts made out in ink. The total money plus the receipts should always equal the imprest amount, in this case one hundred dollars. When the cash becomes low, a check is made payable to the custodian of the fund to "buy back" the receipts on hand. As money is disbursed from the petty-cash fund, the receipt taken in should be marked "paid" so that it won't be fraudulently reused.

There may be a need for several petty-cash funds to accommodate employees who must often put out cash for minor expenses. The publicity director, the properties director, and the production stage manager are logical candidates. Or workers may be asked to spend limited amounts from their own pockets and then be reimbursed periodically upon surrendering receipts. Whichever method is used, cash payments should only be made as . a last resort and only for small amounts.

## Types of Checking Accounts

Money should always be stored at the least cost and at the greatest benefit to its owner, within the boundaries of what is legal and prudent. At the very least, most theatre organizations of any size are able to maintain interest-bearing checking accounts, if not savings accounts and certificates of deposit. Other types of investments carry greater risk and should only be used with extreme caution—never for the storage of deferred income or capital ear-marked for deferred payment.

Any theatre that has income and expenses should establish two types of checking accounts, each with its own checkbook, account number and name. These are:

1. Box Office Account
2. General Operating Account

The box office account should begin each fiscal year with a balance of zero and thereafter receive only the income from ticket sales. In fact, all ticket income should be deposited into this account, so that an exact record of paid ticket sales is maintained. In the case of a single production project, the final balance in the account should be exactly the same as the final total gross shown on the box office statement. For theatres that operate a multi-production season, the cleanest way to maintain records is to transfer (by check) the total weekly gross or individual performance gross out of the box office account and into the general account. At season's end, the box office account should be back to a zero balance (excluding service charges). Of course, management may take a "loan" from box office funds, but the less active the box office account, the less chance there will be of spending deferred income or creating confusion when it comes time to reconcile box office statements with actual income. One fundamental principle should always be observed: all box office income (and *only* box office income) *must* be deposited into a separate box office account before it is disbursed for any reason whatsoever.

The general operating account should be that from which all disbursements are made. It may also be desirable to maintain other checking accounts to handle payroll, payroll taxes, and other such budget categories where an isolated accountability is helpful. When a theatre maintains several checking and savings accounts, it is good practice to use several different banks. This helps establish credit ratings as well as good relations with the local business community. In any case, each checking account should use different colored checks to avoid mistakes and confusion in the business office. All checks should provide space to itemize or describe the transaction. Payroll checks should provide the employee with a detachable stub where gross wages, taxes and other deductions may be itemized.

## PAYROLL PROCEDURES

A paycheck is based on an agreement between an employer and an employee. When this agreement is merely verbal, it is difficult to verify and is subject to all kinds of misinterpretation and ill feeling. It is generally better for both parties if the conditions and benefits of employment are spelled out in a written contract. When this is the case, that contract is the document used by the business office to provide the basic facts necessary for writing the employee's paycheck.

### Special Features of Theatrical Payrolls

Several features of payroll calculation are mandated by law and are standard for all salaried employees in a given state and city; but the preparation of a theatrical payroll often involves additional features that, while not all unique to this profession, do complicate the process. For example, Actors' Equity Association takes upon itself the responsibility for determining a "parts breakdown" regarding the roles and performance functions of its members during the rehearsal period of many Equity productions. If an actor performs two different parts, some special feat such as a pratfall or a slide, or some dangerous feat such as walking a tightrope, the actor may be entitled to more compensation than the base salary in that actor's contract. The same might also be true for a member of IATSE or AFM who is required to work on stage during the performance. While parts breakdowns are not necessary for all productions, they are commonplace when it comes to musicals, variety shows and plays with numerous characters; therefore, payroll information for many Equity shows cannot be complete until the union has determined the parts breakdown.

Royalty payments and percentages—both tied to actual box office revenues—are also common in the professional theatre. This almost always involves stars (who are also on the regular payroll), as well as directors, composers, lyricists, book writers, designers, and producers (who usually receive only fees and/or the royalty payments). Theatres which provided initial tryout or workshop productions that contributed to the development of the work are also on the list of those who receive royalty payments.

Daily or weekly per diem amounts are often paid to employees who are on tour with a production. In some cases these are tied to living-away-from-home expenses, and if such costs exceed a specified percentage of the per diem or the base salary, then the employer must kick in the difference. There may also be travel allotments to pay for air, bus or train tickets; penalty fees to pay when management fails to comply with union travel rules; penalty payments to pay when overtime rates are activated for any number of reasons; or additional pay when performers are involved in a broadcast, recording, taping or filming.

The business office must also scrutinize each performer's contract for special riders that mandate such amenities (and costs) as baby sitters, tutors, traveling companions, dressers, maids, chauffeurs or hairdressers who would also add to the payroll. Other riders may stipulate percentage agreements, food services, dressing room decor and anything else under the sun that the performer's agent is able to sneak into the contract. The process of payroll preparation for a professional theatre company can, indeed, be a complex one.

## Cash Payrolls

When employees are paid in cash, a single check should be drawn from the general account for the total net amount of the cash payroll. The business office may then instruct the local bank (in writing) to divide the total into appropriate cash amounts. The bank may request the organization to fill out pay envelopes, showing each employee's name and the amount of salary, but most banks are willing to insert cash into the individual envelopes. Upon receipt of the envelope, the employee should be required to count the money and then sign a payroll sheet or receipt to indicate that it is correct. In all other ways, the cash payroll process is the same as a standard payroll.

## The W-2 and W-4 Forms

The business office obtains basic payroll information from the W-4 form, required by the federal government, which each employee must fill out and submit to the business office. It requires the employee to state his or her name, permanent address, Social Security number, and the number of exemptions being claimed. This is a mandatory procedure and necessary in order for the employer to prepare payroll tax returns and W-2 forms (showing the gross annual amount earned by each employee) at the end of each year. Both forms are available free of charge from any IRS office. The business manager should also request a copy of the current Circular E or "Employer's Tax Guide" from the IRS. This contains in table format the current amounts of federal payroll taxes the employer must withhold according to the employee's marital status and number of deductions claimed by the employee on the W-4 form. Similar tables are also available for the purposes of computing state and local income taxes (where these exist). In cases where the employee maintains a permanent residence in another state, taxes should still be withheld according to the schedule of the state in which salary is earned. The employee then has the bothersome responsibility of filing income tax returns in all states where income has been earned over a certain minimum amount during a given fiscal year. Exceptions and modifications to this rule can be explained by a local Certified Public Accountant.

## INS Form I-9

The Immigration Reform and Control Act of 1986 attempts to discourage illegal entry into the United States by the denial of employment to illegal aliens. The law requires all employers to do five things:

1. Have employees fill out their part of Form I-9 when they start work
2. Check employee documents to verify identity and eligibility to work
3. Properly complete Form I-9
4. Retain the form for at least three years. If the person is employed longer than that, the form must be retained until one year after employment terminates
5. Present the form for inspection to the Immigration and Naturalization Service (INS) or the Department of Labor upon request.

The I-9 does not have to be completed for employees hired:
Before 11/7/86
After 11/6/86 but terminated before 6/1/87
As occasional domestic workers in a private home
As labor provided by a contractor who provides contract employees
(e.g., employee leasing)
As independent contractors.

Nor does the form need to be completed by people who are self-employed.

## The Independent Contractor

An independent contractor is a person or group paid by a fee from which no tax deductions are made. The responsibility for paying all income taxes, therefore, falls on the independent contractor and not upon the em-

347

**SINGLE** Persons–**WEEKLY** Payroll Period

**(For Wages Paid After December 1989)**

| And the wages are– | | And the number of withholding allowances claimed is– | | | | | | | | | | |
|---|---|---|---|---|---|---|---|---|---|---|---|---|
| At least | But less than | 0 | 1 | 2 | 3 | 4 | 5 | 6 | 7 | 8 | 9 | 10 |
| | | The amount of income tax to be withheld shall be– | | | | | | | | | | |
| $540 | $550 | $98 | $86 | $75 | $64 | $55 | $49 | $43 | $37 | $31 | $25 | $19 |
| 550 | 560 | 100 | 89 | 78 | 67 | 56 | 50 | 44 | 38 | 32 | 27 | 21 |
| 560 | 570 | 103 | 92 | 81 | 70 | 59 | 52 | 46 | 40 | 34 | 28 | 22 |
| 570 | 580 | 106 | 95 | 84 | 73 | 62 | 53 | 47 | 41 | 35 | 30 | 24 |
| 580 | 590 | 109 | 98 | 87 | 76 | 65 | 55 | 49 | 43 | 37 | 31 | 25 |
| 590 | 600 | 112 | 100 | 89 | 78 | 67 | 56 | 50 | 44 | 38 | 33 | 27 |
| 600 | 610 | 114 | 103 | 92 | 81 | 70 | 59 | 52 | 46 | 40 | 34 | 28 |
| 610 | 620 | 117 | 106 | 95 | 84 | 73 | 62 | 53 | 47 | 41 | 36 | 30 |
| 620 | 630 | 120 | 109 | 98 | 87 | 76 | 65 | 55 | 49 | 43 | 37 | 31 |
| 630 | 640 | 123 | 112 | 101 | 90 | 79 | 68 | 56 | 50 | 44 | 39 | 33 |
| 640 | 650 | 126 | 114 | 103 | 92 | 81 | 70 | 59 | 52 | 46 | 40 | 34 |
| 650 | 660 | 128 | 117 | 106 | 95 | 84 | 73 | 62 | 53 | 47 | 42 | 36 |
| 660 | 670 | 131 | 120 | 109 | 98 | 87 | 76 | 65 | 55 | 49 | 43 | 37 |
| 670 | 680 | 134 | 123 | 112 | 101 | 90 | 79 | 68 | 57 | 50 | 45 | 39 |
| 680 | 690 | 137 | 126 | 115 | 104 | 93 | 82 | 70 | 59 | 52 | 46 | 40 |
| 690 | 700 | 140 | 128 | 117 | 106 | 95 | 84 | 73 | 62 | 53 | 48 | 42 |
| 700 | 710 | 142 | 131 | 120 | 109 | 98 | 87 | 76 | 65 | 55 | 49 | 43 |
| 710 | 720 | 145 | 134 | 123 | 112 | 101 | 90 | 79 | 68 | 57 | 51 | 45 |
| 720 | 730 | 148 | 137 | 126 | 115 | 104 | 93 | 82 | 71 | 60 | 52 | 46 |
| 730 | 740 | 151 | 140 | 129 | 118 | 107 | 96 | 84 | 73 | 62 | 54 | 48 |
| 740 | 750 | 154 | 142 | 131 | 120 | 109 | 98 | 87 | 76 | 65 | 55 | 49 |
| 750 | 760 | 156 | 145 | 134 | 123 | 112 | 101 | 90 | 79 | 68 | 57 | 51 |
| 760 | 770 | 159 | 148 | 137 | 126 | 115 | 104 | 93 | 82 | 71 | 60 | 52 |
| 770 | 780 | 162 | 151 | 140 | 129 | 118 | 107 | 96 | 85 | 74 | 63 | 54 |
| 780 | 790 | 165 | 154 | 143 | 132 | 121 | 110 | 98 | 87 | 76 | 65 | 55 |
| 790 | 800 | 168 | 156 | 145 | 134 | 123 | 112 | 101 | 90 | 79 | 68 | 57 |
| 800 | 810 | 170 | 159 | 148 | 137 | 126 | 115 | 104 | 93 | 82 | 71 | 60 |
| 810 | 820 | 173 | 162 | 151 | 140 | 129 | 118 | 107 | 96 | 85 | 74 | 63 |
| 820 | 830 | 176 | 165 | 154 | 143 | 132 | 121 | 110 | 99 | 88 | 77 | 66 |
| 830 | 840 | 179 | 168 | 157 | 146 | 135 | 124 | 112 | 101 | 90 | 79 | 68 |
| 840 | 850 | 182 | 170 | 159 | 148 | 137 | 126 | 115 | 104 | 93 | 82 | 71 |
| 850 | 860 | 184 | 173 | 162 | 151 | 140 | 129 | 118 | 107 | 96 | 85 | 74 |
| 860 | 870 | 187 | 176 | 165 | 154 | 143 | 132 | 121 | 110 | 99 | 88 | 77 |
| 870 | 880 | 190 | 179 | 168 | 157 | 146 | 135 | 124 | 113 | 102 | 91 | 80 |
| 880 | 890 | 193 | 182 | 171 | 160 | 149 | 138 | 126 | 115 | 104 | 93 | 82 |
| 890 | 900 | 196 | 184 | 173 | 162 | 151 | 140 | 129 | 118 | 107 | 96 | 85 |
| 900 | 910 | 198 | 187 | 176 | 165 | 154 | 143 | 132 | 121 | 110 | 99 | 88 |
| 910 | 920 | 201 | 190 | 179 | 168 | 157 | 146 | 135 | 124 | 113 | 102 | 91 |
| 920 | 930 | 204 | 193 | 182 | 171 | 160 | 149 | 138 | 127 | 116 | 105 | 94 |
| 930 | 940 | 207 | 196 | 185 | 174 | 163 | 152 | 140 | 129 | 118 | 107 | 96 |
| 940 | 950 | 210 | 198 | 187 | 176 | 165 | 154 | 143 | 132 | 121 | 110 | 99 |
| 950 | 960 | 214 | 201 | 190 | 179 | 168 | 157 | 146 | 135 | 124 | 113 | 102 |
| 960 | 970 | 217 | 204 | 193 | 182 | 171 | 160 | 149 | 138 | 127 | 116 | 105 |
| 970 | 980 | 220 | 207 | 196 | 185 | 174 | 163 | 152 | 141 | 130 | 119 | 108 |
| 980 | 990 | 224 | 211 | 199 | 188 | 177 | 166 | 154 | 143 | 132 | 121 | 110 |
| 990 | 1,000 | 227 | 214 | 201 | 190 | 179 | 168 | 157 | 146 | 135 | 124 | 113 |
| 1,000 | 1,010 | 230 | 217 | 204 | 193 | 182 | 171 | 160 | 149 | 138 | 127 | 116 |
| 1,010 | 1,020 | 233 | 220 | 207 | 196 | 185 | 174 | 163 | 152 | 141 | 130 | 119 |
| 1,020 | 1,030 | 237 | 224 | 211 | 199 | 188 | 177 | 166 | 155 | 144 | 133 | 122 |
| 1,030 | 1,040 | 240 | 227 | 214 | 202 | 191 | 180 | 168 | 157 | 146 | 135 | 124 |
| 1,040 | 1,050 | 243 | 230 | 217 | 204 | 193 | 182 | 171 | 160 | 149 | 138 | 127 |
| 1,050 | 1,060 | 247 | 234 | 221 | 208 | 196 | 185 | 174 | 163 | 152 | 141 | 130 |
| 1,060 | 1,070 | 250 | 237 | 224 | 211 | 199 | 188 | 177 | 166 | 155 | 144 | 133 |
| 1,070 | 1,080 | 253 | 240 | 227 | 214 | 202 | 191 | 180 | 169 | 158 | 147 | 136 |
| 1,080 | 1,090 | 257 | 244 | 231 | 218 | 205 | 194 | 182 | 171 | 160 | 149 | 138 |
| 1,090 | 1,100 | 260 | 247 | 234 | 221 | 208 | 196 | 185 | 174 | 163 | 152 | 141 |
| 1,100 | 1,110 | 263 | 250 | 237 | 224 | 211 | 199 | 188 | 177 | 166 | 155 | 144 |
| 1,110 | 1,120 | 266 | 253 | 240 | 227 | 214 | 202 | 191 | 180 | 169 | 158 | 147 |
| 1,120 | 1,130 | 270 | 257 | 244 | 231 | 218 | 205 | 194 | 183 | 172 | 161 | 150 |
| 1,130 | 1,140 | 273 | 260 | 247 | 234 | 221 | 208 | 196 | 185 | 174 | 163 | 152 |
| 1,140 | 1,150 | 276 | 263 | 250 | 237 | 224 | 211 | 199 | 188 | 177 | 166 | 155 |
| 1,150 | 1,160 | 280 | 267 | 254 | 241 | 228 | 215 | 202 | 191 | 180 | 169 | 158 |
| 1,160 | 1,170 | 283 | 270 | 257 | 244 | 231 | 218 | 205 | 194 | 183 | 172 | 161 |
| 1,170 | 1,180 | 286 | 273 | 260 | 247 | 234 | 221 | 208 | 197 | 186 | 175 | 164 |
| 1,180 | 1,190 | 290 | 277 | 264 | 251 | 238 | 225 | 212 | 199 | 188 | 177 | 166 |
| 1,190 | 1,200 | 293 | 280 | 267 | 254 | 241 | 228 | 215 | 202 | 191 | 180 | 169 |

$1,200 and over    Use Table 1(a) for a **SINGLE person** on page 22. Also see the instructions on page 20.

Page 25

348

## EMPLOYMENT ELIGIBILITY VERIFICATION (Form I-9)

---

**1** **EMPLOYEE INFORMATION AND VERIFICATION:** (To be completed and signed by employee.)

| Name: (Print or Type)   Last | First | Middle | Birth Name |
|---|---|---|---|

| Address: Street Name and Number | City | State | ZIP Code |
|---|---|---|---|

| Date of Birth (Month/Day/Year) | Social Security Number |
|---|---|

**I attest, under penalty of perjury, that I am (check a box):**

☐ 1. A citizen or national of the United States.

☐ 2. An alien lawfully admitted for permanent residence (Alien Number A _____ ).

☐ 3. An alien authorized by the Immigration and Naturalization Service to work in the United States (Alien Number A _____ .
or Admission Number _____ , expiration of employment authorization, if any _____ ).

**I attest, under penalty of perjury, the documents that I have presented as evidence of identity and employment eligibility are genuine and relate to me. I am aware that federal law provides for imprisonment and/or fine for any false statements or use of false documents in connection with this certificate.**

| Signature | Date (Month/Day/Year) |
|---|---|

PREPARER TRANSLATOR CERTIFICATION (To be completed if prepared by person other than the employee). I attest, under penalty of perjury, that the above was prepared by me at the request of the named individual and is based on all information of which I have any knowledge.

| Signature | Name (Print or Type) | | |
|---|---|---|---|
| Address (Street Name and Number) | City | State | Zip Code |

---

**2** **EMPLOYER REVIEW AND VERIFICATION:** (To be completed and signed by employer.)

Instructions:

Examine one document from List A and check the appropriate box, **_OR_** examine one document from List B **_and_** one from List C and check the appropriate boxes. Provide the **_Document Identification Number_** and **_Expiration Date_** for the document checked.

| List A<br>Documents that Establish<br>Identity and Employment Eligibility | List B<br>Documents that Establish<br>Identity | **and** | List C<br>Documents that Establish<br>Employment Eligibility |
|---|---|---|---|
| ☐ 1. United States Passport | ☐ 1. A State-issued driver's license or a State-issued I.D. card with a photograph, or information, including name, sex, date of birth, height, weight, and color of eyes. (Specify State)_____ ) | | ☐ 1. Original Social Security Number Card (other than a card stating it is not valid for employment) |
| ☐ 2. Certificate of United States Citizenship | | | ☐ 2. A birth certificate issued by State, county, or municipal authority bearing a seal or other certification |
| ☐ 3. Certificate of Naturalization | ☐ 2. U.S. Military Card | | |
| ☐ 4. Unexpired foreign passport with attached Employment Authorization | ☐ 3. Other (Specify document and issuing authority) | | ☐ 3. Unexpired INS Employment Authorization Specify form |
| ☐ 5. Alien Registration Card with photograph | _____ | | # _____ |
| **_Document Identification_** | **_Document Identification_** | | **_Document Identification_** |
| # _____ | # _____ | | # _____ |
| **_Expiration Date (if any)_** | **_Expiration Date (if any)_** | | **_Expiration Date (if any)_** |
| _____ | _____ | | _____ |

**CERTIFICATION: I attest, under penalty of perjury, that I have examined the documents presented by the above individual, that they appear to be genuine and to relate to the individual named, and that the individual, to the best of my knowledge, is eligible to work in the United States.**

| Signature | Name (Print or Type) | Title |
|---|---|---|
| Employer Name | Address | Date |

Form I-9 (05/07/87)
OMB No. 1115-0136

U.S. Department of Justice
Immigration and Naturalization Service

ployer. The independent contractor must, nevertheless, fill out and submit a W-4 form and must sign a statement certifying that he or she is working as an independent contractor. The obvious advantage of this for the employer is that no matching tax or Social Security contributions will be required as they are for other salaried employees. Many artists and consultants who earn large amounts of money work as independent contractors, forming their own corporation into which all their earnings are deposited. In such cases, the fee is made payable directly to the corporation and the corporation then becomes responsible for declaring its earnings and paying taxes at the end of the year. This system often provides an individual with a more advantageous tax situation than working for a regular salary, but only when very large earnings are involved. The employer who pays independent contractor fees must indicate this on Form 1099 when filing tax records with the government at year's end.

Strictly speaking, the Internal Revenue Service does not regard any individual as an independent contractor unless that person is incorporated (such as an accounting firm or a consulting firm) and working for the corporation. This means that all people working under union contracts and all casual or part-time laborers are employees, subject to employee tax laws. If an unincorporated person who is not legally authorized to receive a fee as an independent contractor is discovered, and if that person fails to pay the appropriate taxes, *the employer may be held liable both for the employee wage deductions and the employer's Social Security tax contribution.* And this frequently happens when a non-taxed, ex-employee applies for unemployment benefits.

## Depository Receipts for Withheld Taxes

A federal depository receipt, which is Treasury Department Form 8109, is a record of payroll taxes turned over to the federal government by the employer. The total federal withheld taxes should be paid to the Federal Reserve Bank or to a depository bank at the end of each payroll week. The payment should be made by a check drawn from the general operating account and sent to the bank with a completed Form 8109, which will show the employer's name, address, registration number, and the amount being paid.

## Employer Identification Number

All corporations must have an Employer Identification Number assigned by the IRS. Even nonprofit organizations that have no employees on payroll must comply with this obligation. The number will be used on such documents as union employees' contracts, W-2 forms and the like. It is assigned by filing an Application for Employer Identification Number (Department of

Treasury Form SS-4) with a local office of the IRS, from which the blank form may be obtained.

## Withholding Tax and Social Security Forms

By the end of each month after the close of each calendar quarter, Form 941 must be filed. By January 31 of the following year, law requires that Form W-2 be filed for each employee. To facilitate this, an individual payroll record should be kept for each employee. This may be done by computer or kept on a form such as the one that follows.

There are three ID numbers that must be obtained by the business office or the accountant, and they are frequently used on employee forms and records:

1. Employer's Registration Number
2. Federal Insurance Contribution Identification Number
3. State Unemployment Insurance Identification Number

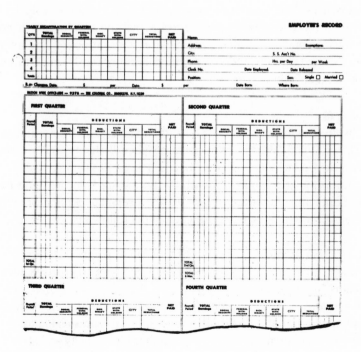

## Unemployment Forms

All states require that employees be furnished with a record of their employment upon termination of that employment. The form on which this information is given varies from state to state: they are obtained from the state Unemployment Insurance Commission. It is wise to attach this form to the employee's final paycheck, as it will be necessary if that person applies for unemployment compensation. When this occurs, the state in which the former employee applies will send a notice to the employer requesting verification of the employment period and salary. This must be returned within a specified number of days, after which time a penalty is imposed on the employer.

## Failure to Submit Withheld Taxes

Late submission of payroll taxes to the IRS carries a 10 percent penalty. Failure to pay such taxes altogether carries a 100 percent penalty plus the employer's tax contributions, if this was done knowingly and intentionally. In fact, the manager is held personally liable for such monies, and even bankruptcy does not discharge that liability in regard to tax payments. To repeat again: at no time should a corporation use withheld tax money for operating expenses. The wisdom of transferring such money to a Federal Reserve Bank at the end of each pay period is that the employer will not then be tempted to budget or use that money for other purposes. The Internal Revenue Service rigorously enforces tax collection and is quick to impose penalties on defaulting corporations.

## Payroll Sheets

Any theatre that maintains a salaried staff and is responsible for administering the payroll should keep its records on payroll sheets or computer spread sheets devised to suit its specific needs. The entries or field will vary, depending upon the state and city in which the theatre is located and the nature of the operation; however, in most cases, a separate column or entry on the payroll sheet will be required for each of the following:

1. *Salary code number:* large organizations may assign a different budget code number to various types of personnel (i.e. artists, technicians, administrators)
2. *Home state, number of dependents, marital status:* this information is obtained from the W-4 form. If an employee claims residence in another state, then exemption is granted from local city and state taxes; this entry would look something like "NY-4-M"
3. *Name of employee:* check W-4 forms to be certain that employee's

name is legal and not assumed

4. *Base salary:* check the contract with the employee to determine the basic contracted salary; if determined according to hours worked, a separate column should be used to enter those hours

5. *Additional salary:* this should include overtime payments, rehearsal pay, vacation pay, extra parts payments and any other earnings that are subject to payroll taxes

6. *Total gross salary:* total of 4 and 5

7. *Social Security:* money withheld for social security, determined as a percentage of the total wages

8. *Federal income tax withheld:* this deduction is based on the gross salary and determined according to Circular "E" (Employer's Tax Guide, IRS Publication Guide No. 15, available from any IRS office)

9. *State income tax withheld:* in those states that require such deductions for state residents

10. *City income tax withheld*

11. *Other deductions:* a double column should give a brief explanation of any other deductions and an itemized list to include such items as union dues, loan repayments, room rent, food charges, etc.

12. *Total deductions:* total of 7 through 11

13. *Net pay:* amount actually paid to employee

14. *Other pay received:* any nontaxable fees given to the employee, such as per diem payments, travel expense reimbursement, rent for performer's own clothing used as costumes and the like

15. *Total amount received:* total of 13 and 14

16. *Check number:* if paid by check, or signature of the employee if paid in cash.

The matter of computing overtime payments can be complicated for a large theatre company. It is essential to keep detailed rehearsal schedules and a record of time worked by all union employees. The stage manager and other personnel supervisors should be required to submit daily time sheets showing the hours worked by union members.

## *The Day to Pay*

Civic and educational institutions usually pay their employees on a monthly or biweekly basis and theatre groups affiliated with them may have no responsibility for salary computation and disbursement. Theatres that employ union laborers, however, will be required to make weekly salary disbursements and to insure that employees receive their pay prior to the commencement of the final weekly performance or work day. This is usually a Saturday or a Sunday. Because banks are not open on weekends, and employees should be allowed to cash or deposit their checks when they receive them, salaries are best paid on the last banking day of the payroll week or period. Actors' Equity Association and other labor organizations require that management offer to cash pay checks at once on the premises where the check is issued or pay by certified check. When this involves keeping a sizable amount of cash on hand, such money should be held for the shortest time possible before being disbursed or redeposited. And, of course, security precautions should be taken—such as requesting a police escort to and from the bank or having an in-house security guard on duty. Also, the employees who transport large cash amounts should be bonded with the theatre's insurance company in a sufficient amount to cover any losses.

Most banks offer special services to corporate customers and can be especially helpful in assisting with the payroll process. For example, if weekly or monthly gross payroll amounts (plus the employer's tax contributions) are deposited with a bank, it may agree to provide the following services:

1. Issue the salaries by check or in cash envelopes
2. Provide a payroll record
3. File the quarterly returns
4. Issue the W-4 forms at the end of the year.

## METHODS OF ACCOUNTING
### The Role of the Accountant

While increases in theatrical production costs over recent decades are largely due to inflation and salary gains, increases related to legal and accounting costs have also been considerable. An accountant or accounting firm, however, is necessary for theatre operations of any size and permanence. As mentioned earlier, the accountant should be directly responsible to the producer or the board of trustees. Nonetheless, the accountant works closely with the business manager in organizing the financial record-keeping system. But rather than paying an accountant or firm to do all the bookkeeping work, it is usually more economical to hire a bookkeeper or train a staff member in those duties. When this is done, the outside accountant will be primarily concerned with filing the necessary tax forms, preparing annual reports, conducting audits of the books and the box office, and reconciling the checkbooks with bank statements. Where problems or discrepancies arise, the accountant reports these directly to the producer or the board, together with recommendations for corrective measures.

NAME
OF
THEATRE

| Clock Number | (A) State<br>(B) Number of Dependants<br>(C) Marital Status | Name | Base Salary | Additional Salary Explanation | Additional Salary Amount | Total Gross Pay | Social Security Tax Withheld | Federal Income Tax Withheld | Philadelphia City Tax Withheld 2% | New York Income Tax Withheld | New York Disability Withheld |
|---|---|---|---|---|---|---|---|---|---|---|---|
| | | | | | | | | | | | |

SHOW _____

THEATRE _____

WEEK ENDING _____

| Maryland Income Tax Withheld | New Jersey Transportation Tax Withheld | New York City Tax | Equity Dues | Other Deductions Explanation | Amount | Total Amount of Deductions | Net Pay | Other Payments Explanation | Amount | Total Pay Received | Signature and Clock Number | Additional Explanation |
|---|---|---|---|---|---|---|---|---|---|---|---|---|
| | | | | | | | | | | | | |

## Bookkeeping Duties

As we have seen, a record should be kept of all financial transactions. This will involve, among other chores, listing all transactions in a journal. A journal is a diary that shows in chronological order all transactions made from checkbooks and petty-cash funds, and also records deposits made. The books may also be kept on an accrual system in which case expenses are recorded when they are incurred and revenues when they are earned, rather than when a check is actually written in payment or when income is actually received. In other words, the expense is recorded when the original invoice is received from the vendor, and the ticket income for a performance is not recorded as income until that performance is over.

Working from the journal entries, the bookkeeper then posts each item or listing into a ledger. Using a chart of accounts (described below), the ledger classifies each transaction, showing, for example, that it pertains to a particular type of expenditure for a particular production (i.e. "makeup supplies, production #3"). Unless one is working with a computer data base, it is helpful to use ledgers that provide numerous columns running across two wide pages.

Based on the information in the ledger, it is comparatively easy to prepare balance sheets, variance reports, and annual financial statements. Active theatre organizations are well advised to prepare weekly or biweekly operating statements that show actual expenses and income to date and how these compare with projections given in the budget. Significant variances should be examined closely and then dealt with by management—hopefully, before they grow into a crisis.

## Balance Sheets

A balance sheet is designed to show the organization's assets and liabilities as of a specified date. It does this according to the following formula:

Assets = Liabilities + Capital

Assets consist of all the cash, material and other resources owned by the business to which a dollar value can be assigned. Liabilities consist of all outstanding financial obligations the business has at the moment. Capital represents the owners' or the nonprofit corporation's equity or proprietorship. Capital equals assets less liabilities. The assets shown on a balance sheet are always equal to the total liabilities and fund balances.

Notice in the sample balance sheet which follows that deferred revenue (money that has already been received, say, for future performances) is shown as a liability. A conservative balance sheet would also show accrued expenses as a liability (materials and services incurred but not yet paid). On the other hand, deferred expenses (which represent prepayments for materials and services not yet received) show up as an asset, as do accounts receivable (which is accrued income, or money earned but not yet received).

### SAMPLE BALANCE SHEET
(Nonprofit Professional Theatre Company)

As of June 30, 19XX

ASSETS:

Cash:

| | | |
|---|---|---|
| Checking Accounts | 26,100 | |
| Savings Accounts | 31,108 | |
| | 57,208 | |
| Marketable securities | 396,997 | |
| Accounts receivable | 1,054,035 | |
| Prepaid expenses | 36,627 | |
| Deferred operating expenses | 90,000 | |
| Total current assets | 1,634,867 | |
| Equipment at cost less depreciation & amortization | 308,840 | |
| | | $1,943,707 |

LIABILITIES &
FUND BALANCES

| | |
|---|---|
| Accounts payable | 150,160 |
| Deferred revenue | 1,428,557 |
| Total liabilities | 1,578,717 |
| Current fund balances | 364,990 |
| | $1,943,707 |

## Depreciation and Amortization

Depreciation is the proportional part of the cost of an asset that has been allocated to a particular period, such as a year. The same is true about amortization, although the latter is generally used for intangible assets such as copyrights, patents, franchises, and good will, whereas depreciation is the allocation attributable to wear and tear on a tangible asset, such as a computer or an automobile. Some financial statements simply show amortization, although depreciation is included. In any case, it is easy to understand that amortization offers a neat way to manipulate figures up and down. For example, an item may be amortized over five years or over twenty, and such allocations can be changed from year to year or even month to month.

## Chart of Accounts

Every financial asset and liability, and every type of income and expenditure for an operation should be assigned a code or line number. The numbering or coding system that is adopted should be tailored to fit the specific organization and, once adopted, should remain uniform throughout the life of that organization. The following list provides one manner in which accounts may be named and coded:

ASSETS:    CODE 100

> To include cash assets, petty cash, accounts receivable from patrons, employees and others, returnable bonds and deposits, prepaid expenses, land, building supplies and machinery

LIABILITIES AND CAPITAL: CODE 200

> To include all accrued withholding and payroll taxes payable, insurance, bonds, accounts and notes payable, mortgages, capital stock, retained earnings, etc.

INCOME:    CODE 300

> To include box office gross receipts, income from interest, concessions, program advertising, income from grants and contributions

CAPITAL COSTS: CODE 400

> One-time expenses to include acquiring and renovating a building, the purchase of major equipment, etc.

ANNUAL OPERATING EXPENSES: CODE 500
> Ongoing costs of operating a facility: paying rent, administrative salaries and costs, marketing, fundraising, legal and accounting costs, etc.

PREPRODUCTION COSTS: CODE 600
> Costs for designing, building and rehearsing stage productions, including artist fees and salaries up to opening night

PRODUCTION OPERATING COSTS: CODE 700
> To include all salaries, fees and royalties for performers, other artists, stagehands, ongoing cost of equipment and costume rental, and, if desired, certain front-of-house costs like ushers, box office personnel and costs, etc.

This system is designed to complement the budgeting system for a professional nonprofit theatre as described in the previous chapter. If this were a seasonal operation, there might be a final code category named "closing costs: 800." Each code in the above system can have one hundred subdivisions, and even more if letters are also introduced (Code 105-a, 105-b, etc.). While coding should be specific, it should not be any more complicated than necessary. The purpose for establishing different accounts and budget lines is to facilitate fiscal analysis and to provide a clear picture of assets, liabilities, income and costs in each area. Multi-production operations should adopt a letter code (A, B, C, etc.) for each production to be used next to the number in codes 600 and 700 above. Hence, "721-C" might quickly translate into "properties rental items for *Tartuffe*." At the end of the season, all the "A" expenses can be tallied, then all the "B" expenses, and so forth, to determine the actual cost of each production. Subdivision items can also be tallied to reveal the total costs in such areas as stage properties, royalties, travel or whatever. Any number of reports and combinations of figures are possible, especially when the record-keeping and reporting system is computerized.

## The Strength in the Numbers

There is a revealing story about an executive who is interviewing an accountant for a staff opening. "How much is 2 and 2?" asks the executive. "How much would you *like* it to be?" answers the accountant!

When figures are made to lie, it is deceitful at best and criminal at worst. Sometimes, however, figures unintentionally present a wrong or misleading picture. And other times figures are manipulated to present a certain impression that supports someone's position or viewpoint but does not constitute an illegal or unethical act. In fact, *whenever* figures are organized in some visible format, they will give a particular impression that would change if they were organized differently. The ironic thing about numbers on a printed page is that we tend to think of them as objective and irrefutable, whereas they are often highly subjective and debatable.

The person who designs the chart of accounts, and even the bookkeeper responsible for coding the ledger entries, makes decisions that will strongly influence the organization's financial profile. For example: How will deferred income be treated? Will production costs and income be averaged out or not? Which expenses will be allocated to which departments? Will anticipated grants and contributions be shown as assets before the money is in hand? Different answers to such questions result in different presentations of the very same sets of figures. And these differences can make the same employee or department look either frugal or irresponsible, either productive or counterproductive, either an asset to the organization or a liability.

While producers and boards of trustees vary greatly, most are result-oriented and most, like the rest of us, prefer good news to bad. This suggests that sanguine financial management should be pessimistic in its projections—always underestimating income projections and always overestimating cost projections; never showing or even crowing about possible grants and contributions until the contract or the check is in hand; always, in short, putting the bad news into the budget so that the annual financial report will look like good news!  In other words, costs will turn out lower than projected, and income will exceed the expectations, and that nice corporate contribution for a new theatre will take everybody's breath away!

## Legal Precautions

All businesses are subject to examination by the Internal Revenue Service in connection with tax liabilities; and all businesses may on occasion be required to present their fiscal records (including receipts, canceled checks and ticket stubs) to insurance companies, arbitration panels or courts of law in order to establish a claim for theft, embezzlement or bankruptcy, or for any number of other similarly depressing reasons. Financial records should always be kept in safe and secure places. Unsold tickets, ticket stubs and receipts should be kept for at least three years before being destroyed, and books of accounts and canceled checks for seven years.

## Annual Financial Reports

Producing companies and theatre organizations are required by law to prepare annual financial reports for distribution among investors, partners, directors, trustees and officers, as well as with state and federal tax agencies. These are often in the form of a year-end balance sheet, as described above. Usually, such reports are prepared by and accompanied by the opinion of a Certified Public Accountant, although these may only be seen by the producer or the board. Even modest community and amateur theatre groups should compile annual reports. The annual report will be a summary of earlier box office reports as well as a statement of current assets and liabilities. It may also include audience attendance figures, production photographs, statements from top board, artistic and management leaders. It may be typewritten or it may be a costly pamphlet in many colors on glossy paper. It may be designed to impress investors or contributors or to attract new ones. Basically, however, it is just a useful business document.

## SUMMATION

There is nothing particularly mysterious about good financial management, but it does require special knowledge and experience. Many techniques of business management can be acquired and handled by people with no special training, provided they have expert supervision. Because so many theatrical producers, artistic directors and even managers are resistant to learning sound economic and accounting practices, a great many poor decisions are made, and a great deal of money is spent unnecessarily to hire consultants, accountants and other specialists. This is not to say, however, that any business that pays taxes should not retain a good CPA to handle and monitor at least the major responsibilities related to financial management.

# 13

# The Box Office
# And Other Sources
# Of Earned Income

A box office is the wallet of a theatre. It must be secure, well-organized and managed with reverence for accuracy and detail. It should
also be regarded as a primary factor in creating the image of the theatre, as
few things are more conspicuous to the public than the box office and the
people who work in it.

## GENERAL BOX OFFICE CONSIDERATIONS

### Design

The design and layout of the box office, even in new theatre facilities,
is often too small and cramped, with steel bars or heavy glass separating the
treasurers from the public, making communication difficult. Such elements
reinforce the suspicion and distrust with which customers often approach a
box office. Perhaps box office design could benefit from the example of the
banking industry. Once built like granite fortresses and decorated with locks,
keys and steel cages for each worker, banks developed a much friendlier
and more open image in the 1960s in order to attract more customers. Most
banks today have open counters between tellers and customers, brightly
lighted interiors, carpeting, live plants and soft music—not to mention such
customer conveniences as drive-up service windows and automatic tellers.
The theatre industry, too, should understand that armed robbers will not be
put off by window bars, but customers will be.

### Location

A box office should be easily accessible to the public, located so that
customer lines do not obstruct the flow of people into the auditorium at per-

formance times and so it can operate independently of the main lobby or other large areas of the building. This often requires that the box office be located off an intermediary lobby between the street and the main lobby. The design should also protect both customers and treasurers from drafts and outside extremes in the temperature.

Ideally, the box office should adjoin the business office or, at least, connect to an inner room without windows or public access that can be used for banking and clerical work. One public window or service counter is generally sufficient to service a five hundred-seat theatre, and more should be added according to the same ratio. Two windows can be useful, however, even for small theatres. One may be used exclusively for advance sales, the other for current performance sales; or an additional window area may be handy for disbursing information or payroll. Drive-up windows would be a plus for some theatres and performing arts centers, and multi-use facilities might benefit from operating one centralized customer service area.

It may also be a helpful marketing technique to operate one or two satellite box offices at convenient locations away from the theatre facility. Or it may be just as effective to offer tickets through local agencies, merchants or telephone ticket services. In any case, the process of buying a ticket should be made as easy as possible for as many people as possible. A checklist of other considerations regarding box office design is provided in Chapter 3.

## Equipment and Supplies

The equipment and supplies required to operate a box office efficiently will be largely determined by the volume of potential sales, the number of people involved in box office work, and whether or not a computerized ticket system is used. The basic requirements usually include:

1. Ticket racks
2. Cash registers, cash drawers or cash box
3. Telephone(s)
4. Typewriter or word processor
5. Adding machine or calculator
6. Safe or vault
7. Work counters
8. File cabinets and storage space
9. Credit card imprinters
10. Computerized ticket sales equipment, if feasible.

Telephone and computer systems can be very costly, so selecting them should be done with care. Whenever possible, managers of other theatres where systems under consideration are being used should be consulted; needs should be carefully analyzed to avoid buying unnecessary services and equipment—however necessary the salespeople may say the equipment is.

Ideally, the equipment should be arranged so that the treasurer need never turn away from the customer and need never take a step. This requires careful design but increases efficiency. Ongoing box office operations should also maintain an inventory of the following supplies:

1. Stationery
2. Box office statement forms
3. Group sales forms
4. Bank deposit forms and deposit bags
5. Credit card charge slips
6. Credit card deposit summary slips
7. Price scales
8. Price multiplication charts
9. Calendars showing performance information
10. Lockable ticket stub boxes for ticket takers
11. Wastebaskets
12. General office and clerical supplies

## Security

Box offices designed in the traditional manner can usually be secured by closing the customer windows and locking a single door. If the box office is designed as a largely open space, sliding panels or metal security gates may be used, or ticket racks and other equipment may be designed to slide into a wall or adjoining room. Obviously, complete security is required for ticket and cash storage. Burglar alarm systems may be installed and even designed to alert the local police precinct in the event of a break-in. Good protection is also realized if the entire box office and the safe are visible from a busy street through a glass wall, in which case lights should remain on all night. In one theatre, where the box office is accessible through the business office, the manager keeps a police officer's hat and club lying casually on a desk where everyone entering the office can see them. Strangers assume there is a police officer nearby! Another inexpensive security device is the installation of a box office microphone wired to an amplifier that can be heard by a security guard, or even in someone's nearby living quarters. When the box office is closed, the system is turned on to pick up the sound of intruders.

When there are no security guards on staff, a police escort or private security agency should be used whenever large cash deposits or payrolls are being transported to and from the theatre. Most managers, however, stop short at keeping guns on hand. Employees should always be instructed not to resist thieves in the event of a robbery. And, of course, as little cash as possible should be kept on hand. Box office income (cash, checks and credit card charge slips) should be deposited in a bank periodically throughout the day if business is brisk, or shortly after the curtain goes up on each performance, using night deposit bank facilities when necessary.

## THE BOX OFFICE TREASURER

### Qualifications

Box office treasurer, unlike a bank teller and most cashiers, is a salesperson. Because of this, treasurers and perhaps the entire box office operation sometimes come under the supervision of the marketing director. More often, the box office is the responsibility of the business manager or finance department. On Broadway, treasurers belong to Local 751 (Treasurers and Ticketsellers) and are contracted by the landlord. Because there is virtually no repeat business for Broadway shows, treasurers are less schooled in polite sales conduct than would be the case where repeat business is important. All treasurers influence which tickets a customer buys, how many tickets are bought and other factors that affect income. Because most seasoned theatregoers have had negative experiences at the box office, treasurers should be closely supervised in regard to customer relations. They should be good salespeople who are also honest, efficient, courteous and well-groomed. Where telephone sales are frequent, treasurers should have good phone voices. While treasurers don't require any special training in theatre, they should have an interest if not an enthusiasm for the productions they are selling (which means they should see a performance as early in the run as possible). To encourage them to feel like valued partners in the enterprise, rather than like prisoners in a cell, treasurers should not only see performances, they should receive copies of all news releases and advertisements, be invited to appropriate staff meetings, and included in social functions. Stars and other artists who earn a percentage of the gross would be smart to introduce themselves to treasurers and increase their enthusiasm for the production—maybe even give them gifts or some other incentive to sell more tickets. Treasurers must be informed about local transportation routes to the theatre, about local parking, restaurants and even hotel accommodations (a surprising number of tourists call ahead to secure their theatre tickets first and then ask for information about lodging).

Management can easily train box office personnel provided they possess the right qualities and potential: sales experience, ability to think and act quickly, dedication to detail and accuracy, and a friendly and helpful attitude toward others are important qualifications. Treasurers with previous experience are not always an asset. They may resist unfamiliar business systems and styles and, regrettably, their experience may include box office embezzlement techniques. It is probably good policy to hire inexperienced treasurers and to replace all box office personnel every year or two. Producers and managers in the theatre should not harbor an optimistic belief in the ability of the average person to resist temptation. Stories about producers who have been surprised by dishonesty range all the way from a famous embezzlement case involving ticket income for the New York production of *The Fantasticks*, to a dinner theatre manager who discovered that her two box office treasurers—both white-haired, retired town librarians—had robbed her blind! There is another true story about a large music theatre in suburbia, at which the center aisle in the orchestra was eliminated by filling it in with new theatre seats. But the producer and the treasurers agreed to keep this fact to themselves and simply pocketed the income earned on the additional seats, until their scam was discovered by the manager of a superstar singer who had played there and, of course, had been cheated out of a portion of his percentage. The culprits were indicted and sent to jail. The theatre went bankrupt and was recently demolished.

## Duties

Treasurers' duties depend on the size of the box office staff and the type of theatre in which it functions. In all cases, one person should be appointed as box office manager, ticket manager or head treasurer, to be directly responsible to the business manager or general manager. A large operation might include the following positions:

> Box office manager (head treasurer)
> Assistant treasurer(s)
> Subscription or season ticket manager
> Mail order treasurer(s)
> Group sales manager

At least two treasurers should be employed in all but the smallest operations and should share responsibilities related to mail orders, telephone orders and information, customer window service, ticket counting, and box office statement computation. Box office hours should fit the convenience of potential customers, and treasurers should give their full concentration to their work. While no box office business should be carried out of the box office, so, too, no other business should be carried into the box office.

Treasurers must be responsible for keeping the box office clean and well organized, because maintenance personnel should never be allowed into the room. Treasurers should also keep themselves well informed about productions so they can provide accurate information to the public. It is never advisable to be vague or dishonest about answering such questions as, "Is it appropriate for children?" "Is it a comedy?" "Is it risque?" And, as mentioned, copies of all press releases, brochures and advertisements should be given to the box office—customer comments, questions or complaints about such material will come to the box office, not to the press office. And the house manager or stage manager should provide the box office with exact curtain times and intermission times.

## THE THEATRE TICKET

The first theatre tickets printed in English were reportedly issued by London's Drury Lane Theatre in 1703. Since then they have served as a convenience for both theatregoers and managers as well as been the object of fraud, theft, speculation and profiteering.

A theatre ticket is a rental agreement that guarantees whatever is printed on it will be delivered. Should the theatre be unable to furnish what is promised on the ticket, it must offer a refund. It may suggest that the ticket be exchanged but it cannot demand this. It is wise to omit the names of productions and performers from the printed ticket and to include the disclaimer "program subject to change," both on the ticket and in advertising, when a series of different attractions is being offered. When this is done, refunds and exchanges will not be necessary when there are program or performer changes, so long as substitutes are offered at the same time, place, date and price as printed on the ticket.

A ticket for an upcoming performance is negotiable. It may be bought or sold anywhere in the world where there is a market for it, although there are laws that regulate where tickets may be sold, by whom and for how much. Such laws are especially stringent in New York State, although they are largely unenforceable. If a ticket is lost or stolen from a box office, it is exactly the same as if money were lost or stolen. The theatre cannot legally reproduce it or duplicate it. If the theatre cannot account for a ticket, it must pay for it: it must declare it as sold and pay royalties, percentages and, where applicable, sales taxes, just as if it had been sold at full price. A box office may contain tickets or computer ticketing systems that represent thousands or even millions of dollars. Treasurers must be impressed with this fact and taught to handle each ticket as if it were a hundred-dollar bill.

### Ordering Theatre Tickets

The two basic types of tickets are reserved tickets and unreserved, or general admission tickets. Unless the theatre prints tickets by its own computer, all tickets should be ordered from a bonded ticket printer, such as Globe Ticket Company (which has a number of offices), National Ticket Company in New York City, Dillingham Ticket Company in Los Angeles, or Quick Tick International, Inc., in Houston. This insures that tickets will be printed on bonded stock as protection against counterfeiting. Unreserved tickets are much less expensive to buy and easier and less costly because customers select their own seats from those that are unoccupied. Unreserved tickets may be ordered in roll form, like those used by most movie theatres, or they may be ordered as separated tickets. They should be numbered (preferably by an automatic printer rather than by hand) from 1 to the capacity number of seats in the house.

Reserved seating tickets may be ordered in a variety of ways. When a series of programs is being offered, and most customers buy the entire series, for example, it will simplify ticket processing to order them in booklet or sheet form (tickets for the same seat at different dates on the series are bound in a booklet or printed together). This saves the box office the considerable work of having to pull individual tickets for a number of performances out of ticket boxes and then having to arrange them in a series. Tickets not sold as a series are eventually separated by the box office and sold for individual performances.

Most reserved tickets come in a standard size (they should fit easily into a wallet) and should include the following information:

Name and address of the theatre
Performance date
Seat number
Row number
Section (orchestra, balcony, etc.)
Performance day (Monday, Tuesday, etc.)
Curtain time
Aisle number (optional)
Title of production (optional)
"No refunds or exchanges" (optional, but good practice)
"Program subject to change" (optional, but good practice).

When ordering tickets, all such information should only be submitted to the printer in writing. The first time reserved seats are ordered from a ticket printing company, the theatre should send a detailed floor plan of the auditorium, clearly showing every seat in the house and indicating seat numbers, rows, sections, and aisles. This is known as a ticket manifest; it is retained by the printer to simplify future orders. The printer sends a confirmatory ticket-order report to the theatre before tickets are printed, to provide a final check against incorrect information. Other factors to consider when ordering tickets are the following:

1. All tickets should be notched or perforated to permit easy and uniform tearing by ticket takers and to make it easier to rubber-band sets of whole tickets

2. Each price category should be printed in a different color. When a single admission price is used for a large theatre, different colors may be used to indicate different sections of the theatre. If there are price differences between matinee and evening, or weeknight and weekend, performances, completely different color sets should be ordered to indicate such differences

3. Ticket colors should be changed from season to season (printing companies keep a record of past color schemes)

4. Tickets should be ordered in pastel colors or white. Printing on dark or vibrant colors is extremely difficult for ushers to read

5. All vital information should appear twice on each ticket, so that both the stub retained by the customer and that retained by the theatre tell the whole story

6. Ticket takers should always tear the ticket at the notch (or so that three-fourths of the ticket remains) and give the customer "the short end of the deal," retaining the longer portion to make stub counting easier for the box office.

## Audit Stubs

The ticket samples that follow show that tickets may be ordered with perforated, detachable portions. These may be left on the ticket for customers to use for parking or coatroom services, or they may be removed by the box office when the ticket is sold. In the latter instance, the audit stub serves as a record of ticket sales. When the ticket is sold, the stub is placed in a locked box, and all stubs are tallied at the end of the day and checked against window income. This system, however, makes ticket refunds, exchanges and discounts very cumbersome. Also, after repeated handling by treasurers, audit stubs tend to loosen and fall off.

## Hardwood Tickets

Special passes used by theatres for special purposes are called "hardwood." The so-called twofer, a publicity gimmick offering two tickets for the price of one, is one type of hardwood. Twofers are distributed throughout the community, to be picked up and, hopefully, exchanged at the box office for actual tickets. Special passes or discount offers may also be handled

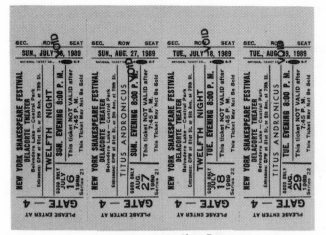

Tickets in Series Sheet Form

A Computer Printed Ticket

Ticket with an Audit Stub

Ticket with Two Audit Stubs

Tickets in Series Booklet Form

Hardwood Ticket Form

A Single Ticket

by giving out a ticket-like card. These might be called a "manager's pass" or "patron's pass" and might entitle the holder to discounted or free tickets as well as such privileges as use of the coatroom, patrons' lounge, a complimentary meal or drink, free parking, and so forth. A hardwood ticket may also be printed as a blank form on which authorized managers or treasurers may fill in the appropriate information and issue it to the customer in lieu of an actual ticket. This allows the box office to retain unpaid tickets that are actually being used and thus eliminates the mistake of counting complimentary tickets as if they had been paid for. And hardwood tickets may be issued for standing room and additional chairs, or when a customer claims to have lost previously purchased tickets (though only when there is a record of that customer's name and purchase). In the latter case, it would be wise to print a disclaimer on the pass to the effect that "this is not a ticket of admission and will be revoked if actual tickets are presented."

To avoid mistakes as well as dishonesty in regard to hardwood, only one or two people should be authorized to issue them; another person altogether should record the names of the recipients and the performance information before actually giving them out. Passes used in lieu of actual tickets should also have a stub that will be detached by the ticket taker and returned to the box office.

## Deadwood

Deadwood is the term used to indicate all unsold tickets that remain after the performance for which they were valid. In the event that actual tickets are substituted by hardwood forms, the actual tickets then become the deadwood—representing "dead" seats that have been assigned but not paid for. When such transactions occur, the actual tickets must immediately be placed in an envelope and marked "dead" so there will be no possibility of selling them.

## Computer-Printed Tickets

Not to be confused with computer box office systems are tickets that are printed in bulk by computers. These may be ordered at very short notice, especially when they are printed from seating plans already in the computer's memory. Such tickets, however, often use a computer printout style that has a rather sterile and mass-produced look, to which some people object.

## COMPUTER TICKET SYSTEMS

Most theatre companies of any size and permanence own at least some computer equipment and, increasingly, this includes a computerized ticket system capable of printing individual tickets on command at the place where they are ordered. Most can also speed and simplify the process of seat selection, ticket accounting and auditing, and the generation of financial and marketing data. Such systems are now standard sales equipment at major sports arenas, performing arts centers, museums, Broadway theatres and road houses.

## Shopping for a System

A theatre organization's box office and business personnel should play an important role in the acquisition of any computer system. They should feel that they have helped put the system in place, not that it was imposed on them by management. As participants in the decision-making that leads to computerization, experienced box office treasurers can help prevent costly mistakes. Their major concern is likely to focus on how to keep the line of customers at the window moving—especially during the rush just before curtain. What about system crashes, backup and accountability? Union treasurers may be especially resistant to computerization and, indeed, they are correct when they argue that they can sell tickets faster the old fashioned way. Just the process of punching in the date, the section, the number of seats, the payment method, and the actual printing of the ticket takes longer than selling pre-printed tickets. For this reason, many treasurers at busy theatres where there is a large amount of walk-up business will mass-print the remaining tickets an hour before curtain, rack them and then sell the deadwood back to the system before closing out. Hence, it is important to acquire a system that includes a "quick sale" mode so that operators can suspend the need to enter the date and select seats from a seating chart—as well as suspend the capturing of name/address and other marketing information. Treasurers often resent having to gather this information, even when time permits. "We were hired to be treasurers," they might say, "not data-entry clerks!" If this is the case, perhaps they would respond in a more positive way to such data entry devices as a light-pen or "mouse." If computer ticketing systems are acquired without the input and support—preferably enthusiastic support—of the box office personnel, they will never be utilized to their full potential.

When shopping for a computer system it is also important to have one computer-literate staff member who will be the "point" person on all technical issues. Computer salespeople are usually sharp and eager to sell things that the buyer might not need. This same staff person logically becomes the system administrator. Even the most elementary systems require an administrator whose salary should be budgeted into the cost of buying and operating the system.

Will the ticket system be the first area of the organization's business operations to be computerized? If so, it should be capable of expansion to accommodate general management needs such as payroll preparation and bookkeeping. If, however, a management system is already in place, then the organization should investigate how it can be expanded to suit box office needs. Particular attention must be paid to the compatibility of a ticketing system with existing hardware and software. For example, does the box office "close out" automatically and post data to the appropriate accounts? If not, can the data be translated to the ledger program or must it be rekeyed? Does the system have the capacity and flexibility to expand along with the organization? For example, is the data storage area large enough to have the theatre's entire season on sale at the same time—or, indeed, to handle ticketing for other theatres and events as a means of earing additional income? Begin by deciding which software meets the organization's needs; then select the hardware on which to run it.

Being a good comparative shopper is necessary when buying technology because advances in both hardware and software are rapid; manufacturers and distributors go out of business with some frequency, and buying the wrong equipment can be a very serious mistake. Several precautions are especially important to note:

1. Get as much advice as possible from a variety of sources: books, articles and sales material; colleagues at other facilities who are using similar equipment (visit them and observe how their system works); consultants, experts and computer salespeople

2. Conduct a thorough analysis of management and box office computer needs. Consult with staff and compose a list of essential computer functions and of others that might be helpful but not necessary. Pay particular attention to how the software will interface between subscriptions or series or other special offers and box office single-sale tickets

3. Insist on thorough demonstrations of equipment before it is purchased and involve employees on the staff who will eventually be using the technology

4. Negotiate the hardware and software contracts with great care. Be certain that they provide protection against any damage that faulty, inadequate or failed equipment may cause to the organization. Be certain contracts cover availability of program codes and information, even if the software company goes out of business

5. Be certain there is an adequate backup system in place, both computerized and manual. Usually a box office system is plugged into an uninterruptable power supply; there is a backup computer in place;

and a manual contingency plan stands ready should all systems fail

6. Be prepared to maintain a manual system concurrently with the computerized system for the first year

7. Beware of donated computer equipment. Box office ticketing programs are the most critical component in a theatre organization's software; they require the most difficult and sophisticated programming and are usually the most expensive. If the box office system crashes or if it is inadequate or ill-suited, there will be serious trouble.

A great many problems can develop with computer systems and most are easy to overlook during contract negotiations. It would be wise to study similar contracts written for other theatre operations. Other factors that shouldn't be ignored when ordering computer equipment include the delivery deadline, preparation of the computer location area, selecting and ordering any necessary telephone tie-in services, and arranging for employee training in computer use. It's an obvious advantage when the system is very user-friendly and can be learned in a few days and mastered in a few weeks.

## Important Functions of a System

A computer ticket system should provide major advantages in three vital areas:

1. Marketing the ticket
2. Selling the ticket
3. Accounting for the ticket

To assist with marketing endeavors, the system should be able to record data about customers and organize it as needed—for example, to generate advance sales reports, to assess the impact of certain sales pieces or media outlets, to create mailing lists, to assemble a profile of high-potential customers, and so forth. Treasurers may be trained to elicit certain information from ticket buyers at the window and over the phone: "How did you learn about this production?" "Have you seen any other performances here?" "May we make dining or lodging reservations for you?" When answers to such questions are keyed into the system, the resulting information quickly becomes an important factor in marketing strategy. It could also increase earned income. For example, mailing lists can be sold or rented; reservations taken for other nearby establishments (parking, restaurants, motels), which may result in sales commissions; and the system may have the capability of printing and distributing tickets for events sponsored by other organizations at other facilities. Also, it should be easy to set up satellite terminals at other locations to transmit and receive data between the computer at the main box office and the terminal operator, thereby creating or servicing off-premises ticket outlets. And a computer ticket system should make it much easier for management to add performances (and tickets) at short notice when demand is high. The instant display on computer screens of statistics about advance sales, date and time of sales, and other such information further helps to monitor and assess marketing efforts. (More on this subject is discussed throughout Part IV of this book.)

A computer ticket system should help to sell tickets by speeding up the process from the customer's point of view and by freeing the treasurer from clerical duties, so that more time can be spent on sales and customer service duties. It should not be assumed, however, that a computer ticket system will require any fewer employee hours than a manual system; time gained by the use of computers will probably be used to redirect the treasurer's duties. For example, instead of counting the deadwood after each performance (because the tickets were never printed and are simply data in the computer's memory), the treasurer may be required to review and report on the day's sales activity ("stormy conditions," "stock market crash," whatever). But time will definitely be saved by eliminating the process of reconciling each treasurer's cash drawer with actual transactions made by that treasurer, because a list of those transactions can be recalled from the computer at the end of each work shift. And time will be saved because banks accept a printout or diskette of credit card transactions, thus eliminating the need to fill out charge slips.

Finally, a computer ticket system will be a major asset to the business manager and accountant because it can so easily track and account for each ticket transaction and, furthermore, provide status reports at any time; this helps to safeguard the assets. Computer systems are themselves vulnerable to schemes of embezzlement and fraud and should be audited against such possibilities, but one safeguard against the unlawful duplication of tickets is the use of printers that can accept unusual card stock as opposed to paper.

Theatres where the volume and frequency of sales is high enough to warrant a computer ticket system should acquire one if possible. But there are many theatre groups for which the cost of this investment cannot be justified. The sections about box office operation that follow in this chapter must, therefore, describe the manual approach to ticket handling—although it will be obvious how a computer system could be substituted.

## SELLING THE TICKET

Before a box office is opened to the public, it should be prepared to operate in the most efficient manner. It should be thoroughly cleaned and dusted; all tickets, correspondence, and other items not related to current operations should be removed; fresh filing cards and systems should be organized; price charts and multiplication charts should be drawn up, together with seating plans and all the necessary forms.

After the tickets have been ordered and received (providing they are the typical, reserved seating tickets), the ticket boxes should be lined up in chronological order and checked against the ticket confirmation order sheet for accuracy of dates, colors, prices and numbering. Once tickets have arrived in the box office, nobody except the people bonded with the insurance company should be allowed to cross the threshold, and the room must be kept either locked or staffed from that point on.

Before placing tickets in the racks, the treasurers should pull all permanent locations—that is, all sets of tickets for special purposes that are to be withheld from sale to the general public. These may include:

1. House seats: seats held for the use of the landlord or producer as authorized by them
2. Press seats: for opening nights and other performances as authorized by the press agent or publicity director
3. Dead seats: tickets that may not be used at all because they offer an obstructed view of the stage, have been removed to make more space for musicians or some other purpose
4. Agency seats: locations permanently assigned for sale by ticket agents, to be paid by the agency or released for general sale at a specified time prior to each performance
5. Special seats: tickets held until a specified time for use by the star, the director or others and paid for by them or by the persons authorized to claim them.

A master seating plan should be drawn up to indicate which seats have been pulled as permanent locations. Most of these should be prime locations in the orchestra within the first twelve rows and on the aisle, where possible. They should also be somewhat scattered, so if most of them are unoccupied at a given performance, they will not leave a noticeable group of empty seats all in the same area.

After pulling permanent locations, series or subscription seats may be assigned, if tickets are sold in this manner. Series ticket buyers should be given the seats of their choice whenever possible and, also, the same seat numbers should be recorded in a card file or in the computer for easy access, in case a customer misplaces the tickets or wishes to exchange them at some point. This record also serves as a basis for processing renewal orders and for serving as a list of most favored patrons.

Once season tickets, permanent locations and advance theatre party orders have been pulled from the ticket boxes, then the tickets are "racked," and the box office is ready to open to the general public.

## Making Up the Customer's Mind

Few people approach a box office with a clear idea of exactly where they wish to sit in the theatre. Their confusion is compounded when they are unfamiliar with the layout of the auditorium. For such reasons, a diagram of the auditorium should be displayed near the box office where customers can study it. Small producing organizations that offer only a few performances of each production might consider adopting what the airlines use in regard to seating selection and maintain a seating chart for each performance. As tickets are sold, they are crossed off on the chart and thereby permit both treasurers and customers to see the unsold seats at a glance. (Or, of course, this may be shown on a computer screen.)

Treasurers should be courteous but firm when discussing seating availability. If, for example, the treasurer asks, "Where would you like to sit?" a long discussion will ensue. If, on the other hand, the treasurer says, "I can give you two excellent seats in the tenth row center," the transaction will proceed more quickly. While treasurers should not mislead customers about seating locations, they should attempt to sell the highest priced tickets. Hence, when the customer asks, "Do you have three for tonight?" the answer might be, "Yes, I can give you three nice seats in the orchestra," with no mention of lower-priced balcony seats unless the customer requests such tickets. When quoting ticket prices, treasurers should always quote the highest price last, since that is the figure the customer will recall first.

As general policy, tickets should be sold on a first come, first served basis, once the permanent locations and group orders have been put aside. Customers should be discouraged from walking into the auditorium to study seating possibilities. The theatre may be poorly lighted, and this may cause accidents, or it may not have been cleaned after the previous performance or a rehearsal may be in progress. The practice also prolongs ticket transactions. After all, the customer is going to occupy a theatre seat for only a few hours, although many behave as if they were going to build a house on the site!

## Dressing the House

When it appears that a performance is not going to sell out, the treasurer should scatter the customers throughout each section rather than pack them together like sardines in a can. Fifty people scattered throughout ten rows appear to be a much larger audience than fifty people squeezed into five rows. Also, when there are empty seats, patrons will move themselves for greater comfort. When dressing the house, however, treasurers should not scatter the audience so much that the *feeling* of audience is destroyed, as this will diminish a unified, group response to the performance.

## Papering the House

A house that is "papered" is one in which a number of seats have been given away. Some producers and managers feel that, when ticket sales are poor, it is better to fill the house with nonpaying guests than to allow numerous empty seats. Others believe this policy will reduce the number of paying customers in the long run, because it may give the impression that business is bad because the production is bad.

Some tickets must be given away for legitimate business purposes—to the press and important visitors, for example. But management is often asked to issue complimentary tickets for no better reason than that the people asking for them simply believe they deserve them. It is difficult to convince some people that the theatre is a business where survival depends upon selling tickets, not giving them away. While they wouldn't dream of asking their friendly grocer for free food or their friendly innkeeper for free rooms, the same people somehow figure they should get free tickets just because they are friendly with the theatre manager or the leading lady. Of course, if local businesses display a theatre's promotional material or provide it with free or discounted services, free tickets might be a reasonable exchange. Nonetheless, "comps" should be given out very sparingly and selectively. When possible, they should also be limited to performances that are not likely to attract a full house of paying customers.

When the decision is made to paper a house, the theatre should look for individuals and groups who can't afford to buy tickets, who are very unlikely to buy tickets or who don't reside in the local community. Comps should also be given out with an eye to their publicity value and the good they might accomplish in terms of community relations. For example, inviting all the secretaries from a nearby corporation or college might create favorable word or mouth that could stimulate higher-ups to buy seats. Or members of the town police department might be given comps just to insure that they will know where the theatre is and, therefore, how to give directions to tourists. Among other groups and institutions a theatre may contact when giving away blocks of seats are senior citizens, noncommissioned military personnel, hospital outpatients, schools and camps.

## Making Change and Handling Cash

Excluding the acceptance of major credit cards, a box office should not extend credit or allow tickets to be charged. An exception to this practice includes the case of a box office that accepts ticket vouchers from authorized ticket agencies for which it is paid later. It may also extend short-term credit to an organization that has agreed to sell a large block of tickets, and it may permit actors and other salaried employed to take tickets, the price of which will later be deducted from their paycheck. But the fewer credits allowed, the fewer the mistakes and problems. Many box offices refuse to accept personal checks from customers (except, of course, mail orders, in which case five-to-ten days may be allowed between the time the check is deposited and the tickets mailed, to be certain the check is valid). Traveler's checks and money orders may be accepted when proper identification is written on the backs, although forgery of such notes does occur. Other helpful practices include:

1. Holding back tickets until payment has been received
2. Leaving any cash payment on the counter until change has been made and checked by the customer
3. Posting a sign next to the box office window that reads "Check your tickets and your change—no refunds or exchanges"
4. Training treasurers to look at a price multiplication chart every time a total ticket price is quoted or entered into a cash register (see the sample that follows).

### SAMPLE TICKET MULTIPLICATION CHART

#### Number of Tickets

| 1 | 2 | 3 | 4 | 5 | 6 | 7 | 8 | 9 |
|---|---|---|---|---|---|---|---|---|
| 35.00 | 70.00 | 105.00 | 140.00 | 175.00 | 210.00 | 245.00 | 280.00 | 315.00 |
| 30.00 | 60.00 | 90.00 | 120.00 | 150.00 | 180.00 | 210.00 | 240.00 | 270.00 |
| 28.50 | 57.00 | 85.50 | 114.00 | 142.50 | 171.00 | 199.50 | 228.00 | 256.50 |
| 30.00 | 60.00 | 90.00 | 120.00 | 150.00 | 180.00 | 210.00 | 240.00 | 270.00 |
| 28.50 | 57.00 | 85.50 | 114.00 | 142.50 | 171.00 | 199.50 | 228.00 | 256.50 |
| 22.00 | 44.00 | 66.00 | 88.00 | 110.00 | 132.00 | 154.00 | 176.00 | 198.00 |

## Credit Card Sales

Most professional theatres can easily arrange to institute a credit card system of payment through their local bank, which will supply any necessary charge slips and deposit-summary forms plus, for a small deposit, the imprinting machine. The bank will credit the theatre's account with the credit card sales and will also deduct a percentage of such sales (usually 4-to-6 percent, depending on the credit card company). The service charge percentage decreases if sales volume is high enough. Individual sales over an amount specified by each card company (often $50) must be approved by telephone with that company, and smaller sales should always be checked against a listing of invalid accounts that is mailed monthly to participating businesses.

Accepting credit charges by telephone gives the customer a secured reservation that does not need to be claimed until curtain time and it gives the theatre the income even if those tickets are never claimed—much better than the policy of holding reservations. And while tickets ordered with credit cards over the phone can be mailed to the customer, it is better to hold them for a signature when they are claimed (and, of course, this saves postage).

When the volume of credit card sales is high, it may be possible to deduct the service charges from the gross on the box office statements so that no royalties, percentages or taxes are paid on that portion of the sale. In any case, service charges can amount to a considerable sum and should always be figured into estimates of income and expenses.

## Taking Ticket Orders and Reservations

Theatres should accept as few unpaid advance ticket reservations as possible, although this may prove unworkable without a system of credit card payments. As a working rule, it can be assumed that at least 10 percent of all unpaid reservations will never be claimed; and, when the weather suddenly turns bad, or sudden events command public attention, that percentage will be much higher. So patrons should be required to claim reservations as far in advance of the performance as possible—an hour, a day, a week, depending on when the reservations are made. The higher the demand for tickets, the more stringent the pick-up policy should be. It is a difficult feat to sell every seat in the house and this may even require taking more reservations than there are tickets available, although this is a risky practice. To sell every ticket, or "go clean," inevitably requires some couples or parties of theatregoers to accept seats separated from each other, or it may involve selling some seats that offer a limited view of the stage. While treasurers should be honest about selling such locations, their sales abilities are of particular importance in selling those last ten or twelve tickets that make it possible to put up the SRO sign.

All ticket orders and reservation envelopes should carry the following information:

Name and address of theatre
Customer's name and initials
The performance date

Matinee or evening performance
Number of tickets ordered
Price per ticket
Time when customer was told to claim tickets.

Theatres with inexperienced treasurers should order ticket envelopes with a preprinted form on the face of them, so that crucial information is not omitted. Ticket envelopes may be ordered from general printing companies or from ticket printing companies, which may provide them without charge if permitted to display their advertising on them. Or the theatre may sell such advertising space itself or print its own ad copy on the envelopes.

Paid reservations being held in the box office should never be sold or given out for any reason—even if they are never claimed. However, as curtain time draws near, it might be wise to check reservations (especially blocks of tickets) that remain in the box office against whatever records exist in the files or in the computer to be certain that a mistake was not made—that the tickets weren't pulled for the wrong date, for example.

Box office telephones should be answered promptly, courteously and efficiently. Transactions should be brief but clear. As many telephone lines should be installed in the box office as required to handle customer calls and as can be properly serviced by the personnel on hand. To avoid the risk of taking orders and then misplacing them, box office telephones should never have extensions outside the box office. An answering device can be used to provide ticket information when the box office is closed. When a large portion of the audience comes from outside the theatre's telephone area code, an 800-line may be made available, although this is a rather expensive service.

## Mail Orders

As with all box office business, mail orders should be double-checked, preferably by two different people. The marketing department should always consult with the box office staff when designing mail order forms for brochures and newspaper ads, to be certain the information being requested is sufficient, correct and efficiently presented. Customers should be requested to include a stamped, self-addressed envelope if they wish to have the tickets mailed. Mail order correspondence should only be opened and processed in the box office or an adjacent work room to avoid losing or misplacing orders. All pertinent information should be written on the order form or letter in red ink: price, number of tickets, total amount, method of payment, performance date, matinee or evening, seat locations, and whether tickets were mailed and on what date, or held at the box office. This should be done even when the customer has already provided such information. All order forms and correspondence should be filed where they are quickly available to the box office. Mistakes and complaints about mail orders will occur and, most likely, will occur during the busy rush just before curtain when treasurers have little time to rummage through ill-kept records and files.

## Series Tickets

The terms "series ticket" and "season ticket" are clear to most customers. But many are uncertain about the meaning of terms like "subscription series" or "patron ticket"; they may assume that patrons and subscribers donate an amount of money to the theatre over and above the cost of the tickets, and in some cases this is true.

Because it is easier and less expensive to sell one hundred tickets once, than to sell one hundred tickets one hundred times, any system that encourages multiple ticket orders is desirable. The more tickets sold in a single transaction the better. When a theatre offers a season of nonrepeating productions, each playing the same number of performances on a uniform schedule of days and times, the business of selling a series ticket is simple. The customer merely selects a day and performance time (Wednesday matinee or Saturday night, for instance) and buys a series of tickets for the same seat for each production in the season. But when a repertory system is the policy, or when performances are scattered unevenly over a long period of time, then confusion is bound to result. Should the theatre select an arbitrary number of performances to comprise a series, or should the customer be allowed the freedom to chose? When the theatre selects the dates in each series, of course, it can beef up the sales for unpopular productions by including these on a series with a blockbuster. Or it may keep the blockbuster off all series and only sell individual tickets to it at full or inflated prices.

When a series of performances extends over a long period, it is a little unreasonable to expect customers not to experience changes in their plans. A liberal policy of ticket exchange may solve this problem to the customer's satisfaction. Or customers may be invited to give tickets they can't use back to the box office as a personal tax deduction. The box office then sells them again and earns a bonus, although accounting for such income is a little tricky, assuming it didn't go straight into the treasurer's pocket! Some theatres sell an "open series" that permits customers to select specific tickets for each production up to twenty-four hours prior to the performance, provided tickets are still available. And there is the membership policy, as practiced successfully by Lincoln Center Theater: patrons pay an annual membership fee of, say, $40, and then, according to ticket availability, are entitled to purchase a specified number of tickets for one show or a number of shows at any time during the season, for a price less than nonmembers would pay.

## Group Sales

Both commercial and nonprofit theatres of any size and permanence obtain much of their business from theatre parties or groups. These  may be drawn from schools, clubs, corporations or special interest groups. They may be organized for purely social reasons; or in order to raise money for some cause or purpose, in which case they are called "benefits," and a tax deductible donation is added to the ticket price and eventually paid, after expenses, to the beneficiary in question. In major theatre cities, there are private companies that serve theatre party clients as brokers in arranging for blocks of tickets and, perhaps, other matters such as dinner reservations, chartered buses and lodging. Naturally, theatres court the agents from these companies by inviting them to performances—sometimes even paying their expenses to see a performance in another city prior to its local engagement. And many companies involved in the tourist industry put together packaged tours. These may be bus companies, airline companies or travel agencies, and they, too, are courted by alert marketing directors who may be able to convince them to include a theatre performance in local tours or, at least, offer it at extra cost to the tour participants.

Most multiple ticket sales, however, result from the efforts of a group sales manager who receives promotional support materials from the marketing department and ticket service from the box office. Group-sales work in the theatre requires coordinated efforts as well as a coordinated policy that clarifies such matters as which shows or performances can be offered at discounted ticket prices, which can be offered for groups at all, which groups should be approached for which productions, and how the agreement between the theatre and the group should be formalized. The sample group sales contract that follows provides a typical model.

## Ticket Agencies

A ticket agency may be operated by the theatre itself (staffed by theatre employees), or independent agencies may be selected by the theatre to serve as authorized ticket outlets. Ticket agencies in many states must obtain a special license from the city or state in which they operate and must conform to a number of laws and regulations. In New York the licensed agent is permitted to charge the customer a service fee over the face value of the ticket (the *same* fee regardless of the ticket price, which is rather unfair to the customer). But while the theatre may pay an agency commission based on its sales, agents may not bribe treasurers with payoffs in exchange for tickets to "hot" shows that they can sell at many times the face value. This is called "scalping," and the practice isn't limited to licensed ticket agents.

STAR THEATRE, INC.
CONTRACT FOR GROUP TICKET PURCHASE:
TERMS

1. Tickets distributed to organization on sale or return basis.
2. One-third deposit of box office price of tickets required.
3. Final payment must be made no later than one week prior to performance date, until which settlement date tickets may be returned for full value.
4. In order to qualify for a discount, discounted value of tickets sold must exceed amount of deposit.

DEPOSIT NOT RETURNABLE WHETHER OR NOT TICKETS
ARE RETURNED

5. Final percentage discount granted is determined by the number of tickets actually sold by the organization.
6. Organizations that sell tickets for more than the price they pay are responsible for the taxation on the excess where taxes apply.
7. In the event of a change in schedule, the liability of the theatre is limited to the return of deposit monies.

Contracting Organization _____
Address _____
Day of Performance _____ Date of Performance _____
Show _____ Settlement Date _____
Agent for Organization _____
Address _____
Phone _____ Date of Contract _____
NO DISCOUNT ALLOWED UNLESS ORGANIZATION SELLS A
MINIMUM OF _____ TICKETS
Accepted for _____ Accepted by _____
(Name of Organization)
Authorized Signature _____ Authorized Signature _____
MAKE ALL CHECKS PAYABLE TO _____

TICKETS RECEIVED BY ORGANIZATION                    Box Office Value
Number of Tickets _____ @ _____                 _____
_____ @ _____                 _____
_____ @ _____                 _____
Total No. Tickets _____ Box Office Value of Tickets _____
Tentative Percentage Discount _____ Deposit Required _____
Tickets Delivered _____ _____ Deposit Received Date _____ Amt. _____
(date)      (by)              Date _____ Amt. _____
Date _____ Amt. _____

| Tickets Received | Tickets Returned | Tickets Sold | Value |
|---|---|---|---|
| _____ | _____ | _____ @ | _____ |
| _____ | _____ | _____ @ | _____ |
| _____ | _____ | _____ @ | _____ |
| | Total Tickets Sold _____ | Total Value | _____ |

CONTRACTING ORGANIZATION _____ Discount at ___ % _____
Discount Value _____
DATE OF PERFORMANCE _____ Deposit Received _____
SHOW _____ Balance Received _____
Date _____
By _____

Haven't you heard of someone who waited in line all night to buy tickets for some superstar rock artist and then walked to the back of the line and sold them at five times their face value?

Where law permits, there are many imaginative places to establish a ticket outlet. Many supermarkets and shopping centers, for example, contain an information or customer courtesy booth that can double as a ticket agency. Many stores may be willing to provide such service merely in exchange for the traffic it will bring in. Tourist information centers, chambers of commerce and even banks are among other possible locations. And there are the computerized telephone ticket services, such as Ticketron. One summer theatre even established a mobile box office that, in the form of a beach buggy, was located in different places on different days of the week on a regular schedule. Because many customers stopped shopping at the box office some years ago, the box office has had to learn how to shop for customers!

Ticket agents of various kinds may be authorized to sell tickets, but they should not be given the actual tickets. These should remain in the box office, and a voucher system should be devised whereby the customer pays the ticket agent, receives a voucher containing the pertinent ticket information and then exchanges this at the box office for the actual tickets. Prior to each performance, the agency must inform the box office of exact ticket sales; then, when this is noted, unsold agency locations are returned to the rack for general sale, and vouchers are reconciled between the box office and the agency for a final settlement. The agency then pays the theatre (on a daily or weekly basis) for tickets it sold. When permanent locations are not pulled and assigned to an agency, the agent may simply phone the box office to conduct a transaction each time a customer walks in.

Booklets of numbered vouchers in triplicate sets should be ordered from a bonded printer and issued to authorized ticket agencies. When a ticket is purchased from an agent, the voucher is filled out and a copy given to the customer for presentation at the box office. The agent submits a second copy that day or at the end of that week when the reconciliation occurs and keeps the third copy for agency records. Needless to say, this whole process would be more efficient if operated as a computer satellite terminal from the main box office.

Appendix G contains a Manual for Box Office Treasurers that provides more operational details in regard to box office management.

SAMPLE AGENCY VOUCHER FORM

---

TICKET VOUCHER        No. 51176

STAR PLAYHOUSE
Main St., Maplewood, MA 577-1000

NAME _____

Performance date_____Eve_____Mat_____

Seat Numbers and Section:
Number of tickets purchased_____at $_____each

Total paid for tickets $_____
Purchase date_____Agent_____
This voucher represents a confirmed ticket order.
Please present it at the box office for actual tickets.
No Refunds—No Exchanges

---

## ACCOUNTING FOR THE TICKET
### Ticket Stubs and Deadwood

Before each performance the ticket taker should be provided with an empty, locked box into which all the stubs torn off customers' tickets can be deposited. The longer portion of the ticket should be placed in the box, the shorter given back to the customer. If there are different price categories for tickets, the stub box might have different slots and compartments for each; this will save time later when the stubs are counted.

The deadwood (those tickets remaining in the box office after each curtain time) are used to determine actual ticket sales; they are subtracted from the capacity of seats at that price, and the difference is entered on the box office statement as the number sold. The ticket stubs should correspond closely to this number, although it is common for a few ticketholders not to show up for any given performance. Obviously, the total deadwood and stubs should never *exceed* the capacity. Tickets should be recounted and statements rechecked until all discrepancies have been resolved. Stubs and deadwood should be counted soon after the curtain goes up and banded in piles of fifty or one hundred. The stub count may or may not appear on the box office statement, depending on the amount of information desired. Each count and computation should be done by at least two people working independently of each other until both can agree on the results. When the statement has been finalized, the stubs and dead tickets should be placed in a box or bag, labeled and stored in a safe place for at least three years.

## Discounted and Complimentary Tickets

The fewer discounts or "specials" that are offered, the less chance for mistakes and dishonesty at the box office. It is difficult to avoid the possibility of enabling a treasurer to charge full price for a ticket, declare it a discounted ticket and pocket the difference. All tickets that are discounted should be stamped or marked so that the returned stubs will indicate which were discounted and to what degree. Treasurers should also keep a written record of all discounts and comps that are issued. When the statement is being computed, this record is compared against all the signed house orders for complimentary and discounted tickets that were given to the box office by the producer, manager or press agent. Box office personnel, of course, should never be authorized to issue either comps or discounted seats without a written order, which should be kept and stored with the tickets.

## Box Office Statements

A box office statement is a financial report that shows the final accounting of tickets and income for a particular performance. Copies of the statement are usually submitted to the producer, the business manager, the accountant, and anyone who is receiving a percentage of box office receipts (playwright, star, and director, or their representatives). Obviously, the information on statements is confidential.

Several types of statements may be desirable for use by the same theatre. These might include:

1. *Master statement*: Shows the capacity number of seats at each price and the total potential ticket income
2. *Daily statement*: Shows actual ticket sales for a specific performance
3. *Weekly box office summary*: Shows a summary of actual ticket sales for a specific week of performances
4. *Seasonal box office statement*: A summation of all box office figures for a given season, as they will also appear in the accountant's annual financial report

5. *Ticket stub report*: This reports the stub count and may be the responsibility of the box office or the house manager

6. *Season ticket sales report*: After series or season ticket sales have ended, a complete record of these must be made for each performance in the series to determine the amount that must be discounted for that performance

7. *Group sales & other discounts report*: When the sale of discounted tickets is frequent and varied, a separate report of tickets for each performance may be required

8. *Advance ticket sales report*: This shows ticket sales for one or more performances in the future. Such reports are easily generated by a computer ticket system; to accomplish them manually would require an audit of every ticket in the box office and is, therefore, not feasible on a frequent basis.

Sample box office statement forms that can be adapted to the needs of different theatres are contained in the appendix.

## Box Office Auditing

An audit of the box office should be conducted at the end of each production or season and any other time a notable discrepancy appears between the number of tickets missing and the amount of income. The audit should be conducted or at least supervised by the accountant and not by the business manager or the treasurers. Essentially, an audit involves counting all the unsold tickets on hand, then making up a box office statement showing income-to-date for all future performances. This total amount, together with income shown on statements for past performances, should be the same as the total of all deposits for ticket sales made into the box office bank account. If income cannot be closely reconciled with the figures shown on the statements, the audit should be done again. It is easy to forget details, like discounted tickets, petty cash money borrowed from the box office, and so forth. Also, the audit will virtually never balance exactly. Even the most honestly and efficiently managed box office may show a 1 to 4 percent discrepancy as the result of honest human error. If a treasurer makes change for thousands of dollars worth of tickets each day, for example, it stands to reason that a few mistakes will be made. In fact, an audit that balances income with tickets sold to the exact penny is more suspicious than one that shows a small discrepancy. An audit system that can be adapted to suit most theatres is provided in the appendix.

## ADDITIONAL SOURCES OF EARNED INCOME

While the business of earning income from sources other than the box office entails additional costs, personnel and problems, few theatres can afford to ignore such potential income. The largest theatre operations often employ such specialists within the marketing department as a merchandizing manager, a concessions manager, an advertising sales manager, and others who generate income in the areas of tours, school programs, and rentals of space to outside groups. Because grants and contributions are subject to a great variety of forces beyond a theatre's control, sources of earned income may provide a more reliable way to supplement ticket income. In small operations, of course, the work of earning this money usually falls to the regular theatre staff. The house manager sells T-shirts during intermissions, for example; the publicity director sells advertising space in the programs; the interns park cars before each performance. This kind of split in responsibilities is unfortunate—like the need for most actors to supplement their income by finding extra employment outside the theatre. But the instinct for survival usually provides the justification for such efforts.

### Advertising Income

Very few theatres fail to generate at least some revenue by selling ads in their printed programs. These may be simple "Compliments of XYZ Hardware Company"-type notices or they may be elaborate display ads. When numerous ads are solicited (perhaps for a souvenir booklet as well as a regular playbill) a full-time ad salesperson may be required for certain periods of the year. Or, of course, the theatre may contract with an outside agency, publisher or printer both to sell the ads and publish the playbills in exchange for a percentage of profits or for a flat fee. This system is common in most large theatre cities and in large performing arts centers where numerous theatres share a common publisher. The playbill comes out on a weekly or monthly basis and contains the same design, general copy and advertising but the performance information differs for each theatre where it is distributed.

Rates for printed advertising of various types are based on the potential number of people who will read the ads, the size of the ad and the prominence with which it is displayed in relation to other advertising. Publishers of other periodicals are already in the business of selling ads and may be anxious to acquire the playbill publication rights to increase their profits at little risk. Theatres that grant such rights, however, must retain full control over all copy that pertains to the theatre and the production at hand and must guarantee that there will always be enough space in each playbill to print the necessary production, cast and staff information. The overall design and content of the playbill may also be a factor for negotiation, since these are important in creating the public image that a theatre projects.

Playbills and souvenir programs provide an obvious place to sell ads, but there are other places where ads may be sold, although the extent to which this is done should be governed by the image the theatre wishes to project. Advertising can easily cheapen the look of a lobby or a playbill unless it is limited and controlled. Nonetheless, here are a few possibilities:

1. *Ticket envelopes*
2. *Printed brochures and performances schedules.* Often, the advertiser will pay the full printing costs of such literature in exchange for being the only advertiser on it
3. *Newspaper ads and media spots.* Corporations may pay for a theatre's media ads in exchange for a mention in those ads, thereby creating a desired association with a cultural activity
4. *Postage imprints.* Private advertising is now permitted on postal imprints; meters may be rented and designed to print short ad messages next to the regular postage imprint. A theatre that puts out large mailings may rent this space to a local restaurant or hotel, for example, in exchange for the postage costs
5. *Lobby display space.* While most theatres avoid blatant lobby advertising, lobby decor may actually be enhanced by renting display space to local art galleries, antique dealerships and boutiques
6. *The fire curtain.* Until the present century, it was commonplace for theatres to paint advertisements on the fire curtain—obviously a prime space that no theatregoer could fail to see. Certain theatres or certain shows may still find this an acceptable practice
7. *Theatre seats.* As hospitals and many public buildings place names of contributors on rooms and pieces of equipment, there is no reason why theatres may not tastefully place the name of a business or a person on the backs or arms of theatre seats to indicate a contribution, to serve as a discreet advertisement, or both.

## Rental Income

Depending on how actively a theatre uses its stage and auditorium, on the availability of other halls and theatres in the community and the terms of the theatre's lease with a landlord, the business of renting a theatre to outside groups can be a lucrative source of income. Most operation and maintenance costs remain constant whether there are five or ten public events in a hall during a given week (unless large numbers of union employees require additional pay for added use of the facility). And when events are sponsored by outside groups, they are likely to attract people to the theatre building for the first time, and this may provide a boost to ticket sales. Of course, outside rentals should not seriously disrupt the theatre's own production schedule or image. Most theatres can be easily adapted to accommodate the following:

1. Stage productions by other theatre groups
2. Films, concerts and recitals sponsored by outside groups
3. Fundraising events, benefits and special events such as lectures and fashion shows
4. Political and municipal rallies and meetings
5. Industrial shows or meetings sponsored in relation to large conventions being held in the area
6. Graduation exercises
7. Recitals by local music and dance schools

## Concession Income

Nickel and dime profits from coin-operated vending machines can amount to an appreciable sum over a period of weeks. Most such machines may be rented or simply used on loan from a vending company, thereby requiring no investment, service or maintenance obligations. These include:

Public pay phones
Candy machines
Soft drink machines
Coin-operated coat lockers
Cigarette machines
Rest room vending machines

Larger concessions that require considerable management and investment but also offer the lure of larger profits include:

Coatroom checking services
Automobile parking lots and services
Restaurants
Alcoholic beverage concessions
Soft drink concessions
Gift shops and boutiques
Art galleries
Candy or baked goods concessions
Souvenir book sales

The inventory and revenue control over such concessions, as discussed in Chapters 11 and 12, is time-consuming when the concession is operated by the theatre, or when the theatre shares profits on a percentage basis. A flat rental fee is sometimes an easier and equally lucrative arrangement. Assuming that a theatre is the primary attraction that brings customers to the building in the first place, the theatre's management must accept overall responsibility for everything that transpires in the building. If a customer is shortchanged in a lobby gift shop, receives poor service in the theatre restaurant or loses money in the lobby pay phone, the complaint will come to the box office—despite the fact that both the theatre and the concessionaire may merely be tenants under the same roof with no other legal or business relationship. So, when the theatre is itself the landlord and leases out concession space, it must devise agreements with concessionaires that protect its own interests. For example, the theatre must reserve the right to evict a tenant concession if it does not maintain certain standards of cleanliness, customer service and product quality. The concessionaire must also be required to carry minimum types of insurance (such as product liability and theft), or such coverage may be attached to the theatre's own policy, which is usually less expensive.

When concessions are used by numerous playgoers, such as coat rooms or parking lots, the theatre ticket may have a detachable stub that entitles the ticket holder to a particular service. Such stubs may also entitle holders to discounted meals in nearby restaurants or other bargains. At the end of each week, the theatre and the managers of those tie-in businesses get together and match the stubs they received with those retained by the theatre. Perhaps the agreement is for the restaurant to pay the theatre a certain cash amount for each stub collected. Or perhaps the box office collects the full amount for a combined dinner and theatre ticket, in which case the theatre periodically pays the restaurant for the stubs it returns.

Sometimes a package deal is created for which customers pay a single price for several services or activities, such as dinner and theatre. The way prices are itemized on package-deal tickets can be important. For example, if both the food and theatre operations are owned by the same company, it may be decided to declare that, out of a $42.50 package price, $27.50 is the food cost and $15.00 is the theatre cost. The lower the theatre income, of course, the lower the payments for percentages, royalties and entertainment taxes. Some theatres even include an automatic service charge on all tickets and never show this portion of the ticket price on the box office statements: the ticket might read, "This price includes a $1.00 parking charge." Of course, this practice is not altogether ethical, as it may shortchange actors, playwrights and others of income that is legitimately theirs.

Many large theatre companies have turned to merchandizing as another source of earned income. Specialty items that carry the theatre's logo or relate to its productions in some way—T-shirts, calendars, cookbooks, tote bags and note paper, to name only a few possibilities—are bought from manufacturers for resale. They may be sold in the lobby, offered through mail order catalogues or used as give-away enticements to attract contributions.

## School and Outreach Income

Most professional nonprofit theatres today operate some kind of school or training program. The reason for this is threefold: such programs may generate additional earned income; they often generate additional unearned income from grants; and they address the urgent need to develop young audiences. In addition, training programs are cost-effective for many theatres because company staff and cast members may be utilized as instructors at little extra cost and the theatre or rehearsal rooms may double as class space. Of course, education programs may also be offered as outreach activities away from the theatre itself, thereby filling both educational and publicity functions. Grants from both public and private sources have long been available for artists-in-schools, artists-in-residence, and a variety of other outreach and touring programs. Yet another approach is for the theatre to associate itself with a nearby college or university. College students may take classes or earn credit for serving internships at the theatre, or the theatre may send artists and staff to conduct classes and workshops on the campus. The possibilities are numerous and, best of all, the college usually handles all the administrative work involved in such joint programs. Theatre companies may also work with local school boards to develop programs in the public schools—and to lobby for more meaningful funding for arts-in-education in general.

The most common training programs sponsored by theatre companies include:

1. *Internships.* These may be in artistic, technical and/or managerial areas and interns may receive college credit, a small stipend or nothing at all
2. *Apprentice programs.* Although "intern" has come to replace the word "apprentice" in most theatre circles, some companies still operate apprentice programs or schools in which the participants pay tuition
3. *Formal training programs.* Many companies offer formal classes— especially acting classes—structured over a period of months and often culminating in a production or series of workshop scenes; often there is a tuition charge. Such programs may be designed either for children or adults

4. *Children's theatre programs.* Some training programs, either involving children or adults, are designed to produce public performances for children and thereby generate both tuition and ticket income

5. *Arts-in-education programs.* Individual artists, groups or whole productions are sometimes engaged to give instruction, performances or both in public and private schools

6. *Workshops and residencies.* Most theatre and dance companies that tour college campuses try to arrange for company members to offer workshops or lecture-demonstrations for appropriate student groups. Or they may arrange a residency that involves company members in instructional duties over a period of days or weeks. Such services are paid by the college (often from a grant given to the campus presenting organization that is sponsoring the company's public performances)

7. *Young audiences programs.* Theatre companies may arrange special performance for young people or school groups, or simply include such groups at regular performances. Special materials may be distributed as classroom instruction aids, company members may visit classroom before or after the performance, or introductory or post-performance discussions may be held at the theatre.

Theatre companies that sponsor extensive education, outreach and training activities will require at least one full-time person to serve as director or administrator, and that person may require support staff. While such activities often generate additional income, they also generate additional responsibilities that should not be taken lightly. It should be remembered that people with talent in one area, such as acting, may have no talent in another, such as teaching.    And while theatre training can enhance theatre appreciation, it can also destroy it.

## Income from Special Attractions

There is no reason why a producing theatre organization cannot also function, at least occasionally, as a presenting organization. There are usually many periods between company-produced performances, productions and seasons when the auditorium is not in use and could accommodate certain special attractions. These should not, of course, be in direct competition with the regular season. But they might be aimed at bringing new audiences to the theatre, together with new sources of earned income.

The process of presenting theatrical and other attractions is described in Chapter 10. It bears repeating, however, that booking and presenting attractions involves risk that can be reduced through experience, but never entirely eliminated. Nonetheless, attractions that may easily be accommodated in most theatres include:

Children's theatre companies
Modern dance companies
Small/medium music ensembles
Solo recitals
Vocal groups
One-person shows
Small touring theatre productions
Films
Lectures

## Miscellaneous Sources of Income

Perhaps the sweetest kind of earned income is that which is derived from the subsidiary rights to a production that a producer or theatre company helped to develop, and quite a few professional nonprofit theatres today are collecting performance royalties from just such plays. The transfer, touring and conversion of productions from nonprofit theatres is discussed in Chapter 6. By comparison with the other items on the following list, income earned from subsidiary rights can be considerable:

Subsidiary rights
Income from interest-bearing bank accounts
Earnings from investments
Equipment rentals
Costume rentals
Scenery rentals
Production services contracted by outside groups

Investing a theatre company's precious capital in stocks, bonds and other financial instruments is very risky and should be avoided in most cases. Interest-bearing bank accounts, however, should be used when possible over non-interest accounts. And the business office should studiously maximize interest earnings by careful management of deposits and withdrawals. If a company's inventory of production equipment and other items can be rented without disrupting the operation, this can bring in additional income. And if production facilities and personnel are sufficient, the theatre may even build production elements for outside organizations.

## SUMMATION

An efficient box office operation requires an especially exacting system of checks and balances, as well as personnel who are both honest and dedicated to detail. Computerized ticket systems have streamlined and simplified box office procedures, although they are still not feasible for all theatres.

Merchandising—whether it involves selling tickets or T-shirts—should be based on sound marketing principles and be conducted according to sound business practices. Increasing the amount of earned income for a given theatre company or organization can be challenging and gratifying, as well as discouraging and frustrating. There are probably few people involved in producing plays and managing theatres who had any inkling, when they first began, that so much of their time would be spent on ostensibly non-theatre business. Hiring bartenders and checking empty bottles, ordering popsicles for the kiddie matinee and filling mail orders for greeting cards are not activities likely to satisfy a love for theatre. But they are often necessary to make theatre possible. The idea for theatre, however, must always remain central. Artistic integrity is compromised when the lobby is overcrowded by unattractive vending machines, when the price of drinks is inflated outrageously, and when barkers selling souvenir booklets make it impossible to enjoy a conversation. When *that* is the marketing policy, one may as well fire the actors and put vending machines on the stage instead.

# 14

# Fundraising And Sources Of Contributed Income

I F philanthropy is the art of giving, then fundraising is the art of getting. The chief function of fundraising is to secure grants and contributions, an activity conducted exclusively within the nonprofit sector. Grants, contributions and in-kind gifts are referred to collectively as "contributed income" or "unearned income." The latter term seems inappropriate because a great deal of work goes into securing this income; a valuable artistic product may result from it and grants are, in fact, contracts to buy specified services. Nor would it be accurate to call such income a gift, as most of it has strings attached. (Remember hearing, "I'll *give* you a dollar, *if* you clean up your room!")

"Development" is often used as a euphemism for "fundraising," which also seems inappropriate. After all, the development department at a film or television company is in charge of writing story treatments and developing screenplays. We also talk about "developing" a theatrical script or production. Nonetheless, "development" is widely used to mean "fundraising."

Some of the larger performing arts institutions have placed fundraising activities under a marketing director or under a director of planning, which may put the responsibility for both earned and contributed income under one manager or department. But whatever title the fundraiser may hold and whoever the fundraiser may report to, he or she is always the poor soul with the empty, outstretched hand.

## GENERAL CONSIDERATIONS

It is rare for a nonprofit arts organization to receive a grant or corporate contribution unless it has been functioning for at least three years. This helps to explain why so many groups start out very modestly and why their initial subsidy comes exclusively from individual contributions—often from the participants themselves together with their relatives, friends and associates. During those first few years of operation, however, it is important to establish and document a track record of artistic accomplishment. This means producing good work before audiences, generating favorable reviews and publicity, and gaining respectful attention within the theatre community itself. Young theatre groups should also practice good accountability in regard to their legal and financial records, and they should collect statistics about ticket sales, outreach activities, contributions, productions, tours, and other matters that will count heavily in their early funding proposals.

Because most individual, corporate and foundation donors operate with little or no staff, they are seldom able to analyze thoroughly the work or the records of the organizations that approach them for funding. The National Endowment for the Arts, the National Endowment for the Humanities, and the state arts councils, however, do usually have sufficient staff to conduct close examination of current and prospective beneficiaries. Hence, their grant awards—however modest—serve as green lights for other funders. It might also be noted that government funding agencies are more likely to support experimental, politically radical and non-traditional projects than private funders. A good illustration of this concerns a theatre company that is dedicated to anarchy and yet receives funding from government arts agencies. "We just walk into those agencies," explains its artistic director, "and say, 'We're here to destroy you—please fund us,' and, you see, they must—if only to prove they are serious about democratic principles and freedom of speech!"

It is sometimes tempting for a theatre organization to permit its funders to influence or even to determine its productions, projects or policies. This is rarely advisable. As emphasized repeatedly throughout this book, artistic ventures of all kinds should be driven by artistic priorities. If these do not agree with a certain funder's priorities, then another funder should be found. At any given time, society in general, and philanthropy in particular, adopts one or two favorite causes and then, it seems, funds them right out of fashion. The arts were a favorite cause in the funding world for ten or fifteen years during the '60s and '70s, but that situation is unlikely to repeat itself for some time. Nonetheless, good trustees and good fundraisers understand that the funds must follow the art, because art that follows the funding has usually lost both integrity and purpose.

## THE FUNDRAISING DIRECTOR

Successful fundraisers invariably possess well-polished communication skills. They must be good writers and editors, and they must also be able to communicate well with other professionals and prominent citizens in a variety of fields and positions. This requires an attractive, out-going personality and, usually, a college education. Like actors, fundraisers must be impervious to rejections and persistent in pursuit of their goals. They must often conduct or supervise research to identify potential funding sources. And, of course, they must have a thorough familiarity with the theatre organization which they are working for as well as the performing arts field as a whole.

Typical responsibilities of a fundraising director—often shared with an associate or full staff—include:

1. Identifying and cultivating potential donors through research and board contacts
2. Preparing or supervising grant applications, appeal letters and funding proposals
3. Designing direct-mail, telephone and other fundraising drives
4. Generating financial reports that account for expenditures, as required by funding agencies
5. Personally soliciting funds and following up donations with progress reports and acknowledgements
6. Conceiving and supervising special fundraising events, galas, benefits and other activities
7. Conducting research into the histories and funding requirements of appropriate agencies, foundations, corporations and individuals
8. Keeping up-to-date records regarding board members, donor histories, volunteer workers, grant deadlines, mailing lists, and the like.

Fundraisers must also keep themselves informed about ever-changing tax laws, government regulations, economic trends and changes in corporate ownership. Reading such publications as *The Wall Street Journal* on a daily basis is a must. And they must constantly up-date their address books, rolodexes and/or data bases as their contacts increase or change.

## SOURCES OF CONTRIBUTED INCOME

There are four basic sources of contributed income: government, foundations, corporations and individuals. A large performing arts organization would have a fundraising specialist for each of these areas.

### Government

Arts funding agencies exist at the federal, state and municipal levels of government. As mentioned, state and local arts councils are a good place for new theatre companies to submit their first funding requests. Most such agencies allocate their funds through a wide range of specified categories or programs, such as theatre, music, dance or performing arts as a whole. They are budgeted on an annual basis, so that once awards have been made there is rarely any surplus from which to grant supplemental funds until the next funding cycle. However, the same nonprofit theatre organization may qualify in several program areas at the same funding agency: for example, theatre and arts-in-education. Also, application deadlines for different programs are often spread throughout the year. All government agencies that fund the arts publish a guide to their programs that also contains an explanation of the application process, and these are available upon request, along with a copy of their latest annual report and other literature.

The National Foundation for the Arts and Humanities is the body that governs the twin endowments, each of which is funded by an appropriation granted by Congress through annual presidential requests, and each is advised by a national council. Under its first chairperson, Roger Stevens, the annual NEA budget grew from $2.5 million in 1966 to $12 million; during eight years under Nancy Hanks, it grew to a little over $100 million annually; and during the next four years under Livingston Biddle III it grew to about $165 million, the approximate level at which it remained under Frank Hodsell in the 1980s. Of course, this is just a fraction of one percent of the total federal budget and puts arts subsidy in the United States at only about fifteen cents per person or sixty-eight cents per taxpayer per year, which is considerably lower than the arts subsidy in most other industrialized nations. Yet Ronald Reagan seriously challenged the very existence of the NEA and the NEH. Only through the lobbying efforts of the arts community, and the congressional leadership of such men as Senator Claiborne Pell and Representative Sidney R. Yates, were the endowments able to survive the '80s. There were no significant budget increases, but neither were there significant decreases. Under President Bush in the '90s with John Frohmayer as head of the NEA, small increases began to reverse this trend, although the agency came under severe criticism by conservative senators and members of Congress.

The NEA awards its grants according to peer panels that base their decisions about applications upon the evaluations and recommendations of the agency's staff. A separate panel for each program is comprised of leading professionals from the appropriate branch of the profession who serve for a limited term on a voluntary basis. While the peer panel system is periodically challenged, it is widely credited as the most non-political method for allocating public funds to the arts. There may, however, be legislative guidelines that mandate the distribution of funds according to population density, voting districts or some other formula. This can present some pretty tough funding choices in states like New York, where one county contains the cultural capital of the world and another seems mainly distinguished for the art of quilt-making—but such is the price of democratic rule.

There are nearly one hundred federal agencies and programs other than the NEA that provide funding and/or assistance to artists and arts organizations; a listing of these is available from the Superintendent of Documents Office in Washington. Fundraisers should apply imagination and logic when approaching government agencies. For example, a prison theatre group and a theatre company comprised of veterans applied to and received funding from the United States Department of Justice. And nonprofit organizations are also eligible to receive government surplus items ranging from office furniture to automobiles. Disbursement of such goods is through state, not federal, agencies, and requests should be directed to the state surplus property official, whose exact title and address is found under the state listings in the phone book. The Department of Cultural Affairs in New York City created a Materials for the Arts program to funnel municipal surplus items to arts groups and this has been used as a model in other cities. Donated items of every description are placed in a warehouse where staff from nonprofit arts organizations can go shopping.

Part of the annual NEA budget is awarded in the form of direct grants to artists and organizations. Another part is divided between the state arts councils, of which there are fifty-six, including Puerto Rico, the Virgin Islands, American Samoa, Guam, the Northern Marianas, and the District of Columbia, and all are members of the National Assembly of State Arts Associations (NASAA). The state arts councils must match their federal allocations with state funds and they, in turn, give some of their budget to municipal and community arts councils—of which there are over two thousand nationwide that are members of the National Assembly of Community Arts Agencies (NACAA)—and their funds are also matched with local tax monies.    In this manner, one federal dollar generates two or three additional dollars. And many other awards made at the different government levels are also given on a matching or challenge grant basis, which specifies that the recipient must raise one or more dollars for each dollar it receives from the funder (grants from the private sector may also be awarded on this basis). In these cases, one tax dollar may generate five or more private dollars in support of the arts—a remarkably productive use of government funds!

Although lobbying, letter writing, demonstrating, picketing and arm-twisting in the halls of government don't seem to be very theatrical activities, no responsible artist or arts administrator can ignore them.  They are the *only* way to insure and increase government support.  There are several national membership organizations, such as the American Council for the Arts (ACA) and the Alliance for Arts Education (AAE), which are primarily involved with arts advocacy. This is also a concern of virtually all professional arts associations unions and service organizations, although nonprofit organizations are legally prohibited from engaging in political lobbying activities. But the individuals who work for those organizations are not.

## Foundations

A foundation is an incorporated nonprofit organization set up to distribute funds or grants to people and projects that meet certain, often very exacting, criteria. There are about thirty thousand private foundations in America, most of which are administered by an attorney, an estate executor or a part-time director and most only award funds within their geographical area. Foundations derive their assets from private estates or corporate earnings; to prevent them from being used merely to shield money from the tax collector, or to funnel untaxed money back into the giver's own pocket, federal law requires that foundations, like other nonprofit organizations, have an IRS-approved mission and further that they serve this mission by giving away at least 5 percent of their assets each year.

Large foundations are headed by a president, chairperson or director and supported by departmentalized staff members. Organizations like the Ford, Carnegie and Rockefeller Foundations resemble large state arts councils, except that their staffs report to boards of trustees rather than to a politically appointed council. And, of course, their interests are not limited to the arts.

There are three broad types of foundations:

*Operating foundations:* established by a business or institution to conduct research, social welfare or other philanthropic activities based on the foundation's stated goals and in-house programs, such as a hospital research laboratory

*Corporate foundations:* established and funded by private or public corporations based usually on a percentage of the annual profits but are otherwise legally separate from the parent corporation, so that the resources of the Ford Foundation, for example, are tied to the profitability of the Ford Motor Company, but its giving policies are not

*Family foundations:* created by gifts from individuals, groups of individuals or family members, like the Rockefeller Brothers Fund or the Donner Foundation; these represent the most numerous foundations, by far.

Fortunately for professional fundraisers and grantwriters from all disciplines, there is a unique national service organization funded primarily by foundations and designed to accommodate research in this field. The Foundation Center maintains major reference libraries and research facilities in Washington, San Francisco, Cleveland  and New York, with ostensibly limitless data about foundations and corporations that can be produced in whatever format one wishes, at the touch of a computer. For an annual fee, frequent users may avail themselves of telephone access, fax service and other time-saving conveniences. Foundation Center Collections are also housed at libraries in a majority of state capitals. Among the invaluable resources at the main centers are:

1. *Form 990-PF*: the IRS information form filed annually by all foundations in the U.S.
2. *Foundation annual reports*: these include full program descriptions and, often, lists of past grantees
3. *Foundation literature*: files containing newsletters, articles, application guidelines and other material
4. *Foundation grant programs by subject*: indexes to current grants of $5,000 or more available on microfiche or computer printouts
5. *General Reference Materials*: the latest editions of such key publications as *The Foundation Grants Index, The Taft Corporate Directory, The Foundation Directory, Source Book Profiles, The National Directory of Corporate Charities*, as well as books and periodicals about fundraising, grantwriting and nonprofit management.

There is also the Grantsmanship Center in Los Angeles and several national membership associations, such as The Council on Foundations, The American Association of Fund-Raising Counsels, The National Center for Charitable Statistics, and The Independent Sector (a national coalition on volunteerism based in Washington, D.C.).

## Corporations

Foundations that derive their assets from corporate profits are themselves independent corporations, outside the control of the hand that feeds them. Still, the amount they are fed each year is directly related to the annual profits of their corporate benefactors. Rather than setting up a foundation, most corporations that make any contributions at all to the nonprofit sector do so directly. Although federal law encourages corporate philanthropy by allowing corporations to reduce their pre-tax earnings up to 10 percent by making contributions to eligible nonprofit organizations, few actually take advantage of this. To help stimulate such giving, the Business Committee for the Arts was formed in 1967. Its membership is comprised of the heads of over one hundred of the nation's largest corporations, and its objectives are to bring the business and arts communities closer together, and thereby encourage increased support for the arts. And indeed, corporate contributions to the arts have shown steady if unremarkable growth in recent decades. In total, they are roughly equal to the NEA budget. But President Reagan's gamble, that corporations could be persuaded to increase their charitable giving as government funding decreased, did not pay off. In fact, there is considerable evidence that corporate giving *follows* government initiatives, both in identifying worthy causes and recipients, and in levels of funding. Major foundations have also provided such leadership through their studying and reporting about certain social, scientific and cultural issues. But corporate philanthropy, traditionally the most conservative, usually prefers to support projects that already carry a stamp of approval.

Decisions about corporate giving are usually made by one of three people: the board president or chairperson, the corporate giving officer, or the public relations officer. Such decisions are often based more on personal contacts and interests rather than on corporate policies, although it is usually hoped that contributions will enhance the corporation's public image, strengthen its influence in its local community and/or directly benefit its employees. Nonetheless, there is rarely much in-house communication about funding activities; if the same funding appeal went to both the giving officer and the public relations director, they might not become aware of the duplication. Besides which, funding from both departments might be perfectly justifiable, although according to different criteria: artistic merit on the one hand, perhaps, and publicity value on the other. Increasingly, corporate support for the arts has come from the public relations or advertising budget: cigarette manufacturers have sponsored cultural events to improve their image, and oil companies have the same goal in their sponsorship of cultural television programming. Many nonprofit theatre companies have benefited from more modest corporate support which, like support from small foundations, is usually restricted to the geographic area of the corporate headquarters.

Corporate contributions come in a variety of forms. Aside from direct cash gifts, corporations often provide subsidy to theatre companies by purchasing tickets, buying a table at a benefit banquet, buying playbill advertising, contributing securities, matching the gifts made by others, underwriting new productions, sponsoring special events or providing loans, and in-kind contributions of goods and services.

"Corporate tie-ins" have also become increasingly common in recent years. These provide cash and/or in-kind contributions that benefit the nonprofit organization, but they also link the names of the donor and the recipient in a very public way: the Kool Jazz Festival, Pepsico Summerfare, and the Texaco Opera Network offer some obvious examples. Or perhaps a clothing designer or retailer pays for an opening night banquet and presents a fashion show of its new line during desert and coffee. Most such tie-ins to date have reflected a certain degree of restraint, although some observers worry that corporate sponsorship of arts programming could one day have undue influence on program selection—by favoring "safe" or "popular" works over new or experimental ones, for instance; or by censoring literary content. Perhaps the most blatant commercial use of an art form is the bold display of brand names on products used in movies in exchange for corporate backing or gratuities. Like any type of patronage, corporate support can seduce its beneficiaries into compromising positions. Good fundraisers and trustees of arts organizations have an obligation to resist such temptation.

Business leaders concerned about good corporate citizenship and the role of corporations in society as a whole have initiated several noteworthy practices: matching the charitable donations of employees is one such policy; lending employees to nonprofit organizations is another. And there are few ways that corporate executives can have a greater impact on the nonprofit sector than by serving on boards of trustees. Several enlightened corporations have even provided special incentives and training to encourage their executives to take on such volunteer service.

Due to the personal nature of most corporate funding decisions, this branch of philanthropy has been severely shaken in recent years by all the personnel displacements resulting from corporate mergers, acquisitions, leveraged buyouts and divestitures. It takes a lot of time and energy to find generous friends and develop funding relationships. With frequent changes in corporate leadership and executive personnel, the number of such liaisons is greatly reduced. But hopefully the business scene will becalm itself, and the dust will settle. When this occurs, however, the corporate world will be much more global in terms of its markets, its personnel, its office and plant locations, and, inevitably, its social and cultural interests. This will undoubtedly affect the nature of corporate funding and place more emphasis on such matters as international touring, cross-cultural programming, and projects aimed at very diverse audiences.

## Individuals

Individual donations given to a theatre organization range all the way from a quarter dropped into the hat of a street mime to a multi-million dollar gift for the construction of a new theatre facility. Of the many billions of dollars that this country recognizes as charitable contributions each year, about 80 percent still comes from individuals, followed by foundations and corporations, in that order. The lion's share of this largess goes to religious organizations, followed by education, health care, human services, and arts and culture, where the share of individual generosity was $6.4 billion in 1987.

This figure contained the lowest increase in charitable giving in twelve years, obviously the result of the 1986 revision of tax laws which eliminated charitable deductions for about 75 percent of the taxpayers who do not itemize their returns. The legislation also reduced tax rates, making charitable deductions less attractive, especially for wealthy donors, and it greatly reduced the tax benefits of gifts of appreciated stock, real estate, and art works (which severely diminished donations of art works to museums, among other things). Nonetheless, individual philanthropy in America has proved to be surprisingly resilient to such change. Wealthy individuals still make large contributions to arts organizations, if not for the tax break then for prestige and the perpetuation of their names. And small donors continue to give their dollar bills simply to perpetuate the arts organizations that bring them joy. For reasons such as these, most nonprofit organizations should spend their main fundraising efforts going after individual contributions—but most do not.

The device by which a solid base of individual donations is accrued is an annual fund drive or donor campaign, as will be discussed below. This may be conducted by any one theatre organization or in cooperation with other arts organizations, as a united fund drive. Another method by which a nonprofit organization may consolidate its fundraising efforts is to estimate its financial needs for two or three years; one fund drive may then be able to cover deficits for the whole period. This cuts down on fundraising costs and bows to the fact that most donors prefer to be approached as seldom as possible. The semiannual or triennial drive may also enable the theatre company to retain the services of a professional fundraising firm or consultant. Those of good reputation provide their services for a set fee, *not* a percentage of the money raised. Generally, they also insist on conducting a feasibility study prior to launching the actual drive. Their assistance can be extremely valuable and should be considered by any nonprofit group that does not have its own fundraising department.

When soliciting a donation from any potential funder, but especially when the request is aimed at an individual, the first rule is this: make the amount requested appropriate to the donor's ability to give. In other words, never ask an "important" person for an "unimportant" sum, or vice versa. The person unable to give the amount requested will give nothing, whereas the person able to give *more* than requested will slyly contribute the pittance and never fork over again!

## METHODS OF RAISING CONTRIBUTED INCOME

There are many different methods and schemes for collecting contributions and, in all probability, a new one is being invented every minute. For most nonprofit organizations, a healthy base of contributed income is a diversified base. Few funders renew their grants or contributions for more than a few years and all are subject to unexpected reversals. A poor national economy can seriously affect government as well as corporate funding; a stock market crash or sudden reversal can affect private funding, and charitable inclinations and preferences in general are always being influenced by what is going on in the nation and the world. So the prudent fundraiser keeps busy cultivating new sources, even while the old ones are still contributing.

## Grants

A grant is a written contract between two parties in which it is specified that one will pay a certain sum to the other in exchange for certain services, such as the staging in San Diego, California, of four new plays by American playwrights. Because the government is not permitted to "give away" its tax-levied funds, government arts agencies can only disburse their appropriations by awarding grants (contracts). Some foundation and corporate donations are also awarded on a contractual basis. This always means that there are strings (conditions) attached to the money. At the very least, it will have to be spent for a specified purpose by a specified time, otherwise it may be denied, timed payments may be terminated, the money will have to be returned or—if you're ready for this—certain goods or property related to the project or organization may actually be confiscated by the funding agency!

These are good reasons for any arts organization to examine closely the guidelines of its potential funders. Are the conditions worth the value of the "gift"?

## Contributions

"Contribution" is the generic term for all types of unearned income. Many contributions, both large and small, are earmarked for specific use: an endowment fund, a capital fund, operating expenses or some special project. One of the more innovative uses of individual donations was pioneered at the Mark Taper Forum, where adult donors bought student subscriptions, or "scholarships," which they could then assign to students of their choice, or others selected by the theatre.

## Annual Fund Drive

An annual fund drive or donor campaign seeks as much money as possible in the shortest time from as many contributors as possible. It may be conducted through the mail, through the media, through special events, over the phone or through any combination of these techniques. After one or two years, it should bring in a fairly predictable amount of money. It should also serve as a method for testing the real strength of audience support, building new audiences and identifying potential major donors. And aside from the concerted effort that goes into an annual drive, individual contributions can be solicited throughout the year by including an appeal for a donation with subscription and other ticket order forms, in playbills, in advertisements, and in public-service announcements.

## Membership Drive

Members may also be subscribers or series ticket buyers, or they may form a distinct category of donors. For example, there may be a guild or friends committee that pays membership dues and also volunteers its efforts to raise even more contributions for the theatre company. Members of either type are customarily entitled to certain privileges: invitations to parties, receptions, rehearsals, discussions and symposia; discounts at local restaurants; free parking, and so forth.

## United Fund Drive

Community arts councils can be especially valuable in organizing local fundraising efforts. More effective results are often achieved when several groups work together. This may also be done through a consortium of companies. Lincoln Center, for example, conducts unified funding campaigns for all its constituents, while each company also continues its individual efforts. The same concept has been adopted by a number of Off-Off-Broadway theatres that just happen to be located on 42nd Street west of Ninth Avenue in Manhattan, an area known as Theatre Row. A fear of losing identity by joining mutual endeavors is understandable, but the old adage that says "there is strength in numbers" still holds.

## Telethon

A telethon is a fundraising campaign conducted on radio or television, its aimed at convincing listeners or viewers to phone in with a pledge to contribute, or an actual contribution by credit card. The cost of air time for a telethon is usually beyond the resources of most theatre companies, unless the time is donated or sponsored by supporters. Telethons become more feasible, however, when conducted as a united effort.

## Benefits and Special Events

A benefit is an attempt to raise money by attracting a group of people to a particular performance or event. Tax laws now require that only that portion of the admission price or amount paid *above the cost of the event and/or items purchased* may be declared by the purchaser as a tax deduction (and only then on itemized tax returns). The IRS is watchful in enforc-

410

ing this regulation, so benefit organizers must account for all costs, and the deductible portion or item-cost should appear in all advertising for the benefit, as well as on the ticket or receipt given to the buyer.

At meal functions, whole banquet tables are often bought by corporations or wealthy individuals as a form of contribution. Sometimes costs of the benefit may be absorbed when a person or corporation underwrites certain expenses, either by paying for them or providing in-kind goods and services.

The possibilities for special events, of course, are only limited by the organizer's imagination. There are auctions, bake sales, group trips, sweepstakes, flea markets, bazaars, parties, whatever. To be successful, they must be appealing, fun, well-organized and well-attended.

SAMPLE BENEFIT INVITATION SHOWING DEDUCTIBLE PORTION

---

ENCLOSED IS $_____FOR_____TICKETS AT $50 each
     ($25 for Arts Organization)       ($25 tax deduction)
     **ALL TICKETS WILL BE HELD AT THE BOX OFFICE**
I CANNOT ATTEND, BUT I AM ENCLOSING
A CONTRIBUTION OF $_____
        R.S.V.P. BY MAY 11, 19XX
     *PLEASE MAKE CHECK PAYABLE TO* **XYZ THEATRE**

---

NAME                      TITLE

---

COMPANY OR ORGANIZATION

---

ADDRESS

---

CITY, STATE, ZIP       TEL. BUS.      HOME

---

## Volunteers

Most nonprofit organizations benefit from the use of unpaid workers (aside from board members). These may be interns, apprentices or students who make a commitment of time over a period of weeks or months, or they may be people who help out on a more limited basis with funding drives and other efforts to raise money. However, if an organization is not prepared to spend considerable time in supervising volunteers, they may turn out to be more of a liability than an asset.

## In-Kind Goods and Services

In-kind gifts are a type of corporate support. They may be in the form of goods or equipment (anything from wine to computers); or services (such as free air travel or free use of the company's copying machines); or expertise (the use of a corporate employee or retiree to provide some type of technical assistance, such as in accounting or welding). Most such gifts gain a tax deduction for the corporation along with good will and publicity, and all at virtually no cost since they are essentially surplus inventory items that the corporation can do without.

## Support From a Parent Institution

Civic, college and university theatres, and certain others operate under the umbrella of a large institution. This parent body often supplies the facility rent-free, plus maintenance, security, staff, supplies, utilities and numerous services, thereby reducing the operating costs for such groups to little more than the money required to build scenery and costumes. On the surface, this may appear to be an enviable situation. Yet sibling theatre organizations are subject to the rules, regulations and discipline of the parent institution—not to mention the bureaucratic red tape required to get things done. They are also subject to whatever political, budgetary, administrative or personnel change or crisis may affect the umbrella institution—and these can be traumatic and debilitating. Also, when receiving grants from outside the institution, the theatre company or project must usually forfeit anywhere from 20 to 60 percent of the grant award to the parent body in the name of "rent" or "service charge." This is usually a legitimate reimbursement for costs absorbed by the institution, but it certainly diminishes the incentive for writing grant proposals and the pleasure of winning awards. A similar "nibbling away" of funds occurs in the flow of budget allocations from their source to particular departments and projects. As once described by the chancellor of a state university, "Getting money from the state legislature, to the university, to the college, to the department, and to the project for which it is intended is roughly like transporting lettuce via rabbit!"

## BASIC ELEMENTS IN SUCCESSFUL FUNDRAISING

### Volunteer Leadership

A professional fundraising firm or consultant hired to raise money for a nonprofit organization looks first at that group's volunteer leadership, which is to say its board of trustees. If this is a "funny board" comprised of the artistic director's family and friends, the job of attracting meaningful contributions will almost certainly be difficult. If, however, the board is comprised of top corporate executives, leading professionals and socially prominent members of the community, *and* if these trustees are willing to use their influence and their contacts to raise funds for the organization, then the job should be much easier. When board membership falls somewhere in between those two extremes, the first step in a serious fundraising campaign should be to strengthen the board with influential and enthusiastically supportive new members. The search for candidates might begin with an examination of subscriber and donor records (which, hopefully, are complete and up-to-date).

## Planning

Fundraising should follow the planning process and invent strategies that will help the organization to realize its goals. At the core of the plan, of course, is the mission statement. As discussed in Chapter 6, a mission statement should be accompanied by a short list of long-term goals and another list of short-term objectives. The former may include the acquisition of a new theatre facility at some time in the future, while the latter may include the production of Shakespeare's history plays during the next season. Goals such as these can be translated into fairly realistic budgets. The projected deficits become the fundraising goals. It may be decided to consolidate all efforts around one funding drive, or to split this into a capital campaign to raise money for the new facility and a membership campaign to raise money for the season. And, of course, government, foundation and corporate sources must be approached as well as individuals.

When short- and long-term planning have not occurred, a professionally directed fundraising effort will reveal this at once and require that it be done before funding efforts even commence. The money should follow the plan. And when the plan—the dream—is a good one, money will follow.

## Management and Administration

While it is up to board members to open doors, it is up to salaried managers and staff to do most of the work. The board member may sign letters to potential contributors, for instance, but the staff researches the titles and addresses of those people and writes the letters. A limited amount of fundraising may be accomplished by one person. Serious efforts usually require two or more full-time specialists. One may be mainly involved with identifying and cultivating potential donors, the other with conducting research, writing proposals and keeping records. Successful fundraising requires that a great deal of solid information be gathered and processed, and this takes time even when the operation is fully computerized.

A board of trustees may form a fundraising subcommittee with its own chairperson, or the board may serve as a fundraising committee of the whole,

413

headed by the board president or chairperson. In either case, one board member should serve as liaison with the fundraising director or consultant. That person then supervises one or more associates and also coordinates funding efforts with other departments, such as marketing and finance. Large organizations often hire a special events manager to work within the fundraising office and to organize and manage benefits, such as auctions and special performances. These, together with wider funding appeals, usually require numerous volunteers, who must be recruited, trained, supervised and thanked—another time-consuming responsibility. And many nonprofit theatres have a junior board, an advisory committee, a friends committee, a donors guild, or some other such group that assists with fundraising and audience development. These special people are also volunteers who require staff support and supervision.

Other management and administration duties in this area are discussed in the above section that describes the responsibilities of a fundraising director.

## Communication

Successful fundraising is conducted on a very human level. It requires written and spoken contact, it requires getting a message across, it requires appeals to the heart, the head, the ego, and, of course, the pocketbook. In short, it requires effective communication skills.

Applications may be sent miles away to the nation's capital, but there can still be phone contact between the fundraiser and the funding agency. Opportunities to meet colleagues and active donors are frequent: benefits, business functions, conferences, cultural events. Personal contacts at both ends of the application process comprise the fundraiser's portfolio—a valuable asset which that person carries from one job to the next.

Few grants or contributions of any size are awarded without personal contact between the contributor and the theatre organization. Often accompanied by a board member, the managing director or the artistic director, the fundraiser must usually visit the potential funder one or more times and be able to present a strong case. When the best known figure at the organization—probably the artistic director—is unable or unwilling to make such visits, raising money becomes more difficult. Contributors like to meet "the main person."

Funding proposals and appeals must also be presented in written form, as will be discussed shortly. This requires the ability to organize often complex information and abstract concepts in a succinct and commanding format. The more fortunate fundraisers are able to tap the resources of their organization's marketing and public relations offices for assistance in preparing funding appeals, campaign brochures and other materials.

## Timing

In order to receive grant awards from government agencies and from many foundations and corporations, the applicant must meet a deadline. Because requests go well beyond the budgetary resources of these funders, a late application almost always means automatic rejection. In fact, the NEA and some state arts councils even require grant seekers to file an "intent to file" notice in advance of the application deadline.

Different corporations have different patterns of relaxed and busy workloads. A knowledge of such patterns helps to determine the most favorable time to approach the board chairperson or the CEO. And it is especially helpful when asking a corporation to provide in-kind gifts, which should always be done well in advance to accommodate the corporation's own priorities.

The time and place where a funding request is first mentioned can also be important. As a general rule, this is best done during business hours in the business place. Few corporate executives, funding officers or wealthy socialites enjoy being buttonholed on the dance floor or over their salmon mousse and lectured about the artistic virtues of the X#! Theatre Company. An exchange of business cards or a request to phone the next day is about as far as that type of introduction should go.

Timing is important when scheduling a funding campaign, a benefit or a special event. Does it conflict with other events? Is it a convenient time, place and date for the people most likely to attend? The Alliance for the Arts in New York City operates an Events Clearinghouse service. For a nominal fee, users can check other events scheduled for a given date and register their own. The LA Planner offers a similar service in Los Angeles, and there are others with different names around the country.

Lastly, there is the timeliness that relates to social issues and causes and to artistic projects: are they in tune with the times? A particular mission or project or play can be of remote interest one day and of enormous relevance the next, depending upon current events. While it's unwise to base artistic planning on such events, it's also foolish not to take advantage when events happen to spark extra interest in artistic projects.

## Follow-Up

Fundraising does not end when the money comes in. Records must be kept regarding pledged, received and deferred contributions; donor records must be updated; receipts and acknowledgements must be sent; and attempts must be made to learn why certain former donors failed to renew their commitments. Grants administration requires even more follow-up after the initial award letter is received. Interim reports that track the expenditure of the award must usually be prepared and sent to the funder; there must be follow-up phone calls and letters to the appropriate program director; final project documentation; and financial accounting.

But perhaps the most important follow-up responsibility—whatever the source of the contribution—is the act of expressing gratitude. Virtually all active fund givers can tell stories about beneficiaries who just took the money and ran, or others who never bothered to communicate between the time they received one contribution and the time they requested another. Corporations that donate in-kind services also like to feel that they've made an important gesture that has been appreciated. When they provide graphic arts services for a theatre company, for example, the appropriate manager from the company should work directly with the corporate graphics person and acknowledge that person's assistance and expertise. Volunteers who work on the telethon or in the costume shop must also be thanked by making them feel like a necessary part of the operation and by rewarding them in some way. And elected officials in the community who have been instrumental in supporting the theatre company—through gestures that perhaps facilitated municipal, county, state, or federal funding, also like to be thanked. The best way to do this, of course, is to support their bids for reelection. Congratulating trustees, donors, volunteers, artists, staff and community leaders on special events or accomplishments in their lives is another way of acknowledging their importance to the theatre company. Saying "thank-you" is a small investment that can reap large returns.

## THE FUNDING PROPOSAL

### Initial Contact

After potential donors have been identified through research and through suggestions from board members, it must be decided:

What to ask for (money, goods, services)
How much to ask for
Who to approach first (the president of the board, the CEO, the program director, the public relations director)
When to make the first contact
How to make the first contact (telephone, letter, in person).

It is best to tailor each request as closely as possible to the specific interest, resources and schedule of the potential funder. Rarely does a single funder pick up the entire tab. By researching the funding history of potential government, foundation, corporate and major individual donors, and by applying common sense and a little imagination, it should be possible to calculate a request that will be realistic from the donor's point of view. And this request—whether it is for money or something else—should usually be made right up front in the initial contact.

Most often, the initial request is made in a one-page letter that is signed by a board member of the theatre organization or the artistic or managing director. This summarizes the project, the request for assistance and the reasons why it should be of interest to the donor being contacted. The letter might also request a meeting during which the project and the support can be discussed in detail. More often than not, such letters gain a negative response—or none at all. This allows staff time and money to be spent more productively on preparing full proposals for those potential funders who *do* express interest in the initial contact letter.

## Standards By Which Proposals Are Judged

Before writing a proposal to capture a grant or contribution, it helps to know how philanthropic agencies and other funders decide which projects to support. While there are many motivations and quirks that distinguish one funder from another, there are certain general standards of evaluation used by most. These include:

1. *Presentation.* The written proposal does not have to be bound (difficult to make copies) or loaded with graphics and printed on color stock (wasteful use of precious funds), nor does the fundraiser have to show up for a meeting in formal dress. Nonetheless, appearances *are* important. Both the proposal and the people representing it should be neat, correct and appropriate. Observance of these matters will communicate a seriousness of purpose in regard both to the theatre company and the proposal, and this aspect of proposal presentation is the first standard by which a judgement is made because it is what the funder first notices

2. *Relevance and Need.* Is the proposal relevant to the funder's interests, as well as to the present needs of the community and society in general?

3. *Originality.* How unique is the project? Is it being duplicated by others who can do it as well or better? Is it a project whose "time is now?"

4. *Potential Benefit.* How many people will benefit from the project (usually, the more the better). How large an audience will there be? Are those who will benefit relevant to the funder (i.e. tax payers in the government funder's constituency, consumers of the

corporation's products, employees of the corporation and their families, etc.)?

5. *Accountability.* Can the organization making the request demonstrate fiscal accountability and responsibility? Does it have a good record of sound management and administration?

6. *Future ability to be self-sustaining.* While it is increasingly understood that the arts can never be fully self-supporting, most funders still believer that the more self-sustaining a particular company or project can be, the better. Also, very few projects receive funding from the private sector beyond a few years.

Being aware of this criterion while developing a proposal is essential. Government funding agencies and some in the private sector usually have their own lengthy application forms that require very specific information;* but all applications include some type of narrative section, and the content of many other proposals is entirely at the discretion of the writer. In either case, imagination and honest inventiveness are often a plus. For example, a small nonprofit theatre company may only perform for an annual audience of ten thousand people—a long way from the ten million who may see an arts program on public television. But perhaps the theatre produces new plays by American writers. If only one of these writers gains national recognition, many millions of people will eventually constitute that playwright's audience.

## Proposal Contents and Support Materials

A funding proposal will vary according to whom it is being sent, from whom and for what. There are a number of acceptable models that may be followed and, of course, style and format differ somewhat with each writer and each organization being represented. But most proposals are contained in a packet of material that includes:

1. *Cover letter.* A straightforward introduction and summation of the proposal, preferably contained on one typewritten page; this may be almost identical to the initial contact letter

2. *Institutional history or background.* A concise, fact-filled narrative history that documents the accomplishments of the organization, defines its relationship and usefulness to its local community and, perhaps, to society in general, and establishes its reputation within the professional theatre world

3. *Project description.* A clear explanation of the project being proposed for support, including a justification, the relevance of the project to the funder, the need for support and the type and amount of sup-

---

*See Appendix J for sample NEA grant application

port being requested

4. *Project budget.* A breakdown of project expenses and income (if any). This may merely give figures related to an isolated aspect of a larger project for which support is being requested; or it may show the figures for the whole project

5. *Support from other sources.* Somewhere, the proposal should list support that has been received from any other sources either for the project at hand or for all of the organization's activities. Also, a list of actual and/or anticipated other sources of support for the project should be shown

6. *Latest audited financial statement.*

7. *Proof of nonprofit status.* Copy of the 501 (c) (3) letter

8. *Board of Trustees list with biographical sketch of each member.*

Depending on the funder and the type of request being prepared, additional material may also be required or included anyway:

1. *Staff listing with biographies.*

2. *Recent brochures.*

3. *Percentage breakdown of earned / unearned income.*

4. *Recent press materials.* These should include good reviews, publicity pieces and several exciting production photographs

5. *Testimonials.* List of awards and citations the organization has received, and copies of genuine letters of praise, though this type of material should be carefully selected and kept to a minimum

6. *Audience demographics.* Statistical profile of the geographical area and the population served by the theatre—perhaps geared to the constituents of greatest interest to the funder.

It is also helpful to include in the proposal a discussion of how the organization plans to meet its goals for the project at hand, why this solution is a realistic one, how the project fits into the short-and long-term goals, how it relates to the mission, how future funding may be developed, and a methodology for project evaluation.

## SUMMATION

As Carl W. Shaver, a respected leader in the fundraising field and president of his own New York firm, has phrased it, successful fundraising is when "the right person asks the right prospect for the right amount for the right reason at the right time!"

Successful fundraising is an exacting business that is built on careful research, reliable information and personal contacts. It is also a very human activity built on personal and professional relationships, whims of artistic preference, perceptions about the role of the arts in society and ideas about priorities. It feeds upon the traditionally generous American view toward charity, although in the field of nonprofit theatre this view remains somewhat impaired by the suspicion that "serious" art is not essential, not suitable for government support, too elitist for general consumption and, in particular, that theatre has been self-sustaining on Broadway and so there's no reason why it can't support itself everywhere else. The growth of the nonprofit professional theatre movement in America, however, has greatly increased the number of those who believe that the commercial approach cannot provide the whole menu of theatre art, nor can this menu be supported without volunteer labor and contributed income. Even more significantly, enough people have now dined off that menu to have whetted new appetites, which they are willing to support through extraordinary means.

Of course, nobody enjoys the feeling of being a poor relation in a rich society, of constantly looking for handouts and free services, counting pennies and always asking favors from friends. The theatre and most of its artists have been poor for twenty-five centuries; poverty has practically been a condition of membership in this profession. While the 1960s saw the dawn of a new era of support for the arts in America, and the decades since then have seen the development of sophisticated new approaches both to fundraising and to fundgiving, an economically secure American theatre is still more of a dream than a reality.

# Part IV

# The Theatre
# and its Audience

# 15

# Marketing Functions

A LTHOUGH words like "publicity," "public relations," "press," and "advertising" are often used synonymously, they are actually different functions in the process of marketing a particular product. Ostensibly, the main product of the theatre industry is live performance. Yet marketing an ongoing theatrical production or company should not end when all the seats to a performance or season have been sold. Long-range marketing objectives should also include selling the idea of theatre, the habit of theatregoing and, in the nonprofit sector, the need for supporting theatre beyond just buying tickets.

## GENERAL CONSIDERATIONS

Merely placing an ad in the local newspaper and distributing posters is not marketing in the full meaning of the word, nor is marketing merely selling, which implies just training and supervising salespeople and taking orders. Marketing involves all the functions required to get goods or services from the production stage to the final user. This is pretty all-embracing, so a theatre's managing director shouldn't be surprised if an aggressive new marketing director asks to have control over box office operations, fundraising, house management, booking, touring and other areas, in addition to the functions more usually associated with promotion. In some organizations this type of arrangement is adopted; however, these last four chapters—which consider the theatre and its audience—will discuss marketing elements, functions and strategies from the more traditional viewpoint.

According to Philip Kotler, the author of several books on the subject, marketing utilizes four basic tools that comprise what he calls "the marketing mix" or the "four P's": product, price, promotion and place. The goal of marketing is exchange—usually (although by no means always) the payment of money in exchange for goods or services. But while the marketing director has control over the four P's, he or she has no control over the general market environment, which includes such factors as the community's economic, political and ethnic profile. The marketing director also lacks control over the product, although he or she can certainly influence how the product is developed, perceived, used and valued.

Successful marketing attempts to accomplish the following:

1. Identify a large number of high-potential buyers for the product
2. Determine how to communicate with them most effectively
3. Price the product to suit the market
4. Motivate the market to want the product
5. Make purchasing the product as easy as possible
6. Make enjoyment of the product as great as possible
7. Create loyal users of the product who will repeat their use and support at increasingly higher levels.

Modern marketing theory and practice were pioneered in America and, depending on one's outlook, may be largely credited or blamed for the conspicuous level of consumerism in our society. Yet despite the successful application of marketing techniques to the sale of almost every imaginable product, the theatre business was late in adopting them. And, strangely enough, it was the nonprofit sector of the arts world that first recognized the value of marketing in the full sense of the term, and that continues to employ the best-trained and most creative marketing directors in the field. Commercial theatres, by contrast, have a long tradition of hiring a press agent to work independently from an advertising agency. But this is beginning to change as marketing experts prove their skills on Broadway as elsewhere in the industry.

In both profit and nonprofit arts circles, there exists a serious concern that aggressively-applied marketing practice will dictate product selection and development, that it will, for example, force artistic directors to produce only safe and traditional plays that appeal to the widest public. And this danger is a real one, especially at board-driven or management-driven companies where most trustees are corporate executives used to basing their decisions on "the bottom line." Artistic personnel at such theatres should be just as aggressive in promoting their priorities. And artistic priorities can survive side by side with well-proven, up-to-date marketing techniques. Marketing research, when joined with evaluations of a company's past marketing performance, can be of great value in making artistic programming decisions—without being the only basis on which such decisions are made.

Producing theatre of high quality is not antithetical to selling tickets, raising money or satisfying all of the theatre's different user groups. Most of the time theatre *must* be of high quality, or tickets won't sell, money won't be raised and users won't be satisfied. This is as true in nonprofit theatre as in commercial theatre. The fascinating paradox is that, in order to make money, commercial theatre must be of high quality and, in order to produce high quality, nonprofit theatre must make money!

## BASIC ELEMENTS OF MARKETING
### *The Market Environment*

The community in which a theatre operates is the immediate family to which it belongs. Wider areas from which it also draws audiences constitute its extended family. It is important to understand both, although a theatre can have more influence over the former. Audiences may be comprised mainly of tourists and bus groups from out of town, but still there is a relatively permanent nucleus of local residents who determine the business, social, cultural, educational and political profile of the community, and whose support of the organization is critical. Theatre managers and artistic directors in large cities deal with complex and continuously evolving power structures and institutions that must be analyzed and understood; in smaller communities, both the power structure and audience tastes may be easier to grasp. But whether located in downtown Los Angeles or in a Kansas cornfield, a theatre company must adapt to its environment if it is to survive. Put another way, a theatre can only exist when a sufficient portion of the local community allows it to exist, so the company must always be mindful of the principle of reciprocity. If the theatre is to get community support, the community must also get support from the theatre.

Chapter 3 discusses factors about community life that a producing organization should consider before establishing a theatre: audience potential, proximity to transportation, the competition, the media, local organizations, the economy, the climate and local attitudes. If such data were gathered and included in a feasibility study, this could also serve as an important research document for the marketing director. Among other things, it should help dictate the structure of a communication network leading from the theatre to the movers and shakers within the community. These people should be identified in terms of their ability to help (or hinder) the success of the venture. Then the theatre operator, members of the marketing staff and others should systematically establish an ongoing dialogue with them. For permanently based theatre companies this will include personal contact with:

1. *Business leaders*: corporate executives, heads of chambers of commerce, bank presidents, heads of local utility companies
2. *Political leaders*: the mayor and other elected and appointed offi-

cials in key municipal positions, elected state and federal representatives, heads of local school boards, community councils and citizens groups

3. *Leading professionals*: college presidents, school superintendents,
   lawyers, judges and other opinion-makers
4. *Media directors*: publishers, editors, critics, journalists and others in
   the print and electronic media
5. *Social leaders*: heads of cultural organizations, directors and administrators of competing performing arts organizations, heads of local
   arts councils and philanthropic groups.

Letters must be sent, appointments arranged, receptions held and personal contacts renewed on a regular basis. To formalize this process, even a
commercial theatre can create one or more advisory boards as a means of
cultivating the friendship and support of local leaders and, importantly, bene-
fiting from their experience and position.

To further nourish its relations with the community, a permanently
based theatre should ask: What local programs, organizations, landmarks and
institutions are most highly regarded by local residents? How can the theatre
use its resources and special know-how to assist these local interests and
endeavors? Here are just a few of the many possibilities:

1. Encourage the sponsorship of benefit performances to raise money
   for local causes
2. Donate use of the theatre facility for meetings and conferences that
   serve local interests
3. Establish a speakers bureau that makes theatre staff and artists
   available to local groups and organizations
4. Arrange for theatre artists, especially celebrities, to participate in local fundraising events (this kind of tie-in provides photo opportunities that will benefit both the event and the theatre)
5. Offer space in the playbill for ads or copy that will benefit local interests
6. Offer lobby space where local charities may hand out information
   or even solicit donations
7. Offer the theatre's mailing list to appropriate, nonprofit organizations
8. Loan properties, lighting equipment and other items to local amateur and nonprofit performing arts groups, though this must be done
   with caution against damage and loss
9. Establish and maintain active membership in local, regional and
   national arts and cultural associations

10. Attend and participate in appropriate non-cultural functions at the community and state levels.

Involvement signifies that a theatre is truly part of the community in which it operates, that it cares about that community and does not ignore the responsibilities of good community citizenship.

## *The Internal Environment*

An analysis of the internal environment of a nonprofit theatre organization begins with its mission statement and stated objectives. What are its goals and what is the likelihood of achieving them in view of the market environment? It is important to assess the competition and then determine how the organization and its product are unique or can best meet the needs of the perceived market. What are the strong points that can be emphasized, and what are the weak points that can be corrected, explained or diminished?

## *Market Research*

Basic research about a given market or community can be conducted inexpensively and quickly by taking advantage of the huge amount of data made available to the public by the Bureau of the Census of the U.S. Department of Commerce. This data is drawn from a population census which is conducted every ten years at the beginning of each decade. It provides demographic characteristics regarding numbers of people, age, sex, race, national origin, family size, employment, unemployment, income and the like. "Current Population Reports" is published annually to update the *Census of Population* and contains the latest information based on births, deaths and human migratory patterns. These and other publications of the Bureau of the Census are available in the business section of public federal depository libraries. Or one may go directly to one of the twelve regional offices of the Census Bureau. Usually in the state capital, a majority of states maintain a state data center that includes these publications as well as additional data on state and local communities. All such resource centers are free to the public, except for minor copying or printout charges. They may be approached by phone, letter or in person, so that in the space of a few hours a researcher can produce the data necessary to draw a very specific profile of a particular community or neighborhood. Statistics are organized on national, state, county, city and town levels and also broken down according to zip codes. And there are numerous other periodicals published by the federal government that are helpful in compiling data for marketing purposes. One of these is *Statistics of Income*, published annually by the IRS of the Treasury Department and compiled from the tax returns of individuals, corporations, sole proprietorships and partnerships.

Initial market research, then, often utilizes secondary source material such as that discussed above. User research, on the other hand, is more specific and involves primary source material—namely, potential, actual and former users. Potential users naturally represent the most amorphous of these three groups because they have yet to have a first-hand acquaintance with the product. It becomes an objective of the marketing department to persuade these people to become users—whether that means buying a ticket, writing a newspaper story, awarding a grant or granting a loan. Then it becomes the objective to persuade these users to repeat and increase their use of the product. When they do not, the objective of the marketing department must be to determine if some aspect of the product (the production, the corporation, the facility, the staff) was to blame and why (poor casting, inadequate parking facilities, rude employees). When market research is purely sales oriented, it often begins with the current audience, because a correct analysis of its profile can lead to marketing communications with potential customers who reflect the same profile. Different methods of studying the audience profile are discussed later in this chapter.

## Target Markets

Targeting a market means identifying some distinct group of people who share similarities of interest, especially in terms of their readiness to exchange time and/or money for a product that promises to satisfy their interests and/or needs. Once the product is analyzed and understood, the marketing department attempts to identify those people most likely to use it. It is a simple matter to target a handful of different markets for the same theatre company, starting with such obvious groups as the board of trustees, current season-ticket buyers, single-ticket buyers, friends and relatives of cast and staff members. With further thought about the particular nature of the product (the season of plays, for example) in relation to the community, additional groups of potential ticket buyers can usually be targeted, such as students, gray panthers, ethnic groups or personnel from a nearby military base. This process is important because no theatre has the resources to engage in blanket marketing. In fact, it is wise to test target markets by making limited approaches to them—by mailing the brochure to five hundred medical doctors, if that is the target, before mailing it to the other ten thousand people in the community.

Aside from markets that are targeted for the purpose of selling tickets, others should be targeted to receive special attention, because they contain users of the theatre organization who influence its success: the press wants to receive news releases in a particular format and in a timely fashion, the government arts councils want to receive grant proposals on time and according to their specifications and so forth. It is important to grasp that the total marketing process comprises exchanges other than the exchange of money for tickets.

## *The Product*

In the Broadway theatre each production is usually marketed separately, even when the same producer is behind a number of different shows, even when these are of the same genre or by the same creative artists. This is also the case with most road shows, even though different shows may play in the same commercial road house in a single season or year. But the majority of theatres—stock, nonprofit professional companies, presenting organizations, opera and dance theatres—offer a series of different productions on a seasonal basis and market them as such. In each case, marketing strategies are applied to create public awareness and understanding of the product, determine which segments of the market most need or desire the product and then convince them to use it. Of course, much of this process depends upon knowing and analyzing the product: the dramatic material, the creative and interpretive artists involved with the production and, when possible, the production in performance. Dramaturgs can be of great assistance in helping the marketing department in this area. In nonprofit theatre the product also includes the institution and its mission. Marketing efforts that are uninformed about the product and its ingredients are seldom so successful as those that are knowledgeable.

Many businesses use market testing or sampling in selected markets before offering new products more widely. In a sense, the theatre has a long tradition of market testing by virtue of the tryout system. The rewrites and other changes made during the tryout period are a response to market testing. Similarly, new films are often tested in limited markets or through the device of sneak previews, then perhaps subjected to further editing. So the creative development of a theatre production is partly a matter of suiting the product to the user—of creating a perfect exchange. The trick is not only to refine the product, but to refine it for the widest number of users. Again this is not to suggest that marketing the arts should dictate the artistic process; it is only to suggest that market research can help the creative team understand the reactions to their work.

Unlike a producer who is trying out a single production, a presenting organization usually has the advantage of booking events that have already been tested, although perhaps not in the local market. But that market is relatively stationary and can be studied over a period of seasons. There are even computer programs that can be used to test market response to a potential booking. These, of course, utilize data taken from the presenting organization's past box office records and other such sources to formulate a history of local audience response to a variety of attractions and marketing strategies. Once again, this illustrates how a marketing tool can help to inform artistic decision-making, but the booking process should take other considerations into account as well.

## Packaging

Packaging begins by wrapping the product in a name. In fact, in the performing arts there are usually several names and titles involved with each event, as with "The Next Wave Festival at the Brooklyn Academy of Music presents Peter Brook's production of *The Mahabharata*." That's a lot of wrapping even for a nine-hour production. Furthermore, each name could stand on its own as a separate product and each conveys something different. Here, however, they are put together in a single package, and because of this they are presumably made more desirable, usable and enjoyable for more people. Interestingly, Brooklyn Academy repackaged itself as "BAM" some years ago in a marketing attempt to become perceived as more user-friendly, a strategy that appears to have worked. The Next Wave Festival is a name that was suggested by a BAM press manager when it was first decided to package a number of unrelated events into a series offering. Eventually, several mini-series were offered within the context of each annual festival; the not-surprising demand for *Mahabharata* tickets, for instance, helped to sell other events made available only as a series. This is a common strategy in marketing performances, although it is not without risk. For example, what if numerous people buy the series but only attend the most popular event, leaving the artists involved in other attractions to face empty houses? This could insult the organization's artistic users and place its future product in jeopardy. Or by combining classical with experimental events in the same series, a high percentage of ticket buyers may decide not to renew their tickets for the following season.

The name selected for a theatre facility, corporation, organization, festival or series—not to mention the artistic work itself—can have considerable impact on how that product is perceived and consequently how it is used. Few products sell themselves, even when they are widely known. Of course there is always a certain amount of impulse buying, and alternatively a certain percentage of loyal customers for any established product, including a theatre, who will buy whatever that business sells or who are loyal consumers due to other facts. For example, some people see each new play by Neil Simon or each new production of *The Mikado*; others automatically renew their subscriptions each year to the local opera or ballet company; and yet others purchase tickets because of a particular performer or director or even a particular performance facility. Nonetheless, these customers rarely provide sufficient support to sustain a theatre operation. Similarly, the loyal users from the media, or philanthropic or artistic communities, are rarely sufficient to sustain the operation in terms of its total needs. So the product must be packaged in some way to serve a variety of users and make it appear unique or especially desirable for all of them.

Standard methods for packaging theatre tickets include subscription or season ticket offers, memberships, series and mini-series offers, group sales and package deals that include the theatre ticket, along with such things as dinner, parking or shuttle bus service. Skillful packaging is aimed at high-potential target markets, so again, it requires a knowledge of the community based on research.

Standard methods for packaging not directly aimed at ticket sales include press releases, press kits, benefit events, funding proposals, job orientation manuals and annual reports.

Packaging, of course, often adds to the cost of the product. This may be the cost of running a shuttle-bus service or the cost of printing the annual report. But if the package meets the needs of enough users, the additional cost may be worth it. Package testing, when time permits, can help an organization avoid costly mistakes by sampling a small portion of a target market before approaching the whole market or by testing several packages in the same market. For example, a single brochure might offer three or four different series of performances for the same groups of events. One might be a series of Friday nights, one might be a series of light entertainments, one might be a series of classical events, and the fourth might be a mixture of different types of events. The response to this kind of offer will quickly determine which series are going to be most popular and which should simply be dropped from future packaging offers.

## Pricing

Ticket pricing is discussed at length in Chapter 13, but it should also be understood that pricing is an integral part of marketing. A product may meet user needs, but if the price is beyond most users' ability to pay, it will fail in the marketplace; conversely, if the product is under-priced, it may be perceived as inferior. Such matters relate to pricing elasticity in relation to the market. How productive in terms of sales and income is it to increase or decrease prices, offer discounts and package deals, and the like? Again, testing or sampling can help answer such questions. And when potential users do not respond to certain price offers, the prices should be changed.

## Promotion

The most basic and widely recognized methods of promoting a product are:

1. *Advertising*: Any type of promotion that is paid for by the second (such as a radio or television commercial), by the line (such as a newspaper ad) or by the service (such as printing a flyer or renting billboard space)
2. *Publicity*: Any mention or coverage about an organization or its products in the media that is not paid for
3. *Public Relations*: General efforts over a period of time that attempt to increase public awareness, interest and support for an organization and its products
4. *Personal Sales*: All non-media personal contact, such as telemarketing
5. *Promotions*: All non-personal communications, such as T-shirts that carry the logo of a particular company or show.

The ways in which these promotion methods are utilized become the marketing strategies or the "how to" of the marketing plan and will be discussed in the next two chapters.

## Place and Distribution

The place where the performance takes place, as discussed in Chapter 3, is always a major factor in determining how the product will be used, how often and by whom. Geographical location, proximity to transportation routes and systems, parking, dining, architectural design, physical condition of the facility and other such auxillary factors are all important and may even help to shape the product itself. Poor acoustics or sight lines, dismal rest rooms or unsightly lobbies are flaws in the internal environment that should be of serious concern to marketing efforts. Such problems have a negative impact on everyone who uses the product, from audience to artists to staff.

Closely related to the place where a product is used is the matter of distribution. A major difficulty in marketing the performing arts is that the product—the performance—is not very mobile. A customer cannot buy it and take it home, like renting a video tape. A customer cannot usually wait for it to be available closer to home, like a current hit movie. While distribution is increased with touring and, occasionally, with cable casting and broadcasting of live productions, these incur such high costs that they are not even options in most cases. Distribution, then, centers around theatre tickets and their accessibility to potential customers. The location and design of the box office, ticketing systems, the behavior of treasurers, and other such elements discussed earlier in this book have a major impact on sales. The goal, of course, is to make ticket buying as easy as possible. This may require that ticket agencies or outlets be established in a variety of locations, that tickets be made available by telephone and that credit card payments be accepted.

## *Evaluation*

A marketing plan and the strategies it employs to sell tickets and provide other services for users of the product should begin by stating a set of goals. A final evaluation of the plan measures end results against those goals. But in the meantime, marketing efforts should be evaluated on a daily basis throughout the implementation period. Contingency strategies should be planned in case initial attempts fail to generate the desired results. Each direct mail piece, each newspaper ad and other promotional effort should be evaluated for its effectiveness. This can be done by coding mailing labels, by coding coupons and order forms and by information obtained orally at the box office. It is reasonable to assume that some promotional strategies will be more effective than others and that some will simply fail. Ongoing evaluation, however, should help to evolve a highly successful marketing plan over a period of time.

## *The Overall Process*

If the basic elements of marketing as discussed above were to be organized in the form of a chart to illustrate the marketing process, they might look like this:

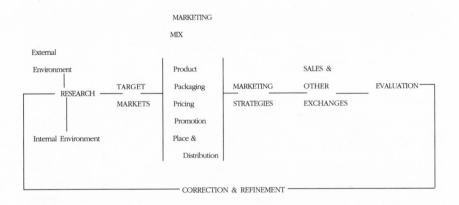

It is helpful to understand the full process and not assume, as many do, that strategies alone constitute marketing or that sales alone constitute success. One should also realize that, while charts are nifty things, they tend toward oversimplification. For example, the chart above doesn't indicate that marketing strategies cannot usually be selected until the marketing budget has been set, or that when income falls below projections even successful strategies may have to be altered or abandoned.

## THE MARKETING BUDGET

What is a realistic assessment of the resources that can be invested in the implementation of a marketing plan? To answer this question will require a close look at the internal environment of the company or organization that is to be marketed. Specifically, one should examine:

1. *Human resources*

   a. Staff: What is the size, training and experience of management and staff members in terms of marketing functions, and how much time can they devote to this area?

   b. Consultants: Is it desirable or necessary to seek outside technical assistance in the market area? What kind? Is it affordable?

   c. Volunteers: How many hours per week can board members and other volunteers be expected to give to marketing efforts, such as letter-writing, telemarketing and conducting surveys?

2. *Financial resources*: A reasonable marketing budget can be set at 20 to 25 percent of the total potential ticket gross, though this will vary in different cases. Is some or all of this amount available now? Can some of this money be gained through contributed income and in-kind services?

3. *Physical resources*: What facilities are available to assist in marketing efforts, such as office space, box office and ticket outlets, spaces for receptions and press meetings? What equipment is available, such as computers, copying machines, telephone systems, fax machines, camera and video equipment?

By listing all such resources—which represent people, money and time—the options available for marketing the organization in question will narrow considerably. For example, a company poor in cash but rich in volunteer labor will have to forego extensive media advertising but can conduct extensive marketing research, outreach and audience development programs, audience education and enhancement activities, telemarketing, and various publicity initiatives. And the age and abilities of available volunteer workers will determine the type of work they are best suited to do: high school students might distribute flyers and posters, college interns might do marketing research, board members might secure in-kind services and seniors might do telemarketing. In the commercial theatre, of course, volunteer labor is more limited—usually to a few apprentices, interns and, perhaps, the board of directors.

A sizable portion of a marketing budget tends to be used up by staff salaries, equipment, printing services and consultants. These costs should always be examined and challenged. The amount that remains after such relatively predictable costs have been budgeted is the amount available to spend on promotional strategies (advertising, publicity gimmicks, press parties and the like). How available resources are allocated to marketing efforts should be decided during the process of formulating a marketing plan. Once a plan has been adopted and implemented, resources may be shifted and reallocated according to how well each strategy seems to be working.

## THE MARKETING PLAN

### Setting Objectives

Marketing objectives should be directly tied to the basic philosophy, mission and goals of the company that is offering the product in the marketplace. If this is a commercial outfit, the leading goal is usually that of making as much profit as possible. Cameron Mackintosh, a commercial producer who takes a keen interest in the marketing of his productions, seems to have proved that even Broadway shows benefit from strong, methodical marketing. *Les Miserables* was a solid hit in London and sold out its eight-week run at the Kennedy Center prior to opening on Broadway, so it benefited from considerable advance publicity. Even so, its $12 million advance sale and the pay-off of its $4.5 million capitalization in only twenty-three weeks was remarkable. By way of contrast, *Cats*—with a similar production history—had a $7 million advance. The difference may well have been in the marketing. Tickets were offered ten months prior to opening (twice as early as *Cats*), there was an aggressive $600,000 advertising campaign, the British cast album was released in America, a new translation of the novel featured the show's logo on its cover and was widely distributed and displayed in bookstores, and other products related to the show were also put on sale. There was nothing new or unorthodox about any of this—except that it was done!

More recently, Jujamcyn Theatres offered all the shows in its five Broadway theatres on a discounted subscription basis—another example of how the commercial theatre is finally adopting more progressive marketing techniques.

Nonprofit theatre organizations face a somewhat more complex marketing challenge in that they must usually deal with an institution (the nonprofit corporation), a performance facility and a number of different productions. The goals articulated in the organization's mission statement must be the core of any marketing plan in this instance. For example, if the mission is to produce new plays that focus on the condition of women in American society, the primary goal of the marketing plan should be identical to that of the mission. Whatever success marketing strategies may have, they will fail if the mission is not accomplished. In this case, practicing American playwrights would be the most important target market because they are the only source of product. They must learn about the theatre's existence and its mission, they must be motivated to submit scripts, they must entrust the theatre with productions and they must want to repeat the process with their subsequent work. Success in achieving objectives such as these entails long-range planning and public relations efforts that continue throughout the life of the organization. Nonetheless, they should be spelled out in a long-range marketing plan that includes a time frame—perhaps three-to-five years—for achieving goals or, at least, making progress in that direction.

Marketing objectives related to ticket sales usually employ short-term strategies that are comparatively self-contained, such as a season ticket campaign. These should be stated in the plan as simply as possible: for example, "increase season ticket sales to 75% of capacity"; or "stimulate broader student participation in theatre department productions"; or "generate group sales of 10% of capacity." Not only might it be a good idea to draw up two marketing plans—one with long-range and one with short-range objectives— it might be wise to have separate plans for each objective, so long as these are compatible with the organization's primary goals and with each other. Eventually, the strategies selected to implement each plan should be translated into a calendar format that shows when each step must be accomplished. A sample is provided on page 439.

## Writing the Plan

In order to get the most out of their available resources, all theatre organizations—even those with no money—should prepare a written marketing plan at least annually. This should include research and sales information from the past one-to-five years, and demonstrate how current marketing strategies and budget allocations are designed to enhance achievements or correct failures of the recent past. It may be a fairly lengthy document containing statistical charts with data drawn from audience surveys and financial reports, as well as evidence reflecting media coverage and advertising results. Or it may be a simple outline that highlights recent accomplishments and failures, lists the available resources, and then states how these will be utilized to accomplish current and future objectives. A typical marketing plan is likely to follow a format and contain information about items such as those in the outline below:

SAMPLE OUTLINE FOR A MARKETING PLAN
I. The Marketing Universe
   A. External Environment
      1. economic
      2. political
      3. educational

        4. social

        5. cultural

        6. the theatre profession

        7. the competition

  B. Internal Environment

        1. mission and institutional objectives

        2. organizational structure

        3. structure and staff related to marketing endeavors

        4. problems and shortcomings

        5. strengths and accomplishments

II. Marketing History & Audience Profile

  A. Five-year season ticket sales history

        1. number of attractions and performances

        2. number of season tickets sold

        3. prices

        4. percentage of capacity and income generated

        5. marketing expenditures

        6. renewal and attrition rates

        7. season ticket telemarketing campaign results

  B. Five-year single ticket sales history

        1. number of attractions and performances

        2. number of tickets sold

        3. prices

        4. percentage of capacity and income generated

        5. marketing expenditures

        6. volume sold through telephone-charge system

        7. volume sold at off-premises agencies

  C. Five-year group sales history

        1. number of attractions and performances involved

        2. number of tickets sold

        3. prices and discounts

        4. percentage of capacity and income generated

        5. marketing expenditures

        6. repeat buyer percentage

  D. Season Ticket Audience Profile

        1. types of services used (series, mini-series, exchanges, donations, etc.)

        2. geographical (zip code areas of residence)

        3. personal profile (education, marital status, age, income, gender, employment, affiliations)

        4. media usage (radio, television, newspapers, magazines)

E. Single ticket audience profile (same as 1 thru 4 above)

F. Group sales audience profile

    1. sales according to types of offers (flat group discount, package deal, senior citizen group offer, corporate offer)

    2. geographical (city and state origins)

    3. affiliations (political, religious, cultural, educational)

G. Total audience profile (combined figures from A,B,C, above)

H. Marketing analysis of last season

III. Opportunities and Problems

A. Opportunities (itemize them)

B. Problems (itemize them)

IV. Marketing Goals and Objectives

A. Marketing philosophy

B. Long-term, mission-related marketing goals

C. Short-term marketing objectives (itemize and prioritize)

D. Research proposals and programs necessary to determine strategies

V. Marketing Strategies

A. Target Markets

    1. service related

    2. sales related

B. Use of Marketing Mix

    1. product

    2. packaging

    3. pricing

    4. promotion

        a. advertising

        b. publicity

        c. public relations

        d. personal sales

        e. promotions

    5. place and distribution

C. Contingency strategies

VI. Marketing Budget

A. Projected expenses (itemize in detail)

B. Projected revenues (itemize in detail)

C. Projected nonmonetary gains (itemize)

VII. Marketing Evaluation

A. Summary of goals and projected results for each marketing initiative

B. Summary of methods by which marketing strategies will be measured and evaluated (such as color coding of brochures)

438

Different organizations, of course, will devise different marketing plans. The important thing is to have one—and use it. Just as with putting together a budget, the planning process should involve nearly everyone within the organization, because they are all users of the product with needs of their own and they all have contact with other users—ticket buyers, vendors, the press and so on—who have still other needs. All major types of users should be targeted in the plan and strategies should be devised to meet their various needs. A good marketing plan will dictate a clear course of action that will usually proceed from research (I and II), to the identification of marketing opportunities and problems (III), to setting objectives (IV), to selecting strategies (V), to composing a budget (VI), to evaluating results (VII).

## Implementing the Plan

After all the research data have been gathered and clearly organized in written form—often the most time-consuming aspect of the marketing process—it must be interpreted and promotional strategies must be selected based on the results. Because resources are always limited, many difficult choices will have to be made. For example, is it best to buy numerous small newspaper ads or a few large ones? Should the staff available for telemarketing be used to sell season tickets or raise contributions for the capital campaign? For each strategy that is selected there might be a separate plan for evaluation. Let's assume that an audience survey of a theatre in Boston shows that a surprising 8 percent of its ticket buyers come from Providence, Rhode Island. Hoping to increase this patronage, the marketing director might initiate a variety of strategies: encourage the board of trustees to recruit a new member from Providence, upgrade and intensify the services provided to the media in Providence; open a ticket outlet there; distribute flyers and discount offers and run a series of ads in the leading Providence newspaper. An evaluation plan for this "Providence strategy" might appear as follows:

| Strategy | Time Period | Cost | Goal | Sales Results |
|---|---|---|---|---|
| "Providence:" Sun. newspaper ads, ticket outlet, flyers, twofers, etc. | Oct - Dec (12 weeks) | $650 per week Total: $7,800 | To increase Providence ticket buyers from 8% to 12% of total audience | Nov 1, Dec 1, Jan 1 |

Only by surveying every person who attends a performance throughout the season could exact results be gathered. However, systematic monitoring of telephone, window and mail-in ticket orders is an effective alternative. If the goal of this strategy is to increase sales by 4 percent over a twelve-week season, one should expect to see results multiply almost from the first week of implementation. If results are disappointing by the end of four or five weeks, the strategy should be analyzed, contingencies considered and changes made. If the entire marketing budget for an organization represents 10 percent of the total potential gross, the ultimate sales objective should be to generate ten dollars in sales for each marketing dollar spent, thereby reaching 100 percent capacity through sales. Beyond this, as discussed earlier, there should also be substantial nonmonetary gains as the result of marketing efforts. Put another way, the cost of the above Providence strategy should bring in $6,500 per week in ticket sales, or $78,000 for the season, plus more favorable attention from the media and heightened awareness of the theatre in the Providence area. Obviously, this equation can be adjusted to suit different organizations, circumstances, policies and needs. But such very specific dollar or percentage goals encourage clear-headed, objective marketing decisions. They help in resisting the often persuasive pitches made by media salespeople, advertising agencies and independent consultants. They help in underscoring where time is well-spent and where it is wasted. And they help in keeping within budget and on target.

## THE AUDIENCE PROFILE

The audience attending a performance provides the primary resource material for research and analysis regarding the product(s) being offered. This may be done informally or through the device of an audience survey.

### Informal Audience Analysis

Often, demographic information can be guessed quite accurately. The audience for a theatre production or even a long season of theatre productions is minuscule in comparison to the audience for a film in national distribution or a network television program, and thus much easier to observe. One can simply stand in the lobby at the beginning or end of each theatre performance and visually estimate the median age, sex, race, income and education of the audience. But more important than socioeconomic data is an understanding of the psycho-aesthetic profile of an audience. What motivations does it have to attend performances (which may be utilized in marketing strategies to attract more patrons)? What perceptions does it have of the production (which marketing may promote or attempt to modify through various communication strategies)? And what would it take to get this audience back into this theatre? With or without formal surveys, theatre managers should be "audience watchers" and make every attempt to understand their patrons, both individually and collectively. Seasoned theatre professionals—including directors, playwrights, producers, and managers—have learned that there is usually a particular spot in a theatre (often where the auditorium meets the lobby) where patrons leaving after a performance will blurt out their initial reactions to the show. In five or ten minutes one can get a brutally candid survey of audience reaction!

There is, of course, a danger in arriving at conclusions informally or intuitively too much of the time. After all, play selection, advertising and many other decisions are made largely on the basis of how an actual or potential audience is analyzed. Many myths and faulty generalizations about theatre audiences have been perpetuated because producers and publicists have always sought quick explanations for poor attendance. "Young people don't go to theatre anymore," "No show can survive a bad review in the *Times*," "People can't afford theatre nowadays," and "Most people prefer light comedies and musicals" are all common statements in theatre circles, although none holds up under scrutiny.

The first comprehensive, nationwide survey of performance arts audiences was conducted by William J. Baumol and William G. Bowen and reported in their 1966 publication, *Performing Arts: The Economic Dilemma*. On the basis of over 24,000 usable survey returns, they found, among other things, that audiences had not changed markedly over previous decades in terms of such characteristics as age and income range, that there was little difference between Broadway and Off-Broadway audiences, and that theatregoers had very high education and income levels. More recent national surveys of audience characteristics have been conducted by the Ford Foundation, Theatre Communications Group, the National Endowment for the Arts, and Louis Harris polls. These studies and others have helped to dispel certain myths about theatregoers, although they tend to be of more use to arts advocacy groups, scholars and arts service organizations than to the marketing director of a local theatre company.

## Audience Surveys

When theatre managers and marketing directors believe they need more than a casual estimation of the audience profile, they frequently conduct a survey of their audiences by means of a printed questionnaire. A common method is to insert the questionnaire into playbills and provide pencils at convenient locations in the lobbies, along with boxes where completed forms may be deposited. If there are several ticket prices and theatre sections, questionnaires can be coded in some way to indicate these differences. This enables the evaluator to learn which sections may or may not object to existing ticket prices, if students or seniors tend to buy certain sections and other correlations between audience characteristics and ticket prices.

An alternate method of survey distribution is to instruct ushers to hand surveys to theatregoers as they enter or during intermission. The most intrusive method is to dispatch a team of interviewers during intermission to conduct oral interviews with a random sampling of the audience. This may guarantee more honest and detailed results, but it may also constitute a serious interruption of the playgoers' evening—as would any kind of curtain speech about the survey.

Providing that questionnaires were distributed to a wide, representative segment of a given group, 20- to 30-percent of those returned would be valid (this excludes questionnaires returned by people who were indignant or joking). Most people like being asked for their opinion and most cooperate to a remarkable degree in giving honest, thoughtful answers.

Survey questions should be designed with the following guidelines in mind:

1. Status questions, such as those regarding the respondents' income, education level, and which media outlets they use, may elicit "guilt" answers that are not entirely reliable
2. The fewer questions on a survey sheet, the better
3. The more precise the questions, the less room there will be for misinterpretation
4. The fewer possible answers to each question, the better (although care must always be taken not to omit possible responses to questions; multiple choice questions should include "other" or "don't know" or "not applicable" among the possible answers, to allow for alternatives that might have been overlooked—otherwise respondents may skip the question altogether and invalidate the results)
5. Only questions that elicit information that is truly valuable (for marketing and other purposes) should be included
6. Instructions should be simple enough for a child to follow.

A common danger in designing a survey is failure to consider all the variables that influence results. Are the questions and answers really measuring what the evaluators *think* they are measuring? For example, results are invalid when the audience surveyed is not representative of the theatre's general audience. If performances are given eight times a week over a twelve-week season, an entire week should be surveyed, because matinee and evening or weeknight and weekend audiences vary greatly—not to mention audiences that result from some group sales effort, such as one that draws in a large group of children or retired sea captains. Also, the week selected for the survey should feature a production that is fairly typical of the theatre's usual attraction. Finally, is each question necessary? Do surveyors really need to know the sex of the respondents, their eating habits or their favorite sports team?

Surveys that result in a sizable number of responses are most easily and accurately tabulated by computer. A key card is designed with a code of punch numbers for each question and possible answer. The responses are then fed into the computer, which can produce a printout showing the tabulated answers in percentiles and in a number of different formats. As an example, let's glance at a single question from a survey conducted by the Brooklyn College Center for the Performing Arts. The first question on the survey appeared as follows:

1. WHERE DO YOU LIVE?
Within 4 miles ( )    Brooklyn( )    Queens( )
Manhattan ( )    Staten Island ( )    The Bronx( )
Nassau/Suffolk ( ) Westchester( )    Other( )

The results appear on the computer printout as follows:

```
1989/90 GUEST ARTIST SERIES/MUSIC AUDIENCE SURVEY

FILE       NONAME            (CREATED 7/13/90)

LIVE
                                  RELATIVE   ADJUSTED   CUM
                         ABSOLUTE   FREQ       FREQ     FREQ
CATEGORY LABEL     CODE    FREQ     (PCT)      (PCT)    (PCT)

NA                  0.      10       0.8        0.8      0.8

WITHIN 4 MILES      1.     799      61.1       61.1     61.9

BROOKLYN            2.     324      24.8       24.8     86.6

QUEENS              3.      72       5.5        5.5     92.1

MANHATTAN           4.      32       2.4        2.4     94.6

S. I.               5.      14       1.1        1.1     95.6

THE BRONX           6.       3       0.2        0.2     95.9

NASSAU SULFOLK      7.      33       2.5        2.5     98.4

WESTCHESTER         8.       6       0.5        0.5     98.9

OTHER               9.      15       1.1        1.1    100.0
                          -----    -----      -----    -----
                  TOTAL   1308     100.0      100.0    100.0

   MEAN     1.753    STC ERR       C.041    MEDIAN    1.306
   MODE     1.000    STD DEV       1.492    VARIANCE  2.226
   KURTOSIS 9.310    SKEWNESS      2.944    RANGE     9.000
   MINIMUM  0.0      MAXIMUM       9.000

   VALID CASES    1308      MISSING CASES    0
```

The same results were then simplified and arranged in numerically descending order on a survey report as follows:

1.  CUSTOMER'S RESIDENCE

| | |
|---|---|
| Within 4 miles | 61.1% |
| Brooklyn | 24.8 |
| Queens | 5.5 |
| Nassau/Suffolk | 2.5 |
| Manhattan | 2.4 |
| Staten Island | 1.1 |
| Other | 1.1 |
| Bronx | 0.2 |

Right away, the experienced statistician would see that there is a flaw in the design of the question. Namely, many respondents could correctly check *both* "Within 4 miles" and "Brooklyn" and invalidate the answer totals. But fortunately, the printout shows under "absolute frequency" the number of responses to each answer, and because the total number of answers exactly equals the total number of responses that were computed (1308), we can surmise that nobody *did* actually check both answers—or that the computer made the necessary adjustments.

To bother the wording of the survey question even further, one might ask: How many people would really know if they live within 4 miles of the college theatre—as opposed to 3 1/2 or 4 1/2 miles? Better wording for the first two answers might have been "Within a 15-minute walk of the campus" and "Within Brooklyn, but beyond a 15-minute walk."

Looking once again at the sample printout, one sees that the responses have been organized into several different categories:

| | |
|---|---|
| *Code*: | the number assigned by the computer |
| *Absolute Freq*: | the actual number of responses to each answer |
| *Relative Freq*: | the percentage from the total sample (1308) responding to that answer |
| *Adjusted Freq*: | the adjusted frequency is not applicable to this survey, but if it had been a more general survey to measure, for example, population, the computer could be programmed with already-known information that it could weigh against the responses to measure the validity of the answers |
| *Cum. Freq*: | the cumulative totals in percentiles from the highest to the lowest answer results. |

Audience surveys are an important marketing tool in theatre management if they are obtained and interpreted with expertise. This might require hiring the services of a consultant or marketing firm. Also, it should be said that surveys are as important in showing the profile of typical as well as atypical ticket buyers. Armed with this kind of information, a theatre may decide, for example, to decrease advertising that reaches theatregoers who have already been "captured" and increase promotional strategies that might attract new audiences.

## Focus Groups

Large performing arts organizations have increasingly used focus groups as a tool in audience research. These are usually comprised of about a dozen people selected randomly from a large target group that the organization wishes to study. Under the discussion leadership of a trained professional, the group meets away from the performance facility and talks about various predetermined issues designed to deepen the organization's understanding of itself and its market. While audience survey results tend to be largely quantative, the results from focus group discussions tend to be qualitative. These are not necessarily representative of the larger group from which they were drawn, yet they may provide deeper insights and help clarify marketing problems and opportunities.

## Hiring Survey Consultants

Most professional theatre organizations have the capability of developing their own questionnaires and conducting their own audience surveys. However, when focus groups are assembled, or external segments of the public are polled, it might be wise to hire a marketing or polling firm, at least to assist in the process and train the surveyors if phone interviews or face-to-face questioning are involved. The credentials of such consulting firms should be checked. Their membership in such professional organizations as the American Marketing Association or the American Association for Public Opinion Research would be a plus.

## SUMMATION

Marketing is a complex process that involves the many steps of getting a product from the production stage to the final user. It is concerned with *all* the people who have contact with the producing organization—the artists, the press, the vendors, the funders, as well as the audience. It is concerned with increasing current audiences, developing new audiences for the future and enriching the enjoyment of everyone who uses the product, as well as simply holding on to current users. Contrary to widely-held thinking in the theatre world, advertising and publicity by themselves do not constitute marketing.

All theatre companies and organizations—large or small, rich or poor—benefit from putting sound marketing principles to work. This begins by conducting research and then formulating a written marketing plan. Measurements should be devised for evaluating each strategy that implements the plan, and these measurements should relate to the organization's long-and short-term goals and objectives.

# 16

# Publicity And Media Relations

THE three little words that theatre people most like to hear are "Standing room only!" A primary objective of most theatrical publicity is, of course, to attract capacity audiences on a regular basis. But ticket buyers are elusive, and many factors influence the success or failure of a theatrical production, making SRO signs a comparatively rare phenomenon. This chapter looks at the basic elements and tools pertaining to theatrical publicity, the aspect of promotion that aims to generate free mention or coverage of a particular product. The chapter emphasizes media relations, because this is the avenue by which to obtain the widest free coverage. To start, let's look at three ingredients that are necessary in all types of promotion.

## THREE REQUISITES OF SUCCESSFUL PROMOTION

### Getting Attention

A newspaper ad, a television commercial, a press release, a personal appearance, a brochure, and all other attempts at promotion must first capture attention before they can promote something. If the reader doesn't *see* the ad, or the editor doesn't *read* the press release, there will be no follow-through, no promotion of the product. There are all kinds of ways to call attention to a particular theatre or production, but whatever strategy is used must *itself* be captivating. The simplest techniques are frequently the most effective. A press release, for example, might be printed on paper with a striking letterhead so that the editor who receives it and whose desk is cluttered with dozens of other press releases will notice it and be less likely to misplace it. The newspaper advertisement with a border around it or with minimal, uncrowded copy will stand out on the printed page. In other words, the ultimate goal of theatrical promotion is to call attention to an organization or production, but the promotional strategy used to do this must first call attention to itself or everything else is for naught.

## Providing Motivation

Once promotional material has captured attention, it must go a second step by gaining the potential user's interest and motivating that person to purchase tickets or follow whatever other course is being advocated—donating money or volunteering services perhaps. Even the most casual observers of hype are aware that they are being appealed to on many levels. Most promotion does more than say, in effect, "buy me." It says "buy me because . . ." The "because" is the promotional element meant to provide enough motivation to convert potential users into actual users. The manipulative and sometimes misleading techniques invented by Madison Avenue to sell Americans everything from pretzels to presidents have been exposed in many studies, including Vance Packard's *The Hidden Persuaders*, Alvin Toffler's *The Culture Consumers* and Theodore White's *The Making of the President*. Yet promotion continues to be effective.

Promotional pieces usually employ what might be called personal motivating appeals: appeals to an individual's (often selfish) needs and desires. The desires to be beautiful, rich, famous and sexy appear to dominate the field. Other more selfless motivating appeals include those to one's sense of honesty, humanity, religion, patriotism and charity. There is nothing wrong with such feelings. What is wrong is that promotion often promises something it can't deliver. How many television commercials, for instance, picture some miserable-looking soul who, upon using a particular product, is miraculously transfigured into the personification of beauty? The people who create such commercials obviously hope that the viewers' emotions will get the better of their intelligence. The most common and probably overused motivating appeal in theatrical promotion is the use of quotations from what the critics have written or said. This supposedly appeals to one's respect for authority and expertise—even though very few critics have much of either. But how honest is it to lift just one complimentary word or phrase from an otherwise uncomplimentary review and use it to reflect that critic's opinion?

## Delivering Satisfaction

Responsible promoters are careful to promise only what their product can deliver, because they want people to use it more than once. And products are usually judged by how they were promoted: do they live up to the promises made or implied about them?  If a play is advertised as an "uproarious comedy hit," that's just what it should be—or the people who see it will feel cheated, will say so to all their friends and, as a result, business will suffer.

While the product should deliver the satisfaction promised by its promotion, promotion material should also provide information satisfaction. If a newspaper ad or a brochure captures the eye, and the copy and/or graphic elements stimulate the desire to attend a performance, then it should also provide the basic information necessary for the reader to follow through, to take action that will convert the reader into a user. Yet strange as it may seem, promotional pieces such as ads and press releases sometimes fail to contain this information, usually because of inexperienced marketing personnel or overworked publicists who neglect to have their work scrutinized and proof read by one or two other people. The failure of promotional material to include such basic information as an address and a phone number usually dooms the material itself to failure. People out there in Consumerland are lazy—the harder it is for them to take action in regard to using a product, the less likely they will be to use it.

Because marketing is a complex process not limited to sales, user satisfaction is an important factor. In the performing arts field this presents some special challenges, because the main product—namely the production–is never the same from performance to performance. This is the very essence of its uniqueness and value, but it is nonetheless a marketing problem. Each audience wants and expects the same satisfaction reported by the critics and general word of mouth. Yet the replacement of a leading performer due to illness, the sudden failure of stage machinery, the rowdiness of two drunks in the third row center, and an infinite number of other occurrences can easily have an adverse effect on audience satisfaction. Good marketing takes this into account by attempting to make audience members partners in solving such problems rather than victims. For example, the audience should not only be informed in advance about cast replacements, but also be asked to give such performers their fair due. Obvious mechanical problems might be announced by the stage manager or even alluded to by a performer in such a manner as to beg indulgence. People seated near the drunks might be asked to help silence them or be patient while they're removed.

Finally, to understand another point about audience satisfaction, let's turn to an old rule about public speaking that says effective speeches tell listeners (1) what they're *about* to hear, (2) what they *are* hearing, and (3) what they've *just* heard. In other words, any message or theme should be repeated at least three times. If theatre managers can somehow tell audiences that they are about to enjoy a production, tell them so again while they are enjoying it, and tell them afterwards that they did enjoy it, the majority will almost certainly feel that they *have* enjoyed it!

## KEY PERSONNEL

As mentioned in the last chapter, even the smallest and poorest theatre organizations need a marketing plan, even if it is drawn up and implemented by volunteers. And to adopt a marketing plan, of course, means to adopt the modern concept of marketing itself. Yet, there is resistance to this in some circles because theatrical tradition long held that, rather than a marketing director and plan, there merely needed to be a press agent or a publicity director. Such specialists are still needed, but they should report to a marketing specialist (even if that person is a consultant), whose job is to focus on all of the organization's goals, resources and opportunities. In small organizations this person may, in fact, serve as publicity director, press agent and public relations director, while also being marketing director. But in large, professional organizations there is usually a press or public relations manager, as well as a marketing director.

Virtually everyone on a theatre's board and staff is a member of the marketing team, because each one is somehow involved in representing, if not actually promoting, the organization to the market environment. Whoever accepts overall marketing responsibility should understand this and attempt to harness all such activities and energies so that they pull in the same direction. More direct supervision should be given to those in the organization who are involved in personal sales, such as personnel in the box office, in fundraising and telemarketing. Then it is often a question of whether to hire a publicist on staff or to engage the services of an outside public relations agency. Each alternative requires a special set of considerations.

### Outside Public Relations Agencies

There are countless independent public relations consultants and agencies across the land. One should remember that the first thing they all have learned in order to survive is to promote themselves! For this reason, as discussed in regard to marketing consultants in the previous chapter, their claims and promises should always be checked with past and present clients. Then there should be lengthy discussions about promotional goals, strategies and the specific services that will be provided. Fees should be openly discussed and checked to be certain they are competitive. Finally, a written agreement should spell out everything that was agreed to verbally. If the agency being retained is comprised of more than one publicist, it is important to know who will have primary responsibility for this particular account. Similarly, the theatre group should designate an in-house staff member to serve as the agency's contact person and liaison.

## Publicity Director

Working under someone responsible for overall marketing policy, a publicity director is a promoter who should be enthusiastic about the product being promoted. This requires an outgoing personality, a sense of conviction and the creativeness to dream up ways to make people sit up and take notice. As with any specialist, an experienced publicity director is much more valuable than one with limited experience. It helps considerably to have knowledge of a particular community, to know members of the press, advertising salespeople and local leaders, and to know such technical matters as how to write a press release, obtain names for mailing lists and design brochures that fit postal regulations. A publicist must have the ability to grasp the essence of a theatre organization or production and translate it in a way that will help the public understand it, want it and support it. When promotion misrepresents the real aims and qualities of a theatre, either intentionally or mistakenly, the damage can be irreparable.

## ATPAM Press Agent

The Association of Theatrical Press Agents and Managers (ATPAM) negotiates minimum employment conditions for press agents, house managers and company managers. Signatories to these labor agreements include the members of the League of American Theatres and Producers, the League of Off-Broadway Theatres and Producers and various independent producers and producing organizations around the nation. The agreement stipulates that any attraction or production in the United States or Canada that is owned, operated or controlled—directly or indirectly—by any signatory must employ a press agent, a house manager and a company manager who are ATPAM members. The press agent must be hired four weeks prior to the first paid New York performance (five weeks before, if the production opens first out of town). On tour (after a production has left New York) or after six weeks of a pre-Broadway tour, the press agent may handle only one production. Other regulations cover part-time press agents, local and associate press agents, apprentices and, of course, minimum salaries, benefits and other types of employment conditions found in most collective bargaining agreements.

## Common Requirements

A publicity, press or public relations director can bring a great deal to a theatre project, but only given a good degree of cooperation and faith on the part of management. Aside from basic tools with which to work (office space, equipment, a budget), the publicist must have easy access to information regarding the history, mission, objectives and accomplishments of the theatre and its personnel. The total marketing budget, as suggested earlier, should be at least 10 percent of the total potential gross, and 15 to 20 percent is more common.

Publicity directors—whatever their exact title might be—should earn salaries that reflect their importance to the success of the organization. These may be in the form of a predetermined fee for specified services, a weekly salary, a percentage of ticket sales or a combination of these. And publicists also need to be given an expense account to cover business entertainment, local transportation and other such costs essential to their work. While ATPAM members are protected against such unfair business practices as nonreimbursement for legitimate expenses, nonunion publicists are not, but when management wants top promotional results, it doesn't allow this type of abuse.

Importantly, the producing organization must permit its promotional directors a fair margin for error. Any type of PR person is expected to be an "idea" person, to invent countless promotional devices and gimmicks and, often, to devise imaginative advertising strategies as well. Not all such ideas will work. In the field of promotion, the following ratio is probably true: out of every one hundred promotional ideas, only ten will be feasible and only *one* will work! This indicates how many ideas a PR person has to come up with—often on a daily basis. If a producing organization rejects too many of these ideas or is too quick to condemn particular strategies, the publicist is denied the leeway and flexibility required to get the job done. Rarely will a single newspaper ad, however expensive, fill the house. A single brochure or flyer seldom brings in sell-out crowds. Repetition, time, and a variety of strategies tied to an overall marketing plan are the fundamental ingredients of successful promotion. And favorable word of mouth is the best indicator that promotion is working and that the product is a good one. No press agent, PR agency or publicity director is a miracle worker (though all have a little P.T. Barnum in their blood). But the best are professional men and women who know how to get the job done effectively and economically.

## THE PROMOTION OFFICE

In order for the publicist to organize and dispense public information, he or she must have access to certain equipment, resources and supplies. Printing, reproduction and mailing machinery or services are expensive, but necessary. Theatre groups that operate under an umbrella institution can usually avail themselves of central printing and mailing services; low budget theatres often rent or borrow reproduction facilities that belong to someone associated with them or that are donated as in-kind services. No matter how the printing needs are solved, the result should be neat, professional-looking literature. Messy, illegible or difficult-to-read material is worthless and should never be distributed under any circumstances. There are simply too many easy and efficient ways to produce and reproduce professional-looking material to allow for any excuses. A busy and well-organized theatrical promotion office should at least possess the following items, adapted to its special needs:

## Publicity Production Equipment and Materials

*Standard Office Equipment*   A direct-line telephone system with answering, intercom and fax capabilities; an electronic typewriter; a complete computer system with printing and graphics capabilities plus the necessary software; a reliable copying machine; if possible, a postage meter; a desktop publishing system; and equipment to collate, fold and staple bulk mailers

*News Release Stationery*

*Regular Office Stationery*

*Photograph Files*   Interior and exterior glossy photos of the facility, resident artists, managers, board members and past productions.

*Glossy Proofs*   Printed on contact paper from glossy photos and called "contact proofs," these should be ordered in the quantity needed for use in newspaper ads and other promotional pieces. Proofs should also be made of the logo, masthead or other frequently used graphic designs of star performers for use in print advertisements, (the subject's head may be silhouetted, and the picture reduced to fit a one-column space)

*Scrapbooks*   All printed publicity and ads should be collected and placed in scrapbooks, arranged by season and by production

*Press Board*   A bulletin board should display all ads, publicity and reviews pertaining to current productions for perusal by staff members and performers before it is removed and arranged into scrapbooks

*Supplies*   An ample inventory of basic supplies, such as poster board, pens, inks and computer software will prevent wasting valuable time on trivial errands

*Biographies*    A computer file should be maintained to store personal and professional biographical data on all artists, board members, and key managers associated with the theatre and its productions

*Artists' Index*  A computer or card file on all previous artists should be updated with each new production, showing the name of the production, dates and role or other artistic function.

## Mailing Lists*

*General Mailing List* (computerized to generate mailing labels for an individual list or any combination of lists)
   Current subscribers/season ticket holders
   Past subscribers who did not renew
   Single ticket buyers and others who have asked to be on the list
   Current board members
   Past board members
   Current contributors (individual, corporate, government)
   Past contributions
   Special advisory groups and volunteers
   Appropriate area organizations (schools, community groups, etc.)
   Appropriate area businesses (hotels, restaurants, etc.)
   Alumni (from any school programs run by the theatre)
   Faculty and administration (for theatre schools)
   Special target groups (seniors, corporate executives, etc.)
   Borrowed or bought lists (from other arts organizations, publishers,
            professional associations, etc.)

*General Press List* (computerized to generate mailing labels for one or more of the following categories):
   Print media
   Electronic media
   Special press lists (drama editors, society editors, etc.)
   Local press list
   Area-wide press list
   National press list
   Opening night invitational list
   Public Service Announcement (PSA) list
   Entertainment listings editors

## A Working Library

   Current editions of all play publishers' catalogues

*See Chapter 17: "Direct Mail Systems"

Copies of all plays in current or imminent production at the theatre

The most recent *Who's Who in the American Theatre*

A good, current dictionary of the English language

A good, current desk encyclopedia

A thesaurus and other word-finder books

New York Critics' Reviews

One or two theatre histories with original production information such as casts, dates, etc.

Playbill collection of all previous productions at the theatre

Area-wide directory of media outlets (giving circulation, listening or viewing statistics and other information. Such directories are available through press-clipping services, or the information may be obtained from the rate sheets available from each media outlet

Map collection of local and general area

Appropriate periodicals (*Variety*, *American Theatre*, local newspapers, professional journals, etc.).

A publicist, like any marketing person, is a strategist. To plan and execute a promotional campaign requires the mind of a field marshal and no small amount of special and ready intelligence. The more preparation that is done in advance of battle, the more intelligence gathered, the more munitions stockpiled, the more contacts made in the field, then the more successful the actual campaign will be.

# GATHERING INFORMATION

## *Historical Data*

Ongoing theatre groups should prepare a well-written narrative history of the company that is updated annually and reproduced in sufficient quantity to distribute to visiting critics and journalists, resident cast and staff members, visiting artists, and others. This simple and inexpensive marketing tool can do wonders in elevating the impression that the organization's users have of it—making them feel privileged to be part of an important artistic endeavor.

To assist in the process of collecting everything about the theatre that appears in print, a news-clipping service can be retained for a monthly reading fee plus, in most cases, an additional charge per clipping. The service will clip all articles and/or advertisements in which the name of the theatre appears and also label each with the publication name, date and circulation. Services can be directed to limit clippings to city-wide, state-wide, area-wide or nation-wide coverage. The clippings quickly alert the publicist as to which publications are using the theatre's press releases and which are not—an important aid in strategic evaluation.

455

Because theatrical press agents and publicists, like publishers and printers, are harried people who usually work in cluttered offices and rarely see
beyond the next deadline, the theatre business has, to an alarming degree,
traditionally ignored the preservation of production records. Every producing organization should assign one person to collect and preserve sample
playbills, posters, articles, press releases and photographs. These should be
safely stored, and a duplicate set of such memorabilia should be deposited
with an appropriate library, museum or theatre collection. It may seem child-
ishly simple to collect such items when a production is current, but a year
later it may be nearly impossible to locate any of them.

## Biographies and Resumes

Most theatres publish brief biographical sketches of performers, other
artists and management personnel in the playbill for the productions with
which they are associated. Often entitled "Who's Who" or "Behind the
Scenes," these write-ups should be literate and interesting, and final copy
approval should be granted to each person included. Resumes and photos
should be obtained as soon as performers and other key personnel are engaged. As well as providing basic information for "bios" and press releases,
these may also give the publicist ideas for feature articles, guest appearances
and one-on-one interviews. The publicity department may even devise a standard news release format to send to an individual's hometown and college
newspapers, stating that so and so ("class of '81" or "daughter of Mr. and
Mrs. Smith of Julesburg") is appearing in a certain production. This is sure-
fire copy for local editors and may stimulate ticket sales for the theatre, even
from very distant customers. David Merrick's long-running Broadway musical,
*Hello, Dolly!* once adapted this technique to audience members and distributed the following card in the theatre lobby:

If you are from out of town, we would like to
notify your home-town newspaper that you
came to see our show, "HELLO, DOLLY!"

Sincerely,

*David Merrick*

NAME  MR & MRS
MR.
MRS
MISS  ...................................................................

ADDRESS................................................................

CITY AND STATE......................................................

HOME-TOWN NEWSPAPER.......................................

*Please give card to usher or drop in box in lobby.*   491

Local newspapers all over the country were soon promoting the show. Other producers have given out free postcards related to their company or production, hoping that audience members would mail these to someone and generate publicity.

## Production Information

Theatre companies fortunate enough to enjoy the services of a dramaturg will be able to rely on that person to do background research on each production, playwright and leading artist involved, and some of this will be very useful in writing press releases, playbill notes and other material; in fact, writing these pieces may be part of the dramaturg's job. Otherwise, this work falls to the publicist. In either case, a major function of marketing is the enhancement of product enjoyment, and helping the audience to understand a production obviously increases appreciation.

## PHOTOGRAPHY FOR THE THEATRE

### Types of Photographs

Theatrical press agents need photographs both for general distribution and specific use. The first case includes photos of the theatre, general production shots, photographs of individual performers out of costume and shots of the leading managers. Photos of visiting VIPS, rehearsals and casual shots of audience members for the society columns have more limited use but are still valuable. The posed photos that performers submit with their resumes are almost invariably of the cheesecake variety—stilted, often touched up by the photographer and frequently taken eons ago. News editors generally favor informal action shots over cheesecake unless, of course, the picture is for inclusion in a paid advertisement or—sorry to mention—an obituary. To obtain casual shots, one usually needs to hire a photographer, unless a photographer is on staff. Hiring a photographer can be expensive, since it usually entails quick photo development and printing, as well as taking the photos in the first place. When a large number of photos are taken, it is best to order a proof or contact sheet (a quickly developed printout of each role of film printed onto a single sheet of paper). The most usable shots can then be ordered in the quantity needed from the contact sheet, which is labeled and filed together with the negatives for possible future use.

### Qualities of Good Theatre Photography

A good photograph has clarity, sharpness, good composition and professional development. Publicity photos are usually intended for reproduction in the print media, so they should be developed with a glossy rather than a matte finish. Dark photographs or those with very dark backgrounds

457

should be avoided because they reproduce badly. Photographs with sharply contrasting light and dark areas and with a predominantly light background are ideal. Also, photos should feature uncluttered subject matter (one to three people, a single building, etc.). Portraits should show the full head and shoulders (or full body) of the subject. Composition and cropping should never eliminate the top of a head or part of a face. Production shots should look dramatic and exciting.

## Uses of Photography

It is still true that a picture is worth a thousand words. When promoting a theatrical company or production, it seems that there are few places where a publicist can't use a good photograph: the brochure, the flyer, the playbill, the houseboard, the poster; the ads, the special displays.

When releasing a photograph to the press, the subjects in it should be appropriately captioned (identified from left to right)—but not in writing scribbled on the back of the picture, as this may press through and mar the face of the photograph. Rather, the caption should be typed on a separate piece of paper that is glued or taped to the bottom back of the photo, then folded so the caption extends several inches over the face of the picture. The caption should also include basic production-related information, such as time, place, price—as well as a brief capsulation of the nature of the place. Editors may pick this up when they have extra space to fill.

Photographic enlargements, or "blowups," of pictures serve as a dramatic means for publicizing a production. The desired size may vary, but 40 x 60 inches is standard for mounting in typical display cases and on sandwich boards. The cost of such enlargements (which may be ordered unmounted or mounted on heavy cardstock) is worth it, if they are put to good use in lobbies, ticket agencies and other places where they may stimulate sales.

Glossy 8 x 10 inch prints of the production and, whenever possible, of each performer should be displayed on a lobby houseboard. This seldom involves much cost, and it is standard courtesy to display a photo of each cast member in the current production, whether there is a contract stipulation that requires this or not.

When the supply is sufficient, photos of individual performers may be autographed and distributed to ticket agencies, group sales directors, volunteer theatre workers and others who may appreciate the gesture.

## THE PLAYBILL

The basic purpose of a theatre program or playbill is to assist the audience in identifying the performers, the roles they are playing, where the action occurs, and the arrangement of dramatic time. Historical background and critical analysis about the play and the production may also be desirable as a tool for audience education and enjoyment. Playbills may be produced in-house on desktop publishing systems (or just typed and reproduced on a copying machine) or they may be elaborately designed, typeset and printed on glossy stock. The full publication responsibility may be assumed by the theatre organization or may be assigned to an independent publisher or printer in exchange for a set fee or a share of the advertising revenues. But whatever advertising appears in the playbill should not completely obscure the standard production information.

## Standard Contents

1. *Title page* often located on the centerfold pages, this should state the name of the theatre, the producer(s) or producing organization, the date(s) of the performance(s) (unless it is an unlimited engagement), the title of the play, the author(s) and any other creative artists (lyricist, book writer), the director, choreographer, musical director and conductor, scenic, costume and lighting designers, and any other artistic collaborators. It should also state if the play is produced or presented "by special arrangement" with a play publisher or other producing organization and, finally, if it is "made possible through the support of" certain corporate, foundation or government sponsors. When performers are union members, their names must usually appear on the title page according to the provisions in their contracts, as discussed later in this chapter

2. *Synopsis of scenes* an outline giving the time and place for each act and scene

3. *Musical numbers* musical productions traditionally list each number by song title, followed by the names of the characters who perform it

4. *Cast of characters* the characters' names are printed on the left, corresponding actors' names on the right, listed in order of speaking or appearance

5. *Biographies* under the heading of "Who's Who" or some other title, there should be brief summations of each principal performer's professional career, if not the entire cast, as well as the director, author, conductor, producer, and leading managers

6. *Production notes*  Background and/or interpretative commentary

7. *Credits*  a list acknowledging people, companies and organizations whose assistance made the production possible

8. *House rules*  brief warnings about such matters as smoking, drinking, eating and taking photographs in the theatre

9. *Production staff*  the people with their titles who worked on assembling the physical production as well as those who run the performances (shop carpenters, seamstresses, stagehands, stage managers, electricians, etc.)

10. *Executive officers and administrative staff*  board of directors or trustees, producers, managers and members of the administrative staff.

Many playbills also contain lists of season ticket buyers, donors, advisory groups, interns, volunteers and others. And, of course, it's desirable to run a promotional article about upcoming productions. Nonprofit theatre companies should also include their mission statement and objectives.

Generally speaking—in both professional and nonprofessional theatres—it is wise to maintain an "everybody or nobody" policy when it comes to listing names in the playbill. Compiling and editing the production-related copy for a playbill is always an in-house responsibility, even when an outside publisher is used. And whoever is assigned to this job must realize that they cannot be too meticulous. Sensitivities run very high when it comes to playbill credits. Mistakes or omissions that seem minor to the editor and general reader can and frequently do evoke tremors of volcanic force from the person with the misspelled name or missing bio.

## Playbill Format and Design

A playbill is an important marketing tool because it is very influential in contributing to the theatre's public image. The design and general look of the playbill together with its contents will speak volumes to the public. The theatre must decide early on whether to invite advertising to defray printing costs (and, perhaps, to earn additional revenue) and, if so, the type of advertising. The job of selling ads for the playbill can be very time-consuming, and the salary for the salesperson may sometimes exceed the revenues.

Among the most commonly used playbill-design formats are the following:

1. *Uniform cover design*  Theatres that offer a series of different productions during the same season should consider designing a single program cover. This can be printed in bulk with contents printed and inserted separately for each different production, thereby reducing cost. The inside of the cover pages can be used for standard information, such as the mission statement, the board and staff lists and a calendar of productions. The drawback is that a uniform cover doesn't permit the reader to distinguish readily between one production and another, though this can be avoided if there is a window in the cover through which the production title or date is revealed as it appears on the first inserted page

2. *Outsize playbill design*  Typical playbills for most professional theatres measure eight by ten inches and audiences have come to accept this as the norm. To help market the unique image of a particular theatre or production, however, playbill designs of unusual shape and size might be considered. Dinner theatre playbills, for example, sometimes resemble large restaurant menus. One professional nonprofit theatre company offered a series of staged readings that it called "brown bag productions." Patrons were invited to bring their lunch, and the program information was typed onto plain white paper, duplicated and slipped into flat paper bags donated by a local department store

3. *Different designs for each production*  This is probably the most desirable option, because each playbill can be designed to reflect the particular nature of each production; but it's also the most expensive option

4. *Multi-purpose playbills*  To cut expenses, it is possible to design a theatre flyer (as a mailer or giveaway piece) that can double as a playbill. Old-fashioned, nineteenth century handbills provide an interesting point of reference for this approach

5. *Souvenir booklets*  Elaborately designed and printed, usually filled with photos of cast members and production shots, souvenir programs may be produced in addition to giveaway playbills and sold as a source of earned income. They may or may not include advertising (if so, the rates are usually higher than for the regular playbill), but printing costs are also higher, so souvenir booklets entail a risk.

Professional photographers, graphic artists, computer specialists, writers and editors can greatly enhance the image projected by a theatre through the medium of print. All such specialists can be hired as part-time consultants, by the job or as full-time staff members. Comparative cost estimations should be compiled to determine which approach will be the most economical and productive.

## PROMOTION GIMMICKS

### Promotion within the Theatre

No member of the audience should leave the theatre without carrying some of its promotional material–if not tickets for future performances. Aside from the playbill, audience members should also be able to pick up a flyer or calendar of events from display racks in the lobby and, perhaps, a button or a balloon bearing the theatre's logo. Giveaway items may be offered in exchange for filling out an audience questionnaire or a mailing list form. Some giveaways can be expensive, but the word of mouth they stimulate may be worth it.

While many theatres rightly feel that announcements and speeches from the stage tend to disrupt the enjoyment of a performance, there are cases in which this is an acceptable manner of publicizing future events. Sometimes there is an especially affable theatre manager, artistic director or performer, whom audiences like to see in front of the curtain before each performance or at the end of intermission to plug upcoming attractions. Or this might be done as part of the curtain calls. The spoken word generally has greater impact than the written word.

If curtain speeches are out, there are still many opportunities to speak personally to customers while they are in the theatre. Box office treasurers can end each transaction by asking if they can make a reservation or sale for the next production. The house manager and ushers can often slip in a few words about upcoming events. The manager and marketing director can be on hand to greet members of the press and other people they recognize and, of course, chat about upcoming events. Personal contact of this kind intensifies word of mouth as well as feelings of loyalty toward the theatre. Ideally, subscribers and other regular users should feel they will be personally missed if they don't attend each and every production.

### Local Tie-Ins and Personal Appearances

Whenever the publicist can somehow connect the theatre, the production or the performers with someone or something else that is of interest to the media, there is a good chance of garnering some free coverage. For example, when performers participate in fundraising efforts for local charities, when the manager speaks at a Rotary meeting, when the theatre runs a benefit for the wildlife refuge and other such tie-ins, the chance for media coverage doubles. And even without such coverage, when well-known personalities associated with the theatre appear at large gatherings (parades, holiday picnics, fairs, large flea markets, shopping centers and the like) this may stimulate word of mouth and sell tickets.On the other hand, it can be argued that, when a celebrity performer is involved, people who see that performer somewhere for free may then not bother to pay for the privilege of seeing the celebrity on stage. If the celebrity not only appears but also performs in some way, this possibility is even greater. And to perform excerpts from a play or participate in a costume parade outside the theatre not only risks overexposure but, what's worse, risks demeaning the theatre and its work. Personal appearances, in short, should be limited to worthwhile occasions where they can be handled with good taste and truly help to elevate the public image of the theatre.

Guest appearances on radio and television talk shows provide a safer and more controllable format for publicity exposure than appearances at large, public gatherings. And because virtually all talk shows are continually seeking interesting guests, it is not difficult for publicists to schedule performers and other suitable theatre personnel. Again, an attempt should be made to use a number of people and not just the leading performer. Radio interviews, of course, can be conducted by phone or prerecorded on tape, which makes scheduling much easier. When setting up interviews, the publicist should provide the host of the program with background information about the person being interviewed and also some basic facts about the production and the theatre. The guest should also be reminded to plug the show. There's nothing more disconcerting for the publicist than to arrange an interview and then witness the guest breeze through twenty minutes of air time without once mentioning the production or theatre that are the objects of the promotion. Yet this happens with depressing frequency.

## Contests, Bargains and Trade-Outs

Bargain tickets or free tickets may be offered through contests or tie-in offers sponsored by local business firms. Banks, for instance, may be persuaded to give "free" tickets that they purchase from the theatre to customers who open new accounts. Other offers may include autographed photos, a personal visit with the star and so forth. Dinner theatres as well as others may devise package offers that include a meal and a show for a single bargain price. This type of combination ticket not only appeals to the customer's sense of economy but, perhaps even more important, appears to make theatregoing easier and more enjoyable by combining several services into one transaction.

Radio and television talk shows, game shows and the like often thrive on contests, call-in participation and giveaways. This presents an excellent opportunity for promotion, since a theatre may provide free tickets as giveaways in exchange for free mention on the show or even free airing of prepared ad copy. Also, when a theatre first runs commercials on a media outlet, it is usually possible to set up an advertising and promotion contract that includes free plugs for the theatre, together with ticket trade-outs and paid commercials.

## Piggyback Promotion

Most large public and private corporations communicate regularly with their customers or shareholders through the mail. And usually their mailings include more than a simple bill or financial statement.

Banks, utility companies and retailers enclose some of their own promotional material and, often, a newsletter or other community outreach literature. Many are also willing to enclose items about local nonprofit arts organizations, either by stuffing a flyer in with their own material or by writing about such organizations in their own newsletters. This is called piggybacking and provides a very inexpensive promotional strategy. And it suggests many possibilities. What about getting the local supermarkets to stuff the theatre's flyers into all the shopping bags as they leave the check-out counters—or printing the theatre's logo onto the bags themselves? What about printing the theatre's production schedule on the place mats at local restaurants, on the bookmarks given out at local bookstores or on the reservation confirmations sent out by local hotels and resorts? Riding piggyback, hitching a ride and jumping onto somebody else's bandwagon in order to further one's own goals are familiar gimmicks that most Americans learn at a very early age.

# LADIES AND GENTLEMEN OF THE PRESS
## Establishing Good Press Relations

Producers, like politicians, will probably never stop arguing about the powers and prerogatives of the press (a term used loosely to include both print and electronic media). Does the press have too much influence and is it unfairly exercised? Should a few journalists with no formal education in theatre have the power to close a show that has taken several years to get from script to stage, costs millions of dollars and employs some of the most respected talents in the business? Harvey Sabinson, former press agent and Executive Director of the League of American Theatres and Producers, once suggested that if producers would just stop quoting critics in their ads, the power of the critics would be greatly diminished. But even if this were to happen, the media would continue to exert an enormous influence on public opinion, and publicists would still have to be hired to court the ladies and gentlemen who create and control media content.

The publicist or other staff member who serves as the main liaison between the theatre and the media should quickly establish a first-name relationship with as many media professionals as possible. This will require personal visits and phone contacts, as well as invitations that might bring these people to the theatre. It entails befriending the publishers and station owners as well as the editors and journalists; knowing who does what, takes orders from whom and when the deadlines are; understanding the style and interests of each media outlet and copywriter. Armed with this type of information, the publicist must try to accommodate each media professional according to his or her particular needs and preferences. This means making that person's job as easy as possible—indeed, practically doing it for them. The closer the publicist comes to accomplishing this, the greater the media coverage will be.

The general press list and its possible subcategories was outlined earlier in this chapter. A copy of this list with corresponding phone numbers, notes about deadlines and other pertinent data should be on line or on hard copy in the publicity office, where it must be updated on a regular basis. Names and addresses of print and electronic media outlets may be taken from the yellow pages of telephone books and from directories published by news-clipping agencies, among other sources. To verify the list and make efficient use of it, a return mail card such as the sample that follows should be sent to each person on the press list. There will be a high rate of return, because editors will quickly grasp that someone is trying to make their job easier.

It is customary to invite drama critics who write for daily publications or programs to opening night performances. Journalists who write for weekly or monthly outlets, feature writers and general editors may be given complimentary press seats for later performances. And a limited number of comps should be given to media people who never write copy but are influential or helpful in terms of the theatre's media relations. Such people as advertising executives, TV cameramen and women, typographers, and layout artists can make all the difference when there is a tight deadline,

It is professionally acceptable for press agents to ask critics or editors to read their reviews to them over the phone before they come out in print or on the air. This may help in creating up-to-the-minute ad copy, preparing the company for good or bad news and, in some cases, deciding whether or not to keep the show running. It is also good professional etiquette, when hosting theatre critics who have deadlines soon after the curtain comes down or who are traveling out of their way to reach the performance to offer them

Dear Editor:

To assist us in sending you news and information in the fastest and most efficient manner, we request that you complete the following form and return it to us.

Do you wish to receive our general press releases?_____

Do you wish to receive photographs from us?_____

Do you wish to receive information only for your entertainment listings or announcements?_____

Do you wish to be informed about special press conferences and interviews held at the theatre?_____

What is your deadline for receiving news copy?_____

To whom should our general news releases be addressed? (Specific editor)_____ (Address)_____   _____

If not the same as above, to whom should information for entertainment listings or announcements be sent?

We look forward to meeting you in person and, if you will contact this office, would be happy to provide complimentary tickets to one of our performances.

Sincerely,

Joseph Smith, Press Representative
Big Sur Playhouse, XX Shore Ave., Los Angeles, CA
Phone: 971-000-1129

transportation and, perhaps, the use of a typewriter and phone after the show. Nor is there any rule against offering to buy visiting members of the press a drink at the lobby bar—although some may refuse such offers for ethical reasons. The press may also be invited to join opening night parties, cast receptions and other such gatherings. And the press agent's expense account should permit individual entertainment of key media people at luncheon or dinner.

## The Press Kit

A press kit is a packet of information assembled for distribution to members of the press. It may be in the form of pages stapled together, or the material may be inserted into an envelope, or it may be arranged in a nice folder. The packaging can be fancy and expensive or simple and cheap. As long as the information is professionally prepared, correct and neatly presented it will be acceptable. Journalists and their colleagues are much more interested in solid information than in packaging.

Every ongoing theatre operation should acquire a supply of envelopes, folders or cover pages to be used for all its press kits over one or more seasons. Brief histories, background sheets, statistics, brochures, production schedules, copies of recent articles and reviews, and photographs should always be available for quick assembly into a kit. In addition, information specific to a particular occasion (such as a press conference, a rehearsal or an opening night) should also be prepared. A member of the press should never leave the theatre or its publicist empty-handed.

## Press Conferences

A press conference is an occasion at which selected members of the press are invited to meet as a group at a specified location for the purpose of gaining newsworthy information. The organization that calls the conference–whether it is the White House or the opera house–hopes that the event will generate media coverage and favorable coverage at that. But while a press conference is a promotional tool, it should never be perceived as pure hype. If this is the case, the press will probably never attend a second conference called by the same organization, and the coverage could easily be negative or nonexistent.

Conferences must be organized around some topic, person or event that is newsworthy: an especially popular performer, the first day of rehearsal, a new artistic or managing director, the unveiling of an architectural model for a new facility, or the like. No exclusivity, no scoop will be gained from a press conference—because everyone there receives the same information;

but those present should be allowed to ask questions and, when the gathering is small enough, to speak personally with the subjects. Early morning conferences should include coffee and pastries and at other times—when informality is desirable—light refreshments. More to the point, a press kit containing background information, photographs and other pertinent material should be given to each media person. As a nice touch, each kit might be labeled with the person's name.

The organization calling the conference must appoint an articulate spokesperson to make opening remarks, introduce those who may also be participating, and then field questions from the press and generally serve as a moderator. Other members of the management staff might be present to assist with hospitality chores and be certain that individual attention is given to each media representative.

## Press Interviews

A press interview is a one-on-one question-and-answer session between a media representative and someone else. These interviews may be done as a live broadcast, taped for later broadcast, taped merely for the convenience of the journalist, or the interviewer may simply take notes. Except under very unusual circumstances, press interviews should be arranged in advance. This gives the interviewer time to do some research and compose a list of questions, and it gives the party being interviewed fair warning, which is especially important if there will be videotaping or still photography involved.

It is never wise to burden busy artists and others with too many promotional chores, such as interviews. They may rightfully get fed up and refuse to do any at all. Whenever possible, these chores should be spread among different members of the company (when too much attention is given to one person, others can easily feel slighted). Also, the publicist must weigh the importance of each interview in terms of potential media coverage and, for example, not waste a busy artist's time on an interview for some small, far-off radio station. Finally, in order to avoid any embarrassing or unprofessional interview behavior, the publicist should check interviewers' credentials when these are unfamiliar. There are as many hams in the media business as in the theatre—maybe more!

## THE PRESS RELEASE

The most common way to feed news and information to the media is by means of a written press release. However, a press release must follow a very specific format and meet certain stylistic requirements, or chances are the editors who receive it will simply chuck it into the nearest wastebasket. A press release is really an attempt to write copy that the editor can publish or broadcast without doing any more editing. To say it again—because this is an important lesson—the publicist is aiming to do other peoples' work for them.

## Stylistic Requirements

1. Releases must be written in the third person, like a news story. Superlatives are unacceptable. The copy must read like information or news reported by an objective observer

2. All essential information (name of theatre, production, performance dates, etc.) should be contained in the first paragraph. Subsequent paragraphs should contain information of progressively decreasing importance. This is because editors traditionally cut copy from the bottom up, unless the article just happens to fit into the space or time available

3. Generally, each press release should be limited to one specific subject, event or idea. Whenever possible, the entire release should be contained on a single sheet of 8 1/2 x 11 inch paper, although 8 x 15 and 8 x 18 are preferable to using two sheets (which might get separated) or to printing on both sides of the same sheet (which prevents editors from using their scissors and hampers other editing techniques)

4. Releases should be typewritten with double spacing and wide margins to allow for editorial notations and changes

5. Releases sent to broadcast media outlets, and public service announcements (PSAs), should be typed entirely in capital letters, triple spaced, and should indicate the reading time (10 seconds, 20 seconds, etc.) at the top of each new paragraph.

Not surprisingly, small media outlets that are starving for copy are more likely to use inferior releases and even to permit the use of superlatives like "hilarious", "sensational," and the like, although never the use of the first person. A release cannot say "We will present . . . "   It must be written in the third person: "The XYZ Theatre will present . . . " Large media outlets, of course, are much more exacting in their requirements than small ones and, in fact, may use press releases only as tip-offs for assigning reporters and critics to cover certain stories and events. A possible exception is when the publicist is known and respected by the media outlet and submits an "exclusive" story or photograph. Exclusives, often written in the style of a feature story, may run longer than news releases and be slanted for use by a particular media outlet as well as a particular column, section or program. The cardinal rule is never to label a story or photo "exclusive to the *Daily Tribune*," or whatever, unless that is really the case.

## Format Requirements

1. News releases should be printed on special stationery designed for that purpose. Along with the name and address of the producing organization, it should carry the word "News" or "News from . . ." or some other phrase that quickly indicates what it is

2. At the beginning of the release should appear the words "For Immediate Release!" or "Release date: . . . " to indicate either that the story should be published as soon as possible or not used until after a specified date

3. Strictly speaking, it is the news editor's job to title all the articles that are printed so that identical headlines will not appear in two different publications. Nonetheless, it is expedient to give each new release (in capital letters) as newsworthy and as attention-grabbing a title as possible to stimulate the editor's interest

4. At the beginning or end of the release, the press agent's name and phone number should appear after the word "Contact:"

5. If a release absolutely must use more than one page, the word "more" or "Continued on page 2" should appear at the bottom of the page and "Continued: page 2" should appear at the top of the second page, perhaps accompanied by the name of the production

6. At the very end of the press release, centered on the page on a line by itself, there should be something to indicate that there is no more copy. The standard editorial symbols are: # # # or -30- or -end-.

## OTHER TYPES OF PRESS ANNOUNCEMENTS
### Public Service Announcements

A PSA usually contains much of the same information and wording as a press release written for the print media, except that it is meant to be read over the air. It is written all in capital letters and the reading time is shown

NEWSNEWSNEWSNEWSNEWSNEWSNEWSNEWSNEWSNEWSNEWSNEWS
from:

THE MIDDLEBORO THEATRE FESTIVAL

Date: 6/12/00                              Middleboro College

Middleboro, OH

For Immediate Release!                            00000

MIDDLEBORO THEATRE FESTIVAL OPENS 8TH SEASON WITH SHAW
COMEDY

The Middleboro Theatre Festival, which offers the only fully professional
summer play series in the Ohio Valley, will celebrate the opening of its 8th
anniversary season on June 21st with ARMS AND THE MAN, George Bernard
Shaw's satire about love and war.  Presented at the Festival Theatre on the
campus of Middleboro College one mile from Exit 9 on the Valley Turnpike,
performances are scheduled through July 10th on Tuesday through Saturday
evenings at 8 PM with matinees on Wednesdays and Sundays at 2 PM.
Information and reservations may be obtained through FestCharge at 000-
333-1111.
Staged by Festival Artistic Director Patricia McVey, ARMS AND THE MAN
features a seasoned cast of actors headed by John Markus and Katrina
Quixote. One of Shaw's most popular plays since its London opening in 1894,
many of the romantic notions it ridicules still persist today.
John Markus, who plays a dashing Swiss captain who appears unannounced
in the bedroom of a young Bulgarian woman, starred as Brick in last season's
festival production of CAT ON A HOT TIN ROOF and has Broadway credits
that include WHAT THE BUTLER SAW and LEGS DIAMOND. On television he
is featured regularly in HOW THE WORLD LOVES.  Katrina Quixote, who
converts the captain into her chocolate cream soldier, has been featured in
many productions at leading regional theatres, including ROMEO AND
JULIET at Washington's Triangle Stage and THE PHILADELPHIA STORY at the
Missouri Rep.
With sets and lighting designed by Harry Ku, ARMS AND THE MAN marks the
fifth Shavian play that Ms. McVey has directed for the festival. The next
production, beginning on July 14th, will be the classic Noel Coward comedy,
PRIVATE LIVES. There is free parking inside the north gate of the campus and
boxed picnics are on sale in the Henry Moore Sculpture Garden before each
performance.

-30-

Contact: O.B.Smith  (000-797-1111)

above each paragraph, with difficult words spelled out phonetically, as in the sample that follows. PSAs sent to television and cable stations may be accompanied by color slides of photographs.

Virtually all broadcasting and cable stations air PSAs, especially those pertaining to nonprofit organizations. These may be announced throughout the programming day or grouped together as a community bulletin board or some similar format. However, stations may want the PSA to follow their own time and format guidelines, and their deadlines for submission may be four or more weeks in advance of airing. Such information must be obtained from each station and, if necessary, PSAs must be prepared individually to suit the requirements of the different outlets.

## Calendar Listings

The vast majority of periodicals include some type of events calendar that lists basic information about entertainment activities in the area. These are similar to public service announcements, although the wording and information are usually even more lean. Again, there are likely to be different deadlines and format requirements for different calendars, so each publication should be contacted; then the theatre organization must set up its own calendar for sending out PSAs and listings in a timely manner. The calendars that appear in Sunday newspapers, chambers of commerce, tourist guides and the like are extremely important because many people save them and refer to them when trying to decide how to spend their leisure time.

## News Tips

A news tip is simply a memorandum sent in writing to appropriate media people, informing them about some special activity that they may consider newsworthy enough to cover in person. This may be the arrival of a star performer at the airport, a performance given for some special audience or any other activity that might provide a photo opportunity for the press and generate some interesting copy for the public (as well as some free publicity for the theatre).

## Column Items

While the number and popularity of gossip columnists is not what it used to be, columns can still provide good opportunities for publicity. The press agent, of course, must be familiar with the general subject and format of each column, must establish at least a telephone relationship with the columnist and must be persistent in offering items for possible use. These usually have to be exclusive items that are not contained in press releases or given to other journalists. Anecdotal items are usually preferred.

SAMPLE PSA

---

PSAPSAPSAPSAPSAPSAPSAPUBLIC SERVICE ANNOUNCEMENT from . . .

THE MIDDLEBORO THEATRE FESTIVAL

Date: 6/12/00

Middleboro College

Middleboro, OH

For Immediate Announcement!

00000

RE: ARMS AND THE MAN

(30 seconds)

THE MIDDLEBORO THEATRE FESTIVAL OPENS ITS 8TH SEASON OF PRO-FESSIONAL THEATRE ON TUESDAY, JUNE 21ST WITH <u>ARMS AND THE MAN</u>, GEORGE BERNARD SHAW'S SATIRE ABOUT LOVE AND WAR. PER-FORMANCES WILL TAKE PLACE AT THE FESTIVAL THEATRE AT MIDDLE-BORO COLLEGE THROUGH JULY 10. CURTAIN TIMES ARE 8 PM TUESDAY THROUGH SATURDAY WITH MATINEES AT 2 PM ON WEDNESDAYS AND SUNDAYS. THE FESTIVAL THEATRE IS CONVENIENTLY LOCATED ONE MILE FROM EXIT 9 ON THE VALLEY TURNPIKE.

(15 seconds)

STAGED BY FESTIVAL ARTISTIC DIRECTOR PATRICIA MC VEY, <u>ARMS AND THE MAN</u> FEATURES A CAST HEADED BY JOHN MARKUS AND KATRINA QUIXOTE (KEY-HO-TAY), WITH SETS AND LIGHTING BY HARRY KU AND COSTUMES BY RAPHAEL PENA (PAN-YA).

(10 seconds)

THERE IS FREE PARKING FOR FESTIVAL TICKET HOLDERS INSIDE THE NORTH GATE OF THE MIDDLEBORO CAMPUS, AND PICNICS ARE ON SALE IN THE HENRY MOORE SCULPTURE GARDEN BEFORE EACH PERFORM-ANCE.

-end-

Contact: O.B.Smith (000-797-1111)

NEWSTIPNEWSTIPNEWSTIPNEWSTIPiNEWSTIPNEWSTIP  NEWS  TIP
from . . .

THE MIDDLEBORO THEATRE FESTIVAL

Middleboro  College

Date:  6/29/00                                    Middleboro,  OH

00000

PHOTO  OPPORTUNITY:   ELNORA  HAYES   BERNHARDT   PRESENTS
AWARD  TO  FESTIVAL

Press coverage is welcome when distinguished stage and screen star, Elnora
Hayes Bernhardt, visits Middleboro and presents the Annual National Theatre
Award for Outstanding Achievement to the Festival's Artistic Director, Patricia
McVey.

DATE:     Thursday, July 10th

TIME:     4:00 PM

PLACE:     The Picnic House at the Henry Moore Sculpture
Garden on the Middleboro College Campus

A cocktail reception will follow to allow interviews with both Ms. Bernhardt
and Ms. McVey.

## Video News Releases

By the 1980s corporate America had developed the use of video news
releases, primarily to introduce new products in the format of a feature story
or the coverage of a pseudo-event. Soon, video news releases came to be
widely used by government, political campaign managers, film companies
and even cultural organizations. Today, television and cable news editors are
inundated with them.

Like a standard press release, a video release attempts to do the TV
news department's work for it. The producers of the video, of course, hope
that it will be shown in its entirely on the evening news–and again on the
morning news. But if only a few "bites" are aired, they may have promoted
their product to millions of viewers. While there are ethical questions about

the media's use of such secondary reportage (especially when its source is not identified, which often it isn't), it appears that the video news release is here to stay and, in fact, that it will gain both in production and air time. Consequently, there is a growing number of private companies that specialize in producing video news tapes at a cost that now averages from $8,000 to $40,000 per tape. The media stations, of course, receive them free of charge. The high cost of video releases keeps them out of reach for most performing arts companies, though, if they are produced in-house or as in-kind service donations, they obviously become more feasible.

## AEA REGULATIONS PERTAINING TO PROMOTION AND ADVERTISING

### Billing Regulations

Collective bargaining agreements negotiated with Actors' Equity Association by the different branches of the industry all contain rulings that cover billing and publicity. Generally, these require that the names of all principal players (those with speaking roles) be displayed on the houseboard of the theatre, either outside or in the lobby. When a principal leaves the cast, the name must be removed, and that of the replacement must be substituted by the day of the replacement's first performance. Similar corrections must be made in the playbill and in all paid advertising controlled by the theatre. Equity actors have the right to approve the biographies that appear about them in all playbills and souvenir booklets. If a mistake or omission occurs, the manager must, upon receipt of written notice, correct this or insert a correction slip into each faulty playbill. In cases where an understudy assumes a role at the last minute, a notice must be placed in the lobby stating the name of the substituting actor and the role being played, and a correction slip to the same effect must be inserted into all playbills; or an announcement must be made from the stage or over the PA system immediately prior to the commencement of the performance. The names of understudies for principal plays must be listed in the playbill.

Other billing regulations are covered in riders written into individual contracts between the actor and the manager/producer. Before any advertising or playbill copy is printed, the publicist at a theatre that employs union artists must carefully check all contracts, note the billing stipulations and then apply these to the composition of the title page in the playbill, on houseboards, posters, in newspaper advertising and other such literature. One must also check whatever agreements may exist between the theatre and the playwright (and other creative artists), between the theatre and another producing organization or between the theatre and a play publishing house (such as Samuel French or Tams Witmark). There will always be a billing clause regarding the author(s). Other credits may also be mandated regarding the original producers or directors of the production.

The more well-known an actor, director or playwright, the more prominently that person's name will figure into the promotional materials, as spelled out in contracts and agreements. As mentioned earlier, some artists are willing to lower their salary demands in exchange for more prominent billing. But it should be remembered that billing takes up valuable space in paid advertisements and, in the long run, may be more costly than paying a higher salary. A simple but typical billing rider in a star's contract might read as follows:

> Actor shall receive sole star billing on a line by himself above the title of the play, wherever that title appears in advertising controlled by the producer, in type that is no less than 100 percent the size, prominence and boldness of the title.

This means, among other things, that the producer may not grant any other performers' billing above the title. A majority of actors in Equity productions have billing riders in their contracts. Some specify exactly where the actor's name must appear in relation to the title and other cast names, others merely specify that the name must appear "wherever the name of the first featured actor appears."   Or the rider may require a name to appear on a line by itself, in a box of a certain size in relation to the title of the play, preceded by a certain phrase (such as "and," "also starring" or "in the role of . . ."), or whatever else the actor's agent dreams up and gets the manager to approve. One publicist got into trouble with an actress whose billing clause read as follows:

> Actor shall receive equal billing after the actor receiving first billing: above the title, on a line by themselves and in the same type, size, prominence and boldness as the other actor.

The playbill was printed as follows:

STAR PLAYHOUSE

presents

| SETH | and | SANDRA |
|------|-----|--------|
| STAR |     | STAR   |

in

Why did Sandra Star throw a tantrum as soon as she saw this? Because she objected to the word "and." " I am not '*and* Sandra Star'," she said quite rightly; "I am 'Sandra Star' "! To give her the truly equal billing promised in her contract, the playbills had to be reprinted before opening night.

Perhaps the most famous battle to obtain equal billing occurred decades ago when two famous headliners refused to appear in the same show together unless their press agents could come up with really equal billing for the playbills and posters. Here is the solution that got the show onto the boards:

Breach of billing requirements can carry stiff penalties for management, sometimes even mandating payment to the actor of one-eighth of the weekly contractual salary for each breach, and for each week the breach continued after notification was received by management.

## Photo Calls

A photo or picture call is when management requires the cast or parts of it to pose for photographs. AEA limits such calls to regular rehearsal periods, certain time limits, only *after* performances and only following a twenty-four-hour notice. Under other circumstances, the manager may be required to pay actors an hourly wage for their services. Actors must also be paid extra if the pictures are used to endorse a commercial product. On the other

477

hand, actors are required to supply management with standard 8 x 10 photographs of themselves at their own expense for display on houseboards and elsewhere.

## Filming, Teletaping and Recording

Actors may usually participate in radio or television commercials at no cost to management, providing these do not include any material from the show being advertised. When it does, actors may have to be paid AFTRA or SAG minimums for such work. If the commercial is over one minute in duration and if it includes material from the show being advertised, all actors involved must be paid the equivalent of one week's salary. If a sound recording is made to cut a record album, or a film is made of the production, all actors involved must be paid either a full week's salary for every day or part-day of recording or filming they do, or AFTRA or SAG minimum rates, whichever is higher. However, actors do not receive compensation when limited footage of rehearsals or performances is teletaped for airing with television reviews or special feature stories about the production, providing the camerawork is done by the TV station itself.

## General Considerations

Both professional and nonprofessional theatre artists should be given the courtesy of a day's advance notice of any promotional activity in which they will be asked to participate, especially when photography is involved. Equity rules concerning personal appearances, press interviews and the like are often purposely vague. It is expected, however, that actors will cooperate and agree to assist the theatre in publicizing the production, whenever the request is a reasonable one. The publicist should at no time require artists to perform in an impromptu manner; nor should they be asked to wear costumes or undertake anything else that might place them in an embarrassing or unprofessional situation. The artists' time and energy should be respected and, of course, they should be reimbursed for any expenses they may incur in relation to promotional activities.

## SUMMATION

The object of publicity is to gain free coverage or to generate favorable word of mouth for a given product. There will, of course, be certain costs involved, such as those for salaries, printing, mailing and the like. But hopefully these will result in the news release being published in local newspapers, the poster displayed at local shopping centers, the mailing list form filled out in the lobby and so forth.

The primary tools of successful publicity include information, communication, technical know-how and imagination. Of the many gimmicks and promotional ideas dreamed up by publicists, only a few should be implemented and only a few of those will work. Effective publicity requires advance planning, a strict adherence to deadlines and meticulous attention to detail. And it requires an ability to understand and interpret the product so that the public will also understand it and, furthermore, want it and buy it. This is to say that publicity must be consistent with the goals and objectives of the production, company, organization and institution being publicized.

Both publicity and advertising are essential strategies in a promotion campaign and both are related to long-term marketing goals. This chapter, then, serves as a basis for the next.

# 17

# Advertising And The Sales Campaign

A DVERTISING is the most expensive element in the marketing mix. It is promotion that one pays for line by line, second by second, stamp by stamp. On the one hand, no theatre has the budget to buy as much advertising as it would like; on the other, no amount of advertising is likely to overcome bad word of mouth. Such facts point to a need for the expert and clear-headed management of any sales campaign. Yet, this may be easier said than done!

While most artists in the theatre world are content to leave business, facility, fundraising and board management to administrators, many are suddenly keen to get involved with managerial decision-making when it comes to promotion. This is because promotion—or their understanding of it—has to do with putting their names in lights. On a less egotistical level, however, artists are rightly concerned that the advertising image projected of themselves and their work be the true image. This concern often translates into serious disagreements over which logo, photograph, ad copy, playbill cover or radio commercial to approve; or how to allocate the advertising budget; or which publicist, graphics designer or advertising agency to hire. Not surprisingly, the image that artists have of their work is often at odds with the image that marketing experts wish to project. Such conflicts can be especially acute in regard to paid advertising, because this is the one marketing element over which management has full control.

## GENERAL CONSIDERATIONS
### Requisite Skills and Services

Few areas of theatre management present as many different options as the design, production and distribution of advertising. In terms of both creativity and economics, it is wise to explore different options and to shop carefully for the requisite skills and services before making decisions. It is also good marketing practice to review existing advertising policy, budgets and vendors at least annually.

A primary step involved in the creation of advertising is that of writing the copy. Obviously, this must directly relate to the nature of the product, the mission of the organization and the overall marketing plan that has been adopted. The copy may be written by the marketing director, the publicist or whoever is assigned to the task. Writing ad copy is a specialty that not everyone can do well. It may be advisable to hire a freelance writer or use an advertising agency if no one within the organization has copywriting experience. And hand in hand with writing the copy is the important task of correcting the final draft and the printer's proof. This, too, requires special skills—in language, grammar, spelling and editing, as well as knowledge of the standard proofreading symbols (#, bf, stet, =/, etc.).

Most theatre organizations need at least the services of a graphics designer to create a logo. Computer-generated graphic designs can be effective, but should also be done by an expert. This may be a one-time expense, but it is worth spending some money to get an effective and professional design. College theatres might call upon the services of the art department. Others might offer a payment or award for a logo or poster design selected from a student competition. Or corporations with graphics departments can be asked to contribute design work as an in-kind service; printing companies as well as newspaper and magazine publishers usually offer their customers various lay-out and design services that may be sufficient to meet the needs of small organizations. Photo offset equipment, for example, can reduce or enlarge photographs, silhouette the subjects in a photograph, and make contact sheets and ad slicks (a camera-ready, glossy proof of a complete print advertisement). Large operations that sponsor numerous events, however, usually find it expedient to hire their own graphics designer on a full-time basis.

Along with most public relations experts, graphics designers are knowledgeable about the alternatives in the printing field, an important factor in keeping the costs within budget. The quality and weight of the paper used for brochures, flyers and posters; the printing method to be used, such as offset or reproduction; whether or not to use color and how; which style of type to use; what quantity to order; which non-printing services to order and which to do in-house, such as folding and stapling—all such matters impact on cost as well as the appearance of printed material.

A great deal of labor (often nonsalaried) may be required to prepare large bulk mailings for the post office or to distribute posters and handbills. This may seem obvious, but it is no laughing matter when thousands of expensive brochures or hundreds of posters are sitting in the promotion office with no help available to process or distribute them.

## Advertising Agencies

Unlike other private agencies that provide technical assistance in such areas as fundraising, marketing and public relations, advertising agencies work exclusively on a commission basis. For most, their income is derived from 15 percent of the cost of all the print and electronic media advertising which they place—and this is paid by the media outlets, just as travel agents receive a commission from the airlines and resorts where they book their clients.

Virtually all Broadway and Off-Broadway productions use ad agencies, as do a great variety of other theatre operations around the country. The traditional method of selecting an agency is to invite at least several to make a presentation, which in essence is a job bid. In the case of a theatrical client, the focus of advertising is usually a particular production, institution or both. The agency will study the subject matter and then prepare several graphics pieces, such as posters, playbill covers and storyboards of proposed television commercials. They may also prepare a written proposal that deals with target markets, promotion strategies and the like. Based upon such presentations, the theatre organization selects an agency. The decision should be based on:

1. The creativity of the concept that the agency presents
2. The past promotional track record of the agency
3. The amount of personal attention the agency is willing to give the account.

While it may seem that ad agencies offer their clients a free ride, there are a few things to be wary about. Because agencies earn their money through ad placements, for example, they are rarely mindful of the other elements in the marketing mix, such as free publicity or personal sales. They would prefer to spend the entire marketing budget on paid advertising. And, because media advertising is more costly, they generally prefer this over print advertising. They may also urge standardized ads or commercials over those that feature frequent changes in copy ("special matinee today," "last ten performances" and so forth), because the latter require close monitoring. On the other side of the coin, agencies often provide excellent graphics and copy writing talent without cost to the theatre organization, they help keep ad salespeople away from the organization's door, they deal with all the placement and deadline details, and otherwise lighten the burden of marketing responsibilities.

## The Budget

Whatever the total marketing budget may be, only a portion of it can be allocated to paid advertising. Again, it is important that advertising expenditures be based on a clear, written marketing plan and not merely on what the competition is doing or what the theatre organization has done in the past.

To access the value of a particular media outlet, one must look at its rating or circulation statistics as well as the profile of its typical users (rock music fans, soap opera addicts, financial news readers, etc.) and then determine which outlets, sections, programs and/or time slots most attract the theatre's own target markets. There is no point in delivering an advertising message to markets that have no interest in it. For instance, the "reach" of a particular city newspaper may be one million readers and the frequency with with these readers might see an advertisement in that paper is daily (or more, if a number of ads for the same product are placed in the same edition). Yet, if less than a fraction of the readership is interested in the product, this newspaper is a very cost-*in*effective place to advertise. So the challenge becomes to find another media outlet or another marketing strategy altogether that is cost-effective.

Repetition is a vital element in successful advertising. Unless a potential user hears or sees the identical message at least three times over the course of a day or two, the message will probably not be communicated. This will also be the case if much time elapses between received messages; it is wiser, for instance, to place twelve radio spots with the same station over two days than over seven days. In addition, the more advertising time or space one buys in the media, the lower the per unit cost, and the cost is further reduced if an organization agrees to purchase a minimum amount of space or time each week over a number of weeks or months.

These are a few general points to keep in mind when allocating limited advertising dollars. They all impact on cost. And it doesn't take much experience in buying ad space to understand how alarmingly costly it is.

## The Time Element

Whoever coined the phrase "time is money" may well have had the promotion game in mind. This is because the more lead time one has to promote something, the more successful the promotion should be. The less time one has, the more expensive the promotion is likely to be. Yet, the theatre business is often handicapped by last minute bookings, cancellations and dashed plans that cause havoc with promotional efforts. Publicity directors and other marketing specialists are not magicians. They cannot speed up postal delivery, stop the presses or reprint the playbills an hour before curtain. They must somehow work within the deadline of opening night as well as within a vast number of media deadlines and the simple time constraints for getting things done. All of which is to say that marketing personnel must have a keen sense of deadline. While budgets and strategies can be controlled and changed, time and its relentless march toward important deadlines cannot. Planning a marketing campaign, then, should include a detailed calendar of deadlines to be followed in the execution of each and every strategy (a sample calendar is included at the end of this chapter). When somebody or something throws a monkey wrench into the works, as often happens, strategies should be changed or adapted to fit the circumstances; it should not seem like the end of the world if a strategy doesn't work—unless nobody bothers to fix it!

## A Focused Message

Limited resources always restrict the size or length of an advertising message—usually to just a few column inches or a few seconds of time. One ad can't sell everything in the department store, as it were. Yet inexperienced copy writers invariably crowd too many messages into this limited space. Just as each press release should focus on a single idea or event, each advertisement should focus on a single message—stated as powerfully as possible, with the fewest words possible. It is usually more effective to concentrate on a single theme or person. A few obvious focal points for theatrical advertising include:

1. A star performer
2. Some well-known artist associated with the production, such as the playwright or director
3. A well-known production title
4. A well-known theatre facility, producer or presenter
5. Quotes from rave reviews
6. Awards, such as a Tony or Pulitzer Prize
7. A bargain or discount offer
8. A limited engagement or limited ticket supply.

Advertising can also focus on one of the motivating appeals discussed in the previous chapter (snobbery, sex, humor and so forth). This is sometimes the best solution when promoting an entire season or series of productions, as illustrated by the New York City Opera advertisement that follows. A 30-second commercial or small newspaper ad obviously can't mention all the performers and events in a long series, so the message must be designed to encapsulate the overall impact that the series is meant to have on its audiences. And all such messages, from PSAs to TV commercials, should answer the 5 W's of good journalism: Who, What, When, Where and Why—as well as How, as in "how to acquire tickets."

Selecting the focus of an advertising campaign should be the responsibility of marketing experts. But whenever the person calling the shots—the producer, the board chairperson, the star, the producer's wife, the star's agent—demands a particular approach to the promotion campaign, it is extremely difficult even for seasoned marketing professionals to say "no." Artists should play prominent roles in the marketing of their work, but they should also trust that people with proven marketing skills usually know the difference between feeding egos and selling tickets.

## Truth in Advertising

The arts by their nature are dedicated to discovering and revealing truth, so it follows that arts marketing should not misrepresent the artistic product. Most managers and their publicists subscribe to this, yet there can be a fine line between honest and dishonest hype. For example, Carol Levine, president of a respected New York theatrical advertising agency, once submitted a presentation bid for a new Broadway musical to be directed and choreographed by Tommy Tune. By any estimation, he was the biggest name connected with the show at that time. The problem was this: how to create a television commercial that featured Tommy Tune without leading viewers to think that he was also performing in the show?

There are, of course, federal laws that deal with ethics in advertising, but they are quite broad. Here's another example. A TV commercial for a Broadway musical was shot outdoors, possibly leading viewers to believe that the entire Shenandoah Valley would be reproduced on stage. Was that ethical? And what about the time producer David Merrick invited people with the same names as the New York critics who had just panned one of his shows to see the show, comment about it, and then permit him to quote their *favorable* remarks in his newspaper ads? (He did, however, also print the addresses of these name-alikes and thereby alerted readers to the hoax.)

Little untruths should also be avoided, like calling a show "hilarious" when it isn't, or "brilliant," "engrossing," or whatever. Such blurbs set the audience up for disappointment and also set the performers up for some rough going.

## Hard Sell vs. Soft Sell

Early in the planning stages of a promotional campaign, it must be decided whether to use an aggressive, hard-sell approach or a seductive, soft-sell approach or something in between. Hard-sell advertising is designed, in effect, to jump off the page and hit the viewer face-on. A soft sell usually

employs understatement, wit and charm and is designed to gently coax the viewer into paying attention. The hard sell commands the consumer to do something; a soft sell relies more on the subliminal. Television commercials, such as those promoting tapes and records of "favorite songs of the '50s," are usually of the hard sell variety. Some of those for designer jeans and perfumes that show curvaceous models in various stages of undress and barely mention the name of the product are examples of soft sell.

Certain types of products have come to be associated with certain styles of advertising. Newspaper ads for automobiles, circus posters and supermarket advertising supplements that are included with the Sunday papers are just a few examples that immediately conjure up specific formats. A certain amount of theatrical advertising also has a sameness of appearance. This can be deadly when trying to get the consumer's attention—although you might attract those who are actually looking for a particular product. Sometimes, then, it may be good strategy to design advertising that goes against tradition—to use hard sell in promoting serious opera, for example, or soft sell in promoting the circus.

## Errors and Misprints

All media outlets occasionally make mistakes in the running of advertisements. All give a rebate, or credit the advertiser and provide additional advertising without charge—but the responsibility for catching errors and misprints falls to the advertiser or its ad agency. This task is easiest if a clipping service has been retained to supply copies of all advertising. Monitoring commercials placed with electronic media outlets is more difficult, although most will provide an advance schedule of approximately when each commercial will be aired. Of course, if the ad copy or layout submitted was faulty to begin with, there is no recourse. When time permits, it is wise to request a proof of each print ad before it is published.

## ADVERTISING COMPOSITION AND LAYOUT
### The Logotype and the Signature

The first task of advertising composition is usually the creation of a graphic image or symbol that visually identifies a specific theatre, production or both. This becomes a trademark that the public may someday automatically associate with the product. When the trademark incorporates the name of the product, it is called a logotype or logo. Or a purely graphic symbol or image may be used. When the logo (or name) of the product is used in combination with the symbol of the product, this is called a signature or a sig.

It is believed that logos and sigs evolved from the picture signs that hung outside medieval taverns and public houses. An establishment known as The Boar's Head Pub, for example, would have a sign simply showing the head of a wild boar. This enabled people who were thirsty but illiterate to find it. Similarly, in Elizabethan days, the public theatres were identified by a picture sign or flag that depicted a rose, a swan, a globe and so forth. Today, despite a somewhat improved literacy rate, we continue to identify many products by means of a familiar symbol or graphic image; just think of cereal boxes, fast food chains and national league baseball teams. The aim is to create a logo that somehow captures the feeling, if not the meaning, of the product it symbolizes. It is a visual statement about the nature of the product. When a new logo is first used in advertising, it should serve as an attention-getting device. As it becomes familiar to the public, it serves as a very economical use of space because it communicates something that would otherwise take much more space. Finally, the logo for popular products—from baseball teams to Broadway shows—may be exploited through merchandising (tote bags, T-shirts and the like).

Some logotypes are superimposed on a picture, placed next to one or designed to incorporate information such as an address and phone number.

SAMPLE INSTITUTIONAL LOGO DESIGNS

**Lincoln Center for the Performing Arts**

Circle in the Square Theatre

Virtually every Broadway and Off-Broadway hit has a widely used logo that the public soon associates with the show. This itself becomes a valuable advertising tool for all future productions of the show. Booking agencies usually supply these to presenters in the form of heralds, ad slicks and 3-sheets, which are discussed in the next section. They may be obtained from the original producers of a particular show; facsimiles of logos for recent hits and frequently produced plays and musicals can be ordered from such companies as the Package Publicity Service in New York City.

SAMPLE SHOW TITLE LOGOS

SAMPLE GRAPHIC SYMBOLS FOR HIT SHOWS

(An image has become sufficiently identified with
a product so that words are not necessary.)

An interesting use of graphic symbols for two shows produced by
Cameron Mackintosh and represented on Broadway by the advertising agency
of Serino-Coyne: *Les Miserables* was already an established hit when *Phantom of the Opera* had its New York opening. The newspaper ads below ran
on the same day and on the same page in the *New York Times*. Obviously,
Cosette is wishing the Phantom a happy opening night!

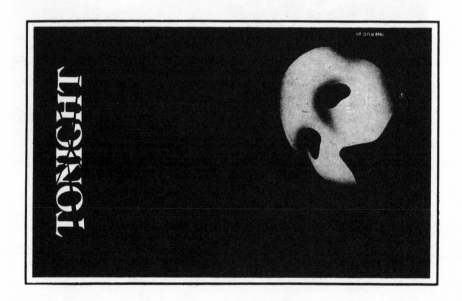

## Types of Display Advertising

Display advertising is any printed promotional piece that uses composition and layout which go beyond straightforward reading material. Rather than text print, it usually employs display type, which is 14 points or larger. Most display advertising incorporates the logo or sig for the product and also—through its composition, layout and graphics—provides further visual and verbal information about the product. Often, the same basic design and copy are adapted for use in different types of display advertising:

1. Ads placed in the print media
2. Brochures
3. Posters
4. Flyers and handbills
5. Heralds (sigs for use at the top of ads, posters, flyers, etc.)
6. 3-sheets (soft-backed sections of an ad for pasting into display frames, such as those on buses and in mass transit terminals)
7. Outdoor billboards

When sketched out on a piece of plain white paper, any ad design looks good. When clipped out of a newspaper and pasted into a scrapbook, it looks even better. But when that same ad appears on a newspaper page, surrounded by a clutter of other ads, photos and news stories, what becomes of it? The same question can be asked about a poster that is crowded into a store window with a dozen other posters. The *context* in which display advertising appears is just as important as the ad itself. Does it stand out beside other display advertising or does it get lost? In regard to the print media, incidentally, the upper right half of the right hand page is considered the optimum positioning for ads (whether in a newspaper, magazine or multipage brochure), because people flipping through a publication seldom look at the left hand page.

Display advertising that contains an ample amount of empty space is likely to be the best attention-getting. While it is important to provide the necessary information about a production or theatre, one must develop a resistance to overcrowding the copy and the composition. Also, letters printed in an unusual yet readable style are attention-getting: script letters, curved letters, letters embroidered with a pattern and so forth. A border that frames the entire ad or a shadow box that draws a heavy "shadow" (usually on the top and right sides of the ad) both help to make an ad stand out on the page. A photograph or graphics design also makes an ad more effective, as does the use of reverse-print typesetting (a graphics device that surrounds the letters with inked space, allowing the letters to be formed by the paper itself).

493

# FESTIVAL THEATRE

**75 MAIN ST. 781-0000**

**Presents**

**NOV. 17, 18, 19, 20, 8 P.M.**

**William Shakespeare's**

# OTHELLO

**Box Office Open 10-5**
**Tickets: $4.00, $5.00, $6.00**
**Phone Orders Accepted**
**Group Rates Available**

1. *Straightforward type and layout.*

**Presents**

**SHAKESPEARE'S**

# OTHELLO

**NOV. 17-20**
**8 P.M.**
**Box Office: 75 Main St.**
**Tickets: $4.00, $5.00, $6.00**
**Phone: 781-0000**

2. *Curved lettering for logo. More white space, less copy.*

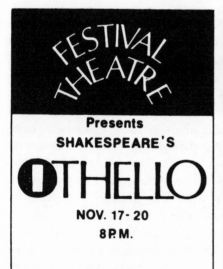

**Presents**
**SHAKESPEARE'S**

# OTHELLO

**NOV. 17-20**
**8 P.M.**

**Box Office: 75 Main St. ( 781-0000 )**
**Tickets: $4.00, $5.00, $6.00**

3. *Reverse-cut logo. Graphic "O" in title.*

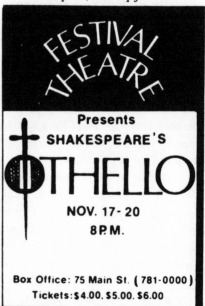

**Presents**
**SHAKESPEARE'S**

# OTHELLO

**NOV. 17-20**
**8 P.M.**

**Box Office: 75 Main St. ( 781-0000 )**
**Tickets: $4.00, $5.00, $6.00**

4. *Shadow box to tie ad together. More elaborate graphic "O."*

These techniques are illustrated by the four display designs for *Othello* that appear on the previous page.

The most striking examples of graphics design for performing arts organizations tend to be those created for dance companies. Perhaps the idea of showing the human condition through body motion inspires the visual artists who design them. In any case, advertising design should not merely follow in the path of tradition, or avoid something new or avoid techniques used by other advertisers in other fields. For instance, one of the advertising methods to become popular recently is the use of postcards—comparatively inexpensive to print and mail and, perhaps even more important in this age of the advertising blitz, very quick and easy to read. Interestingly, the most effective postcards don't merely reproduce the layout and copy from a poster or a newspaper ad; instead, they show a photo or design that, ostensibly, has nothing to do with the performing arts company or production being advertised. They attempt to whet enough curiosity so that one will attend a performance just to discover the connection between the production and the postcard!

The desirability—if not the constitutional right—to locate display advertising in public places such as along highways and on street corners has come under increasing criticism with the growth of environmentalism. Many people feel that visual pollution is as offensive as noise and chemical pollution. Because the arts have always labored to improve the quality of life, arts managers should be sensitive to such issues. Glueing bumper stickers onto cars, inserting flyers under windshield wipers, attaching posters to telephone poles, and leaving handouts where they might blow around should be shunned. Indeed, any method of outdoor advertising should be practiced with restraint, good taste and within legal regulations. However, if permission can be obtained to display street banners, flags, banners towed from small aircraft or other types of advertising display, these might be designed in such a way as to enhance pride in a cultural landmark, help celebrate a local event or commemorate a national holiday.

## Organizing the Information

Before any advertising layout is attempted, it is essential that basic marketing research and planning, as discussed in Chapter 15, be accomplished. Based on that, it is then necessary to select a focused message created to appeal to target markets and then to commission a logo or sig which encapsulates that message in a graphically dramatic way. Ongoing theatre operations should probably focus on the name of their institution—at least through the use of a strong logo—as a unifying factor for all their publicity and advertising. Public loyalty should first be developed toward the institution and then toward the individual productions, so that the nucleus of an audience is there to support whatever productions are offered. When each production is promoted individually, each publicity campaign must build an entirely new audience.Advertising composition must also take contractual billing provisions into account, in the same manner as playbill composition (discussed in the previous chapter).

When the production being advertised is a one-shot deal, as it usually is from Broadway to the local community theatre, incorporating the necessary information into display ads, and then embellishing these ads with a little fancy type or perhaps a photograph, is not too difficult for someone with the right skills. When there is a multi-week, multi-production season or series to advertise, the task is more difficult. And it is most difficult when the season is performed in repertory, which requires presenting a complicated schedule of performance dates that may not adhere to any logical pattern. If productions can be scheduled so that each is at some point in the season offered on a Monday, each on a Tuesday and so forth, then series tickets will at least conform to the same day of the week (although not necessarily every week of the season). Or a series might consist of three or four plays in rapid succession over one or two weeks (an enterprising way to capture playgoers in heavy tourist areas where visitors spend only a week or two). One of the most effective methods of showing a multi-production repertory schedule is to enter the play titles onto a calendar, as shown earlier in the New York City Opera advertisement.

When a play series consists of different productions, each offered for one or more consecutive weeks, the season can be listed in clear, chronological order. Pocket-size schedule cards that customers can keep in a wallet or pocketbook should be printed. Designing the ad copy for this type of season might seem like a simple matter, but compare the four design formats on the following page. The eye can easily follow the chronological order of events in only two of these designs.

It is always wise to test advertising designs on at least a few disinterested readers before going to press. Even experts can develop copy blindness after the subject matter becomes overly familiar—a misspelled name goes unnoticed, the phone number is left out and so forth.

Advertising copy should abbreviate ticket and price information for economy of space, usually the briefer the better. For example:

Ticket Information:
Monday through Saturday at 8:00 P.M.
        Orchestra:    $25.00, $20.00
        Mezzanine: $20.00
        Balcony:      $17.50, 15.00

Wednesday and Saturday matinees at 2:00 PM
        Orchestra:    $20.00, $17.50
        Mezzanine:  $17.50
        Balcony:      $15.00, 12.50

may be reduced to:

Tickets: Mon thru Sat (8:00) $25.00, 20.00, 17.50, 15.00
        Wed & Sat (2:00) $20.00, 17.50, 15.00, 12.50

**1**

| Jan. 4-9<br>The Man Who<br>  Came to Dinner | Jan. 11-16<br>The Fantasticks |
|---|---|
| Jan. 18-23<br>The Odd Couple | Jan. 25-30<br>Dial M for Murder |
| Feb. 1-6<br>The King and I | Ticket Information:<br>———————<br>——————— |

**2**

Jan. 4-9    Jan. 11-16    Jan. 18-23    Jan. 25-30    Feb. 1-6

Ticket Information:

**3**

| Jan. 4-9 |
|---|
| Jan. 11-16 |
| Jan. 18-23 |
| Jan. 25-30 |
| Feb. 1-6 |
| Ticket Information:<br>———————<br>——————— |

**4**

| Jan, 4-9 | ———————<br>——————— |
|---|---|
| ———————<br>——————— | Jan. 11-16 |
| Jan. 18-23 | ———————<br>——————— |
| ———————<br>——————— | Jan. 25-30 |
| Feb. 1-6 | ———————<br>——————— |
| Ticket Information:<br>———————<br>——————— | |

Play promotion customarily includes a descriptive phrase above or below the title of the production being advertised. Sometimes, however, a play or a star is so well-known that such blurbs are unnecessary or even insulting to the reader's intelligence. One need not use a superlative to describe *Death of a Salesman*, for instance, or Dustin Hoffman or Colleen Dewhurst. But in some cases a blurb can provide a clue about the nature of the event, and perhaps motivate people to attend it. Readers like to know if a production is serious or comic, musical or non-musical, new or a revival. This information can be worded into a descriptive phrase, such as "a musical adaptation," "a modern dress version," "a drama of political corruption," "a comedy of gender." Alliteration has been overly used in theatrical promotion, so that blurbs like the following should be avoided: "Marlowe's marvelous melodrama," "Simon's sizzling satire," "Wilde's witty winner!" A straightforward description, a clever play on words, an incisive quotation or a single, strong adjective make the most effective blurbs.

Finally, it should be remembered that different types of display advertising often require different copy and composition in order to speak forcefully to the target market at which they are aimed. For instance, a direct mail campaign may be aimed at three different targets, (1) current subscribers, (2) former subscribers and (3) people who have attended single performances. The brochure or other mailing piece should be adapted to each group. Current subscribers might be given the opportunity of retaining their present seat locations if they renew within a certain period, former subscribers might be offered a special incentive to "return home," and nonsubscribers might be offered a special one-time discount. Similarly, ad copy aimed at seasoned theatregoers can assume that they are more informed about the theatre and its repertoire than others. The more directly and personally an advertising message speaks to the person who receives it, the more effective it will be. But marketing can only achieve this when someone has done the homework.

## DIRECT MAIL SYSTEMS

Direct mail advertising is a proven marketing strategy and often less expensive than media advertising. But the days of the penny postcard are long gone; printing, handling and postage costs are high, so it is now necessary to pay close attention to the validity of each mailing list. This is a three-part process that entails:

1. Creating or obtaining an initial list of correct names and addresses appropriate for specific uses

2. Building on the list by capturing appropriate additions
3. Periodically cleaning the list to eliminate inappropriate names or to correct address information that has changed.

## Creating a Mailing List

The mission, size, and type of organization—together with its marketing policies and strategies—all will influence how its direct mail system is designed. Like planning a budget, the creation of this management tool should involve everyone in the organization who needs to communicate with groups of users by mail on a regular basis. Collecting names for each category of what may be a general mailing list or two (one for sales and fundraising purposes, for example, and one for purposes of media relations) usually begins in-house. The box office should have the names and addresses of all current subscribers, as well as those of recent customers who bought single tickets by mail or credit card. The fundraising office should easily be able to supply correct names and addresses for board members, donors and potential donors. The publicity office should have a basic list of editors and others with whom it communicates regularly. The most valid and valuable lists are those that contain names of current users. But, like all entries on a list, even these should be periodically verified for correctness.

Secondary sources of names for a mailing list may be culled from property tax lists at city hall and acquired from address records kept by chambers of commerce, professional organizations, charity groups and even from the telephone book. However, these should be kept separate from lists of known customers, used less frequently and, as mentioned in a previous chapter, sample tested before being used fully. Finally, one may buy, borrow or rent mailing lists from companies specializing in that business or from publishers, corporations or other cultural institutions. Secondary sources of names, however, are always less valuable than primary sources and—with the high costs of printing and postage—they constitute a gamble that may be little more reliable than slapping money down at the racetrack.

After deciding the types of lists needed and the sources from which they will be compiled, one must decide how these lists should be organized and generated: by zip code, alphabetically, or by user category (alumni, donors, current subscribers, drama editors, and so forth). If a data processing system is not used, the mailing list should be typed onto 3 x 5 cards, color coded by different categories or zip codes, or coded by ink markers of different colors. Hopefully, a computer system is available, and careful thought is given to setting up the field that will determine the various ways in which the list(s) can be generated.

## Capturing New Names

Once a list category has been deemed necessary and has been created with the names of appropriate, known users, additional names of people who fit that category should be added as they are captured. As discussed in Chapter 13, computerized box office systems may often be programmed to capture mailing list information, though this may also be accomplished without computers. Either way, the box office treasurers must cooperate in the endeavor. Ideally, each area or department within the organization will accept responsibility for gathering new names and updating information on captured names to feed into the computer. It is not difficult to do this, but it requires a high level of willingness on the part of those staff members involved.

Another primary source of new names is the audience itself—many of whom may not have had direct contact with the box office. Mailing address forms, such as the one below, can be placed at convenient points in the lobby or stuffed into the playbills.

---

BE THE FIRST TO HEAR ABOUT UPCOMING PRODUCTIONS

(To receive our brochure, please complete this form and place it in the lobby drop box.)

NAME  _____

ADDRESS  _____

_____ ZIP  _____

DAYTIME PHONE: (    )  _____

---

Space might also be provided for the customer to write in the name and address of "a friend who might also like to receive our brochure." Operations attended by tourist audiences should design forms that distinguish between permanent addresses and those that are seasonal or temporary. Theatres that offer different types of attractions should design a form that targets specific programming interests:

---

PLEASE PLACE MY NAME ON YOUR MAILING LIST

I would like to be informed about events in the
categories that I have checked below:

☐ Theatre   ☐ Music   ☐ Dance   ☐ Film   ☐ Children's Theatre

NAME _____

ADDRESS _____

_____ ZIP _____

---

Address forms that are inserted individually into playbills rather than printed as part of them are more likely to be filled out and returned. Attractive desks equipped with pencils and drop boxes should be placed at convenient points in the lobby. The playgoer who is already standing in the lobby is the playgoer most likely to return, so to miss the opportunity of capturing that person's name and address is, at best, shortsighted.

In cases where a single production is being organized (not associated with any ongoing theatre organization), the publicist should attempt to rent or borrow mailing lists belonging to other performing arts companies in the area. One successful Broadway producer, for example, used to deliver flyers about his shows to box office mail order clerks for other shows. Once a ticket was ordered for the other shows, he reasoned, why should the competing producers care if customers received publicity about *his* show?

## Maintaining the Mailing List

If a particular mailing list is used only four times a year at a postal rate of twenty cents and printing costs of eighty cents per piece, one tiny mistake like an incorrect zip code costs the organization four dollars annually. Multiply that by five hundred other tiny mistakes on a list of, say, five thousand names and the organization has an annual loss of two thousand dollars—no longer so teeny! Yet, this type of waste is very common, because so many organizations neglect to maintain their mailing lists in top order.

The first policy decision to be made about list maintenance should concern how current the entries should be—that is to say, how long should the names of inactive users remain on the list? If the list is for sales promotion, and a person on it doesn't purchase a ticket after two mailings, should that person receive a third, a fourth or a fifth mailing? The marketing department should set up a computer program that records the user activity of everyone on every list, giving the ticket buying, contributing, publicity generating and/or volunteering activity of each individual. This enables the organization to track each user and periodically generate special mailing lists for those who didn't renew their season ticket or their annual contribution. Magazine publishers have done this for decades and now, with the advent of inexpensive computers, even small theatre companies can do it, too. But while the computer makes the record keeping simple, the gathering and inputting of information depends on reliable staff members. And even under the best circumstances, it is impossible to track everyone on the list; some active users will always be eliminated because they appear to be inactive. But this is not so serious a problem as repeatedly sending mailers to people who will never respond. And, after all, there is the likelihood that active users who were mistakenly dropped will be recaptured in a brief time.

While bulk postage rates are lower than first class, it may be desirable to use first class so that incorrectly addressed pieces will be returned, although these might also be forwarded to a new address without the knowledge of the sender. The alternative is to send a bulk rate mailing that is labeled "return requested." In this case, incorrectly addressed pieces will be returned with a new address given or an indication of why delivery couldn't be made. The only drawback is that such returns cost nearly twice the amount of first class postage.

When several different mailing lists are being used, there is a good chance of duplication—another possibility for wasted postage.  Duplications may even be found in a single list, because one person's name appears in several ways (John Smith, Jack Smith, J.B. Smith, etc.); the computer may not be able to purge such duplications automatically, so a printout of names in alphabetical order should be made and studied on a regular basis. An easier if more expensive alternative is to print "If you have received a duplicate of this brochure, please hand it to a friend." And, when it is not possible to merge duplicate names that appear on different lists being used for the same mailer, each list might be mailed several days apart so that duplicates won't all arrive in the same mailbox on the same day.

If it begins to sound that creating, building and maintaining mailing lists for an active theatre operation is a full-time job, this is correct—or, at least, it will be part of a full-time job for a data entry person. But the work entailed in keeping correct and up-to-date donor lists, press lists and sales promotion lists of various kinds is an administrative responsibility crucial to the survival of many organizations.

## Mailing Methods

When and how often direct mail lists are utilized depends on the budget available for this purpose and the priorities for communicating with actual and potential users. Current postal rates and regulations are spelled out in booklets available at every post office. Still, rates and regulations change frequently, so it is wise for the manager or marketing director of a theatre to speak personally with the local postmaster. What are the current rates? How should mail be prepared for delivery to the post office? What are the advantages and disadvantages of the various mailing methods?

There are many different bulk (third class) mail rates. Basically, the more post office work done by the sender, the lower the rate. Also, rates are lowest for nonprofit organizations. The three methods of postage payment are:

1. *Precancelled stamps*: these are purchased at the post office and affixed individually by the sender
2. *Postage meter*: the sender must purchase the meter from a manufacturer who also supplies a license application. Then the sender takes the meter to the post office, which sets it as requested and imposes the corresponding postal charge (meters should be capable of being set to the closest one-tenth of 1 percent)
3. *Permit imprints*: a permit number is given by application to the local post office and then printed directly onto the mailing piece at the same time the rest of it is printed; the addressed and sorted bulk mailer is then delivered to the post office together with a mailing statement and the sender pays cash for the corresponding postage

There is an annual mailing fee for the right to use either stamped or imprinted bulk mail methods, and another fee to acquire an imprint number. Permit numbers, however, remain valid indefinitely, providing they are used for at least one mailer a year. All mailings must be handled by the post office where the permit was filed, and each batch must be accompanied by a Statement of Mailing when it is delivered. There is also a Small Volume Bulk Mail Application for mailings that weigh no more than one hundred and forty pounds. The presorting process required for the sender to qualify for bulk rates includes affixing different colored stickers onto the lower left corner of each piece (thereby indicating the destination zone), then banding and sacking pieces for the same zone. Due to the fees and the labor involved in bulk mailing, organizations that send out only one large mailing each year or several small ones may find it cheaper to use first-class postage.

The local post office may be more lenient about regulations than federal rules dictate. As a courtesy gesture, for example, some post offices have even been known to return undeliverable bulk pieces (at least within the local zip code) and ignore the standard additional charge to the sender. In other cases, especially around Christmas, bulk mail may pile up at the post office undelivered—although a few kind words to the postmaster can sometimes hasten its departure.

## Design Considerations

The first decision that must be made when planning a bulk mailer is whether to design it as a self-mailer or as something that will be inserted into an envelope and sealed. The former, of course, is much less expensive to produce and easier to mail—it may be anything from a postcard to a folded and sealed brochure. Whether or not self-mailers are generally perceived as junk mail and generally ignored by recipients is a matter of opinion and, often, design.

Postage rates, of course, increase with the weight of the piece and there are restrictions regarding size and shape. Also, one should be certain that stamps, address labels, typing, handwriting or whatever else might be used will not slip off or rub off, especially when using mailer material such as plastic, Mylar or aluminum. Oversights in this regard have led to some very expensive mistakes!

## Timing

Promotion that is dependent on the United States Postal Service must follow a special clock. Enough time must be permitted to:

1. Prepare, proofread and print the material to be mailed
2. Address sort, label, band, sack and deliver the mailer to the post office
3. Allow for postal delivery
4. Allow for return of any first class ticket orders or other type of RSVP
5. If applicable, allow time for tickets to be mailed from the box office and received by the customer comfortably before the performance date.

If bulk rates are used, a reasonable timetable will require a total of no less than six weeks from beginning to end, and a longer period is usually desirable.

## Hiring a Mailing House

Additional time may have to be added to the schedule when an organization hires the services of an outside mailing house. Such outfits charge according to the amount of mail in each batch and the services they render. They will convert addresses from file cards to computer listings that can generate a printout for periodic checking and revision and adhesive address labels for mailings. It is much more economical when the theatre organization conducts all the list-building and list-maintenance chores, as well as the sorting, bulk mail labeling and bagging chores after the address labels have been printed by the mailing house, although, for an additional charge, the firm would gladly handle the whole process from beginning to end.

It is important to obtain a clear commitment regarding the length of time it will take the mailing house to complete its part of the work. Chances are that the theatre organization will be one of its smallest accounts, so it may not enjoy a very high priority.

## ELECTRONIC MEDIA ADVERTISING

It might be said that we live in the age of the 30-second commercial message. We've become so accustomed to receiving information in this manner that thirty seconds is often the maximum amount of time we're willing to give before we tune out —whether it's the radio or television set, the teacher or the telemarketer, the letter or the brochure. Advertising must express its messages quickly, memorably and often. Advertising in the electronic media must do this with even greater economy of words and images than in print media. It might be said that a media moment is even more fleeting than a moment in the theatre, because it rarely has our full attention and lacks the space or time to build to a crescendo. It is a crescendo out of context. To get the context (which is the whole point of advertising), one must use the product.

Radio advertising is less expensive than television and usually offers the advertiser more production services; radio also provides a simple and fast method for getting a message out to the public and may offer a more specific target market and, therefore, more cost efficiency than newspaper advertising. However, on the down side, radio listeners rarely pay much attention to commercials, often switch to different stations and almost never retain numerical data, such as dates and phone numbers.

Television viewers often *do* pay attention to commercials, represent a much wider audience, and may respond to effective advertising in large numbers because of its dramatic and human impact. Of course, it can take a considerable amount of time, money and talent to produce even a good 10-second TV spot. Few arts organizations can afford the desired frequency needed to insure cost efficiency, and it is often difficult to measure results.

When both radio and television advertising are being planned, the temptation is to create the TV commercial first and then simply turn the audio portion into a radio commercial. But, in view of the above comparisons, it is obvious that the two should be different versions of the same message.

## Radio Commercials

Most radio stations compile demographic information about their listeners and will provide this to potential advertisers. While rates are based on the total number of listeners, the advertiser should be more interested in *who* is listening. Working with a station's advertising rep, a theatre company is likely to buy a package of time that includes a specified number of spots at different periods of the day. Included in this may be trade-outs, introductory discounts for new advertisers, guest participation on certain programs, rudimentary copywriting and production services and the like. To secure the desired time spots, sales contracts should be concluded at least several weeks before the commercials are to be aired, and tapes or scripts of the commercials should be delivered to the station at least a few days before. Most spots are thirty seconds and about seventy-five words long or sixty seconds and about one hundred fifty words long, although 10-second spots may be available at very low rates and aired as fillers at the discretion of the station. It pays to examine the different rates and packages carefully in order to come in on budget and on target.

Unlike writing copy for a press release, writing ad copy—especially for radio and television—can and often should be personalized. The endorsement format in which a well-known celebrity promotes the product is often effective. If there is a star in the production who is willing to make the commercial, this can be effective, or ad copy may be read by an anonymous announcer. The most elaborate commercials are produced on tape and make use of several voices, as well as music and other sound effects. Here is the script for a radio commercial prepared by the Attisano-Levine advertising agency in New York for a Broadway revival of *Born Yesterday*:

BORN YESTERDAY - 60-Second Radio

(Setting: A Congressional Hearing Room.)

(Sound effect: Pounding gavel.)

CHAIRMAN: Order! Order! This Senate hearing regarding the comedy BORN YESTERDAY is about to begin.

SENATOR: Mr. Chairman . . .

CHAIRMAN: Senator, you are out of order!

SENATOR: Mr. Chairman, I believe the American public has a right to know that Edward Asner, who made Lou Grant a household name, and Madeline Kahn, who made me laugh till I cried in "Blazing Saddles" and "Young Frankenstein," are performing certain political acts that we should all investigate.

(Sound effect: Pounding gavel)

CHAIRMAN: Senator!

SENATOR: . . . Allegations of bribery, sexual favors . . .

(Sound effect: Crowd "Oohs")

SENATOR: . . . and corrupt government officials.

CHAIRMAN: Senator, we already know there's some extremely *funny* business going on and Garson Kanin, we believe, is behind it all. But, with a limited number of performances, it's a local matter, out of our jurisdiction. The public will have to judge this for themselves. This show called BORN YESTERDAY, starring Edward Asner and Madeline Kahn, is on its way to Broadway, and we can do something about it then.

SENATOR: Are we to understand, Mr. Chairman, that thousands of people could die laughing and you're going to sit back and watch?

CHAIRMAN: Umm. . as a matter of fact, yes, Senator. I've got front row seats. Ha, ha, ha!

(Sound effect: Pounding gavel.)

VO: BORN YESTERDAY, starring Edward Asner and Madeline Kahn at (name of theatre). For tickets, call 765-4321.

## Television Commercials

Because performing arts events are rarely advertised on television, those commercials that do appear tend to stand out, which, of course, increases their impact. Cost is not the only factor that limits such advertising. Few theatrical producers and managers have much experience with TV advertising and may not be entirely convinced that it is cost effective. Yet there are a number of instances when TV advertising campaigns have greatly increased box office sales and, in some cases, even overcome poor or mixed critical reviews. While the cost of producing a television commercial can rival the cost of producing the show itself, low budget commercials are certainly possible—especially 10-second spots, which can be aired frequently within a cluster of other commercials and can be very effective. Also, if the theatre company places its own television advertising, many stations will deduct the 15 percent commission that would otherwise go to an agency. This is also true of other media outlets and can represent a considerable saving.

The traditional way of developing a concept for a television commercial is to script it out by describing the visual element next to the audio (voice and sound) elements. Then the script may be illustrated on a storyboard, which shows a series of crude sketches depicting the key visual moments and also prints the voice-over or other audio elements directly below them. These are usually arranged on a large, black poster board. The television shooting script followed by the corresponding storyboard of a proposed TV commercial for *Born Yesterday*, prepared by Attisano-Levine, illustrates this technique:

BORN YESTERDAY—30-Second T.V.

| VISUAL | AUDIO |
|---|---|
| (Ed Asner and Madeline Kahn seated at table backstage) | ED: For once, be objective. Which one of us do you think audiences really want to see?<br>MADELINE: Why, me, of course. |
| (Same) | ED: Baloney! Anyway, I've got a bigger part.<br>MADELINE: Yes, but I get more laughs. |
| (Closeup of Ed) | ED: That's debatable. |

| | |
|---|---|
| (Closeup of Madeline, shuffling deck of cards) | MADELINE: Now, why don't we just settle this with a friendly game of cards. |
| (Shot Of Ed and Madeline as she begins to deal cards) | ED: Okay, and whoever wins, gets the biggest dressing room. MADELINE: All right . . . |
| (Cut to "Born Yesterday" logo) | VOICEOVER: See Edward Asner and Madeline Kahn in Garson Kanin's brilliant comedy, "'Born Yesterday" |
| (Cut to closeup of Ed, shiftily eyeing his cards) | ED: Okay, what've you got? |
| (Closeup of Madeline as she lays cards on table) | MADELINE: Four aces. |
| (Closeup of Ed as he eyes cards and puts them on table) | ED: So do I. |
| (Cut to table as we see Ed's hand laying down his aces opposite hers) | VOICEOVER: Edward Asner and Madeline Kahn in "Born Yesterday." |
| (Cut to Ed and Madeline sitting at table arguing) | VOICEOVER: For tickets, call Teletron, 765-4321. |

## TELEMARKETING

The use of the telephone as a marketing tool—telemarketing, as it is called—offers yet another strategy for achieving an organization's declared marketing goals. These often include increasing subscription sales, single ticket sales, group sales, contributions and/or memberships. Like other marketing strategies, telemarketing should be tied to an overall marketing plan and coordinated with other aspects of that plan, such as direct mail advertising and radio commercials. No theatre organization should pour all its marketing resources into a single strategy, however promising it may appear.

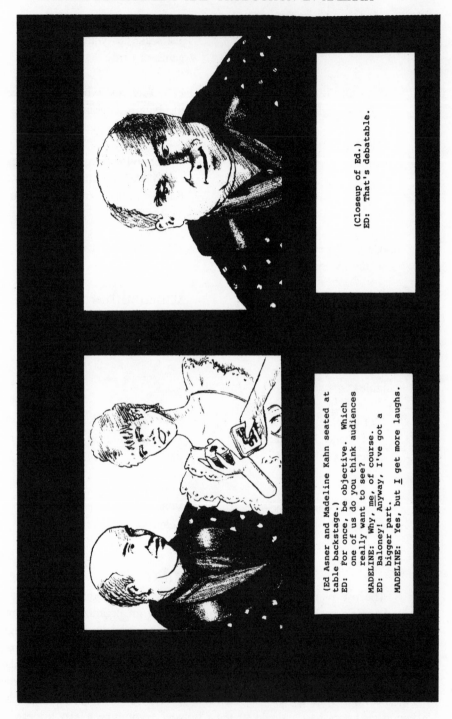

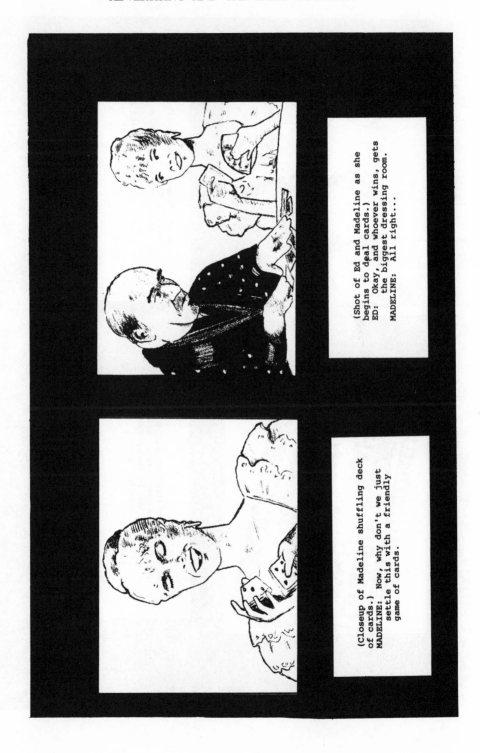

(Shot of Ed and Madeline as she
begins to deal cards.)
ED: Okay, and whoever wins, gets
    the biggest dressing room.
MADELINE: All right...

(Closeup of Madeline shuffling deck
of cards.)
MADELINE: Now, why don't we just
    settle this with a friendly
    game of cards.

Before embarking on a telemarketing campaign, it's a good idea to take a very clear look at some of its problems and disadvantages:

1. Many people regard telephone solicitations as an invasion of their privacy
2. The reputation of an entire institution is being placed in the hands of phone callers who could seriously harm that reputation
3. Poor management of mailing/phone lists can result in annoying calls to current users and multiple calls to the same person
4. Telemarketing is much more expensive than it may at first appear, when one considers costs for personnel, training, equipment, service charges, follow-up and billing
5. Initial results of phone calls are never fully accurate (some people won't honor their commitments)
6. Effective callers, even after careful training, are few and far between.

Telemarketing, like direct mail advertising, has been overused in recent years. Almost anybody with a reasonably permanent address and a phone listing has been inundated by junk mail and an increasing number of junk phone calls. This has decreased the effectiveness of these strategies at best and, at worst, created a backlash against advertisers who use them.

Frustrated by the frequency of wrong numbers, no answers, machine answers, and the like, it wasn't long before telemarketing experts recruited computer dialing and messaging systems to aid their efforts. Computerized telemarketing enables machines to dial countless phone numbers incessantly until they are either invalidated or connected with a human voice. When contact is achieved, the computer can be programmed to activate a recorded message which ends either by asking the listener to call a certain toll-free number (perhaps with a prize or discount as incentive) or puts the listener into direct contact with a live telemarketer. This equipment is out of reach (if not out of character) for most performing arts companies, although it may be used when an outside telemarketing firm is engaged.

Successful telemarketing requires the supervision of a skilled expert. If such an individual is not part of an organization's regular staff, then a consultant should be hired to plan and supervise an in-house telemarketing campaign, or a firm can be hired to handle the whole process, using facilities in-house or conducting the campaign at its own facilities. This last option, of course, means that the theatre won't have to set up the special phone lines and caller work stations required for a sizable telemarketing campaign, although it also means forfeiting direct involvement in the sales process.

## Setting Goals

If a goal of the marketing department is to increase ticket sales for the upcoming season by 10 percent, it might be decided that a telemarketing campaign can achieve half of this. Then, after studying the results of earlier marketing research and such resources as subscriber lists and donor records, target groups should be selected and specific dollar goals determined for each. This may break down as follows:

| | |
|---|---|
| Former subscribers who didn't renew | 1% |
| Single ticket buyers | 3% |
| Names of museum & symphony patrons | 1% |
| Total | 5% |

These percentages, of course, would translate into specific dollar amounts related to ticket prices.

## Estimating Costs

If the decision is made to conduct a telemarketing campaign, it must be decided *how* it will be conducted and *by whom*. Will a private firm or a consultant be hired? What special or additional resources, such as telephones and computer terminals, will be needed? What additional personnel, especially callers, will be needed and will they be volunteers or salaried? And what will be the cost of mailers, postage and other materials related to the campaign? Once the total cost has been determined, this should be compared with the total dollar goal to determine how much it will cost to earn each dollar. This figure can vary enormously. It may even be found that a campaign will cost more than it may reasonably be expected to bring in. A professionally organized and operated telemarketing campaign, however, is likely to cost at least thirty cents of each dollar brought in and as much as eighty cents of each dollar may be justifiable in some cases. After all, it may be even more important to fill theatre seats than to increase income.

## Arranging for Personnel, Equipment and Services

If an outside consultant or firm is engaged, the selection and contracting process should follow that for engaging any other type of outside technical assistance, as discussed earlier in this book. Nonprofit organizations, of course, can seek necessary telemarketing services and equipment in the form of in-kind services. Corporations may be approached, for example, and asked for use of their telephones during evening and weekend hours when they are closed. Or they might provide computer time and services. Telephone companies—now more competitive than ever—might provide free services, especially if they are given credit during each call.

Having professional, paid leadership and support staff is always advisable and it is generally better to employ paid callers rather than use volunteers. Most nonprofit organizations, of course, make extensive use of volunteers and are sorely tempted to involve them in a telemarketing campaign. Yet volunteers tend to be neither as professional—even with good training— nor as motivated as callers who are receiving a salary or hourly wage. And it is even better, in addition, to offer caller teams special bonuses for reaching the goals set for the target group they've been assigned to call. This encourages team work and is more productive than if commissions were offered, based on sales made by individual callers.

## Organizing the Data

As with any promotional effort, success is closely tied to the quality of the research and resulting data. Once target markets have been selected for telemarketing, names and other information must be gathered and organized to make the process as easy, effective and cost-efficient as possible. If the guidelines suggested earlier in this chapter for building and maintaining mailing lists have been followed and if data—such as phone numbers and the history of use in relation to the theatre organization has been captured and recorded, especially from current and recent users—then telemarketing will proceed smoothly. But the data must be correct and up-to-date. Of course the telemarketing process itself will enable the organization to capture additional data, which should then be fed into the user records. Aside from users' names and phone numbers, it is also important to have accurate information about such matters as whether they are past or current subscribers, past single ticket buyers or past or current donors. Telephone scripts are usually based on one or two such assumptions about the users being called.

All this information can be typed onto individual file cards, with a separate file for each target group to be called. Hopefully, the proper merging and purging is done so that no name is contained in more than one file or duplicated within the same file. There should also be space on each card for the callers to record the results of their efforts and also enter comments and new information. Naturally, it is more efficient if these files are contained in a data bank that can be displayed on a terminal in front of the caller and generate whatever forms, payment requests, receipts and late payment notices may be necessary. Or the forms—printed on four or five attached, self-carbon pages—could be generated in advance of the campaign. If printed on 8 1/2 x 11 inch sheets, the top three-quarters of each page might be devoted to (a) data about the user and (b) comments entered by the callers.

The user data should include:

1. Name
2. Home address and phone
3. Work address and phone
4. Name of spouse
5. Spouse's work address and phone
6. Ticket status over past three years (subscriber, etc.)
7. Contribution status over past three years (amounts given and when)
8. Other relationship to organization (board member, volunteer, etc.).

Then there should be simple and clear directions for the caller to enter comments about the following:

1. Date of calls (enter)
2. No answer or person not in (call back)
3. Person moved out of area or died (destroy file)
4. "No, never!" (destroy file)
5. "Not this year!" (retain file)
6. "Maybe." (retain file, send brochure)
7. "Yes!" (enter exact order, including number, location and price of tickets)
8. Amount of additional contribution (enter)
9. Total billing amount (enter)
10. Paid by phone (enter credit card name, number, expiration date, send receipt)
11. Bill (enter billing date, send bill and return envelope)
12. Caller's name (enter).

The bottom third of these form pages might be detachable slips pre-printed with the user's name and address, suitable for inserting directly into business envelopes and of the proper size for the recipient to insert, with payment, into a self-addressed return envelope. If paid by credit card over the phone, the customer merely receives a receipt; if not, a bill is sent. There should also be one or two late payment notices among these forms for use if necessary. This type of system, of course, greatly simplifies the bookkeeping and other paperwork involved in a telemarketing campaign.

## Scripting the Sales Pitch

As with any advertising, telemarketing should be based on an economically worded message that gets the targeted receivers' attention, appeals to them in some way and motivates them to take the desired action. This means that callers should work from carefully developed scripts; however, unlike most play scripts, these must allow for a variety of different responses—like the script for *The Mystery of Edwin Drood*, which allows for sixty-six possible endings depending upon the "whodunit" vote of the audience just prior to the final scene.

A good script will require the caller to accomplish the following:

1. Say "hello" and ask for the appropriate party
2. Identify him or herself by name as well as the organization on behalf of which the call is being made
3. Relate the call to a mail piece recently sent to the listener, if this was the case
4. Relate the listener to the organization, if possible, by using such known data as "current subscriber," "past subscriber," etc.)
5. Make the pitch (for subscription renewal, a contribution, etc.)
6. Offer alternatives, depending on the response, such as a miniseries or lower donation
7. Encourage credit card payment over the phone
8. Confirm all necessary information in detail (name, address, purchase or contribution, credit card information)
9. Conclude the conversation quickly but politely.

Of course the caller may never get beyond the first or second step before the party hangs up in his ear—although experienced callers complain most about reaching lonely folks who try to keep the conversation going for hours. As anyone familiar with improvisational theatre knows, the possible scenarios are endless. The telemarketing script can merely provide a guide for the caller, a reminder to cover all the necessary points and deliver the correct message. Importantly, it should also include within the first thirty seconds an opportunity for the listener to end the call if the product is of no interest. This reduces alienation and can save both parties from wasting a lot of time.

## Training and Monitoring the Callers

Telemarketing involves personal sales techniques, although without any visual component. When selecting the callers, it would be a good idea to interview them over the phone before meeting them in person. Each applicant might be given a script to work with, and the interviewer might create a rating chart that contains five or ten points according to which each applicant is graded. The aim is to select people who have bright, crisp and correct enunciation together with an extemporaneous delivery (the listener shouldn't be able to tell whether the caller is reading or not) and the ability to think quickly.

Telemarketing campaigns are usually conducted over a period of one to four weeks. At least the first day should be devoted to a training session, during which the callers try out the scripts on the supervisors and on each other, then evaluate themselves and the scripts. The personality of each caller should be allowed to modify the scripts, as long as this adds to the effectiveness of the sales pitch. Once the supervisors are confident in the ability of the callers, at least a few sessions should be spent testing the scripts on a segment of, say, 10 percent of the actual target groups. The results should be carefully analyzed. If only a few of the callers are having success, the script is most likely at fault. If only a few of the callers are having *no* success, then *they* are most likely at fault and should receive more training or be eliminated. There should be frequent group discussions during this period. Callers should be encouraged to share their assessment of their successes and failures, and also report on the reactions they're receiving over the phone. The most successful campaigns are run as a group effort, with supervisors serving as coaches, and callers offering tips and encouragement to each other—perhaps to gain a bonus for their particular team.

## Evaluating the Results

Results of a telemarketing campaign should be recorded at least on a daily basis. If these are displayed on a chart for all the callers to see, it may serve as an incentive for increased productivity. Progress charts can also be generated by computer to show a comparison between the number of calls made, the average time spent on a call by each phoner and the average amount of money earned or pledged per call and per hour. When results are superimposed over a chart showing the campaign's daily and weekly dollar goals, it is easy to evaluate the results at a glance. Based on this evaluation together with a system whereby the supervisors monitor the callers and the calls, adjustments and changes should be made throughout the campaign.

## COORDINATING THE SALES CAMPAIGN

This chapter and the previous two have considered the marketing process both in general and in detail. Marketing not only includes promotional activities designed to generate sales, but also includes fundraising and the training and supervision of box office and house management personnel. In a sizable theatre organization, then, marketing responsibilities and activities are extensive and require the work of numerous people. Yet whether two or two hundred people are involved, marketing efforts should be coordinated by one person who is qualified to handle the needs of the project or organization in question. Marketing personnel—from the director to the volunteers—should be aware of the overall marketing plan and how their responsibilities and tasks figure into it. A determined effort should be made to coordinate activities so they will generate the maximum results. When this is not done, people might be working at cross purposes, and one effort might actually compete with or cancel out the effectiveness of another.

Some marketing departments cover an office or conference wall with a huge calendar showing every day of the year or season, with spaces to note activities and deadlines. This may be more effective than merely keeping such a calendar on computer, although both might be useful. A calendar that everyone can see simultaneously is a good tool for use during planning, analyzing and evaluating discussions, because it facilitates decision-making. The sample calendar that follows illustrates how all basic marketing activities for a particular theatre can be placed within a time frame and then studied in terms of cash-flow demands, conflicts, personnel needs, demands on the facility and the relationship of such matters to the production schedule and artistic needs. What this general calendar represents, of course, is the overall, annual marketing plan. The larger and more complex the operation, the greater the coordination must be. In fact, the marketing director may spend most of each day in meetings and conferences that are primarily aimed at—what else—*coordinating!*

Each of the basic marketing activities listed on the sample calendar might have its own more detailed calendar and budget. Both the time frame and the budget estimations should be prepared by the people responsible for executing them, brought to the marketing director, and put on the table for discussion in relation to other marketing proposals and their impact on the budget. It should be expected that most proposals will be revised or rejected, or several proposals may be merged to create a new strategy.

## SUMMATION

Successful marketing is a very creative process and, like the process of creating theatre, is collaborative by nature. It requires that the existence and qualities of a product be communicated in such a way that people will use it. Users include everybody who in some way interacts with the product—whether by helping to make it, fund it, promote it or enjoy it . All such users, together with *potential* users, constitute the market for the product. Marketing, therefore, has many constituencies.

While most of the budget and energies of a marketing department for a theatre will be spent on promotional and fundraising strategies, one should never forget that the end goal of marketing is to enhance the satisfaction and enjoyment of those people who use the product. Artists and administrators

SAMPLE CALENDAR FOR ANNUAL MARKETING ACTIVITIES

**GENERAL MARKETING FUNCTIONS**
Basic market research & analysis
Select concept, focus, targets
Select pricing, packaging
Finish developing budget
Select promotion strategies
Devise calendar of deadlines
Reassessments and corrections
Evaluation
Annual report

**PUBLICITY DIRECTOR (Or Press Agent)**
Teas for focus groups & volunteers
First seasonal press release
Weekly press releases, PSAs, etc.
Playbill copy deadlines
Interviews, guest appearances, etc.
Poster & flyer distribution
Press conferences, luncheons

**ADVERTISING DIRECTOR (Or Agency)**
Mail season brochure
Mail pre-telemarketing letters
Major Sunday newspaper ads
Daily ads in local press
Radio spot announcements
Television commercials
Telemarketing (season tickets)
Mail group sales brochure
Close playbill ad sales
Finalize merchandise orders
Airplane banner-flying

**FUNDRAISING DIRECTOR**
Annual capital campaign event
Individual donor campaign mailer
Individual donor telemarketing
Corporate sponsor performance/banquet
Gov't grant proposal deadlines

WEEKS & MONTHS:

SEPT | OCTOBER | NOVEMBER | DECEMBER | JANUARY | FEBRUARY | MARCH | APRIL | MAY | JUNE - AUGUST

Production #1 | Production #2 | Production #3 | Production #4

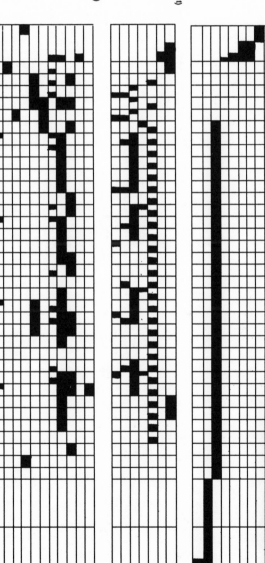

521

should feel pleased about their association with a given production and theatre company, the press should feel confident that they are helping to promote something worthwhile, contributors should feel rewarded for their generosity, and audiences should feel entertained and, if possible, enlightened. There is a great deal more to marketing than placing a few ads in the local newspaper!

# 18

# Facility And Audience Management

THE idea, the artists, the staff, the money, the place and the materials for a theatrical production are brought together and organized for the benefit of an audience. If management has been effective, it will appear that the performance happened of its own accord—like magic! The audience will never know that the roof leaks when it rains, that mechanics are still trying to repair the air conditioning, that the fire marshall is threatening to halt the performance because of inadequate fireproofing on the scenery, or that the manager reached into his own pocket when no other funds were available to buy flowers for the leading lady. The audience arrives, the performance takes place—and nothing unintended should impede audience appreciation. To insure an ideal atmosphere for a performance is the obligation of facility and audience management. This entails two different areas of concern and, often, two different managers: one to manage the physical plant and one to manage the audience.

## FACILITY MANAGEMENT

Most Broadway and Off-Broadway shows as well as most touring productions are performed in theatres that are owned and managed independently from the production company. College and civic theatre organizations may also have little if anything to do with managing the facility in which they perform. On the other hand, most of the professional nonprofit theatre companies as well as stock and dinner theatres do operate their own facilities. When this is the case, a whole new layer of management must be added to the business of producing theatre.

In most cases the landlord—whether an individual, a corporation, an institution or a municipality—assumes responsibility for such basic facility-related matters as:

1. The building itself
2. Building services equipment (plumbing, wiring, heating, cooling and telephone lines) but not the cost of operating it
3. Insurance for the building and its equipment
4. Public liability insurance (the tenant must usually take out additional liability and other types of insurance)
5. Maintenance of the building and permanent equipment.

The company or organization that actually operates the facility—either as tenant or owner—must assume additional responsibilities such as those related to:

1. Janitorial services
2. Building security
3. Purchase or rental of special equipment
4. Purchase and inventory control of building supplies
5. Hiring and supervision of building employees
6. Creation and updating of operations manuals
7. Establishment of emergency equipment, supplies and procedures
8. Supervision and control of facility usage
9. Management and operation of house-operated concessions
10. Contracting and supervision of rented concessions.

Facility management may also include the considerable amount of attention that must be paid when the building as a whole is rented to outside groups. But even when this is not the policy, a busy resident company or multi-purpose facility, such as a campus performing arts center may require careful scheduling to gain maximum use of its available spaces for rehearsals, performances and other in-house activities.

## Setting Policy for Facility Usage

Assuming the theatre organization has full control over its performance facility, it should adopt a set of policies regarding how the facility is to be used and by whom. This will require a close look at the artistic and economic needs of the organizations, as well as the characteristics and use potential of the facility. How much rehearsal time will productions require on the stage itself? How much time will the designers and technicians require on stage? How much time should be allotted to striking each production? Should the theatre be rented for meetings when there is a set on the stage? Answers to such questions will set time limitations on the resident productions and also enable the facility manager to establish a calendar that shows when the theatre and its various spaces are free for rental and other purposes.

If renting space to outside groups is the policy, then the question of whether or not there should be any restrictions on this policy should be settled early on. For example, what if a religious or political organization wishes to rent the theatre? What if a local promoter wants to book in a series of rock concerts? While many theatre companies are sufficiently independent to control such policy decisions, those affiliated with a large institution—like college and civic theatre groups—are often pressured to take in unwanted bedfellows, as it were. What happens when the mayor's office or the college president's office phones and asks to schedule an emergency meeting that would preempt a rehearsal? The board of trustees, together with the chief manager and artistic director should establish the policies that will determine facility usage; neither the facility manager nor some administrator should have to cope with such decisions on a case by case basis. And the more groups or constituents that have access to the facility, the greater the need for clear and prioritized policies will be.

Finally, if outside rentals are permitted, the organization must establish a pricing policy; different rates might be set for different spaces, different times of the day, week or year; and different services included in the rental agreement (such as box office services, the use of a piano or a PA system). Rental rates may be structured as a flat fee, as a percentage of the gross, or according to some other formula.* Based on the pricing policy, a rental rate sheet can be prepared and used by the rental administrator to quote a standard set of fees to anyone seeking that information.

## *The Facility or Operations Manager*

Any sizable facility that accommodates an active theatre organization will require a full-time manager. This person is usually called a facility or operations manager. In some cases, specifically for a presenting organization, the job is combined with that of house manager or hall manager. This chapter deals with facility and audience management separately, although these two areas are closely related and sometimes dealt with as one. An operations manager may also be responsible for the purchase, rental and upkeep of theatrical production equipment, such as stage lighting systems and the power equipment in the scene shop. In yet other cases, the operations person is responsible for the purchase and operation of computer hardware. How the job is defined depends on the resources and needs of the organization and on the skills of the person who is hired.

---

*See also Chapter 10: "Negotiating Booking Fees and Commissions"

## Building Employees

An operations manager may supervise a sizable staff of building employees. Very often, these are unionized workers and, in the case of college- and municipally-operated facilities, their collective bargaining agreement may be such that it's nearly impossible to reassign, retrain or fire them. This presents a major challenge to management. The different types of building employee positions might include:

1. Building engineer
2. Superintendent
3. Heating plant engineer
4. Elevator operator
5. Cleaner (janitor)
6. Ladies room matron
7. Porter (doorman)
8. Groundskeeper
9. Security guard
10. Parking attendant

Some of these jobs may be combined, depending on the nature of the facility. But it is always wise to have at least one person on staff who has solid knowledge and skills in such areas as plumbing, electricity and the mechanics of operating large equipment, in other words, that increasingly rare creature, a jack-of-all-trades. Without this kind of expertise on hand the organization can end up paying high fees for countless service calls made by outside companies.

The hall manager of a presenting organization—who may be responsible for programming as well as facility supervision—would, in addition to the above employees, also hire and supervise the following people:

1. Technical director
2. Stage manager
3. Stage technicians (sound, lighting, etc.)
4. Stagehands
5. Projectionist
6. Box office treasurers
7. House manager
8. Ticket takers
9. Ushers

Or, of course, these employees might be provided by the landlord as part of the rental agreement.

## Operations Manuals

Although discussed in Chapter 4, it bears repeating that there should be an operations manual or "idiot book" for each job in the theatre. These will be especially useful when there is a high rate of turnover in certain jobs, for instance when workers are hired as needed for each performance event or production. It is the responsibility of the facility manager to create these manuals, keep them current and be certain that they are followed in practice. Importantly, manuals should include procedures to follow in the event of an emergency.

## Technical Information Sheets

Any performance facility that rents space to outside groups or that books in guest attractions must prepare several categories of information—and these must be both detailed and accurate. Even when compressed into outline form, the technical information for a 1000-to-3000-seat theatre will probably fill ten to twenty pages. Rental groups and touring attractions depend on this information as a substitute for being at the facility itself, when their productions are being designed and organized. The information should include inventories of available production equipment, diagrams of the stage that show all its dimensions, the house seating plan, and so forth.*

## Architectural Blueprints

Among the most valuable resources in facility management are the architectural blueprints or detailed elevations which were used by the contractors who constructed the facility—as well as blueprints for any subsequent renovations. These should be available at a moment's notice, although stored in a secure place. There should also be copies kept off the premises. Together with engineering plans related, for example, to the electrical system, the telecommunications system or the stage grid system, blueprints can save important time and dollars in the event of a breakdown, emergency or disaster of some kind.

## Security Methods

The security needs at different facilities vary from a good set of lock and keys to an around-the-clock team of security guards and attack dogs. Security is aimed at protecting people and property against assault, robbery and vandalism. The extent to which security precautions are taken will greatly depend on the location of the facility (whether or not it is in a high crime neighborhood, for instance), the nature of the attraction (whether or not it might attract an unruly audience), and a wide variety of special circumstances. Good facility management calls for periodic studies of building security and

*See sample technical information sheet in Appendix D

immediate correction of any perceived problems. A security consultant can often recommend effective solutions to certain problems, although a theatre may also call upon local law enforcement officials for free advice. Many detective units of police precincts employ a security specialist who is available to advise local residents and businesses about crime-prevention techniques.

Basic types of security methods include:

*Protection provided by law enforcement agencies* (the local police, for example, provide armed escorts during transportation of large amounts of cash to and from a bank; the FBI helps investigate bomb threats)

*Protection provided by private security companies* (to conduct a security study, to provide licensed security guards and the like)

*Permanent security equipment* (such as locks, burglar alarm systems, metal detectors and exterior lighting)

*Precautionary security measures* (having performers check all their valuables with the stage manager for safe storage during performances, having all visitors sign in and out of the building with a doorman during certain periods of the day, making employee access to rest room possible only with a key during non-performance hours and so forth).

Usually, a combination of these methods is put into effect. Some should be installed or established on a permanent basis while others will be necessary only under special circumstances. Extra security will be required, for example, if a hugely popular crowd-drawing performer is playing at the facility; if a head of state, popular member of royalty or a famous celebrity is going to be in the audience; or if the material being performed incites certain people to riot or attracts protesters. Management must foresee the need for special security and then take the necessary measures to avoid pandemonium—or worse. Often this entails working with the police, the FBI, the Secret Service, or aids to the personage who is expected to create all the flap. For instance, if the President attends a performance, he must be provided with a special phone line and a security shield in front of his seat. If the Queen of England attends a performance, she must receive a private drawing room with a commode that is equipped with a velvet-covered seat. Such is the breadth of the security business!

## Rental to Outside Groups

Fees earned from renting the facility or spaces within it to outside groups can provide important sources of income. But rentals will also provide additional problems and additional management responsibilities. One of the greatest challenges is to minimize the friction between the resident theatre group or several resident constituents and the rental policy itself. This requires one to understand that most theatre artists want passionately to have a rehearsal/performance space that belongs exclusively to them. Anything less will be regarded as a compromise, a defeat, a betrayal or an inequity. And this is a valid opinion. Everyone who has earned the right to be called a professional has also earned the right to an exclusive work station—the secretary's desk, the manager's office, the scientist's laboratory, the athlete's gymnasium, the actor's performance space. Hence the importance of establishing a rental policy that the resident or primary users of the facility can live with.

Another important matter in relation to rental groups is that of insurance. A theatre organization's insurance policy does not automatically extend to other groups that may use the same facility. So additional coverage must be arranged either by the resident or the rental group, as will be discussed in the next section.

Well before actually renting a facility, the organization should design a standard rental agreement or contract that can be used in all cases. This will require the assistance of an attorney and, preferably, input from each department head in the organization. While a sample rental contract is provided in the appendix, it would also be wise for an organization to study such agreements that have been used by similar operations. Even then, experience with outside rentals will doubtless lead to amendments in the contents of the agreement as time goes on.

## INSURANCE FOR THE THEATRE

When producers, managers or presenters get together, it's not unusual to hear someone ask, "Who does your insurance?" As a matter of fact, insurance brokers are so important to theatre production that they are often given credit in the playbill. However, some producing organizations are not concerned because they are insured through the institution within which they operate or because they are self-insured. Most city and government buildings, for example, carry no insurance, because it is less expensive to absorb damage costs, losses and lawsuits than to pay expensive insurance premiums. Private organizations may be self-insured to a degree, although law requires certain conditions and limitations. And banks require insurance that covers the full replacement value of any property that is mortgaged. Some states operate an insurance pool for small and unusual businesses, thus providing low-rate group protection for participants who are otherwise unable to qualify for coverage. All producing organizations must pay all or part of certain employee insurance, from workers' compensation to any additional insurance mandated by union contracts and agreements.

Like any contract, an insurance policy is only valid in the areas it defines and qualifies. The special jargon used in policies may be difficult for the layman to understand and may even be subject to wide-ranging legal interpretation. The word "occurrence," for instance, provides much broader coverage than the word "accident." While most insurance regulations, including those that govern workers' compensation, are a matter of state law, there are only minor differences from one state to another.

Very often, the producing company does not own the theatre in which it performs. In such cases the landlord probably carries an insurance program to cover the building. This should provide at least 80 percent of the full replacement value (after taking depreciation into account) in the event of destruction. If coverage is written for only one-half of the replacement value, when it should have been written for 80 percent, then a partial settlement would be paid in the same proportion. For example, if a building that should have been insured in the amount of $800,000 was actually insured for only $400,000, and it sustains fire damage which would cost $150,000 to restore, the underwriter would pay only $75,000. While the landlord's insurance usually includes public liability, the typical rental contract between the landlord and the tenant/producing company indemnifies the landlord against any claims related to the company's use of the building. This means that the producer must buy what is known as contractual liability insurance (because it relates to the rental contract). In cases where the tenant is not a corporation and therefore doesn't have the liability protection afforded by corporate status (as is the case with a Broadway show organized under a limited partnership agreement), policies must be carefully written to cover all potential exposures to risk, because the general partners are fully liable out of their own funds. The main risks at many theatres are pilferage, burglary and theft.

Liability insurance rates for a theatre *building* are based on admissions. The premium is first based on estimated admissions and then adjusted by means of an increase or refund at the end of the year when actual admissions are known. Liability insurance rates for a theatre *company* that does not own the building in which it operates are based on the company's total payroll. Insurance brokers usually earn their income from a 5-to-15 percent commission paid by the underwriters with whom they place policies. However, some brokers charge their clients a fee (which amounts to about the same cost as a commission) in order to demonstrate their impartiality in selecting underwriters. Some underwriters, on the other hand, refuse to write policies for less than a certain amount of premium value. Naturally, the cost of the landlord's insurance is handed along through the rental fee and this, together with the cost of the producer's insurance, is handed along through the ticket price. The insurance for a Broadway show—including cancellation of performances due to nonappearance of the star—might cost one-or-two percent of the total gross, although this figure can vary greatly. Writing insurance for an incorporated theatre company that owns its own theatre or is operating under a long-term lease is comparatively simple, because this is a more standard way of conducting a business and thereby understood by more underwriters.

## Selecting a Broker

Because insurance is expensive and lack of sufficient coverage could put an entire operation out of business, it is important to shop carefully for the right broker. According to Robert A. Boyar, whose firm is now a division of Marsh & McLennan, Inc., in New York City, and who is considered the dean of theatrical insurance brokers, the two most important qualities to look for in a broker are integrity and experience. Integrity is required if a broker is to gain a thorough understanding of each client's business, how it works and what the risks are. For this reason brokers are sometimes referred to as risk managers. (Large corporations employ risk managers on their staffs.) They must also exercise integrity in identifying the best underwriter for each policy, which is to say an underwriter who understands the nature of the risks being covered. Without this, the underwriter may refuse the policy, limit the coverage, decrease the commission or increase the premium. A broker who is known and respected by underwriters will also be trusted by them not to misrepresent the true nature of each risk. Like other professionals, brokers tend to specialize in the types of insurance they handle or, at least, the types with which they have real knowledge—medical, maritime, theatrical, whatever. Obviously, theatrical clients should look for a broker with as much experience as possible in the same class or type of insurance—in this case live entertainment and cultural institutions—one with numerous other clients in the same class. Without such experience, the broker won't fully understand the risks, and this will result in higher premiums—sometimes much higher than necessary. But when a theatre organization is one of many theatre clients at the same brokerage, it benefits from all that firm's insurance programs in its class. Incidentally, neither the broker nor the underwriter need be located especially near the client.

Several brokers may be asked to bid for a client's business. This often entails a few long telephone conversations during which the broker attempts to identify the risks to the organization, the amount of coverage it should assume and (a very different matter) the amount it is *willing* to assume. When a broker is selected, there is often an on-site inspection of the place of business or further discussions. Then the broker endeavors to place the policy with an underwriter, who in turn may conduct another on-site inspection. As a result of this process, the client may be asked to make certain improvements or changes in the way business is conducted. Once the policy is in effect, any claims are administered by the brokerage firm; so, once again, it pays to be able to work with a claims manager who is experienced with the class of insurance in question. To expedite insurance claims and provide the best legal protection, the appropriate supervisors of a theatre (company manager, stage manager, technical director and house manager) should be provided with an insurance claim kit that instructs them what to do in the event of accident or other emergency. (See Appendix K)

## Types of Insurance Coverage

Following is a list of the more standard types of insurance related to the operation of a theatre:

*Workers' Compensation:* usually administered by insurance companies, though in some cases by a state-operated fund created by payments mandated for all salaried employees. The law stipulates that employees cannot file suit against employers for work-related injuries (although they may sue any third party that was involved); the benefits for injured workers include various medical services plus, if the person is unable to work, a weekly payment of two-thirds of the worker's salary up to a maximum of $300, a sum that varies somewhat from state to state.

*Employee Pension, Health and Life Insurance:* contributions made by the employer and, often, also by the employee to a pension fund or insurance program; may be voluntary or may be mandated by collective bargaining agreements.

*Disability Insurance:* manditory in certain states, including New York, New Jersey and California.

*Comprehensive Liability Insurance:* covers injuries to the public and also property damage.

*Automobile Liability and Property Damage:* a minimum amount of coverage is mandated by each state; may be extended to include vehicles used but not owned by the company or to cover drivers under age 21; provides coverage for claims against the theatre organization.

*Fire Insurance and Extended Coverage*: to protect buildings and their contents; rate determined by location and condition of the property; mandatory if property is mortgaged.

*Boiler and Machinery Insurance*: coverage for large heating, air-conditioning and other expensive machinery in the building.

*Theatrical Property Floater*: floater policies were first created as a type of marine insurance to cover things that are literally floating around on a boat; a theatrical property floater covers risks to lighting equipment, scenery, costumes, properties, exhibitions or art works in the lobby, etc.; can be extended to cover all such property during a tour.

*Inland Marine Insurance*: to cover risks to canvas tents, movable theatre chairs, etc.

*Business Interruption*: (also called "extra-expense insurance") covers loss of business income as well as expenses incurred under certain conditions, such as destruction of the place of business, of stage scenery or costumes, illness of the star or failure of computerized systems.

*Rain Insurance*: a specific type of business interruption insurance to cover outdoor performances.

*3-D Bond and Theft Insurance*: coverage against dishonest employees, embezzlement, depositor's forgery, forgery, hold-up (whether on the premises or in transit to or from a bank), lost money and securities, etc.

*Fidelity Bond*: covers defalcation by dishonest employees only.

*Personal Effects Insurance*: required by Equity to cover personal property, furs, clothing and jewelry of actors, when such items are in the theatre or with the actor on tour.

*Extraordinary and Ordinary Risk or Peril Compensation*: required by Equity when a performer is asked to execute some unusual physical feat; or just to cover employees for ordinary risks of employment, and thereby provide benefits over and above that guaranteed by workers' compensation.

*Travel Insurance:* Actors' Equity requires that its members be covered with $150,000 in accidental dismemberment and death insurance during travel to meet their contractual obligations.

*Products Liability Insurance:* against public liabilities in relation to concessions products; this should be paid by the operator or lessor.

*Coat Room Insurance:* to protect against loss or theft of checkroom holdings, for which management is held liable (*even when there is a sign disclaiming responsibility for items lost or stolen from the checkroom*).

*Nonappearance Coverage:* to indemnify the producer for expenses in the event a star performer does not appear or a unit attraction does not perform as contracted.

*Copyright Infringement:* although playwrights in theory indemnify producers by claiming that their work is original, they rarely have the resources to pay the legal costs of fighting claims of plagiarism, so the producer or theatre company producing a new work often takes out this type of coverage.

For most of the above types of insurance, the question of deductability will arise. Should fire insurance, for example, cover damage over the first $500 or $1000, or some other figure? Should business interruption or nonappearance of the star exclude the first one or two performances lost, and how many lost performances should be covered? The answers arrived at between the producer and the broker obviously influence the cost of the premiums. It's a vexing process because there is always a temptation to gamble against adversity and take out less than optimum coverage. But when the theatre is in flames or the balcony caves in, when the computerized turntables on stage don't work or the star literally breaks a leg, there is nothing more reassuring than full insurance coverage.

## AUDIENCE MANAGEMENT

### *The House Manager*

On Broadway and at commercial theatres on the road the house manager, as the term implies, works for the house, which is to say for the landlord. The house manager is the landlord's on-site representative responsible for supervising all the other front-of-house employees who are also contracted by the landlord: treasurers, ticket takers, directors, ushers, doormen, matrons and maintenance personnel. A key responsibility of the house manager in commercial theatre is to check and verify the accuracy of each box office statement before the end of the performance. This is done in the presence of the company manager, who is the *producer's* on-site representative. In unionized theatres, both the house manager and the company manager are members of ATPAM.* The majority of professional theatres in America, however, do *not* fall under ATPAM jurisdiction. For this reason, the duties of a house manager vary considerably from theatre to theatre. For example, in college theatres the house manager probably only works for the hour before a performance and during the performance and is only charged with supervising the ushers and dealing with whatever special circumstances may affect the audience. In community, stock, dinner, and small professional theatres the house manager might also fulfill other jobs—perhaps in the press office or the box office. And, as mentioned earlier, the house manager may also be given most of the facility management responsibilities. But the basic duties most often assigned to the house manager in most operations include:

1. Supervise front-of-house personnel:
   a. assistant house manager
   b. ticket takers
   c. ushers
   d. elevator operators
   e. rest room matron
   f. checkroom and other concession attendants
   g. security guards
   h. doorman
   i. parking attendants
2. For payroll purposes, verify the hours worked by the employees listed above
3. Arrange for a house physician to be on call
4. Coordinate ticket taking with box office and ticket-taking systems and needs
5. Supervise cleanliness and sanitary conditions of audience areas
6. Maintain safety and fire laws in audience areas and generally enforce house rules
7. Oversee special customer services (water fountains, rest rooms, concessions, pay phones, etc.)
8. Coordinate curtain times with stage manager through house warning bells and communications with backstage
9. Handle special customer problems regarding seating, disruptions and emergencies
10. Check all audience areas before they are opened to the audience and after each performance

---

*See also Chapter 5

Before each performance, the house manager should tour all the public areas of the building personally *as if with the eyes of a customer seeing them for the first time*. Is the lobby floor clean? Is the furniture dusted and polished? Are curtains, seat covers and draperies neatly arranged? What is the auditorium temperature? Are all the light bulbs working? Are there any accident traps (such as loose carpeting, unlighted steps, insecure railings, or sharp edges on seats)? Theatres tend to use soft interior lighting, and janitorial employees tend toward blindness; so a house manager should make these daily inspections with the critical eye of a disapproving mother-in-law. Older theatres, especially, require scrupulous cleaning if they are to look fresh and neat. And a theatre must be ventilated frequently with fresh air to avoid building up a musky, unpleasant odor—particularly between matinee and evening performances and after long rehearsal periods.

Qualifications for the administrative personnel in theatre have been discussed in Chapter 4; and the behavior of staff members who deal with the public has been described as a critical marketing tool. But the importance of how a theatre staff greets the public cannot be overemphasized. Almost as soon as a visitor walks into a theatre, that person can sense the kind of operation it is. Staff members, from doormen to managers, from ushers to performers, immediately convey an attitude of one kind or another. This invariably emanates from the top manager, if not from the producer or board of trustees. It might be an attitude of confidence, arrogance, vitality, informality, confusion, carelessness, pride, professionalism, amateurism or a combination of these. And it begins to condition the theatregoer's reaction to a performance even before the curtain goes up. The attitude of the staff is reflected in both dress and behavior. Employee uniforms for ushers, ticket takers and others are becoming a thing of the past, at least for small operations; however, in large auditoriums, uniforms are helpful simply by making it easy to identify house employees. When uniforms are not used, some identifying garment may be worn, such as a vest, jacket, apron, sash or even a flower in the lapel. Standards of attire may be changed from production to production in order to reflect differences between them and help prepare the audiences for what they are about to see. Generally, however, it is sufficient if front-of-house employees are courteous, efficient and appropriately attired. But this requires close supervision by the house manager. A well-known general manager at one resident theatre personally lines up the entire front-of-house staff before each performance and checks everyone's grooming, from shoeshine to fingernails.

## The Rules of the House

Virtually every theatre should establish and uphold a series of house rules; these should be printed in the early part of each playbill, and the rules that are especially difficult to enforce should be further emphasized with printed signs in appropriate places. Some rules, such as those regarding smoking, reflect municipal and state laws. Others, such as those prohibiting the taking of photographs or the making of tape recordings during perform-ances, relate to federal laws governing copyright protection and piracy. And others, such as the delayed seating of latecomers, merely reflect the policy of the individual theatre. The most common matters about which house rules might be formulated are:

1. Smoking, eating and drinking
2. Cameras
3. Tape recorders
4. Seating policy
5. Ticket refund and exchange policy
6. Standing room
7. Wheelchair accommodation
8. Lost and found articles
9. Emergency procedures
10. Audience services (checkrooms, phones, drinking fountains, rest rooms, etc.).

## Seating the Audience

The larger the audience, the more supervision and control are required over the flow of human traffic. But even with an audience of only fifty-to-one hundred people, patrons need guidance in getting from the street through the lobbies and into the correct theatre seat. Everything possible should be done to insure that public transportation and automobile parking systems are adequate to handle the entire audience in the hour or half-hour before each performance. Are there comfortable places where early customers can wait? What is the policy regarding latecomers, and have ticket buyers been fore-warned about it? When should the lobbies be opened? When should the auditorium be opened? When should the curtain go up? Questions like these should be settled well in advance. Knowing that a sizable number of theatre-goers will arrive late (due to traffic or parking delays, or some other reason), some theatres maintain a policy of beginning performances ten or fifteen minutes *after* the advertised curtain time. (As a courtesy, media critics and VIPs should be told the exact curtain time.) Other theatres make a point of taking the curtain up on time, exactly as advertised. Lengthy curtain delays, of course, have a negative impact on audience psychology.

The flow of audience traffic should be easy and comfortable, although it is important to aim for a certain crowding effect. Nothing is more deadly than a mere handful of people standing around a cavernous lobby or scattered around a huge auditorium. When this happens, the concept of "audience" is destroyed along with any possibility of group reaction to the performance. An experienced house manager will be able to sense when a crowd of people in a lobby is psychologically ready to assume their theatre seats. A healthy amount of lobby crowding creates an excitement and sense of anticipation which peak at a given moment—and that is the moment when the house should be opened. Theatres that contain restaurants, cocktail lounges and other concessions will find that concession sales decrease as soon as the house opens and, if audiences members are busily patronizing the concessions, should open the house later than theatres without such facilities— or suffer the wrath of some very disgruntled concessionaires!

Along with the attitude of front-of-house staff, theatre lobby activities and concessions help determine audience reaction both to the theatre and to the performance. The types of concessions on hand and how they are managed can enhance or dampen the experience of theatregoing. Lobby ambience and decor are also important. For example, the sound of a piano playing, of glasses clinking, champagne bottles popping, and the sight of a burning fireplace or flashbulbs going off are things that put most people in a festive, relaxed mood. Of course this may not always be appropriate, but some kind of pre-performance atmosphere *is* appropriate, and this should be determined and even fabricated where it does not exist (the fire doesn't have to be real, the staff member exploding flash bulbs needn't use a loaded camera and the champagne bottles being popped needn't contain the real stuff). In short, theatricality need not be confined to the stage.

The architecture of a theatre will dictate how many ticket takers, directors and ushers will be necessary to seat an audience quickly and efficiently. The physical point at which a customer must make a decision about how next to proceed is exactly the point where an usher or director must be stationed. Customers should never have to guess whether they should go upstairs or down, right or left, whether they should proceed or wait for an usher. Most of all, when reserved seating is used, theatregoers should never be left alone to find their own seats. Too many will occupy incorrect seats and create embarrassing problems when people with the right tickets for those seats arrive. There is a peculiar quirk of human nature that seems to compel people to hold their ground once they have established it as their own. Call it "squatter's rights" or "territorial imperative," theatregoers are loath to move once settled in a theatre seat. And, it seems, those most loath to move are those who are asked to do so after the curtain has gone up. It is far easier to seat people correctly in the first place.

Many theatres have adopted the policy of not seating latecomers until

appropriate intervals in the performance. Some productions begin with particularly quiet or sensitive moments, and this situation should always prohibit people from being seated. Theatres with continental seating, where each
row may contain as many as sixty or seventy seats without aisle separations,
almost automatically prohibit seating of latecomers except during scene
breaks or other appropriate moments. When it is the policy not to accommodate latecomers, this should be stated on a lobby sign, on the printed ticket
and, wherever possible, in advertising.

There should be some system for warning the audience that the performance is about to begin or resume. The least expensive and crudest way
to do this is to flash the lobby lights on and off. Better to install an electri-
cally operated gong or bell that can be controlled by the house manager and
heard in all audience areas of the theatre. And there should be a house phone
or cordless system that enables the house manager to speak with the stage
manager at all times. This will prevent the house manager from seating the
audience too early if there are delays backstage and, similarly, prevent the
stage manager from calling "places" if there is a delay in seating the house.
And under no circumstances should the curtain rise before the house manager instructs the stage manager to proceed.

The length of an intermission will vary according to:

1. How many intermissions are scheduled during a given performance
   (usually the more that are scheduled, the shorter they should be; the
   first intermission should be the longest)
2. The length of performance time before the intermission (the longer
   the performance time, the longer the intermission should be)
3. The size of the audience (the smaller the audience, the shorter the
   intermissions should be)
4. The availability of concessions and rest room facilities (not until after  concessions have served all customers and after rest room facilities have emptied should the performance resume)
5. Extenuating circumstances (more intermission time may be required
   for complicated scenic or costume changes; intermissions may be
   shortened or eliminated at certain performances to avoid paying
   union overtime rates, or to allow sufficient time between two closely
   scheduled performances to meet union requirements)

When a playgoer moves from the lobby into the house, the first person encountered should be the ticket taker. To insure that torn ticket stubs
will be obtained from all customers, the first entrance into the house should
be no larger than the width of two standard doors. The ticket taker should

greet each customer verbally and might also instruct each where to proceed next ("inside to your right," "up the stairs to your left," "please wait for an usher to seat you," and so forth). Directors should be stationed at each stairway, aisle or turn to examine ticket stubs and instruct the customers where to go next. It is usually more efficient if patrons wait at the top of aisles for ushers to seat them, and large theatres may station ushers at two or three points progressively further down an aisle. All ushers should keep an eye out for customers who are trying to seat themselves without assistance. One good way to prevent this is to make playbills available only from the ushers. If customers can pick them up behind the last row of seats, they will be more tempted to seat themselves. The house staff should also enforce house rules by being on the lookout for people walking into the theatre with a camera, a drink, a Chihuahua or whatever. In European theatres it is sometimes the custom to reward ushers and box office treasurers with gratuities. When this occurs in American theatres, the employee should be allowed to keep the gratuity.

Before each performance, the ushering staff should be given individual intermission assignments for opening and closing doors, for turning on and off manually operated house lights and other such chores. Similarly, the house staff must be thoroughly familiar with procedures to follow in case of an emergency or unusual occurrence. And it is wise to caution the entire front and backstage staff about deportment during performance hours, emphasizing the following rules:

1. Never run or shout in audience areas because this can cause panic— especially in the event of a real emergency
2. Never use the auditorium to gain access to or exit from the backstage area
3. Performers and backstage personnel should always use the stage door, never lobby or house entrances
4. Backstage employees should always report the presence of strangers or unauthorized visitors
5. Backstage personnel should never be seen in audience areas during performance hours except in cases of emergency.

The best management is usually the least conspicuous management. Theatregoers like to be serviced efficiently but unobtrusively. The front-of-house staff can be friendly without being obnoxious or pushy. The house manager and front-of-house staff really comprise the official host of an event, of an evening out. Like the host at a good dinner party, the house manager must keep things going, keep people moving, cover for any mistakes or deficiencies, try to make each guest feel like the most honored guest, and help each one to go away with the belief that the evening has been a smashing success. This takes sobriety, diplomacy, organization and an awareness of others. The truly accomplished theatrical house manager, like the accomplished host or maitre d', is a rarity.

## SPECIAL AUDIENCE CONDITIONS

Special problems frequently arise during public performances. A latecomer argues with the head usher, someone in the fifth row center becomes ill during the second act, the air-conditioning system develops a case of whooping cough, someone in the balcony begins using a flash camera. These and countless other occurrences are common, and someone with authority on the theatre staff must be present to handle them immediately.

### In Case of Fire

Perhaps the most serious and potentially dangerous threat to an audience is fire. History has recorded a long series of theatre fires that have killed thousands of people and have made the public rightfully aware of danger whenever smoke invades a public gathering place. Following the Brooklyn Theatre fire in 1896, which killed over three hundred people, the actor-manager Steele MacKaye and other innovators developed methods for fireproofing stage scenery and invented folding safety seats for the audience. Modern technology, of course, has vastly improved upon materials, devices and structures to further reduce the threat of fire in public buildings. But the threat has yet to be eliminated, and countless plays continue to be produced in antiquated or wooden buildings that are hardly less susceptible to fire than those in use a hundred years ago. Even the truly fireproof theatre (if it exists) is not immune from the disaster and loss of life that can result from mass panic; for good reason, it is illegal to shout "Fire!" in a public place unless there actually is a fire. All it takes is a smoldering cigarette or electrical wire to cause hysteria and disaster.

Insurance companies and building inspectors are extremely strict about enforcing public safety laws and regulations, but complete enforcement depends upon the theatre management itself. When a producing organizations enjoys a sell-out, for instance, it can be unbearably tempting to place extra chairs in the aisles, to exceed the legal limit of standees and allow people to sit on aisle steps. When stage properties are added at the last minute, or scenery is late in construction, it is easy to overlook fireproofing measures. When stage directions call for a completely dark theatre in order to create or enhance some special effect, there is a temptation to cover or extinguish the aisle and exit lights. In the nation's busiest theatre capitals, a fire inspector virtually sits on the scene designer's shoulder, but this is not usually the case elsewhere. Just as the theatre manager holds the customer's advance sale ticket money in trust, so the manager holds the customer's safety in trust.

While no one likes to anticipate a theatre fire, it would be foolhardy for management not to formulate procedures for the staff to follow in the event of fire or some similar threat to the audience. Fire rules should be posted on the actors' call-board backstage and should be distributed to all personnel. At some time before the first performance, the stage manager should assemble the cast and production crew to review emergency regulations, and the house manager should review emergency procedures with the house staff before *every* performance. Ushers should be stationed at key points throughout the house so that exit doors can be opened quickly during a performance if necessary. Importantly, the stage manager and the house manager should be the only people authorized to institute emergency measures during performance hours and they must communicate any such intention to each other. Obviously, a very cool head is required. When does a threat become a true emergency? What should be done to protect the public, when should it be done, and how should it be done?

It is not unusual in theatre for some harmless occurrence to appear like an impending disaster. For example, a broken fan belt in a heating or air-conditioning system may suddenly flood the air with smoke-like fumes. If cigarette receptacles are not cleaned out constantly, they will begin smoldering. If audience members are not scrutinized as they enter the auditorium, somebody will get through with a burning cigarette or cigar (producers, directors and playwrights nervously puffing away in the back of the house are likely to be the worst offenders).

When an audience *perceives* a threat to its safety, however innocent the cause may be, its fears should be allayed at once. The quickest and most direct way of doing this is for the stage manager to make an announcement from the stage or over the public address system. This should be done in a calm, reassuringly apathetic voice, and the message should minimize the danger: "Ladies and gentlemen, it seems the fan belt that operates our stage revolve has developed difficulty and is creating the odor you smell in the air. But we'll endeavor to go on with the performance while our stagehands repair it, if you'll just bear with us." Much better than: "Don't panic, ladies and gentlemen. There is no fire in the theatre; just a little difficult with some of our machinery." The word "panic" can sometimes cause panic because it suggests danger. If such announcements can be delayed until an intermission or scene break, all the better. The house manager is in the best position to judge the audience mood and determine whether or not such an interruption is desirable, so the stage manager should never take such action alone. As often as not, a situation like that seems much worse backstage than it seems to the audience.

When the emergency is a real one and it is advisable to get the audience out of the theatre quickly, it is even more important to follow a cool and relaxed procedure. If the performers can be alerted to the situation, they will be able to bring the performance to a normal-appearing halt, and the curtain can be brought down as if it were a scheduled intermission or scene break. The house lights should come up at once, and the house manager and staff should immediately open all exit doors. Many people will leave automatically and others can be coaxed out in quick fashion by ushers telling them, "Please clear the auditorium for this intermission—please clear the theatre."

Often a performer is more reassuring than a staff member when it comes to announcing difficulties or emergencies, especially if speaking from the front of the auditorium itself and not from the stage or in front of the stage curtain. It is difficult to say why this is true, but perhaps a complete break from character and the surprise of seeing a performer in the house somehow creates a sense of security among audience members. In any case, it is the exact antithesis of someone running onto the stage during a performance and shouting "Fire!" There is no emergency that requires *that* kind of announcement, but a well prepared staff is the only assurance against such an insane deed.

## Power Failure

The advent of a power failure that plunges a crowded theatre into sudden darkness is a major threat to public safety. New theatre complexes usually have emergency generator equipment capable of supplying the whole electric system if public utilities fail, and all new theatres are required by law to install and maintain emergency lighting devices in the public areas of the building. These may be simple, battery-operated spotlights, or they may be connected to an emergency generator. In either case, they must be rigged to become operative immediately, if normal electric power fails. The presence of emergency lighting precludes the possibility of an audience suddenly being thrown into total darkness.

As Broadway producers found after the famous blackout of 1965, there is no regular insurance or legal recourse for recovering income lost due to the failure of public utilities—or for not paying union employees for work losses during such periods. Small theatres, by stocking up on candles (the type which contain the flame within a glass canister) or battery-operated lights, might be able to continue performances without normal lighting equipment. Large theatres have greater difficulty in protecting audiences and should remember that there are times when the curtain must go *down*. Often, a power failure is of short duration, so a pause or intermission should be allowed to continue for twenty or thirty minutes before any decision is made about sending the audience home. When this happens, the audience should first be instructed to retain their ticket stubs for a refund or exchange. It is unwise to keep on hand the cash equivalent of a night's receipts, so extensive refunds are usually impossible at short notice.

## National Emergency

It is much easier for management to react to a national emergency when it occurs before a performance rather than during one.Whether or not to cancel subsequent performances can be deliberated carefully, and the appropriate people can be consulted. But what if the emergency occurs during the first act of a performance and the audience will be certain to learn about it during intermission? In this case, management has a responsibility to uphold public trust and announce the situation at the conclusion of the act. In the event of a presidential assassination or some other equally momentous occurrence, the audience should be sent home. Refunds will not be required or demanded. The alternative is to inform the audience of the situation and announce that the performance will continue after, perhaps, observing a moment of silence. Management should also remember that the performers are as likely to be affected by shocking news as the audience, so this must also be taken into account. Traditionally, most theatres remain closed on days designated for national mourning.

## Illness of a Performer

The reason for employing understudies is to prevent performance cancellations when performers are taken ill, either before or during a performance. Whenever a performer is replaced, however, an announcement to that effect should be made from the stage (this is a requirement if union performers are involved).* Theatrical tradition dictates that the illness or even the death of a performer shall not, unless absolutely necessary, cause the cancellation of a performance. Understandably, there have been cases when this tradition has been broken. When singer Leonard Warren died during a performance at the New York Metropolitan Opera, General Manager Sir Rudolf Bing stopped the performance and dismissed the audience. More recently— also at the Met—a member of the audience committed suicide by jumping from the top balcony into the orchestra during an intermission of a performance that was being broadcast live to a national radio audience. The audience at the theatre, of course, saw what happened and was eventually sent

*See also Chapter 16

home. The radio audience was never told why the rest of the performance was cancelled, as this might have encouraged other people to seek national attention by disrupting a live broadcast.

A common precaution in regard to the illness of a performer or audience member is to retain a house physician who can be reached quickly if needed. However, it is often quicker and more efficient to rely on the emergency medical units through which paramedics and ambulances may be summoned at any hour.

First aid equipment should be placed both backstage and in some front-of-house location where it is easily accessible. There should be an emergency cot backstage (another union requirement), and a cot or couch in the public lounge area. Also, it is wise for the theatre to invest in a stretcher and a wheelchair, either of which may suddenly be required. Although the Good Samaritan law protects laypeople against prosecution for medical malpractice, only a minimum amount of first aid should be applied until professional help arrives, and a seriously ill or injured person should never be moved more than is absolutely necessary.

### Illness of an Audience Member

If debilitating illness of performers is rare, illness of audience members is quite common. This may be true because so many arrive having indulged in too much food, liquor, sun or tourist activity. Heart attacks, epileptic seizures, drug reactions and upset stomachs are phenomena known to seasoned house managers. When someone becomes so ill during a performance that they must be removed from the theatre, this should be done as quickly and unobtrusively as possible. If no wheelchair is available, several staff members should, if possible, position the victim in a simple, armless chair for conveyance up the aisle and to the lobby until medical help arrives.

When anyone on the theatre premises is involved in an accident, however minor, that person should complete an accident report form.* Theatrical unions and workers' compensation laws require specific forms for this purpose that are available through insurance companies, which will also supply accident report forms for completion by audience members involved in accidents. If such forms are not completed soon after an accident occurs, the theatre may be exposing itself to lawsuits that could have been avoided. Similarly, it is always wise to require an accident victim of any kind to receive immediate medical attention so that the nature of the injury can be legally established at a later time, in the event of a lawsuit or insurance claim.

### Contacting Members of the Audience

If it is necessary for management to locate a member of the audience

---

*See sample in Appendix K

during a performance, some methods for doing this are better than others. When a playgoer who is sitting in the theatre is tapped on the shoulder by an usher and told there is a phone call in the front office, the unexpected nature of this news will make the customer think the worst: the house is on fire, something has happened to the children, someone has had an accident. It is highly probable that the playgoer will react by shouting "What?" or "Oh, my God!" or some similar exclamation. On the other hand, if the playgoer is told that someone outside wishes to speak with him or her, this will probably be regarded as curious but not especially threatening. The point is to get the customer out of the audience before anything is said about a telephone call or before relaying any messages or information.

The biggest problem related to phone calls for audience members is usually that of trying to determine how important the matter is. Frequently, there are phone calls from children or babysitters who are merely frightened about something or can't find something. If the caller is reporting a serious accident, management must try to determine if the playgoer's *immediate* knowledge of it is necessary. Chances are there is nothing the customer can do about it anyway. Deciding whether or not to interrupt somebody during a performance is a matter of weighing an individual's welfare against the welfare of the entire audience. Very few emergencies are great enough to notify an audience member before the next intermission, at which time ushers may be stationed at each exit to page the individual concerned. During a performance or, preferably, before the curtain rises, ushers may also be instructed to page a person orally but quietly as they walk slowly down the aisles. Before this is done, of course, the box office should be checked to see if there is a record of the person's name and seat location. Unlike many movie theatres, live theatres virtually never interrupt a performance to page an individual from the stage.

## Drunks, Druggies and Demonstrators

Unhappily, public exhibitionism in a theatre is not always confined to the stage. Disturbances caused by individuals in the audience are common and varied. As often as not, rowdiness stems from alcohol or drug abuse— and such abusers can be exceedingly difficult to handle. Attempts to reason with such people often increases their antagonistic behavior. And their companions are often not helpful in calming them or removing them from the theatre. An usher might try informing the disruptive person that someone is waiting to see him or her at the back of the theatre. Whatever tactic is used, the situation should be approached with caution, since violent and injurious behavior is a real possibility.

More serious than drunks and druggies is planned or organized disruption of a performance. Foreign artists and touring companies have frequently been the target of protesters who seek publicity by staging a demonstration during a performance. The news media would do a great favor to the cause of culture and international relations by refusing to report such disturbances. Many is the time that audiences have been denied their privilege of enjoying visiting artists because performances are interrupted by hecklers and protesters. Leaflets are thrown from balconies, demonstrators line up to chant slogans from the stage, and even bomb threats are made to terrorize audiences and intimidate managements. When disruptions such as these can be anticipated, it is the obligation of management to arrange for special security guards and police protection. In some cases the State Department has ordered federal agents to accompany and protect foreign artists and, if management expects serious trouble, it should request the best and fullest protection available. No member of a theatre staff is trained to handle organized protesters and none should be asked or allowed to attempt this. As soon as a demonstration of any serious intensity begins, the performance should be stopped and the police called in at once. An intermission should then take place, followed by an announcement that everything is under control and time to allow the audience and the performers to regain their composure. As with drunks and druggies, demonstrators are also incapable of listening to reason. Once such people begin a disturbance, the best and possibly the only course is to get them out of the theatre as quickly as possible. The action taken should be swift and decisive, and absolutely no time should be wasted on trying to placate or calm the disrupter.

## Funny and Unusual Occurrences

In live theatre, as in any other situation involving live human beings, adherence to a formal script or format has its limitations. If someone throws a rotten tomato at a performer, the audience expects the unfortunate victim to react like a living person, not like a mechanical doll or the image on a motion picture screen. When the audience is exposed to some disruption in the house, so is the performer on stage. This often requires theatrical illusion to be broken—a principle that holds equally true for both funny and unfunny occurrences. When a performance is interrupted by the sound of a jet flying overhead or sirens outside, or an actor's trousers accidentally split up the back in plain view of the audience, it is best for the performer to acknowledge the situation with a pause, a knowing look or an *ad lib*. Such acknowledgement is the *only* way to erase the occurrence from the mind of the audience or, at least, to assure the audience that it is not alone in its awareness of the incident.

Sometimes also there are national events that are not emergencies but nonetheless command almost total attention from the public. These include

World Series baseball games, the coverage of space missions or the resignation speech of a President of the United States. The public's compulsion to glue itself to television sets at such times can mean that even paid theatre tickets will go unused. This presents a special challenge to theatre managers. The best solution may just be to acknowledge the greater power of the Monster Box, place a few of them around the lobby, hold the curtain until the event is over, and let as many members of that audience as possible know in advance that this will be the policy.

At other times, an incident will occur in the house just before curtain, in some fashion that excludes the performers from learning about it. This can greatly affect the audience mood and reaction to the performance and, of course, in turn can affect the performers' perceptions of their work. One funny incident once occurred when a little old man was wandering about the aisles visiting with friends just before the curtain rose. At that very quiet moment, an usher demanded to see his ticket stub. He became irate and loudly protested that he knew where his seat was: "Pee on the aisle, lady, pee on the aisle!" he exclaimed. The entire house broke into laugher. And what was worse, every so often during the performance a playgoer would giggle and set off a whole new round of laughter—having nothing to do with the performance. Let's hope that the house manager sent word backstage so the actors didn't all wonder whose costume had split at the inseam!

## When There's No House to Manage

For the most part this chapter concerns itself with house management in relation to traditional indoor theatres. But what about street theatre or performances given in parks and other open spaces? Is a house manager required under these circumstances? The answer is yes, except for instances where the audience is a mere handful of bystanders.

Playgoers watching a street theatre production need guidance about where to stand or sit, and the performers may, at times, need protection from overly enthusiastic or rowdy onlookers. If there are no assigned tickets or seating places, the "house manager" must unobtrusively coax people into the desired positions, telling them that they should sit down so people behind them can see, and so forth. If donations or a collection of money is made, this must be supervised. The outdoor audience manager may have to help assemble an audience in the first place, as when a street theatre troupe arrives at its chosen performance site with little if any advance publicity. In such cases a small group of people might be gathered in front of the playing area to act as decoys for attracting other people. Police officers who come along may need proof that the troupe has received official permission to perform, and other matters will require attention during the performance. Play festivals that are presented in large city parks and recreation areas are more formally organized and may involve near-traditional seating arrangements. But whatever the situation is, some type of audience management will be necessary.

## AUDIENCE PSYCHOLOGY

A theatrical performance creates a special set of psychological requirements. First, the performer must have the attention of the audience, and the audience must usually be polarized to respond as a whole, not merely as a number of different individuals. As already discussed, the way an audience is managed before the curtain goes up can go a long way toward establishing group psychology and oneness of response. Second, it is necessary for an audience to suspend many of the normal standards of reality—it must accept a special kind of theatrical reality regarding such matters as time, place, action, and character. Normal standards and perceptions must be suspended in order for theatre to communicate its perceptions in its unique way.

Paradoxically, live entertainment has come to seem unreal in this media-dominated age. Audiences today—especially new or occasional theatregoers—have difficulty adjusting to the liveness of the event. This is sometimes demonstrated by talking, eating and getting in and out of seats as if those audience members were at home in front of their television screens. Some actually seem unaware that the performers on stage are aware of the audience. Jean Dalrymple, whose long career bridged the onset of the electronic era, decided during the '70s that, at least in musicals, it was necessary to use electronic amplifiers to project the voices of performers and she introduced this now-common technique while she was director of the theatre program at New York's City Center. It wasn't that performers couldn't be heard without amplification, but that their voices sounded too thin, quiet and "unnatural" for listeners usually attuned to an amplified piece of technology. Home media entertainment habits have shortened the attention spans of many people and, with their one-to-one relationship to the viewer, often make it difficult for live performers to elicit a unified group response from a theatre audience. Good audience management, then, must sometimes include audience education—finding ways to teach people that good audience behavior is necessary for the enjoyment of live performance.

Most performers, producers and theatre managers are audience-watchers; they must be, if they are to thrive in their profession. The audience, after all, is the raw material of a performance, so how it is composed, managed and entertained determines the final nature of the product. As discussed throughout this book, there are many factors unrelated to the performance that contribute substantially to audience psychology. One of those that demands close attention is the auditorium temperature.

An ideal room temperature of sixty-eight degrees Fahrenheit should be the aim. It may be necessary, however, to cool an auditorium to a temperature considerably below this before the audience is admitted, since the body temperature of a large group will quickly and substantially increase room temperature. When the temperature is cool, audience response will also tend to be cool. When temperature is allowed to increase slightly along with the increasing intensity of dramatic action on stage, audience response will also become increasingly warm. It may be desirable, then, to allow the temperature to rise as high as eighty degrees toward the end of each act.

Many theatres contain air-conditioning systems that produce a noise audible to the spectators. If this seriously interferes with acoustics, the system should not operate during the performance. When machinery produces a low, steady hum, the noise may be tolerable, but only if it *is* steady. If such machinery is stopped or started during quiet moments in the performance, the noise becomes unacceptably obtrusive. For this reason, the best system is one that can be controlled manually by the house manager at a location where the audience and the performance can be seen and heard. Any mechanical system that cuts on and off automatically presents a major problem that adversely affects audience response.

At the ancient Greek theatre festivals, players and playwrights vying for prizes used to hire claques, groups of spectators who were paid to applaud their work and show disapproval of their competitors' work. Present-day opera stars sometimes cultivate a few of their most enthusiastic fans and support a claque in this manner. In the commercial theatre, at least one famous star is known to station her spouse in the back of the audience for each of her performances so the loyal-husband claque can initiate each round of laughter and applause! The business of manipulating audience reaction is an ancient and, perhaps, not dishonorable one. Indeed, it is quite remarkable how easily audience psychology can be influenced. One good claque standing at the back of the auditorium near the temperature controls can determine audience reaction (for better or worse) almost regardless of what is happening on the stage. An audience is highly susceptible to suggestion. Laughter, silence, coughing and applause are all infectious; when one person in an audience sets a strong example, the majority are likely to follow. But while it is comparatively easy for a claque—official or unofficial—to stimulate laughter and applause, it is very difficult to inspire a restless, coughing, fidgeting audience to settle down. These symptoms are often caused by boredom with the performance, but may also result from an overheated auditorium, or other such factors. They indicate that group response has been broken or was never established. Sometimes, one good "SHHHHHHH!" from the back of the house will do the trick. Or the circulation of cooler air may help. But if the trouble is with the production or the performance, the audience of the moment is simply stuck in a bad situation with little recourse but to walk out of the theatre. There is a little known story about one audience that began leaving the theatre *en masse* as soon as the final curtain came down. As it happened, these were paraplegics from a local veterans' home who had to get into their wheelchairs and leave before others in the audience could follow. But when he saw so many leaving during his curtain call, the temperamental star exclaimed to the actor next to him, "They're walking out! They're walking out on my curtain call! " Of the opinion that the star was getting his just reward and, knowing the makeup of the audience, the fellow actor said, "And *some* of them haven't walked in years!"

## SUMMATION

Good facility management results in a good laboratory where theatre artists can work and where audiences can appreciate the results of this work. Good audience management requires an audience engineer who can manipulate both the components of the facility and crowd psychology in order to enhance that appreciation. All the ingredients required for theatrical production are easy to obtain in comparison with desired audience response. Indeed, a production may run for many performances without once achieving the response hoped for by its director and performers. Or this response may happen only once in every ten or twenty performances. Why? There is no simple answer, although theatre people will never tire of inventing them. It is even more difficult to explain the magic and exhilaration of total audience-performer collaboration when it does happen. All we know is that it happens—once in a while. And if we have shared this uniquely satisfying human experience just once, then we are inspired to seek it out again and again—as a performer, a producer, a manager, a volunteer or a spectator.

# Conclusion

## THE ARTISTIC/MANAGERIAL PARTNERSHIP

The preceding pages describe how the American theatre has been organized in the past, how it operates today and what standard management systems are available to facilitate a theatre's artistic goals. However, a book of this size and scope cannot include every production method, management system or marketing or fundraising tip ever invented. Nonetheless, the basics are here along with guiding principles of conduct that—given imagination, flexibility and commitment—can serve as the foundation for successful theatre production and management.

I would like to devote these final pages to a few general observations, recommendations and thoughts I have about the future of the performing arts in America. Central to all of these is my ongoing concern about the relationship between artists and managers, and my hope that this book will assist in nurturing what I like to call "the artistic/managerial partnership."

Commercial theatre production in America dates back to 1752, although it becomes more recognizable to the contemporary eye with the combination companies of the mid-1800s and the booking and touring systems that developed in the early 1900s. These profit-seeking activities quickly became identified as "show business," and still comprise a considerable amount of production on Broadway and the road. But show business has been effectively matched by nonprofit professional theatre production. This system dates back to models pioneered by Margo Jones and others during the 1940s and '50s, and also owes something to the artistic example of European theatre companies and to the economic example set by symphony orchestras in this country. Today, the two methods—commercial and nonprofit—comprise the bulk of professional theatre activity in America. Yet both systems have become somewhat diluted due to their growing reliance on each other. Economic conditions have forced the commercial sector to rely on its nonprofit counterpart for product, and declining subsidization has forced the latter to become more profit-oriented. Also, there are all kinds of people and organizations (such as agents, unions and the creative and performing artists themselves) who function in both sectors.

Other viable production systems could conceivably evolve from such present-day practices as theatre cooperatives, co-productions, consortiums, investment pooling, or even foreign investment and subsidy. Schemes for financing the arts must adjust to the economic realities of the day. But, for this to happen, managers must possess the same urge for exploration and risk that motivates successful artists and, if I may add, the same willingness to break with tradition. Change is inevitable. And the pace of change is directly linked to what is happening in such fields as communication, technology, economics and government—and in the natural spheres of environment, population and social development. In the United States, rapidly changing demographics alone guarantee that power structures will keep shifting and, therefore, that new ways of doing things will come into being. This means that the way theatre is produced and managed will change along with everything else. Alternatives will be found, for example, to the Limited Partnership Agreement, the joint venture and the 501 (C) (3) models for theatrical financing; entirely new venues in which to present performances will be discovered; as yet untried methods for attracting audiences will be developed. The most successful arts managers, as always, will be those who perceive the changes around them and come up with innovations to accommodate them. To quote Emerson, it is wise to remember that traditions, like institutions—

> . . . are not aboriginal, though they existed before we were born:
> that every one of them was once the act of a single man: every
> law and usage was a man's expedient to meet a particular case:
> that they are all imitable, all alterable: we may make as good; we
> may make better.

Of course, it is a little premature to encourage managerial innovation when many if not a majority of so-called professional theatres in this country have yet to adopt even rudimentary business practices, such as sound bookkeeping and cost control systems. If one is going to depart from tradition, it is best to understand what that tradition and its alternatives entail. This can be learned through both education and experience. As arts management training at various levels is improved and increasingly accepted as a necessary credential for employment in this field, more and more arts organizations will function with greater efficiency. But to get beyond the point of mere survival—no mean feat in itself—to the point of doing work of high artistic merit requires inspired artists as well as management that is driven by more than a quest for balanced budgets. It requires management that can guide the arts safely through the next decades, reinforcing society's perception of the arts as the torchlight of civilization.

Along with "third century managers" who are grounded in the liberal arts and have a humanistic orientation, several other types of arts managers have emerged in recent years. These include those who are more interested in the process of management that in the arts being managed—experts who tend to move frequently from one organization to another mainly to gain salary increases. And they also include top executives who have moved into arts organizations from the corporate sector, whose main focus is likely to be cost-effective production and the bottom line. These managers are especially detrimental to companies that lack strong artistic voices who can keep the focus on the real mission. To help guard against the dominance of such managers, arts management training programs should give preference in admitting mainly to those students with demonstrated interest and background in the arts and should develop a curriculum that gives more than casual attention to the *artistic* aspects of planning and policy for arts organizations. Also, boards of trustees should be encouraged to undergo periodic training and evaluation sessions in order to keep their priorities in the right order. Funding agencies could greatly encourage this type of board development by making such activities a stipulation for their largess. Colleges with arts management training programs could also assist by offering special seminars and workshops for board members as well as practicing arts administrators.

Artists, too, should have more and better opportunities for ongoing training than now exist. Without getting into the question of the quality of arts programs in colleges, conservatories and schools, I would like to touch upon a few less formal possibilities for individual learning and growth.

While most artists dream of finding a home base where they can practice their art meanwhile earning a steady and sufficient income, the few who achieve this—artistic and music directors, for example—often become overworked and over-isolated from the arts community and the world at large. To avoid the early burnout that can result, and thereby avoid losing important artists to other fields, ways must be found to provide regular and, sometimes, substantial time off for them to renew their energies. This could be done by granting paid leaves of absence, subsidizing working vacations, rotating artistic directorships among two or three people, or appointing fulltime co-directors.

The American theatre has ignored the training of its young professional artists for far too long. Although Actors' Equity and other performers' unions publish newsletters, magazines and rulebooks, and provide a few basic services, the value of such activity by itself is minimal—especially for new members. There are no meaningful orientation requirements for new union members and no junior membership or other system for delineating the differences between the neophyte and the seasoned professional. While AEA has invented the journeyman contract and the membership candidate program, these are limited to Equity theatres where the use of nonprofessionals is permitted and are, in effect, little more than labor-organizing tactics for eliminating the nonunion members at those theatres altogether. Other than what they are able to overhear at auditions and what they garner from rulebooks that read as if they were written by ailing attorneys, young performers have little idea of their obligations to management, of management's obligations to them, or of anything resembling what might be called "professional deportment." Unions could easily sponsor orientation meetings and training seminars conducted by senior members, most of whom are known to be generous with their time and flattered to share their knowledge and experience. Furthermore, to insure that actors maintain their technical skills on a par with dancers and musicians, requirements for regular scene practice and acting classes should be mandated in every contract and done largely on the actors' own time and expense.

While on the subject of unions, and Actors' Equity in particular, there are other areas that need to be reviewed with fresh eyes if the art of acting, as well as the welfare of the actor, are to thrive. For instance, Equity's policies regarding showcase and workshop productions need to be liberalized rather than made increasingly restrictive, which has been the trend. Because there is a desperate need to provide as many production opportunities as possible for playwrights, and because performers also need to work and to be seen, nothing could be more shortsighted than to discourage product development—which in the performing arts means talent development. Equity's policies regarding alien actors need to be negotiated with foreign actors' unions, particularly British Equity, with a view to the value of international exchange rather than xenophobic unionism. While Equity's audition and casting policies have improved in recent years—notably the encouragement of nontraditional casting—more flexibility is needed in regard to rehearsal regulations, especially at ongoing resident theatres. Every possible measure should be taken to insure the development of ensemble acting and strong resident acting companies. Equity should also realign its governance structure to provide a more democratic voice for professional theatre companies and their local actors who are based outside New York City and Los Angeles. Among other matters, this would require an increase in the number and clout of regional AEA offices. The question of whether stage managers should belong to Equity or some other collective bargaining group, like their own association or ATPAM, should be examined. And, while there is room for improvement in the quality of theatre management, there is also room for improved union management. To date, both sides have been guilty of communicating with each other only when contract negotiations fall due or when special problems arise. But given an honest, day-to-day mutuality of concern for the art that *both* labor and management are supposed to serve, we could witness a new era of real progress in the professional theatre. Meaningful labor-management partnerships could give birth to joint efforts that would strengthen fundraising, health and welfare plans, arts advocacy, audience development, training programs, production development, national and international theatre exchange, and other matters.

Of course, it will avail the theatre little to put its own house in order only to discover that the house is empty.

Like others in this field, I sometimes daydream about what our society would be like if the arts were given as much support and attention as athletics. Think of it: required weekly if not daily arts practice from primary school through high school; ongoing school funding for arts materials, productions, coaching and intercollegiate competitions; acres of space for arts facilities; and the promise of full scholarships to finance college educations. And just imagine if radio and television regularly devoted a major segment of each and every newscast to the arts, not to mention hours of prime time programming every week!

The fact is, however, that the arts are not a regular part of the curriculum in most schools any more than they are represented by regular media programming. There are almost no arts textbooks available for students at the primary and secondary levels. And arts instruction—where is exists—is often the first item to be struck from the budget when there are cutbacks. Mindful of this situation, a number of brave advocates have lobbied for increased arts education funding. The trouble is that the National Endowment for the Arts has been virtually the only sympathetic ear on the national level. But NEA doesn't have and never will have even a fraction of the money or the muscle necessary to undertake the revolution in American education that is required to create a culturally and artistically literate society. Clearly, this is a job for the U.S. Department of Education in collaboration with several hundred thousand local school boards. Just as clearly, arts education programs—as opposed to arts-in-education programs—divert the NEA's sadly limited funds away from direct grants to artists and arts companies. Better to reward arts projects that are doing their own audience development, and doing it effectively because they are fighting for their survival. This has stimulated artists to go into the schools, the streets and the parks; it has inspired the invention of free ticket programs, pay-what-you-can tickets and ticket scholarships for students; and it has greatly shifted strategies away from the "subscribe now" approach toward a variety of less traditional target groups. These and other strategies must be further developed if the new audiences necessary to sustain live theatre production in America are to be captured and converted into habitual theatregoers.

When the NEA or any other major funder announces that it will award grants for certain types of programs, there will always be a number of applicants who will invent projects just to fit those program guidelines. This demonstrates the great power of funders. But, as we know, power corrupts. In this case it can corrupt artists and arts institutions by seducing them into doing work that they have no business doing. Ideally, then, funders should simply establish criteria for excellence and leave it at that. But such criteria are difficult to formulate, especially by committee. This was amply demonstrated by the deplorable attempt of the United States Congress to censor the NEA in 1989 for awarding several grants that indirectly supported exhibitions which a few senators considered obscene. The subsequent effort by the Congress to define what it meant by obscenity revealed how easily bigotry might become the law of the land, even infringing upon freedom of expression as guaranteed by the First Amendment.

The fact is that politics and the arts have never been comfortable bed partners—in America or any other nation. Yet, even without government patronage, and often in the face of government suppression, the arts have survived to bear testimony to future generations and to speak in a voice that is remembered long after the patronage and/or the politicians are gone. As Shelley once wrote, "poets are the unacknowledged legislators of the world." Because politicians have understood this—especially those who *don't* understand poetry—they have always been wary of artists. So I am usually pessimistic about meaningful increases in tax-based support for the arts; not because we have such overwhelming problems as homelessness, a huge foreign debt, a health care crisis and other phenomena that even politicians can understand; not because Americans seemingly prefer spending their recreational dollars on sports, drugs and guns. The problem is that American politicians do not see a constitutional mandate for the arts and, more to the point, have an aversion to supporting programs which they don't understand but secretly suspect are undermining their fondest objectives. While the absence of government subsidy for the arts in a free society is certainly preferable to subsidy with censorship, perhaps a case of enlightened arts subsidy may some day be made strong enough to convince our elected representatives of its necessity. After all, people who nurture and support those who are less healthy and less fortunate than themselves also require nurture and support— something that the arts provide especially well. Recent polls have shown that Americans would approve modest tax contributions to benefit three areas of national concern—education, the environment *and the arts!* Such factors provide a good foundation for the case that must be built. But a great deal of selfless activism and a small army of articulate and persuasive arts advocates will be required to overcome the conservative and anti-intellectual opinions that have dominated American government and society for so long. While our artists have often done duty as effective spokespeople for the cause, our arts managers must assume an increasingly active leadership role in terms of advocacy and must recruit arts audiences in large numbers and send them into the battle for government support if the arts are to remain an option in our pursuit of happiness.

As the threat of government complacency or censorship is real in every society, other attempts to manipulate artistic expression become apparrant through the practice of corporate patronage in market economies.

Prior to the 1980s, most corporate contributions to the arts were funnelled through a corporate giving officer or even a private foundation funded by corporate profits but otherwise independent from the decision-making back at headquarters. The officers and directors who held these positions usually remained in place for years and developed ongoing contact with numerous fund-seekers and recipients. But with the advent of corporate takeovers, conversions and mergers, corporate personnel of all kinds experienced frequent changeovers. This created a faceless corporate profile and replaced an interest in good corporate citizenship with an urgency to increase profits in order to pay off inflated buy-out costs. Hence, corporate giving to nonprofit organizations began to be funnelled through corporate marketing budgets. This meant that such funds were no longer scrutinized by shareholders or foundation trustees and that they were "given" with strings attached. Corporate sponsorship—as opposed to corporate contributions—is money given with the expectation of getting something in return. This may mean receiving free tickets for corporate employees, adding the name of the corporation to the name of an arts festival, or touring an arts company only to those cities or nations where the corporation conducts business. How long before it will also mean that corporations take an active role in artistic planning for the companies that accept their sponsorship? The performing arts industry must intensify its efforts to adopt and apply good American marketing techniques for itself, rather that forfeit control in exchange for sponsorships that allow others to make major marketing if not policy decisions on its behalf.

Of course, contributions from individuals have always comprised the largest percentage of unearned income for the arts. And of nearly equal importance is the extraordinary amount of time spent by individual volunteers on behalf of nonprofit arts organizations. Interestingly, volunteerism is a concept peculiar to the Western democracies and especially common in America. The capitalist nations in Asia and the emerging socialist democracies have little tradition in philanthropy and volunteerism, as we think of them. But as they assume their place in the international community, these notions are likely to embrace such activities in their own best interests, which could have a major impact on arts production and attendance the world over. Meanwhile, it would help American philanthropy significantly if U.S. tax laws were repealed so that charitable giving of any dollar amount would again benefit all taxpayers who give—both individuals and corporations. Furthermore, there is a need for new national legislation not only to provide direct subsidy to the arts (an amount equal to 20 percent of the entire nonprofit arts deficit in this country is often mentioned as a reasonable goal), but also to provide tax concessions and other indirect benefits widely enjoyed by industries far less vital to national interests than the arts. Importantly, this must include meaningful incentives to encourage research and development, if American arts products are to retain the virtually universal preeminence they now enjoy.

If the theatre is to assume a more central place in our society, it must form partnerships that will improve the status of each practitioner while also strengthening the influence of the industry as a whole. The theatrical unions that began organizing at the beginning of the twentieth century marked a first step in this direction by forcing producers and managers to accept creative and performing artists as partners in the production process. The Federal Theatre Project and the NEA introduced a partnership with government which stimulated the remarkable growth of nonprofit professional theatre, together with greatly increased corporate and individual contributions. We have also seen the establishment of numerous arts service organizations that have helped their members and clients by means of technical assistance programs, coordinated advocacy appeals, access to valuable data banks, and simply by facilitating communication between theatre professionals, as well as between the theatre and outside parties of interest. This type of activity must continue and expand, particularly for the benefit of struggling and emerging companies. Similarly, arts managers' associations of various kinds should reach out with greater frequency to serious but inexperienced colleagues. And all such organizations—together with the unions—should have the guts to establish reasonable criteria for professionalism in the theatre. Only by defining, policing and broadcasting serious professional standards can the theatre in America expect to be taken seriously. This has begun to happen, but we still have a long way to go.

Whenever production costs increase and support diminishes, it is tempting to form partnerships that will lead to reduced costs. This can be both practical and creative, but the danger is that it can lead to over-centralization, as with the creation of touring circuits controlled by a single producer or agency. Having seen how such extremes of control devastated professional theatre in the nineteenth century and again in the mid-twentieth century, we should be watchful for developments that signal the gathering of too much power in too few hands. Real strength, as always, lies in diversity.

One of the difficulties in writing a book of this size and scope is that things are always changing. What is printed today may be out-of-date tomorrow. But while it is important to keep up with union rules, advances in computer technology and the like, it is even more important to keep up with the changing currents of the society in which we are striving, however humbly, to function. This has not been an easy task in recent years, when it often seemed as if history was on fast-forward. One of the most notable happenings, of course, was that the Iron Curtain finally went up—with the same breathtaking effect of a great curtain at the opera house, revealing to the onlookers one stunning *coup de theatre* after another. In fact, much of what occurred politically was fed by theatre works and artists—one of whom even became president of his country. No wonder conservative politicians in America grew fretful—they were probably having nightmares of a Tennessee Williams or a Sam Shepard becoming President of the United States! Even liberal politicians would have difficulty accepting *that* kind of possibility— which says a lot more about what's wrong with the American theatre than what's wrong with American politics. Our theatre has yet to make a partnership with our people. Yet, America is still the New World and is still just at the beginning of its unique experiment as a pluralistic society. Its virgin fields have been planted with the seeds of European, African, Asian and Indian civilizations, and the first great cultural harvest is still a season away. It behooves the theatre and its managers, I think, to further cultivate America's multicultural mission by helping its citizens to revel in the joy of our diversity while also celebrating those characteristics that make us kin.

Finally, a word should be said about the growing importance of American theatre in relation to what is rapidly emerging as a global arts community—so rapidly, in fact, that the next edition of this book may have to be titled *Theatre Management and Production in the World.* Not "around the world," mind you, but within an increasingly interdependent, international community. Given the development of the European Economic Community, the replacement of communist systems with free market societies and the renaissance of Asian influence, the time when it is as easy to do business with Brussels as Baltimore is upon us. Markets for every product, including the arts, are opening with astonishing speed. This opportunity has brought about the emergence of a new specialist—the global arts manager. But, more important, it means that the essentially compassionate message conveyed by the arts will finally reach a percentage of the human race that may even be sufficient to insure its future!

# Appendices

# Appendix A

SUGGESTED SYLLABUS FOR AN UNDERGRADUATE COURSE
IN THEATRE MANAGEMENT

## *Aims of the Course*

This course is designed to provide an introduction to the economic and managerial aspects of American theatre, especially as they apply to nonprofit professional theatre. It is assumed that the student has fulfilled the prerequisites in theatre history and production but is comparatively untutored in economics and business administration. The course aims to relate principles of business management to the theatre, to evaluate theatre management to date and to suggest new directions for the future. Emphasis will be placed on the practical and contemporary aspects of the field.

## *Required Reading*

Langley, Stephen. *Theatre Management and Production in America.* Drama Book Publishers, New York, 1990.

Langley, Stephen and Abruzzo, James. *Jobs in Arts & Media Management.* American Council for the Arts, New York, 1990.

*Theatre Profiles.* (Current edition.) Theatre Communications Group, New York.

## *Units of Study*

(Each unit, except the first, will comprise approximately three hours of classroom lecture and discussion.)

1. Introduction to the course: aims, definitions, scope
2. Capsule history of theatrical producing and management in America
3. Organization and structure: the commercial theatre
4. Organization and structure: the nonprofit theatre
5. Setting goals, long-range planning, board development, leadership
6. Legal procedures: laws, incorporation, nonprofit status, contracts, legal agreements, copyrights, subsidiary rights
7. The theatre facility

8. Planning a season and organizing production requirements
9. Staffing, casting and personnel management
10. Financing, budgeting, cost-controls, ticket pricing and box office operation
11. Fundraising and sources of unearned income
12. Marketing, audience development and sources of earned income
13. Audience and company management
14. Classroom presentation of student term projects
15. Future prospects and directions in theatrical producing and management.

## Written Assignments

Each student will invent a hypothetical theatre company and propose a "dream season" of productions. These must be planned for an actual, existing theatre space, such as the campus theatre or a nearby LORT theatre. Each assignment is due the week after the class discussion to which it relates. All assignments will be reworked according to the instructor's comments and then reassembled in a single packet for final submission on the last day of class. During the previous week, each student will have made a 10-minute oral presentation to the class describing his or her project. The packet should include the following:

1. A one-paragraph mission statement, plus three-to-five goals or objectives for the project or company
2. A list of the first season's productions; a description of the theatre facility to be used, including a ground plan showing the stage and audience areas
3. A line chart that shows all full-time staff positions (artistic, administrative, technical) for the company and their relationship to each other; also a list of all job titles within each of the three areas showing weekly salaries and number of employment weeks for each
4. A production budget for each show planned (including rehearsal costs, scenery, costumes, lighting, props, etc.)
5. A pre-opening budget (excluding production costs) and an ongoing weekly operating budget (again excluding production costs). These should be put together with staff costs and production budgets with sub-totals shown on a summary sheet. Finally, grand totals of all costs, together with seasonal ticket income at both 100% and 60% of capacity. The differential should be shown.

# Appendix B

SUGGESTED CORE OF COURSES FOR A MASTER'S DEGREE
PROGRAM IN PERFORMING ARTS MANAGEMENT

## *First Semester*

*Principles and Components of Performing Arts Management*

An introduction to organizational, fiscal, legal, marketing, funding and artistic policy-making principles and techniques involved in managing the performing arts.

*Computer Applications in the Performing Arts*

Current use and potential applications of computers in relation to administration, stage production, music, choreography and the development of the artistic product.

*Organization Behavior*

History of management thought; individual needs, values, motivation, career development, small groups, formal organization and management processes.

*Background Elective I*

An advisor-approved course dealing with a particular period, movement, artist, genre or philosophy in the performing arts.

*Performing Arts Research and Bibliography*

Introduction to research and computer facilities, including the campus library and other local resources and collections; exercises in writing styles and formats for letters, proposals, reports, articles, news releases and formal papers.

*Performing Arts Management Internship I*

A twenty-hour per week, semester-long internship under academic guidance, with professional supervision.

## *Second Semester*

*The Performing Arts and the Law*
Studies in legal problems and procedures related to the performing arts: profit and nonprofit corporations; contracts; agreements; copyright law; federal and local regulations.

*Business Management of the Performing Arts*
Accounting, bookkeeping, payroll, budgeting and cost-control procedures for performing arts ventures, companies and institutions.

*Marketing the Performing Arts*
Marketing theories and strategies in relation to audience development: advertising techniques, publicity, promotion and press relations.

*Background Elective II*
An advisor-approved course dealing with a particular period, movement, artist, genre or philosophy in the performing arts.

*Performing Arts Management Internship II*
A twenty-hour per week, semester-long internship under academic guidance, with professional supervision.

## *Third Semester*

*Labor and Employee Relations in the Performing Arts*
A study of labor unions related to the performing arts: the collective bargaining process; contract negotiations; labor law; federal, state and local regulations; personnel policies; and legal issues.

*Fundraising Techniques for the Performing Arts*
Study of the philosophy and methodology of raising contributed income for nonprofit professional performing arts companies and institutions: government, corporate and individual sources; grants research, writing and administration.

*Managerial Economics and the Performing Arts*
Examination of decision-making and market equilibrium in performing arts production, based on familiar economic concepts and models. Construction of production and operating budgets in relation to current costs and revenues in the performing arts industry.

*Personnel and Company Management for the Performing Arts*

A study of the psychological dynamics of group behavior and personnel interaction; uses of meetings and group discussions, management intervention, incentive systems; special problems related to personnel on tour; the challenge of managing the artistic temperament.

*Performing Arts Management Internship III*

A twenty-hour per week, semester-long internship under academic guidance, with professional supervision.

## Fourth Semester

*Artistic/Managerial Decision-Making in the Performing Arts*

The dynamics of planning, organizing and realizing performing arts projects, ventures, companies and institutions with special attention to the interrelationships between artists, managers and trustees in the collaborative process of making theatre.

*The Performance Facility: Design and Operation*

Aesthetics and functions of theatre architecture; variations on traditional performance spaces; planning for construction and renovation; working with architects and consultants; the bidding process; zoning, permits, building codes and regulations; fitting the space to the artistic vision.

*Professional Residency and Major Paper*

A semester-long professional management residency with a leading performing arts agency, company or institution: minimum of four months at forty hours per week, resulting in a major paper (in lieu of a thesis) that describes and evaluates both the residency sponsor and the residency experience, with appendices that present samples of the resident's project-related work.

## Notes:

Other courses that might be considered required or elective include:

Stage Management
Artist Representation and Contract Negotiation
Case Studies in Performing Arts Management
Administration of Government and Independent Arts Agencies
The Arts and Society: Politics, Special Interest Groups and Education
The Arts and Education

Public Policy and the Arts
Special Seminars
Visiting Lecture Series

This curriculum can be adapted to a two-or-three-year program lead-ing to an M.A., M.F.A. or M.B.A. degree.

Candidates accepted into this program should be computer literate, have completed at least one undergraduate course in accounting and have an undergraduate major or considerable life experience in at least one of the performing arts. Any deficiencies in these areas should be made up by re-quiring the student to take courses where needed, without credit, prior to the end of the first semester in the graduate program.

Academic programs and requirements should be individually tailored to fit the background, needs and career goals of each student.

Only people with both academic and professional credentials should be utilized as instructors.

Only those institutions of higher education that can offer both on-cam-pus and off-campus internship experiences of high professional quality should offer a graduate program in this field.

# Appendix  C

SAMPLE  AGREEMENT  USED  BETWEEN  A  TOURING
ATTRACTION  (AND/OR  BOOKING  AGENCY)
AND  A  PRESENTING  ORGANIZATION

# THEATRE MANAGEMENT AND PRODUCTION IN AMERICA

## ARTIST/ATTRACTION FIXED COMPENSATION AGREEMENT

Agreement made this        day of                              by and between
(hereinafter called the ''Artist/Attraction''), c/o Manager at                    for the services of
                                                                    (the ''Artist''), and

with its principal place of business at

                                        (hereinafter called ''Presentor'').

1. **Details of Performance(s)** (a) Presentor hereby engages from Artist/Attraction the services of Artist for the Performance(s), on the date(s), time(s) and place(s), and for the compensation all as set forth herein, and Artist/Attraction hereby agrees that Artist shall render such services, subject to the terms and conditions set forth herein.
(b) **Manager** shall mean
(c) **Number of Performances**
(d) **Type of Performance(s), Day(s), Date(s), Time(s) and Place(s)**

SAMPLE COPY

(e) **Rehearsal(s), Date(s), Time(s), and Place(s)**

(f) **Theatre Name, Address, Seating Capacity, Stage Entrance**

(g) **Piano(s), Make and Size Required**

(h) **Persons to Notify on Arrival**
Name
Address

Phone Number
(i) **Presentor's Representative & Phone Number**
(j) **Recommended Hotel and Address**

2. **Compensation** The Compensation to be paid by the Presentor to the Artist/Attraction shall be the sum of $                    (the ''compensation'')

SAMPLE COPY

3. **Payment of Compensation** The compensation hereunder shall be paid by the Presentor to the Manager on behalf of the Artist/Attraction **no later than the intermission of the first Performance.** Payment shall be made only by bank or certified check **made payable to Manager** on behalf of Artist/Attraction.

4. **Letter of Credit** Presentor shall furnish Manager upon the execution of this Agreement with a clean unconditional irrevocable Letter of Credit payable by sight draft drawn on a United States commercial bank in the amount of the compensation. Such Letter of Credit shall be in form and substance acceptable to the Manager on behalf of Artist/Attraction. Sums evidenced by such Letter of Credit shall be immediately payable to Manager on behalf of Artist/Attraction by presentation to such bank of Manager's draft at sight at any time commencing fourteen (14) days prior to the date of the first scheduled Performance and continuing until thirty (30) days after the date of the last scheduled Performance.

5. **House Seats** Number of house seats reserved at the regular price/complimentary for Artist/Attraction per Performance until one (1) hour prior to each such Performance .

6. **Binding Effect:** THIS AGREEMENT SHALL NOT BE BINDING UPON THE ARTIST/ATTRACTION UNTIL EXECUTED BY THE ARTIST/ATTRACTION. IF THIS AGREEMENT IS EXECUTED BY THE MANAGER ON BEHALF OF ARTIST/ATTRACTION, THE MANAGER IS EXECUTING THIS AGREEMENT ONLY AS A MANAGER FOR THE ARTIST/ATTRACTION, IS NOT OBLIGATED TO PRESENTOR HEREUNDER, AND SHALL NOT BE RESPONSIBLE FOR ANY ACTS OR DEFAULTS OF THE ARTIST/ATTRACTION, THE ARTIST, OR FOR THE NON-PERFORMANCE BY THE ARTIST/ATTRACTION OF ITS OBLIGATIONS HEREUNDER. THE NON-ARRIVAL OF THE ARTIST CAUSED BY ANY INCOMPLETE OR INACCURATE INFORMATION FURNISHED BY PRESENTOR AS SET FORTH ABOVE SHALL NOT RELIEVE PRESENTOR FROM FULFILLMENT OF ITS OBLIGATIONS HEREUNDER.

ALL OF THE PROVISIONS SET FORTH AS ''ADDITIONAL PROVISIONS'' AND ALL OF THE REQUIREMENTS SET FORTH IN ANY ADDENDUM ANNEXED TO THIS AGREEMENT ARE HEREBY INCORPORATED IN THIS AGREEMENT WITH THE SAME FORCE AND EFFECT AS THOUGH SET FORTH IN FULL ON THIS PAGE.

**IN WITNESS WHEREOF,** the parties hereto have executed this Agreement the day and year first above set forth.

Presentor (Organization Name)                          Artist/Attraction

By: X                                                  By:        SAMPLE COPY
    Presentor (Name)                                       Manager

                                                       By:
Title

PRESENTOR'S COPY (after being countersigned)                    FCA: REV. B: 8/84 11M

572

# APPENDIX C

## ADDITIONAL PROVISIONS

7. **Requirements**: Presentor agrees to furnish and fulfill the following Requirements as well as those Requirements set forth in any Addendum annexed hereto at its sole cost and expense for each Rehearsal and Performance:

a) A PIANO(s), PROPERLY TUNED, if required.

b) a microphone on the stage of the Theatre and a sound system in good working order, if required.

c) (1) the Theatre, properly lighted, heated, equipped and cleaned; (2) ushers, ticket sellers, ticket takers, all necessary attaches and special police; (3) suitable dressing rooms for the personnel of the Artist/Attraction and space for equipment.

d) (1) any necessary personnel which may be required by Artist/Attraction to unload the vehicles carrying the Artist/Attraction's equipment and property, to bring such equipment and property to such place within the Theatre as the Artist/Attraction's representative shall determine, and after the last Performance to remove such equipment and properties from the Theatre and to return such equipment and properties and load such equipment and properties on the vehicles; and (2) all other personnel which may be necessary in connection with the Performance(s) and Rehearsal(s) including without limitation, stage hands, spot light operators, stage carpenters, electricians, sound technicians, dressers, property men, wardrobe personnel, additional and/or standby musicians, and any other local labor which shall be necessary and required by Artist/Attraction, and/or required by any union having local jurisdiction.

8. **Unions**: The Presentor agrees to adhere to and abide by the applicable rules and regulations of all unions having jurisdiction over the Performance(s).

9. **Presentor's Warranties and Representations**: Presentor hereby warrants and represents to Artist/Attraction as follows: (a) that it has or will have a lease for the Theatre covering the date or dates of the Performance(s) and Rehearsals, that during the Performance(s) the lease will be in full force and effect, and neither Presentor or Theatre will be in default thereof, and that the lease will be exhibited to Artist/Attraction or Manager upon request. (b) that admission to the Performance(s) and seating in the Theatre shall be without regard to race, color, religion or national origin. (c) that the Presentor will be solely responsible for payment of all charges, assessments, royalties or license fees required to be paid for the right to perform all music performed at the Performance(s).

10. **Advertising Material**: Presentor agrees to use only photographs furnished by the Artist/Attraction. Upon Presentor's request Artist/Attraction may, but is not obligated to, furnish such quantities of press materials, heralds, window cards and three-sheet posters as the Artist/Attraction in its sole discretion deems necessary or desirable. Presentor agrees to imprint, distribute and display properly all materials so received without change or alteration. Presentor hereby agrees that Manager on behalf of Artist/Attraction shall have the right to approve the contents of all advertising and publicity materials Presentor wishes to utilize both as to form and substance and such approval shall not be binding upon Manager unless in writing executed by Manager.

11. **Concessions**: Subject to whatever standard house concession is in effect on the date of this Agreement, the Artist/Attraction shall have the right, to have such persons as it may desire sell souvenir program books in the lobby of the Theatre immediately prior to and after each Performance and during each intermission. Presentor shall not directly or indirectly receive any fee, remuneration or other compensation in connection with such sales, agrees to turn over to the Artist/Attraction any such fee, remuneration or other compensation as and when received by it, and agrees to use its best efforts to enable the Artist/Attraction to sell such souvenir program books without cost to it.

12. **Program**: The Artist/Attraction will select and provide the works to be performed for the Performance(s). If the Artist/Attraction has a choice of works, or a variety of programs, the Presentor, on reasonable prior written notice to Manager, shall have the right to select the program or works from such choices. The Artist/Attraction shall furnish Presentor with copy for each program to be performed and Presentor agrees at its own expense to print and distribute for each Performance a sufficient quantity of house programs conforming to the program copy furnished by the Artist/Attraction.

13. **Credit to Manager**: All programs shall carry a credit to Manager, Artist's piano company, and Artist's record company(s), in position and prominence as Manager may specify, either in any Addendum annexed hereto or by prior written notice to Presentor, and shall include such other credit lines as Manager may reasonably request.

14. **Restrictions**: Presentor agrees to prevent the broadcasting, recording, transmission, photographing, or any other transmission or reproduction of the Performance(s) or any part thereof by any means or media now or hereafter known including but not limited to audio, visual, or audio-visual means. Presentor further agrees that unless specifically set forth in this Agreement, the Performance(s) by the Artist/Attraction shall not be in conjunction with the performance of any other performer and that no assisting artist not part of the Artist/Attraction shall perform at a performance without the prior written consent of the Artist/Attraction.

15. **Indemnity**: Presentor hereby agrees to indemnify Artist/Attraction, Artist, and Manager from and against any claim of breach of any of Presentor's representations, warranties and agreements hereunder and from any claims of third parties of any kind, nature, or description for personal injuries or property damage in connection with the Performance(s), except with respect to any claim proven to be due solely to the willful act of Artist or Artist/Attraction, from which claim Artist/Attraction similarly agrees to indemnify Presentor.

16. **Impossibility of Performance**: In the event that the performance of any of the covenants of this Agreement on the part of the Artist/Attraction Artist or Presentor shall be prevented by act of God, physical disability, the acts or regulations of public authorities or labor unions, labor difficulties, strike, war, epidemic, interruption or delay of transportation service, or any other causes beyond the reasonable control of such party, such party shall be relieved of its obligations hereunder with respect to the Performance(s) so prevented on account of such cause. If the Performance(s) shall be prevented for any of the foregoing causes, neither the Presentor nor Artist/Attraction shall be under any obligation to present the Performance at a different time, except that if the Performance(s) shall be prevented for any of the foregoing causes, the Presentor shall use its best efforts to re-engage the Artist/Attraction within a twenty-four (24) month period on the same terms and conditions set forth herein, subject however to the Artist's availability. In the event the Artist consists of persons other than the featured performer and one or more of such persons cannot perform for any reason, Artist/Attraction shall have the option either to use its reasonable efforts to furnish a substitute for each such person, which substitute Presentor agrees to accept; or to perform without such person, in which event the Artist/Attraction shall not be liable for such failure of any such person to perform, or to treat such person's unavailability as an Act of God on the part of Artist and Artist/Attraction.

17. **Notices**: All notices to Presentor and Artist/Attraction shall be in writing addressed, in the case of Presentor, to its address set forth above, and in the case of Artist/Attraction, to Manager at its address set forth above.

18. **Modification, Etc.**: This Agreement contains the entire understanding of the parties, shall be amended or modified only by a writing executed by Presentor and Artist/Attraction, or Manager on its behalf, and shall be construed, governed and interpreted pursuant to the laws of the State of New York applicable to agreements wholly to be performed therein. Presentor shall not have the right to assign this Agreement or any of Presentor's obligations hereunder.

19. **Remedies**: In the event Presentor breaches or defaults in the due performance of this Agreement or any of its warranties, representations, or agreements hereunder, or in the event prior to the date of the first Performance the Presentor has failed, neglected or refused for any reason whatever to perform any obligation under any agreement with any other artist or attraction, or if in the sole opinion of Manager, the financial standing or credit of Presentor has been impaired or is unsatisfactory (and any of such events shall hereinafter be deemed an "Event of Default"), then and upon the occurrence of an Event of Default, Artist/Attraction shall have the right to terminate this Agreement and its obligations hereunder. Presentor acknowledges that Artist/Attraction has refused offers for other performances in order to enter into this Agreement and that Artist/Attraction has incurred substantial out of pocket expenses in connection herewith; and therefore agrees, in an Event of Default, that any and all sums payable to Artist/Attraction as compensation be immediately due and payable, that any and all sums paid to Artist/Attraction or Manager, in its behalf shall be retained by Artist/Attraction as liquidated damages, and that Artist/Attraction shall have the right to present any letter of credit furnished it for payment. Artist/Attraction shall have, in addition and not in lieu of those remedies set forth above, the right, if there is an Event of Default, to exercise all of its rights and remedies against Presentor at law or in equity. All such rights and remedies may be exercised cumulatively, or in the alternative at the sole discretion of Artist/Attraction.

20. **Service of Process**: Presentor hereby irrevocably submits itself to the jurisdiction of the Courts of the State of New York, New York County, and the jurisdiction of the United States District Court for the Southern District of New York for the purpose of any suit, action or other proceeding which may be brought by Artist/Attraction against Presentor arising out of or based upon this Agreement or the subject matter thereof. Presentor hereby waives, and agrees not to assert, in any such suit, action, or proceeding, any claim that it is not subject to the jurisdiction of the above named Courts, that its property is exempt from attachment or execution, that such suit, action or proceeding is brought in an inconvenient form, or that the venue of such suit, action, or proceeding is improper. Presentor hereby consents to service of process by registered mail at the address to which notices are to be given and agrees that such service shall be deemed effective upon Presentor as if personal service had been made upon Presentor within New York State, New York County.

573

# Appendix D

SAMPLE TECHNICAL INFORMATION SHEET
FROM A TOUR PRODUCER TO A PRESENTER
FOR A MUSICAL PRODUCTION FEATURING
A STAR PERFORMER

(Name of Show)  Rider, Part II

## Technical Requirements

The following pages outline the technical requirements for the touring production of (name of show). Your cooperation and advance preparation will facilitate an efficient set-up, run and load-out. We believe that we have covered all areas of concern, but if you have any questions after reading this document please contact us.

AUDIO:  The sound mixing position must be in the orchestra section of the house and will occupy a space 4' by 8' with room behind for two additional 2' by 2' outboard racks and standing room for an operator. The console's height from the operating table is 20", so we recommend a position to the far AUDIENCE LEFT of the orchestra section which is clear of any balcony overhang. Positions under a balcony MUST be avoided to assure good sound quality. The position must be within 175' of the stage and clear of sight or sound obstructions.

Audio also requires two clean 20 amp/110 volt services within 30' of the stage. Although we *may* tie into an existing house sound system by providing the house with a balanced 600 ohms LINE LEVEL output from our system, we always reserve the right to use our own speaker package. Under all circumstances, this production will be allowed to use and run its own multi-cables (snakes) from the audio mixing position to the stage area.

CARPENTRY:  The stage area, wings and backstage areas must be cleared of all obstructions such as pianos, flats and scenery pieces. This production uses massive rolling units. All pipes (battens) must be cleared of all goods or hanging pieces prior to our arrival. If the pipes are not cleared, it will slow down the set-up and make it less efficient and more expensive. Time is of the essence in our set-up; a house that has not been stripped may force us to cut

575

scenic elements from the show and this will lessen the quality of the production.

If loading is done from a street or parking lot, arrangement should be made by the presenter to clear all vehicles and obstructions that could impede loading or unloading.

In a conventional counter weight house (not double purchase), we will need 12,200 lbs. of weight to hang our show. We hang 32 linesets of lighting and scenery in 31'6" of depth from the first available lineset.

We request that the same local crew work the "rail" at each performance.

In the carpentry call numbers, we request that one qualified person be assigned to assist in point rigging for our side lighting towers, each of which is rigged off a truss suspended by two points. This person should be available on both the "IN" and "OUT."

ELECTRICS: We travel with our own full, front-of-house and stage instruments. We will use both your box boom and balcony rail positions. If you have instruments hanging in your front-of-house positions, we will use them, provided they are the right intensity for our production and that they can be patched into our road system. We will never use your instruments on stage, so please clear them.

For Electrics power we require 3 Phase, 4 Wire, with ground, 110 Volt, 600 amps per leg. If any special hook-up is needed, a qualified person must be available one hour into the load-in and immediately following the final performance.

Three followspots are required. If no spots are available at the theatre, they must be rented at the presenter's expense and available the morning of the load-in. Super Troupers are strongly recommended and preferred. We do not supply carbons. We request that the same spot operators (2) work all performances and be part of the load-in crew. Changing operators would seriously compromise the production.

PROPERTIES: We require sixteen music stands, fifteen chairs and twenty stand lights for the pit. It would be very helpful if you could arrange two sets of each, so that one could be used in the lobby for an orchestra rehearsal while the other is being set in the pit.

We require that a newly tuned piano be located in the rehearsal room or lobby on the morning of load-in and that a console upright be located in the pit where it should be tuned in place the day before our arrival. The pit piano must be one of the following: YAMAHA Model U or P series; KAWAI BL-12; YOUNG CHANG U-131; BALDWIN (Hamilton Series). All pianos should be tuned to A-440. The expense of piano tuning shall be that of the presenter.

The piano should be retuned on the morning of the fifth performance. Additional retuning will be at the discretion of the stage manager.

On stage we require four 3' by 6' tables.

WARDROBE: The wardrobe workroom should be large enough (600 sq. feet) to accommodate two workboxes, eight gondolas and six hampers as well as two worktables. We also request that four hanging racks be provided and at least three 20 amp circuits be available in the workroom.

The company consists of thirty performers, musical director, assistant conductor and drummer, two company managers, three stage managers and a crew of eleven. The dressing room requirements are as follows:

One star dressing room
Eight principal dressing rooms
One musical director's room
One chorus room for thirteen males
One chorus room for eight females
One stage manager's office with telephone (backstage)
One company manager's office with telephone (front-of-house)

All performers' dressing rooms must be clean and well-lighted with hanging racks and running water and all must conform to Equity regulations. Each space used by a performer must have a mirror. The wardrobe "IN" starts at 9:00 AM unless specified differently by the wardrobe "White Card" sent to the local wardrobe business agent. The wardrobe show call is earlier than the other running crew calls for each performance. All dressers must be female.

YELLOW CARD CALL: This is a yellow card attraction that requires the following IATSE labor (THIS IS A PRELIMINARY CALL. We will advise about final call at a later date):

| | "IN" | "PERFORMANCE" | "OUT" |
|---|---|---|---|
| Electrics | 12 | 5 | 12 |
| Carpentry | 12 | 8 | 12 |
| Audio | 3 | 0 | 3 |
| Properties | 4 | 3 | 4 |
| Wardrobe | 4 | 5 | 4 |
| | | | |
| Totals | 35 | 21 | 35 |

LOADING & UNLOADING:   Above the yellow card call, four crew members are required to work in the trucks during the "IN" and six members during the "OUT." The loaders on the "IN" should be prepared to stay throughout the day as the trucks may have to be unloaded in shifts and repacked with "empties."

ORCHESTRA:   Fourteen local musicians shall be provided by and paid for by the presenter. They are two first violins and one each of the following: cello, viola, bass (upright), flute (dbl. piccolo), clarinet, oboe (dlb. english horn), bassoon, first trumpet, second trumpet, trombone, harp and french horn.

Because local musicians will be used, a rehearsal is necessary on the day of the opening performance. Under normal circumstances the orchestra will rehearse either in a rehearsal room or in the lobby of the theatre from 11:00 AM to 3:00 PM. The orchestra will then do a sound check with the cast from the pit from 6:00 to 7:00 PM. The presenter will provide an additional piano at the location of the rehearsal.

SECURITY:   Security personnel will be provided for each performance at the presenter's expense. Such personnel will be at the theatre one hour before each performance and remain until the last company member has departed. Security personnel will receive their instructions from the production stage manager.

SPACING AND SOUND CHECK:   Before each opening performance, it is necessary for the performers to have time to familiarize themselves with the new stage facility and run a sound check to set levels and adjust equalization. This procedure will end 1/2 hour before the scheduled curtain time— the audience cannot be admitted into the auditorium until then. Before every performance the performers are allowed access to the stage for warmup from one hour before half-hour until the performance. Any cost for this stage time will be paid by the presenter.

CREW CALL: Before each performance, local heads of each department are called for one hour before half-hour to assist with preshow checks and maintenance. These costs are the obligation of the presenter. On opening night only we require that all running crews be called at one hour before the normal half-hour call to receive instructions.

SHOW INFORMATION: There will be a twenty-minute intermission. If the house needs a longer break, or normally takes a longer break, inform the production stage manager prior to the opening.

HOUSE SEATS AND COMPLIMENTARY TICKETS: The production company shall be entitled to eight pairs of complimentary tickets and ten pairs of tickets for purchase per performance. All such tickets will have seat locations in the center of the orchestra, rows 10 to 15. All seats will be held at the box office until one hour prior to curtain unless released earlier by the company manager. This clause supersedes Paragraph 22 of the contract.

THE STAR'S DRESSING ROOM: The following items must be in the star's dressing room and replenished daily:

| | |
|---|---|
| Perrier water | No-salt seltzer water |
| Cheese and cold cut platter | Diet Coke |
| (brie, blue cheese, ham, | Mixed nuts or cashews |
| pastrami, salami, potato chips) | Fresh fruits |
| Pepsi cola (diet) | Ice |
| Fresh rye bread | Lemon |

The dressing room must be freshly painted and carpeted, contain a comfortable couch and chair, coffee table, and touch-tone telephone (long distance usage shall be paid by the producer). The dressing room must have a make-up area and private shower separate from the sitting area.

TRANSPORTATION: The star shall be provided, at presenter's expense, a luxury sedan and driver for transportation to and from the airport, to and from press and publicity engagements, and to and from the theatre for all rehearsals and performances.

TEMPERATURE: The stage and dressing room areas should be maintained at a temperature of between 68 and 70 degrees Fahrenheit whenever the company is in the theatre.

PRESENTER AVAILABILITY: The presenter or the presenter's representative must be available at all times to the road carpenter and the stage manager from one hour prior to the load-in until the end of the first performance. He/she must be prepared to make decisions on behalf of the local presenter.

AGREED AND ACCEPTED:              AGREED AND ACCEPTED:


_____, G.M.

(Name of Show) Company              Presenter

# Appendix E

SAMPLE LICENSE AGREEMENT FOR RENTING
A THEATRE FACILITY TO AN OUTSIDE GROUP

Brooklyn Center for the Performing Arts
at Brooklyn College

**LICENSE AGREEMENT** made this_____day of _____between the BOARD OF TRUSTEES OF THE CITY UNIVERSITY OF NEW YORK (hereinafter referred to as Licensor), party of the first part, and _____

of_____
for itself, its successors and/or it's legal representatives (hereinafter referred to as Licensee), party of the second part.

**WITNESSETH:** The Licensor does hereby grant to the Licensee permission to use the following space in Brooklyn College (hereinafter referred to as the College) for the following performances (description of space and dates and times of performances):

and rehearsals (it is requested that at least a portion of the period be used to consult with the technical staff before program participants arrive at the licensed facilities):

said premises to be used by the Licensee only and for the sole purpose of

and for no other purpose. The following room(s) will be available for dressing, make-up and/or other agreed purposes:

The Licensee agrees to pay Licensor as a fee for such use, the sum of

        $_____, as follows:

        $_____ on signing of this license agreement

        $_____ Balance on/or before_____

Any other payments:_____

The entire fee and all other sums due Licensor shall be paid to it prior to the time of opening of the door to the premises for the performance, concert, lecture, and/or public meeting contemplated, and time shall be of the essence with respect to such payment. Extra charges for additional rehearsals, extra stage work, overtime, extra rooms, etc., if any, will be payable when billed. Fees are not refundable.

Permission for the above use is made upon the foregoing and following terms, agreements and conditions which the respective parties agree to and observe, keep and perform:

- 1 -

# APPENDIX E

(1) The Licensee agrees that, if any stage work or other special arrangements are permitted, same shall be done only under the supervision of and with the approval of the Licensor, and the Licensee agrees to pay for the same when billed. Licensee agrees that Licensor shall not be liable for any claims or causes of action arising from or out of the acts of any of the employees of Licensee, or their omission to act, and agrees to indemnify Licensor from any such claims or causes of action. Licensor shall provide tickets for all performances and any arrangements for the use of the box office shall be entered into as a separate agreement with the Licensor and is not included in this agreement.

(2) In case all charges and fees due Licensor are not paid prior to the performance, the Licensee agrees that the Licensor may, at its election, collect such fees and charges due hereunder or any part thereof out of the receipts, if any, from the sale of tickets or subscriptions at the box office and said receipts are hereby assigned by the Licensee to the Licensor to the extent of the amount of any charges due by Licensee under this agreement and which may at any time remain unpaid to Licensor.

(3) The Licensor shall not be obliged to furnish possession or the use of the premises involved herein until all payments have been made as described above, and the Licensee hereby specifically agrees that if each and every of the above payments have not been made by the Licensee to Licensor, the Licensor may without further notice of any kind to the Licensee, or to any other person, refuse to open the doors until such payments have been made. Upon any default in payment by the Licensee, the Licensor shall retain any money already paid, and the Licensee shall be and remain liable to the Licensor for any balance remaining to be paid as specified herein.

(4) The Licensee agrees not to permit entrance of any number of persons greater than the number of existing 2,482 (    ) seats in the premises involved herein, and no persons shall be permitted to use or occupy any space as standing room. Any use of the stage made by the Licensee for auditorium or seating purposes shall be only with the written consent of the Licensor upon such terms and conditions as may be specified by the Licensor.

(5) The Licensee agrees that Licensee will not use nor attempt to use any part of the premises for any purposes other than that above specified, nor for any use or proposed use which will be contrary to law. Licensee further agrees that Licensor in its sole absolute discretion, if it deems any proposed or existing performance, concert, lecture, and/or public meeting to be contrary to law, contrary to public safety, or opposed to decency or good morals or detrimental to the reputation of the College, may forthwith terminate this license, and/or interrupt such performance, concert, lecture, and/or public meeting, and dismiss or cause the audience to be dismissed, and if the Licensor sees fit, turn off the lights, and on exercise by Licensor of any such discretion, all rights of the Licensee hereunder shall immediately terminate. In any such event the Licensor shall be entitled to retain or receive any money paid or agreed to be paid to it hereunder; and Licensee agrees to indemnify the Licensor against any claim for damages arising out of any act of Licensor, its agents, or employees, in the exercise of Licensor's discretion under this clause.

(6) The Licensee covenants and agrees that in any performance, concert, lecture, or public meeting of any kind in the College's premises, no language shall be uttered or feature of any kind presented that shall be unlawful, and that every member connected with any such performance, concert, lecture, or public meeting, or other such purpose for which this license is granted, shall abide by, conform to, and comply with all the laws of the United States and the State of New York, all the rules and regulations of any governmental bureau or department and all the local laws of the City of New York, and the rules and regulations of the Licensor for the management of its building, and will not do nor suffer to be done, anything on the said premises during the term of this agreement, in violation of any such rules, laws, or local laws, and if the attention of Licensee is called to such violation of the part of the Licensee, or any person employed by or admitted to said premises by Licensee, such Licensee will immediately terminate, desist from, and correct such violation.

- 2 -

(7) The Licensee covenants and agrees that it will not sell or serve, nor allow to be sold, brought into, or served on the premises, any alcoholic beverages or liquors. And the Licensee also covenants and agrees that no refreshments shall be served, article sold, or smoking permitted, unless a space is designated for such purposes by the Licensor; that no nails, tacks, or screws shall be driven or placed, and that all decorations shall be put up without defacing the building and under the supervision and with the approval of the Licensor, and that in case any damage of any kind shall be done to the said premises or the appurtenances thereof, the Licensee agrees to pay, in addition to the sums above mentioned, the amount of such damage or such amount as shall be necessary to put said premises in as good order and condition as the same were at the commencement of said agreement.

(8) The Licensee agrees not to transfer or assign this license without the written consent of the Licensor first had and obtained, nor suffer any business on the premises other than herein specified. The Licensee agrees not to do or permit anything to be done in said premises or bring or keep anything therein, including the use of flash equipment requiring electrical outlets which conflict with the laws relating to fires, with the regulations of the Fire Department, or with any of the rules or ordinances of the Board of Health.

(9) The Licensee agrees that in the event that motion picture projection or still picture projection be all or a part of the performance, the only position in the theater which is acceptable for the placement of motion picture projectors, stereopticons, slide projectors, any device using a carbon arc light source, and/or any device using a Xenon light source, shall be the house projection booth. No portable projection equipment of any kind with the exception of UL approved television transmission projectors shall be placed or permitted to be placed in any area of the auditorium other than the house projection booth, and at the Licensee's expense. At the sole discretion of the Licensor, a motion picture operator with a current New York City Bureau of Gas and Electricity Motion Picture Operator's License may be procured by the Licensee and at the Licensee's expense to operate projection equipment in the projection booth, but said operator shall, at all times, be under the supervision and approval of the Licensor's chief projectionist. A copy of the projectionist's current operator's license shall be presented to the Licensor prior to the performance date.

(10) It is mutually agreed that no audio or video broadcasting and/or recording will be permitted without the consent of Licensor first had and obtained in writing. The Licensee agrees to assume responsibility for, and to save the Licensor harmless from, any liability upon any claim or cause of action arising out of the utterance or publication of any alleged slanderous or libelous statements, whether in the broadcasting of any radio or television program, from the premises or in any recording or publication of the same, or in any other manner. The Licensee further agrees that should said audio/video broadcasting and/or recording be mutually agreed upon by both the Licensor and the Licensee, the Licensee shall not broadcast or record the performance nor cause the performance to be broadcast or recorded without first obtaining the written consent of each performer or his agent. Standard Broadcast and Recording Clearance release forms will be supplied by the Licensor for this purpose and the completed and signed forms must be presented to the Licensor prior to the first performance playdate named on page one of this contract. An individual form must be submitted to the Licensor for each performer before any broadcast or recording can be made.

(11) The Licensee agrees to secure in advance before the doors are opened, any and all licenses and/or permits that may be requisite for any performance, concert, lecture and/or public meetings given under this agreement; to secure any necessary certificates of electrical inspection from the Department of Water Supply, Gas and Electricity of the City of New York and/or the New York Board of Fire Underwriters for operation of any motion picture or other machine or equipment, and to do all other acts necessary to comply with all laws and requirements of the State of New York, the City of New York, or any department, board or authority thereof governing theaters or amusements, or otherwise applicable to said premises, including certification that stage sets and stage properties to be used by Licensee comply with the flame proof requirements of the New York Board of Underwriters.

- 3 -

(12) In accordance with the N. Y. City Administration Code, Chapter 19, Section 165.1, the Licensee agrees not to use or cause to be used, within the theater, any pyrotechnic device, heat-operated smoke machine, open flame cigar or cigarette without the written approval of the Fire Commissioner, Division of Fire Prevention. It remains the responsibility of the Licensee to inform the performing artists of these legal restrictions. Violations of Chapter 19, Section 165.1 can carry penalties of up to $1,000 per violation and the immediate close down of the performance by the Fire Captain.

(12b) The Licensor, recognizing its obligation to provide reasonable protection to the audience from ear damage, inserts the following Sound Pressure Protection Clause: The Licensor reserves the right to stop the performance should the Sound Pressure Level exceed the safety level of 115db at a distance of 15 feet from any speaker cluster for more than 60 seconds duration. Should this maximum safety SPL be exceeded, the power mains to the amplifiers will be disconnected. The Licensor's house soundman will take readings during the rehearsal and will monitor the performance to determine if average SPL's remain under 115db. A penalty of $500.00 will be imposed on the Licensee should the Licensor be forced to shut down the performance for dangerous Sound Pressure Levels. It remains the responsibility of the Licensee to inform the performing artists of this restriction, and to insure that those performers who use portable sound reinforcement, do not exceed the house Sound Pressure Limit.

(12c) The Licensee agrees to inform the Licensor no less than two weeks prior to the first performance named on page one of this contract of the intent to use any kind of coherent light emission device. At the Licensor's sole discretion, Laser light sources may be permitted to be used within the theater, but only with the following conditions, to which the Licensee agrees: No Class III or IV Laser device as defined by the Bureau of Radiological Health of the Food and Drug Administration (FDA) shall be placed or caused to be placed into operation within the theater without the required FDA written "variance." The FDA variance must be presented to the Licensor at least one week prior to the first performance. No Laser device shall be allowed to operate, even with written variance, if an FDA representative has not first been allowed to inspect the equipment and its installation in the theater prior to the performance, with proof of such an inspection submitted to the Licensor prior to the performance. All Laser devices and their use must conform to the Radiation Control Health and Safety Act.

(13) The Licensee agrees that it shall be the distinct obligation of the Licensee and of all persons connected with the Licensee under this license, not to involve the Licensor in any labor disputes. In the event that such a labor dispute arises, the Licensor has the absolute privilege and right to cancel this license and Licensee shall remain liable for the license fee.

(14) The Licensee agrees to light and heat the premises. Licensor does not guarantee the air conditioning equipment.

(15) The Licensor shall not be liable for any damage to any property in said premises or building at any time caused by any water, rain, snow, steam, gas, or electricity, which may leak into, issue or flow from the pipes or plumbing work or wires, or from any part of the building to which the premises hereby licensed are a part, or from any other place or quarter, nor shall the Licensor be liable to anyone for any loss of property from or on said premises, however occurring, or for any damage done to furniture, fixtures, or other effects of the Licensee, by an employee of the Licensor or any other person.

(16) Should the licensed premises herein described be destroyed either wholly or in part, or injured by fire or the elements, mob, riot, or use of any part of the premises, or performance of any part of this agreement be prevented or interfered with by strikes or any other cause prior to or during the time for which use of said premises is licensed, the Licensor may at its discretion, terminate the said license, returning to the Licensee any payments they may have been made to it for the proportionate period of use prevented, or interrupted, and the Licensee hereby expressly waives any claims for damages or compensation should the license be so terminated. The Licensor shall not in any way be liable for any loss or damage to personal property or other damage, delay, inconvenience, or annoyance to the Licensee arising from or because of strikes, lock-outs, or other labor difficulties, or for any other reason whatsoever.

(17) The Licensor, its officers, agents, and employees shall have the right at all times to enter any part of the licensed premises.

(18) The Licensee agrees to comply with the provisions and requirements of Section 485a of the Penal Law and such other provisions of law that may be applicable to performance by children under the age of sixteen years.

(19) The Licensee agrees that no portion of the sidewalks, entries, vestibules, halls, elevators or ways of access to public utilities of said building shall be obstructed by Licensee or used for any purpose other than for ingress and egress to and from the premises.

(20) Any change, addition or alteration to this license agreement shall not be binding unless made in writing and signed by the Licensor.

(21) This license agreement contains all of the terms of the understanding between the parties hereto and shall not be binding on the Licensor, and the premises referred to herein are not secured for any of the dates mentioned herein until this license agreement has been signed by the Licensor and Licensee, respectively, and a deposit has been made as specified by Licensor.

(22) All fees and all sums due Licensor under the terms of this agreement shall be payable by cash or by certified check or draft on a New York bank.

(23) If Licensee provides tickets, Licensee agrees to provide to Licensor, at least 30 days prior to the date of the performance, a printer's manifest of the house (a notarized, signed statement from the printer of the tickets listing the amount of tickets printed and each price). All tickets shall be printed by a bonded ticket house; e.g., Globe Tickets, Arcus-Simplex-Brown, Inc., National Ticket Co.

(24) The Licensor at its discretion reserves the right to add additional security as needed for the performance to a maximum of $_____

(25) Orchestra seats, Row 0, seat numbers 0-107 thru 0-114 are to be reserved for use by the Licensor for all performances. The tickets for these seats must be surrendered to the Licensor at least 10 days prior to the performance date.

(26) The Licensee agrees that all publicity material in the form of, but not limited to newspaper ads, radio ads, flyers, printed announcements of any kind, or promotional activities which communicate with the public, informing them of the event named on page one, shall be submitted to the Licensor for final approval. The Licensee agrees, also, that no such advertisement, promotion or communication shall use the logo of BCBC and that no advertisement, communication of promotion shall be issued or cause to be issued without the prior consent of the Licensor.

# APPENDIX E

(27) The Licensee shall provide the Licensor with a cash bond in the amount of $_____. Licensee's failure to mount the performance as advertised will result in the forfeiture of as much of the principal sum of the bond as is required to be used by the Licensor to refund advance ticket sales should the Licensee not provide prompt, full and complete refunding services. A service charge of One Dollar ($1.00) per ticket refunded will be deducted from the principal sum of the cash bond. Any additional payments due Licensor arising from Licensee's performance, if not promptly paid, shall also be deducted from the cash bond. Any excess cash shall be returned within a reasonable period of time.

(28) The Licensee agrees to accept the premises "as is" after having inspected the premises and found the premises suitable for the performance outlined above. The Licensee further agrees to indemnify and hold the Licensor harmless against liability claims and suits arising out of such use and occupancy and to provide the Licensor with a Certificate of Insurance with Brooklyn College, Center for the Performing Arts, and the City of New York named as additional insured. The insurance for the scheduled event shall include personal property, real property, and personal injury liability insurance coverage in the minimum amount of Five Hundred Thousand Dollars ($500,000.00). Such liability coverage will include the following:

a) Any personal and bodily injury to persons who attended the scheduled event as well as to persons who are lawfully on the Brooklyn College Campus immediately prior to, during or following the scheduled event.

b) Any personal property damage to persons who attend the scheduled event as well as to persons who are lawfully on the Brooklyn College Campus immediately prior to, during or following the scheduled event.

c) Any property damage to the buildings and other parts of the physical structure or grounds of the Brooklyn College Campus which is proximately caused by the scheduled event.

(29) The Licensee agrees that failure to comply with any of the above provisions by _____ days prior to the performance date, shall render this contract null and void and the deposit shall not be refundable.

**IN WITNESS WHEREOF,** The Board of Trustees of the City University of New York, the party of the first part, has caused this instrument to be signed by its duly authorized agent, and the party of the second part has duly signed this instrument, the day and year first above written.

> **BOARD OF TRUSTEES OF THE CITY UNIVERSITY OF NEW YORK (Licensor)**
>
> BY:_____
>
> _____(Licensee)
>
> BY:_____

Signed and Delivered
in the presence of:

_____

587

# Appendix F

SAMPLE TECHNICAL INFORMATION
BROCHURE FOR POTENTIAL
OUTSIDE RENTAL GROUPS

## Theater Rental Information

**BCBC**

**Brooklyn Center for the Performing Arts at Brooklyn College**

Brooklyn Center for the Performing Arts at Brooklyn College contains two fully equipped proscenium theaters. Walt Whitman is a 2500-seat concert hall and George Gershwin is a 500-seat theater. Both spaces have excellent sightlines and are air-conditioned.

The theaters are suitable for a wide range of programs including classical and popular music concerts, recitals, dance performances, stage plays, opera, film projection, graduations, lectures and meetings. They are also suitable for production work including still photography, film, video and radio.

## Walt Whitman Hall

**Stage**
- Proscenium: 38 feet wide, 20 feet high, 34 feet deep from curtain line to backwall
- Apron: 23 feet from curtain line to front of apron at center line
- Floor: flat finished wood with airspace; black Marley flooring available

**Seating**
- Capacity: 2,482 (Orchestra: 1,074; Mezzanine: 564; Balcony: 844)
- Mezzanine and Balcony can be curtained off

**Lighting**
- Strand-Century Multi-Q computerized lighting system with 64 dimmers
- Standard repertory lighting plot and two Super Trouper follow spots available

**Sound**
- Fully equipped sound system with tape playback
- System can interface with client's outboard equipment
- System has excellent fidelity and ⅓ octave equalization for optimum response
- 4-channel surround system available for special effects

**Technical Equipment and Personnel**
- Single speed 44-line counterweight fly system
- House curtain (vertical operation), black legs and borders, beige travelers, blackout curtain, cyc, black and white scrims
- Motorized screw orchestra lift can play from stage to basement level
- Acoustical shell available
- 35mm projection system with 40-foot CinemaScope screen and Dolby Stereo sound as well as 4-track magnetic quadraphonic sound
- 3∅ 400 amp per leg company switch on stage
- 3∅ 200 amp per leg company switch at loading dock to power remote video truck with separate entrance boxes for audio/video/electrical power
- Full stage crew available

Walt Whitman Hall

# George Gershwin Theater

**Stage**
- Proscenium: 30 feet wide, 16 feet high; 33 feet, 2 inches deep from curtain line to backwall
- Apron: 14 feet, 6 inches from curtain line to front of apron at center line
- Floor: flat finished wood with airspace; black Marley flooring available

**Seating**
- Capacity: 504

**Lighting**
- Strand-Century Micro-Q computerized lighting system with 48 dimmers
- Standard repertory lighting plot available

**Sound**
- Fully equipped sound system with tape and disc playback
- System can interface with client's outboard equipment

**Technical Equipment and Personnel**
- Single speed 45-line counterweight fly system
- House curtain (vertical operation), black borders, legs and travelers, cyc, black scrim
- Motorized screw orchestra lift can play from stage to basement level
- Double 16mm arc projection system with 30-foot CinemaScope screen
- Full stage crew available

George Gershwin Theater

# Appendix G

A MANUAL FOR BOX OFFICE TREASURERS
(Can be adapted for a computerized box office)

CARDINAL RULES OF BOX OFFICE BEHAVIOR

1. *Never* leave the box office unattended.
2. *Never* allow an unpaid ticket leave the box office.
3. *Never* allow anyone into the box office unless they are bonded.
4. *Never* take any box office business across the threshold.
5. *Never* discuss box office grosses or numbers of tickets sold with anyone. (If people inquire about business, your answer should be: "Business is very good," and absolutely nothing more.
6. *Never* show a statement to anyone; never prepare a statement in front of customers; never count money or prepare bank deposits in view of customers.
7. *Never* bring food or beverages of any kind into the box office.
8. *Never* issue free or discounted tickets without a written order from the producer or the manager.
9. *Never* make personal promises to customers or encourage them to deal only with you. Anyone in the box office should be able to help any customer.
10. *Never* tie up the box office phones with personal or unnecessarily long conversations.
11. *Never* hesitate to ask questions if you are uncertain about some policy or problem.
12. *Never* hesitate to hand over all monies in the event of a robbery.

P.S. Remember that you control the lifeline of the theatre. In the eyes of the customers you, more than any other person, *are* the theatre. Remember that a ticket is negotiable and, therefore, must be regarded as cash. Treat each ticket as if it were a fifty-dollar bill.

DAILY DUTIES OF THE TREASURERS

1. Report on time and have the customer windows open and ready for business from the stroke of 10 AM until the stroke of 10 PM.
2. Keep the box office clean and neat at all times. Since the janitor is

not allowed into the room, you will be required to sweep the floor daily.

3. Process all mail orders daily (see below).

4. Maintain and enlarge the mailing list:

    a. *Every* name and address that comes into the box office on a ticket order, check, credit card slip, information request or mailing list form must be checked against the mailing list.

    b. If the name is *not* already on the list, make out a new card, write the year in the upper right corner and file it.

    c. If the name *is* on the mailing list, enter the current date and refile the card.

5. Complete a box office statement for each performance:

    a. Each treasurer will complete their own statement and only then will these statements be compared for correctness. Only when all statements agree may a final copy be given to the business manager: no treasurer will end their time shift until all the statements agree.

    b. Each finalized statement will be signed by the head treasurer who is responsible for its accuracy.

    c. All deadwood, counted and numbered, will be boxed, labeled with the performance date, then given to the business manager.

    d. All stubs will be counted by the house manager and then numbered, banded and given to the business manager to check against the deadwood.

6. "Rack" all tickets by date and keep the current ticket rack filled with the tickets for the next, immediate performance.

7. Make out two daily bank deposits:

    a. One listing mail order checks only.

    b. One listing all other checks, credit card slips and cash (minus the precise amount of cash to be kept on hand for sales and payroll purposes. The business manager will dictate these amounts.)

    c. The treasurer shall also give the business manager a daily "silver and bill" cash order when this is required.

8. "Check out" the returned agency tickets and income each day when the agency treasurer(s) report to the box office. The agency treasurer will not leave the theatre until the daily receipts and cash are correct and accounted for.

9. "Phone in" unsold ticket locations for other theatres and record

unsold ticket numbers which they, if acting as your agent, did not sell. Return these unsold agency tickets to the rack: retain the sold tickets under the name of the agency and mark them "sold."

10. Report any problems, discrepancies or helpful information to the business or general manager.

## GENERAL SALES PROCEDURES

1. Always be courteous—but firm! Keep each transaction as brief and efficient as possible.
2. Every seat in the house is a "good" seat.
3. If phone or window customers ask for tickets and you are SRO, encourage them to return just before curtain time for cancellations.
   a. Cancellation lists are started an hour and a half before curtain time.
   b. Customers must be in the lobby and remain there to get on the list (no phone listings).
   c. Write the name, number and price of tickets desired and where the customer is waiting.
4. All ticket reservation envelopes shall carry the following, clearly written information:
   a. Customer's name and initials.
   b. Performance date: matinee or evening
   c. Number of tickets: price per ticket (2 x $4.95). Do not ever write the total amount due.
   d. Write the *exact* time when you told a customer that tickets, if not claimed, would be canceled.
5. Any ticket that is reserved *and* paid for will be held eternally.
6. Unpaid reservation policy:
   a. If the order is made more than a week in advance of the show, encourage the customer to send a check and, if the customer agrees, write "Ck. in mail" on the ticket envelope.
   b. Otherwise: we hold unpaid tickets until 12:30 (matinees) or 6:30 (evenings) on the performance day. If customers can't claim tickets by then, they must phone again to reconfirm the reservation. Then say that we hold tickets until 2:00 (matinees) or 8:00 (evenings) NEVER longer.
   c. Cancel and return to the rack all unpaid reservations not claimed within ten minutes after the "hold" time. This policy will be carried out whether we are sold out or not.
7. All tickets are to be sold on a "first come, first served" basis.
8. "Dress the house." Don't pack 'em in unless necessary.

9. Double check every transaction. *Handle only one transaction at a time.*

10. Traveler's checks and personal checks in the exact amount due are always acceptable, with driver's license or other identification on back. Master Card or Visa are also accepted at the window and by telephone.

11. Credit is never extended; unpaid tickets never leave the box office.

12. Press and complimentary tickets will be issued on numbered hardwood forms provided by the business manager and the actual tickets then placed in the "*dead*" rack. Record the number printed on the hardwood form on the back of the corresponding theatre ticket.

13. When making change:
    a. Don't give out tickets until the money is in your hand.
    b. Leave the customers' money on the counter until they have their change in hand.

14. Until one half hour prior to curtain, only the producer or general manager may assign or use house seats. At half-hour, the head treasurer may release the remaining house seats for general sale.

15. Do not put house seats on sale until the last feasible moment. If they are needed to cover an emergency or mistake, only the head treasurer may authorize their use.

## PROCEDURE FOR HANDLING MAIL ORDERS

1. All mail must be processed daily.

2. All mail work must be kept in a separate place, away from other business.

3. Wire baskets will be provided to hold "Information Requests," "Unprocessed Ticket Orders," "Problem Orders," "Mailing List Additions," and "Checker Basket."

4. Open each piece of mail and:
    a. Staple all contents to the customer's envelope with the check on top—throw nothing away!
    b. Separate ticket orders from information requests.
    c. Stamp the order form with the PAID stamp and enter the amount of the check in the "mail order income" box.
    d. Record customer's name and address on the check if it does not appear on it already.
    e. When all letters have been opened and checks removed, make out the bank deposit and place it, along with the checks, in the safe.

5. Process each piece of mail individually as follows:

    a. Read entire letter or form and underline in red: date, number of tickets and location desired.

    b. Pull the tickets, giving the customer what he wants if possible, and write the date of the tickets, location and price per ticket on the letter in red. Be certain he has sent in the right amount for the tickets.

    c. Stamp and address an envelope to the customer.

    d. Attach all this together and place in the "checker" basket.

6. Checker duties:

    a. Reread each letter.

    b. Check order against tickets pulled.

    c. Write "tickets mailed" and today's date on letter.

    d. Place tickets in envelope, blanket them, weigh envelope to determine postage, scotch-tape the envelope seal, place envelope in outgoing mail box.

    e. Place the customer's letter or order in "mailing list" basket.

7. After customer letters have been checked against the mailing list, file them alphabetically in the "customer correspondence" file.

    a. If a customer phones to inquire about an order, check this letter file immediately.

    b. If customers complain that they didn't get what they asked for, locate their order. Chances are they forgot what they ordered.

## POSSIBLE MAIL ORDER PROBLEMS AND POLICY REGARDING THEM

1. If check is insufficient to cover tickets ordered:

    a. Pull the tickets anyway.

    b. Deposit the check.

    c. Hold tickets and notify the customer of the balance due.

2. If the check is for *more* than the amount due:

    a. Process mail as usual, enter refundable amount on letter.

    b. Mail the tickets.

    c. Enclose a letter signed by the head treasurer saying that "upon presentation of this letter at box office, a refund will be made."

3. If tickets are sold out for the performance requested by customer:

    a. Return the letter and the check to the customer.

      b.  Notify the customer when tickets are available.

4.  If the customer returns tickets by mail for a refund, refer the case to the business manager for a decision.

5.  If the mail order is incomplete and does not include all the necessary information:

      a.  Place the letter and check in the "problem" basket.

      b.  Notify the customer of his or her negligence (by phone, if a local call, otherwise by postcard).

6.  When possible, use the postcard form shown as follows to notify the customer when an order cannot be filled:

---

We are unable to complete your ticket order for the following reason:

_____ We are sold out for the (price) (date) you requested.
_____ Seats available, but not the specific locations.
_____ Incorrect payment. You sent \$_____Should be \$_____
_____ Failed to state date_____matinee_____evening_____
_____ Check returned for signature.
_____ Number of tickets and price were not indicated.
_____ Tickets requested not available until_____
_____ The performance you requested is not scheduled.
_____ We are returning your check.
_____ We are holding your check for further instructions.
_____ We are holding your tickets at the box office.

---

PROCEDURES FOR ANSWERING THE BOX OFFICE PHONES

1.  Salutation: "Good morning. Playhouse box office."

2.  If the call is not box office business, refer it to the correct number. Do not take messages or accept nonbusiness calls.

3.  If you are speaking on one line and another line rings:

      a.  Ask your party to "hold on, please" and push the hold button.

      b.  Nest, push the flashing button, ask that person to "hold on, please." Customers phoning long distance will probably tell you, in which case deal with them immediately.

      c.  Push hold button again, return to original call and finish that before going on to the next.

4.  Long distance calls take priority over local calls.

5.  Phone calls take priority over window customers.

6. Learn immediately how to give clear directions (car and public transportation) to the playhouse from all points within a fifty-mile radius.
7. When an order is taken, repeat the number of tickets, location and date and *emphasize* the cancellation time.
8. If a customer requests your name, give your first name only.
9. Keep yourself informed about the intermission and show break times.
10. Make a note about the seat numbers occupied by doctors. Inform the manager if any VIP or celebrity ticket orders are made.

## PROCEDURE FOR HANDLING CREDIT CARD ORDERS

1. At the box office window:
   a. Fill out a blank credit card duplicate slip with: today's date, date of performance, matinee or evening, number of tickets ordered, price per ticket, total price, ticket locations.
   b. Insert customer's card under the dupe slip in the imprinter and slide handle. CHECK TO BE CERTAIN THAT THE IMPRESSION IS LEGIBLE.
   c. If order totals more than amount specified by credit card company, phone the toll-free credit number to get an authorization.
   d. Check all other card numbers against the current published list of invalid numbers.
   e. Ask customer to sign the slip and "please press down."
   f. Give tickets and customer copy of slip to customer.
   g. Write customer's permanent address on back of the theatre copy of the slip for mailing list.
   h. Place the theatre copy and deposit copy of slip (still attached) in "today's CC orders" box.
2. Over the telephone:
   a. Write customer's name and address on the duplicate slip, preprinted with the theatre information by the imprinter.
   b. Write the credit card number and company initials.
   c. Fill in ticket information and price as per above instructions.
   d. Write "PO" for "phone order" where customer's signature would otherwise go.
   e. Repeat all information for customer to verify.
   f. Inform customer there is now a paid reservation that will be held until claimed.

    g. If customers request that tickets be mailed, ask them to send a stamped, self-addressed envelope.

    h. Place the entire dupe slip together with tickets pulled in "CC Check" basket. (Prior to the performance, a treasurer will be assigned to check all credit card numbers, check accuracy of written information against the tickets pulled, file tickets and customer's copy of slip in envelope under the appropriate performance date.)*

## PROCEDURE WHEN CUSTOMER HAS LOST TICKETS

1. If tickets were ordered by mail:

    a. If they were season tickets, check customer's file card and issue a pass for correct locations, signed by head treasurer.

    b. Check mail file and issue a pass for correct locations, signed by head treasurer.

    c. If there is no record of customer's order, head treasurer may cross-examine customer and use his or her own judgement as to whether or not a pass should be issued.

2. If it was a credit card order, check the file of credit card duplicate slips (filed by performance date).

3. If correspondence shows that the tickets ordered were for another performance than the one remembered by the customer, issue a pass for that performance only.

4. Always issue passes for lost or stolen tickets by writing the locations on a ticket envelope, not on hardwood, as that would represent a duplicate ticket if the actual ticket shows up.

5. Always clearly explain to customers that, if a pass is issued for lost or stolen tickets and they arrive at their seats to find someone sitting in them with the real tickets, the customer with the pass must relinquish the seats.

6. No theatre staff member is to enter into any dispute between customers in regard to found or stolen tickets: this matter is strictly between the two customers.

*Note: Theatres with a high volume of telephone credit card orders may find it easier to hire a special phone operator to handle such calls. In this case exact ticket locations are not given to customer; rather the order forms are given to a treasurer who periodically pulls the tickets, completes the information on the order slip and files the tickets under the performance date.

# Appendix H

## AN AUDIT SYSTEM FOR THE
## NONCOMPUTERIZED BOX OFFICE

1. Clean out all money due box office (by check from regular account; include I.O.U.s, petty cash advances, etc.).
2. Prepare a statement of all money due the box office for tickets (from agencies, benefit groups, etc.) *if* the actual tickets are in the hands of the agent.
3. Deposit all checks and monies on hand (except required cash for change).
4. Transfer all "tax admission" monies from box office account to tax bureau, if there are any such taxes.
5. Compute the checkbook balance; deduct all checks paid out. Deduct all refunds made through the last performance.
6. Compute total gross forward (minus tax) to last performance.
7. Arrange to pick up bank statement and canceled checks of box office account on the Friday prior to audit; notify bank in advance. Reconcile these with checkbook balance as of audit date.
8. Count all cash on hand (include cash box advances to ticket agencies).
9. Count all UNPAID tickets on hand, both in rack and reservation envelopes.
10. In counting tickets, each group must be checked by another counter. Recount where there are discrepancies.
11. Prepare audit statement as follows:

ADD COLUMN

1. Advance sales monies received from agencies and credit card orders
2. Advance monies due from agencies for actual tickets in their hands
3. Cash on hand
4. Agency cash on hand (if loaned from box office)

SUBTRACT COLUMN

1. Any monies due box office, *not* already paid to box office account
2. Beginning-of-the-season box office balance

COMPUTE

Add column, minus the subtract column will equal the advance sales for the remainder of the season. Add this to the price represented by all

UNPAID tickets on hand and you *should* get the total potential gross for the remainder of the season. This is, of course, only if you have transferred all monies from the box office account as determined by the gross shown on statements up to the last performance. Your remainder, then, should equal the cash sales advance you have just computed.

Prepare a statement as follows:

Calculation of Box Office Shortage or Overage
Per Reconciliation performed on_____.

at_____(AM) (PM)

| | |
|---|---|
| Box office checkbook balance (including deposit in transit) | $XXXXX |
| *Add:* Cash fund left in box office | XXXX |
| *Add:* Accounts receivable (agencies, hotels, I.O.U.s, etc.) | XXXX |
| | |
| Total Adjusted Cash Balance | $XXXXX |
| | |
| Capacity of house (in printed tickets for last week) | $XXXXX |
| *Less:* Unsold tickets on hand (in racks, at agencies, reservations unpaid for) | XXX |
| | |
| Net Advance Sales of Last Week | XXXXX |
| | |
| Cash Over or Under Advance Sales | $_____ |

AUDIT MANAGER_____

ASSISTING:

_____

_____

_____

DO NOT DEPOSIT ANY OF NEXT YEAR'S TICKET SALES INCOME, BUT KEEP IN SEPARATE FOLDER OR BANK ACCOUNT, PENDING COMPLETION OF BOX OFFICE AUDIT.

# Appendix I

SAMPLE BOX OFFICE REPORT FORMS

SAMPLE 1
BOX OFFICE REPORT

DATE:_____  cc: _____

ATTRACTION:_____  DATE OF PERFORMANCE _____

THEATRE_____  CURTAIN TIME _____

| Location | Capacity | On Hand | Sold | Price | Total |
|----------|----------|---------|------|-------|-------|
| _____ | _____ | _____ | ____ | ____ | ____ |
| _____ | _____ | _____ | ____ | ____ | ____ |
| _____ | _____ | _____ | ____ | ____ | ____ |
| _____ | _____ | _____ | ____ | ____ | ____ |
| _____ | _____ | _____ | ____ | ____ | ____ |

Specials:

_____          ____  ____  ____
_____          ____  ____  ____
_____          ____  ____  ____
_____          ____  ____  ____
_____          ____  ____  ____

Less Credit Card Charges:
Less Subscription Discounts:
Less Agency Charges:
Totals____  _____  _____  _____  _____
                          (total used)
                          Gross forwarded: _____
                          Gross to date:   _____

Remarks:


Total receipts transferred or credited to:

## SAMPLE 2
## BOX OFFICE STATEMENT

DATE ........................ ATTRACTION ..................

EVENING ..................... MATINEE .....................

| Capacity | On Hand | Sold | Gross Per Ticket | Gross Amount | Tax Per Ticket | Tax |
|---|---|---|---|---|---|---|
| Orch .... | ......... | ......... | 4.09 | ......... | .31 | ....... |
| Orch .... | ......... | ......... | 3.50 | ......... | .25 | ....... |
| Orch .... | ......... | ......... | 2.36 | ......... | .14 | ....... |
| Balc. .... | ......... | ......... | 3.50 | ......... | .25 | ....... |
| Balc. .... | ......... | ......... | 2.36 | ......... | .14 | ....... |
| Balc. .... | ......... | ......... | 1.45 | ......... | .05 | ....... |

Matinee luncheon special:

.................. ................... .............

Other specials:

.................. ................... .............
.................. ................... .............

*Less:* Supscription discount:
*Less:* Credit Card Charges:

.................. ................... .............

Standees .......... ......... ......... .........

       Gross this performance      ............... .......
       Gross forward      ............... .......
       Gross to date      ............... .......

## SAMPLE 3
## BOX OFFICE STATEMENT

ATTRACTION _____

DATE_____MATINEE_____EVENING_____

WEATHER:  SUNNY_____CLOUDY_____STORMY_____

| CAPACITY | ON HAND | SOLD | TICKET PRICE | GROSS AMOUNT |
|---|---|---|---|---|
| Orch. _____ | _____ | _____ | 4.75 | _____ |
| Orch. _____ | _____ | _____ | 3.95 | _____ |
| Orch. _____ | _____ | _____ | 2.75 | _____ |
| Balc. _____ | _____ | _____ | 3.95 | _____ |
| Balc. _____ | _____ | _____ | 2.75 | _____ |
| Balc. _____ | _____ | _____ | 1.75 | _____ |

Dinner Theatre Specials _____          _____

Matinee Luncheon Specials _____          _____

Other Specials _____          _____

_____          _____

LESS Season Ticket Discount: _____          _____

(For Use on Playhouse Copy Only)   Gross this performance _____
Mail Order Income Today _____   Gross forward _____
Window Income Today _____

Agency Income Today _____   Gross for this
Attraction to date _____

Total Bank Deposit Today _____

SAMPLE 4
BOX OFFICE STATEMENT

_____ PERF. OF _____ DATE _____ MAT EVE

WEATHER _____SERIES _____ DAY _____

| | ORCH. | BALC. | PRICE EACH | TOTAL |
|---|---|---|---|---|
| SUBSCRIPTION | | | | |
| REG. SALE | | | | |
| CO-OP SALE | | | | |
| GROUP | | | | |
| GROUP | | | | |
| GROUP | | | | |
| COMP | | | | |
| STUDENT COMP | | | | |
| DEADWOOD | | | | |
| TOTAL | | | | |
| CAPACITY | | | | |
| DIFFERENCE | | | | |
| TOTAL PAID THIS PERF. | | | | |
| PREVIOUS TOTAL | | | | |
| TOTAL TO DATE | | | | |

ATTENDANCE _____

_____
TREASURER

REMARKS:

## SAMPLE 5

BOX OFFICE STATEMENT_____THEATRE.  SHOW_____

DAY_____DATE_____AT_____PM.  WEATHER_____

| Price | Capacity | Theatre | Agency Allot. | Pass | Spec | Total Dead | Sold | Amount | Loc. Tax | Fed. Tax |
|---|---|---|---|---|---|---|---|---|---|---|
| | | | | | | | | | | |
| | | | | | | | | | | |
| | | | | | | | | | | |
| | | | | | | | | | | |
| Total | | | | | | | | | | |

SPECIALS: (Seasons, Industrials, Groups, Disc.)

| | Price | No. Sold | Amount | Loc. Tax | Reg. Price | Disc. % | | | | |
|---|---|---|---|---|---|---|---|---|---|---|
| S e a s o n | | | | | | | | | | Total |
| G r o u p s | | | | | | | | | | Total |
| D i s c s. | | | | | | | | | | Total |
| I n d u s t | | | | | | | | | | Total |

THEATRE PARTY AGENTS' & BROKERS' FEES
AGENCIES:

| | Price | Sold | Amount | Loc. Tax | Agency Dead | | | | |
|---|---|---|---|---|---|---|---|---|---|
| | | | | | | | | | |
| | | | | | | | | | |
| | | | | | | | | | |
| Total | | | | | | | | | Total |

HARDWOOD:

| | Price | Sold | Amount | Loc. Tax | Serial Numbers | | | | |
|---|---|---|---|---|---|---|---|---|---|
| | | | | | | | | | |
| | | | | | | | | | |
| | | | | | | | | | |
| | | | | | | | | | Total |

We hereby certify that the
undersigned have personally
checked the above statement
and it is in every respect correct.

This Performance _____

    Total to Date _____

        Total _____

TREASURER_____

    Adjustment _____

MANAGER_____

      TOTAL _____

SAMPLE 6

THEATRE                                    WEEK ENDING

### WEEKLY SUMMARY OF BOX OFFICE STATEMENTS

| | Admissions | Amount | Tax | Show |
|---|---|---|---|---|
| Theatre | | | | |
| Seasons | | | | |
| Industrial | | | | |
| Groups | | | | |
| Agencies | | | | |
| Hardwood | | | | |
| Adjustments | | | | |
| Total This Week | | | | |
| Less Commissions-A | | | | |
| Total This Week - 1 | | | | |
| This Week's Total | | | | |
| Plus Commissions | | | | |
| Grand Total This Week | | | | |
| Total Carried Forward | | | | |
| Grand Total to Date | | | | |

*Bank Deposits this week        $ _____        Net of Refund

Bank Deposits to date             _____        Net of Refund

Grand Total Bank Deposits       _____        Net of Refund

*Do not include re-deposits

**Must correspond to Ticket Account Report
for this week**

**Includes Weekend Deposit**

# Appendix J

(Available with instructions for completion from the National Endowment for the Arts)

OMB No. 3135-0055 Expires 12/31/89

| Theater Fiscal Year 1989 | Organization Grant Application Form NEA–3 (Rev.) |
|---|---|

Applications must be submitted in triplicate and mailed to: Information Management Division/TH, 8th floor, National Endowment for the Arts, Nancy Hanks Center, 1100 Pennsylvania Avenue, N.W., Washington, D.C. 20506

| I. Applicant Organization (name, address, zip) | II. Category under which support is requested: | III. Period of support requested: |
|---|---|---|
| | | Starting _____ |
| | | month  day  year |
| | | Ending _____ |
| | | month  day  year |

**IV. Summary of project activity (Complete in space provided. DO NOT reduce copy or continue on additional pages.)**

**V. Estimated number of persons expected to benefit from this activity.**

**VI. Summary of estimated costs (recapitulation of budget items in Section IX)**

|  | | Total costs of activity |
|---|---|---|
| A. Direct costs | | |
| Salaries and wages | _____ | $ _____ |
| Fringe benefits | _____ | $ _____ |
| Supplies and materials | _____ | $ _____ |
| Travel | _____ | $ _____ |
| Permanent equipment | _____ | $ _____ |
| Fees and other | _____ | $ _____ |
| | Total direct costs | $ _____ |
| B. Indirect costs | _____ | $ _____ |
| | Total project costs | $ _____ |

**VII. Total amount requested from the National Endowment for the Arts**   $ _____
(Total amount requested from NEA as a % of total proposal costs in VI. above = _____ %)

| VIII. Organization total fiscal activity | 1987–88 season | Estimated for 1988–89 season |
|---|---|---|
| A. Expenses | 1. $ _____ | 2. $ _____ |
| B. Revenues, grants, & contributions | 1. $ _____ | 2. $ _____ |

**Do not write in this space**

IX. Budget breakdown of summary of estimated costs

2

A. Direct costs

1. Salaries and wages (INCLUDE ARTISTS' COMPENSATION IF PAID ON A SALARY BASIS)

| Title and/or type of personnel | Number of personnel | Annual or average salary range exclusive of incidentals | % of time devoted to this project | Amount $ |
|---|---|---|---|---|
| | | | | |
| | | | | |
| | | | | |
| | | | | |
| | | | | |
| | | | | |
| | | | | |
| | | | | |
| | | | | |
| | | | | |
| | | | | |

Total salaries and wages $ _____
Add fringe benefits $ _____
Total salaries and wages including fringe benefits $ _____

2. Supplies and materials (list each major type separately)

Amount
$

| | |
|---|---|
| | |
| | |
| | |
| | |
| | |

Total supplies and materials $ _____

3. Travel

Transportation of personnel

| No. of travelers | from | to | Amount $ |
|---|---|---|---|
| | | | |
| | | | |
| | | | |
| | | | |

Total transportation of personnel $ _____

Subsistence

| No. of travelers | No. of days | Daily rate | $ |
|---|---|---|---|
| | | | |
| | | | |
| | | | |
| | | | |

Total subsistence $ _____
Total travel $ _____

**IX.  Budget breakdown of summary of estimated costs (continued)**

**3**

4.  Permanent Equipment

Amount
$

| | |
|---|---|
| | |
| | |
| | |

Total permanent equipment    $ _____

5.  Fees for services and other expenses including incidental
expenses for artists (list each item separately)
(INCLUDE ARTISTS' COMPENSATION IF PAID ON A FEE BASIS)

Amount
$

| | |
|---|---|
| | |
| | |
| | |
| | |
| | |
| | |
| | |

Total fees and other    $ _____

B. Indirect costs
Rate established by attached rate negotiation agreement with
National Endowment for the Arts or another Federal agency
Rate _____% Base $ _____

Amount

$ _____

**X.  Contributions, grants, and revenues (for this project)**

A. Contributions

Amount

1. Cash

$ _____

2. In-kind contributions (list each major item)

| | |
|---|---|
| | |
| | |
| | |

Total contributions    $ _____

B. Grants (do not list anticipated grant from the Arts Endowment)

$

| | |
|---|---|
| | |
| | |

Total grants    $ _____

C. Revenues

$

| | |
|---|---|
| | |
| | |
| | |

Total revenues    $ _____
Total contributions, grants, and revenues for this project    $ _____

**4**

XI. Final Reports

Have you submitted required Final Report packages on all completed Arts Endowment
grants since (and including) Fiscal Year 1984?

_____Yes  _____ No. If no, please mail immediately, under separate cover, to Grants Office/Final Reports Section to
maintain eligiblity. Do not include with your application package.

XII. Certification

We certify that the information in this application, including all attachments
and supporting materials, is true and correct to the best of our knowledge.

Authorizing official(s)

Signature                     X _____ Date signed _____
Name (print or type)          _____
Title (print or type)         _____
Telephone (area code)         _____

Signature                     X _____ Date signed _____
Name (print or type)          _____
Title (print or type)         _____
Telephone (area code)         _____

Project director

Signature                     X _____ Date signed _____
Name (print or type)          _____
Title (print or type)         _____
Telephone (area code)         _____

*Payee (to whom grant payments will be sent if other than authorizing official)

Signature                     X _____ Date signed _____
Name (print or type)          _____
Title (print or type)         _____
Telephone (area code)         _____

* If payment is to be made to anyone other than the grantee, it is understood that
the grantee is financially, administratively, and programmatically responsible for
all aspects of the grant and that all reports must be submitted through the grantee.

BE SURE TO DOUBLE CHECK THE "HOW TO APPLY" SECTION UNDER THE APPROPRIATE CATEGORY FOR ALL
MATERIALS TO BE INCLUDED IN YOUR APPLICATION PACKAGE. LATE APPLICATIONS WILL BE REJECTED. IN-
COMPLETE APPLICATIONS ARE UNLIKELY TO BE FUNDED.

Privacy Act
The Privacy Act of 1974 requires us to furnish you with the following information:

The Endowment is authorized to solicit the requested information by Section 5 of
the National Foundation on the Arts and the Humanities Act of 1965, as amended.
The information is used for grant processing, statistical research, analysis of
trends, and for congressional oversight hearings. Failure to provide the requested
information could result in rejection of your application.

OMB No. 3135-0055 Expires 12/31/89

## FY 1989 Professional Theater Companies Supplementary Information Sheet

**Name of Organization:** _____

If event was booked in, indicate with **one** asterisk; mark co-productions with **two** asterisks. Indicate number of public performances on "Title" line between parentheses. Provide 1989–90 season information only if it is reasonably firm.

**I. SEASON INFORMATION**　　　　**1986–87 Season**　　　　**Artistic Director:** _____

| Title | 1. _____ ( ) | 5. _____ ( ) | 9. _____ ( ) |
| Author | | | |
| Director | | | |

| Title | 2. _____ ( ) | 6. _____ ( ) | 10. _____ ( ) |
| Author | | | |
| Director | | | |

| Title | 3. _____ ( ) | 7. _____ ( ) | 11. _____ ( ) |
| Author | | | |
| Director | | | |

| Title | 4. _____ ( ) | 8. _____ ( ) | 12. _____ ( ) |
| Author | | | |
| Director | | | |

**1987-88 Season**　　　　**Artistic Director:** _____

| Title | 1. _____ ( ) | 5. _____ ( ) | 9. _____ ( ) |
| Author | | | |
| Director | | | |

| Title | 2. _____ ( ) | 6. _____ ( ) | 10. _____ ( ) |
| Author | | | |
| Director | | | |

| Title | 3. _____ ( ) | 7. _____ ( ) | 11. _____ ( ) |
| Author | | | |
| Director | | | |

| Title | 4. _____ ( ) | 8. _____ ( ) | 12. _____ ( ) |
| Author | | | |
| Director | | | |

**1988-89 Season**　　　　**Artistic Director:** _____

| Title | 1. _____ ( ) | 5. _____ ( ) | 9. _____ ( ) |
| Author | | | |
| Director | | | |

| Title | 2. _____ ( ) | 6. _____ ( ) | 10. _____ ( ) |
| Author | | | |
| Director | | | |

| Title | 3. _____ ( ) | 7. _____ ( ) | 11. _____ ( ) |
| Author | | | |
| Director | | | |

| Title | 4. _____ ( ) | 8. _____ ( ) | 12. _____ ( ) |
| Author | | | |
| Director | | | |

**1989-90 Season**　　　　**Artistic Director:** _____

| Title | 1. _____ ( ) | 5. _____ ( ) | 9. _____ ( ) |
| Author | | | |
| Director | | | |

| Title | 2. _____ ( ) | 6. _____ ( ) | 10. _____ ( ) |
| Author | | | |
| Director | | | |

| Title | 3. _____ ( ) | 7. _____ ( ) | 11. _____ ( ) |
| Author | | | |
| Director | | | |

| Title | 4. _____ ( ) | 8. _____ ( ) | 12. _____ ( ) |
| Author | | | |
| Director | | | |

# FY 1989 Professional Theater Companies Supplementary Information Sheet (Page 2)

**Name of organization:** _____

**II. GENERAL INFORMATION**

|  |  | Actual 1986–87 | Actual 1987–88 | Current Year 1988–89 | Next Year 1989–90 |
|---|---|---|---|---|---|
| Capacity of theater(s) | 1. | | | | |
| | 2. | | | | |
| | 3. | | | | |
| | 4. | | | | |
| Top single ticket price | | | | | |
| Top subscription price | | | | | |
| Lowest single student discount price | | | | | |
| Number of performance weeks | | | | | |
| Season (starting month—ending month) | | | | | |
| Season tickets sold | | | | | |
| Total attendance | | | | | |
| Percentage of capacity | | | | | |
| Number of employees | | | | | |

Salary or salary range per <u>week</u>/ #weeks employed
(use listing that approximates your staff titles)

| | Actual 1986–87 | Actual 1987–88 | Current Year 1988–89 | Next Year 1989–90 |
|---|---|---|---|---|
| Artistic Director | | | | |
| Managing Director | | | | |
| Development Director | | | | |
| Marketing Director | | | | |
| Technical Director | | | | |
| Costume Supervisor | | | | |
| Properties Supervisor | | | | |
| Actors in performance | | | | |
| (exclusive of incidental expenses) | | | | |
| Actors in rehearsal | | | | |
| (exclusive of incidental expenses) | | | | |

Fee range, per production
(exclusive of incidental expenses)

| | Actual 1986–87 | Actual 1987–88 | Current Year 1988–89 | Next Year 1989–90 |
|---|---|---|---|---|
| Directors | | | | |
| Designers: Sets | | | | |
| Costumes | | | | |
| Lights | | | | |
| Artist incidental expenses | | | | |
| Housing: Total expenditure | | | | |
| # artists served | | | | |
| Transportation: Total expenditure | | | | |
| # artists served | | | | |
| Other: _____ | | | | |
| Total expenditure | | | | |
| #artists served | | | | |
| Total actor employment weeks* | | | | |
| Average weekly actor salary* (gross) | | | | |
| Rehearsal period (weeks per production) | | | | |
| Type of A.E.A. contract, if any | | | | |

Plays toured (name)

States toured (name)

* See page 43 for instructions
(continued on next page)

## FY 89 Professional Theater Companies Supplementary Information Sheet (Page 3)

Name of Organization: _____

NOTE: Expressing dollar figures as a percentage of total expenses is optional. Round off to nearest percentage.

### III. FINANCIAL INFORMATION

Fiscal Year Ends (Month) _____

| | Actual 1986–87 | | Actual 1987–88 | | Current Year 1988–89 | | Next Year 1989–90 | |
|---|---|---|---|---|---|---|---|---|
| | $ | % | $ | % | $ | % | $ | % |
| **EXPENSES** (All Funds) | | | | | | | | |
| Artistic personnel | / | | / | | / | | / | |
| Technical personnel | / | | / | | / | | / | |
| Administrative personnel | / | | / | | / | | / | |
| Production expenses | / | | / | | / | | / | |
| Marketing expenses | / | | / | | / | | / | |
| Fundraising expenses | / | | / | | / | | / | |
| Occupancy expenses | / | | / | | / | | / | |
| Administrative expenses | / | | / | | / | | / | |
| **Sub-Total** | / | | / | | / | | / | |
| Capital expenses | / | | / | | / | | / | |
| Other expenses _____ | / | | / | | / | | / | |
| | / | | / | | / | | / | |
| | / | | / | | / | | / | |
| **Total expenses** | /100 | | /100 | | /100 | | /100 | |
| **EARNED INCOME (All Funds)** | | | | | | | | |
| Box office income | / | | / | | / | | / | |
| Other earned income | / | | / | | / | | / | |
| **Total earned income** | / | | / | | / | | / | |
| **EARNINGS GAP** | ( )/ | | ( )/ | | ( )/ | | ( )/ | |
| **CONTRIBUTED INCOME** (All Funds) | | | | | | | | |
| NEA—Theater—Companies | / | | / | | / | | / | |
| —Other: _____ | / | | / | | / | | / | |
| —Opera-Musical Theater Program | / | | / | | / | | / | |
| —Dance Program | / | | / | | / | | / | |
| —Expansion Arts Program | / | | / | | / | | / | |
| —Inter-Arts Program | / | | / | | / | | / | |
| —Challenge or Advancement Program | / | | / | | / | | / | |
| —Other Program _____ | / | | / | | / | | / | |
| Other Federal sources | / | | / | | / | | / | |
| State government sources | / | | / | | / | | / | |
| Local government sources | / | | / | | / | | / | |
| Individuals | / | | / | | / | | / | |
| Corporations | / | | / | | / | | / | |
| Foundations | / | | / | | / | | / | |
| United Arts Fund | / | | / | | / | | / | |
| Other contributions | / | | / | | / | | / | |
| **Sub-Total** | / | | / | | / | | / | |
| Capital contributions | / | | / | | / | | / | |
| **Total contributed income** | / | | / | | / | | / | |
| **SURPLUS OR (DEFICIT)** | / | | / | | / | | / | |
| **Fund balance beginning of year** | | | | | | | | |
| **Fund balance end of year** | | | | | | | | |
| **Net current assets (liabilities) end of year** | | | | | | | | |

# Appendix K

## SAMPLE INSURANCE CLAIM KIT

TO THEATRE ADMINISTRATORS AND SUPERVISORS

This claim kit has been prepared to assure standardization of processing all insurance claim matters. Prompt and careful attention will insure that all claims will receive proper and efficient consideration by the insurance company.

GENERAL INSTRUCTIONS
1. Each claim, of whatever nature, should be reported promptly, using forms provided with this kit or furnished by the insurance company.
2. Liaison should be established with the office of our insurance company. Other information is furnished elsewhere in this kit. Arrangements have been made for a representative of the company to contact you, to discuss procedures and to provide for close cooperation.
3. Should unusual difficulties arise with respect to any claim, notification should immediately be made to John Doe, Claims Supervisor of our insurance company, tel: 000-555-0001.
4. In the event that any claim appears to be of a serious nature, verbal contact should be made immediately with the insurance officer. This should be followed by the regular written report.
5. Additional copies of all report forms may be obtained from the insurance officer.
6. Feel free to consult with the managing director of the theatre with respect to any claim matter.
7. Supervisors should be careful not to commit themselves on liability matters (injuries to patrons), nor to commit themselves for any expenses on their compensation cases.
8. Insurance company offices and representatives:
    1._____
    2._____
    3._____

SPECIFIC INSTRUCTIONS

A.  EMPLOYEE INJURIES (WORKMEN'S COMPENSATION)

1.  Employees should be directed to report any injury during the course of employment to the manager immediately.
2.  All bills for treatment of injuries should be forwarded to the insurance company, attention: John Doe, and should contain the following information:
    a.  Name of employee
    b.  Place where injury occurred
    c.  Date of injury
3.  Classes of Employees:
    a.  Performers are considered to be New York State employees and are subject to New York State laws. Forms provided for New York should, therefore, be used and distributed as set forth later in this kit.
    b.  Nonperformers are considered to be employees in the state where employed. Forms provided for the state in which your theatre is located should be used and distributed as set forth later in this kit.
4.  It is vital that a copies of all reports be forwarded to the insurance company.

B.  INJURIES TO PATRONS

1.  First aid should be rendered as quickly as possible.
2.  Employees should be directed to report any injury sustained by a patron, no matter how minor, to the manager.
3.  Manager should obtain all data pertaining to the accident, including area where accident occurred, names and addresses of witnesses, if possible, and all information pertinent to the injured patron.
4.  Report should be prepared as quickly as possible and distributed as follows:
    a.  Original to servicing office
    b.  One (1) copy to the insurance company
    c.  One (1) copy to the manager
    d.  One (1) copy for your file.
5.  Details of injuries of an apparently serious nature should be telephoned to the insurance office as soon as possible. Written report, distributed as above, should follow.

## C. AUTOMOBILE ACCIDENTS

1. Report of accident should be prepared as quickly as possible, on forms provided, and distributed as follows:
   a. Original to servicing office
   b. One (1) copy to the insurance company
   c. One (1) copy to the manager
   d. One (1) copy for your file
2. State reports, when required, should be prepared and forwarded as follows:
   a. Proper state authority, as indicated on forms
   b. Copy to the manager
3. Where damage to vehicle, either theatre-owned or leased or other party's, or injury to parties, appears to be of a serious nature, immediate telephone report should be made to insurance office. Written report should follow.
4. Where damage to theatre vehicle is involved, report should contain information as to where vehicle may be inspected.

## DIRECT DAMAGE TO THEATRE PROPERTY

1. All information pertaining to direct damage to theatre property should be reported to the manager immediately.
2. With respect to burglary or vandalism claims, report at once to local police, giving all details except with regard to values or extent of dollar loss sustained.
3. Great care should be taken to protect undamaged property when a loss occurs, and losses should be reported promptly.

## PERFORMERS

1. All performers are considered to be New York State employees.
2. Use Form C-2 to report all injuries to employees in this category: form should be completed as fully as possible.
3. All bills should be sent to the insurance company, attention: John Doe, containing information as set forth previously in this kit.

# Appendix L

## AN ANNOTATED GUIDE TO SELECTED NATIONAL AND REGIONAL ARTS SERVICE ORGANIZATIONS

ACRONYM      NAME OF ORGANIZATION HOME OFFICE, FUNCTION

AAI

**AFFILIATE ARTISTS, INC.**  New York City
Provides artists with professional experience by offering 3-year residency programs. Publishes *Catalyst*, a quarterly magazine, and *The Affiliate Artists Residency Handbook.*

AAE

**ALLIANCE FOR ARTS EDUCATION**  Washington D.C.
(c/o John F. Kennedy Center for the Performing Arts)
A network of organizations that links state-level efforts to promote high quality arts education; holds a biannual conference, offers fellowships for arts teachers and technical assistance for educational organizations, sponsors the American College Theatre Festival at the JFK Center and publishes *Interchange*, a bimonthly newsletter.

**ALLIANCE FOR THE ARTS**  New York City
Conducts research and policy work, and offers information services and workshops in relation to all types of cultural institutions in NYC; publishes *The Events Clearinghouse Calendar*, a bimonthly listing with related phone service regarding fundraising events in NYC.

ART/ Boston

**ALLIANCE OF RESIDENT THEATRES**  Boston, MA
Publishes a monthly catalogue of all theatre, dance and music performances in Boxton, offers a ticket sales service and provides other programs and services for member organizations in the area.

ART/ New York

**ALLIANCE OF RESIDENT THEATRES**  New York City
Provides programs to member organizations in the city to

increase managerial strengths in such areas as marketing, development and finance; offers research and consulting on real estate matters; publishes several guides and *Theatre Times*, a bimonthly magazine

AAA **AMERICAN ARTS ALLIANCE** Washington, D.C.
Lobbies congress and federal agencies on behalf of nonprofit professional arts organizations nationwide.

ACA **AMERICAN COUNCIL FOR THE ARTS** New York City
Organizes seminars throughout the country on arts policy and management issues, provides an arts education program, does research to improve arts legislation and serves as a facilitator in bringing originating artists together with arts organizations. Publishes the monthly magazine, *Vantage Point*, and is a major publisher of books in the field.

ADA **AMERICAN DANCE GUILD** New York City
A membership organization to promote dance; offers various services to dance teachers, performers and choreographers; holds annual conference; bimonthly newsletter.

ASOL **AMERICAN SYMPHONY ORCHESTRA LEAGUE** Washington, D.C. A service and educational organization to promote the development of American symphony orchestras and the cultural vitality of the communities they serve; operates Orchestra Management Training Program of one-year internships; publishes *Symphony Magazine* bimonthly.

ATCA **AMERICAN THEATRE CRITICS ASSOCIATION** Evansville, IN Membership organization of American drama cirtics to promote skills, ethics and knowledge in this field; fall meeting in NYC, spring meeting in other theatre city; affiliated with the International Federation of Theatre Critics.

ABC **ARTS AND BUSINESS COUNCIL** New York City
Provides advice on various aspects of business management for individual artists and arts companies; publishes *Winterfare*, an annually updated list of cultural institutions and companies in the arts.

**ARTS INTERNATIONAL**   New York City (c/o Institute of International Educators)   To encourage international cultural exchange, provides programs for artists and arts administrators going abroad; lists programs in *FYI*, a publication of the New York Foundation for the Arts.

**ARTS MARKETING ASSOCIATION**   Portland, OR
Membership organization for marketing directors and departments of nonprofit performing arts groups nationwide.   Publishes monthly magazine.

AM

**ARTS MIDWEST**   Minneapolis, MN
Created by the merger of Affiliated State Arts Agencies of the Upper Midwest and the Great Lakes Arts Alliance; serves IL, IN, IO, MI, MN, ND, OH, AK, WI; arranges tours for performing artists, provides a fellowship program and a jazz program; offers arts management information services.

ARCL

**ARTS RESOURCE CONSORTIUM LIBRARY**   New York City
A collection of published materials on arts management, law, advocacy, policy, education and other concerns of arts organizations and individuals; operated by ACA and VLA.

AAAE

**ASSOCIATION OF ARTS ADMINISTRATION EDUCATORS**
New York City (c/o American Council for the Arts)
Membership organization (most are heads of graduate-level arts management programs) that provides a forum for communication and advocacy of educational standards; compiles *Survey of Arts Administration Training Programs*  published biannually by ACA.

AHA

**ASSOCIATION OF HISPANIC ARTS**   New York City
Collects and disseminates information about Hispanic arts events, mostly in NYC; publishes *AHA*, a monthly magazine in calendar form.

APAP

**ASSOCIATION OF PERFORMING ARTS PRESENTERS**
Washington, D.C. (Formerly ACUCAA, the Association of College, University and Community Arts Administrators)
Membership organization mainly comprised of individual and

621

institutional presenters; conducts seminars and workshops and a major annual conference each December in NYC; publishes *Inside Performance* and *The Bulletin*, both quarterly.

ATHE    **ASSOCIATION OF THEATRE IN HIGHER EDUCATION** Evansville, IN    A membership organization for theatre educators and students on the college level; conducts annual summer conference.

BOMI    **BOX OFFICE MANAGEMENT INTERNATIONAL** New York City    Membership organization that provides information and services; holds major annual conference and several regional conferences each year; monthly newsletter.

BCA    **BUSINESS COMMITTEE FOR THE ARTS** New York City Raises money for the arts from corporate membership fees; advocates corporate sponsorship; monthly newsletter.

CC    **THE CANADA COUNCIL** Ottawa, Ontario Awards grants to Canadian arts organizations and artists of all disciplines; publishes a handbook of grants information and various brochures.

CCA    **CANADIAN CONFERENCE OF THE ARTS/CONFERENDE CANADIENNE DES ARTS** Ottawa, Ontario Supports arts and culture in Canada by a variety of communication, consultation and research activities; publishes the annual *Directory of the Arts*.

COS    **CENTRAL OPERA SERVICE** New York City Provides job notices for members in opera management and artistic positions, works as an information agency in the field; holds an annual national conference, publishes the quarterly *COS Service Bulletin* listing national and international opera events; also *Survey of Opera in the United States*, and directories of U.S. and foreign opera events.

CMA    **CHAMBER MUSIC AMERICA** New York City Membership organization of professional chamber ensembles, presenters, organizations and individuals involved in chamber music; provides technical assistance, offers low cost instrument insurances; provides information and promotes funding; annual conference.

**CONSORTUIM FOR PACIFIC ARTS AND CULTURES**   Agana, GU   Provides booking and informational services serving Alaska, American Samoa, CA, Guam, Hawaii and the Northern Mariana Islands.

**THE COSTUME COLLECTION**   New York City (c/o Theatre Development Fund)   Collects costumes and rents them to nonprofit organizations on a sliding scale based on seating capacity and number of performances.

**COUNCIL ON FOUNDATIONS, INC.**   Washington, D.C. Membership organization to assist corporations in making grants; publishes quarterly magazine, has NYC branch.

CCF   **CULTURAL COUNCIL FOUNDATION**   New York City Private organization that provides fiscal and managerial services to clients and consultations to nonclients; arranges workshops for nonprofit arts organizations; monthly newsletter.

DNB   **DANCE NOTATION BUREAU**   New York City National and international organization for choreographic documentation through notation; serves as the certifying body for professional notation teachers; provides awards and fellowships; semiannual newsletter.

DTW   **DANCE THEATRE WORKSHOP**   New York City Provides services for members, including rehearsal space rentals, a nationwide mailing list service, a quarterly newsletter and a National Performance Network office that does touring consultations.

**DANCE/ USA**   Washington, D.C. Provides data reports regarding the finances and management of dance companies; serves as an advocate for the field; provides an outreach program; bimonthly newsletter.

**THE DENVER PARTNERSHIP**   Denver, CO
Advocacy and management organization for local business concerns; lobbies on behalf of business members for the revitalization of downtown Denver, partially through arts events.

**THE FOUNDATION CENTER**   New York City
A major reference library and research facility for date regarding foundations and corporations; key facilities in Washington, D.C., Chicago and New York. Foundation Center Collections are also housed at libraries in a majority of state capitals.

FEDAPT   **THE FOUNDATION FOR THE EXTENSION AND DEVELOP-MENT OF THE AMERICAN PROFESSIONAL THEATRE**   New York City   Provides management consulting, technical assistance and information to the field; offers programs, workships and seminars; publishes books, work papers and a newsletter.

**THE GRANTSMANSHIP CENTER**   Los Angeles, CA
Offers training programs and workshops to nonprofit organizations for preparation of grants proposals; publishes the handbook, *Program Planning and Proposal Writing*.

HAI   **HOSPITAL AUDIENCES, INC.**   New York City
Organizes free tickets to film and theatre performances for outpatients and visits of performances to health facilities; annual newsletter.

HOLA   **HISPANIC ORGANIZATION OF LATIN ACTORS**   New York City   Bridges the gap between professional hispanic actors and directors, casting agents and theatre companies; annual festival of plays in NYC each May; monthly newsletter and directory.

**THE INDEPENDENT SECTOR**   Washington, D.C.
Consists of corporate, foundation and volunteer organizations; aimed at promoting a national forum to encourage giving and volunteering to all kinds of nonprofit initiatives; publishes newsletter and reports.

IAAM   **INTERNATIONAL ASSOCIATION OF AUDITORIUM MANAGERS**   White Plains, NY
Membership organization for upper level managers and univer-

sity faculty involved in management of public assembly facilities; provides services and information, publishes the magazine, *Auditorium News*.

ITI/US      **INTERNATIONAL THEATRE INSTITUTE OF THE UNITED STATES**    New York City     Service and information agency to promote and facilitate international exchange of professional theatre companies and individuals; quarterly newsletter.

IOD      **THE INSTITUTE OF OUTDOOR DRAMA**    Chapel Hill, NC Provides planning, organizing and consulting services for groups wishing to produce outdoor performances; quarterly newsletter.

**LEAGUE OF CHICAGO THEATRES**    Chicago, IL Advocates and helps market the performing arts locally and on tour; services approximately 120 theatres; sponsors the International Theatre Exchange; publishes *Promoters Guide*.

LHAT      **LEAGUE OF HISTORIC AMERICAN THEATRES**    Washington, D.C.    Membership organization for theatres, arts centers, cultural facilities and individuals involved in theatre restoration and preservation; provides consultants and information; annual conference; newsletter.

**LITERARY MANAGERS AND DRAMATURGS OF AMERICA** New York City    Provides communication among literary managers and dramaturgs and promotes growth of this discipline.

M-AAA      **MID-AMERICA ARTS ALLIANCE**    Kansas City, MO Provides presenting and touring information and services to AK, KS, MO, NB and OK; cosponsors Midwest Regional Booking Conference each September.

M-ASAC      **MID-ATLANTIC STATES ARTS CONSORTIUM**    Baltimore, MD    Regional agency that serves presenters in DE, MD, NJ, PA, VA, WV, D.C.; publishes two directories: *Performing Arts Sponsor/Presenter Directory* and *Performing Artists Organization Directory;* also operates the Arts/Information Exchange Program (AIEX), mailing to organizations and artists.

**NATIONAL ALLIANCE OF MUSICAL THEATRE PRODUCERS**
New York City
Comprises of about 70 member organizations of professional
(Equity) opera, operetts and musical theatre companies; aims
to assist members in preserving and extending American musical theatre through a festival, joint development of original
works, shared productions, management services and a newsletter. National conference on the east coast in the fall and another on the west coast in the spring for members only.

NALAA **NATIONAL ASSEMBLY OF LOCAL ARTS AGENCIES**
Washington, D.C.    Serves as a cohesive force between state
arts councils and arts organizations in 50 states; facilitates networking and assistance in providing quality arts programming
at the community level.

NAAO **NATIONAL ASSOCIATION OF ARTISTS ORGANIZATIONS**
Washington, D.C.    Provides a network of support and communication between artists and organizations working in contemporary art.

NASAA **NATIONAL ASSEMBLY OF STATE ARTS AGENCIES**
Washington, D.C.    Provides information about state arts councils and federal or state partnership programs; conducts conferences and workwhops.

NAPAMA **NATIONAL ASSOCIATION OF PERFORMING ARTS
MANAGERS AND AGENTS**    New York City
Assists in touring arrangements between performing groups and
presenters; involved in conferences, workshops and panels
dealing with a variety of concerns in the performing arts.

**NATIONAL CORPORATE THEATRE FUND**    New York City
Approaches corporations for funding on behalf of leading U.S.
theatres; publishes annual report.

NEA **NATIONAL ENDOWMENT FOR THE ARTS**    Washington, D.C.
Independent agency chartered and funded by the U.S. Congress
that supports American art and artists through awards, grants
and policy advisement; strives to make the arts more accessible
to the community; publishes *Art Revies, Guide to the NEA,
Annual Report* and a variety of special papers and reports.

626

NEH      **NATIONAL ENDOWMENT FOR THE HUMANITIES**
Washington, D.C.     The twin agency of the NEA established
to promote understanding of American culture; provides grants
to individuals and organizations in the areas of history, philosophy and language as well as arts-related areas.

NFAA      **NATIONAL FOUNDATION FOR ADVANCEMENT IN THE
ARTS**   New York City and Miami, FL
Aims to identify, encourage and support emerging artists
through various nationwide programs.

     **NATIONAL INSTITUTE FOR MUSIC THEATRE**    Washing-
ton, D.C. (c/o Kennedy Center for the Performing Arts, Education Department)    Support organization for opera and musical theatre of all types; provides grants and fellowships to individuals in the field.

NJSO      **NATIONAL JAZZ SERVICE ORGANIZATION**    Washington,
D.C.    Provides information and services to ensembles, organizations and individuals involved in creating, performing, teaching, presenting and perserving jazz music.

NOI      **NATIONAL OPERA INSTITUTE**    Washington, D.C.
Supports and encourages the growth of opera in the U.S.; offers grants to opera companies and singers as well as apprenticeships in opera administration and production; arranges the
sharing of sets and costumes between companies.

NSFRE      **NATIONAL SOCIETY OF FUNDRAISING EXECUTIVES**
Alexandria, VA
A network of 10,000 professional fundraisers who offer education   programs to help organizations and individuals become
efficient fundraisers; houses the Library of National Fund Raising,
Foundation for Fund Raising Scholarship and publishes NSFRE
quarterly as well as a semi-monthly newsletter.

NEFA      **NEW ENGLAND FOUNDATION FOR THE ARTS**
Cambridge, MA    Grant-giving organization connecting audiences and artists in CT, ME, MA, NH, RI, VT; promotes touring by
subsidizing presenters and provides guide to programs.

NYFA **NEW YORK FOUNDATION FOR THE ARTS, INC.**
New York City      One of the largest providers of grants to
individual artists and arts organizations in NY State and elsewhere; awards fellowships, residencies and loans; publishes *FYI*
quarterly.

**O'NEILL THEATRE CENTER**    New York City
Offers summer training program to college students as well as
conferences for playwrights, cirtics and musical theatre performers and directors throughout the year; has permanent theatre
facilities in Connecticut.

OA **OPERA AMERICA**    Washington, D.C.
Established to support professional opera companies in North,
Central and South America.

PACT **PROFESSIONAL ASSOCIATION OF CANADIAN THEATRES**
Toronto, Ontario
National trade and service organization for professional, English
language theatres in Canada; provides advocacy with federal
government; works as a collective bargaining association; publishes bimonthly magazine, *Impact,* a monthly employment
bulletin and *Canada on Stage,* an annual monthly yearbook.

PAMI **PERFORMING ARTS MANAGEMENT INSTITUTE**
New York City      Offers a three-day seminar each November in
New York and each May in Los Angeles covering various aspects
of arts management.

PARC **PERFORMING ARTS RESEARCH CENTER**    New York City
(c/o New York Public Library, Museum of the Performing Arts,
Lincoln Center)      A research facility and noncirculating library
of books, artifacts, recordings, video tapes and films; the world's
largest collection of information about the performing arts.

**PERFORMING ARTS RESOURCES, INC**    New York City
Organization offering support services to the performing arts,
including workshops and seminars, a personnel network, a
research center and The Technical Assistance Program (TAP),

628

which relates to production and personnel issues; publishes *Dance Floor Anthology*, and a variety of manuals.

PAS **PERFORMING ARTS SERVICES**   San Francisco, CA
A membership organization that provides marketing, mail room and ticketing services; runs STUBS, ticket sales outlets at various locations in the city; also offers half-price, special audience and free ticket programs.

**THE PITTSBURGH CULTURAL TRUST**
Pittsburgh, PA
A planning service for the arts in Pittsburgh and beyond; aims to promote the growth and expansion of the arts; TIX BOOTH offers full and half-price tickest; publishes newsletter and operates research library at the Fulton Theatre.

PMI **PUBLIIC MANAGEMENT INSTITUTE**
San Francisco, CA      A publishing and research facility with books on corporate giving and "how to" books in the arts; awards grants and is involved in direct giving; recently published 8th edition of a catalogue listing the top 500 corporations that donate to the arts.

**SAN DIEGO THEATRE LEAGUE**   San Diego, CA
Membership organization that promotes and markets theatre in the San Diego area; provides ticket services and advertisement discounts; publishes *San Diego Live*, a listing of member theatres and their current productions.

SAF **SOUTHERN ARTS FEDERATION**   Atlanta, GA
Provides touring programs, activities and long-term technical assistance to presenters in AL,FL, GA, KY, LA, MS, NC, SC, TN; supports developing arts organizations in the region.

SWAP **SWAP NORTHWEST**   Seattle, WA
An organization of over 300 arts presenters from Canada and the Northwest U.S.; coordinates booking and provides information; publishes a newsletter and presenters directory for subscribing groups.

TAP      **TECHNICAL ASSISTANCE PROGRAM**    (See Performing Arts Resources, Inc.)

     **THE ARTS EXCHANGE**    Austin, TX
Touring arts program aimed at expanding and cultivating the performing arts in Texas.

TBA      **THEATRE BAY AREA**    San Francisco, CA
A multi-resource communications organization for area theatre workers and companies; publishes the monthly *Callboard* and the biennial *Theatre Directory of the Bay Area*.

TCG      **THEATRE COMMUNICATIONS GROUP**    New York City
Established to support and promote nonprofit professional theatre throughout the nation; provides computer network; operates ArtSearch to publicize employment opportunities in professional and educational theatre; publishes the monthly magazine *American Theatre*; serves as a major book publisher.

TDF      **THEATRE DEVELOPMENT FUND**    New York City
Offers half-price tickets, ticket subsidy programs, non-subsidy programs, voucher programs and operates ticket outlets to support audience expansion for both commercial and nonprofit theatre, music and dance productions

T/LA      **THEATRE LOS ANGELES**    Los Angeles, CA
Member organization designed to facilitate performing arts production; offers workshops, grants, information and networking services for directors; monthly newsletter.

TM      **TICKET MASTER**    Denver, CO
A computerized ticket service for theatres and presenters in the Denver area; works on a contract and fee basis.

     **TOUR ARTS**    San Francisco, CA
Provides tour management and travel arrangements for all disciplines in the performing arts in the San Francisco area.

SMA      **THE STAGE MANAGERS ASSOCIATION**    New York City    A membership organization founded by and for Equity stage managers; publishes member directory.

USIA **UNITES STATES INFORMATION AGENCY**   Washington, D.C. Deals with the presentation and upholding of the reputation of the U.S. abroad; awards grants and acholarships and has an exchange program for teachers and students.

USITT **UNITED STATES INSTITUTE FOR THEATRE TECHNOLOGY** New York City   Membership organization for theatre designers, technicians and administrators; sponsors spring conference plus workshops and seminars related to technical advancements and products; newsletter and magazine, *Theatre Design and Technology*.

VLA **VOLUNTEER LAWYERS FOR THE ARTS**   New York City Provides legal assistance to artists and arts organizations (free to those who can't afford fees); conducts seminars and maintains reference library; publishes *The Columbia-VLA Journal of Law and the Arts*. There are similar organizations in nearly two dozen cities including Chicago, Washington, D.C., Atlanta, Philadelphia and Seattle; a national conference is organized periodically.

**VOLUNTEER: THE NATIONAL CENTER**   Arlington, VA Resource organization working with nonprofit centers to promote volunteerism in the U.S.; annual conference; publishes *Voluntary Action Leadership* quarterly.

WAAA **WESTERN ALLIANCE OF ARTS ADMINISTRATORS**   Azuza, CA   Membership organization that promotes interaction between the east and west coasts; hosts annual conference for arts administrators.

WESTAF **WESTERN STATES ARTS FOUNDATION**   Santa Fe, NM Provides fee support to presenters for touring companies and artists in AZ, CO, ID, MT, NE, NM, OR, UT, WA, WY; also provides promotion and marketing assistance; publishes guides of available tours for presenters.

# Appendix M

## THEATRICAL LABOR UNIONS AND GUILDS

| Acronym | Full Name | Home Office |
|---------|-----------|-------------|
| AEA | Actors' Equity Association | New York City (with regional office in Los Angeles, San Francisco and Chicago) |
| AFM | American Federation of Musicians | New York City |
| AFTRA | American Federation of Television and Radio Artists | New York City |
| AGAC | American Guild of Authors and Composers | Hollywood, CA |
| AGMA | American Guild of Musical Artists | New York City |
| AGVA | American Guild of Variety Artists | New York City |
| ASCAP | American Society of Composers, Authors and Publishers | New York City |
| APATE | Asociacion Puertorriquena de Artistas y Technicos del Espectaculo | Santurce, PR |
| ADC | Associated Designers of Canada | Toronto, Ontario |
| ATA | Association of Talent Agents | Los Angeles |
| BMI | Broadway Music, Inc. | New York City |
| CAEA | Canadian Actors' Equity Association | Toronto, Ontario |
| DGA | Directors Guild of America | New York City & Los Angeles |
| DG | The Dramatists Guild of America | New York City |
| HAU | Hebrew Actors' Union | New York City |
| IATSE | International Alliance of Theatrical Stage Employees and Motion Picture Operators of the United States and Canada | New York City |

| IBEW | International Brotherhod of Electircal Workers | New York City |
| | International Brotherhood of Teamsters, Chauffeurs, Warehousemen and Helpers | New York City |
| OE | International Union of Operating Engineers (Local 30) | New York City |
| IAU | Italian Actors' Union | New York City |
| LTE | Legitimate Theatre Employees Union | New York City |
| PACT | Professional Association of Canadian Theatre | Toronto |
| PG | The Publicists' Guild | New York City |
| PUC | The Playwrights Union of Canada | Toronto |
| SAG | Screen Actors' Guild | Los Angeles |
| SEIU | Service Employees International Union<br>Local 9<br>Local 54 | <br>San Francisco<br>New York City |
| SSDC | The Society of Stage Directors and Choreographers | New York City |
| TPU | Theatrical Protective Union | New York City |
| TWA | Theatrical Wardrobe Attendants Union | New York City |
| USA | United Scenic Artists | New York City |
| WGA | Writers Guild of America West, Inc. | Los Angeles |

# Appendix N

## MANAGEMENT ASSOCIATIONS
(Contact AEA or CAEA for names and
addresses of current presidents)

| Acronym | Full Name of Association |
|---------|--------------------------|
| ADI | American Dinner Theatre Institute |
| ATLAS | Associated Theatres of Los Angeles |
| BAT | Bay Area Theatres |
| CAT | Chicago Area Theatres |
| CORST | Council of Resident Stock Theatres |
| COST | Council of Stock Theatres |
| HAT | Hollywood Area Theatres |
| | League of American Theatres and Producers |
| | League of Off-Broadway Theatres and Producers |
| LORT | League of Resident Theatres |
| NATR | National Association of Talent Representatives |
| OMS | Outdoor Musical Stock Association |
| PLOTYA | Producers' League of Theatre for Young Audiences |
| RMTA | Resident Musical Theatre Association |
| U/RTA | University/Resident Theatre Association |

# Bibliography

A selected bibliography of books and periodicals related to performing arts management and producing in America.

KEY

   I. Background Reading
  II. Government and the Arts
 III. Studies of Individual Theatre Regions, Companies and Managers
 IV. Theatrical Producing and Management: General
  V. Structure and Management of Nonprofit Organizations
 VI. The Board of Trustees
VII. The Arts and the Law
VIII. Economics and the Arts
 IX. Financial Management
  X. Marketing, Publicity and Audience Development
 XI. Fundraising and Philanthropy
XII. Community Theatre
XIII. Theatre, the Arts and Education
XIV. Theatre Architecture
 XV. Directories and General Reference Books
XVI. Career Guidance
XVII. Bibliographies
XVIII. Periodicals and Annuals

Note: "American Council for the Arts," "Association of Performing Arts Presenters" and "Drama Book Publishers" are used below to indicate publishers previously named "Associated Council of the Arts," "Association of College, University and Community Arts Administrators (ACUCAA)" and "Drama Book Specialists (Publishers)" respectively.

## I. BACKGROUND READING

The American Assembly. *The Future of the Performing Arts.* New York: The American Assembly, Columbia University, 1977.
*The Arts: A Central Element of a Good Society.* New York: American Council for the Arts, 1965.
*The Arts: Planning for Change.* New York: American Council for the Arts, 1966.
Bernheim, Alfred. *The Business of the Theatre: 1750-1932.* Reprint. New York: Benjamin Blom, Inc., 1964.

Brockett, Oscar G. *The Theatre: An Introduction. 5th Edition.* Boston: Allyn and Bacon, Inc., 1987.

Billington, Michael, consulting ed., *et al. Performing Arts: A Guide to Practice and Appreciation.* New York: Facts on File, 1980.

Boardman, Gerald. *American Musical Theatre: A Chronicle.* New York: Oxford University Press, 1986.

DiMaggio, Paul. *Managers of the Arts.* Cabin John, MD: Seven Locks Press, 1987.

Dorian, Frederick. *Commitment to Cultural Arts Patronage in Europe. Its Significance for America.* Pittsburg: University of Pittsburg Press, 1964.

Engel, Lehman. *The American Musical Theatre: A Consideration.* New York: CBS Legacy, 1975.

FEDAPT. *The Challenge of change: Papers and Presentations from the 15th Annual National Conference.* New York: Foundation for the Extension and Development of the American Professional Theatre, 1987.

Gard, Robert E. and Marston Balch and Pauline Temkin. *Theatre in America: Appraisal and Challenge.* New York: Theatre Arts Books, 1968.

Golden, Joseph. *The Death of Tinker Bell: The American Theatre in the 20th Century.* Syracuse, NY: Syracuse University Press, 1967.

Greyser, Stephen A. *Cultural Policy and Arts Administration.* Cambridge, MA: Harvard University Press, 1973.

Hirsch, E.D., Jr. *Cultural Literacy, What Every American Needs to Know.* Boston: Houghton Mifflin Company, 1987.

Hofstadter, Richard. *Anti-intellectualism in American Life.* New York: Alfred A. Knoph, 1963.

Krawitz, Herman with Howard Klein. *Royal American Symphonic Theatre: A Radical Proposal for a Subsidized Professional Theatre.* New York: Macmillan Publishing Company, Inc., 1975.

London, Todd. *The Artistic Home: Discussions with Artistic Directors of America's Institutional Theatres.* New York: Theatre Communications Group, 1988.

Lowry, W. McNeil, ed. *The Performing Arts and American Society.* Englewood Cliffs, NJ: Prentice Hall, 1978.

MacDonald, Dwight. *Against the American Grain: Essays on the Effects of Mass Culture.* New York: Random House, 1962.

Manoff, Robert Karl, ed. *The Buck Starts Here: Enterprise and the Arts.* New York: Volunteer Lawyers for the Arts, 1984.

McLuhan, Marshall. *Culture Is Our Business.* New York: McGraw-Hill, 1970.

———. *Understanding Media: The Extensions of Man.* New York: Signet, 1964.

Mitchell, Arnold. *The Nine American Lifestyles: Who We Are and Where We're Going.* New York: MacMillan Publishing Company, Inc., 1983.

NEA. *The Arts in America. A Report to the President and to the Congress.* Washington, DC: National Endowment for the Arts, 1988.

Reiss, Alvin H. *Culture & Company.* New York: Twayne Publishers, Inc., 1972.

Rockerfeller Panel Report. *The Performing Arts: Problems and Prospects.* New York: McGraw-Hill, 1965.

Toffler, Alvin. *The Culture Consumers: A Study of Art and Affluence in America.* New York: St. Martin's Press, 1964.

Veblen, Thorstein. (1899). *The Theory of the Leisure Class.* New York: Macmillan (New American Library), 1953.

Von Eckardt, Wolf. *Live the Good Life: Creating a Human Community Through the Arts.* New York: American Council for the Arts, 1982.

Wilson, Robert N., ed. *The Arts in Society.* Englewood Cliffs, NJ: Prentice-Hall, 1964

## II. GOVERNMENT AND THE ARTS

Adams, W. Howard. *The Politics of Art.* New York: American Council for the Arts, 1966.

*Americans and the Arts: A Survey of the Attitudes Toward and Participation in the Arts and Culture of the United States Public.* New York: American Council for the Arts, 1975.

Arian, Edward. *The Unfulfilled Promise: Public Subsity of the Arts in America.* Philadelphia: Temple University Press, 1989.

Biddle, Livingston. *Our Government and the Arts.* New York: American Council for the Arts, 1988.

Buttita, Tony, and Barry Witham. *Uncle Sam Presents: A Memoir of the Federal Theatre, 1935-1939.* Philadelphia: University of Pennsylvania Press, 1982.

Field, Alan I. and Michael O'Hare, J. Mark Davidson Schuster. *Patrons Despite Themselves: Taxpayers and Arts Policy.* New York: New York University Press, 1983.

Heckscher, August. *The Public Happiness.* New York: Atheneum, 1962.

Kreisberg, Luisa. *Local Government and the Arts.* New York: American Council for the Arts, 1978.

Larson, Gary O. *The Reluctant Patron: The United States Government and the Arts, 1943-1965.* Philadelphia: University of Pennsylvania Press, 1983.

Lowry, W. McNeil, ed. *The Arts and Public Policy in the United States.* Englewood Cliffs, NJ: Prentice-Hall, 1984.

Mulcahy, K.V., and C.R. Swaim, eds. *Public Policy and the Arts.* Boulder, Co: Westview Press, 1982.

Netzer, Dick. *The Subsidized Muse: Public Support for the Arts in the United States.* New York: Cambridge University Press, 1978.

O'Connor, Francis V., ed. *The New Deal Art Projects: An Anthology of Memoirs.* Washington, D.C.: Smithsonian Institution Press, 1972.

Purcell, Ralph. *Government and Art.* Washington, D.C.: Public Affairs Press, 1953.

Ritterbush, Philip C. *Cultural Policy in the United States.* New York: Publishing Center for Cultural Resources.

Taylor, Fannie, and Anthony L. Barresi. *The Arts at a New Frontier.* New York: Plenum Press, 1984.

Waits, C.R., and W.S. Hendon, H. Horowitz, eds. *Governments and Culture.* Akron, OH: Association for Cultural Economics, 1985.

Wyszomirski, Margaret Jane, ed. *Congress and the Arts.* New York: American Council for the Arts, 1987.

## III. STUDIES OF INDIVIDUAL THEATRE REGIONS, COMPANIES AND MANAGERS

Atkinson, Brooks. *Broadway.* New York: Macmillan Company, 1970.

Bentley, Joanne. *Hallie Flanagan: A Life in the American Theatre.* New York: Alfred A. Knopf, 1988.

Bing, Rudolf. *5000 Nights at the Opera.* New York: Doubleday & Company, Inc., 1972.

————. *A Knight at the Opera.* New York: G.P. Putnam and Sons, 1981.

Bloomfield, Arthur J. *The San Francisco Opera: 1923-1961.* New York: Appleton-Century-Crofts, 1961.

Brustein, Robert. *Making Scenes: A Personal History of the Turbulent Years at Yale: 1966-1979.* New York: Random House, 1981.

Carson, William G.B. *Managers in Distress: The St. Louis Stage, 1840-1844.* Reprint. New York: Benjamin Blom, n.d.

Chinoy, Helen Krich. *Reunion: A Self-Portrait of the Group Theatre.* Lanham, MD: University Press of America, 1983.

Churchill, Allen. *The Great White Way: A Re-Creation of Broadway's Golden Age of Theatrical Entertainment.* New York: Dutton, 1962.

Clapp, William Warland. *Record of the Boston Stage.* Reprint. New York: Benjamin Blom, 1968.

Clurman, Harold. *The Fervent Years.* New York: Knopf, 1945. (Republished by Hill & Wang, 1964.)

Crowley, Alice Lewisohn. *The Neighborhood Playhouse: Leaves from a Theatre Scrapbook.* New York: Theatre Arts Books, 1959.

Cox, Bill J. "Katz Productions, Ltd.: A Management Residency Report." Unpublished M.F.A. Dissertation, Brooklyn College, Department of Theatre, 1984.

Deutsch, Helen, and Stella Hanau. *The Provincetown: A Story of the Theatre.* New York: Farrar and Rinehart, 1931.

Donaldson, Frances. *The Actor-Managers.* Chicago: Henry Regnery Company, 1970.

Donohue, Joseph W., Jr., ed. *The Theatrical Manager in England and America, Players of a Perilous Game: Philip Henslowe, Tate Wilkinson, Stephen Price, Edwin Booth, Charles Wyndham.* Princeton, NJ: Princeton University Press, 1971.

Eaton, Walter Prichard. *The Theatre Guild: The First Ten Years.* New York: Arno Press, 1926.

Elliott, Eugene C. *A History of Variety-Vaudeville in Seattle from the Beginnings to 1914.* Seattle, WA: University of Washington Press, 1944.

Enders, John. *Survey of New York Theatre.* New York: Playbill, 1959.

Fishkin, Daniel L. "An Internship with Columbia Artists Management, Inc." Unplubished M.F.A. Dissertation, Brooklyn College, Department of Theatre, 1978.

Flanagan, Hallie. *Arena.* New York: Duell, Sloan and Pearce, 1940.

Fox, Ted. *Showtime at the Appolo.* New York: Holt, Reinhart and Winston, 1983.

Freedley, George. *Broadway Playhouses.* New York: New York Public Library, 1943.

French, Ward. "The Story of the Organized Audience Movement." Unpublished Article, Columbia Artists Management, Inc., Community Concerts Division.

Frick, John, W. *New York's First Theatrical Center: The Rialto at Union Square.* Ann Arbor, MI: UMI Research Press, 1985.

Gard, Robert E. *Grassroots Theatre.* Madison, WI: University of Wisconsin Press, 1955.

Goldman, William. *The Season: A Candid Look at Broadway.* New York: Harcourt, Brace & World, Inc., 1969.

Gottfried, Martin. *Jed Harris: The Curse of the Genius.* Boston: Little, Brown and Company, 1984.

Graham, Philip. *Showboats: The History of an American Institution.* Dallas: University of Texas, 1951.

Green, Abel and Jope Lurie Jr. *Show Biz.* New York: Henry Holt Company, 1951.

Greenberger, Howard. *The Off-Broadway Experience.* Englewood Cliffs, NJ: Prentice-Hall, Inc., 1971.

Greenwald, Jan Carol. "The Independent Booking Office: A Management Residency Report." Unpublished M.F.A. Dissertation, Brooklyn College, Department of Theatre, 1985.

Guither, Peter S. "Katz Productions: A Management Residency Report." Unpublished M.F.A. Dissertation, Brooklyn College, Department of Theatre, 1985.

Harding, Alfred. *The Revolt of the Actors.* New York: William Morrow & Company, 1929.

Harrison, Harry P. *Culture Under Canvas: The Story of Tent Chautauqua.* New York: Hastings House, 1958.

Henderson, Mary C. *The City and the Theatre.* Clifton, NJ: James T. White, 1973.

Hodge, Francis. *Yankee Theatre.* Austin, TX: University of Texas Press, 1964.

Houghton, Norris. *But Not Forgotten: The Adventures of the University Players.* New York: Sloan, 1951.

Ireland, Joseph N. *Records of the New York Stage: 1750-1860*. Reprint. New York: Benjamin Blom, 1968.

James, Reese David. *Cradle of Culture: 1880-1810, The Philadelphia Stage*. Philadelphia: University of Pennsylvania Press, 1957.

Johnson, Charlie H., Jr. *The Central City Opera House: A 100 Year History*. Colorado Springs, CO: Little London Press, 1980.

Johnson, Stephen Burge. *The Roof Gardens of Broadway Theatres, 1883-1942*. Ann Arbor, MI: UMI Research Press, 1985.

Kendall, John S. *The Golden Age of the New Orleans Theatre*. New Orleans,LA: Louisiana State University Press, 1952.

Laufe, Abe. *Anatomy of a Hit: Long-Run Plays on Broadway from 1900 to the Present Day*. New York: Hawthorn Books, 1966.

Leavitt, M.B. *Fifty Years in Theatrical Management*. New York: Broadway Publishing, 1912.

Lee, Douglas Bennett, and Roger L. Meersman, Donn B. Murphy. *Stage for a Nation: The National Theatre, 150 Years*. Lanham, MD: University Press of America, Inc., 1986.

Levine, Mindy N. *New York's Other Theatre: A Guide to Off-Off-Broadway*. New York: Avon Books, 1981.

Little, Stuart W. *Off-Broadway, The Prophetic Theatre*. New York: Coward, McCann, 1972.

Loney, Glenn, and Patricia MacKay. *The Shakespeare Complex: A Guide to Summer Festivals and Year-Round Repertory in America*. New York: Drama Book Publishers, 1975.

Ludlow, Noah. *Dramatic Life As I Found It*. Reprint. New York: Banjamin Blom, n.d.

MacKay, Constance Darcy. *The Little Theatre in the United States*. New York: T. Holt, 1917.

Marcosson, Isaac F., and Daniel Frohman. *Charles Frohman, Manager and Man*. New York: Harper, 1916.

Martin, Ralph G. *Lincoln Center for the Performing Arts*. Englewood Cliffs, NJ: Prentice-Hall, 1971.

McAvay, Gary S. "Columbia Artists Theatricals Corp.: A Management Residency Report." Unpublished M.F.A. Dissertation, Brooklyn College, Department of Theatre, 1982.

McCleary, Albert, and Carl Glick. *Curtains Going Up*. Chicago and New York: Pitman, 1939.

McLean, Albert F., Jr. *American Vaudeville As Ritual*. Lexington, KY: University of Kentucky Press, 1965.

Merkling, Frank, and John W. Freeman, Gerald Fitzgerald. *The Golden Horseshoe: The Life and Times of the Metropolitan Opera House*. New York: The Viking Press, 1965.

Moody, Richard. *The Astor Place Riot*. Bloomington, IN: Indiana University Press, 1958.

Moore, Jonathan D. "The Independent Booking Office: A Management Residency Report." Unpublished M.F.A. Dissertation, Brooklyn College, Department of Theatre, 1984.

Nelson, Stephen. *"Only A Paper Moon:" The Theatre of Billy Rose.* Ann Arbor, MI: The University of Michigan Press, 1987.

Newton, Michael, and Scott Hatley. *Persuade and Provide: The Story of the Arts and Education Council in St. Louis.* New York: American Council for the Arts, 1970.

Novick, Julius. *Beyond Broadway: The Quest for Permanent Theatres.* New York: Hill and Wang, 1968.

The Ontario Theatre Study Report. *The Awkward Stage.* Toronto: Methuen Publications, 1969.

Patrick, J. Max. *Savannah's Pioneer Theatre: From Its Origins to 1810.* Atlanta, GA: University of Georgia Press, 1953.

Pollock, Thomas Clark. *The Philadelphia Theatre in the Eighteenth Century.* Philadelphia: University of Pennsylvania Press, 1933.

Prevots, Naima. *American Pagaentry.* Ann Arbor, MI: UMI Research Press, 1990.

Price, Julia S. *The Off-Broadway Theatre.* New York: Scarecrow Press, 1962.

Rubin, Stephen E. *The New Met in Profile.* New York, Macmillan Publishing Company, Inc. 1975.

Salem, Mahmoud. *Organizational Survival in the Performing Arts: The Making of the Seattle Opera.* New York: 1976.

Selznick, Irene Mayer. *A Private View.* New York, Knopf, 1983.

Smith, Patrick J. *A Year at the Met.* Alfred A. Knopf, 1983.

Smith, Sol. *Theatrical Management in the West and South for 30 Years.* Reprint. New York: Benjamin Blom, n.d.

Smither, Nelle. *A History of the English Theatre at New Orleans: 1806-1842.* Reprint. New York: Benjamin Blom, 1967.

Sobel, Bernard. *Broadway Heartbeat: Memoirs of a Press Agent.* New York: Heritage, 1953.

Sokok, Martin L. *The New York City Opera: an American Adventure.* New York: Macmillan Publishing Company, Inc., 1981.

Stagg, Jerry. *The Brothers Shubert.* New York: Random House, 1968.

Straight, Michael. *Nancy Hanks: An Intimate Portrait.* Durham and London: Duke University Press, 1988.

Taper, Bernard. *The Arts in Boston, An Outsider's View of the Cultural Estate.* Cambridge, MA: Harvard University Press, 1970.

Willard, George O. *History of the Providence State 1762-1891.* Providence, RI: The Rhode Island News Company, 1891.

Young, Edgar B. *Lincoln Center: The Building of and Institution.* New York: New York University Press, 1980.

Zeigler, Joseph W. *Regional Theatre: The Revolutionary Stage.* New York: DeCapo Press, 1973.

643

## IV. THEATRICAL PRODUCING AND MANAGEMENT: GENERAL

Barrell, M.K. *The Technical Production Handbook: A Guide for Sponsors of Performing Arts Companies on Tour.* Denver, CO: Western States Arts Foundation, 1977.

Conolly, L.W., ed. *Theatrical Touring and Founding in North America.* Westport, CT: Greenwood Press, 1982.

Cullman, Marguerite. *Occupation Angel.* New York: W.W. Norton, 1963.

*Cultural Resource Development: Preliminary Planning Survey and Survey and Analysis.* New York: New York State Comission on Cultural Resources, 1973.

Dilker, Barbara. *Stage Management Forms and Formats.* New York: Drama Book Publishers, 1979.

Eaton, Quaintance. *Opera Production I: A Handbook.* New York, DaCapo Press, 1974.

_____. *Opera Production II: A Handbook.* Minneapolis, MN: University of Minnesota Press, 1974.

Ellfeldt, Lois, and Edwin Carnes. *Dance Production Handbook.* Palo Alto, CA: Mayfield Publishing Comapny, 1971.

Engel, Lehman. *Planning and Producing the Musical Show.* New York: Crown Publishers, 1967.

Eustis, Morton. *B'way, Inc! The Theatre as a Business.* New York: Dodd, Mead, 1934.

Farber, Donald C. *From Option to Opening,* 3rd ed., revised. New York: Drama Book Publishers, 1977.

_____. *Producing Theatre: A Comprehensive Legal and Business Guide.* Drama Book Publishers, 1981.

Gassner, John. *Producing the Play.* New York: Dryden Press, 1953.

Golden, Joseph. *Help! A Guide to Seeking, Selecting and Surviving an Arts Counsultant.* Syracuse, NY: Cultural Resources Council, 1983.

Graf, Herbert. *Producing Opera for America.* New York: Atlantis Books, 1961.

Gruver, Burt, Revised by Frank Hamilton. *The Stage Manager's Handbook.* New York: Drama Book Publishers, 1972.

*How To Do It "Kit": Airs for Volunteer Administrators.* Washington, D.C.: National Center for Voluntary Action, 1976.

Jeffri, Joan *The Emerging Arts: Management, Survival and Growth.* New York: Oraeger Publishers, 1980.

Jones, Margo. *Theatre-in-the-Round.* New York: McGraw-Hill Paperbacks, 1965.

Langley, Stephen, ed. *Producers On Producing.* New York: Drama Book Publishers, 1976.

Lewis, Philip C. *Trouping: How The Show Came to Town.* New York: Harper & Row, n.d.

Manoff, Robert Karl. *The Buck Starts Here: Enterprise in the Arts.* New York: Volunteer Lawyers for the Arts, 1984.

Moskow, Michael. *Labor Unions and the Arts.* New York: American Council for the Arts, 1970.

Pick, John. *Arts Administration.* New York: E. & F.N. Spon in association with Methuen, 1980.

Plummer, Gail. *The Business of Show Business.* New York: Harper and Brothers, 1961.

*Presenting in America.* Kansas City, MO: Mid-America Arts Alliance, 1988.

Pravots, Naima. *American Pagaentry.* Ann Arbor, MI: UMI Research Press, 1990.

Raymond, Thomas C., and Stephen A. Greyser, Douglas Schwalbe. *Cases in Arts Administration.* Revised ed. Cambridge, MA: Arts Administration Research Institute, Harvard University, 1975.

Reiss, Alvin H. *The Arts Management Reader.* 2nd Revised ed. New York: Law-Arts Publishers, 1979.

Shagan, Rena. *Road Show: A Handbook for Successful Booking and Touring in the Performing Arts.* New York: American Council for the Arts, 1985.

Sikes, Toni Fountain, ed. *ACUCAA Handbook: Presenting the Performing Arts.* Washington, D.C.: Association of Performing Arts Presenters (formerly the Association of College, University and Community Arts Administrators), 1984.

Stanton, Sanford E. *Theatre Management.* New York: Appleton-Century, 1929.

Stern, Lawrence. *Stage Management.* Boston: Allyn and Bacon, Inc., 1974.

Taylor, Fannie. *Negotiating and Contracting for Artists and Attractions at Educational and Nonprofit Institutions.* Washington, D.C.: Association of Performing Arts Presenters, 1982.

Visser, David. *Hitting the Road: Planning a Performing Arts Tour.* New York: Theatre Communications Group, 1982.

Wolf, Thomas. *Presenting Performances: A Handbook for Sponsors.* Cambridge, MA: New England Foundation for the Arts, 1977.

## V.  STRUCTURE AND MANAGEMENT OF NONPROFIT ORGANIZATIONS

Clifton, Roger L., and Richard L. Reinert, Louise K. Stevens. *The Road to Success: A Unique Development Guide for Small Arts Groups.* Boston: Massachusetts Cultural Alliance, 1988.

Conrad, William R., and Willima R. Glenn. *The Effective Voluntary Board of Directors: What It Is and How It Works.* Chicago: Swallow Press, 1975.

Connors, Tracy D., ed. *The Nonprofit Organization Handbook.* New York: McGraw-Hill, Inc., 1980.

Crimmins, James C., and Mary Kiel. *Enterprise in the Non-Profit Sector.* New York: American Council for the Arts, 1983.

Dougherty, Carol. *How Full of Briars: The Organizational Structure of the Non-Profit Theatre Corporation.* Orlando, FL: Orlando Publishing, 1983.

Horwitz, Tem, and Thomas R. Leavens. *Arts Administration: How to Set Up and Run a Successful Nonprofit Arts Organization.* Chicago: Chicago Review Press, 1977.

Oleck, Howard. *Nonprofit Corporations, Organizations and Associations.* 3rd ed. Englewood Cliffs, NJ: Prentice-Hall, 1974.

Peterson, Eric. *Nonprofit Arts Organizations: Formation and Maintenance.* Berkeley, CA: Bay Area Lawyers for the Arts, 1977.

Setterberg, Fred, and Kary Schulman. *Beyond Profit: The Complete Guide to Managing the Nonprofit Organization.* New York: Harper & Row Publishers, 1985.

Vogel, Frederick B., ed. *No Quick Fix (Planning).* New York: Foundation for the Extension and Development of the American Professional Theatre, 1985.

Volunteer Lawyers for the Arts. *New York Not-for-Profit Organization Manual.* New York: Volunteer Lawyers for the Arts, 1982.

Wolf, Thomas. *The Nonprofit Organization.* Englewood Cliffs, NJ: Prentice-Hall, 1984.

## VI. THE BOARD OF DIRECTORS

Crawford, Robert W. *In Art We Trust: The Board of Trustees in the Performing Arts.* New York: Foundation for the Extension and Development of the American Professional Theatre, 1981.

Duca, Diane J. *Nonprofit Boards: A Practical Guide to Roles, Responsibilities and Performance.* Phoenix, AZ: Oryx Press, 1988.

*The Key to Effective Trusteeship of Arts Organizations: The Board Chairman and His Challenge.* University Park, PA: Pennsylvania State University, 1976.

Kurtz, Daniel, L. *Board Liability: Guide for Nonprofit Directors.* New York: Volunteer Lawyers for the Arts, 1988.

O'Connell, Brian. *The Board Member's Book: Making a Difference in Voluntary Organizations.* New York: The Foundation Center, 1988.

Paquet, Marion A. with Rory Ralston and Donna Cardinal. *A Handbook for Cultural Trustees.* Waterloo, Ontario, Canada: University of Waterloo Press, 1987.

Rauner, Judy. *Helping People Volunteer.* San Diego, CA: Marlborough Publications, 1980.

Trost, Arty, and Judy Rauner. *Gaining Momentum: For Board Action.* New York: American Council for the Arts, 1984.

U.S. Chamber of Commerce. *Association Bylaws.* Washington, D.C.: U.S. Chamber of Commerce (Association Department), n.d.

U.S. Chamber of Commerce. *Association Committees*. Washington, D.C.: U.S. Chamber of Commerce (Association Department), n.d.

## VII.  THE ARTS AND THE LAW

Council of New York Law Associates. *Getting Organized: A Guide to Acquiring and Maintaining Corporate and Tax-Exempt Status for Non-Profit Organizations*. New York: Volunteer Lawyers for the Arts, 1984.

Farber, Donald C. *Actor's Guide: What You Should Know About the Contracts You Sign*. New York: Drama Book Publishers, 1971.

_____., ed. *Entertainment Industry Contracts*. 4 Vols. Albany, NY: Matthew Bender & Company, 1987.

_____. *Producing Theatre: A Comprehensive Legal and Business Guide*. New York: Drama Book Publishers, 1981.

Golden, Joseph. *On The Dotted Line: The Anatomy of a Contract*. Syracuse, NY: Cultural Resources Council, 1979.

*How To Apply For and Retain Exempt Status*. (Publication #557.) Washington, D.C.: The Internal Revenue Service, n.d.

Jacobs, Milton. *Outline of Theatre Law*. New York: Greenwood, 1972.

Kurtz, Daniel L. *Liability: Guide for Nonprofit Boards of Directors*. New York: Noyer-Bell Limited, 1988.

Lidstone, Herrick K., and R.J. Ruble. *Exempt Organizations and the Arts*. New York: Volunteer Lawyers for the Arts, 1976.

Rudell, Michael I. *Behind the Scenes: Practical Entertainment Law*. New York: Law & Business, 1984.

Taubman, Joseph. *Performing Arts Management and Law*. 4 Vols. New York: Law-Arts Publishers, Inc. 1972.

U.S. Chamber of Commerce. *Association Legal Checklist*. Washington, D.C.: U.S. Chamber of Commerce (Association Department), n.d.

Volunteer Lawyers for the Arts. *The New York Not-for-Profit Organization Manual of the Conference Sponsored by the Council of New York Law Associates, Volunteer Lawyers for the Arts*. New York: Volunteer Lawyers for the Arts, 1978.

Volunteer Lawyers for the Arts. *VLA Guide to Copyright for the Performing Arts*. New York: Volunteer Lawyers for the Arts, 1988.

## VIII.  ECONOMICS AND THE ARTS

*The Arts as an Industry: Their Economic Importance to the New York/New Jersey Metropolitan Region*. New York: Cultural Assistance Center and The Port Authority of New York and New Jersey, 1983.

Baumol, William J. and William G. Bowen. *Performing Arts: The Economic Dilemma*. New York: The Twentieth Century Fund, 1966.

Blaug, Mark, ed. *The Economics of the Arts*. Boulder, CO: Westview Press,

1976.

DiMaggio, Paul, ed. *Non-Profit Enterprise in the Arts.* New York: Oxford University Press, 1986.

Ford, Neil M. and Bonnie J. Queram. *Pricing Strategy for the Performing Arts.* Washington, D.C.: Association of Performing Arts Presenters, 1980.

Grant, Nancy K. and William S. Hendon, Virginia Lee Owen, eds. *Economic Efficiency and the Performing Arts.* Akron, OH: Association for Cultural Exonomics, University of Akron 1987.

Hendon, W.S., and N.K. Grant, D.V. Shaw, eds. *The Economics of Cultural Industries.* Akron, OH: Association for Cultural Economics, University of Akron, 1984.

Hendon, William S. and Harry Hillman-Chartrand, Harold Horowitz. *Paying for the Arts.* Akron, OH: Association for Cultural Economics, University of Akron, 1987.

Hendon, M.A., and J.F. Richardson, W.S. Hendon, eds. *Bach and the Box: The Impact of Television on the Live Arts.* Akron, OH: Association for Cultural Economics, University of Akron, 1985.

Hendon, W.S., and J.L. Shanahan, eds. *Economics of Cultural Decisions.* Akron, OH: Association for Cultural Economics, University of Akron, 1983.

Hendon, William S., and J.L. Shanahan, A.J. MacDonald, eds. *Economic Policy for the Arts.* Cambridge, MA: Abt Books, 1980.

Hendon, W.S., and J.L. Shanahan, I.T.H. Hilhorst, J. van Straalen, eds. *Economic Research in the Performing Arts.* Akron, OH: Association for Cultural Economics, University of Akron, 1983.

Hendon, W.S., and J.L. Shanahan, I.T.H. Hilhorst, J. van Staalen, eds. *Market for the Arts.* Akron, OH: Association for Cultural Economics, University of Akron, 1983.

McNulty, Robert H. and R.Leo Penne, Dorothy R. Jacobson. *The Economics of Amenity: Community Futures and the Quality of Life.* New York: Partners for Livable Places, 1985.

Moore, Thomas Gale. *The Economics of the American Theatre.* Durham, NC: Duke University Press, 1968.

Owen, V.L., and W.S. Hendon, eds. *Managerial Economics for the Arts.* Akron, OH: The University of Akron, 1985.

Perloff, Harvey S., ed. *The Arts in the Economic Life of the City.* New York: American Council for the Arts, 1979.

Poggi, Jack. *Theatre in America The Impact of Economic Forces, 1870-1967.* Ithaca, NY: Cornell University Press, 1968.

Shaw, Douglas V., and William S. Hendon, C. Richard Waits, eds. *Artists and Cultural Consumers.* Akron, OH: Association for Cultural Economics, University of Akron, 1987.

Throsby, C.D., and G.A. Withers. *The Economics of the Performing Arts.* New York: St. Martin's Press, 1979.

Vogel, Harold L. *Entertainment Industry Economics.* Cambridge: Cambridge University Press, 1986.

## IX.  FINANCIAL MANAGEMENT

*A Portrait of the Financial Condition of Presenting Organizations.*  Washington, D.C.: Association of Performing Arts Presenters, 1987.

Anthony, Robert T., and Regina E. Herzlinger.  *Management Control in Nonprofit Organizations.*  Homewood, IL: Richard W. Irwin, 1975.

Beck, Kirsten.  *How To Run a Small Box Office.*  New York: The Alliance of Resident Theatres/New York, 1980.

Ferber, Henry.  *Reserved Seat Box-Office.*  New York:  National Ticket Company, n.d.

*The Finances of the Performing Arts: Volume I.*  (A Survey of 166 Professional Nonprofit Resident Theatre, Opera, Symphony, Ballet and Modern Dance Companies.)  New York: Ford Foundation, 1974.

*The Finances of the Performing Arts: Volume II.*  (A Survey of the Characteristics and Attitudes of Audiences for Theatre, Opera, Symphony and Ballet in 12 U.S. Cities.)  New York: Ford Foundation, 1974.

Gross, Malvern J., and William Warshauer, Jr.  *Financial and Accounting Guide for Nonprofit Organizations.*  3rd ed. New York: John Wiley & Sons, 1983.

Jeffries, Joan.  *Arts Money: Raising It, Saving It and Earning It.*  New York: Neal Schuman Publishers, Inc., 1983.

Messman, Carla.  *The Art of Filing.*  New York: Volunteer Lawyers for the Arts, 1988.

Nelson, Charles A., and Frederick J. Turk.  *Financial Management for the Arts: A Guidegook for Arts Organizations.*  New York: American Council for the Arts, 1976.

Taubman, Joseph, ed.  *Financing a Theatrical Production.*  New York: Federal Legal Publications, Inc., 1964.

Turk, Frederick J., and Robert P. Gallo.  *Financial Management Strategies for Arts Organizations.*  New York: American Council for the Arts, 1984.

Wehle, Mary M.  *Financial Management for Arts Organizations.*  Cambridge, MA: Arts Administration Research Institute, Harvard University, 1975.

_____.  *Financial Practice for Performing Arts Companies: A Manual.*  Cambridge, MA: Arts Administration Research Institute,Harvard University, 1977.

Wharton, John F.  *A Fresh Look at Theatre Tickets.*  (Report to the Legitimate Theatre Industry Exploratory Commission.)  New York: League of New York Theatre, 1965.

_____.  *Some Forgotten Facets of Theatrical Financing.*  (A Report to the Legitimate Theatre Industry Exploratory Commission.)  New York: League of New York Theatres, n.d.

## X.  MARKETING, PUBLICITY AND AUDIENCE DEVELOPMENT

Alexander, J.H. ed.  *Early American Theatrical Posters.*  Hollywood, CA:

Cherokee Books, n.d.

Arnold, Mark. *Dialing for Dollars: Subscription Sales Through Telemarketing.* New York: Theatre Communications Group, 1982.

Barry, John F., and Epes W. Sargent. *Building Theatre Patronage.* New York: Chalmers Co., 1927.

Biegel, Len, and Aileen Lubin. *Mediability: A Guide to Nonprofits.* Washington, D.C.: Taft Products, 1975.

Blimes, Michael E., and Ron Sproat. *More Dialing, More Dollars: 12 Steps to Successful Telemarketing.* New York: American Council for the Arts, 1986.

Breen, George Edward, and A.B. Blankenship. *Do-It-Yourself Marketing Research.* 2nd ed. New York: McGraw-Hill, 1982.

Capbern, A. Martial. *The Drama Publicity.* New York: Pageant Press, Inc., 1968.

Cole, Robert S. *The Practical Book of Public Relations.* Englewood Cliffs, NJ: Prentice-Hall, 1981.

Frank, Susan with Mindy N. Levine. *In Print: A Concise Guide to Graphic Arts and Printing for Small Businesses and Nonprofit Organizations.* New York: Alliance for Residnet Theatres/ New York, 1984.

Foundation for the Extension and Development of the American Professional Theatre. *Subscription Guidlines.* Rev. ed. New York: FEDAPT, 1977.

Kotler, Philip. *Marketing for Nonprofit Organizations.* 2nd ed. Englewood Cliffs, NJ: Prentice-Hall, 1983.

————. *Marketing Management: Analysis, Planning and Control.* 4th ed. Englewood Cliffs, NJ: Prentice-Hall, 1980.

Laundy, Peter, and Massima Bignelli. *Graphic Design for Nonprofit Organizations.* New York: American Institute of Graphic Arts, 1980.

Levine, Mindy N. with Susan Frank. *In Print: A Concise Guide to Graphic Arts and Printing for Small Businesses and Nonprofit Organizations.* Englewood Cliffs, NJ: Prentice-Hall, 1984.

Maas, Jane. *Better Brochures, Catalogs and Mailing Pieces.* New York: St. Martin's Press, 1981.

MacIntyre, Kate. *Sold Out: A Publicity and Marketing Guide.* New York: Theatre Development Fund, 1980.

McArthur, Nancy. *How To Do Theatre Publicity.* Berea, OH: Good Ideas Company, 1978.

Melillo, Joseph V. *Market the Arts!* New York: The Foundation for the Extension and Development of the American Professional Theatre, 1983.

Metropolitan Cultural Alliance. *Getting in Ink and on the Air: A Publicity Handbook.* Rev. ed. Boston: Metropolitan Cultural Alliance, 1978.

Mitchel, Arnold. *Marketing the Arts.* Menlo Park, CA: Stanform Research Institute, 1962.

Mitchel, Arnold. *Professional Performing Arts: Attendance Patterns, Preferences and Motives.* 2 Vols. Washington, D.C.: Association of Performing Arts Presenters, 1984.

Mokwa, Michael, and William N. Dawson, E. Arthur Prieve, eds. *Marketing the Arts*. New York: Praeger Publishers, 1980.

Morison, Bradley G., and Julie Gordon Dalgleish. *Waiting in the Wings: A Larger Audience for the Arts and How to Develop It*. New York: American Council for the Arts, 1987.

National Endowment for the Arts. *Audience Development: An Examination of Selected Analysis Prediction Techniques Applied to Symphony and Theatre Attendance in Four Southern Cities*. New York: Publishing Center for Cultural Resources, 1981.

National Endowment for the Arts. *Surveying Your Audience*. New York: Publishing Center for Cultural Resources, 1985.

Newman, Danny. *Subscribe Now! Building Arts Audiences Through Dynamic Subscription Promotion*. New York: Theatre Communications Group, 1977.

Parkhurst, William. *How To Get Publicity*. New York: Times Books, 1985.

Ries, Al, and Jack Troot. *Positioning: The Battle for Your Mind*. New York: McGraw-Hill, 1981.

Rossie, Chuck, ed. *The Media Resource Guide: How To Tell Your Story*. 4th ed. New York: Gannett Foundation, 1985.

Skal, David J., ed., and Robert E. Callahan, designer. *Graphic Communications for the Performing Arts*. New York: Theatre Communications Group, 1981.

Tedone, David. *Practical Publicity: How To Boost Any Cause*. Boston: The Harvard Common Press, 1983.

Warwick, Charles A., and Donald P. Lininger. *The Sample Survey: Theory and Practice*. New York: McGraw-Hill, 1975.

## XI. FUNDRAISING AND PHILANTHROPY*

Bergin, Ron. *Sponsorship and the Arts*. Evanston, IL: Entertainment Resource Group, 1990.

Brentlinger, Marilyn E., and Judith M. Weiss. *The Ultimate Benefit Book: How To Raise $50,000-plus for Your Organization*. Cleveland, OH: Octavia Press, 1987.

Brownrigg, W. Grant. *Effective Corporate Fundraising*. New York: American Council for the Arts, 1982.

Chagy, Gideon. *The New Patrons of the Arts*. New York: Harry N. Abrams, Inc., 1973.

_____. *The State of the Arts and Corporate Support*. New York: Eriksson, 1971.

Chamberlain, Marjorie. *The Art of Winning Corporate Grants*. New York: Vanguard Press, 1980.

Cummings, Milton C. Jr. and Richard S. Katz, eds. *The Patron State*. New York: Oxford University Press, 1987.

Cummings, Milton C. Jr. and J. Mark Davidson Schuster, eds. *Who's To Pay?* *(The International Search for Models of Arts Support)*. New York: American Council for the Arts, 1988.

Daniels, Ellen S. *How to Raise Money: Special Events for Arts Organizations.* New York: American Council for the Arts, 1977.

Eells, Richard. *The Corporation and the Arts.* New York: Macmillan, 1967.

Gingrich, Arnold. *Business and the Arts.* New York: Paul S. Eriksson, Inc., 1969.

*Grants for Arts and Cultural Programs.* New York: The Foundation Center, 1987.

Grasby, William K., and Kenneth G. Sheinkopf. *Successful Fundraising: A Handbook of Proven Strategies and Techniques.* New York: Charles Scribner's Sons, 1982.

Keller, Mitchell, ed. *The KRC Guide to Direct Mail Fund Raising.* New Canaan, CT: KRC Development Council, 1977.

Mark, Charles C. *Federated Fund Raising by Arts Councils.* New York: American Council for the Arts, 1965.

*Partners: A Practical Guide to Corporate Support of the Arts.* New York: Alliance for the Arts, 1982.

*People in Philanthropy.* Washington, D.C.: The Taft Corporation, 1988.

Plinio, Alex J., and Joanne B. Scanlon. *Resource Raising: The Role of Non-Cash Assistance in Corporate Philanthropy.* Washington, D.C.: The Independent Sector, 1986.

Porter, Robert, ed. *Guide to Corporate Giving in the Arts 4.* New York: American Council for the Arts, 1988.

Reiss, Alvin H. *Cash In! Funding and Promoting the Arts.* New York: Theatre Communications Group, 1986.

Sikes, Toni F., ed. *Fundraising Letter Idea Book.* Washington, D.C.: Association of Performing Arts Presenters, 1984.

*Source Book Profiles,* 2 Vols. New York: The Foundation Center, n.d.

Stopler, Carolyn L. and Karen Brooks Hopkins. *Successful Fundraising for Arts and Cultural Organizations.* Phoenix, AZ: Oryx Press, 1989.

*United Arts Fundraising.* New York: American Council for the Arts, 1987.

Wagner, Susan, ed. *A Guide to Corporate Giving in the Arts.* New York: American Council for the Arts, 1978.

Watson, John H., III. *Corporate Support of the Arts.* New York: National Industrial Conference Board, 1970.

White, Virginia. *Grants for the Arts.* New York: Plenum Press, 1980.

Wyszomirski, Margaret, and Pat Clubb, eds. *Private Arts Patronage: Patterns and Prospects.* New York: American Council for the Arts, 1988.

Wyszomirdki, Margaret and Pat Clubb, eds. *The Cost of Culture* New York: American Council for the Arts, 1989.

Young, Donald R., and Wilbert E. Moore. *Trusteeship and the Management of foundations.* New York: Russell Sage Foundation, 1969.

## XII.  COMMUNITY THEATRE

Bilowit, Ira J.  *How To Organize and Operate a Community Theatre.*  New York: American National Theatre and Academy, 1964.

Burgard, Ralph. *Arts in the City: Organizing and Programming Community Arts Councils.*  New York: American Council for the Arts, n.d.

Cavanaugh, Jim.  *Organization and Management of the Nonprofessional Theatre.*  New York: Richard Rosen Press, Inc., 1973.

Clark, Barrett H.  *How to Produce Amateur Plays.*  Boston: Little, Brown and Company, 1925.

Cutler, Bruce.  *The Arts at the Grassroots.*  Lawrence, KA: University of Kansas Press, 1968.

Dalrymple, Jean.  *The Complete Handbook for Community Theatre.*  New York: Drake Publishers, 1977.

Daniels, Ellen S., and Robert Porter.  *Community Arts Agencies: A Handbook and Guide.*  New York: American Council for the Arts, 1978.

Gard, Robert E., and Gertrude S. Burley.  *Community Theatre.*  New York: Duell, Sloan and Pearce, 1959.

Gibons, Nina Freedlander.  *The Community Arts Council Movement: History, Opinions, Issues.*  New York: Praeger Publishers, 1982.

Golden, Joseph.  *Olympus on Main Street: A Process for Planning a Community Arts Facility.*  Syracuse, NY: Syracuse University Press, 1980.

Green, Joann.  *The Small Theatre Handbook.*  Boston: The Harvard Common Press, 1981.

Legat, Michael.  *Putting on a Play.*  New York: St. Martin's Press, 1984.

McCalmon, George and Christian Moe.  *Creating Historical Drama: A Guide for the Community and Interested Individuals.*  Carbondale, IL: Southern Illinois University Press, 1965.

Pearson, Talbot.  *Encores on Main Street: Successful Community Theatre Leadership.*  Pittsburgh, PA: Carnegie Institute of Technology Press, 1948.

Seldon, Samuel, ed.  *Organizing a Community Theatre.*  Cleveland, OH: National Theatre Conference, 1945.

Stern, Lawrence.  *School and Community Theatre Management.*  Boston: Allyn & Bacon, 1979.

Young, John W.  *The Community Theatre: A Manual for Success.*  New York: Samuel French, 1971.

## XIII.  THEATRE, THE ARTS AND EDUCATION

Abbs, Peter.  *Living Powers: The Arts in Education.*  Philadelphia: Taylor and Francis International Publishers, 1987.

Arts, Education and Americans Panel.  *Coming to Our Senses: The Significance of the Arts for American Education.*  Reprint. New York: American Council for the Arts, 1988.

*The Arts and the University.* New York: Council on Higher Education in the American Republics, Institute of International Education, 1964.

Blafe, Judith H., and Joni Cherbo Heine. *Arts Education Beyond the Classroom.* New York: American Council for the Arts, 1988.

Bernardi, Bonnie, and Beverly Grova, Nancy Meyberg, Valerie Wolf. *Partners in the Arts: An Arts in Education Handbook.* Sant Cruz, CA: Cultural Council of Santa Cruz Count, 1983.

Bloom, Kathryn. *Arts Organizations and Their Services to Schools: Patrons or Partners?* New York: The JDR 3rd Fund, 1974.

Carnegie Commission on Higher Education, *The Rise of the Arts on the American Campus.* New York: McGraw-Hill, 1973.

Clifford, John E. *Educational Theatre Management.* Skokie, IL: National Textbook Company, 1972.

Courtney, Richard. *The Dramatic Curriculum.* New York: Drama Book Publishers, 1980.

Davis, Jed H., ed. *Theatre Education: Mandate for Tomorrow.* New Orleans, LA: Anchorage Press, 1985.

Davis, Jed H. and Mary Jane Evans. *Theatre, Children and Youth.* New Orleans, LA: Anchorage Press, 1982.

Educational Facilities Laboratories. *The Arts and Surplus School Space.* New York: Educational Facilities Laboratories, 1981.

Fowler, Charles. *Can We Rescue the Arts for America's Children? (Coming to Our Senses 10 Years Later).* New York: American Council for the Arts, 1988.

Holtje, Adrienne. *Putting On a School Play.* New York: Parket Publishing Company, 1980.

Katz, Jonathan, ed. *Arts and Education Handbook.* Washington, D.C.: National Association of State Arts Agencies, 1987.

McLaughlin, John, ed. *A Guide to National and State Arts Education Services.* New York: American Council for the Arts, 1987.

Morrison, Jack. Foreword by Clark Kerr. *The Maturing of the Arts on the American Campus.* Lanham, MD: University Press of America, Inc., 1985.

National Endowment for the Arts. *Toward Civilization: A Report on Arts Education.* Washington, D.C.: National Endowment for the Arts, 1988.

New England Foundation for the Arts. *The Arts Go To School: An Arts-in-Education Handbook.* NewYork: American Council for the Arts, 1983.

Ommanney, Katherine. *The Stage and the School.* Reprint. New York: Harper and Company, 1982.

Remer, Jane. *Changing Schools Through the Arts.* New York: McGraw-Hill, 1982.

Schubart, Mark. *Hunting of the Squiggle: A Study of a Performing Arts Institution and Young People, Conducted by Lincoln Center for the Performing Arts.* New York, Praeger, 1972.

Sterling, Carol, and Mary Jane Bolin. *Arts Proposal Writing: A Sourcebook of Ideas for Writing Proposals for Any School Program.* Princeton, NJ: Educational Improvement Center Press, 1982.

Willis, Jerry. *Negotiating and Contracting by Educational and Other Non-profit Institutions.* Washington, D.C.: Association of Performing Arts Presenters, 1980.

Wolf, Thomas. *The Arts Go To School: An Arts-in-Education Handbook.* New York: American Council for the Arts, 1983.

## XIV.  THEATRE ARCHITECTURE

American Theatre Planning Board. *Theatre Check List: A Guide to the Planning and Construction of Proscenium and Open Stage Theatres.* Rev. ed. Middletown, CT: Wesleyan University Press, 1983.

Armstrong, Leslie, AIA., and Roger Morgan. *Space for Dance.* Dallas: Publishing Center for Cultural Resources (for the National Endowment for the Arts), 1984.

*The Arts in Found Places, A Report.* New York: Educational Facilities Laboratories, 1976.

Athanasopoulos, Chrestos Georgiou. *Contemporary Theatre.* New York: John Wiley and Sons, Inc., 1983.

Beranek, Leo L. *Acoustics.* New York: McGraw-Hill Book Company, 1954.

————. *Music, Acoustics and Architecture.* New York: John Wiley and Sons, inc., 1962.

Brown, Catherine R., and William B. Flessig, William R. Morrish. *Building for the Arts: A Guidebook for the Planning and Design of a Cultural Facility.* Rev. ed. Denver, CO: Western States Arts Foundation, 1989.

Burris-Meyer, Harold., and Edward C. Cole. *Theatres and Auditoriums.* Rev. 2nd ed. Huntington, NY: Robert E. Krieger Publishing Company, 1975.

Burris-Meyer, Harold., and Lewis S. Goodfriend. *Acoustics for the Architect.* New York: Reinhold Publishing Corp., 1957.

Burris-Meyer, Harold, and Dorothea Mallory, Lewis S. Goodfriend. *Sound in the Theatre.* 2nd ed. New York: Theatre Arts Books, 1979.

Cogswell, Margaret, ed. *The Ideal Theatre: Eight Concepts.* New York: American Federation of the Arts, 1962.

Collison, David. *Stage Sound.* London: Cassell, 1982.

Department of the Army. *Design Guide for Music and Drama Centers.* (DG 1110.3.120.) Issued by Engineering Division, Military Programs Directorate, Office of the Chief Engineers, U.S. Army, 1982.

Egan, M. David. *Concepts in Architectural Acoustics.* New York: McGraw-Hill, 1972.

Elder, Eldon. *Will It Make a Theatre.* New York: Alliance for Resident Theatres/New York, 1979.

Finelli, Patrick. *Sound for the Stage. A Technical Handbook.* New York: Drama
    Book Publishers, 1989.
Friedman, Daniel, and Joseph Valerio. *America's Movie Palaces: Renaissance
    and Reuse.* New York: Educational Facilities Laboratories, 1982.
Izenour, George C. *Theatre Design.* New York: McGraw-Hill, 1977.
Joseph, Stephen. *New Theatre Forms.* New York: Theatre Arts Books, 1968.
Knudsen, V.O., and C.N. Harris. *Acoustical Designing in Architecture.* New
    York: John Wiley and Sons, 1950.
Leacroft, Richard, and Helen Leacroft. *Theatre and Playhouse: An Illustrated
    Survey of the Theatre Building from Ancient Greece to the Present
    Day.* London: Methuen, 1984.
Mayer, Martin. *Bricks, Mortar and the Performing Arts.* New York: Twentieth
    Century Fund, 1970.
McNamara, Brooks, and Jerry Rojo, Richard Schnecher. *Theatres, Spaces,
    Environments: 18 Projects.* New York: Drama Book Publishers, 1975.
Mielziner, Jo, and Ray Smith, eds. *The Shapes of Our Theatre.* New York:
    Clarkson N. Potter, Inc., 1970.
Mullin, Donald C. *The Development of the Playhouse: A Survey of Theatre
    Architecture from the Renaissance to the Present.* Berkeley, CA:
    University of California Press, 1970.
National Endowment for the Arts Grant Recognition Program. *Design Arts
    Places and Spaces for the Arts.* New York: Municipal Arts Society of
    New York, 1981.
*New Places for the Arts: A Scrapbook.* New York: Educational Facilities
    Laboratories, 1976.
Penn, Herman J. *Encyclopedic Guide to Planning and Establishing an
    Auditorium, Arena, Coliseum or Multi-Purpose Building.* Greenville,
    SC: Penn-Fleming, 1963.
Robinson, Horace W. *Architecture for the Educational Theatre.* Eugene,
    OR: University of Oregon Books, 1970.
Schubert, Hanne Lore. *Modern Theatre Buildings: Architecture, Stage Design,
    Lighting.* New York: Praeger, 1971.
Snedcof, Harold. *Cultural Facilities in Mixed-Use Development.* Washington,
    D.C.: Urban Land Institute, 1985.
Steward, H. Michael. *American Architecture for the Arts.* Dallas, TX: Handel
    & Sons Publishing, Inc., 1978.

## XV. DIRECTORIES AND GENERAL REFERENCE BOOKS

*A Guide to National and State Arts Education Services.* New York: American
    Council for the Arts, 1987.
Boardman, Gerald. *The Concise Oxford Companion to American Theatre.*
    New York: Oxford University Press, 1987.
Bowman, Walter P., ed. *Theatre Language: A Dictionary of Terms in English.*
    New York: Theatre Arts Books, 1961.

Cahn, Julius. *Official Theatrical Guide.* 20 Vols. New York: Empire State Building, 1896-1921.

Christensen, Warren. *National Directory of Arts Internships.* Los Angeles, CA: National Network of Artists Placement, 1987.

Coe, Linda C., and Rebecca Denney, Anne Rogers. *Cultural Directory II: Federal Funds and Services for the Arts and Humanities.* Washington, D.C.: Smithsonian Institution Press, 1980.

Cornelison, Gayle. *A Directory of Children's Theatres in the United States.* Lanham, MD: University Press of America, 1983.

*Directory of Matching Gift Programs for the Arts.* New York: Business Committee for the Arts, 1985.

Ewen, David. *Complete Book of the American Musical Theatre.* New York: Holt, Rinehart and Winston, 1970.

_____. *Encyclopedia of the Opera.* New York: Hill & Wang, Inc., 1955.

*Federal Funding Guide.* Arlington, VA: Government Information Service, 1985.

Finley, Robert. *Who's Who in the Theatre.* 15th ed. New York: Pitman Publishing Company, Inc., 1972.

*The Foundation Directory.* New York: The Foundation Center, 1987.

Free, William and Charles Lower. *History into Drama: A Source Book on Symphonic Drama.* New York: Odyssey Press, 1967.

*Grants for Arts and Cultural Programs.* New York: The Foundation Center, 1987.

Hartnoll, Phyllis, ed. *The Oxford Companion to the Theatre.* 4th ed. Oxford: Oxford Press, 1983.

Horowitz, Harold, *et al,* eds. *A Sourcebook of Arts Statistics: 1987.* (Prepared for the National Endowment for the Arts.) Rockville, MD: Westat, Inc., 1988.

Lewis, Jack, ed. *National Directory for the Performing Arts.* 4th ed., Volume I: "Performing Arts Organizations and Facilities." Santa Fe, NM: National Directory, 1988.

Lewis, Jack, ed. *National Directory for the Performing Arts.* 4th ed., Volume II: "Performing Arts Education." Santa Fe, NM: National Directory, 1988.

Lounsbury, Warren C. *Theatre Backstage from A to Z.* Rev. ed. Seattle, WA: University of Washington Press, 1967.

Millsaps, Daniel, ed. *National Directory of Arts and Education Support by Business. Corporations.* Washington, D.C.: Washington International Arts Letter, 1983.

_____., ed. *National Directory of Arts Support by Private Foundations.* Washington, D.C.: International Arts Letter, 1983.

_____., ed. *National Directory of Grants and Aid to Individuals in the Arts.* Washington, D.C.: International Arts Letter, 1983.

*New York Times Directory of Theatre.* NewYork: Arno/Quardrangle, 1973.

Odell, George C. *Annals of the New York Stage.* 15 Vols. New York: Columbia University Press, 1927-1949.

Packard, William, and David Pickerting, Charlotte Savage, eds. *The Facts on File Dictionary of the Theatre.* New York: Facts on File, Inc., 1989.

Pride, Leo B., ed. and comp. *International Theatre Directory.* New York: Simon and Schuster, Inc., 1973.

Primus, Marc, ed. *Black Theatre: A Resource Directory.* New York: The Black Theatre Alliance, 1973.

Rae, Kenneth, and Richard Southern, eds. *International Vocabulary of Technical Theatre Terms in Eight Languages.* New York: Theatre Arts Books, 1960.

Rigdon, Walter, ed. *The Biographical Encyclopedia and Who's Who of the American Theatre.* New York: James H. Heineman, Inc., 1966.

Sharp, Harold S. and Jarjorie Z. Sharp. *Index to Characters in Performing Arts.* 2 Vols. New York: Scarecrow Press, Inc., 1966.

Veinstein, Andre, and Rosamond Gilder, George Freedley, Paul Myers, eds. *Performing Arts Collections: An International Handbook.* New York: Theatre Arts Books, 1960.

## XVI. CAREER GUIDANCE

Dumler, Egon, and Robert F. Cushman. *Entertainers and Their Professional Advisors.* Homewood, IL: Dow Jones-Irwin, 1987.

Langley, Stephen and James Abruzzo. *Jobs in Arts and Media Management: What They Are and How To Get One!* New York: American Council for the Arts, 1989.

Minier, Sarah, ed. *The Arts Administrator: Job Characteristics.* (New Edition) Washington, D.C.: Association of Performing Arts Presenters, 1988.

Prieve, E. Arthur, ed. *Survey of Arts Administration Training: 1989-1990.* New York: American Council for the Arts, 1989.

## XVIII. BIBLIOGRAPHIES

Baker, Blanch M. *Theatre and Allied Arts: An Annotated Bibliography.* Reprint. New York: Benjamin Blom, 1968.

Coe, Linda and Stephen Benedict, eds. *Arts Management: An Annotated Bibliography.* Washington, D.C.: National Endowment for the Arts, Cultural Resources Development Project, 1980.

Gohdes, Clarence. *Literature and Theatre of the States and Regions of the USA: An Historical Bibliography.* Durham, NC: Duke University Press, 1967.

Howard, John T. *A Bibliography of Theatre Technology.* Westport, CT: John T. Howard, Jr., 1982.

Nakamoto, Kent, and Kathi Leven, eds. with 1983 ed., H. Perry Mixter. *A Selected and Annotated Bibliography on Marketing the Arts.* Washington, D.C.: Association of Performing Arts Presenters, 1983.

Ortonali, Benito, ed. *International Bibliography of Theatre: 1982-1986.* 5 Vols. New York: Publishing Center for Cultural Resources, 1985-1990.

*Performing Arts Books 1876-1981 Including an International Index of Current Serial Publication.* New York: R.R. Bowker Company, 1981.

Prieve, E. Arthur, and Daniel J. Schmidt. *Administration in the Arts: An Annotated Bibliography of Selected References.* Madison, WI: Center for Arts Administration, Graduate School of Business, University of Wisconsin-Madison, 1977.

Stratman, Carl J. *Bibliography of the American Theatre Excluding NYC.* Loyola University Press, 1965.

Waak, William L., ed. *Careers and Career Education in the Performing Arts: An Annotated Bibliography.* Lanham, MD: University Press of America, Inc., 1983.

Whittingham, Nik-ki. *Arts Management in the '90s.* Chicago, IL: Enaaq Publications, Inc., 1990.

## XVIII. PERIODICALS AND ANNUALS

*ACA Update.* (Monthly), American Council for the Arts, 1285 Avenue of the Americas, New York, NY 10019

*Affiliate Artists Newsletter* (Quarterly), 1515 Broadway, New York, NY 10036

*American Theatre* (11 issues per year), Theatre Communications Group, 355 Lexington Avenue, New York, NY 10017

*Annual Report / National Endowment for the Arts* (Annual), National Endowment for the Arts, Public Information Office, 1100 Pennsylvania Ave., Washington, D.C. 20506

*Art and the Law* (Quarterly), Volunteer Lawyers for the Arts, 1285 Avenue of the Americas, 3rd floor, New York, NY 10019

*Arts Bulletin* (Bi-monthly), Canadian Conference for the Arts, 141 Laurier Ave. W., Suite 707, Ottawa, Ontario K1P 5J3, Canada

*Arts International* (Quarterly), Institute of International Education, 1400 K Street NW, Washington, D.C. 20005

*Arts Management* (5 issues per year) (The National News Service for Those Who Finance, Manage and Communicate the Arts), 408 West 57th Street, New York, NY 10019

*Arts Review* (Quarterly), National Endowment for the Arts, U.S. Government Printing Office, Superintendent of Documants, Washington, D.C. 20402

*Artsearch* (Bi-monthly), Theatre Communications Group, 355 Lexington Ave, New York, NY 10017

*Auditorium News* (Monthly), International Association of Auditorium Managers, 500 North Michigan, #1400, Chicago, IL 60611

*Backstage* (Weekly), 330 West 42nd Street, New York, NY 10036

*BCA News* (Bi-monthly), Business Committee for the Arts, 1775 Broadway, New York, NY 10019

*Billboard Magazine* (Weekly), Billboard Publications, 1515 Broadway, New York, NY 10036

*BOMI Newsletter* (Quarterly), Box Office Managers International, 500 East 77th Street, #1715, New York, NY 10162

*The Bulletin* (11 issues per year), Association of Performing Arts Presenters, 1112 16th St., Washington, D.C. 20036

*The CC Flash* (Monthly), Cultural Council Foundation, 625 Broadway, New York, NY 11212

*The Catalog of Federal Domestic Assistance* (Annual with supplements), U.S. Office of Management and Budget, Superintendent of Documents, U.S. Government Printing Office, Washington, D.C. 20402

*Columbia-VLA Journal of Law and the Arts* (Quarterly), Volunteer Lawyers for the Arts, 1285 Avenue of the Americas, 3rd floor, New York, NY 10019

*Connections* (Quarterly), National Assembly of Local Arts Agencies, 1625 I Street #725A, Washington, D.C. 20006

*COS Bulletin* (Quarterly), Central Opera Service, Metropolitan Opera Association, Lincoln Center, New York, NY 10023

*Dance Magazine* (Monthly), 33 West 60th Street, New York, NY 10023

*Design for Arts in Education* (Bi-monthly), Heldref Publications, 4000 Albermarle Street NW, Washington, D.C. 20016

*Dramatics* (9 issues per year), International Thespian Society, Cincinnati, OH

*Dramatists Guild Quarterly* (Quarterly), The Dramatists Guild, 234 West 44th Street, New York, NY 10036

*Equity News* (Monthly), Actors' Equity Association, 165 West 46th Street, New York, NY 10036

*Facility Manager* (Quarterly), International Association of Auditorium Managers, published by P.M. Haeger & Associates, 500 North Michigan Ave #1400, Chicago, IL 60611

*Ford Foundation Letter* (6 issues per year), Office of Reports, 320 W 43rd St., New York, NY 10017

*Foundation Giving Watch* (Monthly), The Taft Group, 5130 MacArthur Blvd NW, Washington, D.C. 20012

*The Foundation Grants Index Annual* (Anually), The Foundation Center, 70 Fifth Avenue, New York, NY 10003

*Foundation News* (Bi-monthly), Council on Foundations, Inc., 1828 L St NW, Washington, D.C. 20036

*The Foundation Reporter* (Anually), The Taft Corporation, 5125 MacArthur Blvd. NW, Washington, D.C. 20016

*Fundraising Management* (Monthly), Hoke Communications, Inc., 224 Seventh St., Garden City, NY 11530

*Grants Magazine* (Quarterly), Plenum Publishing Company, Journals Department, 233 Spring Street, New York, NY 10013

*Grantsmanship Center News* (Bi-monthly), Grantsmanship Center, 1031 South Grand Ave., Los Angeles, CA 90015

*Horizon* (10 issues per year), 1305 Greensboro Ave, Tuscaloosa, AL 35401

*Inside Performance* (Quarterly), Association of Performing Arts Presenters, 1112 16th St., Washington, D.C. 20036

*Institute of Outdoor Drama Newsletter*, IOD, University of North Carolina, Chapel Hill, NC 27514

*International Arts Manager* (Bi-monthly), Barkol Ltd, 20 Horsford Road, London SW2 5BN, England

*ISPAA Performing Arts Forum* (Bi-monthly), International Society of Performing Arts Administrators, University of Texas, Box 7518, Austin, TX 78712

*Journal of Arts Management and Law* Heldref Publications, 4000 Albemarle St. NW, Washington, D.C. 20016

*Journal for Cultural Economics* (Bi-anually), The University of Akron, Department of Urban Studies, Akron, OH 44325

*Lighting Dimensions* (Monthly), Lighting Dimensions, 135 Fifth Avenue, New York, NY 10010

*Musical America International Directory of the Performing Arts* (Annually, plus supplements, including the annual "Festivals" directory), Musical America, 825 Seventh Ave., New York, NY 10019

*NASAA News* (Bi-monthly), National Association of State Arts Agencies, 1010 Vermont Ave NW #920, Washington, D.C. 20005

*Northwest Arts* (Bi-weekly), 538 98th Street, Seattle, WA 98115

*Opera America Bulletin* (Monthly), Opera America, 633 E St. NW, Washington, D.C. 20004

*Opera News* (17 issues per year), Metropolitan Opera Guild, Inc., Lincoln Center, New York, NY 10023

*Performance-Management* (Bi-annually), Brooklyn College, Performing Arts Management Program, Brooklyn, NY 11210

*Playbill* (Monthly), 71 Vanderbilt Ave., Suite 320, New York, NY 10169

*Players Magazine* (22 issues per year), National Collegiate Players, Dekalb, IL 60115

*Source Book Profiles: Facts on Foundations* (Quarterly), The Foundation Center, 888 Seventh Ave., New York, NY 10106

*Stern's Performing Arts Directory* (Annually), Robert D. Stern & William Como, Publishers, 33 West 60th St., New York, NY 10023

*Talent and Booking Directory* (Annually), Somerset Communications, Berwin Entertainment Complex, 6525 Sunset Blvd Studio A, Los Angeles, CA 90028

*Theatre Crafts Magazine* (10 issues per year), 135 5th Avenue, New York, NY 10010

*Theatre Design and Technology* (Quarterly), U.S. Institute for Theatre Technology, Inc., 10 West 19th Street, New York, NY 10011

*Theatre Directory* (Annually), Theatre Communications Group, 355 Lexington Ave., New York, NY 10017

*Theatre Journal* (Quarterly), University/College Theatre Association, Johns Hopkins University Press, 701 W 40th St. #275, Baltimore, MD 21211

*Theatre Magazine* (3 issues per year), Yale School of Drama, 222 York St., New Haven, CT 02520

*Theatre Profiles* (Annually), Theatre Communications Group, 355 Lexington Ave., New York, NY 10017

*Theatre Three* (2 Issues per year), Department of Drama, Carnegie Mellon University, Pittsburgh, PA 15213

*Theatre Times* (8 issues per year), Alliance for Resident Theatres/New York, 325 Spring St. #315, New York, NY 10013

*Theatre Week* (Weekly), 28 West 25th St. 4th floor, New York, NY 10010

*The Drama Review (TDR)* (Quarterly), Tisch School of the Arts, New York University: published by MIT Press Journals, 28 Carleton St., Cambridge, MA 02142

*USITT Newsletter* (Quarterly), U.S. Institute for Theatre Technology, 10 West 19th St., New York, NY 10011

*Variety* (Weekly), 475 Park Avenue South, New York, NY 10016

*Vantage Point* (5 issues per year found in *Horizon*), American Council for the Arts, 1285 Avenue of the Americas, New York, NY 10019

*VLA News* (3 issues per year), Volunteer Lawyers for the Arts, 1285 Avenue of the Americas, 3rd floor, New York, NY 10019

# Index

# INDEX